IDEOLOGY AND MEANING-MAKING UNDER THE PUTIN REGIME

MARLENE LARUELLE

IDEOLOGY AND MEANING-MAKING UNDER THE PUTIN REGIME

STANFORD UNIVERSITY PRESS
STANFORD, CALIFORNIA

Stanford University Press
Stanford, California

© 2025 by Marlène Agnès Laruelle. All rights reserved.

No part of this book may be reproduced or transmitted in any form or by any means, electronic or mechanical, including photocopying and recording, or in any information storage or retrieval system, without the prior written permission of Stanford University Press.

Printed in the United States of America on acid-free, archival-quality paper

Library of Congress Cataloging-in-Publication Data
Names: Laruelle, Marlène, author.
Title: Ideology and meaning-making under the Putin regime / Marlene Laruelle.
Description: Stanford, California : Stanford University Press, 2025. | Includes bibliographical references and index.
Identifiers: LCCN 2024025741 (print) | LCCN 2024025742 (ebook)
 | ISBN 9781503631397 (cloth) | ISBN 9781503641594 (paperback) |
 ISBN 9781503641600 (epub)
Subjects: LCSH: Putin, Vladimir Vladimirovich, 1952- | Russia (Federation) | Russia (Federation)—Politics and government—1991-
Classification: LCC DK510.763 .L373 2025 (print) | LCC DK510.763 (ebook) | DDC 320.94709/04—dc23/eng/20240824
LC record available at https://lccn.loc.gov/2024025741
LC ebook record available at https://lccn.loc.gov/2024025742

Cover design: Daniel Benneworth-Gray
Cover photograph: Miguel Á. Padriñán / Pexels

CONTENTS

List of Figures   vii

Acknowledgments   ix

Introduction   1

PART I
THE REORDERING OF IDEOLOGY   13

1. Actors, Networks, and Structures   15
2. The Sedimentation of Ideology   39

PART II
FROM LEARNING TO UNLEARNING THE WEST   73

3. The Painful Relationship to a Polysemic West   77
4. Byzantium: The Christian Europe   97
5. Spiritual Security: Statism, Patriotism, History   109
6. Russia's Imperialness and the Fight for Ukraine   126

PART III
RUSSIA'S COUNTERREVOLUTION   147

7. Civilization: Rejecting Western Universalism   151
8. Conservatism: Russia's Answer to Liberalism   170
9. Katechon: Reaction and Eschatology   193

PART IV
RUSSIA'S GEO-IMAGINARIES — 211

10 Eurasia: The Transcontinental Space — 215

11 The Russian World: From Messianism to Irredentism — 231

12 Anticolonialism: Russia as a Global South Power — 245

Conclusion — 265

Notes — 287

Selected Bibliography — 345

Index — 363

LIST OF FIGURES

FIG. 2.1 Mentions of "ideology" in presidential speeches, 2000–2023   60

FIG. 3.1 Presence of the universal values, prosperity, and identity in presidential speeches, percentage of sentences per year, 2000–2023   82

FIG. 3.2 Mentions of "democracy" (when associated with "Russia") in presidential speeches, 2000–2023   83

FIG 3.3 Mentions of "fascism" and "Nazism" in presidential speeches, 2000–2023   94

FIG. 5.1 Mentions of "statehood" in presidential speeches, 2000–2023   112

FIG. 5.2 Mentions of "patriotism" in presidential speeches, 2000–2023   113

FIG. 6.1 Mentions of "empire" (when associated with "Russia") in presidential speeches, 2000–2023   135

FOG 6.2 Mentions of tsars by name in presidential speeches, 2000–2023   136

FIG. 6.3 Mentions of "history" and "culture" in presidential speeches, 2000–2023   141

FIG. 7.1 Mentions of "civilization" in Russian presidential speeches, 2000–2023   159

FIG. 7.2 Russia's civilizational identity(ies) in presidential speeches, 2000–2023   161

FIG. 8.1 Mentions of "conservatism" in presidential speeches, 2000–2023   175

FIG. 8.2 Mentions of traditional values in presidential speeches, 2000–2023   177

FIG. 10.1 Mentions of "Eurasia" in presidential speeches, 2000–2023   221

FIG. 11.1 Mentions of "Russian World," "compatriots," "Donbas," and "Novorossiya" in presidential speeches, 2000–2023   243

FIG. 12.1 Mentions of "colonialism" in presidential speeches, 2000–2023   253

FIG. 12.2 Mentions of "colonialism" and "multipolarity" in Russian media, 2000–2023   254

ACKNOWLEDGMENTS

As I finalize this book in spring 2024, two years after the beginning of the Russo-Ukrainian War, I want to express my gratitude to all the colleagues and friends who have supported me in this endeavor at a time of deep rethinking of the Russian Studies field. The Institute for European, Russian, and Eurasian Studies at The George Washington University has been, as always, a wonderful place for stimulating intellectual exchange. A fellowship at the IWM in Vienna, Austria, allowed me to revise and complete the manuscript in an inspiring environment.

This book would not have seen the light of day without the help of many colleagues and friends who spent time discussing my hypotheses and arguments with me and reading prior versions of it: Juliette Faure, Jules Sergei Fediunin, Ivan Fomin, Ivan Grek, Maria Lipman, Adam Lenton, Guillaume Sauvé, Gulnaz Sibgatullina, Robert Otto, and Julian Waller. Other colleagues working on similar themes, such as Mikhail Suslov, Paul Robinson, Helge Blakkisrud, Pål Kolstø, and Matthew Blackburn, have exchanged ideas with me on these topics over the years. I am also grateful to Dylan Royce and Jarlath McGuckin for their research assistance, to Christopher Ellison, Ellen Powell, Keary Iarussi, Taylor Margvelashvili, and Erik Piccoli for their editing at different phases of the project, and to Aleksei Medved, Maria Popova, and Sergei Tikhonov for their work on the Kremlin speeches database.

As always, my husband and daughter have offered me the emotional support needed to pursue such an endeavor in difficult times.

IDEOLOGY AND MEANING-MAKING
UNDER THE PUTIN REGIME

INTRODUCTION

Any major political actor controls reality through the imaginary.
GEORGE BALANDIER, *Le pouvoir sur scènes*[1]

HOW DID THE RUSSO-UKRAINIAN WAR become possible, and what role did ideology play in enabling it? This book reclaims the study of ideology as an unavoidable component of the tools we use to render the world intelligible: ideology is a collective language constitutive of social life. The book thus hopes to contribute to the political science debate on the interaction between ideas and policy decisions, as well as to the field of political theory by taking a deep dive into the Russian case study. The trend among Western observers to look at Russia's ideological construction as purely artificial, irrational, and unsustainable limits our capacity to comprehend both the resilience of the regime and its appeal to part of Russian society—and to some constituencies abroad. The Russian regime *does* offer an ideological construction that has internal plausibility and coherence—whatever one thinks of its contents. To capture it, one must take a careful and granular look at how concepts are deployed and operationalized, their place in the ideological structure offered by the regime, their inner articulation, their evolution, and their promoters. That is the aim of this book.

LOCATING THE PLACE AND ROLE OF IDEOLOGY IN THE PUTIN REGIME

To ensure its hegemony, the Putin regime relies on three mechanisms of governmentality: material (redistributing prosperity, at least partly), ideational (generating consensus), and repressive (silencing dissident voices). It has crafted an intelligent policy of material support for those social classes that constitute its main electorate and has pioneered a sophisticated values-based legitimation strategy. For many years, the third pillar, repression, was minimal compared to the other two: the authorities targeted members of the political opposition, activists, and those who spoke about taboo topics (e.g., Putin's family and wealth, his relationship with Chechen head of state Ramzan Kadyrov, high-level corruption) but were careful to let the large majority of the society live without fear of political repression. This situation has gradually changed, to the point that it is now challenging to know the extent to which fear plays a role in the population's acquiescence to the social and political order.

The first two pillars of governmentality—the material and the ideational—have long resulted in a cocreational regime in which a large part of the population, whether actively or passively, supports the directions the Kremlin dictates to the country. In spring 2021, a survey asked a nationally representative sample of Russian citizens: "Does Russia need a state ideology?" Seventy-nine percent of respondents said yes, 14 percent said no, and 7 percent were unsure.[2] One may, of course, wonder how self-censorship affects this approval, and interrogate the gap between attitudes and behavior, but at least in their public expressions, a majority of citizens do share the regime's language. What, then, is this ideology that the population appears to support?

Much ink has been spilled in an effort to pin down Russia's ideological characteristics. One can identify several schools of thought. A first argues that ideology is not a salient component of the regime's construction, contending that the latter has been purely instrumental and opportunistic.[3] Yet the Russian regime has been profoundly and genuinely engaged in a political project for the country: The terrible evidence of going to war against Ukraine, even at the price of destroying a large part of the elite revenues accumulated in the West, confirms that the Kremlin is animated not solely by kleptocratic strategies but also by a set of beliefs regarding the best path for the future of the country.

Providing a more nuanced analysis while maintaining that the regime has no ideology, Sergey Guriev and Daniel Treisman contend that the Kremlin is, first and foremost, a skilled propaganda operator.[4] Andrey Makarychev prefers to present these ideological articulations as void of "ideological authenticity" and amounting to mere "moral rhetoric."[5] However, it is problematic to decry elites' supposed hypocrisy: ideology does not require deep-seated beliefs among citizens so much as the reproduction of certain practices and rituals. The connection between the ideas a politician espouses professionally and their personal ideology is complex, and there is always a pragmatic calculation that a policy decision or a declaration will secure success for the one making it.

A second school contends that ideology reveals the very nature of the regime and a decision-making process that is animated mainly through it. It sees Putin's regime as a totalitarian, fascist, neo-Stalinist institution motivated by militarism, revanchism, nationalism, and imperialism. In this view, deeply entrenched ideological convictions explain all of Russia's actions on both the international and the domestic fronts. Charles Clover's *Black Wind, White Snow*, Marcel van Herpen's *Putin's Wars*, and Michel Eltchaninoff's *Inside the Mind of Vladimir Putin* are good representatives of this insistence on Russia's ideological "grand design."[6] This analysis has skyrocketed in the Western media since the full-scale Russo-Ukrainian War, with narratives about Russia's immanent belligerence presented as an atemporal feature that cannot be changed until it is totally destroyed. A central argument of that school relates to the use of the label *fascist*.[7] The most prominent voice expressing this view, Timothy Snyder, contributes to promoting terms such as *rashizm* (a portmanteau that combines fascism and Russia) coming mostly from the Ukrainian media world.[8] Mikhail Epstein prefers to employ *schizofascism*,[9] a notion that Snyder shares, as he sees the conflict between Russia and Ukraine as a situation of "actual fascists calling their opponents 'fascists' "[10]—that is, where Russia accuses Ukraine of its own sins.

A third school, to which I belong, claims that ideology is an important but not exclusive part of the regime's governmentality toolkit. It advances a more nuanced view that reads ideology not as a binary opposition—that is, as either a cynical cover for material interests or a set of immutable deep beliefs—but as a context-sensitive process of meaning-making. This interpretation encompasses three levels of analysis. First, the regime's ideological construction has evolved slowly, with gradual sedimentation, and chronology therefore matters over the quarter-century of Putin's reign. Second, the regime's relationship with Russian society is much more than simply authoritarian: it is cocreational, based on an implicit social contract with the population that is continuously renegotiated and limits the authorities' options. The regime's ideological construction should, therefore, be read as part of the nation-building process and not simply as a search for an immediate political status quo. Third, the internal configuration of the regime has long resembled a conglomerate of competing opinions. This manufactured discursive chaos has reluctantly moved toward a more cohesive—and repressive—ideology: the scope for improvisation, along with the bottom-up dynamic underpinning the cocreational nature of the regime, has largely, but not entirely, been erased.

A rich field of English-speaking literature on Russia's ideological construction has sprung up over the years. Without delving into great detail, one can mention a well-developed but now aged literature on Eurasianism built in the 1990s and 2000s.[11] A more recent subfield focuses on Russian conservatism, with seminal works by Paul Robinson, Mikhail Suslov, Glenn Diesen, Kristina Stoeckl, Dmitry Uzlaner, and David Lewis.[12] State language has been studied in depth by Olga Malinova.[13] The centrality of memory wars and the cult of the Great Patriotic War have been investigated by several scholars, among them Jade McGlynn, Nina Tumarkin, and Nikolay Koposov.[14] On the foreign policy side, Russia's vision of the world stage and its interpretation of its changing status have been explored in depth by Andrey Tsygankov, Richard Sakwa, and Andrej Krijkovic, to name just a few.[15] The place of the Russian Orthodox Church in coauthoring some of the state language alongside the regime—in both its domestic and international aspects—has been studied in several works.[16] Messianism and the notion of a Third Rome have also been subject to their fair share of studies.[17]

These great works do not necessarily engage with the question of the regime's ideology as a whole, nor do they try to define it. Three landmark books do try to do so. In *The Code of Putinism*, Brian Taylor explains insightfully that "Putinism is more like 'Thatcherism' or 'Reaganism' than like 'Marxism'—it is not a fully developed, all-encompassing ideology, but a system of rule and a guiding mentality, a personality and an historical moment."[18] Elena Chebankova's *Political Ideologies in Contemporary Russia* argues that the Russian state limits itself to balancing among different political ideologies that exist in society.[19] Mikhail Suslov's *Putinism: Post-Soviet Russian Regime Ideology*, on the contrary, sees Putinism as a state ideology with some forms of coherence.[20] In addition to these, one can also mention Gulnaz Sharafutdinova's *Red Mirror: Putin's Leadership and Russia's Insecure Identity*, which uses social identity theory to explain the popularity of Putin;[21] Cheng Chen's *Return of Ideology*, which compares Russia and China;[22] and Bo Petersson's *The Putin Predicament*, which posits the regime's ideological eclecticism.[23]

To these works can be added lively discussions and analyses from Russian colleagues in the form of classic academic literature, op-eds or blogs, and social media posts. Even in a context of a drastically reduced scope for expressing themselves freely and/or while grappling with the challenges of emigration, scholars such as Ilya Budraitkis, Ivan Fomin, Ilya Kalinin, Ivan Kurilla, Andrey Kolesnikov, Maria Lipman, Andrey Melville, Alexander Morozov, Nikita Savin, and Ilya Veniavkin, among others, continue to study the regime's ideological evolution, bringing nuances, insider expertise, and a more grassroots perspective that remain invaluable.

RUSSIA AS A LENS FOR GLOBAL IDEOLOGICAL PARADIGM SHIFTS

Russia's ideological production cannot be understood as a manifestation of Russia's exceptionalism or "ungraspability" (*neob"iatnost'*), a notion well developed by the many Russian intellectual schools looking for the country's unique *Sonderweg*. It should, on the contrary, be reconnected to worldwide trends. The tendency of Western pundits to present the Russian president as an archvillain and absolute Other of the West obscures the many bonds that connect Russia's evolution to the rest of the world. I see Russia not as the nemesis of the West but as a *micro-world*, in that it contains the central contradictions of today's world order. Far from any "end of ideology," the liberal-democratic framework that was long considered the main compass against which other normative constructions were judged is now being challenged and weakened. The most powerful antagonist and alternative to the Western universalism of liberal-democratic discourse can be labeled under the broad umbrella of illiberalism. By that term I define a cluster or an aggregation of different ideological families that articulate a rejection of some or all of the different scripts of liberalism and blend diverse intellectual traditions and policy norms and practices that promote majoritarianism, sovereignism, and traditional hierarchies (social, sexual, gender, cultural) and recognize the right to particularism and some forms of exclusivity.[24]

In the early 2000s (if not before), Russia became the first European country of size to experience a massive backlash against liberalism precisely because it had experienced an authoritarian liberalism, both political and economic, that had deeply shaken the foundations of the societal order in the 1990s. Simultaneously, Russia's international prestige had decreased, with the post–Cold War order relegating the country to second-class status. While the regime mainly responded to the decline of the country's international status, the citizenry reacted mostly to the violence of political and economic liberalism—a top-down and bottom-up encounter that has produced "Putinism." What was originally a situational ideology rapidly reconnected with older roots, namely a long conservative tradition anchored in nineteenth-century intellectual thought and forms of moral conservatism and anti-Westernism dating back to the Soviet era that could easily be reframed for this new context.

The Putin regime has since been able to stay in tune with the evolution of the international scene, inspiring those who challenge the liberal hegemony in all its aspects: political, societal, economic, and geopolitical. It has taken the lead in denouncing a crusading US universalism during the neocon era; in defending authoritarian sovereignty against external interference in the so-called Global South; and in criticizing progressivism in national, family, sexual, and gender matters and in defending a Christian/Western/white civilization that is supposedly under attack.[25] Based on a strategy of niche soft power, the regime has microtargeted some specific audiences (e.g., Western far-right and some far-left groups, Christian and Muslim traditionalists, the Latin American left and right, pan-Africanist movements), speaking to some well-identified constituencies whose features predispose them—at least theoretically—to Russia's grand narratives. This strategy has emerged from the Kremlin's awareness of its limited outreach capacity compared to US soft power, both financially and in terms of its potential to export Russian culture and brands worldwide.[26]

As we will see later, the Russian regime has exploited all the contradictions of the West, both as a geopolitical hegemon and as a normative model, to promote transgression and subversion. The rebellious aspect of this ideological export is nothing new: since the nineteenth century, Russia has been exporting revolutionary ideologies—from Populism and leftist terrorism to Communism—to challenge what has been seen as Western hegemony. What the Russian regime offers today in terms of ideology is immeasurably less structured doctrinally than Communism, but it is better adapted to today's postmodern conditions of ideological bricolage and fluidity. Underestimating Russia's status as a brand representing rebellion or resistance to "the world as it is" is mistaken, as we have seen with Western miscalculations regarding Moscow's capacity to retain its partners in the non-Western world. Yet there also have been limits to that soft power: Tucker Carlson's long interview with Putin in February 2024 demonstrated that shared values between American Trumpists and the Russian leadership are not enough to produce explicit political and policy cooperation based on well-articulated ideological arguments.[27]

THE BOOK

This book proposes a critical reconstruction of the regime's intellectual genealogy: it posits that one can make sense of Russia's ideological construction in all its diversity and uniformity, capturing its inner coherence along with its contradictions, ambiguities, and omissions. It takes this construction seriously and does not dismiss it because it does not fit what is supposed to be "our" (read: Western liberal) vision of reality. In this approach, the book relies on a rich literature on ethical considerations when it comes to taking religious beliefs seriously[28] or analyzing conspiracy theories not as logic-defying but as expressions of popular mechanisms for making sense of the world.[29]

The book interprets Russia's ideological construction as a reordering process aimed at the decontestation of fluid semantic spaces, to follow Michael Freeden's language.[30] This is why the book title links ideology with *meaning-making* and not with propaganda. Propaganda is the communication strategy used to spread meanings. I focus here on the creation of meanings, not on how they spread—mass media strategies are not part of my research and already have been well studied by colleagues.[31] While writing this book, I remain concerned with the risk of a retrospective surrationalization of ideology and take seriously the bias of logocentrism—that is, of overemphasizing words and seeing in them a fundamental expression of an external reality. I do recognize that the regime's ideological construction has been in many ways nondiscursive. Indeed, approaches that solely try to seize, define, and then typologize the regime's doctrinal content partly miss the point: it remains important not to stress doctrine over worldview, textuality over pop culture, content over style, and solitary eccentric thinkers over structure without considering the toolkit of behaviors, habits, and technologies of governmentality.

In this book, I argue that the Putin regime does have an ideology—aggregated from multiple repertoires and doctrinal stocks—but cannot be restricted to it: as a regime, it pursues a set of governmentality practices that may not always articulate well with the ideological realm. This means that ideology may or may not inform the decision-making process: sometimes it does precede and inspire it, sometimes it is called upon to provide *a posteriori* legitimation, and sometimes there is no direct link between the two. Ideological production can therefore be proactive or reactive. If the authorities do have a consistent and coherent global view of their political project, based on a set of beliefs, a mental apparatus, this does not imply that ideology systematically informs every decision but rather that there has been a process of mutual reinforcement between decision-making and ideology. As Jade McGlynn neatly explains in the realm of memory policy, "Russia does not prioritize the political threat posed by external actors' embrace of antithetical narratives where there is no apparent political will to use the memory to challenge Russian geopolitical ambitions and/or identity."[32]

To explore Russia's ideological construction, I borrow from political science, political philosophy, history, cultural studies, and critical geopolitics. In the tradition of strategic empathy—looking at issues through the perspectives of others, especially when they are strategic adversaries[33]—I study Russia's ideological construction based on emic notions, those used by the regime itself. As such, I do not attempt to project a Western interpretative framework onto Russia: this is why the book explores "civilization," "patriotism," "conservatism," "Eurasia," and other concepts, as opposed to external interpretative tools like "imperialism," "nationalism," and "militarism," even if I obviously articulate them in my analysis. Similarly, I do not attach any label of authenticity: I do not seek, for instance, to decide whether the regime merits the title of "conservative" or is usurping it, as that would suppose an identifiable essence to the concept, but rather to study how references to conservatism are used and have evolved.

Methodologically, the book is based on multiple approaches, mostly qualitative but also quantitative, ranging from content and discourse analysis to big data. It is based on a two-decade-long study of the ideological field, reading Russian publications, interviewing Russian experts, and conducting annual fieldwork. It encompasses large corpora of presidential speeches, official documents, and ideological texts produced by actors and institutions in "orbit" around the Kremlin.

To complement what is mostly a qualitative study, I looked in a more systemic way at presidential speeches from January 2000 to December 2023, as available on the website of the Presidential Administration, kremlin.ru.[34] This is not the first time a scholar has proposed taking a quantitative approach to the regime: Olga Malinova has been working with granularity on several aspects of presidential speeches;[35] Oksana Drozdova and Paul Robinson have examined Putin's rhetoric over the years;[36] Alicja Curanović has used the approach to look at the issue of messianism;[37] and Adriana Cuppuleri looked at 7,000 speeches and statements from the Russian president and the minister of foreign affairs.[38] However, it is the first time, to my knowledge, that the quantitative evolution of several key strategic narratives and repertoires over the twenty-four years of Putin's reign has been explored.

This approach brings with it several methodological and epistemological issues. First, the corpus of about 12,500 presidential speeches includes those given by Dmitry Medvedev during his presidency (2008–12); while the speeches given by Vladimir Putin at this time, when he was prime minister, are not included. Second, it is a matter of debate whether one should look at the absolute number of instances that the president uses a given term in speeches or assess this discourse in a more proportional way. I decided to go with a simple numbering of occurrences. Third, the semantic space has shifted over time, with the result that the same term may be deployed over the years but be understood differently. Fourth, a quantitative approach is problematic in that it gives the same value to texts of different natures. But it is easy to guess that an address to the nation has more political and symbolic weight than a small speech to inaugurate a new institution, and that Direct Line—a heavily scripted annual live TV program in which Putin spends several hours answering citizens' questions[39]—has a different narrative logic than a long, uninterrupted monologue in front of the Duma.

Speeches can indeed be constructed with different strategies in mind: Ivan Fomin has shown, for instance, that content diverges depending on whether the goal is "ideological proclamation (when the regime declares its core values), ideological indoctrination (when the regime seeks to promote its ideology explicitly), declarative justification (when the regime presents decisions for implied silent popular approval), and mobilizing invocation (when the regime seeks people's active participation)."[40] Despite these limitations, the corpora still offer fascinating insights. Indeed, Western experts tend to stress certain Putin quotations without looking at the whole picture of his speeches or of the entirety of state language, hence the need for a more quantitative approach that allows patterns to emerge and avoids singling out nonrepresentative components.

Yet this book is not Putin-centric—far from it. The Russian president is obviously a central piece of the whole political architecture, but this book does not try to "get inside Putin's head" and does not pretend Putin is a deep political thinker. Instead, it places the Russian president in the broader context of different strains of strategic culture, ideological interest groups, and intellectual history; looks at figures who embody more moderate or more radical versions of the presidential narrative; and stresses the diversity of actors, structures of production, and discourses around him.

The book focuses on the "Putin regime"—a reductive but convenient terminology that encompasses the more than two decades of Vladimir Putin's rule. It also uses "Russian regime" to describe a broader period that includes the Yeltsinian decade of the 1990s in those cases where I see continuity with the Putin years. To describe a political system as a "regime" implies that it is a nondemocratic system with no political alternation. While this is true of Putin's Russia, I use "regime" in a more neutral way, seeing it as interchangeable with "government," "authorities," or other problematic terms such as "the Kremlin." But I do differentiate between the Presidential Administration as the core of the system; the government as its bureaucratic organ; the Duma and Federation Council; and myriad institutions that belong, whether integrally or peripherally, to the various ideological ecosystems.

The book looks at ideological construction as conducted by the political mainstream. This includes the many groups and entrepreneurs of influence that find themselves "in orbit" around the Kremlin but excludes people, institutions, and narratives that are seen by the regime as in opposition, either liberal or ethnonational. I also distinguish between the Russian *establishment* and Russian *elites*. The establishment is the political and intellectual mainstream, those who have some official status in state structures, while elites are all those with financial or social-cultural capital—a much more diverse group that includes oligarchs and intellectuals, some of whom disagree with the regime and are now repressed by it.

The first part of the book provides a comprehensive overview of the Russian regime's ideological production. It explores it in a structuralist way, looking at its ecosystems and main mechanisms of engineering ideational content (chapter 1). It retraces the gradual sedimentation of ideology by a Kremlin long reluctant to formalize too much doctrinal content, preferring to play with a multiplicity of floating signifiers and ensuring shared social practices (chapter 2). A second part investigates the meaning of "the West"—an eminently polysemic term—in Russia and how the regime went from borrowing from the "West" to challenging it, decoupling from it, and eventually fighting against it (chapter 3). To position Russia in relation to the West, the regime has recrafted a narrative of Russia as the Second Europe, the Byzantine one (chapter 4). It has also engaged in a colossal process of securitizing national history and space (chapter 5), as well as rediscovering Russia in its historical continuity and its imperial and White past, in particular with regard to its obsession with Ukraine (chapter 6).

The third part of the book researches the regime's counterrevolutionary script, formulated around three notions: civilizationism to refute a universalism associated with Western normativity (chapter 7); conservatism to deplore what is seen as excessive, degraded, and morally corrupt Western liberalism (chapter 8); and *katechon*, translated as bulwark, shield, or gatekeeper of order against chaos, a more eschatological and reactionary understanding of the counterrevolutionary script (chapter 9). The fourth part delves into the regime geo-imaginaries, shaped by Russia's spatial realities and the tradition of seeing itself as a pivot of a broader space, be it Eurasia (chapter 10), the Russian world (chapter 11), or as the leader of the anticolonial resistance against Western neo-imperialism (chapter 12). The conclusion briefly explores the content-manufacturing aspect of the regime and how Russian society accepts, cocreates, adapts, or rejects this intense ideological engineering.

PART I
THE REORDERING OF IDEOLOGY

THE SOVIET NARRATIVE OF a bright Communist future began collapsing in the 1970s, if not earlier, among certain Soviet constituencies. In the interstices of a post-totalitarian system grew the myth of the West as the realm of all things desired—as a symbol of freedom, money, travel, consumerism: what Alexey Yurchak calls the "imaginary West."[1] Ever since the turbulent years of perestroika and the early 1990s, when Soviet narratives were dismantled, the authorities have worked to create a new identity language that makes sense of Russia's history and current situation and of its relationship to the real and imaginary West, with the aim to generate a new national consensus.

Until the Russo-Ukraine War of 2022, the regime had been reluctant to commit to an official state ideology. Article 13 of the Russian Constitution of 1993 prohibits it: "Ideological plurality shall be recognized in the Russian Federation. No ideology may be instituted as a state-sponsored or mandatory ideology."[2] But over the years, ideology became a symbol of "cognitive independence" from the West and a key piece of the regime's approach to cultivating and maintaining a distinctly Russian worldview. And while the war has relaunched debates about abolishing Article 13 of the Constitution, the authorities have remained cognizant that such a project would face two major difficulties. First, Russian society has grown more diverse and fragmented in terms of lifestyles and ideological preferences: reinstating a program of forced indoctrination the way that this was done with Marxism-Leninism would be challenging. Second, imposing ideological constraints entails the corresponding development of a large-scale repressive apparatus to certify the application of dogma and punish the recalcitrant, including among the elite. The Putin team itself is a product of the fragmentation and globalization of

Russian society: it remembers the failure of the Soviet tools of repression in the last decades of the USSR, as well as the exorbitant costs associated with maintaining such a granular coercive system.

The challenge thus became: How to promulgate a new ideology without overtly assailing a fragmented society? How to develop a consensual "national idea" without officializing it as a new "state ideology"? For a long time, the solution devised by the Presidential Administration involved, firstly, saturating the public space in a bid to marginalize dissenting opinions, all the while manufacturing a wide ideological diversity within a space that follows the rules of a competitive marketplace of ideas. The different concepts launched in the public space had their own ideological exchange rates, and a whole world of ideological entrepreneurs, producers, and subcontractors took shape. The regime also limited its interference in society at large and did not force its ideational products on citizens, letting individuals manage their lives with their own sets of values—in what Levada Center sociologist Boris Dubin calls the "nonintrusive state" (*gosudarstvo, kotoroe ne dostaet*).[3]

Although this strategy worked for a long time, gradually the authorities felt the national consensus was weakening as some constituencies began showing an antiregime mindset, and with this, engaging in the search for alternative, counterhegemonic narratives. This pushed the authorities to move toward a more coherent program of doctrine-building, accompanied by a revival of Soviet-inspired indoctrination mechanisms and a more repressive policy toolkit—a dynamic that has been accelerating since the full-scale invasion of Ukraine.

ONE

ACTORS, NETWORKS, AND STRUCTURES

Russia needed a new political lexicon for communicating to ourselves and the external world images and meanings essential for the nation's historical subjectivity.

VLADISLAV SURKOV, 2007[1]

THERE HAVE BEEN SEVERAL goals of state ideological production: securing consensus for the political status quo by showing the validity of the current social order, sidelining any forms of opposition deemed as capable of causing dissension and chaos, and making it impossible to project an alternative future to that of the current regime. These goals have largely worked: the state has become a central purveyor of meanings for a large part of the Russian population, and Vladimir Putin has been seen as both personifying the country's destiny and simultaneously unaccountable for its everyday problems.[2] In this sense, the regime's production of ideology as not only textual and visual messages but also social practices fits the Althusserian vision of ideology as the "imagined existence of things."[3]

DEFINING AND TYPOLOGIZING IDEOLOGY

The lack of consensus on a definition of ideology contributes to the multiplicity of contradictory analyses of the Russian regime's relationship to the ideational realm. There are indeed several possible definitions, ranging from ideology as a worldview to ideology as a doctrine.[4] Some are broad, such as that of John Gerring, who sees it as "a set of idea-elements that are bound together, that belong to one another in a non-random fashion."[5] More precise definitions focus on ideology's social function, insisting on its class or group aspect: for Teun van Dijk, for instance, "ideologies are the fundamental social cognitions that reflect the basic aims, interest and values of the group,"[6] while Andreas Fagerholm sees ideology as "biased thoughts related to the organization of power and status in a society."[7]

A large part of the existing literature on ideology, especially in political science, has been limited by two assumptions. The first contends that ideology is produced by elites and functions in a top-down manner. Fagerholm presents it, for instance, as "a coherent set of biased political ideas that is distributed by elites and well-rooted in the minds of the (super)majority."[8] Yet a growing school proposes viewing ideology as a cocreation by society and its elites. Jost, Federico, and Napier, for instance, insist on the existence of a bottom-up ideology, of individual ideological proclivities that may or may not fit the elite-produced ideology and that are genuinely believed because they are cognitive processes that help make sense of the world[9]—a perspective I share.

As a second limitation, ideology is often projected on "Others": nondemocratic countries would have an ideology, but not liberal democracies. As the anthropologist Clifford Geertz observes, it is "one of the minor ironies of modern intellectual history that the term 'ideology' has itself become thoroughly ideologized."[10] Some scholars have brought nuance to this discussion, however. For instance, Juan Linz states that only totalitarian states have ideologies, while authoritarian regimes have "mentalities," which refers to a more flexible doxa spread throughout society.[11] Another difference would be that in a totalitarian regime, the center of gravity is the ideology itself, rather than the leader, and the main goal or ambition is not to keep the leader in power so much as to "remake society and the state in the image of that ideology."[12] While this makes a central distinction on the place of ideology in society (and places Russia in the authoritarian, not totalitarian, category), it is still founded on a restricted definition of ideology having to do with state propaganda.

Yet semiotics, anthropology, and cultural studies—all of which insist on the meaning-making effect of ideology—have shown that ideology exists in every political context, including democratic ones. In *Mythologies*, Roland Barthes describes myths as a metalanguage to make sense of the world, thereby helping to naturalize particular worldviews and power relations.[13] For Clifford Geertz, ideologies are symbolic systems that serve as a roadmap for a person in a complex social reality: they result in a creative adaptation by each of us.[14] The notion of narrative grammar proposed by French-Lithuanian semiologist Algirdas Greimas, according to which each narrative displays "plots linked to sequences of events, characters that operate as protagonists, and a set of moral imperatives and behavioral injunctions," stresses the importance of the storytelling aspect of ideology.[15]

Michel Foucault has shown that discourses, as "practices that systemically form the objects of which they speak," contribute to normalizing and legitimizing power relations and operate in both democratic and authoritarian contexts.[16] Following this tradition, I believe ideology is not limited to nondemocratic countries: every society shares some mainstream ideology (or is polarized around two clusters of ideologies, conservatism and progressivism, like the United States). What differs between a democratic and nondemocratic setting is whether citizens have the right to a plurality of ideologies and face different degrees of pressure exerted by dominant institutions, whether state or private, to enforce one ideology over others.

To take into consideration the contribution of semiotics to the research on ideology, I choose here Teun van Dijk's definition of ideology based on four criteria: it has internal structure as forms of shared social cognition; it controls socially shared attitudes on important social issues (such as immigration, abortion, the death penalty); it has foundational texts such as manifestos; and it is present in the everyday discourse, interaction, and practices of members of the ideological group and not only among politicians.[17] This definition combines ideology as a structure with some philosophical coherence, a global overview of the proper order of society, and a more political or policy-goal-oriented implementation aspect.

In this definition, ideology covers both elite and grassroots realities, as well as both ideational projections and practical or organizational aims. It therefore complements Geertz's elegant view that, even if ideologies may function as "disguises for ulterior motives" (mostly at the elite level), they are always "maps of problematic social reality" that attempt to "render otherwise incomprehensible social situations meaningful, to so construe them as to make it possible to act purposefully within them."[18] As mental maps, ideologies enable us to navigate the world and, therefore, should be seen as offering both *thought* and *behavior* patterns. This last point is crucial in the Russian case, where practice and rituals are central to signaling ideological conformity: the authorities are not so much interested in the thought aspect (that is, in who does or does not genuinely believe in what they express outwardly) as they are in the behavioral realm of what citizens display in the public space.

Agreeing on a definition of ideology does not dry out another piece of the debate, which relates to the categorization of ideologies (identifying, typologizing, and naming them) and their inner architecture. In Van Dijk's definition, which I share here, racism, antiracism, patriarchy, feminism, nationalism, socialism/communism, fascism, neoliberalism, and environmentalism, among others, are ideologies, while liberalism, conservatism, and illiberalism are meta-ideologies or aggregate clusters of ideologies in different combinations depending on the historical moment and the country's political culture.[19] The Russian state ideology should therefore be read as a cluster of ideologies, in the plural, rather than as any one single ideology in the conventional sense.

One of the limitations of this hierarchy, as with the majority of conceptual works around ideology, is that it interprets the ideational realm mostly through traditional textual culture. However, "thick" ideologies, as defined by Michael Freeden, are a product of classical modernity that belong to the past. The postmodern world, with its inherent ideological fluidity or liquidity (as framed by Polish sociologist Zygmunt Bauman[20]) may only produce "thin" ideologies. In a fragmented world based on the idea that knowledge is intersubjective and self-referential, the definition of ideology has been fundamentally transformed. Textual realities are partly disappearing, replaced by more visual and globally more sensory ones—a shift that remains largely understudied and will impact the way we define, name, and categorize ideologies.

Post-Soviet Russia offers a textbook case for the study of ideology: it exhibits both myriad doctrinal corpora as well as flexible grand narratives; its ideological construction is developed mostly for domestic audiences but in deep interplay with the international scene and foreign-policy strategies; and the regime has secured its hegemony through saturation of the discursive space and through practices of both co-option and repression. Disentangling ideology from action, and what is *downstream* from what is *upstream* from policy action, is obviously challenging. All our decisions are made according to our reading of the world: they are situational, adapted to changing contexts, and we can reconstruct a posteriori logics or arguments that were not explicit at the time of the facts. Is ideology feeding the regime's decisions, or arriving a posteriori to justify the decisions made?

To answer this question, one needs to recognize ideology as a puzzle with multiple pieces and layers that fit together. Going from the broader and vaguer to the more precise and bounded, I see at least three levels in the regime's ideological grammar. First, there exists a doxa or zeitgeist, meaning a nonhomogenous set of opinions, popular prejudices, and general presuppositions. This doxa is implicitly formulated and based on *Erfahrungsraum*, the "realm of experience" that shapes a society's interpretation of the world at a certain moment. It is deeply ingrained in the society's lived experience, the "thickness" of everyday social life, transgenerational memory, and horizontal pressures. I argue that the Russian regime relies on a doxa, or a core set of principles, formulated in the mid- to late 1990s, before Putin's rise to power, and which have not evolved much since. This set of principles can be summarized as follows: (1) Russia should not collapse as did the Soviet Union; (2) Russia should be recognized as a unique great power to be secured; and (3) the state embodies the Russian nation, hence society should be supportive of the regime and accept the prioritization of state interests over individual rights.

Second are metanarratives or strategic narratives structuring the regime's evolutions. They operationalize the three principles of the doxa to make then "commonsensical" in different, rapidly evolving, contexts.[21] These discursive constructs offer coherent and credible plots whose aim is to make sense of the political and social order. They are similar to what Marianne Kneuer calls "missions": unlike ideologies, missions, being "substantially flexible and modularly constituted," are constantly adapted to fit changing conditions.[22] They are produced in a reactive manner to changes in context. One can for instance identify five major strategic narratives that have now stabilized in state language: Russia as a civilization-state, Russia as katechon, Russia as defender of traditional values, Russia as the antifascist power, and Russia as the leading anticolonial force. These strategic narratives can be found in presidential discourses, major political figures' speeches, and official documents from the various ministries and state bodies.

Third are *topoi*, or ideologemes—small, key semantic units such as *gayropa* (a portmanteau of "gay" and "Europe"), "Ukronazism" (a portmanteau of "Ukraine" and "Nazism"), the "collective West," "Russophobia," "genocide," etc., that have pullulated in the public space. Their diffusion is particularly noticeable at the lower echelons of state production: they proliferate in institutions such as the Duma (Russia's parliament), and in media, especially television—Russia's infamous political talk shows have become launching pads for new ideologemes, one after another. Yet the chaos of ideologemes should obscure neither the coherence of the mental apparatus nor the roots of the displayed repertoires in intellectual history. Table 1.1 summarizes the three layers of the regime's ideological construction.

TABLE I.I.   Main layers of Russia's ideological construction.

Core Beliefs	Metanarratives	Ideologemes or *Topoi*
Russia cannot afford a new collapse	Russia as civilization-state	Such as
	Russia as katechon	Gayropa
Russia's should reassert itself in the world		Cultural codes
	Russia as defender of traditional values	Greater Eurasia
		Ukronazis
State has priority over citizens		Collective West
	Russia as the antifascist power	Russophobia
		Genocide
	Russia as the leading anticolonial force	

Source: Author

AN OPEN-ENDED IDEOLOGY

In Russia's ideological construction, chronology matters. The full-scale invasion of Ukraine is such a watershed that it pushes us to reread history through the eyes of a traumatized present. However, projecting onto the past the reality of today distorts the analysis.

One should first ask whether the regime of the past two decades can be envisioned as a single, unified phenomenon. Despite major evolutions, elements of continuity are numerous. At a human level, Putin and key members of his entourage have formed a relatively stable group since the early 2000s, even going back to the 1990s for those in his core inner circle with whom he worked during his time in Anatoly Sobchak's administration in St. Petersburg.[23] The regime has obvious difficulty renewing itself: looking at the sixty most famous Russian politicians, Nikolay Petrov concludes that their average age, as of January 2024, had risen to sixty-four.[24] This does not mean there are no new faces emerging, but when they do, they are often children or relatives of members of the inner circle, as best exemplified by Dmitry Patrushev: the agriculture minister and now deputy prime minister for agriculture is the son of Nikolay Patrushev, the former director of the FSB (the successor to the KGB) and the powerful Security Council of Russia, and now aide to the president. This continuity is also visible among the broader political elite in the middle and lower ranks of the *nomenklatura*; about 60 percent of them have a Soviet background, that is, either they or their parents had worked in the Soviet state system.[25]

At an ideological level, continuity is also visible. The Russian leadership's core set of principles has not evolved over the years, remaining anchored in the experience of the collapse of the Soviet Union and the chaotic 1990s. As we will see later, these core elements were expressed early on in Vladimir Putin's Millennium Manifesto of December 31, 1999, in which he insisted on the idea of Russia as a civilization unto itself, which cannot simply repeat Western models and which is shaped by greatness, statism, and national unity.[26]

While the three core principles have remained stable, their interpretation has evolved. Putin has, for instance, always believed that his mission was to restore Russia's status as a great power—this is a stable element of his geopolitical grammar. But the means of achieving this have changed, and with them, the strategic narratives: in the 2000s he believed that this great-power status could be reacquired by Russia with the approval, in good times and bad, of the West, and the integration of Russia into the global economy. Gradual failures to obtain this recognition (which, for Moscow, means a right of review over the former Soviet space) have fostered the idea of a great power that must reassert itself no longer *with* the West but *against* it. The definition of "against" has evolved too, from the sense of growing competition with the West on the international stage to the sense of being at war with the West through Ukraine as proxy. Just as important, the regime's public policy toolkit has significantly evolved over the years, from a genuine "honeymoon" between Putin and the population in the early 2000s into a much more repressive regime today. Fear of mass repression has indeed increased: according to the independent Levada Center, after decreasing in the 1990s and 2000s, fear of state repression has risen again, reaching a high of 51 percent in 2021, before going back down to 37 percent in January 2024.[27]

For a more granular approach to the continuities and discontinuities of the regime's ideological construction, one can divide it into three main eras: early Putinism, from Putin's taking office on December 31, 1999, to his return to the presidency in March 2012 after the Medvedev interlude; late Putinism, from the beginning of his third presidential term in 2012 to the full-scale invasion of Ukraine in 2022; and war Putinism, which has characterized his regime ever since. Obviously, this three-part division remains schematic and can be refined into many subdivisions. One can discuss, for instance, whether Medvedev's presidency in 2008–12 should be considered a part of early or late

Putinism: it was a genuine transition, promoting some forms of modernization and liberal thinking while simultaneously inaugurating the conservative turn and especially the Russian Orthodox Church's entry into state institutions.[28] Another element of continuity over these three eras is that wartime Putinism is doctrinally rooted in the 2020 constitutional amendments, as well as in the two texts published by Putin in 2020 and 2021 on interpretations of the Second World War and the alleged unity between Russians and Ukrainians.[29]

Reading the regime's ideological construction as both having core beliefs *and* being a set of evolving strategic narratives is essential if we want to avoid any teleological view of Russia, reading backward from the current reality. Yes, there is continuity over the quarter-century of Putin's power, yet there were always a multitude of possible futures other than the war against Ukraine. It was not predetermined in the regime's DNA that the Russian president would take such action. Putin's Ukrainian obsession is in some respects a given (see chapter 6), but in other ways it has been constructed by the regime's more global evolution, its interaction with the West, and could have evolved differently. Therefore, it is essential to identify the turning points that influenced the directions the regime took and reduced the possibility of alternative futures. It should also be remembered that for the Kremlin, the "special military operation" was supposed to resemble what happened in Budapest in 1956 or Prague in 1968, and therefore not generate an earthquake on the scale we know today. But once the war had become a reality on the ground, the regime was able to draw on both narratives and indoctrination methods that were already in place but which had not been fully deployed. It was therefore able with relative ease to adapt its ideological, indoctrination, and legal arsenal to the idea of a great civilizational war with the West.

IDEOLOGICAL PRODUCTION AS A SYSTEM AND A HIERARCHY

The regime's plurality in ideological production has been a built-in mechanism of its adaptation: the assemblage of discourse is a strategic tool in and of itself. Ideological products are encouraged and then downgraded regularly so the regime can stay flexible and adapt in a changing strategic environment. Gleb Pavlovsky, the father of political communication in Russia and the main image-maker of early Putinism (see below), coined one of the best descriptions of this survival toolkit: "The Kremlin's politics looks like a jazz group:

an uninterrupted improvisation as an attempt to survive the latest crisis."[30] Indeed, as in jazz, there is an established common theme or point, but each authorized player is allowed to improvise at will.

It would thus be a mistake to see this construction as slapdash or random: its major scripts have an inner logic, and the main cultural mythologies offered for consumption have been tightly routinized. The regime's ideological production has been founded on the postmodern idea of an eclectic bricolage of notions made available for broader consumption: polyphony and polysemy are by design and not by default. Floating signifiers are amalgamated from different language registers, and some notions are so furtive that they are difficult to capture, as Mikhail Suslov et al. demonstrate for the idea of pan-Slavism.[31] Fuzziness and interpretative elasticity are key elements of the functionality of this ideational system: ideological volatility, discursive shifts, reconfigurations, and repackaging are the norm. Consequently, the narratives promoted are contingency-specific. There is both ideological opportunism (the ability to adapt to a new context) *and* stability in the core set of beliefs.

For years, the different components of this ideological bricolage could coexist without extensive articulation: the aim was to test ideas and see what would stick. As Juliette Faure explains, "State support for ideology production . . . was not aimed at implementing a specific ideological program but rather at cultivating a set of lines and narratives opening up policy courses."[32] While the state has long manufactured a multiplicity of voices as long as they were not too explicitly oppositional, the room for expressing divergent views has gradually contracted into the production of a more uniform and rigid framing of domestic and international affairs. It would thus be wrong to see this polyphony as a cacophony: There is order in it, as the famous "vertical of power" also functions in the ideational realm. With the full-scale war, the "special military operation" is accompanied by a "special ideological operation," which is aimed at forcing unanimity within Russian public opinion, with new indoctrination mechanisms in place that echo those of the Soviet Union.[33]

As in all authoritarian regimes, the leader's personality matters and compensates for the lack of institutionalized divisions of power. Vladimir Putin obviously sits at the top of the pyramid, with some key figures around him representing different embodiments of the president, some more radical than Putin and others more moderate.[34] In the ideological realm, as in the other decision-making domains, Putin remains the supreme arbiter between different groups and visions. He is the center of the system in every sense of the word: the top of the chain to whom everyone turns, implicitly or explicitly, but also the ideological center in the sense that he cultivates a median position that speaks to different audiences. His voice is thus central in two dimensions: in the sense of being the core—the embodiment—of the system and in the sense of being in the middle, the centrism of the political landscape.

Putin's speeches are thus both the top of the pyramid and the tip of the iceberg: they should be read as both an upstream process (that is, resulting from a long process of crafting that takes into consideration several agencies and institutions with competing interests before producing an official, "final" version that all should agree on) and a downstream mechanism (that is, informing how other actors should position themselves and how the media should comment on them).

Although central, his speeches do not represent the language of the state in its entirety. Government agencies and official figures may bring nuances—more moderate or more radical—into a polyphonic narrative. The Russian president is said to have a genuine interest in history and to be an avid reader of history books, especially memoirs of prominent figures in Russian history and literature, but not of thinkers per se.[35] But he is not an ideational producer, nor the kind of ideologue who would spend hours reading philosophical texts, let alone writing them. He has a whole team around him, responsible for "digesting" various doctrinal texts and choosing the themes, even the quotations, that will populate his speeches. It is difficult to know whether he intervenes directly in the process, even if he may himself refer to some of the great names of Russia during his Direct Lines (even if this is a scripted event).

While there is no cult of personality in today's Russia on the level seen in totalitarian regimes, there has been a branding of the president as the embodiment of the nation. The Presidential Administration built up Putin's masculine virility identity in a flamboyant way in the 2000s and early 2010s. The glamorous and macho image of the president cultivated by the PR machine has contributed to the consolidation of a traditional manliness on the basis of three notions: physical bravery (Putin tranquilizing a Siberian tiger, hunting and fishing in the wilderness, and practicing extreme sports), technological mastery (Putin playing the role of fireman during the 2010 Moscow forest fires, riding a Harley-Davidson motorcycle, driving military trucks, and piloting military jets), and machismo (Putin pin-up calendars, "Putin girls" who present themselves as the president's virtual lovers and sing phrases such as "I want a man like Putin").[36] Putin's personal image-making has thus contributed to the widespread acceptance of gendered clichés on men and women's traditional roles. With the president's aging, the macho image has been partly replaced by Putin as the living expression of Russia's deep-seated national interests, the country's *longue durée* encapsulation, captured by Vyacheslav Volodin's crisp formula: "There is Putin—there is Russia; there is no Putin—there is no Russia."[37] This ontology of power has only consolidated since the full-scale war, which has seen Putin transform into a military commander and take on the role of a savior protecting the nation from an existential threat.

Around Putin, one can identify some political figures who play a greater role in the regime's ideological parlance than others. In his inner circle, for instance, neither FSB director Alexander Bortnikov; Sergey Ivanov, former head of the Presidential Administration and now special representative of the president; former minister of defense Sergey Shoigu; nor Rosneft chief Igor Sechin has expressed a sophisticated ideological position. By contrast, Nikolay Patrushev, whom we already mentioned as a key figure of the regime, and Sergey Naryshkin, former chief of the Presidential Administration of Russia, former chairman of the Russian State Duma, and now director of the Foreign Intelligence Service, have been vocal and prolific in their two decades in power with Putin, as has former president and current deputy chairman of the Security Council of Russia Dmitry Medvedev.

The three men in this latter group have published several articles that reflect their own interpretations of the regime's ideological core, each with their own nuances and stresses. As analyzed by Martin Kragh and Andreas Umland, both Patrushev and Naryshkin very early represented a more radical version of Putinism than Putin himself, displaying an obsession with anti-Americanism, Ukraine's submission to Russia, and the need for a multipolar world arrayed against the West. While Patrushev has been infatuated with the danger of "color revolutions," Naryshkin has focused on historical policy.[38] For his part, Medvedev has come to specialize in ultra-provocative social media statements against the West. The trio represent aggressive incarnations of Putin's more centrist and moderate positions, and have been key contributors to the Kremlin's infatuation with pseudoscience.[39] To them should be added figures who are said to be influential and close to the president but who do not express themselves publicly, chief among them probably Yury Kovalchuk. A billionaire reputed to be "Putin's personal banker," and a fervent supporter of mystical Orthodoxy and Russian imperialism, Kovalchuk is said to have inspired the president to pursue the war and seek the annexation of Ukraine.[40]

COMPETING IDEOLOGICAL ECOSYSTEMS

Moving beyond personalities, one can identify institutions and networks producing ideology, which I have called "ideological ecosystems." Unlike the Soviet regime, today's Russia does not have an institutionalized Politburo: it functions in a more flexible, patronal, and transactional way. Each of these ecosystems forms a specific realm made up of institutions, funders, and patrons, identifiable symbolic references, ideological entrepreneurs, media platforms, think tanks and discussion clubs, and civic organizations in constant motion, all making continual readjustments to maintain their equilibrium. Each has its own boundaries, but all are plastic and mobile, with lines of connection to and from other such ecosystems. These ecosystems partly overlap with the notion of Kremlin "towers" used to describe the different factions of the regime: above all, the "mobilization coalition" (the military-industrial complex and security services) and the "modernization coalition" (government "liberals" and private business).[41] These two "towers" exist in the ideological realm: looking at several tens of texts published by the regime's main figures, Ivan Fomin identifies a large spectrum of opinion going from "radical statism" to "radical liberalism (eleuthericism)," confirming that the Russian establishment was organized along two main poles of statism and liberalism and therefore far from ideologically monolithic, at least before the war.[42]

At the center of the regime one can find the Presidential Administration, which has a dual identity: it is an ecosystem in its own right, *and* it oversees the other ecosystems and their interaction. Since its creation in 2000, it has been the institutionalized apparatus in charge of producing, spreading, and checking ideological products. But for a long time it focused mostly on managing Putin's own branding and curating state media and on outsourcing ideological and doctrinal production to external actors and segments of civil society through, for instance, presidential grants.[43] Over the years, it has become increasingly involved in crafting new concepts itself, and in building its own doctrinal stock through its in-house institutions (see below).

Outside of the Presidential Administration, three major ecosystems exist inside the Kremlin: the military and security services, the political Orthodoxy, and the so-called "systemic liberals." The military-industrial complex encompasses all power agencies or *siloviki*: the FSB, the Ministry of the Interior and its security services, the National Guard, as well as the Ministry of Defense and the large military industries, both public and semiprivate. It is far from a unified ecosystem, and the struggles within it are intense, with the FSB leading the ideologization of public policy, while other institutions, especially the military, have a tradition of depoliticization.

This ecosystem shows the most continuity with the Soviet regime, for obvious structural reasons: it defends geopolitical and industrial interests that have not dramatically evolved, except insofar as they have had to adapt to a market economy and, in some cases, readjust their strategic calculus. At the human level, its main figures are mostly aging Soviet civil servants and high-ranking military officials. All of the military-industrial complex's actors believe in a traditional, Soviet-inspired system that molds individuals as "healthy patriots" and raises youth with a patriotic-military education. Over the years, a hardcore faction that pushes for more radical indoctrination has become more vocal—we can identify these as the hawks of the regime, or the "party of war."

The Orthodox realm is centered around the Russian Orthodox Church and its administrative body, the Moscow Patriarchate, surrounded by a looser network of groups promoting a more or less radical political Orthodoxy. One of its core places for blending church and state is the World Russian People's Congress, led by Patriarch Kirill. Created in 1993, it unites high-level clergy, the whole constellation of political Orthodoxy figures and institutions, and representatives of state institutions and Duma MPs (Putin and several ministers speak at its annual forum). All representatives of this ecosystem insist on Orthodoxy as the spiritual backbone of Russia, yet they should be differentiated from one another: the church's main goal is the re-Christianization of the country, while the political Orthodoxy groups interpret Orthodoxy as a political ideology more than a religious faith. If the patriarchate's mainstream position is conservative, some figures such as Metropolitan of Crimea and Sevastopol Tikhon (Shevkunov), rumored to be a potential successor to Patriarch Kirill, are pushing for the church to take the lead on a more reactionary agenda. A prominent cleric and best-selling writer often presented as Putin's personal confessor (something neither man has confirmed, although it is true that they meet often), Tikhon emerged from Orthodox fundamentalist circles: he was one of the initiators of the movement against electronic barcodes[44] before coming around to the patriarchate's view, though he has kept his radical vision of a reactionary Orthodoxy. Outside of the church, there coexist different antiliberal civil society groups: some apocalyptic ones that refer back to the medieval autocratic regime, some more classically monarchist groups nostalgic for the nineteenth-century Romanov tsars, and the modernists who promote a monarchism better adapted to today's conditions and who focus on reactionary family policy inspired by the US Christian right.[45]

The third ecosystem is that of the "systemic liberals" (*sislibs* in Russian). This term groups the technocratic elite that emerged during the late Yeltsin through early Putin eras and formed at that time a core cluster of the regime, especially visible during the Medvedev administration. They were supportive of Russia's reassertion on the global scene but read this reassertion through Russia's normalization and integration into the world order. Since then, their place in the regime's global balance has diminished, to the advantage of the *siloviki*, and they have been gradually confined to the economic and finance realm. With the full-scale war, some have become very cautious and even kept silent, such as former minister of finance and chairman of the accounts chamber Alexey Kudrin. Others have remained loyal to the regime and played an integral part therein while continuing to distance themselves from the party of war, such as Central Bank Governor Elvira Nabiullina and Moscow Mayor Sergey Sobyanin. A third group has embraced the new course: Dmitry Medvedev epitomizes this transformation from a modernizer to a virulent hawk, whose public role is now to produce the most provocative statements. A similar path has been taken by first deputy chief of staff of the Presidential Administration Sergey Kiriyenko, now in charge of managing Ukraine's occupied territories and crafting new mechanisms for ideological indoctrination.

Even after identifying the Kremlin's main ideological ecosystems, we are still lacking a complete picture of the whole intermediate layer of institutions and actors—both public and private, at the national and local levels—whose job is to create and disseminate ideological products in Russian society and abroad. What is the role of the establishment in building ideology? It is challenging to decipher what is genuine cocreation from what is *cueing*, "a process by which highly placed individuals carefully read Kremlin signals and adopt policies that mirror those of the top leadership."[46]

The latest survey of Russian elites conducted by Hamilton College in early

2020 show them to be mostly focused on domestic issues and worried about Russia's inability to solve its own domestic problems, yet more ready than before to send troops abroad to help friendly regimes. The *siloviki* segment was notable for its greater anti-Westernism and conspiracy mindset than in the cases of its civilian counterparts, but the number of elites favoring a Russia-Ukraine unification was then at its lowest, even among *siloviki*.[47] From this snapshot one can suppose that there is both cocreation of some broad set of principles or values, for instance on anti-Americanism,[48] and cueing on specific strategic decisions made by Putin and his inner circle, for instance on the full-scale invasion or the theory of the "absorption" of Ukraine.

We also have no good measure of the role in producing ideologies played by the two national legislative chambers, the Duma and the Federation Council, or by the consultative Civic Chamber.[49] As Julian G. Waller suggests, the production of narratives to feed the regime's ideological needs "can best be understood as an entrepreneurial behavior by lower-tier elites signaling loyalty and usefulness to the regime center."[50] We know even less about what goes on at the bureaucratic level. As in other fields, the government and ministries work mostly as executive bodies in charge of implementing what has been decided, though they are not themselves the decisionmakers. But what are the mechanisms, institutions, and places of production, and who are their agents and in-between actors, that allow ideas to trickle down and upward with regard to bureaucratic production? How do we get from intellectuals' "big discourse" to the "small discourse" of politicians, lawyers, and policymakers, and vice versa?

IDEOLOGICAL ENTREPRENEURSHIP

To solve part of this puzzle, it is worth developing the notion of entrepreneurial behavior and its relationship to ideational production. The Russian regime blends the idea of the state as the main provider of support to the most fragile social groups, on the one hand, and a neoliberal strategy of outsourcing work to nonstate actors to reduce the costs related to administering a massive bureaucracy, on the other. This neoliberal element means that public and private actors work together, due either to clientelism (private actors receiving privileged access to public funding and bidding on state contracts) or to a more intimate mixing (such as the same person having both a position in the civil service and a private business—a practice that is by no means unique to Russia). In the Russian context, the ideological market is an opportunity to generate not only revenue but also social capital: funding from a state institution is less significant as a source of financial revenue than as a source of political revenue that guarantees connections inside the system and access to a pool of potential patrons.

This neoliberal structure has given birth to what I have called entrepreneurs of influence—individuals without official status in the state administration who nevertheless have a patron inside the system and have been able to build for themselves a niche of activities that they oversee using their own funds.[51] They may, of course, attempt to get state funding of different kinds, but they function through privatized mechanisms of influence. They take the risks of their actions; they often tap their own financial and social capital to invest in a sector, hoping that the Kremlin will provide a return on their investment (financial and/or political), but knowing that they may fail and be disavowed by the authorities or become a casualty of their competitors' settling of scores.

The notion of an entrepreneur of influence is grounded in a large body of literature that has documented the inner machinery and logistics of Russian power since the collapse of the Soviet Union. During the turbulent 1990s, violent entrepreneurship dominated the shift toward a market economy, epitomized by the infamous "thieves-in-law" (*vory v zakone*—big mafia bosses with patrons inside the political system and law-enforcement agencies).[52] Some entrepreneurs of influence offer "violent influence," among them the infamous Chechen leader Ramzan Kadyrov and the late Yevgeny Prigozhin, who have provided paramilitary services to the Russian regime; others, such as the tycoon Konstantin Malofeev, occupy the niche of moral values entrepreneurship and can be defined as an ideological entrepreneur of influence because they use their own capital to advance a relatively coherent ideological agenda.

POPULAR CULTURE

Another tool of the regime's consolidation of its hegemony has been the successful use of popular culture.[53] One has to remember that at the end of the presidential campaign that elected Putin in March 2000, the newspaper *Kommersant-Vlast'* ran a front-page story titled "Stierlitz, Our President"—a direct reference to the hero of the Soviet cult television series *Seventeen Mo-*

ments of Spring.⁵⁴ The series' hero, Maksim Isaev, who operated under the name Max Otto von Stierlitz, became the iconic Soviet version of James Bond—but while Bond is a man of action, Stierlitz embodies an intellectual spy trying to preserve honesty and authenticity in a corrupt world. As film critic and screenwriter Maya Turovskaya notes, "*Seventeen Moments of Spring* structured the late Soviet imagination with respect to fascism with greater force than the well-known ideological stereotypes or extremely sparse historical literature."⁵⁵ This blending of fiction and reality, with the analogization of Putin to Stierlitz, has initiated a trend that continues to this day, with the regime investing massively in cultural production.

Indeed, the state has since poured massive sums into supporting the entertainment sector and pushing it to produce more patriotic content, a process supervised and channeled through such agencies as the Presidential Council for Culture and the Presidential Directorate for Social Projects, among others. Obviously, television has been key: politics and entertainment have merged in the tradition of political talk shows as "infotainment," propelled by their popular hosts, such as Dmitry Kiselyov, Vladimir Soloviev, and Olga Skobeeva.⁵⁶ But television series, pop music bands, sports, as well as youth subculture (rap and hip-hop, graffiti, gaming, etc.), have not been forgotten. There are many important players behind these scenes. For visual entertainment, Konstantin Ernst, the CEO of Channel One Russia, as well as world-famous film director Nikita Mikhalkov, have led the patriotic and conservative cultural turn in cinema and miniseries, handing out lavish funding for projects that align with their ideological orientation.

The 2024 Kremlin leaks revealed by the Baltic investigative journalist platform Delfi have offered a window into this construction: to prepare for the March 2024 presidential election, the Presidential Directorate for Social Projects spent hundreds of billions of rubles to produce creative works insisting on traditional values and positive changes in Russians' lives. Among the main structure in charge of funding this entertainment sector has been the Institute for Internet Development, created in 2015 and led by Alexey Goreslavsky, which now finances mostly movies and television shows. However, here too there are cocreated mechanisms, as the authorities seem to claim ownership of every successful film or series, even when film directors themselves have not been informed that their productions were considered part of regime promotion.⁵⁷

WHEN POLIT-TECHNOLOGY BLENDS WITH INTELLECTUAL HISTORY

One can discuss how much of the "software" of today's ideological production is the result of Soviet-era legacies or a byproduct of the post-Soviet period. The Soviet regime featured a highly developed ideational toolkit. Ideology was omnipresent in many aspects of everyday life, even if largely discredited and seen mainly as an exercise in conformity in the public space.[58] This paradox shaped late Soviet culture, which is the intellectual cradle in which today politicians and ideologues were trained and socialized. The Moscow Methodological Circle, for instance, emerging in the 1960s and led by Georgy Shchedrovitsky (1929–1994), gave rise to a second generation of thinkers who drove post-Soviet ideological construction. Called the "methodologists" (*metodologi*), they have been instrumental in spreading among the establishment the ideas of managerial governance and social engineering,[59] and have been often denounced—unfairly—as a kind of pseudoscientific sect resembling Scientology. But dissident intellectual production has its own legacy too: several underground circles of bohemian intellectuals and artists from Moscow and Leningrad, such as the Yuzhinsky-Golovin circle, have inspired contemporary ideologues such as Alexander Dugin, who have stayed connected to countercultural circles and the conservative avant-garde.[60]

This Soviet legacy, both official and dissident, has accentuated the high sensibility of the whole Russian political class to everything semantic and semiotic, up to the point of creating the notion of polit-technologies—sophisticated political marketing and ideational creativity around politics.[61] In the early 1990s, a huge range of public relations firms emerged, often with sponsors or links to US firms interested in supporting the liberals in their transformations, as well as in making money on a new market of potential consumers.[62] The phenomenon was so massive that it became a Russian term in itself: *piar* (PR, in Russian). This spin-doctoring offered easy enrichment to thousands of communication and marketing specialists—often with a professional past in the agitprop world—and played a major role in replacing "real" politics with an illusory one. Polit-technologists proceed indeed from the idea that power is just a managerial technique with an ideological façade and that societies can be engineered technocratically.[63] The responsibility of this PR community in failing the young Russian democracy has been masterfully framed by Viktor Pelevin, one of the leading contemporary Russian writers, in his novel *Generation P*, which denounces the cynicism of these political technologies.⁶⁴

A central figure of the polit-technology culture was Gleb Pavlovsky (1951–2023), a former dissident inspired by leftist theories and science fiction from the Strugatsky brothers, Arkady and Boris. Ivan Krastev aptly describes his polit-technology as "a Molotov cocktail of French postmodernism and KGB instrumentalism."⁶⁵ At the peak of its influence in the later 1990s and early 2000s, Pavlovsky was the regime's primary image-maker, and his Foundation for Effective Politics (FEP) oversaw PR strategies and image campaigns for the Kremlin and some regional authorities. He was also one of the first to see the potential of the internet and launched dozens of online papers and news portals that would become influential in the 2000s, incubating prolific "idea factories" where intellectuals and polit-technologists would cross paths.⁶⁶ In search of a new values language, Pavlovsky foresaw nationalism, conservatism, and the Russian World as central repertoires for Russia, before gradually retreating and taking a more critical position on the regime's evolution.⁶⁷

In the 2000s, the Kremlin managed to launch new clusters for a more bureaucratic production of ideas. Western-inspired think tanks such as the Valdai Club and the Russian International Affairs Council (RIAC), came to complement analytical centers working internally, close to the security services, such as the influential Council for Foreign and Defense Policy headed by Sergey Karaganov, and the Russian Institute for Strategic Studies (RISI).⁶⁸ With regard to domestic policy, the Presidential Administration has had its own in-house think tank, the Institute of Socio-Economic and Political Research (ISEPI), influential mostly in the mid-2010s. It seems now to rely more on the Social Research Expert Institute (EISI), in charge of several new war-related ideological projects. Not in-house but connected to state structures are the Institute for National Strategy, led by Mikhail Remizov, and the Center for Strategic Research, formerly led by liberal finance minister Alexey Kudrin. The revival of academia after the difficult 1990s also helped to revitalize intellectual production: IMEMO (Institute of World Economy and International Relations) and MGIMO (Moscow State Institute of International Relations) have pursued their Soviet-time specialization in international affairs; Moscow State University and the Higher School of Economics elaborate domestic and "conceptual" policy; and the Institute of History at the Academy of Sciences and the Russian State Archives deal with historical policy.

Part of the complex picture of Russia's ideological construction relies on the relationship between public intellectuals and classic academics, on the one hand, and the authorities, on the other. This relationship is ambivalent: the former may be seen by an external observer as working at the service of the Kremlin—though this negates their own perception of autonomy, as well as their resentment or delusion regarding how the authorities adopt, steal, and/or reframe their intellectual contributions.[69] The notion of a *discursive habitat* is probably the most useful to encapsulate the many layers of intellectual production that enable the regime to produce ideology. As Elias Götz and Jørgen Staun explain, this discursive habitat "circumscribes how government officials understand the world, enabling some policy avenues while closing down others."[70] The question of Russia's knowledge-power nexus, as well as of academia as enabler of violence—the intellectual and academic responsibility in creating an ideological habitat that made the war possible—will remain central moving forward.

A LARGE DOCTRINAL POOL TO DRAW FROM

While the regime has been able to produce an impressive amount of ideational content, it has also demonstrated an incredible capacity to absorb. This is visible in the way the authorities have co-opted, integrated, and transformed doctrines. Here I define "doctrines" as textual corpora that offer ideological coherence to a higher degree than the state-sponsored strategic narratives and are developed by identifiable authors or institutional propagators outside of public administration. To feed its ideational constellation, the regime relies on a large pool of already existing cultural mythologies. Aliaksei Kazharski summarizes it tidily: "Discursive practices are dependent on the sum of preceding textualities that are available for recycling. Looking at this dependency implies studying how texts are 'made possible' by other texts."[71] Therefore, it is critical to understand the morphology of textualities and the pool of ideas already available to capture how new layers are structured. This does not mean promoting a path-dependency theory rooted in a primordialist vision of Russia which would indicate that the country and its elites have merely reproduced a preexisting worldview: the regime is profoundly in tune with the globalized world and inspired by it.

I identify at least seven main doctrines in today's Russia from which the regime cherry-picks. Two of them are theology-based, generated by religious institutions: that of the Russian Orthodox Church and that of the Islamic muftiates. The church can mobilize a strong image of spiritual continuity and rootedness in the past that favors the regime's search for national consensus, and the muftiates reverberate similar symbolic politics to their own constituencies. While both play a central role in supporting state ideology, they remain autonomous from it thanks to their religious missions, which are broader in time and space than the Kremlin's state-centric ideology. They struggle to find an equilibrium between being seen as the state's right hand in religious matters and retaining legitimacy in the eyes of their respective communities of believers. Areas of tension or divergence can be seen in terms of mores and family values (the church and the muftiates are more conservative than the state); in terms of memory policy (the church is more critical of the Soviet regime's atheism and mass violence than is the state, even if this cautious stance has been diminished gradually); in terms of national identity (the church is more ethnonationalist than the state, while the muftiates are more concerned with promoting Islamic identity and local ethnic identities than the state); and in terms of foreign policy (both the church and the muftiates are less aggressive than the state and are internally divided on Russia's foreign policy).[72]

A third doctrine that contributes to the state kaleidoscope is what may be referred to a "Russian Communism," represented by the Communist Party of the Russian Federation (CPRF) and its intellectual and political figures. It predated the state in combining Marxism-Leninism and Russian nationalism, in particular Stalinist National-Bolshevism and the rehabilitation of Orthodoxy.[73] It advances a stronger Soviet nostalgia than the state's and employs more leftist political language, insisting on social justice, a welfare state, and renationalization, while criticizing privatization and neoliberalism. It has its own audience and constituencies (mostly elderly and provincial voters, but has also captured part of the younger middle class who can express opposition to the establishment through it), who may both support the regime in principle and yet still compete electorally with the presidential party United Russia.[74] The Kremlin has gradually reintegrated into its constellation several doctrinal components from the Russian Communist school, including social justice and a Russocentric reading of Soviet doctrine. Moreover, when it comes to foreign policy, the state has endeavored to present Russia to its Chinese partners as the legitimate heir of the Soviet Union and Marxism by having Communist Party leader Gennadi Zyuganov participate in high-level diplomatic exchanges between the two countries.

Three other doctrinal schools revolve around those whom Katharina Bluhm calls "conceptual ideologues"—intellectual figures who promote a certain political agenda and undertake organizational activities around their ideas.⁷⁵ Their intellectual production targets more the regime than public opinion. These are members of the imperial-Eurasianist school, which proposes a messianic and aggressive ideology for Russia (exemplified by the writings of Alexander Dugin and Alexander Prokhanov);⁷⁶ the Young Conservative school, which advanced a more moderate, European-inspired conservatism and favors a civilizationist isolationism for Russia (with Mikhail Remizov and Boris Mezhuev as key figures); and the monarchist and "White" school, which defends a vision of Russia inspired by late tsarism and the White emigration, with the reactionary thinker Ivan Ilyin (1883–1954) as its major intellectual point of reference. The latter school is led by the media tycoon Konstantin Malofeev and brings together mainly cultural figures such as film director Nikita Mikhalkov.⁷⁷

A new seventh doctrine, which one might describe as "Z-patriotism," is still in formation at the time of writing. Born of the war experience, it is developed by military bloggers who have become key opinion leaders in an increasingly uniform public space.⁷⁸ "Z" doctrine is intimately linked to state ideology (many military bloggers work for or at least cooperate closely with the Ministry of Defense) but retains autonomy from it. Populist in nature, it denounces the elites for their corruption and lack of willingness to defend Russia, a criticism that has resulted in the repression of its key figures by the state: first Wagner leader Yevgeny Prigozhin, who was killed in a plane crash in August 2023 in what many believe was a Kremlin-plotted assassination in response to his failed mutiny in June, and then former Donbas warlord and Russian nationalist Igor Girkin-Strelkov, who is serving time in jail.

This "Z" doctrine stands out from other corpora because it does not offer classical doctrines in the sense of long, sophisticated texts—even if one can identify more classic ideologues such as writer Zakar Prilepin. Represented mostly on social media, it features shorter texts (in the form of blogs, as well as poetry, memoirs, and diaries of soldiers) and has strong visual (memes, photos) and musical components. Yet it can be considered a doctrine in the sense that it offers a full-scale vision of what the social order should be. Similar to the Communist, church, and muftiate doctrines, the "Z" doctrine has its own audience and is embedded in social life through networks of veterans and volunteer groups supporting the front.

These intellectual traditions are rediscovered, reinterpreted, and instrumentalized when needed, often in a very opportunistic way, by the regime (table 1.2). They are not directly *informing* it. For example, it is neither the late reactionary émigré philosopher Ivan Ilyin nor the contemporary far-right ideologue Dugin who *inspire* the Kremlin's vision of Russia. It is rather a vision of Russia that emerged in lived experiences by Putin's inner circles and more broadly the establishment, which then looked for intellectual soil and a better-articulated doctrine to justify and nurture itself. These nuances are fundamental if we are to capture what is downstream and what is upstream in the Kremlin's ideological production. Indeed, existing scholarship tends to conflate the two movements: upstream are those feeding ideational products to the Kremlin (which are then read by the Presidential Administration's departments in charge of narrative-framing), and downstream are those amplifying the narratives put out by the Kremlin. Many actors of the Russian ideological realm function both upstream and downstream. As Juliette Faure shows, the regime's interaction with the broad field of ideological actors is thus a two-way street, and this cocreational nature should thus be emphasized if one wants to understand the regime's ability to adapt.[79]

The regime's current ideological construction is both more flexible and more organic than the Soviet doctrine and is capable of adapting to quickly evolving realities. An eclectic patchwork of diverse, sometimes contradictory narratives, it has core parts but no standardized identifiable sources, whereas

TABLE 1.2. Main actors and institutions of ideological production.

Kremlin's ecosystems	Presidential Administration, *Siloviki*, Orthodoxy, "systemic liberals"
Main think tanks	Council for Foreign and Defense Policy, Institute of Socio-Economic and Political Research (ISEPI), Social Research Expert Institute (EISI), Institute for National Strategy, Center for Strategic Research, Valdai Club, etc.
Doctrine-producers and entrepreneurs of influence	ROC and Muftiates, "Russian Communism," Young Conservatives, Izborsky Club, White Russia, "Z" patriotism

Source: Author

Marxism-Leninism offered a full teleological interpretation of the world with highly codified symbols and state-sponsored rituals. At least until the full-scale war against Ukraine, producers of ideology had transactional relationships with state structures—a neoliberal marketplace of ideas in which to buy and sell. With the onset of the war, the recentralization trend has accelerated, and more Soviet-style mechanisms have reappeared, yet without reaching the same level of internal cohesion and top-down circulation. Indeed, more important than the structure of the content itself, Soviet ideology was taught through a huge web of vertically organized higher education institutions, agitprop schools, and trade union structures, with cells in every workplace and every leisure organization, making it deeply embedded into the social life of every citizen, which is not the case—at least so far—for the current ideology.

TWO

THE SEDIMENTATION OF IDEOLOGY

Today we do not have a monopoly on ideology; however, we have thrown out the baby with the bathwater.
VLADIMIR PUTIN, 2012[1]

DEBATES ABOUT THE EXISTENCE of an official ideology in Russia have largely revolved around the question of the regime's ideological evolution over more than two decades under Putin's reign. Some argue that the Russian president has had an established ideology ever since he took office, while others see a gradual construction that has been reactive to events. Both interpretations can be true and compatible if we dissociate abstract goals to be achieved from the tools or means for reaching them. The current regime has always had three main *goals*, formulated since Putin's Millenium Manifesto of December 1999: stability at the state or regime level (state and regime are conflated, from the Kremlin's point of view); consensus at the societal level; and recognition of Russia's strategic sovereignty by the West, and in particular by the United States, at the international level. What has changed over the years is not the goals but the *ideational toolkit*, as well as the *policies* made available for achieving those goals. That is why I use the notion of sedimentation to analyze Russia's ideological evolution and present here a brief chronology of this evolutionary process, divided in three broad periods of early, late, and war "Putinism."[2]

REBUILDING POLITICAL HEGEMONY: THE BIRTH OF CENTRISM (1994–1999)

The often-mentioned personality and policy contrast between Boris Yeltsin and Vladimir Putin should not obscure major continuities. Presidentialism in Russia has been institutionalized since the adoption of the 1993 Constitution, such that the prime minister has never played a major role in the formulation of state policies. The same applies in the ideology-related realm: Putin has embraced and systematized the conclusions drawn from the dynamic of weakening ideological polarization that preceded him. "Putinism" cannot be understood without connecting it to its legacy of political centrism under Yeltsin's second term, even if, obviously, some ideational products were reinterpreted over the years.

The 1993 Turning Point

From the last years of perestroika until 1994, the Russian elite engaged in a discourse that advocated for the establishment of a "normal country" (read: Western), revealing how they were anxious to make up for what was seen as lost time and to terminate as soon as possible the development path taken by the Soviet Union. The conservative putsch of August 19, 1991, which ousted Mikhail Gorbachev from office for three days, did not enjoy popular support; rather, it served to discredit proponents of the status quo and strengthened the reformers' position. The supporters of liberal "shock therapy" gathered around Boris Yeltsin, who was elected chairman of the Supreme Soviet of Russia in March 1990 and then president of Russia on June 12, 1991. In the midst of this pro-Western consensus, only a few dissenting voices asserted themselves: those of the Communist Party of the Russian Federation (CPRF), which was formed from the ashes of the old Communist Party of the Soviet Union and led by Gennadi Zyuganov; the ill-named Liberal-Democratic Party of Russia (LDPR), led by the far-right eccentric Vladimir Zhirinovsky; and the Moscow Patriarchate (the administrative body of the Russian Orthodox Church [ROC]). All sought continued consideration of Russian civilization's specific character, thought to be unassimilable into the Western model, and the need for Russia to remain a respected great power on the international scene.

After the Soviet Union was dissolved in December 1991, however, the violent impact of social and economic change was such that the widespread support enjoyed by what was seen as the march toward a dual process of Westernization, both economic and political (the introduction of a market economy and the establishment of a parliamentary system), weakened quickly. Soaring prices, the loss of savings accumulated during the Soviet period, the collapse of living standards, massive closures of factories and businesses, the elimination of social benefits (especially for pensioners), and late payment of salaries—all broke the pro-Western consensus in 1992 and 1993. A brutally impoverished society, the wild privatization of large industrial enterprises, and the birth of a privileged class enjoying social success based on its control of the shadow economy—all deeply offended a population accustomed to Soviet uniformity in its way of life.

Unlike in Central Europe, in Russia the Communist *nomenklatura* was the main agent of the transition to a market economy. While former dissidents were largely absent from the post-Soviet political scene, former Communist Party members easily benefited from privatization, fueling the view that the Soviet collapse had been programmed and plotted by elites who had betrayed the egalitarian ideal of the regime.[3] As a result of these unprecedented changes, "democracy" was equated with the ravages of capitalism and gradually became a negative, even insulting, term in a system that refused to recognize the oligarchs' pillaging of wealth for what it was: the Russian word *dermokratiya*, revealingly coined around this time, mixes the words for "democracy" and "shit." The discourse on the absence of a new ideology for the country was also seen as hypocrisy. The presence of Western donors was interpreted as a proof of "Western economic diktat," and liberalism, especially in economic terms, was perceived as a new ideology imposed by force. References to the "European example" faded, and political rights were considered secondary to dealing with the material problems of individual survival and social justice.

The first political shock to hit the fledgling Russian democracy came in the fall of 1993, after Yeltsin won a hard-fought referendum on continued reforms (though he garnered 58 percent of the vote, turnout was only 53 percent). Yeltsin presented a draft constitution to the Supreme Soviet, then dominated by Communists and nationalists, which rejected it. He then decided to dissolve parliament, which responded by voting for his impeachment. A state of emergency was declared on September 24, and military troops loyal to the president stormed the parliament building on October 4, officially leaving more than 150 dead. This bloody event has played an important role in the collective memory of post-Soviet Russia, as it seemed that the democratic project ended in bloodshed, and the country nearly descended into civil war.

The event also marked the beginning of the presidentialization of the regime: the self-proclaimed democrats and liberals—supported by Western countries—endorsed the use of violence against an elected parliament and supported the December 12 referendum that favored a new constitution with weaker legislative powers and a stronger executive.[4] To avoid what was perceived as a step backward, they backed Yeltsin in his muscular demonstration of power and demonization of the Communist opposition. They propagated the idea that in its march toward the West, Russia needed to maintain an authoritarian regime—which was legitimate because it supported liberal values—that would disregard the defiant, "red-brown" coalition of Communists and nationalists, branded as an existential danger to democracy.

1994–1995: Decreasing Political Polarization

After such a moment of tension, it became clear that the liberal reforms would be conducted in a less intensive and less ideological manner. As early as February 1994, the Duma granted amnesty to the August 1991 putsch planners and the October 1993 insurgents, thus enabling figures like Ruslan Khasbulatov and Alexander Rutskoy to return to political life.[5] In April, the Kremlin proposed a civic agreement whose signatories thereby vowed not to overthrow the constitutional order or organize massive, extra-parliamentary regime-change movements. More than two hundred associations signed it, including the LDPR, the liberals, and Democratic Choice of Russia, while the CPRF and the Agrarian Party refused, seeing it as a restriction on their freedom. President Yeltsin, in his annual address, called for the country's problems to be resolved through a "new conception of co-citizenship (*sograzhdanstvo*) of the nation."[6] That same year, Yeltsin's visit to an exhibition of the nationalist painter Ilia Glazunov caused a scandal among liberals, who were confounded by the president's symbolic validation of one of the major figures of Soviet antisemitism (Yeltsin then commissioned him to redecorate some of the Kremlin Palace).[7]

Shocked by the unexpected popular support enjoyed by the opponents of reform, some liberals began to view the ideological polarization of the country as an excessive price to pay for the establishment of democracy and a market economy, especially in the context of the First War in Chechnya, which shook the foundation of the new Russian Federation. The fiftieth anniversary of the end of the Second World War in May 1995 offered the opportunity to exult in Russia's prestigious past and reaffirm the importance of national sentiment. While the CPRF tried to capture the event by linking Soviet patriotism to Zyuganov personally, the Kremlin played the card of reconciliation between "Whites" (anti-Bolsheviks) and "Reds" (Bolsheviks) around the cult of the military.[8]

On May 9, 1995, a large memorial park commemorating the war was inaugurated in Poklonnaya Gora, an inner-ring suburb of Moscow. A statue of Marshal Zhukov, who had accepted the surrender of Berlin at the end of the Second World War, was restored on Manege Square near the Kremlin, and a new sculpture representing the historic victories of Russia over the Mongols, Napoleon, and Nazi Germany was built on Kutuzovsky Avenue. Stamps commemorating Stalin, Roosevelt, and Churchill were issued. The discourse on repentance for past crimes—especially those of Stalin—which had been a driving force of perestroika, slowly faded. On March 15, 1996, the Communist-dominated Duma repealed its recognition of the Belovezha Accords, signed on December 8, 1991, and approved by the Supreme Soviet, which validated the dissolution of the Soviet Union. The Duma also bestowed legality on the referendum of March 17, 1991, when 70 percent of the population voted to maintain the Soviet structure.

Despite the Kremlin's efforts to reappropriate patriotic symbols of the motherland, the defeat of the liberals in the 1995 legislative elections was even more sweeping than in 1993. They failed to receive even 20 percent of the votes, with the party Our Home-Russia, headed by Prime Minister Chernomyrdin, receiving 10 percent; the social-democratic party Yabloko, led by Grigory Yavlinsky, at 7 percent; and Democratic Choice of Russia, led by Gaydar, receiving a mere 3.9 percent. Facing them, so-called patriotic forces won almost half of the voting-age population (23 percent for Zyuganov and 11 percent for Zhirinovsky). Confronted with Zyuganov's immense popularity, a sick and weakened Boris Yeltsin became concerned about his prospects for reelection, which were in no way guaranteed. He then decided to campaign on more centrist issues rather than the continuation of reforms. His readiness for pragmatic compromise was demonstrated by his insistence on closer ties with Belarus and the formation of a Russian-Belarusian union reminiscent of the Soviet Union.

In order to weaken the Communist candidate, the Kremlin brought on board General Alexander Lebed (1950–2002), governor of the Krasnoyarsk krai, who had received 14.5 percent of the vote in the first round of the presidential elections and then joined the incumbent president in the second round, bringing with him votes that would otherwise have gone to Zyuganov. Thanks to the media's demonization of the CPRF, which was presented as the "party of the past," the inflation of a "red-brown" peril, and huge support from American PR consultants,[9] Boris Yeltsin won the election with nearly 55 percent of the vote but with little popular enthusiasm. Surveys confirmed the majority feeling among Russians that there had been a lack of choice and that they had voted according to the logic of the "lesser evil."[10]

1996: The First Call for a New National Ideology

Once reelected to his second term, Boris Yeltsin immediately set about promoting Russian national identity and quickly lifted the ideological ban that had been imposed on patriotic themes.[11] In 1995, the chairman of the Federation Council, Vladimir Shumeyko, and the press secretary for the president, Vyacheslav Kostikov, began invoking Russia's need for "democratic patriotism." This term was also employed in the president's statement to the National Assembly on "Strengthening the Rule of Law in Russia,"[12] in which he mentioned the formation of a civic Russian identity and the need for a strong state, as well as the importance of reintegrating the post-Soviet space around Russia and reaffirming the country's unity and indivisibility.

On June 12, 1996, the national holiday celebrating the adoption of the Declaration of Sovereignty of the Russian Federation in 1990, Boris Yeltsin raised the possibility of forming a new national ideal: "There were different periods in Russia's twentieth-century history—the monarchy, totalitarianism, perestroika, and the democratic path of development. Each era had its ideology. We do not have one." He concluded by explaining that "the most important thing for Russia is the search for a national idea, a national ideology."[13] This statement raised concerns among some politicians and intellectuals, who pointed out that Article 13 of the Constitution stipulated that the state was prohibited from establishing an official or mandatory ideology.

Nationalist opponents of Yeltsin interpreted the presidential remarks as an indirect validation but also as an attempt to usurp a topic that had never belonged to the liberals. In October, the Duma Committee for Geopolitics, headed by the LDPR, organized parliamentary readings on the "Russian Idea" and the need to provide the country with a new ideology. Members of the LDPR and the Congress of Russian Communities (KRO), a small structure inspired by Alexander Solzhenitsyn's idea and led by Dmitry Rogozin that emphasized the need to protect Russian compatriots abroad, called on the Duma to vote in favor of an ethnic definition of Russianness and criticized the rise of neo-Eurasianism as promoted by "red-brown" ideologists Alexander Dugin and Alexander Prokhanov.[14]

President Yeltsin's speech calling for a new ideology for the Russian Federation was followed by a series of official initiatives: a study group was established, headed by presidential advisor and director of the sociological center INDEM, Georgy Satarov, who was known for his commitment to perestroika and rapprochement with Europe.[15] This group never reached an agreement on any final text and simply organized the publication of an anthology of key articles on the topic. In January 1997, the government newspaper *Rossiiskaia gazeta* launched a contest in search of a new Russian Idea, gathering hundreds of slogans from readers. The Institute of Sociological Analysis organized a poll on the issue, although its authors were obliged to point out that no consensus view was obtained, with the majority of respondents classified as "post-Soviet individualists."[16] Several official meetings took place between the Moscow Patriarchate and the Ministry of the Interior, as the church attempted to present itself as the only institution capable of offering a prescriptive ideology for public opinion.

A few months after Yeltsin's statement, Igor Chubais, brother of then deputy prime minister Anatoly Chubais, published a book entitled *From the Russian Idea to the Idea of a New Russia*, which had a great impact on public debate at the time, especially among the ruling elite. After recapitulating the old debates, the author went on to endorse the idea of a new ideology, arguing that "where there are no ideas, there is no country."[17] He criticized shock therapy and privatization, which strengthened the power of the nomenklatura instead of dispossessing it, and called for a new consensual Russian identity combining spirituality, collectivism and individualism, social democracy, civic identity, pride in the national past, and linguistic purism.

The work appeared in a collection called *Novye vekhi* (New Milestones), a direct reference to the founding role of the collection *Vekhi* (Milestones), a manifesto against the ideology of the radical intelligentsia by some of the biggest names in Russian philosophy in the early twentieth century, including Nikolay Berdyaev, Sergey Bulgakov, Peter Struve, and Semyon Frank. Published in 1909, *Vekhi* called on the revolutionary intelligentsia to promote the primacy of the spiritual over the material, to strive toward a merger of faith and reason, and to restore the role of religious philosophy in the intellectual and spiritual development of Russia.[18] The message of the *Novye vekhi* collection was therefore unambiguous: a segment of the elite rejected the liberal radicalism promulgated on their behalf and called for a more consensual development, one more in tune with the "Russian Idea."

Many liberals criticized this interpretation of Yeltsin's statement about the need for a national idea. For them, the crucial issue was not the creation of a new ideology in the Soviet sense of the term but a collective reflection on the Russian Idea, which was then defined not as a corpus of texts imposed from above but as a fruitful interrogation of the society they wished to build. Economists such as Vladimir Filatov and Sergey Fateyev, as well as researchers on military issues like Andrey Kokoshin, sought to equate the Russian Idea with a defense of the country's interests. For the former, this Idea could only exist in a competitive, free-market economy, while the latter believed in the necessity of a powerful state with a strong army and foreign-policy decisiveness.[19]

The Second Half of the 1990s: Building Political Centrism

Between 1994 and 1996, the idea of great power (*derzhavnost'*) reemerged vividly in the Russian public space.[20] There was a consensus among analysts—even among liberals—that Russia was in critical condition. The state was weak, destitute, unable to finance an army, without influence in the international arena, and without clearly defined geopolitical interests. Domestically, the central government was in perpetual decline with respect to the concessions being demanded and obtained by ethnic republics. The Khasavyurt Accords signed with Grozny in August 1996, which put an end to the First Chechen War, were seen as a humiliation that had been inflicted upon great Russia by little Chechnya. Explicit comparisons were made with the 1905 defeat of tsarist Russia by Japan—the first victory of a non-European country against a European power.

During his second term (1996–99), President Yeltsin moved the political cursor toward a more centrist political positioning. Alexey Podberezkin, one of the key ideologues of the Communist Party at that time, has described how Yeltsin managed to appropriate the notion of "healthy patriotism" from the Communists and put together a coalition of reformers, leftists, and nationalists.[21] This patriotic centrism was perceived at the time as the most logical choice between what were then defined as two extremisms: the backward-looking Communism and imperial nationalism of the main opposition parties, CPRF and LDPR, and the pro-Western liberal experiment of the first

Yeltsin administration. Former presidential candidate Alexander Lebed encapsulated that mindset with his book, *Ideology of Common Sense*, published in 1995.[22] With Lebed, two other key figures embodied this new ideological combination: Moscow mayor Yuri Luzhkov (1936–2019) and minister of foreign affairs and later prime minister Yevgeny Primakov (1929–2015).[23] All three called for Russia to preserve its strategic interests in the post-Soviet space without returning to a Soviet or an imperial logic; to develop a distinct stance in the international arena and build a multipolar alliance with China and India without reverting to Cold War patterns of confrontation with the West; and to restructure Russia domestically by reaffirming the role of central power without recreating an ideologically based regime.

These centrist figures strengthened the patriotic discourse and marginalized the last liberals and their pro-Western discourse by claiming that Russia needed to be a strong state domestically and a great power internationally. In the legislative elections of 1999, the idea of a specifically Russian path of development was agreed upon even within parties that were considered liberal: all critically analyzed the country's situation and saw a need for more authoritarian policies that could meet the Chechen security challenge. The new presidential party, Unity, deftly played on these sentiments, co-opting the electoral niche established by Primakov and Luzhkov's rival Fatherland (Otechestvo) party. It was able to transform the new prime minister Vladimir Putin (interim director of the FSB and secretary of the Security Council of Russia), still totally unknown to the public, into the embodiment of national consensus and security. The notion of conservatism was not named as such, but the idea of centrism as a third way between reform and reaction was its equivalent and would become the ideological backbone of "Operation Successor"—the nickname of the PR campaign to elect Putin.

Putin's Millennium Manifesto: A Balancing Act

Putin's first article, "Russia at the Turn of the Millennium," often referred to as the Millennium Manifesto, was published on December 31, 1999, just before he became acting president following Yeltsin's resignation. In his resignation speech that same day, Yeltsin did not hide his disappointment with the past decade: "I said that we would leap from the gray, stagnating totalitarian past into a bright, prosperous and civilized future. I believed in that dream, I believed that we would cover the distance in one leap. We didn't."[24] Putin's manifesto was crafted by German Gref, then head of the Center for Strategic

Development and a figure who would provide Putin with his main economic ideas for the next decades.

The manifesto succeeded in appropriating competing ideologies and building a long-awaited third way that was supposed to rally different sides—a first step toward political and ideological hegemony.[25] Putin emerged as the figure in which Westernism and *pochvennichestvo* (an intellectual trend of the late nineteenth century insisting on the notion of being rooted in one's own soil) could merge. The article announced many of the future features of the regime, and Putin spelled out what he saw as his mission for the country:

> The experience of the 1990s vividly shows that our country's genuine renewal without any excessive costs cannot be assured by a mere experimentation in Russian conditions with abstract models and schemes taken from foreign textbooks. The mechanical copying of other nations' experience will not guarantee success, either . . . I am against the restoration of an official state ideology in Russia in any form. There should be no forced civil accord in a democratic Russia. Social accord can only be voluntary. That is why it is so important to achieve social accord on such basic issues as the aims, values, and orientations of development, which would be desirable for and attractive to the overwhelming majority of Russians. [These values are:] belief in the greatness of Russia (*derzhavnost'*) . . . statism (*gosudarstvennichestvo*) . . . and social solidarity.[26]

While Putin explicitly opposed a state ideology in the sense of a new Marxism-Leninism doctrine as a top-down process, he believed in a voluntary "social accord" or "social solidarity" that would manifest as horizontal unity around a new national idea. As this new national identity or consensus could not be established by decree, it would have to emerge through an organic process in which "universal human values and primordial Rossian (*iskonnye rossiiskie*) values that have withstood the test of time" would slowly merge. This is a central point to stress: the Kremlin hoped for an organic consensus from the bottom up. Over the years, the gradual feeling that this consensus did not emerge or that it existed but was weakened by certain societal forces (the liberals, the future "foreign agents," and whoever would then be identified as external to the national consensus), had forced the regime to go back to the idea of a top-down, coercive ideological consensus, which was never the favored option.

In terms of values, the Millennium Manifesto already contained the three aforementioned goals of Putin's reign: stability for the regime and the state, societal consensus around the regime, and recognition on the international stage. It celebrated the idea of Russia's unique identity (*samobytnost'*), its civilizational values, the centrality of the state, and the importance of collectivism. As Sanna Turoma and Kåre Johan Mjør argue, with the manifesto "Putin thereby rejected the idea of state ideology to present, instead, an idea of the state as an ideology."[27]

While these three goals were a genuine Thermidorian reaction to the 1990s, they were also rooted in continuity with the Yeltsin era. Indeed, Putin had to deal with the fundamental ambiguity of his own legitimacy: embodying the counterrevolution to the Yeltsin decade while at the same time being a product of it. The original Putinism of the Millennium Manifesto recognizes the 1990s not as a new "Time of Troubles," as it would be presented later, but as a foundational act for a new Russia, a solid ground upon which to build a new order. As we will see in chapter 3, Putinism has kept parts of this original ambiguity: criticizing political, cultural, and geopolitical liberalism while never challenging the economic legacy of the 1990s in terms of privatization, the embrace of neoliberalism, and globalization—only with the Russo-Ukrainian War have some forms of questioning of privatization emerged.

The patriotic centrism established in the mid-1990s was shared by all the main political structures born of the Yeltsinian establishment: Unity (the future United Russia) as well as the Union of Right Forces (UFR) and its then leaders Sergey Kiriyenko and Anatoly Chubais. In a crucial piece published in 1999 entitled "The Right Turn," another UFR leader, Alexey Ulykaev, explained that the right is the new center, the new consensus between reforms and counterrevolution, between liberalism and statism, and between pro-Westernism and patriotism.[28] The main terms of what would later become the regime's hegemonic discourse were all set.

EARLY PUTINISM: 2000–2011

Upon taking office, the new president insisted on presenting himself as non-ideological and in charge of offering Russia a new sense of normalcy.[29] His job was to be a good technocratic captain of the ship—a metaphor to be used regularly—and navigate it safely through troubled waters. For Ivan Krastev, Russia at that time offered a postideological, managerial, and technocratic type of thinking.[30] This depoliticized stance was built as a direct continuation of the previous administration's centrism, seen as the pragmatic politics of common sense, while simultaneously establishing hegemony and closing the political space.

In practice, Putin's first term (2000–2004) was organized around stabilization and recovery, with themes such as order, authority, and state effectiveness, which were embodied in two slogans: the power vertical and the dictatorship of the law. Russia became a "managed democracy": the president recentralized disparate powers given to republics and regions, secured oligarchs' loyalty or their dismissal (with the seizure of Mikhail Khodorkovsky's Yukos Oil holdings being the most symbolic case of punishing political dissidence among oligarchs), restricted the political landscape, redistributed raw material rents, and reasserted the country on the international stage.[31]

At the ideational level, the focus of this first period of Putinism was centered on patriotism, which was seen as the obvious way to end ideological polarization at both elite and societal levels. This patriotism was manifested in three ways: the reintegration of Soviet symbols into the new nation-building; the creation of historical continuity for Russia over its political disjunctures; and a shift from portraying the Soviet Union's collapse as the birth of a new Russia to being a disruption of Russia's statehood. Putin also heavily stressed the country's weakened demographic outlook as a matter of national security,[32] a prefiguration of the future traditional-values agenda, and was already complaining about the lack of political and moral conscience among the elite and in general society. The main spin doctor for the Kremlin at that time was Gleb Pavlovsky, author of the idea of "Putin's silent majority." In 2003, the authorities discussed the creation of a Council for National Ideology to be convened by major intellectual and cultural figures; however, the project never led to anything concrete and aroused little enthusiasm within state bodies.[33]

Soviet Nostalgia Lite as a Pathway to Consensus

As Julie Deschepper notes, early Putinism has been marked by "multiple reinvestments of the Soviet-era heritage."[34] The normalization of the Soviet legacy was interpreted by the regime as a central element of social consensus. The rehabilitation of Soviet symbols encapsulated the creation of a new political language in tune with the nostalgia for the late Soviet period expressed by a large part of the population. In December 2000, a new law on the flag, emblem, and anthem of the Russian Federation helped to bring about a new ideological compromise in reconciling the three major eras: the tsarist regime, the Soviet Union, and independent Russia. The government selected as a new national flag the white, blue, and red tricolor, the symbol of Russia's young democracy under the provisional government of 1917. The coat of arms appearing on its national seal combines elements of the two previous regimes: the red background represents the Soviet period and the double-headed golden eagle at its center symbolizes the imperial era, while also complementing the color scheme of the Soviet-era flag.

The Soviet anthem was brought back to replace a nineteenth-century anthem composed by Mikhail Glinka that had been reinstituted in the early 1990s. The music of the anthem remained unchanged, but its lyrics were amended to remove references to Communism. In 2000, the former red flag of the Soviet Army was also reintroduced as the flag of the Russian Armed Forces. In 2003, it was redesigned with a double-headed eagle to symbolize tsarism, the four five-pointed stars that Trotsky had proposed, and the slogan "Motherland, Duty, Honor," as used by the tsarist armies in the eighteenth century. In 2007, the Federation Council approved a law allowing the Soviet flag with the hammer and sickle to be used once more at major ceremonies, such as the victory celebrations held on May 9. However, the Duma voted in favor of the red star flag without the hammer and sickle, leading to dissension between the two chambers.

After re-officializing tsarist and Soviet symbols, the Kremlin turned to the issue of holidays and commemorative days. Although festivities related to the anniversary of the May 9 victory in the Second World War have always been the biggest national holiday, the authorities decided to rehabilitate the Day of Russia's Sovereignty on June 12. The Soviet tradition of professional holidays was expanded with a 2006 presidential decree introducing fourteen new days to revive national military traditions and the prestige of army service. The Kremlin also reinforced the celebration days of Russia's military glory, which are marked on the calendar, though employees do not get these days off from work.

With these dates established, the debate over commemorations turned to the issue of finding a replacement for November 7, the anniversary of the Bolshevik Revolution. Following a 1996 presidential decree, the celebration of the Bolshevik Revolution was transformed into a Peace and Reconciliation Day. In 2004, the Interreligious Council of Russia proposed to mark the events of November 1612, whose celebration date is roughly equivalent to that of the Bolshevik Revolution. The proposal was backed by Patriarch Alexy II and the Duma voted overwhelmingly in favor of introducing November 4 as People's Unity Day.

The new holiday commemorates the 1612 victory of Moscow residents over the Polish-Lithuanian Commonwealth. With neither tsar nor patriarch, the Russian civilian population, led by Kozma Minin and Dmitry Pozharsky, managed to stop Polish expansion in its tracks. This victory finally brought an end to the Time of Troubles (1598–1613), when, due to a lack of a reigning dynasty (the Rurikids had died out), the Russian state itself nearly disappeared. The November 4 commemoration therefore officialized a double parallel: first, between the Time of Troubles and the Yeltsin era, both of which are seen as symbols of peril to the nation; and second, between the enthroning of the first Romanov, Mikhail, in 1613, and Vladimir Putin's nomination— the two saviors of the nation guaranteeing continuity at the chief executive leadership level.[35]

The pragmatic narrative of the Russian authorities, supposedly nonideological, soon found itself challenged by the color revolutions, particularly the 2004 Orange Revolution in Ukraine. While references to liberalism and the Western model had become intermittent in the public arena after the failures of the Yeltsin era, the rise of political contestation in the name of democracy in Russia's near abroad induced the Kremlin to react.[36] Moreover, on the domestic front, the authorities had to face up to the large popular demonstrations in 2005, which took them by surprise and showed that social contestation was still possible.[37] Just as unexpected was the dissent of the nationalist Rodina Party (heir of the Congress of Russian Communities) led by Dmitry Rogozin. As Rodina had been created with the support of the Presidential Administration, it was therefore expected to show total loyalty to the president, but its dissent convinced the government that political puppets can still possess their own degree of agency.[38] The bloody hostage-taking at a school in Beslan (in North Ossetia, along the border with Georgia) in September 2004 also stoked popular fears and increased demands for security in the context of the Second Chechen War.

In an address to the Federal Assembly in 2005, Putin made his own vision of the past particularly clear by claiming that "the collapse of the Soviet Union was the greatest geopolitical catastrophe of the century."[39] The formalization of this widely held view (more than three-quarters of Russians approved of this statement[40]) that had long been regarded as politically incorrect closed the first cycle of the reintroduction of former tsarist or Soviet symbols. With it grew the framing of the 1990s as an awful decade that robbed Russians of confidence in the future, which was meant to be contrasted with the 2000s. As Olga Malinova explains, the "wild 90s" came to be used as a metalanguage of loss and trauma, the counterexample of what Russia should be.[41] A push for an increase in structured ideological content emerged within the presidential administration. In 2006, the publication of a book by Alexey Chadaev, entitled *Putin: His Ideology*, provoked a stir within Kremlin circles.[42] While some supported the move toward recognizing the need for an ideology, others did not hide their lack of enthusiasm for the idea.

Vladislav Surkov's Blueprint on Ideological Construction

Vladislav Surkov, deputy head of the presidential administration from 1999 to 2011 and Putin's longtime *éminence grise*, embodied the paradoxical, postmodern attitude of the state elites toward ideology—he later inspired Giuliano da Empori in his *The Wizard of the Kremlin*.[43] Replacing Pavlovsky as the Kremlin's main spin doctor, Surkov organized the repackaging of the regime during Putin's second term in office and became the major creator of a new "image factory" (*fabrika obrazov*), playing with concepts, symbols, metaphors, and visuals. He supplied the regime with the most refined tools, inspired by marketing and public relations techniques from the private sector. Coming from the left, like Pavlovsky, and having been inspired by the Neo-Soviet leftist movement, Surkov was deeply inspired by myriad countercultures, including rap, hip-hop, and street art, which he used as a source of inspiration and sometimes of co-optation.[44]

Among his core polit-technological activities, Surkov organized the pro-presidential youth movement Nashi; worked closely with the United Russia party's youth branch, Young Guard; launched Russia Today (RT), the Russian television channel aimed at foreign audiences, destined to become a central tool of the Russian voice abroad; and was involved in the creation of A Just Russia–For Truth, a loyalist center-left social alternative to the presidential party United Russia. With his right-hand men, Alexey Chesnakov and Konstantin Kostin, the deputy chiefs of the domestic policy department of the Presidential Administration, Surkov funded several new media enterprises such as vzglyad.ru, pravda.ru, elektorat.ru, politonline.ru, politgeksogen.ru, and regnum.ru. Through these, he pursued a strategy of saturating the media space with new voices in order to marginalize those of the opposition, moving from the televised realm, which was already under control, to the mushrooming Russian-speaking internet, or "Runet."[45] Surkov excelled in co-opting public intellectual figures close to the regime and giving them space to express their own opinions and develop their own projects. After the 2012 conservative turn, his team members would take divergent positions, with some continuing to accompany the regime in its ideological evolution and others moving toward the opposition.

Surkov will go down in Russian political history as the father of the slogan "sovereign democracy," crafted as Russia's answer to Western pressures to democratize and its neighbors' color revolutions.[46] The idea asserts that Russia will find its own sovereign path of political development without "external management," while still belonging to a universal model of democratic development. Similarly, in the economic sphere, Russia would modernize according to neoliberal principles, though the state would play a central role in that modernization. The regime's rising authoritarianism was explicitly formulated: the Russian way of democracy would be marked by "the striving for political wholeness and centralized power, the idealization of goals, and the personification of politics."[47]

On the international scene, Surkov's vision for Russia's role in the world was one of embracing globalization by creating a specific Russian brand or voice that would make the country an attractive great power with an economy on its way to modernization, strengthened by soft-power tools.[48] Surkov was highly critical of those who looked back to the Soviet experience and who felt attracted by the idea of a Eurasian or Asian destiny for Russia.[49] The "sovereign democracy" argument has remained Russia's key rhetorical line and was incorporated into United Russia's program statement, even if the concept itself was never used by Putin. Although Surkov gradually lost his central role in the Presidential Administration–led political scene, he put together a remarkably intricate blueprint for engineering ideological diversity and has remained to the present day a perceptive reader of the Kremlin's evolution.

United Russia as a Testing Ground for Ideology

Political hegemony through the crafting of a new ideological language has developed not only at the level of the Presidential Administration but also of the president's party. United Russia quickly understood that political contestation could emerge both within the so-called liberal camp and to the party's left—a space where the focus was on topics of a more nationalist and socialist nature. If the president's party wanted to leave its stamp on domestic political life for the coming decade, it would no longer be able to limit itself to glorifying the president's person and a nonideological managerialism: it would have to formulate a more coherent ideological posture.⁵⁰

This ideological process had in fact began much earlier. Already in 1999, the website of the party Unity, the direct predecessor to United Russia, contained the rubric "Our Ideology," which referred to conservatism. The director of the Center for Development of Programmatic Documents of the Unity party, German Moro, a recognized researcher on conservative theories, saw in conservatism the "only system of ideas capable of saving Russia" and defined it as a way of thinking that "is based on eternal social and moral values: respect for one's own tradition, trust in the tradition of one's forefathers, and priority given to the interests of society."⁵¹ As studied by Sergey Prozorov, in the early 2000s many parties and figures began identifying themselves as conservative "in order to be distinguished from both the dominant 'liberal-democratic' political orientations and the oppositional strands," among them the Conservative Party of Lev Ubozhko, the "New Force" of Sergey Kiriyenko, and the political commentator Andranik Migranyan.⁵²

In the mid-2000s, once consolidated as the hegemonic party representing the president, United Russia was shaken by calls for more internal debate and the formation of ideological wings.⁵³ Boris Gryzlov, then United Russia's president and Duma speaker, lambasted the principle of revolution and charged it with having caused Russia a great deal of damage and slowing the country's modernization—both in the 1910s and in the 1990s. In his view, Russia's modernization could only be realized through a process of gradual reforms that would proceed without inducing devastating social effects, endangering the state's stability, or borrowing from foreign ideologies, whether Marxism or liberalism. The ideology of the party, according to Gryzlov, was "the support provided to the middle class and the actions undertaken in the interest of that class, which has no need of a revolution of any kind whether financial, economic, cultural, political, orange [color revolutions, *ML*], red [Communist], brown [fascist] or blue [homosexual]."⁵⁴ He then intervened to try to systematize United Russia's viewpoint by asserting that the party had only one ideology, namely "social conservatism."⁵⁵ By this term, he meant to define the party's centrism, its pragmatism in economic matters, and its desire to dominate the entirety of the political landscape.

Two political wings were allowed to take shape inside the president's party. One of these, termed "conservative liberal," was led by Vladimir Pligin, who had previously worked as a lawyer for the mayor of St. Petersburg, Anatoly Sobchak; and Valery Fadeev, then editor-in-chief of the magazine *Ekspert*, president of the Institute for Social Forecasting, and copresident of the association Business Russia. The conservative-liberal current included several figures who had begun their political careers in the Union of Right Forces before allying with United Russia. It was backed by close associates of Dmitry Medvedev, who on several occasions claimed that he hoped for a classic European right-wing ideology with economic liberalism as a core principle to develop within United Russia.[56] The rival current, called "social conservative," was directed by Andrey Isaev, formerly head of the Federation of Independent Unions of Russia before siding with Luzhkov and Primakov's Fatherland; and Yury Shuvalov, formerly in charge of relations with the media and society for the Presidential Administration.[57]

The conservative-liberal current called for the Kremlin to deal resolutely with economic matters and to put an end to the bureaucratic pressures that privileged large state-run corporations but impeded the burgeoning of the private sector. It also encouraged the country to commit itself to policies of economic diversification and support for the private sector. In contrast, the social-conservative current represented a more leftist tradition, advocating for a bigger state role in the national economy.[58] These two currents were not recognized as official factions or wings, but instead expressed themselves in discussion clubs: the November 4 Club for the liberal conservatives and the Center for Social Conservative Policy for the social conservatives.

In 2007, while debates pitting the currents against each another were raging and preparations for the legislative campaign fueled internal conflict over the question of a new term for Vladimir Putin, a third group emerged under the label "patriotic conservatism."[59] Led by Ivan Demidov, a shrewd expert of the televised scene before he himself became involved in TV production (he worked for military channel Zvezda and the Orthodox channel Spas), this third position presented itself as Christian conservative but also as more nationalist. It was embodied by the "Russian Project" (*Russkii proekt*), born from the desire to shift the meaning of conservatism in Russian from a leftist, economy-centered narrative toward a more nationalist reading, and was backed by the two social-conservative leaders themselves, Andrey Isaev and Yuri Shuvalov. They aimed to attract voters of more nationalist sensibilities who were supporters of Dmitry Rogozin's Rodina, the first party at that time calling for a political project molded on the European far right.[60]

At the project's launch, Demidov stated: "United Russia is ready to revive the terms of nationalism, nation and Russian, which have been privatized and discredited by organizations such as the Movement Against Illegal Immigration."[61] The use of "Russian" (*russkii*), to the detriment of "Rossian" (*rossiiskii*), was not neutral: the Russian project was not a project for Russia, but a project for ethnic Russians. It was closely linked to the Russian Club, a small discussion group whose focus was organizing conservative meetings, rehabilitating the classics of Russian philosophy's Silver Age, supporting the patriarchate in its request to introduce courses on Orthodox culture in schools, and advocating for strict control over migratory flows. One of its leading intellectuals was Yegor Kholmogorov, who would become an important voice within conservative-reactionary intellectual circles (see chapter 9).

The Russian Project's heritage was later transformed into a State-Patriotic Club, a much more respectable version of itself that was less overtly linked to ethnonationalism and more open to conservatism, and influenced by the émigré reactionary thinker Ivan Ilyin and world-famous dissident writer and Nobel Prize winner Alexander Solzhenitsyn (1918–2008). The club's activities were focused on the promotion of patriotic education, the diffusion of moral values, and respect for military institutions. It called for a unifying conservative ideology, and its formulations, such as "our common civilization can be variously called: East European, Eurasian, Russian Orthodox, Post-Soviet," were destined to become the new mainstream in the 2010s.[62]

The question of ideology again took center stage during the presidential election of 2008 and the transfer of power from Putin to the man who had been serving as his prime minister, Dmitry Medvedev. During the December 2007 legislative elections, Putin made a point of criticizing the United Russia party for its lack of ideology: "Has United Russia proven to be an ideal political structure? Quite obviously not. It has no formed ideology, no principles for which the majority of its members would be ready to do battle and on which to stake its authority."[63] The establishment of a Putin-Medvedev diarchy in 2008 strengthened the space for increased ideological content inside the presidential party itself. The party then decided to forge ahead by formalizing the existence of its internal ideological currents and instituted a "Charter of Political Clubs."[64]

The Medvedev Interlude: More Modernization, More Conservatism

In 2008, Dmitry Medvedev became Russia's new president, and Vladimir Putin his prime minister. Medvedev's taking office thwarted many Western predictions: Putin may not have respected the spirit of the Constitution, but he complied with the letter of it by rejecting calls to serve a third consecutive presidential term. Although Medvedev had been a part of Putin's inner circle since the 1990s, his election was not a pure political fiction. By becoming prime minister, Putin risked losing control of his protégé and finding himself unable to return to power in the next election. He was careful, however, to transfer the essential functions previously exercised by the president (supervision of the Ministries of the Interior and Defense, FSB, etc.) to his new role as the head of the government.

For four years, the Medvedev-Putin diarchy worked in tandem to direct the general political system.[65] With Putin positioned as the head of both the government and the presidential party, these two institutions suddenly gained increased media visibility and policy credibility. Members of the government more clearly emerged in the public eye as figures with their own personalities, and the presidential party, which had until then essentially functioned as an electoral machine, became more structured. The gap between the *siloviki* and the civilian, technocratic bureaucracy became more visible, with the range of conflicting interests widening, especially around the balance between opening to foreign direct investment and closing for security reasons.[66]

Once elected, Medvedev advocated for a modernization agenda, mostly economic and technological, but also one with political potential, under the slogan "Russia forward" (*Rossiia-vpered*).[67] Yet the project did not result in any substantive institutional reforms, and even its flagship projects like Skolkovo—billed as "Russia's Silicon Valley"—failed to live up to expectations. The new president promoted a liberal think tank that functioned outside of the presidential party's framework, the Institute of Contemporary Development (INSOR), led by Igor Yurgens, who served as vice president of the Russian Union of Industrialists and Entrepreneurs (RSPP). The institute published several provocative reports asserting the need for Russia to make far-reaching reforms not only of its economy but also its political structure, questioning the usefulness of regional bodies like the Collective Security Treaty Organization (CSTO) for promoting Russia's role in its near abroad, and openly debating possible Russian membership in NATO.[68] INSOR was probably created not so much to develop concrete policy recommendations but to open new spaces for discussion, analyze reactions from public opinion and various interest groups, and foster the formation of a modernization lobby.[69]

While often presented as the peak of Russia's modernizing trend, Medvedev's presidency also prefigured the ideological evolutions to come: a conservative turn with a new role given to the Russian Orthodox Church, the first steps toward the securitization of national history (see chapter 5), and a growing anti-Westernism. In 2009, he himself declared that the Soviet Union "was in a certain way ideologized; however, on the whole, the experience was positive."[70] His presidency is also the time when then prime minister Putin articulated the first denunciation of US-led liberal internationalism and Russia's refusal to comply with it during his famous Munich speech.[71] In August 2008, Russian intervention in Georgia, following President Mikheil Saakashvili's ill-fated decision to attempt to retake by force the two secessionist regions of South Ossetia and Abkhazia, only further confirmed that "frozen conflicts" from the early 1990s were far from being settled and capable of heating back up.[72]

While one can debate what was initiated by Putin and the *siloviki* and what was genuinely coming from Medvedev and the more technocratic groups, one can clearly identify Medvedev's own input on the side of conservative values and the leadership role given to the church.[73] At Patriarch Kirill's enthronement in 2009, Medvedev called the church the historical and future source of "the moral forces of the Russian nation."[74] And indeed during his term, the church was promoted as a legitimate partner in discussing societal—and especially family—relations, causing perspectives on morality to become an intrinsic part of any discussion on "modernization."[75] Medvedev also supported the idea of introducing the teaching of religion in school. Heavy resistance from the Ministry of Education and the teachers' unions eventually resulted in parents being offered the choice between several components of "Fundamentals of Religious Cultures and Secular Ethics," some more overtly religious (Orthodox or Islamic) and some more secular (secular ethics or introduction to world religions), for their children.[76]

Then first lady Svetlana Medvedeva, too, played a critical role in promoting the church by making openly anti-abortion statements and playing the role of mediator between religious figures who served as confessors for the president and his inner circle, such as Metropolitan Tikhon, Father Vladimir Volgin, and Father Kiprian. She associated herself publicly with a variety of Orthodox causes such as the restoration of the New Jerusalem Monastery;

she established the Day of the Family, Love, and Fidelity to instill in young people the importance of family values; and she chaired the management council of the program "Spiritual and Moral Culture of the Younger Generation of Russia," created with the blessing of Patriarch Alexy II.[77] Medvedev's advisor on family policy was Yevgeny Yuriev, the CEO of the investment fund ATON, a member of the Orthodox Church's Commission on Family, and the main author of the Federal Program of State Support for Multi-Child Families of 2008–15. All the elements of the future conservative turn were already there.

As we can see from figure 2.1, references to the term "ideology" were much more numerous during Medvedev's presidency than during Putin's first two terms and even the third one. They seem to have grown again since 2020, but of course the semantic space of ideology has expanded so much that many other terms implying the same content are now being deployed.

FIG. 2.1. Mentions of "ideology" in presidential speeches, 2000–2023.

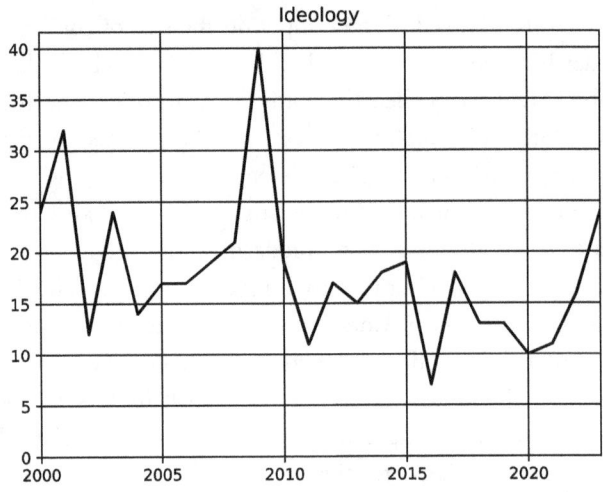

Source: Author's compilation based on Kremlin.ru.

LATE PUTINISM: 2012–2022

Late Putinism began with Putin's return to the presidency in March 2012. His third term promised to be difficult, as it started with the biggest protests the country had seen in twenty years, the Bolotnaya protests. When Putin and Medvedev revealed, in September 2011, that they were about to exchange their respective offices and had decided they would do so as early as 2008, the active segment of public opinion ignited. Critics denounced the contempt for voters displayed by the presidential duo, the sham elections with their predetermined outcomes, and the widespread corruption of the system. Between the December 2011 parliamentary elections and the March 2012 presidential election, tens of thousands of people took to the streets almost every week in Moscow and other major cities. At the height of the protests, in late February 2012, crowds of over a hundred thousand people were on the streets chanting anti-Putin slogans, demanding the resignation of the Electoral Commission and members of the government, and calling for transparent elections.[78] The lawyer and blogger Alexei Navalny (1976–2024) emerged as a leading figure embodying the denunciation of corruption, labeling Putin and his United Russia as the "party of crooks and thieves." In his heyday, his blogs—among the most widely read in Russia at the time—punctuated the protests.[79] Navalny's peak of public visibility would come in 2013 when he was authorized by the regime to run for mayor of Moscow and garnered an unexpectedly high 27 percent of the vote.

Reacting to Bolotnaya: The Conservative Turn of 2012–2013

While the scale of the demonstrations had taken the Kremlin by surprise, the response was fairly swift. The regime's relationship to ideology evolved on three levels. First, it took a more structured, content-related turn, with a stronger emphasis on Russia's anti-Western and antiliberal stance, the country's greatness, and the eternal infallibility of Russian/Soviet state leaders. The equilibrium between diversity and unity was partly disrupted: a statement of faith in the monopoly of the state on the ability to represent the nation's interests became dominant. Second, the Kremlin became more repressive against those who were advancing a competing agenda from the liberal side. Some prominent opposition figures were harassed, persecuted, and prosecuted, and some academics and opinion leaders were pressured to leave their jobs or even the country.

Third, the government developed a toolkit of new laws and decrees—though it applied these very selectively—that gave state organs more coercive powers to suppress patterns of behavior deemed inappropriate. This included new legislation on "foreign agents" (2012), first targeting institutions, then individuals, receiving foreign money; the Dima Yakovlev law, which sanctions US citizens involved in "violations of the human rights and freedoms of Russian citizens," banning them from entering Russia or adopting Russian children (2013); a law banning "gay propaganda," purportedly to protect children (2013); a law on "undesirable organizations" that are accused of undermining national security and suspends their activities on Russian territory (2015); and an anti-extremism law with an extensive yet ambiguous definition of what could qualify as extremism (2016). Attempts at moralizing the public space accelerated too: a new law was adopted to protect religion and religious believers from blasphemy and defamation,[80] and the Duma held contentious debates on whether or not to open casinos in Sochi and annexed Crimea.

In Putin's circles, Surkov's project of a "managed democracy," his postmodernity, and the liberal interlude of Medvedev's presidency were all interpreted as failures that had led to the Bolotnaya mass protests. Western-style modernization had failed at reforming the country, pushing the Kremlin toward more backward-looking sources of inspiration to determine Russia's future path. Surkov was replaced as deputy chief of staff of the Presidential Administration by Vyacheslav Volodin, who ended his predecessor's eclectic ideological games and organized a more rigid ideational production. The authorities took advantage of the Pussy Riot affair (a scandal wherein Pussy Riot, a political punk rock band, sang anti-Putin songs in the Cathedral of Christ the Savior in Moscow)[81] to marginalize the progressive urban middle classes and their oppositional mood in the name of a provincial silent majority that shared the regime's conservative and patriotic stance—the Russian version of the US "silent majority" that supports the Republican Party.

Gradually, the authorities rebuilt a welfare state favoring their core electoral and ideological constituencies. The regime's patronage mechanisms have since overlapped with the drift toward conservatism.[82] As Gulnaz Sharafutdinova explains:

> The main target audience of Putin's "moral" leadership was the more socially conservative, parochial, and nationalist segments of the Russian public: those who saw themselves as the main losers of the Soviet collapse; those who made a living in struggling industrial cities and monotowns; those who

held a grudge against oligarchs and the new Russians with their lavish, cosmopolitan, glamorized lifestyles; and finally, those who had sought a refuge in religion from the cynicism and material values of post-Soviet life.[83]

Debates surrounding the need for a more structured ideology reemerged. In 2012, chief Kremlin spokesman Dmitry Peskov commented that "[Putin] is thinking about ideology . . . Patriotism is very important. Without dedication from people, without trust of people, you cannot expect a positive impact of what you are doing, of your job."[84] At the 2013 Valdai summit, Putin declared that "questions about who we are and who we want to be are increasingly prominent in our society," and openly called for "a new national idea."[85] And for the first time in his annual address to the nation, Putin referred positively to the *Moral Code of the Builder of Communism,* a set of twelve "commandments" adopted by the 22nd Congress of the Communist Party of the Soviet Union in 1961, which he saw as a "primitive excerpt from the Bible."[86]

But some wanted to go further than simply referring to the need for a national idea: Elena Mizulina, then chairwoman of the Duma's Committee on Family, Women, and Children and known for her conservative views on morality, proposed an amendment to the Constitution stating that Orthodox Christianity is the basis of the cultural and national identity of the Russian Federation.[87] Yevgeny Fedorov, a provocative ultranationalist MP from United Russia who has been in charge of elaborating some ideological products, proposed abolishing Article 13 of the Constitution, which prohibits a state ideology.[88] None of these proposals were accepted.

The Crimean Euphoria and Its Gradual Fading

The Euromaidan revolution in Ukraine in the winter of 2013–14 suddenly offered the regime a unique strategic opportunity to seize. Moscow supported pro-Russian figures and movements in Ukraine and over the course of a few days captured Crimea and supported warlords in Donbas pushing for secession from the government in Kyiv. Crimea's formal annexation by the Russian Federation in March 2014 proved to be a unique moment of unity and enthusiasm, with Putin's approval ratings reaching their highest, at over 80 percent.[89] As a result, the regime was able to secure a rally-round-the-flag moment that calmed the dissatisfaction expressed in 2011–12 and offered a few more years in favor of the status quo. The regime took advantage of this unanimity to consolidate its repressive legislative apparatus, marginalize what remained of public dissident voices and spaces, and recentralize its security apparatus.

Several official documents pushed for more rigidly codifying Russia's "national idea," such as the 2016 Information Security Doctrine, which discussed how to defend the Russian information space against the falsification of history. The Presidential Administration organized a series of educational seminars for officials on ideological issues such as conservatism and patriotism.[90] The Ministry of Culture under Vladimir Medinsky became the leading institution in charge of this codification. A longtime member of United Russia and a passionate historian (he received a PhD in history that has been denounced for its plagiarism),[91] Medinsky has been described as a "nationalist enamored of classicism and traditional values."[92] He gained attention for his role on the presidential commission to combat the falsification of history (see chapter 5) before becoming one the ideologues-in-chief of the regime and author of numerous books denouncing foreign myths about Russia.[93]

Charged with revising the 1992 Law on Foundations of the Cultural Policy of the Russian Federation, Medinsky and his team drafted a new text, quite radical and inspired by the Soviet instrumentalization of culture, stating that culture is a tool for societal unity and shaping a spiritual-cultural matrix for the nation. The Presidential Administration, uncomfortable with the draft's language, blocked its adoption and developed a revised document, passed by presidential decree in 2014, which established a more sober and less politicized view of Russian cultural policy.[94]

Even though Medinsky's text was amended, the tone displayed in public evolved with the Crimean euphoria of 2014–15. Reactionary public figures were given preference in terms of direct or indirect state support or media presence, such as Nikolay Starikov, a bestselling writer of nationalist and conspiracy-mongering books and organizer of the Great Fatherland Party; the neo-imperialist duo of Alexander Prokhanov and Alexander Dugin; and the monarchist Orthodox line of the world-famous film director Nikita Mikhalkov. In 2016, a new Law on the Fundamentals of the Prevention of Offenses against the Russian Federation authorized the regime to prevent so-called antisocial behavior, vaguely defined as "violating generally accepted norms and morals, the rights and legitimate interests of others."[95] Many public figures tried to capture the new niche of values framing. Alexey Chadaev, who had already authored a first book on Putin's ideology in 2006, took the lead once again by laying out the ten values that would define Putin's

Russia[96]—foreshadowing the future presidential decree listing Russia's "traditional values."

The post-Crimea ideological effervescence gradually faded, and the regime had to refocus on the country's socioeconomic issues. In 2016, the Kremlin decided to reintegrate political figures with a more liberal agenda. Former finance minister Alexey Kudrin was named deputy chief of the president's Economic Council, and his Center for Strategic Research was charged with drawing up a new economic strategy for Russia. After ten years as the head of the Rosatom State Atomic Energy Corporation, Sergey Kiriyenko became deputy chief of the Presidential Administration. With his arrival, the pendulum swung somewhat away from the conservatism promoted by his predecessor Volodin and toward a more centrist and technocratic position. In 2017, the Presidential Administration decided to provide grants to associations registered as foreign agents, halted direct funding for the infamous vigilante motorcycle club, the Night Wolves, and repressed Orthodox fundamentalists who were prepared to engage in street violence against the film *Matilda*, which they considered blasphemous.

In spring 2017, the country again witnessed the eruption of mass protests. These occurred mostly among the younger segments of the population in large urban centers following the release of the investigative film *He Is Not Dimon to You*, put out by Alexei Navalny's Anti-Corruption Foundation (FBK), which denounced Medvedev's suspected role in corrupt practices. While the protests were smaller than those of 2011–12, they were the first of such scale since the rally-round-the-flag moment of Crimea's annexation. Another source of dissatisfaction and public protests was motivated by the planned demolition of apartment buildings from the 1960s, the *khrushchevki*, seen by the population as a way to generate a new, more expensive housing market.[97] The mismanagement of pension reforms, which provoked mass protests in June 2018, also sent a signal that welfare policies remained a central element of the population's acquiescence to the regime. A vivid and vocal urban activism took shape in Russia's main megalopolises, as well as in more remote regions, especially in ethnic republics, revealing a new generation of active citizens who did not engage in directly confrontational politics but who wanted to participate in shaping their local future by forcing municipal and regional authorities to demonstrate accountability.[98]

Despite a renewal of socioeconomic tensions, the 2018 presidential election proved the regime's success at managing public opinion even in a context of decline of the post-Crimea consensus. Putin was able to obtain his highest vote share ever, 76.6 percent of votes cast in the first round. Even if there were obvious cases of electoral fraud, this feat was made possible by securing the votes of Russia's big cities: the typical display of low voter turnout by the middle classes was reversed, and this time, they massively turned out to vote for him.[99]

Though electorally in control, the regime appeared to be slowly losing its political grip over the population and its capacity at renewing itself. No new faces emerged close to that of the president: Putin's entourage was being gradually reduced to its most hawkish figures, especially FSB director and secretary of Russia's Security Council, Nikolay Patrushev.[100] The Russian political system became increasingly punitive for second-tier elites, with about 1.5–2 percent of regional elites facing prosecution annually.[101] At the same time, a new generation of technocrats in their thirties and forties was promoted. Well-trained in managing a modern and neoliberal state, totally unknown to the public, and not directly connected to Putin, they were loyal to the system as a whole. The idea of a "Putinism without Putin" slowly took shape. And indeed, the regime seemed to arrive at a point where its natural death by inertia appeared to be a plausible scenario, symbolized by what some saw as Putin's likely last term in office.

The 2020–2021 Turning Point

What appeared to have been a slow, steady decay of the political system was shaken by several external factors, both domestic and international, which helped the regime to regain the initiative. The Covid-19 pandemic allowed the Kremlin to accentuate its control over society. In July 2020, the authorities organized a referendum, widely supported (officially with 79 percent approval), to validate amendments to the Constitution, the main goal being to authorize the president to run for several new consecutive terms, potentially until 2036. In exchange, the amendments mandated that the state take charge of several social provisions, including regularly indexing pensions and social benefits to inflation and guaranteeing a minimum wage at or above the poverty line—measures that were widely publicized to ensure popular support for the constitutional reforms.

Amendments also enshrined a revised version of the nineteenth-century tsarist formula "Orthodoxy, Autocracy, Nationality" in Russia's supreme text: marriage can only be between a man and a woman; any actions in favor of the "separation of a territory" (*otchuzhdenie territorii*), including calls for separatism, are forbidden (particularly intended to refer to Crimea, as well as to the Kuril Islands, disputed with Japan); dual citizenship is banned for those seeking elected office; the memorialization of Russia's heroic role in the Second World War is sacred and cannot be challenged without legal consequences; and so on.[102] While not explicitly establishing religious faith as mandatory, the amendments also mentioned the importance of "trust in God, transferred by ancestors," and made Russian "the language of the state-forming people, being a part of multinational union of equal nations of Russia."[103]

The pandemic also isolated Putin, literally: afraid of contracting the coronavirus, the president spent almost two years isolated from his staff and cabinet members, limiting his travel within Russia and reducing in-person interactions. Mikhail Zygar, a Russian journalist who has closely studied the president's "court," stated that Vladimir Medinsky and Yury Kovalchuk were practically the only ones able to spend time with the president.[104] This physical isolation is likely to have accentuated the bias in the information delivered to Putin by the FSB through classified documents—his only window into society and the world.

Repression against the opposition hardened and remaining spaces for expression faded. In August 2020, Alexei Navalny was poisoned with the Novichok nerve agent and hospitalized in serious condition in Germany. Multiple investigative teams confirmed the role of the FSB in the poisoning.[105] Navalny returned to Russia in January 2021 only to be arrested and jailed for parole violations before being sentenced to nine, and then nineteen, years in a maximum-security penal colony after being charged and found guilty of large-scale fraud and contempt by a Russian court.[106] Pressures relating to official memory and history issues escalated, symbolized by the closure of Memorial, the oldest and most respected Russian association working on Soviet state crimes and contemporary human rights.

On the international scene, tensions with the West accelerated and Ukraine loomed even larger as a crystallizing point of friction. The Kremlin had hoped that Volodymyr Zelensky, elected in 2019, would be a compliant partner for Russia, ready to implement the Minsk II agreements. This was not the case: the Ukrainian government took several actions (forbidding Soviet symbols in the public space, banning Ukrainian televisual channels belonging to oligarchs judged too close to Russia, making Ukrainian language compulsory, etc.) that Moscow interpreted as a disruption of their bilateral tacit agreement, triggering an ideological hardening. In March and April 2021, Russia began amassing thousands of personnel and military equipment near Russia's border with Ukraine, but partially withdrew them later. In June, Putin published his infamous article on the unity between Russia and Ukraine, which was seen as the ideological justification for a possible war (see chapter 5).[107] Still, he continued throughout the year to send contradictory signals to the West about Moscow's lack of interest in an armed conflict and insisted on being open to negotiations with the United States about Europe's global security architecture.[108]

WARTIME PUTINISM: SINCE 2022

With the full-scale invasion of Ukraine on February 24, 2022, the Russian state faced its biggest crisis since the collapse of the Soviet Union. The power vertical gradually constructed over two decades had annihilated any intermediary institutions that could have challenged the decision to launch the so-called special military operation. The Security Council convened on February 21, and television broadcasts showed its immobilized if not terrified members listening to the president's decision and acquiescing out of fear.

Unprepared and uninformed, Russian elites seemed at first to panic, but they rapidly stabilized and reconsolidated around the Kremlin. Two and a half years after the beginning of the full-scale invasion, we have seen almost no defections from the elite, with only a few minor exceptions of already marginalized figures (such as Anatoly Chubais and the oligarchs Mikhail Fridman and Petr Aven). Yet this does not imply genuine support, but passive acquiescence. The unique scale of the sanctions launched by the West only further reinforced elite consolidation, thus discouraging potential defectors from any kind of break with the regime. The so-called systemic liberals, the technocratic elites in charge of managing state finances and the economy, have remained not only loyal but have excelled at adapting state spending and the budget to the war context. Yet the war has relaunched intra-elite fights: several high-level businessmen or CEOs of big firms have been killed, "suicided," or died in strange accidents, both at home and abroad—likely a sign of property rights readjustments among different vested interest groups.[109]

The regime's equilibrium has moved toward the more hawkish side, with an increasingly vocal party of war that encompasses all security services and defense-related institutions, as well as myriad ideological and media entrepreneurs. "War correspondents" (*voenkory*: that is, journalists embedded within the Russian Army and paramilitary groups on the frontlines) have become new opinion leaders within an increasingly repressive political system. Some of these military bloggers—among them WarGonzo and Grey Zone—have hundreds of thousands of followers on Telegram; others, like Operatsiia Z, have more than a million.[110] Many of them consider today's war and the annexation of new Ukrainian territories to be the long-awaited continuation of unfinished business from 2014. They have the capacity to criticize the regime for its lack of effectiveness at organizing the army, preparing troops, and mobilizing society at the level the current stakes require, and offer an efficient populist safety net to the authorities.

Closely interconnected to the rise of prowar opinion leaders was the consolidation of warlord-like figures, personified by the late Yevgeny Prigozhin, who used the war and the successes of his Wagner Group on the frontlines to try to win a place among the established elites. As Julian Waller states, "The rise of political-military barons—that is, these political figures with personal control over real military resources and favored, clientelist connections to the apex executive—is an important change" in the history of Russia's political regime.[111] Prigozhin's death on August 23, 2023, confirmed the renewed grip of the Kremlin over any potential dissident voices and the limitations of these populist stances.

Political parties, both United Russia and the so-called systemic (that is, loyal) opposition (the Communist Party, LDPR, Just Russia-For Truth), now spend most of their time on creative ways to signal their loyalty and utility, with heightened competition to incubate new repressive legislation. The regime has also moved to increase coercion within society. The implicit social contract that the regime made with private citizens, of providing for their security and social benefits in exchange for their noninvolvement in politics, has been partly broken. This was caused not so much by the war itself as by the September 2022 mobilization that, due to its disorganization, gave the impression that every family could be impacted and might have to send its men to the front.

To secure the society's acquiescence, the Duma passed the highest number of laws ever, more than six hundred over the course of the year.[112] Among the main ones, the March 5 law considers any so-called fake information on the "special military operation" and the Russian military to be treasonous. This was followed by a series of laws that expanded the number of conditions that could lead someone to being labeled a foreign agent (with the dubious notion of "being under foreign influence" as one such potential criterion). The state agency Roskomnadzor restricted internet freedom, with approximately 400,000 websites blocked in 2022 and 880,000 in 2023.[113] The Russian economy has been put on a war footing, with state orders given priority over commercial contracts. Between February 2022 and early 2024, about 20,000 people protesting against the war had been at least temporarily detained (four-fifths of them in February–March 2022), more than 5,000 people had been fined for "discrediting the Russian forces," and more than 900 criminal cases had been opened against antiwar dissidents.[114] Opposition figures such as Ilya Yashin and Vladimir Kara-Murza received extremely harsh sentences, and Alexei Navalny died in an Arctic jail on February 16, 2024.

The war has also revived debates over Article 13 of the Constitution prohibiting the adoption of an official state ideology. The elite showed a divided opinion on the matter at the Eleventh St. Petersburg International Legal Forum, held in 2023. Some—chief among them Investigative Committee head Alexander Bastrykin and other *siloviki*, presidential adviser Vladimir Medinsky, current deputy chairman of the Security Council Dmitry Medvedev, and justice minister Konstantin Chuychenko—have called for repealing Article 13 and reinstating a state ideology, while others (especially the famous jurist Valery Zorkin, president of the Constitutional Court) have opposed this. The former group argues that to prevent Western ideas from penetrating Russia, the state should formulate a new state ideology based on the presidential decree of November 2022 extolling spiritual values. Tatyana Gurova, a pro-Kremlin media manager, has argued that the lack of an ideology is "akin to the ban on having an army after a defeat."[115] For the latter group, however, a national idea is enough, and the 2020 constitutional amendments have already defined the contents of this national idea, so there is no reason to convene a Federal Assembly to change the Constitution to make it legally binding.[116] As of the writing of this book in spring 2024, this debate continues, unresolved.

Over the more than three decades since the collapse of the Soviet Union, the Russian authorities, first under Yeltsin and then under Putin, have gradually retaken control of the ideological marketplace. This marketplace went from being an ultra-polarized field in the early 1990s, which pushed the country close to civil war, to being a pluralistic field that was diversified and neoliberal but still with the state as a hegemonic player from the mid-1990s to the early 2010s. On that front, there is a genuine continuity between the late Yeltsin era and early Putinism, an important point to remember when analyzing the long-term transformations of the Russian regime. For a long time, the Presidential Administration has continued to support or launch competing, and sometimes even incompatible, ideological projects. With the advent of late Putinism and wartime Putinism, the ideological field has become increasingly solidified, with the state regulating ideological production, punishing divergent ideological strains, and building a more coherent language. While there is no state ideology in the legal sense of the term, there is now an official ideology, eclectic and contradictory though it may be, which is in a hegemonic position.

PART II
FROM LEARNING TO UNLEARNING THE WEST

IN MARCH 2000, PUTIN, having just been elected president, declared to the BBC: "Russia is part of the European culture. And I cannot imagine my own country in isolation from Europe and what we often call the civilised world . . . So it is hard for me to visualise NATO as an enemy."[1] Twenty years later, we live in a markedly different geopolitical reality. But the quote remains fascinating because it reveals the polysemic nature of the "West" and announces the painful learning of this polysemy by Russian elites. What should they do if Europe as a culture does not overlap with the West as a political and strategic reality? With whom should they partner if Europe is no longer the embodiment of a "civilized world"? Sorting these notions out is crucial if one wants to understand the political construction of the Russian regime, where the West is rejected in the name of a certain formulation of Europe, where modernity is promoted over postmodernity, where conservatism is associated with old-fashioned liberalism, and where modernization has shifted from being Western-centric to being non-Western or even anti-Western.

Every identity is situational, based on our perception of others, our public image (how others see us), and the need for some form of inner coherence with our system of values. Nationhood follows a similar model, with strategic narratives constructed both to create consensus among domestic audiences and to brand the country on the international stage.[2] In Russia, the relationship to the West/Europe has always been the gravitational point of national identity, its main constitutive Other.[3] But the notions of "the West" and "Europe" are so polysemic that Russian political and intellectual elites have spent a great deal of time trying to figure out what these terms cover, what to take as inspiration, and what to reject. As Ella Shohat and Robert Stam show, these terms refer not to a geographic or political location but to an epistemic position: "Eurocentric thinking attributes to the 'West' an almost providential sense of historical destiny. Eurocentrism, like Renaissance perspectives painting, envisions the world from a single privileged point."[4]

Taking a Braudelian *longue durée* view of history, Russia's status as an epigone of Europe has molded the intellectual and political history of the country. In the Late Middle Ages, the growing power of the Moscow principality against both the Golden Horde and its local competitors—from Kyiv to Novgorod—was built on the myth of its being a Third Rome (see chapter 4). In early modern times, key figures, from historian Nikolay Karamzin (1766–1826) to Empress Catherine the Great, framed the Russian Empire as a European power, even though it would achieve European status only with the Congress of Vienna of 1814–15, which followed the defeat of Napoleon's continental imperial system. The Soviet experience transformed the country from epigone to peer competitor. Soviet Russia was not a European periphery, but the leader of one-third of the world, offering a powerful Communist messianism that spoke to parts of world public opinion for decades. With the collapse of the Soviet Union, however, Russia returned to its peripheral status. The liberal international order has consigned Moscow to a minor role: at best it is a second-tier actor that must accept the West's normative supremacy, at worst it is positioned as a rogue state on par with North Korea and Iran.

One might thus read Russia's history as that of a country transformed according to foreign blueprints coming from Europe since the eighteenth century and throughout the Soviet period, given that Marxism was born in Europe and intended to be applied to developed industrial economies. In more recent history, the end of Communism was perceived to have ushered in Western norms, but the idea that the reproduction of Western ideological and economic standards, especially neoliberalism, will bring modernity created resentment and disappointment. The results of this belief have shaped Russia's political course, especially given that contemporary elites were socialized under late socialism, where the "imaginary West" was the ultimate gold standard, a land where everything to which Soviet citizens aspired was freely available.

In the nineteenth century, Russian intellectuals wrestled with the question of whether their country ought to follow a Western model of civilization (as the Westernizers, or *zapadniki*, advocated) or develop along its own specific path (the point of view of Slavophiles, all their followers, pan-Slavists, *pochvenniki*, and Byzantinist proponents).[5] But no one was debating Russia's Europeanness, and for good reason: all of them understood Russia as part of a European civilization, referring above all to their shared Christian roots and humanistic culture. For the anti-*zapadniki*, Western Europe represented only one way of understanding European identity, while Russia offered another interpretation of it. This division was anchored in the history of Christianity: from one Christian root had sprung two traditions—Catholic (and later Protestant) and Orthodox; and two empires—Roman and Byzantine.[6] As Fyodor Dostoyevsky declared: "We Russians have two homelands: Russia and Europe—even in cases when we call ourselves Slavophiles. . . . The greatest of all the great missions that the Russians realize lies ahead of them is the common human mission."[7]

For all Russian intellectuals of the era, Russia had to be understood as the bastion of European or Christian civilization against the Asian or non-Christian world. For the *zapadniki*, this destiny was a burden: they saw it as having impeded Russia's progress as compared to its Western European neighbors. For the anti-*zapadniki*, by contrast, it was an opportunity, a blessing that had enabled Russia to maintain a Byzantine interpretation of Europe. Although Russia was understood to be on the borders of Europe geographically, all participants in the debate considered Russia to be part of Europe by virtue of its history, faith, and culture. The rapid expansion of the Russian Empire during the nineteenth century did not fundamentally challenge this perspective, since all the major European powers of the time were pursuing colonial policies that involved conquering territories on other continents. Indeed, Russia's colonialism was seen as an expression of Russia's innate civilizing mission to bring European enlightenment to Asia.[8] It was only at the turn of the twentieth century—and then with the rise of the Eurasianist movement during the interwar period—that the conceptualization of Russia as lying outside of European civilization took shape.

This brief historical detour illuminates both parallels with and differences from the current situation. In present-day Russia, the terms of the identity debate are no longer binary (Europe versus non-Europe, the "West" versus the "rest") but trinary: Russia can be seen as both European and Western; European but not Western; neither European nor Western. These three narratives reproduce different strategies of social identity: mobility (aspiring to join nations seen as having a higher status—that is, primarily Western countries), competition (acquiring new tools to change Russia's place in the rankings and upgrade itself), and creativity (rejecting such comparisons and proposing alternative rankings that would position Russia outside of the Western/European-centric hierarchy).[9]

Of the three views, the first (that Russia is both European and Western in nature) was supported by the Kremlin only briefly, from the time of perestroika to the mid-1990s, as reflected in Mikhail Gorbachev's call for Russia to rejoin the "common European home" and to become a "normal" (read: Western) country.[10] In his memoirs, Gorbachev repeatedly stressed that the Soviet elites of the time were imbued with European culture.[11] The "path to the West" gradually closed in the first years of independent Russia.[12] It did not disappear entirely from state discourse, but became intermittent, visible mostly in economic and financial policy circles among those who would become the "systemic liberals."

From the 2000s, the second view of Russia's belonging (a European but anti-Western Russia) gained official status as the most viable option for Putin's Russia, at least until the full-scale war in 2022. The representation of Russia as a better Europe—one that does not follow the Western path of development but represents the original and "real" Europe—overlaps almost entirely with the conservative posture discussed in Part III. Once again, today's official narratives echo nineteenth-century debates: Western Europe is decried for its liberalism, materialism, and consumerism, while Russia is celebrated for its conservatism, humanism, and spirituality.

The third option (of Russia being neither Europe nor the West) was long marginal in the Russian establishment but has gained prominence since 2022, with the full-scale war and decoupling from the West. It has taken multiple forms: the radical Eurasianism of such well-known figures as Alexander Dugin (who see Russia as the anti-West *par excellence*); discourses on Russia's "civilizational autonomy" (which frame Russia not necessarily as an anti-West but simply as a non-West); and discourses on Russia as the embodiment of anticolonialism, in solidarity with the Global South (which may position Russia as either anti-West or non-West—see chapter 12).

Even if Russian political and expert circles firmly believe that Asia's rise demonstrates that Westernization is no longer needed for modernization, Asia itself never appears as the yardstick of Russia's identity. Even when negated, Europe remains the focal point for Russia's self-representation, showing that one can be anti-European and Eurocentric at the same time. This painful relationship to an existential but polysemic Other has dramatically influenced the regime's gradual shift toward the culturalization of Russia's identity and history. This securitization trend has allowed the gradual blending of two divergent interpretations of Russia, the imperial and the Soviet.

THREE

THE PAINFUL RELATIONSHIP TO A POLYSEMIC WEST

Of course, Russia is a very diverse country, but we are part of Western European culture. No matter where our people live, in the Far East or in the south. We are Europeans. [But] if they push us away, then we will be forced to find allies and reinforce ourselves. What else can we do?
VLADIMIR PUTIN, *First Person*[1]

SCHOLARSHIP EXAMINING RUSSIA'S IDEOLOGICAL construction tends to search for identifiable "others" in Russian state language, whether nationalism, great-powerness, anti-Westernism, conspiracism, or conservatism. The often unspoken (and sometimes genuinely unthought) argument here is that Russia is inherently opposed to a democratic, liberal, progressive, unified West. Back in the Cold War era, Harvard professor Richard Pipes, one of the leading scholars on the Soviet Union, placed special emphasis on Russia's "un-Western" traits—an approach that has become more acute since the 2010s, with the steady otherization of Russia by Western commentators. The lack of reflexivity regarding the implicit *us* in the study of Russia has contributed to a trend in scholarship that insists on discussing what makes Russia's ideologies different (implicitly, from *us*) rather than understanding what makes them similar to *us*, or similar to non-Western experiences. Accordingly, this chapter begins with an exploration of the placement of universal values, modernization, and liberalism in the Russian official language, which serves to illuminate the extensive overlaps between the Russian regime and the West in terms of ideational repertoires.

The notion of "the West" is indeed closely interconnected with other semantic clouds—universal values, modernization/modernity, progress, and civilization—which are themselves extremely equivocal. Seen from Russia, the West includes both the United States and Europe; it is represented by transatlantic institutions—primarily NATO—and the Western liberal international order. The notion of Europe is more complex and contains at least three overlapping identities: the European Union construct; a wider Europe, including non-EU countries, that maintains a dialogue with close neighbors such as Russia, Turkey, and the Mediterranean Basin; and a cultural heritage and philosophical background. This more cultural/philosophical layer is itself diverse, referring variously to Christianity, the Enlightenment, liberalism, modernity, or postmodernity.

The term "universal values" is usually deployed to describe broad respect for human beings and to denote "civilization" as opposed to "barbarism." It tends to be associated with democracy and human rights but can also be brandished by authoritarian regimes to justify their right to diverge from Western norms. Modernization has a complex philosophical subtext that relates to the notions of modernity—itself contested—and of progress. The semantic space of modernization, modernity, and progress is often connected to a material, economic, or technological interpretation but may also, implicitly or explicitly, relate to the political or social nature of a country. Finally, liberalism covers a wide semantic spectrum extending from political liberalism (individual political rights and institutional checks and balances) to societal liberalism (inclusiveness), and from economic liberalization to neoliberalism.

Notional and chronological granularity is crucial here, as the Russian regime has positioned itself differently toward each term at different periods of time. As we will see, Moscow has historically targeted its disapproval primarily at the Western liberal international order, which positions Russia as a rule-taker, not a rule-maker. Criticisms of political and societal liberalism emerged much later, as a byproduct of this disapproval; the core issue here has historically been geopolitical, not ideological. The Putin regime has gradually juxtaposed a geopolitical West marked by societal liberalism, globalization, postmodernity, and secularity, with Russia, a land of "old-fashioned" liberalism, classic modernity, conservative values, sovereignty, and spirituality. This chapter proposes to disentangle these conceptual nodes by examining the four stages of Russia's relationship to the West: sharing, challenging, unlearning, and fighting.

SHARING WITH THE WEST: UNIVERSAL VALUES, MODERNIZATION, AND ECONOMIC LIBERALISM

As discussed in chapter 2, Putin's reign is rooted in ambiguity toward the Yeltsinian legacy. The regime has gradually constructed an image of the 1990s as the countermodel, a new Time of Troubles the repetition of which should be avoided at any cost.[2] Yet it has remained loyal to the Yeltsin era's main economic achievements: the privatization of the national economy and the right to private property. The Russian political scientist Leonid Polyakov noted as early as a 2000 article entitled "The Liberal Conservative" that Putin's socioeconomic reform program is liberal, and therefore in tune with Yeltsin's presidency, even if situationally and stylistically conservative.[3] To comprehend this blend, it is worth recalling that neoliberalism arrived in Russia less as an economic tool than as a global political project: as leading Russian reformers Anatoly Chubais and Yegor Gaidar openly state, "shock therapy" was aimed at weakening the nomenklatura and making a return to Communism impossible.[4]

Since then, the Russian regime has protected the market economy and private assets and maintained a high degree of oligopoly, even if private entrepreneurs face intrusive state intervention for political reasons. The security apparatus has also been heavily involved in extracting resources in a neoliberal manner.[5] In addition, society has been encouraged to gain autonomy from the state and organize itself along neoliberal lines, with citizens responsible for their own well-being and happiness.[6] Over the years, the government has implemented broader neoliberal measures to reduce state spending on public services by outsourcing them to private companies (all with connections inside the "system"). The social and healthcare realms, too, have been largely outsourced to private actors, in particular the Russian Orthodox Church,[7] up to the embrace of "philanthrocapitalism."[8] Although this has gone largely unstudied by the Western literature, Russian scholarship has noted the deep connections between economic neoliberalism and conservatism in terms of values—a tandem inspired by the US and British traditions of conservatism. Aleksandr Bikbov and Ilya Budraitkis explore, for instance, how neoconservatism and neoliberalism have blended in new neoliberal urban projects that capitalize on the Soviet cultural model of (neo)classicism.[9]

Moreover, the Russian authorities have been building a state-of-the-art school of technocrats in the macroeconomic and financial sectors that has succeeded in keeping Russia in fiscally advantageous conditions. The idea that globalization and international competition is good for Russia because it "cancels out" the West's normative advantage—an idea first crafted by Vladislav Surkov[10]—has continued to shape the mindset of Russia's financial elite. Economic policies have gradually shifted from general openness to Western actors to greater restrictions in the name of security concerns,[11] but the globalized nature of the Russian economy has not been questioned. Indeed, the Russian establishment has accepted Russia's peripheral status in the world economy as a place for raw material extraction much more easily than it has accepted its status as a secondary great power. As Ivan Timofeev, director general of the Russian International Affairs Council and one of the leading figures of IR in Russia, accurately summarizes:

> Economic factors were secondary for the "Russian rebellion." In theory, Russia can be considered dissatisfied with its peripheral status in the global economy and its role as a raw materials appendage. In practice, Russia has become very deeply integrated into the international division of labour. However, compared to the stories about democracy, sovereignty and foreign policy, Russia's dissatisfaction with its place in the world economy was articulated in a very weak way.[12]

During the first two years of the Russo-Ukrainian War, the regime's technocrats demonstrated their capacity to ensure that state budgets remained afloat.[13] However, the full-scale invasion of Ukraine has, for the first time in thirty years, challenged at least some aspects of the regime's commitment to economic liberalism. Indeed, the government seems resolved to question the long-sacrosanct privatization of the 1990s. Several big private companies have lost legal proceedings, likely for a variety of reasons: strategic (renationalizing companies that were under foreign control, as an answer to Western sanctions), economic (controlling and reorienting production for the war economy), and simple competition (settling scores between members of the establishment). While Putin has ruled out a complete deprivatization,[14] representatives of the business community, among them Alexander Shokhin, head of the powerful Russian Union of Industrialists and Entrepreneurs, have nevertheless expressed concerns about this growing trend of nationalization.[15] For the political analyst Nikolay Petrov, "It is probably more correct to talk not about de-privatization, but about an ongoing large-scale redistribution of property in which de-privatization is only one of the tools."[16]

On top of rolling back, state spending has been reoriented. The government has launched a new "military Keynesianism" that provides massive state support for military-industrial production and generous financial packages to men who go to the front and their families.[17] The war has thus accelerated the trend of societal dependence on state support: more than 40 percent of the Russian population now receives revenue, a salary, or a pension from the state.[18]

To capture what the Putin regime has historically shared or continues to share with the West, I traced the presence of themes such as universal values, modernization/modernity, and liberalism in presidential speeches. To that end, I analyzed the twenty-three annual presidential addresses to the nation delivered by Russian presidents since 2000. I found that a total of 1,836 terms appeared at least ten times. Following Putin's Millennium Manifesto, which delineates how Russia should combine its different legacies, I then classified these terms into three categories: universal values (including such terms as democracy, elections, rights, freedom, justice, equality, progress, and general sociopolitical modernization); prosperity (including such terms as economy, business and the market, sectorial development, private sector, demography, education, science and technology, labor, health, and housing); and identity (including terms such as law and order, dictatorship, stability, criminality, corruption, law and justice, security, the military, and the full spectrum of national-conservatism: tradition, values, morality, spirituality, culture, history, and nation).

As figure 3.1 shows, these three metanarratives have maintained more or less the same balance since 2000, with minor adjustments. This is an important and unexpected finding that invites us to examine in greater detail the perception that presidential speeches have gradually securitized, as well as the image of a Putin increasingly obsessed with identity and law and order. Notably, issues related to prosperity, economics, and well-being remain the leading grand narrative of the state, before universal values and identity-related topics. The idea that the core element of the social contract is that the state should deliver the material conditions for improving Russian citizens' standard of living has persisted. This confirms Ivan Fomin's finding that "when Putin seeks to mobilize the nation, the promises of happiness, prosperity, and welfare appear to him more reliable than just the rhetoric of patriotic statism."[19] This language relies heavily on the notion of social justice, which remains central to political language and to which the Russian population is highly sensitive.

The "universal values" narrative, which was important during Putin's first

FIG. 3.1. Presence of the three metanarratives (universal values, prosperity, and identity) in presidential speeches, percentage of sentences per year, 2000–2023.

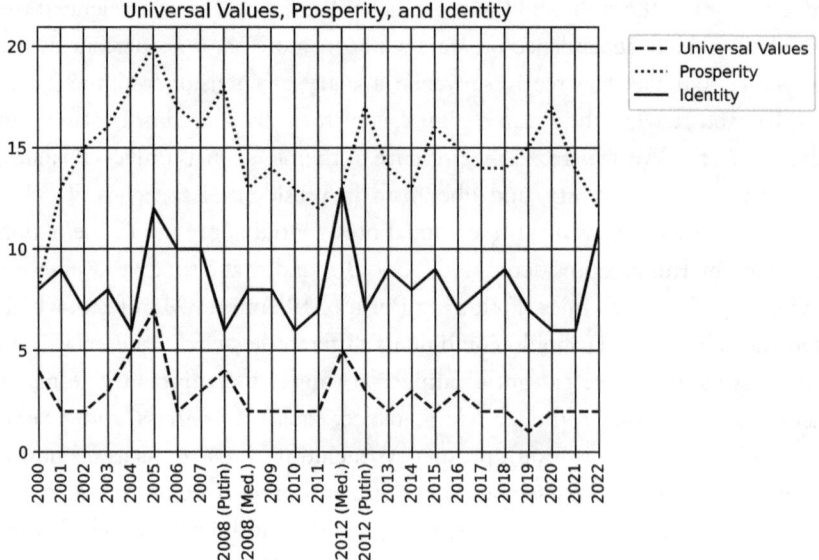

Source: Author's compilation based on Kremlin.ru.

term, has unsurprisingly decreased since 2013, though it has not entirely disappeared. As shown in figure 3.2, the concept of "democracy" has faced a more abrupt decline since 2011 than any other notion discussed in this book. Its meaning has also evolved: democracy has come to be used not to discuss voting processes but to express something related to legality more broadly (*zakonnost'*).[20] And as we might expect, the identity metanarrative has recurrently peaked at moments of crisis: in 2005 after the Orange Revolution in Ukraine, in 2011–12 during the Bolotnaya protests, and in 2022 with the onset of war (fig. 3.1).

The regime's liberal conservatism or conservative liberalism, which was dominant in early Putinism and has faded—yet never disappeared—with late Putinism, is closely linked with the idea that reforms should be state-led. The notion of a reformist state imposing reforms on a reluctant, backward-looking society has deep roots in Russian history.[21] The country has gone through several cycles of modernization and reaction since the seventeenth century:

FIG. 3.2. Mentions of "democracy" (when associated with "Russia") in presidential speeches, 2000–2023.

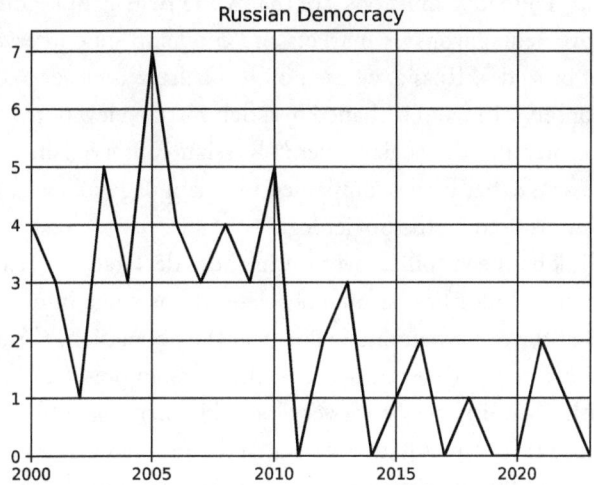

Source: Author's compilation based on Kremlin.ru.

Peter the Great's forced modernization/Europeanization, the Bolshevik revolutionary project, and the Yeltsinian decade of forced liberalism were all violent moments of state-led reformism imposed in an authoritarian way. This top-down reformism tradition partly explains why the Russian liberal and Western-oriented intelligentsia tends to feel a deeply rooted contempt for the population.[22] An illustrative example comes from Boris Nemtsov's *Testament of a Rebel*, in which he plainly declares: "The Russian people, for the most part, is divided into two uneven groups. One part is the descendants of serfs, people with a slavish consciousness. There are very many of them and their leader is V. V. Putin. The other (smaller) part is born free, proud and independent. It does not have a leader but needs one."[23] With the 2022 war, this contempt has been accentuated, with unfortunate comments from the liberal opposition in exile promoting the idea that "good Russians" have moved abroad while "bad Russians" have stayed at home.[24]

For a long time, a core goal of the Putin regime was to avoid polarization between conservatives and liberals in favor of a pro-reform synthesis of the two groups. This political centrism allowed the regime to merge the ideas of a Russia moving toward Western political values and economic and social modernization, on the one hand, with a form of conservative leftism that insisted on consolidating the state and restoring basic principles of social justice, on the other.[25] Here, one must observe that while British and American conservative movements favor free markets and condemn state intervention, the same cannot be said of Russia, whose political culture is closer to continental European conservatism and is shaped by a Schmittian view of the state as the main actor protecting the social order.[26] Russian conservatism is thus more leftist in the sense that it is accompanied by a language of social justice and redistribution inspired by the Soviet legacy.

A lot of ink has been spilled over Putin's 2019 declaration to the *Financial Times*: "The liberal idea has become obsolete. It has come into conflict with the interests of the overwhelming majority of the population."[27] Yet when one looks at the last two-and-a-half decades, the Russian president has not been obsessed with liberalism per se for very long. He mentioned liberalization in a positive sense three times between 2001 and 2003, and it was only a decade later, in 2013, that the term reemerged in his speeches with a negative connotation, condemning "people with liberal views who criticize everything"[28]— and even then he continued to use the term to evoke economic liberalization (a positive in his mind). A more pronounced semantic turn occurred in 2014, when Putin first identified "liberals" as a political group and decried the "liberal defense" of homosexuality.[29] However, the term still bore some positive connotations: Putin referred to himself that year as "a real liberal," going on to say that "I support liberal views."[30] As we will see later (in chapter 8), Putin presented himself as conservative around the same time. One conclusion might be that his self-presentation is purely situational, if not opportunistic or cynical; however, a more logical conclusion is that the terms were not mutually exclusive in his view.

While Putin has continued to stress the importance of economic modernization and has never totally abandoned references to universal values, the shift from supporting liberalism, at least in some discursive aspects, to denouncing it wholesale has been a major change. This is the tip of the iceberg when it relates to the Russian regime's perception of its relationship to the polysemy of the West and all its implied subtexts. In this evolution, Russia's place on the international scene has been the fundamental issue: the rejection of liberal internationalism has been the driver of Moscow's movement away from liberalism.

CHALLENGING THE WEST: THE REJECTION OF LIBERAL INTERNATIONALISM

A core element of the conflict between Russia and the West relates to the world order's normativity and its scripters.[31] The international scene has evolved dramatically since the collapse of Communism, with the domination of a liberal internationalism defined by multilateralism, supranational institutions, a trade-based vision of peace, and the right to engage in humanitarian intervention on the grounds of universal human rights.[32] The ambiguity of this liberal world order is that in addition to open multilateralism and rules-based cooperation, there is, as Princeton professor John Ikenberry states, "an expectation that a liberal international order will move states in a progressive direction, defined in terms of liberal democracy."[33] I therefore share Andrej Krickovic's and Richard Sakwa's explanation that the Russia-West conflict is an ontological conflict between two contending principles: on Russia's side, the idea that the world order should be based on rules of coexistence such as sovereignty, noninterference, and balance of power; on the West's side, that the expansion of the liberal community is the main guarantee for peace and stability.[34]

Mikhail Gorbachev and the perestroika-era elites around him genuinely believed the Soviet Union was going back to its "European home" and would become the equal cofounder of a new pan-European political community.[35] As Richard Sakwa argues, the Russian elites wanted to join a *transformed* West, not an *expanded* one.[36] The collapse of the Soviet Union was interpreted as a recognition by Moscow of the West's success, but not as a capitulation to the West. As the Russian establishment has come to realize that Russia will not be given the status of cocreator of a new European order, they have therefore gradually distanced themselves from the existing transatlantic institutions. Moscow has thus been guided much more by concern about its status in the world (and regime stability at home) than by any deeply rooted ideological opposition to liberal democracy per se.[37] As Alicja Curanović explains, "The conservative turn in Russia's foreign policy should be viewed as a reaction to Russians' perception that they have failed to achieve the desired recognition as an equal to the major powers, in other words, the West."[38]

The Russian establishment has vocally denounced liberal internationalism since at least Putin's famous Munich speech of 2007. Since then, political language has radicalized but has not dramatically transformed. As the Russian foreign policy establishment interprets the international scene through the lens of realism—the theory that, by nature, states are selfish organizations that defend their own strategic interests[39]—it sees liberal internationalism as a cover for US imperialism and military hegemony, which denies the legitimacy of other political systems and their cultural contexts. Moscow has thus pointed out the contradiction between the US's rhetorical support for a rules-based order and its regular flouting of international rules in practice (by invading Iraq and Libya, violating Serbia's territorial sovereignty to support Kosovo's independence, supporting color revolutions, orchestrating regime change in the Middle East, forcing exogenous nation-building in Afghanistan, etc.), as well as its refusal to sign such major international treaties as the Rome Statute, which established the International Criminal Court.[40] Western interventionism has thus played a central role in Russia's critiques of the liberal world order: Sergey Karaganov, head of the influential Council for Foreign and Defense Policy and professor at the Higher School of Economics, contends that democracy "was made a caricature by Western attempts to spread it forcefully across the globe, using it as a dogmatic rhetorical token in political argument, and imposing where it was not appropriate or necessary."[41]

In denouncing US liberal internationalism as a destructive force that creates global disorder, the Russian regime thus opposes not *internationalism* per se but its *liberal* version, and calls for a *sovereign* internationalism. Sovereignism stresses defending national sovereignty as a key element of both domestic politics and the international order. Moscow advances this sovereignism across three domains: political, cultural, and economic. Political sovereignism asserts that only nation-states command political legitimacy, as this is the only level at which citizens express their will through elections (even if these elections are neither free nor fair), and therefore that powers properly belonging to the nation-state should not be delegated to unelected supranational institutions. US interventions in the Middle East have, for instance, been viewed by the Russian political establishment as a process of de-sovereignization.[42] Yet Russia does not call for a full-fledged Westphalian order in which all states would enjoy equal sovereignty: great powers are seen as more legitimate than small countries, and Moscow believes in alliances between countries or "civilizations," which may voluntarily weaken (but not delegate) their sovereignty in the name of cooperation.[43]

Cultural sovereignism centers on an essentialist definition of the nation—who it includes and what its core cultural features should be. In this view, at the heart of each nation-state is a core nation entitled to promote its culture, while foreigners, migrants, and minorities must accept a second-tier status and recognize the supremacy of the majority. This is what the Russian authorities promote in their media directed at European and American constituencies, as well as what they proclaim at home, where the ethnic Russian core is given symbolic and—in some sectors, such as culture, history, and language—practical supremacy.

The Russian regime is more ambivalent toward economic sovereignism. It supports the idea of state control over strategic sectors and avoiding excessive interference by foreign interests, and has criticized financial capitalism, as well as the "dictates" of the International Monetary Fund and the World Bank. But as we saw, neoliberal integration into a globalized economy remains the norm for Moscow, embodied by international trade, the search for technological modernity, foreign direct investments, and Russia's upward mobility in Western-centric "doing business" indexes. The idea of Russia as a country open to the world has thus dominated throughout Putin's reign. Now that the decoupling with the West has become a long-term trend, these globalization processes have come to center on the so-called Global South.

The sovereign internationalism for which Moscow pushes is ambivalent.[44] Sometimes the regime calls for a return to a Yalta order in which Russia and the United States would talk to each other to resolve international tensions—with China added into the mix, making the binary relationship into a triangle but retaining the idea of "gentlemen's agreements" between the great powers determining outcomes for the rest of the world. At other times, Russia calls for a more multipolar system in which different "civilizations" (see chapter 7) would be recognized as the subjects of international politics and the US would be demoted as a key partner.[45] Whereas the US-Russia relationship is central to the "status quo ante" solution, it is marginal in the "new world order" solution. For Russia, the latter approach would further entail changing its self-perception from an old-fashioned great power to that of a global power—that is, one center of influence among many others.

While Russia brands itself, alongside China, as one of the leading nations of the sovereign internationalist coalition, it has also carved out for itself the position of a joker or trickster on the international stage—an architect of destabilization and chaos. The figure of the trickster was central to Soviet culture, as in this closed society people were accustomed to operating in contradictory normative systems. The Russian regime has been able to upgrade the popular image of the trickster to global status, defined by liminality and transgression. As Xymena Kurowska, Vyacheslav Morozov, and Anatoly Reshetnikov explain, "Russia lacks the capacity to transform the West-dominated international system. Destabilizing it from within is more affordable and addresses their concerns related to both security and status."[46] This "joker policy" is well encapsulated by RT and Sputnik's emphasis on providing an alternative to the established outlets (referred to as "mainstream media"); they exalt their own irony, sarcasm, and sensationalism, which have the clearly formulated goal of demystifying the West and its values.[47]

Moscow has therefore been promoting a postliberal, antiliberal, or illiberal (depending on how these concepts are defined) vision of the world that aligns better with its strategic interests than does liberal internationalism. As the research director of the Valdai Club and chief editor of the influential journal *Russia in Global Affairs* Fyodor Lukyanov states, since "Russia has failed to find a place for itself in the liberal order, it thinks it might be able to achieve a more advantageous position in the world order that comes to replace it."[48] The Russian authorities have thus played around with different policy toolkits simultaneously: normative opposition, by working inside international institutions to oppose Western influence; rebellion, by playing the joker on the international stage (interference in elections, disinformation campaigns, "hybrid" warfare); and exit from the West in all its definitions (political, economic, cultural) in pursuit of non-Western global alternatives.

UNLEARNING THE WEST: REDEFINING RUSSIA'S IDENTITY

During early and late Putinism, the regime vacillated between a narrative of social competition (Russia as a superior alternative to the West or Europe) and one of social creativity (Russia as the anti-West or the anti-Europe). The Russian establishment long regarded Russia as part of a broader Western community, understood by Putin as "the most advanced states in the world,"[49] with the idea that the differences between Russia and the West, especially economically, were relative, not essential. Yet the synonymity between the West and modernity/modernization was challenged by China's rise to power and the 2007–8 and 2014 economic crises that particularly affected Western economies. Since then, many voices in Russian expert circles have expressed the idea that Westernization is not the only way to achieve economic modernization, instead looking East—not only to China but also to such Asian tigers and dragons as South Korea and Singapore—for models from which to draw inspiration. In 2015, Sergey Karaganov spoke frankly about this turn away from the West: "We all lived in a world in which we saw ourselves and the world order to a significant degree through the eyes of the West and through the prism of theories to which the West gave birth, including those that explain international relations. These theories no longer work."[50]

Since the 2012–14 turning point, the regime has moved more definitively toward social creativity, impelling the Russian establishment to conceptualize the country's "civilizational" identity as *essentially* opposed to almost everything defined as Western, understood as a synonym for liberalism. In this worldview, the West, in all its definitions, is problematic. As we have seen, the primary issue has been with the geopolitical script of liberalism, which remains the fundamental point of disagreement for the Kremlin. But over time, this rejection of geopolitical liberalism has grown to be associated with a critique of cultural liberalism. Domestically, this shift has served to consolidate the "silent majority" against the liberal opposition, who stand accused of wanting not only to cede Russia's sovereignty to the "West's diktats" but also to morally corrupt Russian society by importing multiculturalism and gender politics (see chapter 8).

This disappointment in what the West has become heralded the end of what Ivan Krastev and Stephen Holmes call the "age of imitation."[51] Some prominent Russian cultural figures have crafted provocative formulas to describe the need to unlearn the West. The eminent film director Andrey Konchalovsky depicts, for instance, Western media as a "Ministry of Truth" that has the power to nominate villains and saviors but always exonerates the economic and political order constructed by, and in the interests of, the "Anglo-Saxon West."[52] Theatre director Konstantin Bogomolov, known for his fiery positions and a longtime liberal critical of conservative figures, has shifted his views and now frequently lambasts Western political correctness. In an inflammatory 2021 article entitled "The Rape of Europe 2.0," he denounces the "new ethical Reich" in which the progressive left, represented by an "aggressive mix of queer activists, fem-fanatics, and eco-psychopaths," is shutting down the ability for society to maintain a plurality of views.[53]

But it was not until Putin's 2019 declaration to the *Financial Times* on the obsolescence of liberalism that a clear shift in mindset could be observed. The shift was probably shaped not only by the rigidification of the regime domestically but also by the victory of several far-right / national-conservative /

populist figures in Europe and the US, and the globalization of culture wars. At the 2022 Valdai summit meeting, Putin referred ten times to liberalism, neoliberalism, liberal elites, and the US-style neoliberal world order, all in a negative way. The shift away from philosophical liberalism, said to have forgotten its own principles, became complete. He asserted:

> The liberal ideology itself has changed beyond recognition today. If classical liberalism initially understood the freedom of every person as the freedom to say what you want, to do what you want, then already in the 20th century liberals began to declare that the so-called open society has enemies—it turns out that an open society has enemies—and the freedom of such enemies can and should be limited, or even cancelled. Now they have completely reached the point of absurdity, when any alternative point of view is declared subversive propaganda and a threat to democracy.[54]

In many respects, what Russian official language now denounces is not the classical liberalism that was a product of the Enlightenment, but today's progressive liberalism embodied by identity politics—the reformulation of the citizenry through individual and group identities, with the promotion of differences (in terms of race, ethnicity, sexual orientation, and gender) and rising discourses of victimhood.[55] Nikolay Patrushev himself gave vent to tirades on the alteration of traditional Western values by postmodernity:

> The entire structure of traditional Western values has been so thoroughly altered that the catalogue of its current "universal" norms has virtually nothing in common with the former, more familiar to us, value system of European civilization . . . New Western values have turned into the imposition of an alien worldview on the world.[56]

In this framework, Russia is presented as holding onto—real, imagined, or idealized—classic modernity against the postmodernity of the West.[57] Sergey Karaganov formulates this idea neatly when he affirms that "while the West pursued 'post-European values,' Russia turned to 'traditional European' values, such as 'sovereignty, a strong state, Christian ethics and moral norms.'"[58] Russia therefore seeks to preserve the modernity of original liberalism, before the arrival of identity politics.[59] The idea of a "first modernity" that needs to be rescued is neither new nor unique to Russia: conservative thinkers such as Leo Strauss, Thomas Molnar, and Eric Voegelin likewise shift the debate on the idea of the "crisis of the West" to focus on the idea that there exists a true Western heritage rooted in a rejection of some forms of modernity.⁶⁰ Russian conservative language frequently borrows from the conservative West, and has integrated themes and strategies that have their origins in US culture wars⁶¹—in this sense, the "age of imitation" has not ended.

FIGHTING THE WEST: FASCISM, RUSSOPHOBIA, AND GENOCIDE

Moving Russia's political culture away from references to the polysemic West could have been accomplished as an economic and institutional "exit" from the West rather than as an entrance into a direct conflict or even war with it. But over the years, anti-Westernism has grown into a central metanarrative on the Russian political landscape, one that is intrinsically associated with conspiracy theories.

Before the full-scale war began in 2022, there were major nuances in the Russian perception of the political West. The Kremlin and state media targeted the US more than European countries, criticizing the EU for subjugating itself to US interests but remaining milder in their rhetoric toward individual European countries, especially those who were key economic partners. Generally speaking, Western European countries such as Germany, France, and Italy were better treated than those seen as being at the forefront of anti-Russian policies, such as the UK, Poland, and the Baltic states. With the 2022 turning point, the idea of a "collective West," which lumps all Western countries together and blends geopolitical and cultural liberalism, has become a central trope of state language. Previously marginal notions, such as the use of the term "Anglo-Saxon countries" to describe the US, the UK, and Canada—countries considered to be spearheading international support for Ukraine—have penetrated the mainstream and can now be found in official state speeches: the Foreign Policy Concept of 2023 refers, for instance, to the "US and other Anglo-Saxon states as the main inspirers, organizers and executors of the aggressive anti-Russia policy of the collective West."⁶²

Over the years, another semantic field has grown: that of "Russophobia." The term is now used by the Russian authorities not only to denounce punitive actions by some Central and Eastern European states against Russian citizens or acts of "cancellation" of Russian culture in the West but also to criticize all those who disagree with Moscow. Coined by the Russian poet and diplomat Fyodor Tyutchev in 1867 to complain about the European refusal to recognize Russia's moral exceptionalism,⁶³ the term reappeared in Stalinist propaganda and during the Cold War years to denounce the perceived Russophobia of US diplomatic policy toward the Soviet Union.[64] Long used within the Russian nationalist *belles-lettres* realm—for instance, by the dissident mathematician and antisemitic writer Igor Shafarevich (1923–2017) in his infamous pamphlet *Russophobia: The Jewish War against the Russian People*—the notion reemerged in official language after 2014 to condemn Western criticisms of Russia. Since 2022, the term's popularity has skyrocketed in the media realm and has even reached a more official level, with the Ministry of Justice developing in 2023 a bill that would provide a legal definition of Russophobia.[65]

The Russian authorities' use of the Russophobia argument is closely tied to the structuring of an argument claiming that "genocide" is being committed against the Russian people.[66] This term likewise has a long history in Russian nationalist circles: it was evoked by Soviet-era dissidents to denounce the regime's destruction of traditional peasant life and disregard for the environment.[67] It was then reactivated in the early 1990s by ethnonationalist groups, which denounced the lack of status of the twenty-five million Russians who found themselves in new countries and who were being mistreated—really or imaginarily—by the newly independent authorities. In 1998, Sergey Glazyev, then associated with the Congress of Russian Communities and its irredentist agenda, published the book *Genocide* to call out the supposed world oligarchy's policy of destroying Russia.[68]

The term first became mainstream in 2008, when Moscow justified its military actions in South Ossetia and Abkhazia as protecting the local population against the "genocide" being perpetrated by the Georgian authorities,[69] and then grew in scale with the war in Donbas in 2014. Since then, the authorities have built a narrative around the idea that "genocide" is being committed by Ukrainian troops in the Donbas region. This narrative places particular stress on the children killed, to whom the "Alley of Angels" memorial was built in Donetsk. This notion took on a legal and judicial character when Russia utilized UN institutions in an attempt to demonstrate the "genocide" of the Donbas population.[70] In his February 24 speech justifying the full-scale invasion of Ukraine, Putin explained that the purpose of the "special military operation" was "to protect people who, for eight years now, have been facing humiliation and genocide perpetrated by the Kiev regime."[71]

Yet it is the deployment of the notions of fascism and Nazism that represent the epitome of efforts to depict the West as Russia's eternal enemy.[72] In the Soviet tradition, as in today's Russia, the term *fashizm* does not refer to a set of abstract principles related to the nature of a political philosophy but rather embodies a very concrete enemy of the nation: Nazi Germany. The Great Patriotic War and the May 9 victory are indeed watershed events in Russia's history, as well as in Russians' memories. Over the course of two decades beginning in the mid-1960s, the Soviet state constructed a powerful epic around the nation's uniquely high contribution to the war and proclaimed the victory over Nazi Germany as legitimizing the socialist regime in its competition with the capitalist world. Yet some elements of Nazi culture, mostly its aesthetic, also circulated among some segments of Soviet society. As Mischa Gabowitsch observes, "The very solemnity of Soviet antifascism, and its centrality to the country's political identity, also led to the emergence of a different kind of irony about fascism, one that is perhaps best described as *stiob* [parody, ML]."[73]

The nation's foundational myth since the 1970s, the "war against fascism" is today still understood in Russia as an event of mythic proportions: larger than life, it exemplifies the highest human values of courage and sacrifice, elevating the Russian people to the double status of martyr *and* hero. As stated by minister of foreign affairs Sergey Lavrov at the 2005 Victory Day celebrations, 1945 was "the victory of life over death."[74] The war conveys such a profound meaning that it continues to form the backbone of social consensus in Russia—manifesting today's nostalgia for late-Soviet culture and Soviet welfare. Yet for the regime, Russia's struggle against fascism is not confined to the past; the crusade is ongoing. Vladimir Putin revealed this mindset as early as 2005, declaring that the "imperishable lesson from the war is [still] today very actual and important."[75] The president has indeed regularly warned citizens that fascism could return and Russia may once again be called to rescue itself—and the world—from this evil.

Long before the first war with Ukraine in 2014, the notion of Russia as *the* antifascist power *par excellence* was already written in stone in both elite discourse and public opinion. Since then, "fascism" has become one of Russia's major strategic narratives, used to justify its intervention in Ukraine and its reading of Western support for the Ukrainian authorities. As shown in figure 3.3, both notions of fascism and Nazism first peaked during Medvedev's presidency, when Central and Eastern European countries launched their own memory wars around the interpretation of the Second World War; Russia responded with the creation of the Presidential Commission against the falsification of history (see chapter 5).[76] While the notion of fascism has regular peaks (around May 9 celebrations in particular), it is worth noting that it has

FIG. 3.3. Mentions of "fascism" and "Nazism" in presidential speeches, 2000–2023.

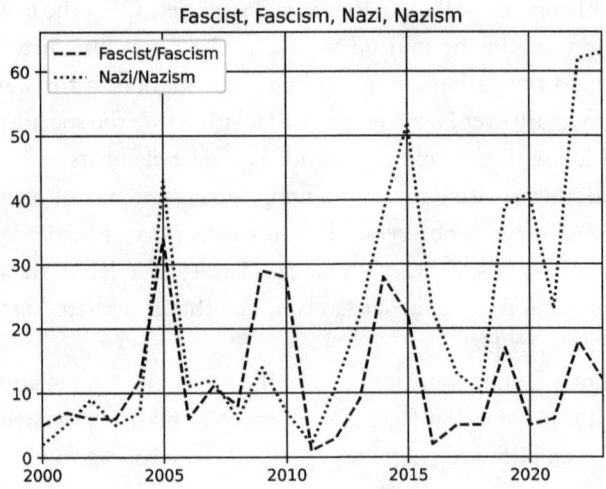

Source: Author's compilation based on Kremlin.ru for *fashizm/fashist, natsi/natsizm*.

been declining in use, replaced by that of (neo)Nazism, which has gradually won out in presidential speeches, a sign of the acuity of the historical parallel drawn by Russia between Nazi Germany and Western-supported Ukraine.

In the Russian vision, today's fascists are people who want to destroy Europe: those who deny the Yalta order by equating Communism with Nazism and those who promote postmodern theories that deconstruct collective identities. Conservatives, meanwhile, are those who want to rescue the "real" Europe: those who promote conservative values, defend classical Western civilization (in the sense of both antiquity and state sovereignty), and support a conventional reading of the Soviet victory in the Second World War. In this *Weltanschauung*, the European far-right forces that Moscow has courted for years find themselves in the conservative camp, not the fascist one, thereby allowing for strategic alliances with them: that is what the Russian media imply when, for example, they present Marine Le Pen as the heir of de Gaulle's worldview and not as a representative of the far right.[77]

The label of "who is fascist" thus determines what the ideal Europe should be. If Russia is fascist—if the Putin regime can be typologized as fascist, or if the Soviet past that the Kremlin does not want to denounce is the equivalent of Nazism—then Russia is to be excluded from Europe and portrayed as its antithesis, the constituent "other" of all the values embedded in the notion of Europe: liberalism, democracy, multilateralism, and transatlantic commitment. If, on the contrary, Moscow declares that Europe is itself once again becoming "fascist"—if the ideological status quo concerning the 1945 victory is contested and Europe's so-called traditional values are under attack—then Russia points the way toward the "real" Europe—Christian, conservative, geopolitically continental, and nation-centric—to be recovered. The current fight to identify who is fascist is thus a struggle to define the future of Europe, and it is the key question of Russia's inclusion or exclusion that draws the dividing line. With the 2022 war in Ukraine, framed by the Russian regime as a reenactment of the Great Patriotic War, the positioning of Europe as neo-fascist or neo-Nazi because it has become "Russophobic" has reached its fateful peak.

The conflict between Russia and the West is based on situated identities. For Russia, the crisis has been produced by the West's refusal to offer Moscow the status of cocreator of the new world order, which resulted in EU and NATO expansion into a space Russia considered to be in its sphere of strategic interest. For the West, Russia is responsible for disrupting the European order by not accepting the strategic autonomy of its neighbors and for openly violating Ukraine's internationally recognized borders.[78] The West and Russia are therefore impervious to each other's arguments, as they relate to different periods of reference. For Russia, "normalcy" refers to the Cold War decades, during which the country enjoyed the status of a respected great power that was consulted on all major international issues, deeply influential on the European stage, and considered the victorious ally of the United States against fascism. For the West, "normalcy" refers to the early 1990s—when Russia aligned with the West's main geopolitical interests, did not oppose EU expansion, and was very critical of its Soviet past.

Over the past three decades, the Russian establishment has been shifting its viewpoint on the relationship with the West in all its semantic dimensions. The Kremlin has continued to share references to universalism and humanism, prosperity, modernization, and economic liberalism—one may obviously dispute whether it has succeeded at implementing them, but it has not abandoned them rhetorically. Yet it has gradually moved from challenging the

West in its embodiment of liberal internationalism to condemning the West as a political, cultural, and moral order that crusades against all those who refuse to adopt its set of values. The idea has taken root that Russia needs to unlearn the West in order to take the lead of what Ivan Timofeev calls the "rebellion of the discontented."[79] Nevertheless, as we will see in the next chapter, there is no consensus among the Russian establishment regarding Russia's relationship to Europe identity-wise. The debate is far from over, even in the context of war.

FOUR

BYZANTIUM
The Christian Europe

Crimea bear[s] an enormous civilizational and sacral meaning for Russia, just as the Temple Mount of Jerusalem does for those who profess Islam and Judaism.
VLADIMIR PUTIN, Address to the Nation, March 18, 2014[1]

EVEN IF THE RUSSIAN regime has evolved in its interpretation of the West, the idea that Russia remains, against all odds, a European country culturally, even if anti-European in its policies, constitutes a cornerstone of the regime, just as it represents a key tenet for the majority of the political and intellectual elite. Over the years, the narrative of Russia's belonging to Europe has taken on a more religious or at least spiritual color, with state language insisting on Russia's Christian faith and its rootedness in Greco-Roman culture.

The geopolitical imaginary epitomizing these European roots is that of Byzantium, a historical and cultural metaphor that allows Russia to present Eastern Christianity as more faithful to the original spirit of Christ than Western Christianity, and therefore Russia as the real Europe as opposed to the decadent West. The myth of being the new Constantinople or the Third Rome also supports several of Russia's strategic and foreign policy goals, as seen in Syria and Ukraine: by reviving its Pontic identity (from Pontus, the Ancient Eastern Mediterranean), Russia anchors Crimea within the national body politic and consolidates its footprint on the Black Sea and Eastern Mediterranean shorelines.

BYZANTIUM, AN OLD RESERVOIR FOR CULTURAL METAPHORS

The "imagined community" with Byzantium has been largely reconstructed over several centuries of Russian history, as documented by the Byzantinologist Sergey A. Ivanov.[2] Russia's embrace of Eastern Christianity under Prince Vladimir in 988 and the marriage of Ivan III and Zoe Paleologue, niece of the last Byzantine emperor, in 1472 constitute the two central bonds between Byzantium and Russia. The first is spiritual, through the choice of the Eastern Orthodox version of Christianity by Prince Vladimir/Volodymyr of Kiev/Kyiv; the second is political and geopolitical, as Ivan III consolidated autocratic rule and led the "reassembly of Russian lands" (*sobiranie russkikh zemel'*), opening the path for the Moscow principality to become the Russian Empire.

First crafted in the early sixteenth century by the monk Philotheus from the Belozersky Monastery under the slogan "Moscow—Third Rome," the metaphor of Russia as the third Rome and therefore the second Byzantium was recorded in the Founding Deed of the Moscow Patriarchate in 1589. The myth was revived in the eighteenth century, when imperial Russia under Catherine the Great sought to defeat the Ottoman Empire and restore Constantinople to its past splendor, and again in the nineteenth century to legitimize Russia's pan-Slavist ideology and its foreign policy of building protectorates in the Orthodox Balkans.[3] Russia as the heir of Constantinople was epitomized by the main figures of Russian conservative thought at that time: Konstantin Leontyev (1831–1891), in his *Byzantinism and Slavdom* (1875), crafted a specific Russo-Byzantine civilization. Leontyev never hid his disappointment with Slavophiles, who, according to him, "have always seemed to me to be people with the most common, European and moderate liberal way of thinking."[4] Criticizing their idealization of the peasantry, he endorsed a monarchist, rather than populist, brand of Orthodoxy.

For Leontyev, Slavonic civilization was nothing without the heritage of Byzantium, as the latter offered a set of precepts whose nature was at once political (the most absolute autocracy and the symphony of powers, *sobornost'* in Russian), religious (the Orthodox faith), and cultural (a patriarchal sense of family and the principle of a peasant commune). Hence, only Byzantinism could be opposed to European modern ideas of equality and liberty and define the Slavs against the Romano-Germanics. Leontyev thus invited Russia to forget about the emancipation of the Slavs—a modern revolutionary and nationalist idea—and focus on liberating Constantinople and reviving its theocracy. *Tsargrad* (the Russian name for Constantinople, meaning "the city of the tsar") would be not simply one of the empire's new administrative regions but a personal possession of the tsar and, like Rome, a double capital: that of Russia and of the Orthodox world.

An outspoken philhellenist, Leontyev was also (impressively for his time, when the Russian elites harbored very explicit anti-Ottoman feelings) quite a Turcophile: he claimed that Russians and Turks were much closer to one another than they were to Westerners and argued that Russia needed "more Asian mysticism and less rationalizing European Enlightenment," making Russia's relations with Turkey the "most natural and the most faithful."[5] The father of Russia's Byzantinist ideology also prefigured a nascent Eurasianism, dreaming of a Russian Empire that would constitute a third world stretching "from the shores of China and of Japan to the Mediterranean and Egypt."[6] He further foreshadowed anticolonial sentiments, stating: "Salvation is in Asia. If we, the Russians, do not take it upon ourselves to create a unique culture, then the 'millions of other Asians' will do so."[7] Fyodor Dostoyevsky (1821–1881) seconded Leontyev's call, declaring that "Constantinople must become Russian."[8]

In Soviet times, Byzantium was initially criticized for its backwardness; it was seen as symbolizing everything the Bolshevik regime wanted to destroy. It was, however, gradually rehabilitated during Stalinism's national-Bolshevik synthesis and then in the 1960s as a historical and cultural legacy that highlighted the *longue durée* of Soviet Russia's distinctness from the capitalist West. From Andrey Tarkovsky's film *Andrey Rublev* (1966) to Sergey Averintsev's classes on Byzantine esthetics at Moscow State University, the legacy of Byzantium was reintegrated into the national pantheon concurrently with the rediscovery of the anti-Bolshevik White movement from the Russian Civil War and the first signs of nostalgia for the last tsar, Nicholas II.[9]

NEO-BYZANTINISM: RUSSIA'S CULTURAL CENTRALITY IN EUROPE

With the Soviet collapse, Byzantium became a powerful source of messianic metaphors for all those trying to make sense of the dramatic changes and to discern paths for the future. It was brandished by the Russian Orthodox Church and conservative forces such as Zyuganov's Communist Party, as well as by Alexander Dugin, who sought to merge references to Byzantine autocracy, Eurasia's geopolitical mission, and Traditionalist authors such as René Guénon and Julius Evola.[10] In the cultural realm, the New Academy of Timur Novikov (1958–2002), which included prominent figures in Russian cultural life, was founded in the early 1990s on the idea of Russia as the guardian of European Christian identity, promoting a new Russian classicism operating within archetypes of ancient culture. As Novikov explains:

> Preserving the classics is especially important to us Russians. After all, following the collapse of the Byzantine Empire it was Rus' that preserved the values of Byzantine civilization, and today, when throughout the century-long "modernization" of European culture Russia alone has not yet undergone a humanitarian catastrophe, we once again must take upon ourselves the function of guardians of the classical European culture to which our country turned three centuries ago.[11]

In the political realm, one of the early and tireless proponents of this Byzantine legacy has been Nataliya Narochnitskaya, one of the least studied yet most prolific and articulate Russian nationalist intellectuals.[12] Narochnitskaya has served as an MP in the Duma, as a representative of co-opted nationalist parties such as Rodina, and as a public diplomacy figure—she worked for a decade as director of the Paris-based Institute for Cooperation and Democracy. Her main work, *Russia and the Russians in World History* (1996), has been reedited several times.[13] She has also been an active contributor to the Presidential Commission to Counter Attempts to Falsify History to the Detriment of Russia's Interests (see chapter 5) and runs her own Historical Perspective Foundation.

Narochnitskaya has been an outspoken supporter of an Orthodox vision of Russia, rehabilitating nineteenth-century pan-Slavism and calling for the unification of all Orthodox nations, and a reinforced solidarity with the Balkans. Updating the old Slavophile theme of a Europe divided between the Romano-Germanic world (now the Anglo-Saxon one) and the Slavic realm, she considers Russia's path to have diverged from that of Western Europe in the fifteenth century, when Russia avoided the Renaissance and the birth of individualism and secularism. She advocates for using the notions of empire and tsardom (*tsarstvo*) to define Russia, as well as engaging with Russia's multiethnic character not through the notion of Eurasia but through that of its being a "post-Byzantine space,"[14] and sees in the legacy of the Third Rome the signs of Russia's moral superiority over the rest of Europe.

However, Naronichtskaya has been quite isolated in her pan-Slavist reading of the Byzantine legacy. As discussed by Mikhail Suslov, pan-Slavism in today's Russia remains a strictly marginal ideology that is far from fully deployed except in the case of the country's relations with Serbia, where brotherhood in Slavness, in faith, and in geopolitical positioning overlap.[15] The old idea of Slavs as the age-old victims of Western aggression has been activated only in the case of Serbia, which has seen the dismemberment of Yugoslavia, followed by the independence of Kosovo, and has been governed by the "outsider" regimes first of Slobodan Milošević and then of Aleksandar Vučić. Otherwise, the Russian political landscape has more often articulated pro-Orthodox narratives than pan-Slavic ones, visible in Moscow's support for Greeks (with frequent mentions of the famous Mount Athos, which is important in Russian religious culture due to housing a cluster of Orthodox monasteries), Cypriots, Abkhaz and South Ossetians, and Balkan nations more than for Slavs per se.

Less nostalgic for pan-Slavism than Narochnitskaya, Mikhail Remizov, one of the leading figures of the Young Conservative movement (see chapter 8), has advanced a better-articulated vision of what Byzantium represents politically for Russia. Russia's Byzantine connection cements its status as a cofounder of European civilization, yet dissociates itself from a post-Christian Europe:

> If we understand civilization in terms of its roots—antiquity, Christianity, a certain Jewish component through Biblical thought, plus Slavic, Celtic, German, Indo-European roots, myths—then we are quite close to Europe. We have common roots. And our cultural codes are also similar.[16]

> Russia should in no way position itself as part of Asia or a conditional "non-Europe." Such a position will play on Russia's separation not only from its potential allies in the Western world, but also from its own cultural roots. Russian culture is one of the standard European cultures, rooted in the common heritage of Christianity and antiquity. An important thesis is the connection of Russia with the Eastern Roman Empire—Byzantium. The very fact of this connection and historical continuity forbids Russia to be "thrown out" of the European field . . . The Byzantine heritage . . . is a very serious argument that allows Russia to position itself as an equal partner in the debate about European values. Of course, along with the baggage of Russian culture proper, this allows the conservative community in Russia to maintain a healthy dialogue with Europe—not as "students of the West" and not in confrontation with it, but from the position of one of the co-authors of European civilization.[17]

Neo-Byzantinism has also been advocated by Leonid Reshetnikov, who worked for decades for the Foreign Intelligence Service and headed the Russian Institute for Strategic Studies (RISI), the Foreign Intelligence Service's think tank, from 2009 to 2017. During his years leading RISI, Reshetnikov oriented the think tank toward a monarchist stance, which was expressed, for instance, when it sided with the church on the issue of the remains of Tsar Nicholas II's family.[18] Fascinated by anti-Bolshevik White émigrés even during Soviet times, Reshetnikov published the first biographical article on Ivan Solonevich (1891–1953), a reactionary White thinker, as early as 1990. In 2019, he released *Going Back to Russia*, a book calling for a return to prerevolutionary Russia as the civilization of Christ.[19] Since then, he has played a key role in reviving the memory of White Russian émigrés in Bulgaria, Serbia, and Greece. His association, Russian Lemnos, the name of a Greek island that hosts a Russian cemetery, has been active in restoring churches, repairing monuments linked to White Russian émigrés, erecting commemorative plaques and statues, and so on.[20] It was banned from Bulgaria in 2019 for espionage activities.

The peak of the metaphor of Russia as the second Byzantium and its near-officialization in state language was reached in 2008 with the pseudo-documentary film *The Destruction of an Empire: Lesson from Byzantium*. Directed by then bishop, future Metropolitan Tikhon, the film was aired on national channels several times, offering a pastiche of history full of factual mistakes and presentisms. The obvious goal was to compare Byzantium to Putin's Russia, framing the two states as facing the same eternal external enemies—the West (with the historical analogy to the Western Crusades) and terrorism (with the historical analogy to the Islamic conquest of Byzantium)—and domestic enemies (oligarchs and liberal forces).[21] The film generated huge public debate, both positive and negative, and was even criticized by Patriarch Alexy II for overstating the similarities between the two cases.[22] It has apparently become a must-see in military circles, with copies distributed by the General Staff of the Russian Armed Forces as anniversary gifts.[23]

The public passion for Byzantium revived in 2014 with the annexation of Crimea, but in a deeply transformed way. Suddenly, Russia was shown as a core participant in European life. Putin argued that Prince Vladimir converted to Orthodox Christianity in the city of Khersones before ordering the official baptism in Kiev.[24] In 2015, a small Byzantine Club was launched within the Institute for Political Research, an official think tank led by Sergey Markov; members included such notable nationalist politicians as Sergey Baburin, as well as Byzantinologists like professor Sergey Karpov of Moscow State University, who is president of the National Committee of Byzantinologists.[25] The club presents itself as "asserting and reinforcing the values of Eastern Christian civilization within the modern world. The Byzantine Club is a forge for new ideas, ideas that shape new approaches to national politics based on a historical continuity with Byzantium."[26]

But this neo-Byzantinism has been much more than a tool of political rhetoric. It has fundamentally reshaped Russia's cultural policies, bringing about what Maria Engström has called a new "Russian renaissance," cherishing European heritage and Western Christian culture.[27] With the annexation of Crimea, Russia's cultural exhibition policy stressed the country's ancient European heritage through a range of cultural events, among them blockbuster exhibitions by the country's main art museums—the Hermitage, the Russian Museum, the Tretyakov Art Gallery, and the Pushkin Museum of Fine Arts—including an impressive exhibition of the Vatican's Pinacoteca masterpieces. This vision of a Russia inscribed in the European classical humanities also inspired the aesthetic reassessment of Soviet cultural classicism, both architectural and painterly, as an integral part of European modernism.[28] Moscow's desire to appropriate the classical humanist traditions that have shaped Russian culture for centuries was encapsulated in the Mariinsky Orchestra's open-air concert conducted in liberated Palmyra, in Syria, in May 2016.[29] Under the title "Pray for Palmyra: Music Revives Ancient Ruins," it recalls the nineteenth-century Slavophiles for whom links with ancient Near Eastern cultures, from the Hittites to the Sumerians, were a sign of Russia's destiny to reconcile Noah's three sons: Japheth (representing the Indo-European peoples), Shem (the Semitic ones), and Ham (the African ones).[30]

This policy of reappropriation of Europe's legacy dating back to antiquity was pursued with the television series *Sophia* (2016), funded by both the Ministry of Culture and the Ministry of Defense. Based on the life of the Byzantine princess Zoe "Sophia" Palaiologina, wife of Ivan III, who laid the foundations of Russia's imperial statehood, the series celebrates both Muscovy's participation in the life of fifteenth-century Europe and the cultural tradition of the Italian Renaissance that the princess brought to Moscow. The metaphor of Byzantium has since continued to be used to define Russia's alternative Europeanness. Metropolitan Tikhon boasted of the idea of creating a historical park celebrating Crimea's Byzantine past;[31] although this was never realized, the historical re-creation "Russia, My History," behind which he was a driving force, insisted heavily on Russia as Byzantium's heir.[32] Around Tikhon, other figures such as the monarchist tycoon Konstantin Malofeev likewise play on the Byzantium parallel: the cover image on the first volume of his book *Imperium* blends St. Basil's Cathedral in Moscow with the Hagia Sophia in Istanbul.[33]

PONTIC RUSSIA: THE PIVOT TOWARD THE EASTERN MEDITERRANEAN AND BLACK SEA REALM

Used at home to defend the regime status quo through historical analogies, the Byzantium repertoire has also been deployed in a specific foreign policy realm: Russia's turn to the Eastern Mediterranean and Black Sea. Since the 2014–15 turning point of Crimea's annexation and war in Syria, Moscow has aimed to secure as much control as possible over the Black Sea: together with the Balkan region, the Black Sea forms one of the key lines of tension with the West, covering NATO members (Turkey, Bulgaria, and Romania) along with five NATO partners (Armenia, Azerbaijan, Georgia, Moldova, and Ukraine); the secessionist Georgian regions of South Ossetia and Abkhazia; and obviously Ukraine.[34] Partial hegemony over the Black Sea allows Russia to project greater military force in the Eastern Mediterranean, guaranteeing its security against NATO and allowing it to help its Syrian ally and others in the Middle East who may need Moscow's support.[35] With the full-scale war, the Black Sea has become a critical space of tensions, with the Ukrainian army winning some major victories against the Russian fleet deployed there.

This pivot toward Russia's southwestern flank should be understood as a structural and long-term reorientation by Moscow toward the country's Pontic roots. This Pontic axis has been accompanied by a demographic trend favoring Russia's south: the Southern and the North Caucasus Federal Districts have grown by more than three million inhabitants in the three decades since the collapse of the Soviet Union; they now account for 18 percent of the country's population (compared to 15 percent in 1991) and are home to such booming cities as Krasnodar, located just east of Crimea.[36] This demographic dynamism reinforces the geopolitical weight of Russia's own Black Sea facade.

To this should be added, obviously, the annexation of Crimea, which dramatically shifted the Russian regime's political and strategic (as well as financial) calculus. In the hope of making any return of Crimea to Ukraine impossible, Moscow has invested massively in linking the region to the rest of Russia, not only in terms of logistics and administration but also at the symbolic level. The Kerch Strait Bridge—inaugurated by Putin in May 2018, seven months ahead of schedule—is a visual reflection of the peninsula's reconnection to Russia's main territorial body, and a key strategic object for the war against Ukraine. The unique status given to the region is reflected in the fact that Sevastopol has been elevated to a federal city on par with Moscow and St. Petersburg, while Sochi has been transformed into one of Russia's capitals, hosting high-level summits and personalities with a frequency eclipsed only by Moscow and St. Petersburg. The Russian authorities have also made an array of symbolic gestures: reshaping the logo of the Crimean republic for tourism purposes; integrating the peninsula and Sevastopol into the new banknotes; funding a massive rebranding of Crimean products, from wine and jams to soaps and teas; securing preferential procurement from state institutions, etc. Donetsk and Luhansk did not get such preferential treatment but are now in the process of integrating the pantheon of Russia's nationhood, while the other annexed regions of Kherson and Zaporizhzhia are less celebrated.

Other telling examples of that Pontic identity were both the screenization of Russia's Europeanness during the opening ceremony of the 2014 Sochi Winter Olympics and the new Italian-style Gorky Gorod ski resort in Sochi, which combines a Roman-inspired amphitheater and Spanish seaside-style architecture. In a similar vein, the Russian Geographical Society funded an archaeological expedition to Akra, a sunken city in the waters of the Kerch Strait between the Black Sea and the Sea of Azov, which was seen as a way to celebrate Russia's reunification with its Bosphorus legacy via Crimea. The branding of the sunken city as a "Crimean Atlantis" epitomizes the mythological process currently underway around Russia's rediscovered Pontic identity. At least the expedition looks more serious than the orchestrated "discovery," by a scuba-diving Putin himself, of two alleged Greek urns on the floor of the Black Sea in 2011, a brazen propaganda move ridiculed by the Russian blogosphere.[37]

Eastern Orthodox Christianity plays a pivotal role in this new Mediterranean entrenchment. A privileged and centuries-old relationship to the Greek and Pontic realms, as well as the protection of Eastern Christians since Ottoman times, are powerful historical memories that have been easily revamped by the Russian Orthodox Church. Russian institutions have, for instance, used and abused Russia's Pontic identity as a soft power tool in relation to Greece and Cyprus. The Russian-Greek businessman Ivan Savvidis has promoted the idea of Russia as the savior of the Orthodox world and a power spiritually linked to Mont Athos to support Russophile movements in Greece.[38]

Last but not least, the Syrian Civil War has pushed the Moscow Patriarchate to display Orthodox solidarity with Levantine Christians. As Dmitry Adamsky puts it, "In Syria, the Orthodox Church became a tool of genuine strategic influence."[39] In the first year of the civil war, the ROC published a statement calling "upon the world community, religious leaders and all public forces to develop a mechanism for the defense of the Middle East Christian communities."[40] Patriarch Kirill visited Lebanon, Egypt, and Syria, where he was received by President Bashar al-Assad himself in Damascus. In 2013, Putin received the primates and representatives of Middle Eastern Churches for the 1,025th anniversary of the Baptism of Rus'.[41] That same year, the ROC lobbied for Moscow to grant Russian citizenship to 50,000 Syrian Christians from the Qualamun region.[42] ROC spokesman Nikolay Balashov saw this request as proving Russia's "great authority" in the Middle East, declaring that Middle Eastern Christians "have known for centuries that no other country would look after their interests in the same way Russia would."[43] In 2014, the ROC organized a meeting with the fourteen existing autocephalous Orthodox churches on the fate of Levantine Christians. The Antioch and Jerusalem patriarchs regularly praised Moscow for its defense of Christians, while sharply criticizing the West for its lack of action in this regard. The ROC also established a dialogue with the Vatican through joint statements on the need for a unified effort to rescue Eastern Christians and stop the violence in the Middle East.[44]

The joint positioning of the Kremlin and the ROC on Russia as the geopolitical protector of Eastern Christians and Byzantium was unexpectedly challenged by the Russian-Ukrainian religious schism. In 2018, the Constantinople Patriarchate decided to recognize the autocephaly (self-headed nature) of the Orthodox Church of Ukraine (OCU), prompting the Moscow Patriarchate to abruptly cut ties with one of the most respected, if geopolitically minor, patriarchates. The full-scale invasion of Ukraine and the pressure from the Ukrainian government to exclude the Ukrainian Orthodox Church of the Moscow Patriarchate (UOC-MP) from the national religious landscape has only aggravated the geopolitical division of the Orthodox realm.

This move toward a major new schism has to some degree weakened Russia's recently rebuilt legitimacy as a Pontic power.[45]

Russia's Byzantine identity crystallized between 2008 and 2014 at a strategic moment for the country's military involvement in the Black Sea and Eastern Mediterranean, as well as for a domestic shift toward the country's southern regions, which enjoy increasing demographic and political importance. Even in the context of the war and decoupling from Europe, the vision of Russia as intrinsically connected to European identity has not disappeared. As Fyodor Lukyanov asserted in 2023:

> The Russia of the future, as long as it is populated by those who live there now, has been, is and will be a country of European culture and European tradition. Regardless of whether it confirms it or denies it, whether it struggles with it or rejoices, it does not matter. Our worldview is shaped by the influence of Europe and by the perception of Europe as a landmark.[46]

The reference to Byzantium meshes well with the regime's counterrevolutionary script, will be discussed in Part III. It has been easily revived as the spatial embodiment of Russia's moral claims to be a conservative power in the face of a Western Europe that has lost its way. Here too, the war has not totally stopped the strategy of appealing to the conservative West. In 2023, a group of scholars published an article in *Russia in Global Affairs* calling on Russia not to forget about its membership of European civilization and indeed to use this as a bridge to speak to conservative Europeans:

> Russia undoubtedly belongs to the European cultural space. At the same time, modern Europe, which has come to a civilizational crisis of values as a result of the imposition of the left-liberal model across the globe, cannot serve as a worthy guide. The preservation and restoration of values characteristic of genuine Europe is an important civilizational task. These are the traditional values whose significance is outlined in Russia's state strategic documents. When setting an example for Europe, Russia should not forget that the Western cultural and political space is not homogeneous and has enough potential allies. Working with them to achieve the common goal of creating a healthier world in the future is the most important task.[47]

Many of the arguments used to promote Russia's exit from the West while belonging to Europe are thus simultaneously present in the Byzantium and Eurasian (see chapter 10) aspirational projects, with two different spatial representations: outside Europe for the second one, inside a revised Europe for the first one. Thus, unlike many other countries that reject the West as a norm-giver and try to offer a competing narrative (pan-Asianism in Asia, neo-Ottomanism in Erdoğan's Turkey), Russia proposes an alternative to the West *in the name of Europe.*

FIVE

SPIRITUAL SECURITY
Statism, Patriotism, History

True sovereignty for Russia is absolutely necessary for survival.
VLADIMIR PUTIN, Address to the Federal Assembly, 2014[1]

TO DEAL WITH THE West in all its semantic diversity, the Putin regime has gradually built what it defines as "spiritual security" (*dukhovnaia bezopasnost'*), with the state as the major cornerstone of this securitization. While the regime long presented a strong state as the best guarantee of normalcy and the embrace of modernization and globalization, it has gradually shifted to a more backward-looking and essentialist definition of what constitutes the state—and the nation behind it. This essentialist turn results directly from the lack of an institutional political space for expressing opinions: it erases debates over sociopolitical issues and primordializes politics as an identity question, giving a para-religious or philosophical depth to a depleted political life. As the Levada Center sociologist Boris Dubin explained as early as 2007: "What is presented as national is the condition allowing the depoliticization of the public space."[2]

The essentialization of the state makes history a political language in itself. This explains the regime's tenacious will to reorder history and memory to fit a teleological vision that makes it the only legitimate voice to explain what Russia should be. Paralleling George Orwell's famous adage "He who controls the past controls the future. He who controls the present controls the past," the Russian historian Yury Afanasyev contends that, in Russia, "The attitude toward the past is the central element of any ideology."[3] To become the undisputed guardian of a statist vision of history, the regime has had to work hard to design a suitable past—a perilous exercise given Russia's convoluted political history and the plurality of memories and infrastructures of remembrance that exist in the society.[4]

Memory is always a selective process: some components are highlighted, others are obscured, still others are silenced. While the prerevolutionary period has to some degree been rehabilitated, the national pantheon remains heavily inspired by the Soviet legacy: to this day, the historical figures most celebrated by the state and best known by the public are those who occupied the pantheon in Soviet times, among them Alexander Nevsky battling against Western invaders, Dmitry Donskoy defeating the Mongols, Peter the Great and his top-down modernization, Yuri Gagarin conquering space, and a whole array of world-famous literary and cultural figures.

The shift toward history accelerated with Putin's third term in 2012 and became one of the central components of his discourse, increasingly detached from everyday realities. Many close observers of the Presidential Administration have indicated that with age and isolation, the president has been diving into Russia's history in search of his own historical legacy.[5] The phenomenon is broader, however. Since 2012, a special section of the Presidential Administration has been dedicated to patriotic education and strengthening the country's so-called spiritual values, heavily investing administrative resources in shaping public memory and discourses around national history. The regime's presentism (interpreting past events in terms of modern values and concepts) is nothing new or specific to Russia. But Moscow's level of securitization of history against the "West" in all its semantic scope has reached unprecedented levels in recent decades.

PATRIOTISM AS STATE-CENTRISM

In the Russian ideological construction, the state is portrayed as the leading actor in Russian history, and service to the state is a key political virtue because, as William Pomeranz reminds us, the state "remains the only institution that has traditionally held the country—and empire—together."[6] This statism can be expressed as *derzhavnost'* (greatpowerness), *gosudarstvennichestvo* (statism), or *gosudarsvennost'* (statehood). Whatever their nuances, these terms all express the idea that Russia exists mainly through its state, which should be the benchmark of everything. The nation and the people are subordinated to it, as they cannot exist except under the protective state umbrella. If the state is weak, Russia is weak; if the state is strong, Russia is strong. Challenging the regime therefore means challenging the state, and thus challenging Russia itself—hence the ideological articulation that opponents of the regime are traitors to the nation. Putin himself declared in 2013: "Too often in our nation's history, instead of opposition to the government we have been faced with opponents of Russia itself. . . . And we know how it ended, with the demolition of the [Russian] state as such."[7] As figure 5.1 shows, and in contrast to many concepts at which we look in this book, presidential mentions of "statehood" were more prominent during early Putinism, declined to a low around 2010, and only later regained some visibility.

The semantic space of statism has taken two primary forms. The first is expressed by the notion of sovereignty as the absolute value of the international scene and interstate relations that we previously discussed. The second revolves around the idea of Russia's "one-thousand-year statehood." What matters here is the historical continuity of the state (*preemstvennost'*) beyond the many changes to the country's borders over time and its two main political disjunctures of 1917 and 1991. As the state embodies the nation, the continuity of leadership is crucial, reflected in the emphasis on state leaders over more cultural figures as personifications of Russia. As early as 2008, the state TV show *Name of Russia*, launched to determine the most notable figure in national history through a nationwide vote, selected nine statesmen and only three cultural figures.[8] In 2017, the government unveiled the Alley of Rulers, comprising thirty-three statues of historical figures who have ruled Russia since the ninth century, from Rurik, the founder of the first state, to Lenin and Stalin and their opponent Alexander Kerensky, the head of the Provisional Government liquidated by the Bolshevik Revolution, to personify Russia's historical continuity.[9]

This statehood should be read as nationhood too: It is the way the Kremlin institutionalizes nation-building language, used to define what Rogers Smith calls "stories of peoplehood,"[10] or a long series of events pertaining to the national group, from foundational moments to the present. The opening and closing ceremonies of the 2014 Sochi Olympics, for instance, visually represented Russia's millennial history, showcasing its central historical moments and the country's main cultural contributions to the world.[11] This insistence

FIG. 5.1. Mentions of "statehood" in presidential speeches, 2000–2023.

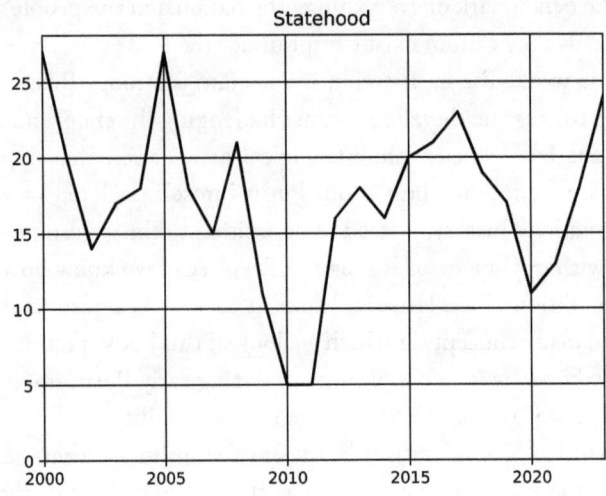

Source: Author's compilation based on Kremlin.ru.

on state continuity is not specifically Russian; France's *roman national* is likewise built on the continuity between the French monarchy and its enemy, the French republic born from the revolution, which are portrayed to young pupils as representing the same state entity regardless of political identity.

The Russian state has actively launched mass cultural heritage promotion to cultivate a shared sense of peoplehood. This includes intensive funding for the cinematographic and televisual production of Russian history, with several blockbusters (but also several commercial failures) devoted to leading historical figures. The government has erected many statues and monuments to shape the urban landscape, allowing regional authorities and sometimes patriotic civil society to develop their own projects. Some of these initiatives are decidedly top-down, like the Alley of the Leaders, while others try to involve the public, as with the vote to name Russia's airports after national heroes—a competition that engaged more than five million citizens.[12] All of this memory frenzy contributes to saturating the public space with historical references—yet, as Alexander Etkind notes, these monuments "do not blame, do not protest and do not explain the past."[13]

The centrality of statism to the Russian political construction has also resulted in patriotism being presented as the core value for citizens. The government launched a state program for the patriotic education of citizens of the Russian Federation as early as 2001, and its budget has grown over the years. Between 2006 and 2015, the authorities contributed between 70 and 130 million rubles annually to the program; this number jumped to 350 million rubles a year between 2016 and 2020 and then increased tenfold to 3.5 billion rubles in 2021.[14] Coordinated by several ministries, mostly Education and Defense, the program covers a wide range of activities offered to citizens and especially to youth (e.g., historical reenactment clubs, military history tours, festivals, and outdoor sports activities).[15]

Centered around the notion of defense of the fatherland and sacrifice for the motherland (*otechestvo* and *rodina*, respectively), patriotism has followed the securitization of Russian history by offering an increasingly militarized understanding of patriotism.[16] Unsurprisingly, the notion has been on the rise over the years (notwithstanding impressive declines, such as that between 2017 and 2019), and has peaked at moment of crisis, in 2014 and since 2020 (see fig. 5.2).

In the context of full-scale war, this military patriotism has grown into a mass phenomenon, with tens of thousands of events organized across the country.[17] In December of that year, the authorities launched the Movement of

FIG. 5.2. Mentions of "patriotism" in presidential speeches, 2000–2023.

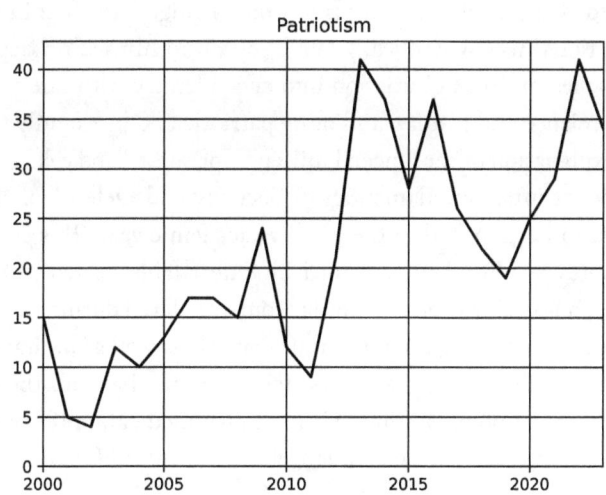

Source: Author's compilation based on Kremlin.ru.

the First, a patriotic youth movement for children from the age of six, which claims a (likely inflated) three million members.[18] The goal of the movement is to inculcate in these young people a worldview "based on traditional Russian spiritual and moral goals." The parallel with its Soviet predecessor is explicit: the movement was created for the centenary of the Young Pioneers, which young Soviet citizens joined before entering the Komsomol.[19]

The movement complements the Young Army (Iunarmiia), created in 2015 and which gathers a wide array of state military-patriotic movements, the Suvorov military boarding schools, and cadet corps into a single organization. Wearing gray uniforms and red berets, Young Army members (of whom there are officially 1.5 million) can choose from an extensive portfolio of activities: (1) dual-use activities inspired by scouting culture (e.g., orienteering in the natural environment, setting up camp and building a fire, providing first aid to victims); (2) physical activities and sports, including participation in several national sport and talent competitions, mostly with a military component; and (3) familiarization with military preparation and techniques, with weekend and summer camp options for artillery training, as well as opportunities to visit military expos and locations and to learn skills from active military personnel.[20]

Beginning in September 2022, all schools were instructed to hold a flag-raising ceremony every week (let us recall that this is the norm in many countries, including the US) and were directed to implement new extracurricular classes called "Conversations about Important Things." The first in this series of "conversations" was symbolically taught by Putin himself on September 1, 2022.[21] These lessons blend initiation into civic identity with safety and security norms, science and history, and more patriotic and pro-family themes, as well as an explanation of the "special military operation" and celebration of its heroes. A new course, Fundamentals of Security and Defense of the Motherland, is set to be launched in the 2024–25 academic year. This course is the heir of the previous Fundamentals of Life Safety (abbreviated in Russian as OBZh), which is itself the heir of similar courses offered during the Soviet era covering basic disaster preparedness and survival, as well as military training and weapons-handling. The new course will provide a basis for the more systematic familiarization of children with military-medical, military-scientific, and military-technical knowledge, as well as the rules of civil and military safety.[22]

Beyond the decisions made by the Ministry of Education, which are implemented across the whole country, early militarization of children (or resistance thereto) is partly left at the discretion of school directors and teachers. More zealous schools may organize mourning rituals for soldiers, offer military games to children as young as five or six, and serve as volunteer centers that help gather equipment for soldiers at the front and send them letters of support—all activities in which school pupils participate.[23] Some others try to do the minimal lip service. For instance, in a rare case, the mayor of Penza suggested not hanging commemorative plaques in schools for those who have died in the "special military operation," evoking their psychological impact on children—a proposal that generated a negative reaction from the political class.[24] This militarization is also visible at the human level: veterans of the "special military operation" will be able to teach the new course on security and defense of the motherland, as well as classes entitled "Lessons of Courage." In the future, they may become coteachers of all instruction related to civic education and a teacher-training center for veterans opened in 2023.[25]

THE STATE'S GRIP ON MEMORY OF THE SOVIET CENTURY

The securitization of Russia's history, understood as the need to reach a unified, mainstream narrative legitimizing the state in any context, was a gradual process. Upon coming to power in 2000, Putin immediately declared his disapproval of the country's multiplicity of historical narratives and history textbooks, seeing this as a sign of weakness and chaos that impeded citizens from feeling connected to their homeland. The government thus launched a commission to review the contents of existing textbooks and remove those considered too anti-Soviet from the officially approved list.[26] In 2005, prime minister Dmitry Medvedev was put in charge of the standardization of education, one of four national projects sponsored by the Presidential Administration.

In view of the need for a more unified narrative, the Ministry of Education released in 2007 a manual for teachers (not a student text), *The History of Russia, 1945–2007*, which aimed—albeit without success—to promote a unified discourse on twentieth-century history (taught in eleventh grade, the final year of high school). Such attempts to control textbooks' historical narrative have focused primarily on how the Stalin era should be interpreted: the teacher's manual famously advanced a positive assessment of Stalinism overall alongside a moderate view of Stalin's political repressions, describing him as "an effective manager."[27] This reflects the general tendency in Russian historiography to explain political repression as a necessary, if regrettable, phenomenon.[28] While this state initiative failed, at the time, to create a monopoly on the "usable past," it influenced textbook production: new works increasingly conformed to the state-backed storyline "through a combination of oblique signaling, selective endorsements, and self-censorship."[29]

The securitizing trend accelerated in 2009–10, when national history issues entered the international scene and became a central component of the memory wars with Central and Eastern European countries. For the Baltic states, Poland, Ukraine, and, to a lesser extent, Moldova and Georgia, rewriting their national histories of the twentieth century, particularly the Second World War, has been intimately connected with reaffirming their European destiny and influencing what Maria Mälksoo describes as the "European mnemonic map."[30] For the "new Europeans" of Central and Eastern Europe, the previous consensus narrative on the alliance between the Western powers and the Soviet Union against Nazi Germany contradicted the lived experience of being passed from Nazi to Soviet domination and excluded from European integrationist efforts for four decades.[31] As then Lithuanian president Valdas Adamkus bluntly put it, for the Baltic countries, May 9, 1945, was the day "we traded Hitler for Stalin."[32]

Newly articulated Central and Eastern European memory narratives have thus claimed the right to equate the Soviet regime with the Nazi regime, calling for transitional justice, punishment, or at least recognition of both perpetrators' guilt; the establishment of restitution and compensation policies; the creation of truth commissions; and the opening of archives. The Russian authorities have responded to what they see as historical revisionism by building a rival narrative and creating legal and historiographical tools for criminalizing this new memory scheme. Moscow decided, for instance, to make explicit its position on Russia's status as the legal continuation of the Soviet Union. In 2010, Russia's leading lawmaker, Konstantin Kosachev, proposed a comprehensive "set of principles, a 'historical doctrine' of sorts" to define once and for all Russia's (ambivalent) status toward the Soviet Union: As the USSR's continuator state, the Russian Federation fulfills all its international obligations, but it does not recognize any moral responsibility or legal obligation for crimes committed by the Soviet authorities.[33]

At the historiographical level, the authorities took several steps to securitize the official storyline. The primary measure involved an attempt to develop a "reverse lustration" policy that would punish anyone who advanced a revisionist historiographical agenda. After several preliminary discussions, this strategy took the form of the Presidential Commission to Counter Attempts to Falsify History to the Detriment of Russia's Interests, announced by President Medvedev in 2009. The commission, led by then director of the Presidential Administration Sergey Naryshkin, comprised twenty-eight members appointed by the president, of whom only five were professional historians. The commission's powers were more restricted than envisaged by the bill that created it. In addition, it provided no legal definition of the term "falsification"; in fact, the critical element in its title was not "falsification" *per se* but actions taken "to the detriment of Russia's interests." The commission was designed to judge not classical revisionism, such as the denial of the gas chambers, but "misleading" interpretations of the victory of 1945. Faced with international and domestic criticism, Naryshkin defended the commission by emphasizing that it would not review historical academic works and therefore played no censorship role; instead, it only addressed attempts to undermine Russia's international prestige.[34]

The commission was disbanded in 2012, leaving behind a mixed record. It had failed obviously to impose memory norms on its neighbors, but facilitated the establishment of broad censorship mechanisms for domestic historiographical production. For instance, it pushed many institutions, such as the archives and the Russian Academy of Sciences, to align with state narratives and produce new content in tune with the official line. One of the only concrete products of the commission was Article 354.1 of the Penal Code, "On the Rehabilitation of Nazism," which criminalizes—without any way of punishing—Baltic and Ukrainian historiographies that rehabilitate collaborationist groups. It also penalizes—this time with the tools for doing so—any new Russian historical research that offers evidence of war crimes committed by the Soviet army, on the grounds that these were not mentioned in the Nuremberg Trials.[35]

Accompanying this securitization, Putin has resurrected the imperial Russian Military Historical Society, led by Vladimir Medinsky, and the Russian Historical Society, led by Sergey Naryshkin, with Putin himself as head of the latter's board of trustees. Both institutions' primary mission has been to take over historical narratives and memory activities and align them with the regime. Both have, for instance, worked on a new unified standard for teaching history that all history textbooks published since 2016 must follow.[36] As in other fields, state institutions continue to work closely with an array of nonstate institutions whose leaders are entrepreneurs of influence with their own ideological agendas, such as Natalia Narochnitskaya's Historical Perspective Foundation, which takes a more Orthodox and Pan-Slavic line, and Alexander Dyukov's Historical Memory Foundation, which specializes in fighting the Baltic States' historiographies of the Second World War.

The securitization of Russian history resulted in a unified ideological line: that the state is always right concerning its own population, even when this means repressing it, and hence the Gulag and mass repressions should be "de-memorialized."[37] This state supremacy implies that the leader is always right, and therefore that Stalin should be at least partly rehabilitated.[38] On this topic—a highly controversial theme during the perestroika years and the 1990s—the state took time to find its footing. In 2010, for instance, Medvedev declared on several occasions that "there can be no justification for the repressions"; used the term *totalitarianism* to refer to the Stalinist regime; and explained that Stalin's massive, organized crimes against his people "cannot be pardoned."[39] But such plain language was rapidly rolled back in favor of more ambivalent statements: the Stalinist regime committed terrible mass violence, but this was "excused" by the need to quickly industrialize and modernize a backward country and prepare it for war with Germany; and that the 1945 victory "confirmed" the wisdom of Stalin's painful policies and justified them *a posteriori*.

However, the Stalinist past and its violence have not been wholly silenced. Putin himself has visited several sites of political repressions, such as the Norilsk Gulag in 2002 and Butovo, a major memorial site near Moscow devoted to the victims of the Stalinist purges, in 2007.[40] The Duma adopted a new law on victims of Soviet political repression in 2015; a Wall of Grief monument dedicated to the victims of political repression was inaugurated in 2017;[41] and the Gulag History Museum, the official institution on the topic, enjoys the patronage of the government. Memory work on Stalinist violence has now largely been transferred to the Russian Orthodox Church, the only institution able to mourn without judging or identifying perpetrators and to redeem the past without affecting the vision of the present.

Indeed, from the state's perspective, the victims of Stalinism can be mourned so long as this process does not entail challenging the historiographical and memory status quo that touts the defeat of the Nazis as the Russian people's ultimate achievement. As a result, the authorities have gradually targeted, banned, and criminalized independent historians and nongovernmental organizations, such as the prestigious Memorial, that connect the study of the past with social activism on current issues. At the symbolic level, the closure of Memorial, Russia's oldest human rights organization, by the authorities in December 2021 was the gesture that made the full-scale invasion of Ukraine imaginable.[42] Since then, the dismantling of plaques installed by the Last Address project (a grassroots initiative that erects memorial plaques on the houses of those killed by state repression) has accelerated, along with the liquidation of memorials to repressed Poles and Lithuanians in several regions of Russia.[43]

The gradual closure of narratives around state violence committed during Stalinism is intrinsically connected to the memory of the Second World War and the issue of Soviet-occupied territories. The Medvedev presidency saw a thaw on this topic: a few weeks after the air disaster that killed Poland's president, Lech Kaczynski, and a large part of the Polish government, Medvedev allowed the publication on a government website of archival documents recognizing Soviet responsibility for the 1940 Katyn massacre, in which 22,000 Polish officers and soldiers were killed by the NKVD, the Soviet secret police; the Duma formalized this recognition.[44] However, this move toward recognition stopped almost as soon as it had begun: the Kremlin relaunched a series of historical explanations and archival justifications to excuse or negate crimes committed by the Soviet state during the war, especially in occupied territories. In parallel, several institutions have been charged with publishing and digitalizing archives that provide evidence of crimes committed by Polish, Baltic, and Ukrainian forces during the Second World War to fit the state narrative on the profound nazification of Central Europe.[45]

The securitization of history accelerated in the final years before the full-scale invasion of Ukraine. In 2020, Putin published "The Real Lessons of the 75th Anniversary of World War II," an article in which he formalized Russia's official reading of the Second World War and of the Ribbentrop-Molotov Pact: he denounced Central Europeans' equation of Nazism and Communism; asked the West to share historical responsibility for letting the Second World War happen; and called for recognition of Russia's role in the victory of 1945.[46] A few weeks later, constitutional amendments—validated by referendum in the middle of the pandemic—enshrined in Russia's highest text the duty to protect "historical truth."[47] The following year, the National Security Strategy made explicit that the defense of historical memory represented a national priority.[48] A new law was passed that prohibited drawing comparisons between Nazism and Stalinism or denying the "decisive role the Soviet people played in countering the Third Reich" and the "humanitarian mission of the USSR in the liberation of European countries."[49]

With the full-scale invasion has come another achievement: the completion of the long-awaited unified textbook for the history of twentieth-century Russia. Authored by Vladimir Medinsky, historian from the Academy of Sciences Alexander Chubaryan, and MGIMO rector Anatoly Torkunov, the unified textbook has been in use since September 2023. Denounced by part of the historian community as counterfactual propaganda and a very ahistorical vision of history, the textbook presents Ukraine's independence as an "anti-Russia project," sees the 1956 Hungarian revolution as a "color revolution," and condemns dissident culture and the perestroika years, as well as the "strategic mistake" of Soviet troops' withdrawal from Eastern Europe in the early 1990s.[50] Revised history textbooks for other classes are planned for the 2024–25 academic year, as are new atlases showing recently annexed territories as part of Russia.

A new university course has also been launched. Known as "Foundations of Russian Statehood," the course—which is quite analogous to the Soviet-era course on Scientific Communism—is mandatory for all first-year students. The textbook identifies "value constants" characteristic of Russia's identity, explaining that "throughout Russian history, a strong central government has been of paramount importance for the preservation of national statehood."[51] With Foundations of Russian Statehood, the Russian authorities have succeeded at connecting the dots between the main ideologemes and repertoires they have produced over the years, For this enterprise, Sergey Kiriyenko recruited a large part of his former team at the State Atomic Energy Corporation Rosatom. Three key figures have emerged. First is Alexander Karichev, a chemist by training who worked in military academies and then in the Presidential Administration, where he covered political work in the regions, before joining Kiriyenko's team at Rosatom and then becoming, in 2018, head of the Presidential Administration's department in charge of the State Council. Close to Karichev is Andrey Polosin, a psychologist by training who worked for years as a "polit-technologist" for different political parties before joining the Presidential Administration and then following his patron to Rosatom. In 2022, Polosin, then teaching at the Higher School of Economics, was promoted to rector of RANXiGS (the Presidential Administration University) to launch the project "Russia's DNA," which would result in the new textbook.[52]

A third central figure is Alexey Drobinin, a diplomat by training, who assumed a leading position in the strategically important International Planning Department of the Ministry of Foreign Affairs, in charge of formulating the new foreign policy language.[53]

While Karichev, Polosin, and Drobinin supervise the administrative contours of how ideology is articulated, another group of authors is responsible for producing their contents: Sergey Karaganov, who represents the academic version of the perspectives held by *siloviki*, for the foreign policy section; Vladimir Medinsky for the history section; Mikhail Piotrovsky, director of the prestigious Hermitage Museum, for the values section; and physicist Mikhail Kovalchuk (brother of Yuri) for the section on Russia's future. The director of the Kurchatov Institute, Russia's leading research and development institution in the field of nuclear energy, Mikhail Kovalchuk is known for his eccentric and pseudoscientific declarations on creating a new Homo sapiens, building new genetic weapons that would attack only one nation, brain manipulations, and many other conspiracy theories.[54]

Multiple institutional initiatives have followed on from the Presidential Administration's new ideological endeavors: the Russian Military Historical Society, for instance, has launched a new journal entitled *Ideology of the Future* that offers different iterations of the state's justification for the "special military operation" in the name of the fight against a renewed, Western-sponsored Nazism in Ukraine. A so-called "Front Philosophy" (*Frontovaia filosofiia*) has been launched by a number of state academic and cultural institutions. Among the most prominent has been the Zinoviev Club: the legacy of Alexander Zinoviev (1922–2006), a Soviet thinker who published in samizdat, emigrated in the late 1970s, and came back to Russia in 1999 to join conservative forces, fits well with the state-promoted cherry-picking approach toward the Soviet past. Zinoviev has become one of the key figures recently rehabilitated by state institutions since he stressed Russia's conflict with the West and the dangers of Western-led globalization.[55]

The new Front Philosophy has been promoted by figures from state media RIA Novosti and Russia Today, Moscow State University, the Higher School of Economics, the Institute of Philosophy of the Academy of Sciences, the Moscow University of the Interior Ministry, and others. A whole Front Philosophy literature has grown since the first Donbas war, which represents a new genre that completes the "war literature" and "war poetry," along with diaries and memoirs related to the 2014 conflict, that have filled Russian bookstores.[56] The new Front Philosophy is reminiscent of Soviet-era initiatives and mechanisms, when state institutions were meant to serve political needs. And indeed, one of the repeated complaints from Front Philosophy supporters is the lack of commissioned works (*goszakazy*) that would affirm the state's readiness to support a higher level of ideological production.

PUTIN THE GEOGRAPHER: RUSSIA AS A SPATIAL IMAGINARY

History is not the only discipline to be enlisted in the regime's statehood project: geography has not been forgotten. If historical continuity is conventionally seen as the cornerstone of nationhood narratives, space also plays a central role in the country's national image and rebranding for both domestic and international audiences. The celebration of Russia's geographical scope—the largest country in the world, covering about one-eighth of the surface of the inhabited continents—its incredibly diverse landscapes, and its wilderness have become routine among political elites. Putin's involvement in extreme outdoor sports and his 1,300-mile cross-country journey behind the wheel of a Lada in 2010 confirm the heavy symbolism with which Russia's spatial features are imbued.

The mission of valorizing Russia's territory has been assigned to the Russian Geographical Society, originally established by Nicholas I in 1845. At its grand reopening in 2009, then prime minister Putin explicitly linked the greatness of Russia as a state and a culture to the size of its territory: "When we say great, a great country, a great state—certainly, size (*mashtab*) matters. . . . When there is no size, there is no influence, no meaning."[57] Completely rebranded and modernized following a model directly inspired by the US National Geographic Society, the Russian Geographical Society now enjoys a monopoly on the production of public geographical knowledge, including approving geography textbooks. It has quickly become highly influential, thanks to generous funding that supports a wide range of seminars, exhibitions, expeditions, and book publications. The society's unique leadership makes this activism possible: It boasts Putin as chairman of the board of trustees (the Russian president speaks at the organization once a year) and minister of defense Sergey Shoigu as its president. For its part, the board of trustees comprises about a dozen oligarchs as well as the leading representatives of the Presidential Administration—a revealing sign of the political nature of this renewed passion for geography.[58]

One of the most representative components of this new state-led spatial imaginary has been the Arctic, rediscovered by the authorities in the late 2000s and now celebrated as reconnecting Russia with the Soviet past.[59] The "Red Arctic" myth, developed in the 1930s during High Stalinism, has been revived; the High North is once again framed as a space for Russia to conquer nature and achieve new technological feats.[60] State television has widely promoted the Arctic and subarctic regions through documentaries. The Russian Geographical Society devotes significant revenue to multidisciplinary Arctic expeditions, which include both military and civilian research components, and display symbolic gestures, such as erecting memorial monuments to Russian and Soviet conquests of the region and planting Russian Orthodox crosses on Svalbard and Franz Josef Land.[61]

In recent years, federal and regional leaders have also promoted national territory through big exhibition parks—a Western trend that Russia has rapidly made its own. The "Wild Nature Festival of the Golden Turtle" is a pioneering example: launched in 2006, it promotes awareness of nature and ecology through art projects (mostly photo and painting awards), with more than 100,000 projects submitted over the course of a decade and annual exhibitions in several cities. Awareness of nature and biodiversity is presented as part of the "patriotic education and improvement of Russia's image in the international community."[62] Another example is "Pristine Russia": an annual exhibition funded by a presidential grant, which celebrates Russia's nature and takes visitors on a virtual tour of the country's national parks and protected areas through state-of-the-art documentary films and photos that showcase Russia's animal life.[63]

In Moscow, the Zaryadye Park has replaced the Rossiya Hotel that once sat between Red Square and the Moskva River. A new cultural attraction with a glass bridge over the river, the park is divided into four landscape zones representing Russia's varied climate and diverse territories (forest, steppe, meadow, and northern landscapes). In addition to a sample of regional flora and fauna, it features educational and recreational places such as a greenhouse florarium, an ice cave, a concert hall, and a cinema with a panoramic screen. The park allows the authorities to display their mastery of new green technologies, such as drainage systems for collecting rainwater, automatic drip irrigation, and vacuum debris removal, and to confirm the extraordinary rethinking of urban landscape and public spaces currently underway in Russia's megalopolises.

These welcome decisions cannot hide one of Russia's critical ambivalences: if the country's greatest legacy to the planet is its role in biodiversity and wilderness preservation, it has failed to advance effective environmental legislation and has gradually lowered the status of environmental protection.[64] Against this bleak backdrop, a notable exception has been the expansion of the protected area system: a new law on the status of protected habitats and nature reserves was enacted, with the creation of several new national parks in Karachay-Cherkessia, Kamchatka, Krasnoyarsk Krai, and the Yamalo-Nenets autonomous district. But this appears an easy way to "greenwash" national policy by protecting some territories from human exploitation without any compulsion to address energy inefficiency and pollution in the country's industries. The numerous exhibitions honoring Russia's unique nature also avoid discussing the dysfunction of the country's environmental policies.[65]

The emphasis on Russia's territories reflects the authorities' willingness to address the country's infrastructure challenges. Profound changes in the spatial organization of the territory have marked Putin's long tenure. Myriad measures have been taken to modernize infrastructure and develop the most sensitive and strategic regions.[66] Still, concrete inequalities between regions in terms of transportation infrastructure and accessibility continue to weaken the country's logistical unity. Many of the exhibitions discussed here praise not only Russia's nature but also its infrastructure projects that allow regions to develop, such as the Kerch Bridge to Crimea, the Vladivostok Bridge, and the repair of airports and roads. They promote these costly infrastructure projects to sway public opinion and secure consensus around the regime's approach to addressing territorial and logistical issues.

This trend of celebrating Russia's territory underlines the geopolitical goal of loudly reaffirming the country's legitimate place in the concert of nations. The decolonizing strategies of former Soviet republics, which seek to cast off Russia's historical domination and nationalize their own territories and histories, have only accentuated the Kremlin's impression that Russia's global relevance is being challenged. To resist this trend, Putin decided in 2018 to commission a new atlas of the world that would reestablish "historical and geographical truth."[67] Not only will the Western names given to some remote Russian territories be Russified—the president explicitly mentioned that some Siberian and Arctic territories had been named for famous Western explorers when they already had a Russian name—but the atlas would also fight against the "de-Russification" of names backed by Russia's neighbors in the post-Soviet space.

Creating a coherent narrative of Russia's history has been challenging for the Kremlin. The Russian elite are divided in their vision of the primary historical references, with a majority favoring late Soviet references (the Brezhnev era), a minority remaining loyal to either Stalin or Lenin, and another minority, particularly vocal, being pro-tsarist. In such a context, few historical figures can generate consensus: Lenin, Stalin, and Solzhenitsyn are all problematic in their own ways and incur some form of protest or condemnation both at the elite level and in society more broadly. More than thirty years after the collapse of the Soviet Union, the national pantheon established in Soviet time remains the easiest to promote and the one that offers the largest sense-making dimension, fed primarily by a widespread nostalgia for the Soviet cultural "Golden Age" of the Brezhnev years.[68]

To compensate for the lack of an easily definable and useable past, the regime has played the broader card of insisting on Russia's "one-thousand-year" statehood and historical continuity. It has securitized Russian history around the idea that the state is the absolute value against various external and internal enemies, the most dangerous of which come from the West. It has also built a sophisticated emotional language around heroes and victims sacrificing their lives for the sake of their motherland as a way to silence any alternative reading of history.[69] Soviet history has been sanitized to generate the broadest possible consensus and merge with popular nostalgia for Brezhnev's "Golden Age." This securitization closely follows the sedimentation of the regime: it took years to be formalized into a coherent language and to be implemented via structured policies of indoctrination, mainly targeting younger generations. It also implied that in parallel with Soviet rehabilitation, Russia's imperial past and identity have rejoined the national pantheon.

SIX

RUSSIA'S IMPERIALNESS AND THE FIGHT FOR UKRAINE

Peter the Great waged the great northern war for 21 years. It would seem that he was at war with Sweden, he took something from them. He did not take anything from them, he returned [what was Russia's]."
VLADIMIR PUTIN, June 9, 2023[1]

THE LATEST STEP IN the process of securitizing Russia has been an intense culturalization of national identity. The authorities have primordialized it around vague notions such as Russia's "cultural codes" that frame cultural identities and productions as atemporal realities with no clearly identifiable social actors and agency. In this way, the obsession with Ukraine is no longer a component of the regime's repertoire but the core itself, reactivating the imperial undertones of state language. This has resulted in transforming a strategic issue—the relationship to NATO expansion—into a new identity project for the regime—forcing Ukraine to rejoin Russia or else be destroyed. This new page in the sedimentation of the regime's ideology blends imperial and irredentist themes. It is imperial when it argues that Ukraine should rejoin Russia because it was historically part of it (with a growing rehabilitation of the White past); irredentist when it calls for the defense of the Russian population in Ukraine.

TSARIST AND SOVIET RUSSIA AS A SINGLE HISTORICAL CHAIN

Until the 2022 war, the securitization of the historical narrative went hand in hand with the Kremlin's desire to maintain a broad palette of historical references, aiming at a "pick and choose" policy to achieve elite and societal consensus. As long as the state's continuity across centuries and beyond its various political and territorial embodiments was respected (which implied, in the regime's logic, rejecting Western-inspired liberalism), almost all interpretations of history were accepted. Indeed, except for certain crucial events, such as the Second World War and Russia's territorial expansion and conquest of other peoples, Russia's historical policy showed a high level of diversity and plasticity. It offered, for instance, several historical products for collective consumption. Citizens could be nostalgic for the Soviet Union or the tsarist empire; they could regard Ivan the Terrible, Nicholas II, Stolypin, Lenin, Stalin, Gagarin, or Putin himself as the most important hero of national history. The country's monument policy has reflected this plural historical policy: the government erected a statue of Prince Vladimir the Great, who Christianized the country, as well as one of the infamous Ivan the Terrible, while busts of Stalin have been mushrooming all over the country in recent years, especially since the military invasion of Ukraine.[2]

While the Second World War narrative generates massive consensus, discourses about pre-Soviet times are more ambivalent. In 1993, Boris Yeltsin described the October Revolution as a catastrophe for the young democratic Russia, born in February 1917 with the collapse of tsarism, and framed the Bolshevik Revolution as having diverted the country from its European path of development.[3] This radical critique of the October Revolution as a wrong turn in Russian history rapidly softened with the failure of liberal reforms: in competition with popular Communist Party leader Zyuganov, a weakened Yeltsin decided in 1996 to promote a more consensual reading by renaming November 7 the Day of Concord and Reconciliation.[4] This compromise—keeping the date of the revolution a holiday while dissociating it from its Communist content—was considered a path to reconciling "Reds" (pro-Soviet) and "Whites" (anti-Soviet). Many other political actors shared this vision, including General Alexander Lebed, who proposed simultaneously reinterring Nicholas II and Vladimir Lenin as symbols of the nation's reconciliation with its controversial past.[5]

In 2015, minister of culture Vladimir Medinsky articulated a more refined proposal for a Red and White reconciliation: recognition of the continuity of Russian history, from the tsarist empire to the Soviet Union to today's Russian Federation; recognition of the trauma of social divisions born from the Civil War; respect for both Reds' and Whites' memories and a recognition that both camps were animated by genuine patriotism; criticism of the ideology of revolutionary terror; and condemnation of external powers' decision to get involved in Russia's internal conflicts.[6] Sergey Naryshkin draws a bold parallel between the 1917 revolutions and today's "color revolutions" and "regime change" policies. On the centenary of the 1917 revolutions, he notes:

> A jubilee of this kind . . . is necessary not for celebrating events, nor for festivities, but above all for rethinking deeply the events of the previous century. And, more importantly, for formulating the main lessons not only for our country but for the world . . . the value of unity, of civic consensus, the ability of society to compromise and to not allow the extreme division of society in the form of civil war.[7]

The state's reluctance to remember what Olga Malinova dubs an "embarrassing centenary"[8] was well formulated by Dmitry Peskov, press secretary of the Presidential Administration. Asked about the state's quasi-silence about the one-hundredth anniversary of the February and October Revolutions, he flatly responded, "And in relation to what would it be necessary to celebrate?,"[9] an unambiguous statement that, from the Kremlin's perspective, there was nothing to celebrate. Sergey Naryshkin expanded on this, indicating that the Russian state would "note" the event, not "celebrate" it.[10]

Russia's historical policy toward the centenary of 1917 thus comprised several parallel strategies: diminishing the meaning of the event to avoid requiring the head of state and government figures to take a stance; outsourcing commemorative events to many institutions, with no preplanned grand design; developing a reconciliatory narrative on the Reds and the Whites; and allowing other actors to take the stage and promote a plurality of contradictory readings of the events.[11] As the outcome of the Kremlin's tergiversations, Putin remained silent on the centenary, making no public declaration or address to the nation as part of the commemoration for either revolution (nor did he comment on the August 1991 putsch). On November 7, 2017, the authorities limited themselves to a military parade on Red Square; however, this commemorated not the Bolshevik Revolution but the heroic defense of Moscow against Nazi troops on November 7, 1941. It was accompanied by historical reenactments of Moscow's resistance in 1612 and the battle against

Napoleon in 1812. The Bolshevik Revolution was, therefore, absent from the only official event of the day.

While imperial times have been reintegrated into Russia's *longue durée* history, there has been no rehabilitation of tsarism per se. References to the Romanov dynasty were common in the early 1990s, when the Yeltsin team used them to criticize the Soviet regime and its supporters and to reconnect with a past that sounded ostensibly more European.[12] Since then, the government has emphasized the dynasty as part of Russia's history and statehood and as a time of prestige and expansion for the empire, playing down any setbacks, such as the defeats in the Crimean War of 1856 and the Russo-Japanese War of 1904–5. As part of this, the authorities supported the reburial of Nicholas II and his family and the legal restoration of their status. They accepted the registration of the Imperial House's Chancellery as a nonprofit organization that works as the informal embassy for the imperial family.[13]

Beyond this symbolism and a celebrity-like presence, however, the authorities have not been keen to give the Romanov heirs any specific status. They use tsarism's symbolic values only to claim the right to an autocratic regime that would reject both West-inspired liberalism and a return to Communism. Several hawks enjoy referring to tsarism: Duma speaker Vyacheslav Volodin, has, for instance, evoked the need to be inspired by the tsarist educational system to reform Russian schools.[14] Some emphasize the last tsar, Nicholas II, as a figure who can redeem Russia from its sins. The murder of the imperial family by the Bolsheviks in 1918 under murky circumstances indeed helped create an aura of mushy sentimentality around the last Romanov emperor.[15] Yet nostalgia for the tsar and regret about his murder do not generate popular support for a monarchist project: the tsar may be welcome as a cultural symbol of a mythical antebellum Russia, but he is not endowed with political legitimacy and must share the Russian public's sympathy with the Soviet leaders who executed him. A minority, mainly within the church, are convinced that monarchy is Russia's natural political state, but for many, tsarism is useful mostly as a tool for advocating for an autocratic regime.[16] In this case, the metaphor of tsarism does not necessarily reveal monarchist convictions but accommodates any lifelong authoritarian presidential regime: As Malofeev explicitly states, Putin should be "the new tsar."[17]

This ambivalence toward tsarism and its collapse is reflected in Putin's own narrative. The president espouses a storyline that is highly critical—more than the Russian authorities as a whole—of the Soviet Union's founding fathers. For instance, he declared several times that the Bolsheviks betrayed the nation by signing the 1918 Treaty of Brest-Litovsk with the German enemy and losing large portions of Russian territory. In 2014, at the Seliger camp, an event that brought together patriotic youth movements, he insisted that the "Bolsheviks wished to see their Fatherland defeated," adding that "this was a complete betrayal of national interests."[18] In 2016, once again asked his opinion of Lenin, he accused him of "having put a bomb under the building named Russia, and it collapsed."[19]

Of all of Putin's history-related speeches in 2012–18, except those on the Great Patriotic War, he most actively actualized the pre-Soviet past,[20] a sign that imperial Russia gradually became an ideological reference for him before he made direct use of it to justify the war in Ukraine. However, on several occasions Putin has mocked those who seek a return to monarchism. Half-jokingly, he has commented on his reluctance to return to pre-revolutionary Russia, where his ancestors worked as serfs[21]—an open rebuke to all those who would romanticize tsarism. In 2017, Dmitry Peskov reacted to the comments of the head of the Crimean Republic, Sergey Aksenov, about the need to restore monarchism: "Putin regards this idea without any optimism. He has been asked the same question several times these last years . . . and very coldly relates to these discussions." A few days later, Putin himself declared, "Thank God we do not have a monarchy, but a republic."[22]

Russian state structures remain generally friendlier to the Red narrative than Putin himself, both due to bureaucratic inertia and because a pro-Soviet line is easily accepted by the population. Yet this pro-Soviet posture is ambivalent, as the state refuses to celebrate the revolutionary moments in which the Soviet Union was born and accommodates it only in its later forms, once it became a solid and unified state. Ironically, while the authorities are friendlier to the Red narrative, their obsessive fear of any popular protest or color revolutions in fact fosters the indirect rehabilitation of tsarism. As political analyst Alexey Makarkin nicely summarizes, "The radical rejection of revolutionism by the Russian intellectual class has led to a glorification of state restoration."[23]

This position was encapsulated by the film *Union of Salvation*, a supposed blockbuster released in late 2019 depicting the Decembrist riots of 1825—an uprising by Russian officers who demanded liberal reforms against the tsar Nicholas I. The movie displays the Decembrists—cult figures in Soviet historiography—as ideologically inconsistent and weak, if not psychologically unstable, because they dared to question the tsar's legitimacy. It concludes by depicting their supposed dangerous attitude, which paved the way for the left-wing terrorism that would shake the Russian empire in the run-up to the 1905 and 1917 revolutions. The storyline should be read as a metaphor for the dangers of street uprisings and the need to maintain the status quo. The idea for the movie indeed emerged during the anti-Putin protests in the winter of 2011–12, when Konstantin Ernst, the CEO of Channel One Russia and a key figure in the on-screen adaptation of the regime's ideology, compared the protests with the 1825 riots.[24] By defending a statist position at any cost, even against progressist movements that have been celebrated in Soviet history, the Putin regime contributes to legitimizing the most reactionary movements that see in tsarism a future for Russia.

THE REHABILITATION OF WHITE IDEOLOGY

The regime's relationship to the White movement appears even more paradoxical. The prestige and cultural legacy of Russian emigration abroad have been broadly reappropriated as part of the national pantheon and celebrated as an integral component of Russia's tumultuous political heritage. The idea of "closing the Soviet parenthesis" and pacifying contradictory memories has succeeded: intellectual and cultural production in today's Russia has fully reintegrated the Civil War and interwar emigration.

This policy is inscribed in a broader strategy of Europeanizing Russia's memory. By honoring the White General Anton Denikin (1872–1947), who was leading the Whites forces in Russia's South during the Civil War and then emigrated to Paris, the Kremlin can celebrate Russia's European destiny at a time when it is being strongly challenged on the ground. It can also insist on the naturalness of the empire, as Denikin vehemently opposed the Bolsheviks' acceptance of the secession of Finland, Poland, and Ukraine. Other leading White protagonists condemned by the Soviet regime face less certain posthumous destinies. They are not associated with the prestigious heritage of emigration to Europe, and the authorities are reluctant to pardon them, as this would mean revoking the original Soviet judicial decision.

Yet these figures tend to be rehabilitated culturally, best epitomized by the posthumous destiny of Admiral Alexander Kolchak (1874–1920), the White leader based in Siberia: although he has not been legally pardoned, he has become the object of growing enthusiasm and benefits from a genuine popular cult, especially through movies. In a third category stand all those whose status cannot be restored legally or culturally. This includes those Whites who collaborated with Nazi Germany, especially Cossacks, and therefore found themselves on the anti-Soviet side during the Great Patriotic War. The strong consensus regarding the role of the Soviet Union in achieving victory in 1945 does not permit favorable judgments of the Soviet Union's enemies.[25]

As we can see, all memory sides are given room—albeit unequally—in a hierarchical pyramid that maintains at its apex the post-1945 Soviet Union. In this pyramid, both Whites and Bolsheviks can be viewed as genuine patriots or traitors to the motherland, depending on one's perspective. A pro-White stance is accepted when it denounces the Bolsheviks as unpatriotic internationalists and dangerous revolutionaries, but it is rejected if it questions the Soviet Union in its entirety and entails support for the Nazi side during the Second World War. A bold pro-Bolshevik viewpoint is accepted only if it recognizes that a consolidated Soviet state rapidly addressed Lenin's original mistakes. While Putin seems to dislike a tsarist regime that failed to reform itself and a weak Nicholas II who led his country to defeat and partition, he has a soft spot for conservative tsar Alexander III (1845–1894) and for White general Denikin and his anti-Ukrainian statements. Putin indeed admires White officers as glamorous patriots: they can be pardoned for fighting against dangerous revolutionaries, but they should then have supported Soviet leaders' reconsolidation of the state.

Yet more than being about historical continuity, the reclamation of the White political legacy comes with a specific political agenda, made explicit in the rehabilitation of the reactionary thinker Ivan Ilyin. Ivan Ilyin rose to preeminence in 2005, when his remains were reburied near those of General Denikin in Moscow's Donskoy Monastery and his grave visited by Putin. As studied by Mikhail Suslov, in the mid-2000s Ilyin was quoted broadly by mainstream political figures,[26] and under Vyachesvav Volodin, the Presidential Administration even distributed Ilyin's main work, *Our Tasks* (as well as Berdyaev's *Philosophy of Inequality* and Vladimir Soloviev's *Justification of the Good*), to regional governors and senior members of United Russia.[27] Since then, the émigré thinker has been quoted by the president about ten times in his speeches, including in his September 30, 2022, address announcing the annexation of four regions of Ukraine. Supporters of Ilyin proliferate around the church and in Putin's inner circles: film director Nikita Mikhalkov, media tycoon Konstantin Malofeev, or, less visibly, Yuri Kovalchuk, as well as, in the state administration, former minister of culture Vladimir Medinsky.

Ilyin embodies a reactionary, autocratic agenda for Russia, one that also offers a theological justification of violence. His central text, *On Resistance to Evil by Force*, can indeed be read as an extra-canonical Russian Orthodox doctrine of just war looking for a divine authorization for coercive violence.[28] Ilyin also sided with the United States against the Soviet Union: in 1947, at the beginning of the Cold War, he even declared that Russian patriots should side with the US if war were to break out between it and the Soviet Union.[29] He very vehemently argued that the Soviet Union was not Russia and that there cannot be, per essence, any "Soviet patriotism."[30]

But one of the critical points of tension in Ilyin's legacy relates to his relationship to fascism and Nazism. Indeed, the émigré thinker saw Italian fascism as a spiritually imperfect form of White ideology. In 1928, he wrote that "fascism is an Italian secular variation of the White movement. The Russian White movement is more perfect than Italian fascism because it has a religious ethos."[31] In 1933, he published an article praising Hitler and the Nazis for stopping "the process of Bolshevization in Germany and thereby rendered the greatest service to the whole of Europe."[32] Ilyin would renew this analysis in his pamphlet "On Fascism" from 1948, criticizing the "mistakes" of Nazism such as hostility to religion and obsession with race, but celebrating the political project, its antisemitic elements, and praising the fascist regimes in Spain and Portugal.[33] This is at the very least an embarrassing legacy to deal with, given the regime's focus on antifascism and vocal anti-Americanism.

This spreading of Ilyin's works by his supporters is undoubtedly oriented "upward" to the inner circles of elites around Putin, with very little time and energy spent trying to promote it "downward" to a broader audience. Moreover, Ilyin's cult does not generate full consensus, as seen by the resistance organized by students and leftist activists close to the Communist Party against the opening of a new "Ivan Ilyin Higher Political School" led by Alexander Dugin at the Russian State Humanities University (RGGU) in 2024. Yet at the state level, the embrace of Ilyin has been more commonsensical, taking from him citations that could have come from more or less any other Russian philosopher on Russianness, state-centrism, and patriotism. The Presidential Administration, as well as Putin himself, have built a much more plural pantheon of ideological references in which Ilyin is a central but not exclusive figure.

RUSSIA'S "IMPERIALNESS" AS A GRADUAL RECONSTRUCTION

This brings us to the question of Russia as an empire. Indeed, by stressing state-centrism, "one-thousand-year" historical continuity, memory of White ideology, and space as major criteria defining Russia's atemporal identity, the regime—implicitly at first and now more explicitly—has been playing with the image of Russia as an empire.

This notion functions in an ambiguous semantic space in Russian: *imperiia* is a neutral term describing a state whose structures are imperial; *imperkost'* is positively connoted and closer to "imperiality" or "imperialness"; and *imperializm* is always negative, linked to colonialism (see chapter 12) and associated with the West. Russia may thus have *imperkost'* but not *imperializm*. The authorities inherited from the Soviet Union an ambivalent vision: the empire was criticized for its backward political and economic nature—as an autocracy with a nascent capitalist system—but was also seen as an integral part of the teleological process toward socialist modernity, with a Russian working class leading backward nations toward a glorious future. The Soviet official pantheon celebrated Peter the Great and Catherine the Great for their modernizing pushes but criticized nineteenth-century tsars; by contrast, late Soviet culture, especially movies and music, romanticized certain features of the late empire.[34]

In the post-Soviet period, references to the empire were long left to the radical fringes—Zhirinovsky or Dugin—and not articulated by the Kremlin. In early Putinism, Anatoly Chubais evoked the future Russia as a "liberal empire,"[35] showing that the term was not then connected to an authoritarian government, but his proposal garnered no interest from the establishment. The notion of being an empire was indeed rarely operationalized positively: Russia's historical expansion and multiculturalism have instead been presented as the product of a "civilizational choice" whereby the non-Russian peoples voluntarily chose to pursue a common historical destiny (see chapter 7). The only positive reading of Russia's "imperiality" was related to territorial expansion: The patriotic historical park "Russia, My History" epitomizes this vision in a simple coloring scheme: in red are the periods of history when Russia's territory contracted, and in green, those when Russia's territory expanded.[36]

It is only with time that the Kremlin gradually *reinvented* Russia as an imperial power because other forms of great power expression—economic attraction and soft power—had failed to deliver what the authorities had hoped for: the right to shape the post–Cold War order in Europe and Eurasia. A search of presidential speeches from 2000 to 2023 (see fig. 6.1) shows, for instance, that the theme of empire became more prominent after 2011, with peaks during the crisis years of 2011–14 and 2021–22.[37] As expected, during his presidency, Medvedev referred less to empire than Putin, although he did participate in relaunching the theme from around 2011.

FIG. 6.1. Mentions of "empire" (when associated with "Russia") in presidential speeches, 2000–2023.

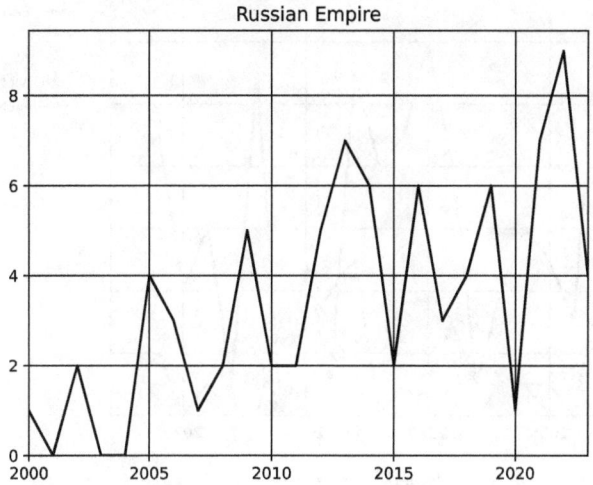

Source: Author's compilation based on Kremlin.ru.

Looking at which tsars Medvedev and Putin have referenced (see fig. 6.2), one notes the unchallenged preeminence of Peter the Great, with twenty-two mentions before 2011 and forty-two afterward. The other tsars receive episodic mentions, and all have drawbacks in terms of Putin's self-vision: Alexander II was too liberal, which cost him his life; Nicholas II was weak, failed to resist the forces of revolution, and abdicated. Even the most autocratic leaders had shortcomings: Nicholas I lost the Crimean War and Alexander III was more isolationist than expansionist.

Over the years, the meanings of the references to Peter have evolved, following the regime's ideological sedimentation. They peaked during Putin's first term, during which he celebrated the modernizer who opened the famous "window on Europe." A 2003 Putin quote is emblematic of that vision: "Peter I dreamt of a country strong, dynamic, and open to the world. And he didn't only dream. He did open Russia to the world, and the world to Russia."[38] Peter then went unmentioned during the first three years of Medvedev's presidency; it was not until 2011 that Medvedev mentioned him as the "creator of a strong and open power (*derzhava*)."[39] From 2012, Putin's references to Peter's reformist role discarded the "window on Europe" theme, instead emphasizing Peter's status as a *derzhavnik*—one who believes in state greatness.

FIG. 6.2. Mentions of tsars by name in presidential speeches, 2000–2023.

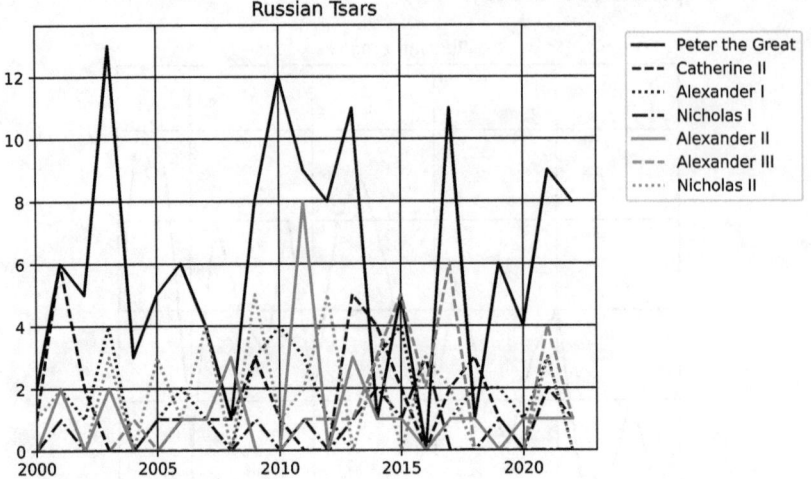

Source: Author's compilation based on Kremlin.ru.

Putin associated his name with ideas of defense, a robust northern fleet, military schools and procedures, and laws and procurators. In his June 9, 2022, speech, he even praised Peter the Great's policy to "return and consolidate" Russia's territories taken by Sweden and stated that his mission was to emulate the Russian emperor.[40] The quote reveals a new reading of Peter as having conquered new territories—in parallel with Putin's annexation of Ukraine's territories—and, therefore, indirectly, an understanding of the empire as a territorial expansion mechanism. We can also presume that Peter the Great's forty-three-year reign is gratifying to Putin, who likewise seems to envision remaining in power until his death.

UKRAINE FROM A STRATEGIC TO AN IDENTITY PROJECT

It is obviously in relation to Ukraine that Russia's rediscovered "imperialness" has crystallized. The regime has always had an obsession with its main neighbor: losing influence over Kyiv was considered an unacceptable sign of weakness vis-à-vis the West even during the Yeltsin era. To avoid Ukraine leaving Russia's orbit, Moscow deployed a wide spectrum of strategies, including economic pressure, soft power, and "hybrid warfare," ensuring that pro-Russian voices were heard in Ukraine, that pro-Russian interests were defended by Ukrainian oligarchic networks, and that anti-Russian groups were labeled nationalist, far-right, or fascist. These techniques likely slowed down Ukraine's distancing from Russia in the 2000s and 2010s, but they did not stop it.[41] The risks of losing Ukraine strategically and having it join the Western world—and therefore its military alliances (both as a potential NATO member and as a potential EU member, as the EU also has a military solidarity component)—was long the Kremlin's main concern. Over time, however, the identity component of the competition with the West over Ukraine also became central.

The entanglement between geopolitics and identity developed gradually. It seems quite evident that Putin and a large segment of the Russian foreign policy elite have always believed that the other post-Soviet nations were only partially legitimate, in the sense that their sovereignty was *de facto* limited, even if it was *de jure* equal to Russia's. But a lack of belief in their agency and requests for their geopolitical loyalty did not initially translate into plans to invade and annex their territories. What began as a rejection of Ukraine's geopolitical agency steadily evolved into a more global argument that Ukraine's very identity was illegitimate. Once the logical connection was made between the absence of geopolitical autonomy and illegitimacy as a nation, there ensued an ideological "sublimation" to demonstrate the supposed unity of the Russian and Ukrainian nations, as presented in Putin's infamous article of 2021.

The regime's identity project toward Ukraine is based on two deep-seated beliefs. The first relates to Ukraine as a nation: the Russian and Ukrainian nations should be at best closely linked (the "brotherhood" trope, which was for long dominant), if not blended into one unified nation (the "triune" trope—with the Belarusian nation being the third, which arrived only recently in the Kremlin's language). The second belief relates to Ukraine as a state: the country's borders are supposedly illegitimate because they were set by the Soviet regime. This narrative was long promulgated by irredentist groups inspired by Solzhenitsyn but not articulated directly by the Kremlin. It did, however, crop up in the official discourse periodically, as in 2008 after the NATO Bucharest summit, where Kyiv and Tbilisi were half-promised membership. According to the Russian press, a furious Putin declared, "Ukraine is not even a state! What is Ukraine? Part of its territory is Central Europe, the other part, the most important part, we gave it!"[42]

But the idea of a territorial conquest of parts of Ukraine was left unspoken by the Kremlin until it saw the opportunity to seize Crimea during the Euromaidan revolution. This first annexation inspired the dream of bringing Ukraine's southeastern regions—the Novorossiya conquered by Catherine the Great from the Ottoman Empire—"back" into the Russian fold, which resulted in fostering secessionism in Donetsk and Luhansk. A direct territorial threat to Ukraine was formulated in Putin's 2020 article on the interpretation of the Second World War, in which he explicitly asserted that "when you leave, take what you brought with you"[43]—that is, if Ukraine leaves Russia's orbit, it cannot take territories that were "given" during the Soviet era. In his article on the unity between both nations, Putin was even more explicit: "Russia was robbed, indeed," by the Soviet leaders who gave territories to Kyiv.[44]

Putin's anticommunist language reached its apogee in his February 21, 2022, speech announcing the full-scale invasion. In it, he argued that the Bolsheviks created the Ukrainian state at the expense of the Russian heartland. Not only did the Ukrainians have the Bolsheviks—and then Stalin and Khrushchev—to thank for having established their artificial statehood, Putin stated, but they also had post-Soviet Russia to thank for not claiming the territories that became Ukraine under the Soviet decision. "And today, the 'grateful progeny' has overturned monuments to Lenin in Ukraine. They call it decommunization. . . . We are ready to show what real decommunizations would mean for Ukraine," concluded Putin.[45] Here, Putin posits the Russian empire as the opposite of the Soviet Union: the Soviet nationalities policy promoted republics to the detriment of the colonial center, while the empire forces the peripheries to merge with the center.

To read the entirety of Putin's presidency as projecting Russia as an empire *by design* thus appears analytically mistaken: the empire has gradually gained dominance *by default* from a pool of many other possible repertoires and foreign policy strategies because alternative projections of great-power status have failed. Consequently, interpreting the quest for territorial expansion in Ukraine as a kind of absolute and permanent imperialism for the sake of growing larger is misguided. The regime's strategy has always been to resort to territorial aggression only after having lost political control over its contrarian neighbors. Moscow was more interested in keeping political control over Kyiv than in invading the country. Moreover, its "special military operation" was modeled on the Soviet interventions in Budapest in 1956 and Prague in 1968—short-term military actions to install a puppet regime.

And indeed, the territories conquered after February 24, 2022, were initially perceived as bargaining chips to be given back to Ukraine in exchange for its strategic neutrality—as we know from the failed Istanbul agreements of spring 2022.[46] It has thus been only gradually, once negotiations failed and Ukraine showed that not only would it not surrender but it would also fight to regain its 1991 borders and was moving decidedly toward NATO and the EU, that the Kremlin embraced the "old-fashioned" imperialist strategy of annexing the new territories.

Moreover, the revival of this imperial strategy is focused obsessively on Ukraine (and potentially Moldova, although the symbolism here is much less attractive). Not every Soviet territory is seen as worth reconquering—the Kremlin is not interested in reintegrating Central Asia or the South Caucasus. Instead, the reintegration quest responds to strategic and normative challenges posed by the West and entails recreating a mythical Russia in which historical junctures and territorial discontinuities are erased or repaired. Ukraine finds itself the central piece of both components of the blend: it embodies Russia's failure to be attractive enough to keep Kyiv in its orbit in the face of Western competition *and* it symbolizes the historical and territorial disjunctures that have broken the mythical East Slavic unity.

Within this blend, the "imperialness" combines elements of territorial greatness (Russia has been cut off from territories that are historically and culturally meaningful), historical continuity (Russia should reconnect with its one-thousand-year statehood to remain strong and protected from external influences), and regime ideology (Russia can exist only as an autocracy). Yet the regime does not entirely embrace any of these imperial components: it does not aim to reconquer the whole of the Soviet Union or the Russian Empire, to restore the imperial stature of Russia as part of the European concert of nations, or to rehabilitate tsarism per se. Russia as an empire thus conflates state projection abroad, nation-building language, regime securitization, and Putin's self-vision of a ruler whose historical role will not be questioned by the future leadership.

RUSSIA'S "CULTURAL DNA" AND THE BIOPOLITICIZATION OF THE WAR

Last but not least, the securitization of Russia has taken the form of an extreme culturalization of national identity. The latter is understood as a reified product of history that individual citizens cannot challenge or force to evolve as values and identity are cross-generationally transferred. The tip of the iceberg of this culturalization has involved growing references to history and culture in presidential speeches, as shown in figure 6.3: "history" is mentioned between 100 and 300 times per year (substantially more than other notions explored in this book), with peaks late in Medvedev's presidency and then since 2020. "Culture" has followed the same trend, albeit at a lower level. In 2014, for instance, the Presidential Administration used the term "history" more than it had in the past two decades combined, to the point that "Russian history" outpaced all themes related to Russian culture, such as literature (*literatura* or *slovesnost'*), classical music, cinema, composers, thinkers, folklore, and tradition.[47]

Reifying the nation has the obvious objective of decontesting politics: in 2019, Vladislav Surkov, more marginal than a decade ago but still a significant figure in the Russian public space, captured the regime's mindset in a text called "Putin's Long State." In it, Surkov revives the mystical bond between the tsar and the people that was at the core of imperial Russia, asserting that Putin can capture and interpret the needs of the "deep people" (*glubinnyi narod*) better than anyone:

> There's no deep state in Russia, everything's out in the open, but there is a deep people. . . . With its gigantic supermass the deep people create an insuperable force of cultural gravitation, which unites the nation and brings the elite down to earth. . . . *Narodnost'*, however defined, precedes statehood, predetermines its form, limits the fantasies of theoreticians, and forces practitioners to take certain steps. . . . An ability to hear and understand the people, to see through it to its depths, and to act accordingly, is the unique and primary quality of the Putin state.[48]

This reification has been epitomized by the growing use of the notion of "cultural code" to express Russia's identity. What this cultural code means remains vague: the only definition that attempts to encompass it is the list of so-called "traditional values" now enshrined in a presidential decree (see chapter 8) as well as in the new university textbooks released in 2023 (see below). The "cultural codes" ideologeme has also developed hand in hand with increased use of biological metaphors to describe geopolitical tensions, including Duma chairman Vyacheslav Volodin's comment on the West's "genetic rejection of Slavs."[49] A similar metaphor can be found in Kiriyenko's new course for university students, which began its life under the slogan "Russia's Cultural DNA" (DNA here signifying "Spiritual-Moral Culture" in Russian) before taking on the more neutral title of "Foundations of Russian Statehood."[50]

FIG. 6.3. Mentions of "history" and "culture" in presidential speeches, 2000–2023.

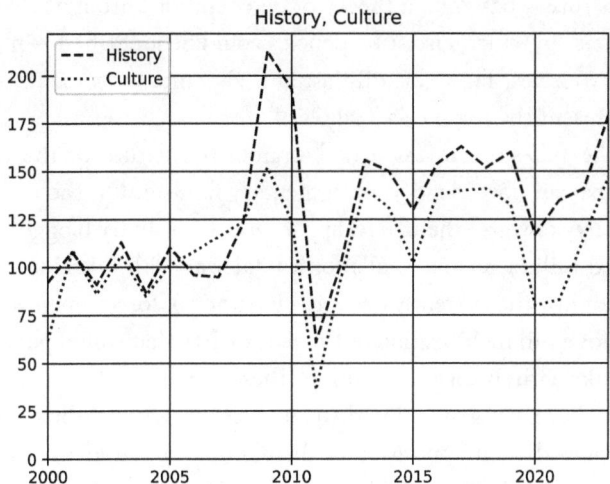

Source: Author's compilation based on Kremlin.ru.

A rich academic literature has interpreted Putinism as an intense biopolitical regime.[51] The main aspects of this biopoliticization of state language and policies include the emphasis on declining demography as a threat to national security, inviting women to return to their reproductive role, denouncing the denaturation of the Russian language by migrants, naturalizing Ukrainian citizens in occupied territories, and deporting and forcibly adopting Ukrainian children to increase the pool of new citizens. All these policies presuppose, in one way or another, an implicit vision of the nation as having a biological identity. But the regime has also promoted a more inclusive vision of the nation, generously granting citizenship to post-Soviet citizens and naturalizing migrants from Central Asia and the South Caucasus.[52]

The debate on Russia's biopolitical regime connects directly to the debate as to whether or not the regime is fascist. The American philosopher Jason Stanley is right to say that it is easier to identify fascism as a collection of tropes and narratives than to identify fascism as a fixed, institutionalized mode of government.[53] Before the full-scale war, the regime could be defined as conservative, illiberal, and authoritarian, but not fascist, as fascism necessitates a utopia, the belief that war is the only way for a new Man to emerge by making a *tabula rasa* of the past. The pre-2022 regime did not have a utopian vision of its future based on a theory of regeneration through violence: there were "pockets" in which fascist tendencies could be identified—in particular, paramilitary circles, far-right militias, and vigilante movements—but these did not represent the regime as a whole.[54]

With the full-scale invasion of Ukraine, the nature of the regime has changed; one can now identify a fragmentary fascism. On the one hand, the so-called party of war—the *siloviki* apparatus, the military bloggers, the paramilitary and militia realms—calls for a total war with Ukraine (conquering Kyiv and not just the currently occupied territories), for an open war with the West, and for a full mobilization of Russian society that would put culture and economy alike entirely on a war footing. These groups do share a fascist imaginary: they believe in regeneration through violence, with all the aesthetics that fascism implies. But in opposition to them, one can still identify a large part of the political establishment (the technocratic part) that wants the special operation to remain just that, "special"—that is, without any implications for the country as a whole. These actors wish for Russian society not to be dragged into the war, prefer demobilization to mobilization, and hope that the middle classes and elites can be protected and that economic and cultural life can continue to exist in a civilian space parallel to the war realm.

The regime appears as a two-headed Janus: one side wants more violence (toward both Ukraine and Russian society) and calls for a spiral toward total war, while the other side wants less violence and a return to "normalcy." There are obviously bridges between the two faces of this Janus. Sergey Kiriyenko's Presidential Administration is, for instance, curating the technocratic side of the state while supervising occupied territories and their integration into Russia. At the beginning of the invasion, Putin himself made some speeches that evoked the need for the Russian society to "self-purify" from "scums and traitors" in order to "be[come] stronger."[55] These rhetorical components, rooted in a totalitarian vision of the healthy body politic, can be associated with fascism, but they also recall many Soviet tropes: denazification, for instance, brings to mind Stalin's policy of de-kulakization, along with other repressive social-engineering projects. Medical metaphors of purity and contamination, as well as dehumanization of enemies, were classic tools of Soviet Orwellian language,[56] and denouncing opponents as a fifth columnists and "national traitors" is likewise nothing new.[57]

The same can be said of Putin's cult of masculinity and the construction of the Russian president as a brand for the man-soldier, the man-defender of the nation, but also potentially the man-aggressor.[58] His metaphor of Ukraine as a beautiful woman who must endure what she dislikes in the context of the implementation of Minsk II ("Like it or not, my beauty, bear with it"[59])—a metaphor with decided undertones of rape—is revealing of Putin's deeply entrenched gendered vision of strength and weakness on the international scene, but this has broader ideological roots than just fascism.

Another feature of the regime's discursive radicalization has been the return of antisemitism. Although Putin worked for years to promote philosemitic and pro-Israel language and policies, the war has rapidly reopened the Pandora's box of antisemitism. He himself has invoked the Jewishness of Volodymyr Zelensky, alleging that the Ukrainian president would use this identity to "cover up freaks, neo-Nazis."[60] He has also relaunched the accusation that oligarchs who have left Russia, such as Anatoly Chubais, are in fact traitors to Russia because of their Jewish identity.[61] Since then, many official figures have emphasized Zelensky's Jewish roots as a sign of his submission to the West and betrayal of genuine Ukrainian culture. Sergey Lavrov drew the ire of the international community by asserting that Hitler, like Zelensky, had Jewish roots,[62] and talk-show anchors such as Vladimir Soloviev and Dmitry Kiselyov have invested deeply in this antisemitism.[63]

While biological or genetic references to Russian identity are almost nonexistent in official discourse on Russia, they have been more bluntly expressed with regard to Ukraine. A radical rhetoric with genocidal tones of this was, for instance, formulated by Timofey Sergeytsev, a PR specialist who participated in the electoral campaigns of several Russian and pro-Russian Ukrainian politicians, and who now works as a columnist at the state news agency RIA Novosti. In the article "What Russia Should Do with Ukraine," released just after the revelation of the Bucha massacres of spring 2022, Sergeytsev proposed the methodical eradication of Ukraine as a nation and a state on the grounds that Ukrainian identity is "an artificial anti-Russian construct with no civilizational content of its own, a subordinate element of an alien [read: Western] civilization."[64]

To achieve this goal, Sergeytsev advanced a set of measures to be assigned to a state agency in charge of the mass lustration (exclusion of specific categories of people from civil service positions for ideological reasons) of Ukrainian institutions, the carrying out of death sentences, and collective re-Russification of Ukraine over more than one generation: "At least one generation should be born, educated, and reach adulthood under the conditions of denazification."[65] Ukrainians would be typologized based on their political stance: the most active "Nazis" would be tried and sentenced to prison or death, less active supporters would be sentenced to forced labor, and average citizens would be reeducated as to their Russianness. The final goal is that "the name of Ukraine itself cannot be preserved."[66]

Sergeytsev's cold and methodical argument belongs more clearly to the fascist repertoire than anything else published by the Russian authorities to date. But here one confronts the key problem of how representative one article is of a regime as a whole. Might it not simply be a sign that hardliners were pushing for the Kremlin to stay firm with regard to its ideological objectives? The latter reading seems to fit better with what we know: disappointed by Moscow's decision to readjust its military strategy to more modest objectives focused on the Donbas and the Sea of Azov; abandon the battle for the capital, Kyiv; and jettison the "denazification" point in Russia's demands during the Istanbul talks, the article likely represents the position of the hawks, but not the central official line. There was indeed evidence of such dissatisfaction among the war party in angry and disappointed discussions on Telegram channels.[67] One can therefore identify the party of war as the faction closest to fascism within the Russian political system, but it should not be interpreted as representing the entire state structure.

Since then, scholars and experts have been collecting evidence of what are called the five "D's" of incitement—demonization, delegitimization, dehumanization, denial, and disinformation—to document verbal (and of course physical) violence against Ukrainians as a recurrent trend in official statements as well as among the occupational authorities.[68] What was initially one-size-fits-all Russian propaganda toward Ukrainians has had to adapt to realities on the ground, better dissociating between Ukrainians living in occupied territories and those in free Ukraine and trying to promote narratives that can accommodate their experiences.[69] Depending on the sources at which one looks, one can therefore identify both pure violence and a more nuanced strategy attempting to win the "hearts and minds" of Ukrainians.

Among Russians, meanwhile, Kiriyenko's project of a new indoctrination has succeeded in maintaining a bureaucratic vision of what ideology should be. None of the radical voices, such as Dugin, are quoted in the *Foundations of Russian Statehood* textbook, and they appear to be seen by the Presidential Administration as spouting "gibberish" (*mut'*).⁷⁰ The textbook remains pretty mild compared to what Russian political talk shows express, and even includes some American sources, as well as Russian scholars living abroad, among them the Helsinki-based political scientist Vladimir Gelman.

Even in the war context, the competitive process through which idea-producers seek recognition from the Kremlin is far from settled. With the ongoing war, a new generation of ideologues and technocrats responsible for ideational production has emerged, with worldviews that are deeply Soviet-inspired, conservative, and bureaucratic. The tsarist past has joined, to a certain degree, the national pantheon, and imperial undertones have grown in state language, yet without calls for a fascist-type revolution becoming the norm. Once again, the state structure has preserved a certain equilibrium between radical calls for violence and regeneration and a technocratic authoritarianism that seeks to remain in power at a lower repressive cost. In this balance, the image of Russia as an empire can be read as both reactionary (restorationist and nostalgic for something that disappeared) and revolutionary (as a utopian vision of Russia's postwar future).

PART III
RUSSIA'S COUNTERREVOLUTION

THE PUTIN REGIME HAS a Thermidorian nature: it sees its mission as stabilizing a postrevolutionary situation born out of the collapse of the Soviet Union and the emergence of independent Russia, which had never existed as a nation-state or within its current legal borders. This stabilization must be effected without reverting to either Soviet or tsarist times while still blending past and present. This reaction is based on two divergent yet overlapping trends. At the societal level, it was born as a backlash against the many political, social, and economic traumas involved in the rapid transformations of the 1990s: in an environment marked by hasty cultural changes, the desire for order, stability, and predictability makes sense. At the regime level, it was founded on the idea that revolutionary changes were dangerous for the political order—as the 1917 and 1991 revolutions resulted in state collapse and foreign interference—and therefore reforms should be conducted in a top-down, not bottom-up manner.

What was previously a situational reaction across a large part of society in the face of so many transformative changes has been progressively built up into a coherent ideology. But far from being only about regime survival—which is, obviously, a nonnegligible component of the ideological construct—this state-backed reaction is also rooted in a genuine ontology. This ontology maintains a pessimistic view of human nature, seeing humankind as driven by negative forces and in an overall decline. It thus favors conservative political philosophy, which holds that humans have features that cannot be easily challenged or denied by means of individual willpower, and that identity (be it national, sexual, or gender) is not a mere social construct that can be changed simply because an individual feels dissatisfied with it.¹ From this standpoint, "excessive" progressivism is seen as destabilizing to the ontology of man.

Russian conservatism thus promotes traditional social institutions, emphasizes stability and continuity, and believes in notions such as traditions and natural law. Beyond this core, it remains highly situational. It does not oppose all change as a matter of principle: on the contrary, in today's Russia conservatism has developed alongside economic and social modernization. Changes are acceptable if they are slow enough for society to adapt and arise "naturally," which, in this context, means not copy-pasted from the West but implemented in a local way (whatever that means in practice). Indeed—and this is key to the analysis—Russian conservatism thinks of itself as counter-hegemonic, opposing the liberalism imported to Russia in the early 1990s and the post–Cold War liberal international order that demoted the country from its great-power status.

This conservatism is therefore memory-based at the national level and status-signaling at the international level. But it does not name explicitly a precise time in the past to be "conserved." As shown in chapter 3, as long as the 1990s are condemned, the choice of the historical period to be celebrated is flexible. Until the Russia-Ukraine War, the Kremlin did not claim to be hearkening back to any particular time: It defended a "no return" (to the Soviet past) policy and embraced the post-1991 realities, from globalization to the (limited) independence of its neighbors. As Sergey Prozorov neatly puts it, for the main figures representing conservatism in today's Russia, "Postcommunist Russia . . . has already generated enough that is worth conserving."[2]

This counterrevolution relies on three main repertoires. One is civilizationism, an emphasis on the diversity of the world, which is to be respected and even celebrated, and a refusal to see the West as the main civilizational benchmark to be emulated. The second repertoire is conservatism, represented by the metaphor of a tree, which cannot grow unless its roots are strong. This has gradually become the main body of language used by the state to express political decisions domestically, as well as Russia's stance on the international scene. The third repertoire is reaction, a language of eschatological thinking and legitimation of violence. The three languages are all spoken simultaneously, but there is still an internal chronology to them. Civilizationism was the expression of the mild and equivocal conservatism during early Putinism, best embodied politically by Vladislav Surkov's "sovereign democracy." Since the 2010s, civilizationism has been steadily integrated into a more theoretically consolidated conservatism, this time with direct policy implications (repressive laws targeting those who transgress traditional values, be it sexual minorities or political dissidents). Following the full-scale invasion of Ukraine, this conservatism has seen growing ideological rigidity and the increasing use of reactionary language.

SEVEN

CIVILIZATION
Rejecting Western Universalism

[We aim to] preserve Russia as a civilization founded on its own identity, on century-old traditions, on the culture of our people, values and traditions.
VLADIMIR PUTIN, Address to the Federal Assembly, 2019[1]

A KEY CONCEPT IN Russia's counterrevolution is that of civilization: by presenting the world as offering numerous paths to modernity, civilizationism denies the existence of a unique yardstick by which to judge other civilizations, and therefore allows Russia to present itself as a unique civilization that rejects Western normative pressures. Although the concept is prominent in Russia's political language and intellectual history, it is far from specific. Civilization narratives have indeed reemerged all over the world, deploying three main metaphors: the "clash of civilizations" to read new international tensions following the disappearance of Cold War bipolarity; the "dialogue of civilizations" to positively frame globalization; and the "civilizational global order" to support a new multipolar or polycentric world moving away from Western supremacy.[2] Having spread around the world, this civilizational language is both locally conceived *and* globally projected.

As with many of Russia's repertoires, the civilizational one is remarkably plastic, but it stands out perhaps more than others for its intrinsic polysemy: civilization can indeed be understood both as a universalist tradition of humanism against barbarism (in its singular use) and as a set of closed worlds seeking autonomy from each other (in its plural use). Although Russian state language uses civilization in both these meanings, it emphasizes the second. It presents Western universalism as both a philosophical threat to the God-given diversity of the world and as a political lie propagated by the West to obfuscate its strategic interests and hegemonic status. Meanwhile, the regime has continued to play on diverse civilizational repertoires: for a long time, it presented Russia as having civilizational features similar to Europe's and some forms of Western culture, yet at the same time as following its own distinctive course of development. It then gradually moved more decisively toward claiming full "civilizational autonomy." Whatever its position with regard to Europe or the West as a benchmark of civilization that is to be accepted, negotiated with, or rejected, one core element of Russia's civilizational ideal has remained: its emphasis on ethnic and religious pluralism as evidence of the country's unique cultural identity, which gives it license to reject the imposition of foreign norms.

A CONCEPT ROOTED IN RUSSIAN THOUGHT

Western European civilizational thinking has its own well-charted genealogy. *The Decline of the West* by German philosopher Oswald Spengler (1880–1936), published in two volumes from 1918 to 1922, put forth a cyclical theory of the rise and decline of civilizations. It was followed by *A Study of History*, a twelve-volume analysis of the rise and fall of civilizations published from the 1930s to the 1960s by the British historian Arnold J. Toynbee (1889–1975). More recently, the American political scientist Samuel P. Huntington's *The Clash of Civilizations and the Remaking of World Order*, released in 1996 (based on an essay originally published in 1993), stated that the end of Cold War ideologies had relaunched older, religion- and culture-based patterns of conflict.[3]

While some Western scholars such as Israeli sociologist Shmuel Eisenstadt developed the theory of "multiple modernities" to challenge Westernization as the unique modernization experience, in the Global South as in Russia, civilizational analysis has grown closer to a culture-based epistemology.[4] Indeed, Russia has its own intellectual genealogy of civilizational analysis that precedes the modern Western European one, deeply influenced by German Romanticism's *Naturphilosophie*. The ideas advanced by Johann Gottfried von Herder (1744–1803) have been fundamental in Russian intellectual life: cultures should remain themselves in their incommensurability; universalism emerges out of the concrete diversity of the world rather than from the abstraction of Man as being everywhere the same. In this view, every civilization has a transcendent idea of its own and is the bearer of a portion of divine truth; should such a unique character disappear, all of mankind would be left impoverished.[5] This influence from German Romanticism has contributed to Russian philosophy emphasizing the concept of "wholeness" (*tselostnost'*) and therefore favoring monist theories of unity versus duality.[6]

Throughout the nineteenth century, a large part of Russian belles-lettres (*publitsistika*) and philosophy debated the idea of Russia's civilizational uniqueness and its "special path" (*osobyi put'*)—the Russian translation of the German *Sonderweg*. At the end of the nineteenth century, several conservative thinkers inspired by late Slavophilism, or pan-Slavism, such as Nikolay Strakhov (1828–1896), Nikolay Danilevsky (1822–1885), and Konstantin Leontyev, explored the notion of civilization in depth.[7] Danilevsky offered the most sophisticated theory of Russian civilizational identity in his *Russia and Europe*.[8] As a fervent opponent of Darwinism, Danilevsky refuted the idea of progress and believed in the circularity of history. He pioneered the use of biological metaphors in the comparison of cultures, considering civilizations as a form of biological species and defining them as "historic-cultural forms." For him, each civilization should be judged by its own cultural and developmental laws (*zakonomernost'*), not by any external yardstick, because they are all "unique and incommensurable."[9]

Among the eleven civilizations Danilevsky distinguished,[10] his emphasis was obviously on the Slavic one and its relationship to the so-called Romano-Germanic civilization. According to him, the Nile was the origin of two major civilizations: one was "celestial and divine," which, via Jerusalem and Constantinople, led to Russia; the other was more terrestrial, which, via Athens and Rome, led to European countries. The Romano-Germanic and Slavic civilizations were therefore born from the same cradle but interpreted the world differently, and Russia was called upon to reunify these two worldviews. While European civilization was said to be old and declining, the Slavic one was claimed to be in its youthful stage and would rise, with Constantinople as its capital. In line with his time, Danilevsky also believed in the colonial mission of the main civilizational centers: Europe over Africa, the Near East, and India; the United States over the entirety of the Americas; and Russia over the whole of Asia.

This civilizational thinking was pursued and theorized in the 1920s by the founding fathers of Eurasianism (see chapter 10). Prince Nikolay Troubetzkoy (1890–1938) deployed Herderian thought through the tale of the Tower of Babel to explain that the variety of languages and therefore of civilizations was God's intention. According to him, pushes for universalism could result only in spiritual emptiness, as they go against God's will, while celebrating the diversity of languages and cultures fits higher, transcendent purposes and helps humankind to be aware of its divine origin.[11] In the late Soviet period, the cultural historian Sergey Averintsev (1937–2004) was the first to rehabilitate Spengler, hitherto considered by Soviet historiography as being too close to Nazi ideology, and connect him with Herder, Hegel, and Marx—i.e., with an interpretation of history fitting Soviet standards.

More dissident but nonetheless influential was the late Soviet historian Lev Gumilev (1912–1992), whose notion of "ethnos" parallels that of civilization: ethnos would be "not a sum of people, but a complex systemic totality,"[12] a closed structure stable in its features over centuries and unable to adopt external elements without destroying itself.[13] Inspired by the natural sciences and especially cosmology, Gumilev advanced a bold determinism, declaring that mankind depends on his entire cosmic and terrestrial environment, of which territory is but a minor part. In his socionatural history, each ethnic group is said to be born from a burst of energy coming from the Earth (this can be geological and mineral activity, circulation of energy in the living realm, or solar activity).[14] What separates them is their level of "passionarity"—their ability to absorb the energy of their living environment to do things that go beyond primordial physical needs. For example, culture, religion, politics, and war are outputs of passionarity.[15] Each group, said to have a lifespan of 1,200–1,500 years, has a different level of passionarity depending on its age and of its relationship to the environment. Obviously, Gumilev believed in the existence of a Russian-Eurasian superethnos whose passionarity would be extraordinarily high.

With the collapse of Marxism-Leninism, civilizational thinking blossomed in Russian academia. The delegitimation of Marxist historical materialism and dialectical materialism taught to every Soviet citizen at school and university was half-replaced, half-perpetuated by a "civilizational approach" (*tsivilizationnyi podkhod*) to world history, no longer as a pathway toward Communism but instead toward full civilizational "awareness" (*samosoznanie*). This trend was exemplified by the Georgian-born scholar Miran

Mchedlov (1928–2007), who contributed to the late-Soviet civilizational turn of Marxist thought.[16] In the 1990s, this turn also took shape under external influences: translated into Russian in 1996, Huntington's *The Clash of Civilizations* initially received a mixed reception, before going on to become a classic point of reference. Russian academia and politicians widely accepted the assumption of a "clash of civilizations," by which they understood that new conflicts in the world arena can be explained by cultural disagreements, though their views diverged on the civilizations that exist and where the key cleavages lie. The main dividing line regarded Russia's own civilizational identity. Some agreed with Huntington that Russia is located on a fault line where several civilizations grind against each other, while others denied that Russia is a fault-line state, insisting that Russia-Eurasia should instead be recognized as a civilization in its own right.[17] This second reading rapidly became the mainstream one.

To replace a vanishing Marxism-Leninism, Russian universities introduced civilizationalism through the newly launched discipline of "culturology" (*kul'turologiia*).[18] In it, culture is understood in an organicist, holistic, and essentialist manner as the new superstructure explaining world history. By extension, teachers of Marxism-Leninism became culturologists, continuing to apply a unilinear interpretation of history as one of conflicts between civilizations with a growing addition of conspiracy theories. Among the main champions of this civilizational analysis were several conservative and/or nationalist authors reproducing old Slavophile clichés on Russian civilization as spiritual and collectivist and Western civilization as materialist and individualistic. Among them were Oleg Platonov, who launched a publishing house and later the Institute of Russian Civilization; and Yevgeny Troitsky (1928–2013), an author trying to synthesize pan-Slavism, Eurasianism, cosmism, Slavic socialism, and racialism.[19]

Among all these figures of early post-Soviet civilizational analysis, Alexander Panarin (1940–2003), who taught in the Philosophy Department of Moscow State University, is likely the one who has had the most lasting influence. His trajectory is representative of Russia's major transformations: first emerging as a pro-Western figure defending the young parliamentary democracy, Panarin gradually grew disillusioned; by the end of the 1990s, he had joined the more conservative camp, affirming that Russia's salvation lies in a strong presidential regime and a return to autocratic traditions. Among his many books was *The Revenge of History* (1998), which, as its name indicates, was intended as a response to Francis Fukuyama's famous end of history thesis.[20] He contributed greatly to the revival of civilizational thinking and formulated it very early as a geopolitical project of multipolarity against US unipolarity.[21]

Panarin promoted the classical view of civilizations as central actors in history. According to him, universalism can only be the result of the hegemony of one particular culture, that of the West, which colonizes other civilizations from within by offering them a Eurocentric and therefore inevitably distorting yardstick, which is "dangerous for the moral health of peoples, because it instills a complex of nonachievement, debasing their own values."[22] Hence the inherent "multivariate nature (*mnogovariantnost'*) of history" according to which civilizations cannot "catch up" with others, as the developmental differences between them are due to their "essence" rather than a "lag."[23] For him, civilizations remain ahistorical: their internal structure is impervious to evolution; they represent unchangeable forms of social construction. Yet contrary to Platonov and others, Panarin was cautious about speaking of "Russian civilization": it was a project for future development, not an existing reality, which could materialize only if the Russian state could revitalize both Orthodox culture and Eurasian geopolitics.[24]

Panarin's major contribution to modern Russia's civilizational debate can be summarized as follows. First, he explicitly links Russia's messianism to being a global safeguard of polycentrism: by its very existence, Russia demonstrates that the West is not the sole driving force of development. As he explains: "In many ways, the future of the post-industrial era depends on Russia's future. If Russia becomes the Third Rome once again, post-industrial society will have better chances of becoming an alternative to the industrial ghetto."[25] Second, he blends eschatology, ecology, and faith. According to Panarin, "Globalization creates a democracy limited to a small group of privileged, extraterritorial people, the rest of humankind being relegated to low-intensity conflicts and a permanent 'ecocide.'"[26] Resistance to globalization will therefore be built on asceticism and repentance in the industrial world, meaning that once Man grasps the necessity of curbing his own consumerism for the sake of higher moral goals, Russia will enter the new era with a unique asset: high spirituality. One can see how this language resonates with the rhetoric of today's Russian officials.

With time, the theme of civilization became central to many works of *publitsistika* and invaded the media world.[27] Even Gleb Pavlovsky contributed to the notion in a premonitory text, echoes of which can be found today: "Russia remains a specific civilization that masters all civilizations with its concise complexity, permeability, and powerful vocal and intellectual capacity that appeals to all human beings."[28] We find similar language in the work of Russian international relations scholars. Already in 2014, a survey conducted among them identified as the foremost Russian thinkers Danilevsky, Leontyev, Panarin, Gumilev, the philosopher Nikolay Berdyaev (1874–1948), and the Eurasianists Troubetzkoy and Savitsky—all figures associated with civilizationist thinking.[29] Over the years, this civilizationist reading of the international scene has become accentuated in the foreign policy realm and has also penetrated academia, with a growing number of PhD dissertations giving legitimacy to the state's use of civilizational language.[30]

THE CIVILIZATIONAL TURN OF THE RUSSIAN STATE'S LANGUAGE

This civilizational reading, both of the world as a place where multiple civilizations coexist and of Russia as a unique civilization, has indeed penetrated the state's language, gradually making its way into official documents during Putin's second term. It was first tested by United Russia: in 2005, the party's leader, Boris Gryzlov, explained: "Russia is not the East, Russia is not the West. . . . To preserve territorial integrity, it is no longer enough to refer to historical victories, Russia needs a civilizational breakthrough, primarily through economic growth and economic diversification."[31]

This civilizational language was then officialized in the 2008 Foreign Policy Concept of the Russian Federation, which explicitly stated: "For the first time in modern history, global competition has acquired a civilizational dimension, and it is manifested in the competition of various value reference points and models of development . . . The cultural and civilizational multiplicity of the contemporary world is becoming more obvious."[32] Since then, civilizational language has become securitized, with the notion of "civilizational security" (*tsivilizatsionnaia bezopasnost'*) invading state language and official documents regarding both foreign and internal affairs.[33]

On the domestic front, Russia's civilizational identity was closely associated with another notion, that of "cultural codes" (*kul'turnye kody*), as expressed in a 2014 presidential decree on the "Basics of State Cultural Policy," written by Vladimir Medinsky's team. It defines culture as a system of values that must be protected by institutions to keep Russia's "civilizational originality" (*tsivilizatsionnaia samobytnost'*), as well as to unify the "mentality of Russia's people." A legislative initiative put forward in 2017 by the Ministry of Culture that aimed to rewrite the federal law "On Culture" associated civilization with the need to preserve cultural features: "Today, more than ever . . . there is a need for legislation that looks at culture as a societal phenomenon that allows for the transmission to future generations of the system of values and an understanding of the morals and ethics characteristic of Russian civilization."[34]

On the international front, the different iterations of the Foreign Policy Concept have all reworked the argument that Russia's civilizational mission is an answer to Western-led globalization.[35] The 2016 version added a Spenglerian accent in discussing the decline of the West, while the 2023 edition is the most lengthy and explicit:

> More than a thousand years of independent statehood, the cultural heritage of the preceding era, deep historical ties with traditional European culture and other Eurasian cultures, and the ability to ensure harmonious coexistence of different peoples, ethnic, religious and linguistic groups on one common territory, which has been developed over many centuries, determine Russia's special position as a unique country-civilization and a vast Eurasian and Euro-Pacific power that brings together the Russian people and other peoples belonging to the cultural and civilizational community of the Russian world.[36]

In 2023, Alexey Drobinin, director of the Department of Foreign Policy Planning at the Ministry of Foreign Affairs and a key figure in the construction of a post-February 24 ideology, published an article bundling cultural-civilizational identity and concrete foreign policy goals. According to him, Russia's civilizational identity can be put into practice through absolute sovereignty, self-sufficiency in economic and geographic terms, and the existence of "our own philosophy of development."[37]

Civilizationism has invaded presidential speeches too (see fig. 7.1). Yet its use has been irregular: spiking around 2005 before collapsing under Medvedev, rising again during Putin's third term before decreasing in 2017–20, and rebounding since. Over the course of 542 references between 2000 and 2023, more than half (303) use *civilization* in the sense of a singular world civilization, associating it with terms like "human," "modern," "world," "human progress," "higher stage of," "cultural achievements," "fundamental foundations," etc. Threats to civilization are often mentioned in reference to Nazism, usually in speeches related to the May 1945 Allied victory over Germany, or to international terrorism. About 15 percent of references (82) evoke civilization in relation to a country, usually as a synonym of "culture" (for instance, the celebration of "Italian civilization" during a trip to Rome), or while discussing the need for "dialogue among civilizations." More than a quarter of all references (157) were about Russia's own civilizational identity.

From this overview, which does not take into account the use of the term by many other senior Russian officials, one can see that the boundaries and content of what is understood by the term *civilization* remain vague: it can be the humanist, universalist tradition of describing world history and progress; it can belong to the contemporary culturalist narrative that classifies countries by civilization; and it can be a way of saying something about Russia's role in the world and interaction with its neighbors, primarily in Europe. At the 2022 Valdai summit, for instance, Putin quoted Leontyev and Danilevsky, insisting that "respect for the ways and customs of peoples and civilizations is in everyone's interest."[38]

To analyze how the regime frames Russia's civilizational belonging, I typologized mentions of "civilization" in presidential speeches, dividing them

FIG. 7.1. Mentions of "civilization" in presidential speeches, 2000–2023.

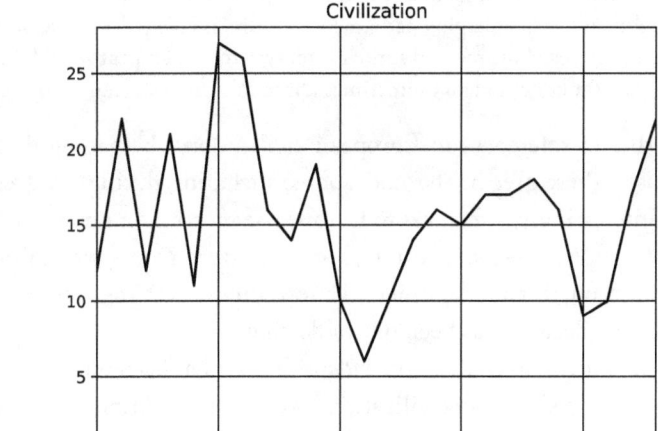

Source: Author's compilation based on Kremlin.ru.

into four categories: Russia as part of European civilization; Russia as part of Christian civilization; Russia as a Eurasian civilization; and Russia as a civilization unto itself (fig. 7.2). Note that Russia is never presented as uniquely part of Asian civilization.

Identifying Russia with European civilization has been a central leitmotif of Russian presidents, with 43 mentions out of 157. References to Russia's European identity were frequent during Putin's first two terms. The particularly high numbers in 2001 and 2003 can be explained by Orthodox commemorations and the tricentennial of the founding of St. Petersburg, respectively, which all emphasized Russia's shared identity with Europe. Globally, the vocabulary used to describe this belonging is always very plain: "Russia is an indivisible part of European civilization"; "Russia's cultural roots are in European civilization"; Russia as a "branch of European civilization"; etc. On some occasions, the vocabulary was ambiguous, like in Putin's 2005 Annual Address to the Federal Assembly, in which he asserted that "above all else Russia was, is and will, of course, be a major European power," which can be read as an imposition of Russia's voice over the European concert of nations. Also in 2005, however, Putin proposed a more political reading of this European belonging:

> Achieved through much suffering by European culture, the ideals of freedom, human rights, justice and democracy have for many centuries been our society's determining values. For three centuries, we—together with the other European nations—passed hand in hand through reforms of the Enlightenment, the difficulties of emerging parliamentarianism, municipal and judiciary branches, and the establishment of similar legal systems . . . I repeat we did this together, sometimes behind and sometimes ahead of European standards.[39]

The number of references to European civilizational belonging dramatically decreased thereafter in the mid-2000s, including during Medvedev's presidency. Interestingly, references to Europe rise mostly at moments of high tensions with the West—2008, 2011–12, 2014, and since 2022—when Russian presidents insist on Russia's legitimate Europeanness. Yet the overall trend over the past two decades has been one of decline.

Part of this European civilizational identification has been replaced by the notion of Russia as a Christian civilization (twenty-one mentions in presidential speeches), which became more prominent between 2013 and 2018. Before that period, this religious reference was mostly deployed to celebrate Orthodox Christianity as Russia's cultural basis, whereas since then it has been used to present Russia as the guardian of an authentic European identity.

FIG. 7.2. Russia's civilizational identity(ies) in presidential speeches, 2000–2023.

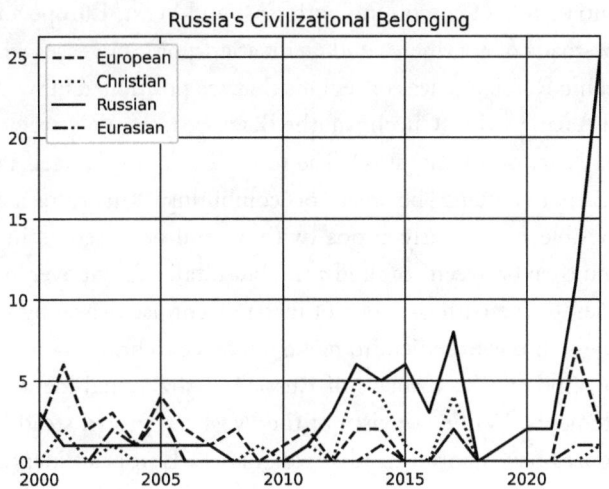

Source: Author's compilation on Kremlin.ru.

References to Russia as a Christian civilization have also been instrumental for Putin to insist on the triune nature of Eastern Slavs. In his address announcing Russia's annexation of Crimea on March 18, 2014, he declared that Grand Prince Vladimir's adoption of Orthodox Christianity a millennium ago had laid the "civilizational foundation" that today keeps Russia, Ukraine, and Belarus united.[40] A similar idea was expressed in 2015 during the official commemoration of the Christening of Rus' that took place all over Russia under the slogan, "The Civilizational Choice of Prince Vladimir."

Russia's Europeanness has been gradually replaced—yet not completely—by the idea of Russia as a civilization unto itself with a dominant 84 mentions out of 157 in presidential speeches and a massive peak since 2020. This notion of a Russian civilization per se appeared in official language in the early 2000s as a generic term to describe Russia's status when compared to other major civilizations, but since 2012 it has stood alone, becoming the main way of describing Russia. The vocabulary accompanying it gives a good overview of its semantic space: "powerful" (*moshchnaia*), "unique" (*unikal'naia* and *samobytnaia*), "multinational" (*mnogonatsional'naia*), and also as a "country-civilization" and "state-civilization" (*strana-tsivilizatsiia* and *gosurdarstvo-tsivilizatsiia*).

Russia as a Eurasian civilization appears just a total of fourteen times and irregularly, mainly on two types of occasions: (1) when the president insists on the country's role of combining both East and West, Europe and Asia, of being a crossroads of continents and civilizations; or (2) in cases when he celebrates specific Russian places or regions that are positioned between the European and Asian worlds (Chechnya, the Black Sea, the Volga region, Kazan, Astrakhan, Tuva, or Vladivostok). The term "Eurasian" is itself rarely used, the emphasis put on being "between" or "combining." This Eurasian narrative was quite visible in the early 2000s (with several occurrences in 2000 and 2004–6), and then between 2011 and 2014, but totally absent over long periods of time. Overall, the pattern is one of intermittent use driven by specific occasions for which it is expedient to make reference to bridging or combining.

One can find similar displays of Russia's civilizational identity in many official statements. While criticism of the West has grown steadily, Russian political figures have continued to stress Russia's European identity, at least until the 2022 war. On several occasions, they have unequivocally presented Russia as a "Third West" alongside America and Europe. One of the first texts calling for building a new ideology for Russia, published in 2006 by Pavlovsky, emphasized, for instance, the common values that Russia shares with Europe: "Russia's opting for Europe is not a fashion or a result of political circumstance. It is the natural result of several centuries of state and societal development."[41] For Vladislav Surkov, who was vehemently opposed to any kind of Eurasian destiny, the need for Russian national identity to be forward-looking was intimately linked to identification as a "second Europe."[42] Speaking in Washington, DC, in 2011, minister of foreign affairs Sergey Lavrov defined Europe, the United States, and the Russian Federation as "the three pillars and three branches of European civilization."[43]

Similar narratives were particularly visible among Russian politicians inspired by the European far right, for whom Russia's European, Christian, and even "white" identity constitutes a fundamental element of their worldview. For instance, Dmitry Rogozin, who represents an ethnonationalist tendency extending back to Alexander Solzhenitsyn, has made this clear on several occasions, such as when he said in 2010:

> For me the question of Russia's belonging to Europe is a question about whether Russians are a European nation. And I answer affirmatively. . . . Russia has always been an inalienable part of a united political culture of historical Europe, European civilization. The West expresses the Vatican's

culture, Russia has continued the history of Byzantium. Moreover, Europe and Russia are united not only by their past, but by their future.[44]

However, these rhetorical nuances between Europe and the West have not been systematically respected. In 2014, at the height of tensions with the West over Crimea, the draft of the new Law on Culture proposed by then minister of culture Vladimir Medinsky, known for his blunt comments, stated that "Russia is not Europe."[45] Yet the text explains that Russia's civilizational roots are to be found in Byzantium, not Rome—affirming what has been the Kremlin's rhetorical line for years but missing the point of Byzantium as being the second Europe. As discussed in chapter 4, even with the full-scale war, projecting Russia as the real Europe has not disappeared, but the idea of the country's isolationist (from the West) destiny now dominates.

CIVILIZATIONISM AS A MEANS OF MANAGING RUSSIA'S MULTIETHNICITY

In presidential speeches, Russian civilization is always *rossiiskaia*, never *russkaia*, to insist on the multinational nature of the country. Indeed, asserting Russia as a unique state-civilization has direct implications on how the regime frames the country's ethnic and religious pluralism. This relationship goes both ways: in order to justify Russia's specific civilizational identity against that of the West, it needs to have some domestic depth of its own—including, if not a sphere of influence in relation to neighboring states, at least a domestic "other" represented by the country's citizens who are not ethnically Russian. Conversely, within the narrative of Russia's being its own civilization, it makes sense for the regime to articulate a language that speaks to the country's ethnic minorities, whatever the status of the country's relationship with the West or Europe may be. Ambivalences in the definition of the nation—*russkii*/Russian, that is, ethnocultural; or *rossiiskii*/Rossian, that is, civic—have been constitutive of the post-Soviet construction: Russia defines itself as an asymmetric federation of a "multinational people" composed of 80 percent of ethnic Russians and 20 percent indigenous minorities.

The constitutive place of multiethnicity in the state-civilization argument was developed at length relatively early, set out in Putin's 2012 article on the national question published in *Nezavisimaia gazeta*. In it he denounced both Europe's failed multiculturalism—which he claimed had dissolved the national core into atomized ethnic groups—and Russian ethnonationalists calling for the right to self-determination. He declared that Russians (*russkie*) had already achieved self-determination by becoming the "state-forming" nation of Russia: "Self-determination for Russians—that is a poly-ethnic civilization held together by a Russian cultural core . . . . The great mission of Russians is to unite and cement this civilization."[46] For him, Russia's civilization is expressed by a cultural code shared by all the ethnic groups living in Russia, which, while multiethnic, are still united because the "Russian people and Russian culture are the linchpin, the glue that binds together this unique civilization."[47]

The presidential discourse on Russia as a civilization is therefore not anchored in ethnonationalism; on the contrary, the regime (and especially Putin) has been vocally opposed to this type of nationalism, seen as a destructive force from within and a threat from outside that seeks to bring about the collapse of Russia. Reading presidential speeches, one can count more than fifty mentions of "nationalism," all with negative connotations except for a few. "Internal" nationalism—that found inside Russia, either among ethnic minorities or among Russian radical nationalist groups—is systematically described as a regressive force associated with extremism and xenophobia that undermines Russia's unity. Putin has even called it a "virus."[48] A second iteration of nationalism is "external," representing anti-Russian forces, and this theme was increasingly stressed in relation to Ukraine, where it became associated with "Nazism." This usage has become dominant ever since Putin's 2021 essay on Russia-Ukraine unity, and he mentioned Ukrainian nationalism some seventeen times in his February 21, 2022, declaration in the lead-up to the war.[49]

Putin's references to nationalism as something positive are rare. At the 2014 Valdai summit, the president did evoke nationalism constructively, calling himself "the main nationalist in Russia."[50] He reiterated this in his 2015 Direct Line annual show: "In this sense I have said that the righteous, the most authentic nationalist is me."[51] At the 2018 Valdai summit, he again insisted: "I am the most proper and true nationalist and a most effective one too."[52] But since the full-scale invasion of Ukraine, Putin has been more vocal than ever about Russia's ethnic pluralism, presenting it as confirmation of the country's anti-Western identity. On March 2, 2022, he declared, "I am a Russian (*russkii*) person . . . but when I see examples of heroism such as the feats of the young Nurmagomed Gadzhimagomedov, from Dagestan, a Lak ethnically, and our other fighters, I want to say: I am Lak, I am Dagestani, I am Chechen, Ingush, Russian, Tatar, Jewish, Mordvin, Ossetin."[53]

One may obviously interpret this celebration of Russia's multiethnicity as a simple obfuscation of Russia's imperial identity and silence on the violence committed by the Russian state against colonized peoples over centuries. In practice, the cultural autonomy of nonethnic Russians has been shrinking over the years. Yet attempts to frame nationhood as an inclusive process of ethnic groups joining a core are nothing new and can be found in the majority of Western European countries, where civic identity is articulated more or less explicitly with the idea of peaceful and voluntary assimilation of both ethnic and regional groups, as well as a newcomers, into a national cultural core. While the nationhood mechanism of blending civic and ethnic identity is not unique to Russia, the Russian case is nonetheless unique insofar as the country has been built through an exceptional level of territorial expansion. It is not newcomers in the sense of immigrants that are to be assimilated into the Russian (*russkii*) core, but indigenous people living on their native lands.[54]

This essentialist pluralism is constructed around the *matryoshka* (nested doll) principle: each ethnic group is allowed to have its own local subcivilizational history, as long as it fits into the Russian supra-ethnic or supranational one. There is therefore an asymmetric pyramid of belonging, with ethnic Russians at the top and ethnic minorities "below" them. And indeed, the civilization argument has been developed around the line of a shared, common destiny of the peoples living on the territory of Russia: all those who adhere to a certain set of culturally conditioned historical myths, such as having voluntarily joined the Russian state as it expanded, are welcome. Young conservative thinker Mikhail Remizov formulates this partnership in a clear-cut way:

> Russia was formed not as a civic nation but as a historical project of a specific union of peoples, with the Russian people at its core. This union is the real basis of the political nation of Russia. The Russian nation is a community made up of those with an interest in the building of the Russian nation and state. The Russian people are the organic nucleus of this community, and the indigenous peoples loyal to Russia are its rightful participants.[55]

This civilizational language has also embraced the multireligious identity of Russia, and in a sense even more easily than the country's multiethnic identity. While ethnic identities have often been contentious (explicitly in the 1990s,[56] more implicitly since then), official religious identities are keen on maintaining the status quo. As the country's second religion, Islam has been celebrated as an intrinsic component of Russia's civilizational state, as well as, to a lesser extent, Buddhism and Judaism. This celebration does not preclude, in parallel, the securitization of religion, especially of Islam, and excludes from the national consensus religious groups considered security threats, which are labeled as extremist or terrorist, proselytizing groups, or simply as foreign.[57]

On several occasions Putin has emphasized the place of Islam in Russia's national identity. For instance, in 2013 he declared: "Islam is a bright element of Russia's cultural code, an integral, organic part of Russia's history. We know and remember many names of Muslims who constitute the glory of our Fatherland."[58] But it would be wrong to think of Muslim institutions, politicians, and thinkers as mere pawns in the regime's narrative-construction; they, too, have used the civilizational framework to legitimize themselves and put forward a reading of Russia's identity that fits their own goals.

Far from being a new phenomenon of the Putin era, this theme of a civilizational unity of Russia's Muslims has a long history. During the Brezhnev years, the different Spiritual Administrations of Muslims worked hard on a notion of Soviet Islam that would make Muslim cultural identity and Communism compatible through a focus on social justice, social harmony, and world peace.[59] While Islam as a secularized identity was the main framework of interpretation, minority groups pushed for a more religious and political reading of Islam. For instance, the underground Islamic Renaissance organization, which sprang up in Tajikistan in the 1970s before spreading to different Soviet Muslim constituencies and becoming a political party in 1990, carried the idea of an Islamic revolution across the Soviet Union.[60] Though it quickly collapsed, it provided a pool of cadres for efforts to craft an Islamic civilizational project for Russia.

In the 1990s, in line with the liberalism of the Yeltsin era, Tatarstan took the lead in promoting the concept of "Euro-Islam"—an Islam that would align neatly with the pro-European stance of then Russian elites while stressing the uniqueness of the Volga-Urals region within the federal structure. The movement failed to gather support outside of the Tatar world and was seen by many Muslim figures as too Russified and pro-Western to be legitimate.[61] In the early 2000s, the theory of "Islamic humanism," launched by Taufik Ibragim, a scholar from the Russian Academy of Sciences, was adopted by the Moscow Muftiate to advocate for a universal, liberal Islam, but there too the project failed.⁶² Neither Euro-Islam nor Islamic humanism was able to gain major popular support among Russia's Muslims or secure backing at a sufficiently high political level to be imposed from the top down, but there were other, more relevant intellectual projects for an Islamic version of Russia's civilizational idealism.

In the 2000s, support voiced by Muslims for the concept of Russia as a unique civilization has picked up with the gradual submission of muftiates to state narratives and to the church's symbolic dominance.⁶³ In 2015, the Kazan Muftiate released a "Social Doctrine of Russia's Muslims," inspired by the ROC's Social Doctrine, explaining how being a "good Muslim" means being an obedient citizen of a secular Russian state. The muftiates have tried hard to present themselves as a national "church for Islam," an Islamic version of the ROC that would be a unique institutional intermediary between believers and the secular state. As Gulnaz Sibgatullina notes, because Islam is interpreted using an Orthodox vocabulary and increasingly in the Russian language, there is a growing convergence at the ideological, and even semantic, level.⁶⁴

Beyond the basic pragmatic cooperation between representatives of the two faiths, one can also see a certain blending of Russian Islam with the church's heavy symbolic politics. The chief mufti of the Ufa-based Central Spiritual Administration of Muslims, Talgat Tadzhuddin, has, for instance, never hidden his friendship with the late Patriarch Alexy II, whom he considered the country's supreme spiritual leader. Tadzhuddin has created for himself the title of "Mufti of All Russia," an obvious echo of his Orthodox counterpart's designation as "Patriarch of Moscow and All Rus'." Similarly, he has publicly engaged in a Muslim version of some Orthodox rituals, such as sprinkling objects with holy water.⁶⁵

Several ideological projects have competed to become the Muslim version of Russia's civilizational language. The most obvious has been the idea of a common Eurasian civilization shaped by a cultural blend of Eastern Orthodox and Islamic influences—specifically a Slavic-Turkic fusion. There have been several iterations of this narrative. First came a Volga-Ural-centric one: in the 1990s, Tadzhuddin rehabilitated the notion of the Bulgars (indigenous Turkic Muslims who lived alongside Russians) as the original people of Tatarstan before the arrival of foreign Tatar-Mongols. Later, in the 2000s, Tadzhuddin partnered with the main neo-Eurasianist ideologue, Alexander Dugin, joining his Eurasia Party and then his International Eurasian Movement, though this failed to produce a legitimate Muslim Eurasianism that could gain widespread popularity.[66]

The second iteration, launched by Tadzhuddin's competitor, Ravil Gaynutdin, and his young deputy, Damir Mukhetdinov, has been more successful in two respects: it did away with the Volga-Ural-centrism of the first iteration, taking a pan-Russian Muslim Eurasianist rhetorical line, and dissociated itself from Dugin to follow the more official, state-sponsored, Eurasian project.[67] Since then, Gaynutdin and Mukhetdinov have insisted on Russia's Muslims as the "Eurasian foundation of Russian civilization" and the Eurasian Economic Union as a "Muslim Union."[68] They have fine-tuned their rhetoric to harmonize with the official anti-Western agenda: Mukhetdinov, for instance, portrays Russia's Muslim community as grounded in "anti-globalism, defense of traditional values, traditional multiculturalism, and moderate conservatism."[69]

A third iteration can be found in the model of Ramzan Kadyrov's dictatorial regime in Chechnya, which offers yet another—radical and caricatural—interpretation of Russian civilizationism, blending a militant patriotism that encourages support for President Putin and classic references to Russia as an Orthodox and ethnically Slavic country, on the one hand, with an ultraconservative Islam inspired by Gulf puritanism and strong anti-Westernism, on the other. Kadyrov likes to pepper his speeches with trendy historical allusions, such as Russian national heroes (he even dressed up as Ilya Muromets, the knight-errant of Russian folk tales), makes great displays of the Russian flag on social media, and celebrates the capacity of Islam itself to embody Russian civilization. In 2014, Kadyrov was received by Patriarch Kirill at the Danilov Monastery in Moscow, a powerful symbol of recognition of the Chechen leader's federal stature and his ability to get the country's highest dignitaries to call on him—at the same time showing that ethnic minorities are a constitutive part of Russia's civilizational identity.[70]

The Russian regime, having played with multiple civilizational repertoires simultaneously, is now gradually shifting toward the "uniqueness" argument of Russia as a state-civilization unto itself. This civilizational claim can result in diverging policies, both expansionist (Russian civilization should include territories outside of Russia's legal borders) and autarkic (to survive, Russian civilization should close itself to the rest of the world). As always, the regime refuses to make a choice between these different options, preferring to keep the full menu available. This narrative of being a civilization per se does not preclude interactions with others and some forms of shared destiny: language about Russia's Europeanness reappear on some occasions, especially when linked to a shared Christian heritage and traditional values promotion, even in the current context of profound decoupling with Europe.

Even if they are rarer, evocations of Russia's civilizational partnership with Asia have also grown: though Russia is never presented as an Asian civilization per se, it is seen as sharing some civilizational values—meaning polycentrism and rejection of Western hegemonic normativity—with Asian countries. Three key *longue durée* components have been put forward to justify Russia's claim to being a civilization in its own right: its geographical size, its ethnic pluralism, and its conservative "cultural code." The last component has been developed at length in Russia's ideological construction.

EIGHT

CONSERVATISM
Russia's Answer to Liberalism

Conservatism is [not] a form of isolation and refusal to develop. Healthy conservatism entails the use of everything best, new, and promising to guarantee gradual development.
VLADIMIR PUTIN, Valdai summit, 2014[1]

THE CIVILIZATIONIST LANGUAGE OF Russian politics is intimately tied up with the promotion of conservatism, the ideological cornerstone of the regime. The Kremlin advocates for what can be defined as an ecumenical conservatism: almost all versions of conservatism are welcome and find room (that said, they are allotted different sizes and statuses) under its protective umbrella.[2] One can define at least four such strains of conservatism: (1) the state-promoted one, presented as moderate and embodied intellectually by state-sponsored projects such as the journal *Essays on Conservatism* and the (now disbanded) circle of the Young Conservatives; (2) liberal conservatism, stressing the importance of economic reforms but in a conservative political context, surviving nowadays mostly among economy and finance technocrats; (3) the Russian Orthodox church's brand of conservatism, more oriented toward religion and moral values, with activist groups focused on family policies; and (4) reactionary conservatism, whose rhetoric may sometimes overlap with more mainstream forms of conservatism but which instead pushes for revolutionary transformations, while more mainstream conservatives favor the status quo (see chapter 9).

CONSERVATISM, A DEEPLY ROOTED RUSSIAN PHILOSOPHY

Russia has been a conveyor of conservative ideologies since the nineteenth century and throughout the twentieth century. One can briefly summarize three sources that influence today's forms of conservatism: not only the obvious conservative thinking expressed during the tsarist regime and among dissidents in the Soviet Union but also the often-implicit social conservatism of the Soviet project, as well as the emphasis placed on morality during perestroika. It is only by combining these different components that one can capture why conservatism could easily be imposed as the solution to what is perceived as liberalism's failures.

Back in the nineteenth century, tsarist Russia presented itself as the bulwark against a revolutionary Europe. After the Napoleonic conquests, Tsar Alexander I played a major role in the counterrevolutionary Congress of Vienna of 1814–15 and the Holy Alliance, based on monarchism and antisecularism. Close to him was Nikolay Karamzin, one of the founders of Russian imperial historiography and an icon of Russian conservatism. Alexander's successor, Nicholas I, continued the idea of liberating Europe from parliamentarianism and anarchism. His minister of national education, Sergey Uvarov (1786–1855), crafted the motto "Autocracy, Nationality, Orthodoxy" as an answer to the French republican *liberté, égalité, fraternité*. Uvarov's Triad promoted a conservative policy based on autocracy in government, Orthodoxy in religion, and the state-founding role of the Russian nationality[3]—and thus its all-important role in the whole imperial tradition. After the liberal reign of Tsar Alexander II, his son Alexander III revived the conservative tradition, which was embodied by Konstantin Pobedonostsev (1827–1907), the chief spokesman for reaction and the tsar's *éminence grise*, who was also in charge of supervising the church.

But it would be wrong to see today's conservative renewal as a simple reconnection with the nineteenth-century past and in no way rooted in the Soviet experience. Conservative groups nested inside Soviet state structures, especially the Communist youth movement, the Komsomols. Labeled the "Russian Party," these groups were marked above all by ethnonationalism, virulent antisemitism, and the idea of ethnic Russians as victims of the Soviet regime.[4] They called for the revalorization of Russian cultural elements against Bolshevik internationalism and Nikita Khrushchev's rhetoric about all the Soviet peoples merging into one unified Soviet nation. Their conservatism was expressed in two ways. Some vehemently rejected everything related to socialism and the Soviet experience and supported the revival of the prerevolutionary past. One prominent example was the "village prose" movement, which idealized in a Slavophile way the peasant lifestyle that was on the verge of disappearing under Soviet transformations and the attendant industrial conquest of agricultural lands.[5] Others, meanwhile, integrated elements of nineteenth-century political culture into their interpretation of the Soviet experience and were nostalgic for Stalin's national-Bolshevism and its rehabilitation of Russian nationalism.[6]

In dissidence and in exile, several groups were promoting conservative values, too. The All-Russian Social-Christian Union for the Liberation of the People (VSKhSON), the main dissident organization of the 1960s, which brought together many young intelligentsia figures, sought to create a Social-Christian ideology based on a form of Orthodox fundamentalism. Inspired by the reactionary Russian émigré ideologue Ivan Ilyin, VSKhSON called for the creation of an anticommunist movement that would lead a clandestine war against the godless regime, counting on the inevitable collapse of the Communist state and its replacement by a Christian system.[7] Other groups were inspired by Alexander Solzhenitsyn, exiled from the Soviet Union in 1974. For him, late imperial Russia had succeeded in an endogenous modernization that, had it not been interrupted by the two 1917 revolutions, would have combined the pursuit of an autocratic regime with the tsar as the embodiment of the nation with elements of modernity and local self-government, the *zemstvo* assembly.[8] Solzhenitsyn called on Russia to give up on imperial or messianic missions and refocus on its culture from the early seventeenth century, a time that Solzhenitsyn believed contained more natural national values.

More broadly, conservative values and practices were inherent in Soviet everyday social practices. Throughout the life of the Soviet Union, the party-state rhetorically emphasized its adherence to the idea of progress and its focus on the future and youth. Yet allegiance to left-wing ideas—such as Marxism-Leninism, atheism, and socialism in politics and economics—was also combined with right-wing social/cultural conservatism. A notable element of state-sanctioned Soviet values was a kind of prudishness, manifest in the preaching of "high morals," the condemnation of adultery (wives complained about unfaithful husbands to Communist Party officials), criticism of premarital sex, and the criminalization of homosexuality. State censorship monitored art, film, and literature for moral and political impropriety, even imposing a virtual ban on mentioning or depicting sex in any of these media.[9] The popular phrase "There is no sex in the USSR" became one of these mottos used to mock official prudishness. In addition, morality mattered in foreign affairs, as capitalism was described as deeply immoral—one can find here the main root of today's official rhetoric about perverted liberalism.

Finally, although the perestroika years are typically remembered in the West as a blossoming of liberal thinking, the moral aspect of that liberalism often goes unnoticed. As Guillaume Sauvé shows, Russian liberalism rose on the premise of a moral revolution against an immoral Soviet regime: liberalism was a means, not an end, for a moral society. But the experience of the 1990s, with its criminality and wild capitalism, destroyed the moral legitimacy of liberalism in the eyes of many Russians, pushing many hitherto liberals to embrace a situational conservatism. The moral corruption of the Yeltsin-era elites, their admiration for everything Western, and their open contempt for the people would become a key leitmotif of the Kremlin's conservative language.[10] Morality has remained the end goal, this time to be achieved through conservatism.

During the perestroika years, conservative movements rapidly took shape, born out of two legacies: one, underground dissident circles calling for a Christian conservative future for Russia, and two, from the Soviet official apparatus, with those opposing Gorbachev's reforms who would come to be known as "red-brown" for their combination of nostalgic references to Communism and radical nationalist sentiment.[11] In the early 1990s, conservatives positioned themselves in direct opposition to the Yeltsin government. The ROC was the first institution to shift its language from one of democratization and pluralism to a narrative of conservative values and the need to protect Russian identity in the face of globalization.[12] The Moscow Patriarchate quickly found political allies among those blaming Yeltsin and his team of reformers for the precipitous collapse of the state, the decline of Russia's status on the international scene, and the criminal takeover of the national economy by oligarchs and mafia groups.

The new Communist Party of the Russian Federation crafted a political language combining Communist, Eurasianist, and Orthodox values. It called for the revival of Russia's great-power status and a reconnection with its unique spiritual legacy.[13] The alliance between Communist forces and the ROC was forged by two key figures: Alexander Prokhanov and Alexey Podberezkin. Together they formulated a new ideological strand that merged references to Orthodox spirituality, nostalgia for the Soviet regime, and a sense of Russia's greatness that transcended historical discontinuities. The ROC also courted Zhirinovsky's LDPR to celebrate Russia's unique spirituality in the face of a decadent West.[14] A plethora of small political and civil society movements representing conservative forces also orbited the church, Communists, and LDPR. Several Orthodox movements, among them the Transfiguration Brotherhood, Foundation of Saint Andrew the First-Called, and Russian Zemstvo Movement, engaged the country's then powerful governors and other high-ranking regional officials to turn their conservative ideals into concrete political reforms and social experiments at both local and federal levels.[15]

CONSERVATISM ENTERS THE STATE'S LANGUAGE

As we saw in chapter 2, conservatism entered the political mainstream under the label of centrism during Yeltsin's second term in office, before penetrating the United Russia party in the early 2000s. The first genuine conservative discussion forum was the Seraphim Club, founded in 2003 by three commentators (Mikhail Leontyev, Maxim Sokolov, and Alexander Privalov) from the political talk show *Odnako* ("However") on Russia's Channel One, as well as the editor-in-chief of the business journal *Ekspert*, Valery Fadeev. In their belief that Russia needed to avoid ideological dualisms to succeed, they felt largely alone at the time. As they explained, "The Third Russia [they call for, ML] has practically no patriots, at least among the elite, which is still divided between patriots of the US (or 'citizens of the world,' which is the same thing) and patriots of the USSR."[16]

The language of conservatism penetrated state institutions and the presidency just a few years later. "Conservative" as an adjective (*konservativnyi*) first appeared in presidential speeches in 2008, when Dmitry Medvedev refused to define himself as either a liberal or a conservative, and declared that Russia's foreign policy could not be defined as one or the other.[17] The term reappeared in 2012, this time as something to be proud of, when Medvedev defined United Russia's position as "conservative-centrist," and Alexey Kudrin, then minister of finance, as a "right-conservative" (*pravokonservativnyi*),[18] thereby reiterating the previous usage of conservatism as a synonym for centrism.

It was only in 2013 that Putin used the term conservatism in a more political-philosophical sense, describing himself as "a pragmatic with a conservative leaning (*uklon*),"[19] an supporter of a "conservative approach (*podkhod*),"[20] and "a man with conservative values (*tsennosti*)."[21] In the 2013 Annual Address to the Federal Assembly, he declared, "Obviously, it is a conservative position [that I share]," and quoted the theologian and philosopher Nikolay Berdyaev: "The sense of conservatism is not that it hampers the move forward and up, but in that it hampers the move back and down."[22] At the 2014 Valdai summit, Putin elaborated on his own view of conservatism:

> It does not mean at all conservatism is a form of isolation and refusal to develop. Healthy conservatism entails the use of everything best, new, and promising to guarantee gradual development. . . . This is why I would ask colleagues not to speculate that, when we talk about conservatism, this means that we want to conserve ourselves (*zakonservirovat'*); this has nothing to do with reality or with our plans.[23]

As shown in figure 8.1, "conservatism" in presidential speeches peaked first during the early years of Medvedev's presidency and then with Putin's return to power between 2012 and 2014. After the watershed year of 2014, Putin used the term more sparingly, only to define United Russia's posture

FIG. 8.1. Mentions of "conservatism" in presidential speeches, 2000–2023.

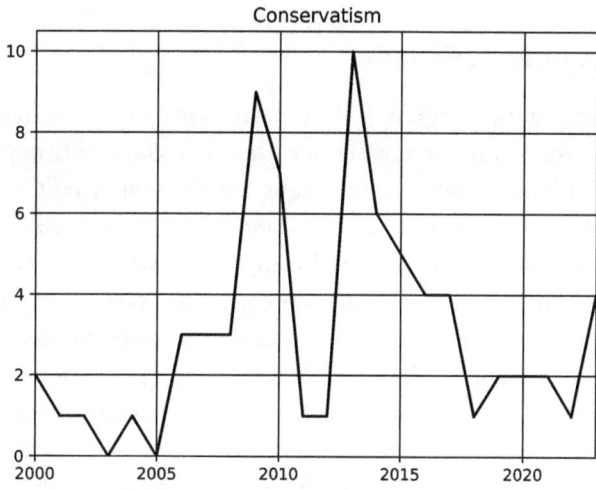

Source: Author's compilation based on Kremlin.ru.

and to acknowledge the coexistence of liberal and conservative readings of the 1917 revolutions.[24] The term even almost disappeared from presidential speeches between 2017 and 2020 before Putin came back to it in 2021, with a massive thirteen mentions in that year alone. Commenting on the West's moral decadence at the Valdai summit that year, he insisted on the need for a "moderate conservatism" not to be conflated with reaction:

> I have already mentioned that, in shaping our approaches, we will be guided by a healthy conservatism. . . . when the world is going through a structural disruption, the importance of reasonable conservatism as the foundation for a political course has skyrocketed—precisely because of the multiplying risks and dangers, and the fragility of the reality around us.
>
> This conservative approach is not about an ignorant traditionalism, a fear of change or a restraining game, much less about withdrawing into our own shell. It is primarily about reliance on a time-tested tradition, the preservation and growth of the population, a realistic assessment of oneself and others, a precise alignment of priorities, a correlation of necessity and possibility, a prudent formulation of goals, and a fundamental rejection of extremism as a method. And frankly, in the impending period of global reconstruction, which may take quite long, with its final design being uncertain, moderate conservatism is the most reasonable line of conduct, as far as I see it. It will inevitably change at some point, but so far, do no harm—the guiding principle in medicine—seems to be the most rational one.[25]

TRADITIONAL VALUES AND FAMILY POLICIES AS RUSSIA'S MORAL LEADERSHIP

Simultaneously, other notions from the same semantic field have become much more common in presidential speeches than conservatism per se: spirituality (*dukhovnost'*), national traditions (*natsional'nye traditsii*), authentic roots (*iskonnye korni*), moral values (*moral'nye* and *nravstvennye tsennosti*), cultural code (*kul'turnyi kod*), moral compass (*moral'nyi sterzhn'*), spiritual bonds (*dukhovnye skrepy*), cultural sovereignty (*kul'turnyi suverenitet*), and, of course, the notorious traditional values (*traditsionnye tsennosti*). A rather poorly defined concept, the latter has become a centerpiece of state language, seen by the authorities as more useable than conservatism: whereas the *-ism* in conservatism implies an intellectual construct, "traditional values" can be understood in a more intuitive (and hollow) way, which makes it harder to pin down, versus conservatism's clear meaning of conserving. As we can see in figure 8.2, "spirituality" has dominated over even "traditional values," while other notions have enjoyed less visibility.

The notion of conservatism, largely abstract, was thus rapidly operationalized through its moral dimension. It is not that this moralistic rhetoric had been entirely absent from Kremlin rhetoric in the 2000s, but nation-building was at that time mostly confined to generating political consensus and patriotism, while moralism became central to the regime after 2012.[26] At the 2013 Valdai summit, Putin made a declaration of faith on what moral conservatism meant to him and how this had become Russia's new political identity:

> We can see how many of the Euro-Atlantic countries are rejecting their roots, including Christian values, which form the basis of Western civilization. They are trying to deny moral principles and their traditional identity: national, cultural, religious, and even sexual. They put in place policies that equate large families with homosexual families, and make faith in God equal to belief in Satan. . . . In many European countries, people are embarrassed to talk about their religion. . . . I believe that this opens a direct path to degradation and primitivism, leading to a profound demographic and moral crisis. What else but the loss of the capacity to reproduce could be the best evidence of this moral crisis? Today, almost all developed nations are no longer capable

FIG. 8.2. Mentions of traditional values in presidential speeches, 2000–2023.

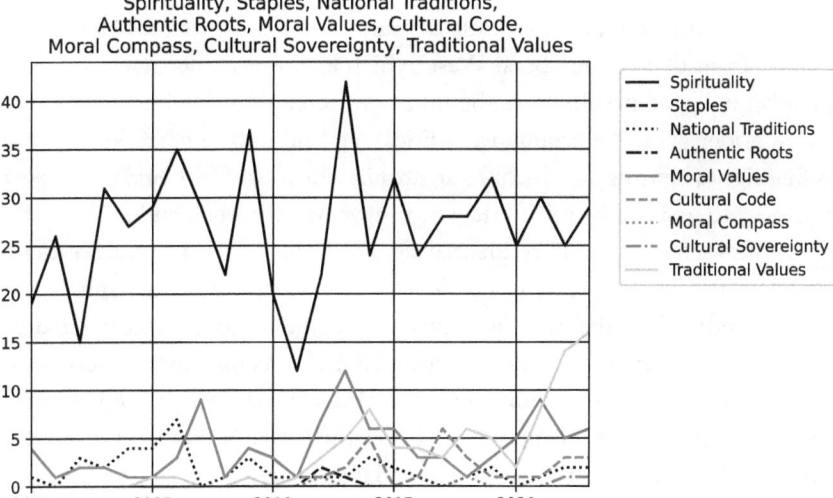

Source: Author's compilation based on Kremlin.ru.

of assuring demographic renewal, even with help from immigration. Without the values present in Christianity and the other religions of the world, without the moral standards that have formed over thousands of years, people inevitably lose their human dignity. We see it as right and natural to defend these values. It is necessary to respect the right of each minority to be different, but the rights of the majority should not be called into question.[27]

Since the 2011–12 conservative turn, the context in which this already-existing language is used has changed. First, the tone of the rhetoric evolved. Going back to Putin's earliest speeches, spirituality was celebrated as the main driver of Russia's revival in all spheres, a constructive element for the country's progress. In 2012, however, Putin lamented the "manifest deficit of spiritual bonds in Russian society."[28] First exalted as a tool for reconstruction, a decade later "traditional values" came to be seen as under siege, something to be protected. Second, this language became more abrupt and acquired concrete targets: Putin's 2013 statement about tolerance being "neutered and barren"[29] illustrates the shift toward repressive policies and, as we discussed in chapter 2, the Duma adopted a series of laws to put these conservative values into practice.

Third, the securitization of this terminology has accelerated, peaking in 2015 with the new Russian National Security Strategy, which listed "the preservation and augmentation of traditional Russian spiritual and moral values" as one of the "strategic aims to ensure national security."[30] Traditional values are presented in the Strategy both as something that distinguishes Russian culture from that of the liberal West (which is, however, not referred to explicitly) and as something that should be protected from the influence of the latter. Along with the economic, political, and military spheres, spirituality is highlighted in this document as an area in which Russia should develop its potential to "expand its role in the polycentric world in the making."[31]

In November 2022, a presidential decree on the "Fundamentals of State Policy to Preserve and Strengthen Traditional Russian Spiritual and Moral Values" codified for the first time seventeen such traditional values: life; dignity; human rights and freedoms; patriotism; civic consciousness; service to the fatherland and responsibility for its fate; high moral ideals; a strong family; creativity; the priority of the spiritual over the material; humanism; mercy; justice; collectivism; mutual assistance and mutual respect; historical memory and intergenerational continuity; and unity of the peoples of Russia.[32] As we can see, these values cover a large spectrum of human sentiments that are hardly unique to Russia, combined with some notions more clearly oriented toward the status quo, such as national unity, respect for elders, and duty toward the state.[33]

Not all these seventeen values are equally celebrated. In tune with the general "culture wars" atmosphere also present in the West, the regime has emphasized family, gender, and sexuality issues as a flagship for the defense of so-called traditional values. Note that the debate on homosexuality and the need for pronatalist policies has taken place against the backdrop of Russia's demographic decline, especially its low life expectancy for men, which Putin has been presenting as a danger to the country's very survival since 2000.[34] Here, I side with Novitskaya et al. on the necessity to fine-tune our analysis and dissociate the state's language on women's rights from that on LGBTQ+ rights.[35] On the latter, the state's language has been radically conservative, in line with the Soviet legacy of pathologizing and criminalizing homosexuality and gender nonconformity. Homophobia has been weaponized by the Kremlin since 2012–13, becoming instrumental in Russia's competition with Europe, decried as *gayropa*.[36] This reached new levels in 2023 with the Russian Supreme Court's decision to ban the alleged "LGBT international movement" for extremism.[37] The fact that this supposed movement is *international* is almost as important, if not more, than its pro-LGBTQ+ policies per se, feeding the regime's belief in conspiracies connected to foreign involvement in morality issues.

On women's rights and gender equality issues, meanwhile, the Russian regime advocated a more moderate conservatism, in line with Soviet views, which were progressive (except during the Stalinist years) yet stereotypical on gender roles.[38] However, since the full-scale invasion of Ukraine, the highest-level officials have adopted a more radically conservative tone: motivated by the idea that in wartime women should prioritize reproduction, the government is pushing more openly for multi-child families and an antiabortion policy.[39] If the latter were to be enacted and abortion banned, it would be the biggest state intrusion into private life in post-Soviet Russia's history.

This cult of traditional values should be read as a retrotopia—the projection of a future modeled on something from the past. Russian society is indeed more conservative than those in Western Europe (although no more than some Central European societies or segments of the American public) in terms of declared values on heterosexuality, abortion, divorce, and transgenerational links; however, it is less conservative in its practices, as well as in its high rates of single-parent families, drug and alcohol consumption, and suicide, not to mention the world's highest age-adjusted mortality rate due to external causes (i.e., those not related to disease).[40] The traditional-values agenda should thus also be read as the regime taking credit for the social improvements over the past two decades in terms of the decrease in male mortality, as well as in the rates of suicide, divorce, abortion, alcoholism, etc., and searching desperately for "demographic normalcy."

The traditional-values agenda has also a crucial dimension of "othering" the West and creating a civilizational border with liberal Europe. As Boris Mezhuev has accurately pointed out: "We desperately need to emphasize our difference from this [Euro-Atlantic] civilization by pointing to the hard ideological line that runs between communities that have agreed to remove traditional taboos and those that refuse to remove those taboos, including by virtue of their allegiance to religious norms."[41] Putin's meeting with Pope Francis in November 2013 was then celebrated by conservative figures such as Natalia Narochnitskaya, whose statement thereafter accurately reflects the official perception of a Western assault on Christian values:

> The current situation shows that in Europe, our common Christian civilization, there is an avalanche of such tendencies as de-Christianization, change of guiding principles, the confusion of sin and virtue, beauty and ugliness, truth and lies. . . . The times set new tasks before Catholics and Orthodox people: to unite in order to preserve the great Christian legacy and its values and morals, primarily those such as faith, motherland, honor, duty, and love. All the values that were born through the Christian idea and were incorporated into the life and history of European nations are under great pressure nowadays.[42]

The latest development in the traditional-values agenda has been Putin's appropriation of the West's—and especially the American Right's—language about "cancel culture." Take his remarks at the 2021 Valdai summit, where he shared a very resolute interpretation of societal changes happening in the West:

> Countering acts of racism is a necessary and noble cause, but the new "cancel culture" has turned it into "reverse discrimination," that is, reverse racism. The obsessive emphasis on race is further dividing people, when the real fighters for civil rights dreamed precisely about erasing differences and refusing to divide people by skin color. . . . In a number of Western countries, the debate over men's and women's rights has turned into a perfect phantas-

magoria. . . . Zealots of these new approaches even go so far as to want to abolish these concepts altogether. Anyone who dares mention that men and women actually exist, which is a biological fact, risks being ostracized. . . . Not to mention some truly monstrous things when children are taught from an early age that a boy can easily become a girl and vice versa. That is, the teachers actually impose on them a choice we all supposedly have. They do so while shutting the parents out of the process and forcing the child to make decisions that can upend their entire life.[43]

THE RUSSIAN ORTHODOX CHURCH AND MUSLIM INSTITUTIONS' CONTRIBUTIONS TO CONSERVATISM

The state is not the only producer of an official brand of conservatism: both the ROC and, to a lesser extent, the muftiates have been working to frame a conservatism that combines state-sponsored language and religious overtones. Religion matters in state-sponsored conservatism not as a transcendent question but as a set of habits and values that confirm the collective identity of citizens. In his 2012 article on the national question, Putin already appealed to religious communities, calling for "active involvement of Russia's traditional religions in the dialogue [about the formation of national policies]. The foundations of the Christian Orthodox Church, Islam, Buddhism, Judaism—with all their differences and peculiarities—include basic shared moral, ethical, and spiritual values: compassion, reciprocity, truth, justice, respect for elders, family and labor values."[44]

While the Russian state has been undergoing a postliberal counterrevolution, the church has seen a counterreformation of its own, taking action against the liberalization of both the clergy and the laity. Over the years, the ROC has become increasingly vocal about its desire to be recognized as a key partner in any state-society interaction and to actively reform the laity.[45] This alliance should not hide points of divergence between the regime and the church: the regime needs institutions that come with strong symbolic power to secure the political status quo, while the patriarchate aims to re-Christianize Russians and bring them back under the tutelage of the church. Still, they do share many concrete objectives, even if the church's submission to the state causes some tensions among the clergy, which does not necessarily favor submission to temporal power. The most successful area of cooperation has likely been the foreign policy realm, where the patriarchate has become the right hand of the Kremlin.[46]

On the domestic scene, the results of this alliance have been more nuanced. The church has become what Kristina Stoeckl calls a central "norm entrepreneur," playing an active role in the military, education, healthcare, family legislation, culture, and state ideology,[47] as well as taking the lead on restricting access to abortion.[48] It has developed its own list of so-called traditional values, published in 2011 as "The Basic Values—Fundamentals of National Identity" by the Moscow Patriarchate's Synodal Department of Church-Society Relations, including faith, justice, peace, freedom, unity, morality, dignity, honesty, patriotism, solidarity, mercy, family, culture and national tradition, prosperity, diligence, self-control, and devotion.

Despite such activism, the church has not won citizens back to its parishes: if a large majority of ethnic Russians identify with Orthodoxy, this is confined to a sense of cultural belonging. The level of Orthodox religious belief has long been stable at around 40 percent, while the share of those who regularly attend religious services is as low as in Western Europe.[49] Nor has the church met with a particularly warm reception in educational institutions. School classes on the "Basics of Orthodox Culture" as one of the options offered under the broad umbrella of "Fundamentals of Religious Cultures and Secular Ethics" did not live up to the church's expectations. Since its introduction in 2010, only about one third of parents have selected the class on Orthodoxy for their children—a disappointing number for the patriarchate, more of them preferring to select Secular Ethics or the Introduction to World Religions classes as alternatives (the Islamic option is selected by less than 5 percent of the population, i.e., less than the share of Russian citizens who come from a Muslim background).[50] This course has been demoted in fall 2024 to reintegrate history classes.

The church has been more successful at the legislative level. Protected by the monarchist media mogul Konstantin Malofeev, a conservative moralist cluster has worked closely with two major state institutions to reshape Russia's family policy: the Duma's Committee on Family, Women, and Children; and the Russian Commissioner for Children's Rights, or Children's Ombudsman, both of which act as go-betweens for the ROC and policymakers.[51] The Duma's Committee was long personified by Yelena Mizulina, its chair from 2011 to 2015, now a senator. Mizulina took the lead in advancing the most conservative law and bills (many of which did not pass the Duma) related to homosexuality, so-called "pedophile lobbies," abortion, domestic violence, juvenile justice, etc. Her daughter, Ekaterina, has followed in her footsteps and is fond of attacking social media for promoting "perverted ideologies." She has been a vocal advocate of banning social media not registered in Russia, as well as Wikipedia, and taxing social media for "deconstructive content."

Another key figure on the Duma Committee on Family, Women, and Children is deputy chairman Vitaly Milonov, who is known for attacking foreign pop culture icons for promoting "perverted" values. In 2012, he criticized concerts held by Madonna and Lady Gaga in Russia, who supported Pussy Riot and the gay community. Milonov organized small protests in St. Petersburg, but none of his claims against the two singers were upheld by the courts. That same year, he sued the German band Rammstein for violating Russia's law forbidding homosexual propaganda targeting minors.[52] In 2019, following a concert in Moscow's Luzhniki Stadium during which the band expressed support for the Russian LGBTQ+ community, Milonov declared: "They considered it possible to behave in this way, [and] we should consider it possible to shield ourselves from this rubbish. If they want to kiss, they can kiss in Ukraine. In Ukraine, they are ready to lick them from head to toe just because they came from Europe."[53] He then tried to get the band's frontman, Till Lindemann (who was accused of sexual abuse in Europe), banned from performing in Moscow in 2021.

Milonov has also attempted on several occasions, although without success, to launch a "vice squad." In the spring of 2014, he suggested organizing a "vice police force" to deal with so-called dysfunctional families and address juvenile delinquency, prostitution, and homosexual relations between minors, as well as what Russian legislation terms "totalitarian sects."[54] Just in time for the start of the 2018 FIFA World Cup, hosted by Russia, Milonov again raised the issue, suggesting that Cossacks should be involved in this initiative: "Volunteer squads are a good idea. I think the Cossacks will help us with this . . . Here you have both a voluntary organization and believers."[55] He floated the idea again in 2020, this time also advocating an identifying stamp in the passports of male prostitutes. In November 2022, he introduced a bill (which has since become law) forbidding gender change, as well as any propaganda in favor of gender reassignment.[56]

Controlled by the same conservative Orthodox moralists, the powerful position of children's ombudsman initiates legal and administrative proceedings in the sphere of child protection. Three figures with a strong reactionary pedigree—Pavel Astakhov (2009–16), Anna Kuznetsova (2016–20), and Maria Lvova-Belova (2020–present)—have held the position in recent years.

Astakhov has denounced what he calls "pedophile lobbies," calling for control over the internet and criticizing the international adoption of Russian orphans. Kuznetsova's and Lvova-Belova's trajectories are emblematic of the presidential party's co-optation of conservative actors firmly embedded in their local milieu, and of women's representation on family-related policies. Kuznetsova is a mother of seven, while Lvova-Belova has five biological and four adopted children, besides being the legal guardian of thirteen disabled children. Their husbands are both Orthodox priests. In 2008, the two women cofounded their first charity association, Blagovest (dissolved in 2020), in Penza Region before climbing the political ladder.

As children's ombudsman, Kuznetsova created a register of sexual predators and pedophiles and instituted several controversial policies related to foster care legislation. Lvova-Belova is often presented as "Kuznetsova II." After working with Kuznetsova at Blagovest, she founded several charity organizations in support of people with disabilities and the elderly, including the first boardinghouse in Russia for young people with disabilities. Since 2021, she has served simultaneously as children's ombudsman, a member of the Federal Council Committee on Social Policy, and senator for Penza Region.[57] Many patriotic and family-oriented initiatives have originated with Kuznetsova, including the new school subject of "Family Knowledge" (*sem'evedenie*), which became part of the official school curriculum in 2021 (one hour a week for nine years).[58] For her part, Lvova-Belova has, since Russia's full-scale invasion of Ukraine, vocally promoted the "adoption" of Ukrainian children from occupied territories by Russian families (she has adopted one such child herself).[59] The International Criminal Court (2023) in The Hague has issued a warrant for her arrest for the war crime of unlawful transfer of children.[60]

The Kremlin's conservative turn has also been supported by Russia's Muslims, who have applauded, and sometimes even anticipated, the regime's gradual officialization of conservatism, given their own Islamic or even Sharia-based mores and values.[61] Russia's muftiates were, for instance, vocal during the discussions around the 2020 constitutional amendments so that heterosexual marriage would be enshrined in the Constitution. The leader of Tatarstan's Spiritual Administration of Muslims, Kamil Samigullin, declared that the Russian Constitution should strengthen "traditional moral values," the central one being that a family can only be constituted "by the union of a man and a woman."[62] The Bashkortostan branch launched "courses on preparation for family life," delivered at the mosque for young people ready for marriage.[63] In the North Caucasus in particular, customary law (*adat*), as well as, in some cases, Sharia law, is increasingly accepted as an integral part of an informal legal system, alternative to the official courts, while not reporting religious marriage (*nikah*) to state authorities has become a widespread practice, as a way to bypass Russian legislation's nonrecognition of polygamy.[64]

Each time the ROC has advocated a more religiously attuned conservatism against secular or liberal segments of society, it has been able to count on the support of the muftiates, a willing partner in these new culture wars. In 2017, for instance, Muslim institutions joined Orthodox radicals in decrying the film *Matilda*, which depicted the (well-documented) love story between the young Nicholas II, still only a tsarevitch (crown prince) at the time, and ballerina Mathilde Kschessinska. The muftiates took their blasphemy accusation against the film very seriously and were more repressive than many nonethnic regions: Tatarstan banned the film from public theaters (though not from private ones),[65] while local authorities in Chechnya and Dagestan, with the support of Moscow's main mufti, Albir Krganov, asked for the film to be banned in their regions and called for a replacement film that would show the last tsar in a better light.[66]

As always, Chechnya stands out for its radical interpretation of state ideological directives and often precedes and exceeds them. The regime in Grozny promotes a form of so-called traditional Islam inspired by Chechen folklore and Sufi tradition, which is much more conservative in its interpretation of religious norms. Mixing *adat* and Sharia, Chechnya has, for instance, introduced a second, "spiritual" passport in which clan ties (*toukhoum* and *teip*) and religious brotherhood (*vird*) are codified—which is illegal in the rest of the Russian Federation.[67] This conservatism is not Salafi, in the sense that it does not confine itself only to the Quran and Hadiths of the Prophet Muhammad, though it claims to take its cues from Sharia law on issues of manners and mores: alcohol consumption is prohibited, gambling is officially banned, and the broadcasting of Western music is controlled. As part of a so-called "moralization program," it is now almost obligatory for women to wear the veil in public places. Chechnya leader Ramzan Kadyrov himself has stated that women are inferior to men, called for honor killings or reprisals to be made legal, and spoken out in favor of polygamy.[68]

INTELLECTUAL CONTRIBUTIONS TO RUSSIAN CONSERVATISM

Russia's official brand of conservatism should not be thought of only as an opportunistic product built by the regime to sustain itself. As we have seen, it relies on a deep-rooted political and intellectual tradition that has been reappropriated and rethought by new generations of thinkers. Two major contributions to conservative thought—leaving aside reactionary thought, which is discussed in the next chapter—can be identified as having grown with the more or less explicit support of state entities.

The only substantial state-sponsored theoretical contribution to the political-philosophical realm has been the quarterly *Essays on Conservatism* (*Tetradi po konservatizmu*), published since 2014 by one of the Kremlin's main think tanks, the Institute for Socio-Economic and Political Studies (ISEPI), led by Dmitry Badovsky.[69] The journal defines conservatism as "not only a political philosophy, but also an ideology [that] is not unique [to any one country] but global and expresses national specificities. . . . Russian conservatism is a reasonable combination of tradition and innovation, with a forward- rather than backward-looking orientation toward the experience of past eras."[70]

With more than nine hundred articles published between 2014 and 2023, *Essays on Conservatism* has brought together a large group of Russian academics and experts to feed the discussion and dialogue with European and Global South iterations of conservatism. Among the most prolific contributors to the journal one can find the main voices of Russian conservatism today: three key figures from philosophy at Moscow State University (Vasily Vanchugov, Mikhail Maslin, and Sergey Perevezentsev) and another trio formerly known as the Young Conservatives (Boris Mezhuev, Mikhail Remizov, and Yegor Kholmogorov; see below).

In its quarterly releases, *Essays on Conservatism* offers excursions into European and American neoconservatism, but they mostly explore classic Russian conservatism, with central figures such as nineteenth-century thinkers Mikhail N. Katkov (1818–1887), the first to express the idea that a civilized state can only be a national state; Konstantin Leontyev, whose theories of Russia as a fundamentally conservative great power were inspired by the Byzantine model; turn-of-the-century philosophers Nikolay Berdyaev and iconic Silver Age philosopher (not to be confused with the TV anchor) Vladimir Soloviev, published for their religious philosophy and sense of Russia's uniqueness; and émigré reactionary thinkers Ivan Ilyin and Ivan Solonevich, recognized for their virulent anticommunism and belief in Russia's Orthodox and imperial destiny. More contemporary thinkers include Alexander Solzhenitsyn and, prominently, Vadim Tsymbursky (see chapter 9).

Orbiting more distantly around the Kremlin, another school has been producing what is probably Russia's main contribution to today's conservatism: the Young Conservatives (*mladokonservativy*).[71] It brought together thinkers (all born in the 1970s) who found themselves disappointed with the backward-looking patriotic ideologies dominant in the 1990s, whether Soviet nostalgia (as represented by Alexander Prokhanov and the newspaper *Zavtra*) or esoteric imperialism (as represented by Alexander Dugin, whose worldview they denounce as a fantasy that is as eccentric in its imperial imagination as it is occult in its intellectual references). They wanted to promote a more pragmatic, "healthy" conservatism, closer to the European one (for instance, to Germany's Christian Democrats), which can come up with concrete, actionable projects for the new Russia. Paul Robinson describes members of this school as "conservative democrats," distinguishing them from "radical conservatives" like Dugin.[72]

For almost two decades now, key intellectual figures such as Mikhail Remizov and Boris Mezhuev (and around them Yegor Kholmogorov and Konstantin Krylov, as well as a group of lesser-known thinkers) have been developing ideological products contributing to a rebranding of Russia as a conservative power defending Christian and European traditional values. The movement emerged at the end of the 1990s, associated with the website "Russian Doctrine," one of the first uses of a digital platform for a conservative project on the Russian internet. At that time, the movement was competing not only with Dugin's neo-Eurasianist theories but also with the rise of neo-paganism within nationalist circles, and therefore made Orthodoxy one of the cornerstones of its understanding of national identity.

Once conservatism went mainstream in the mid-2000s, the Young Conservatives saw significant expansion (and several schisms) and began working closely with Gleb Pavlovsky and his Foundation for Effective Politics (FEP), Stanislav Belkovsky's Institute for National Strategy, and the Analytical News Portal (APN.ru). Thanks to the quality of their analysis, Remizov and Mezhuev rapidly made APN.ru the go-to Young Conservative platform. In this era of intellectual flourishing, they created their own discussion club, the Conservative Assembly, which elaborated a doctrine for the movement: *The Counter-Reformation: Report of the Conservative Assembly*, released in 2005.[73]

An alternative constitution, to replace that of 1993, was also published: it proclaimed the legal and historical continuity of the Russian state, from the medieval Kievan Rus' to the Soviet Union and contemporary Russia, with official status granted to the Russian Orthodox Church.

Collaborating with several Orthodox circles, especially Vitaly Averyanov's Center for Dynamic Conservatism, the Young Conservatives' discussion club jointly released *Serge's Project*.[74] The reference to Sergius of Radonezh (1314–1392), one of Russia's most popular saints, confirms the distinctly Orthodox tone of the document, which received significant support from the Moscow Patriarchate. The text was presented as the successor to the famous *Vekhi* of 1909, but it equally merits comparison with the neoconservative foreign-policy think tank Project for a New American Century. Another manifesto, *Imperatives of National Renaissance: Manifesto of Russian Conservatives*, was published in 2006 with a slightly different group of Young Conservative signatories.[75]

Pavlovsky subsequently invited Remizov to become the editor of the *Russian Journal*, a forum that catapulted Remizov and his team to the forefront of Russia's ideology-crafting. In the mid-2000s to mid-2010s, core Young Conservatives worked closely with the Presidential Administration, though they were to be disappointed. Some other members of the movement moved toward a more oppositional position: Konstantin Krylov (1967–2020) promoted a more ethnic form of nationalism and became one of the key intellectual figures in the *Natsdem* (national-democrat) movement, of which late dissident leader Alexei Navalny was also a part.[76] Yegor Kholmogorov moved toward the most reactionary groups (see chapter 9).

Both Remizov and Mezhuev replicated eighteenth-century British conservative philosopher Edmund Burke's emphasis on the particular over the universal, denying the legitimacy of political positions based on abstract knowledge devoid of real-world context. Although their positions can be compared in many respects to the neoconservatism that emerged in the 1980s in the US and the UK, they denounced neoliberalism as a philosophy of extreme individualism and globalization. Economically, Russian conservatives are predominantly leftist—Remizov even speaks of a "leftist conservatism."[77] This leftist strain has been theorized and partly implemented by Sergey Glazyev, former presidential advisor on regional economic integration and one of the architects of the Eurasian Economic Union, who has published several articles calling for Russia to move away from a liberal economy and back toward a more socialist one.[78] The Young Conservatives thus updated the Soviet tradition of seeing capitalism as a major source of social ills, while advocating for Keynesian policies like moderate protectionism, state-led industrial and innovation policy, a large role for the government in providing public services, and the renationalization of some sectors that were illegally privatized in the 1990s.[79]

Unlike the Prokhanov-Dugin movement, which defends an expansionist policy, the Young Conservatives were generally isolationist.[80] As a genuine follower of Tsymbursky (see chapter 9), Mezhuev has been calling for an isolationist strategy since as early as 2001.[81] With the 2022 Russia-Ukraine War, he found new arguments in favor of what he calls Russia's "civilizational indifference," in particular toward Europe, as the best strategy for the country.[82] Remizov, too, has criticized any form of messianism: "One can say this country gave the best years of its life to mankind . . . and not to itself. This must never happen again."[83] He therefore calls for Russia to opt out of Western globalization: "One cannot be victorious over globalization; one can only exit it."[84] Isolationism is considered the best way to avoid conflict with the West, especially over Europe: if Russia retreats from competition, it can hope to live more peacefully in a semi-dissident position vis-à-vis the world order. In the eyes of the Young Conservatives, Russia can no longer afford to dream of being an alternative superpower: "We simply do not have the resources to legitimize an imperial/supranational power . . . We have no need to either dispute or lighten the US hegemonic burden, turning [America] into a sparring partner in the global ring."[85] The solution for Russia is thus, more modestly, to project itself as "a rebel province of the global empire."[86]

Also contrary to the Prokhanov group, which openly expresses nostalgia for the Soviet Union, the Young Conservatives do not look backward to the Soviet Union as a model. In the Russian context, being conservative means championing a "conservative evolutionism" and distrusting the tradition of borrowing models from abroad. Given this memory of failed liberalism in the 1990s, conservatism is interpreted as forward-looking. The only possible way for Russia to enjoy a "restoration of the future" (*restavratsiia budushchego*), to keep its future options open and avoid being trapped in the past by the US-led liberal international order, is to become a conservative stronghold.[87]

For Kholmogorov, the pairing of conservatism with liberalism should not be read as one of status quo and reaction, on the one hand, and progressivism, on the other; instead, it should be understood as a choice between rootedness and universalism. Conservatism supposes that individuals enjoy some continuity with past generations and are anchored in their homelands (what Kholmogorov presents as a "call to belonging": *appelatsiia k prinadlezhnosti*), while liberalism advocates an abstract universalism. *The Manifesto of Russian Conservatives* defines conservatism as:

> Faith in oneself, in one's historical and spiritual path, and the ability not to submit to foreign influences while remaining open. . . . Conservatism is always national: national conservatism is above all the love of one's historical identity and the recognition of the creative force of one's people.[88]

The belief that conservatism is the only possible path for a forward-looking Russia is articulated in one of the Young Conservatives' most interesting doctrinal contributions: their interpretation of the relationship between conservatism and liberalism. They proclaim, contrary to conventional wisdom, that although liberal ideologies may be progressive in some respects domestically, they are oriented toward the status quo, since their proponents currently dominate the world and therefore wish to stay in power and not be challenged. Conservatism, by contrast, finds itself on the side of resistance, rebellion, or even revolution, owing to its desire for change. Within the current world order, this places conservatism on the side of change and liberalism on that of resistance to change. The same reversal of the standard interpretation is made with regard to democracy/authoritarianism. For the Young Conservatives, deeply shaped by the traumatic decade of the 1990s, liberalism was imposed on Russia in an authoritarian manner, while the Putin regime, with its significant popular support, should be seen as genuinely democratic, even if how it exercises power is not.

Remizov brings another noteworthy point to the discussion: in today's conditions, conservatism means defending classical modernity against postmodernity. Classical modernity was born from the fruitful combination of the Enlightenment and its opponent, political Romanticism, which made "conservatism the coauthor of the *moderne* of the contemporary epoch."[89] The West has since moved from modernity to postmodernity with the trend toward moral liberalization beginning in the 1960s and 1970s, while conservatism has continued defending the original meaning of modernization, as it had been classically understood. Remizov elaborates:

> If earlier conservatism defended the institution of the decaying agrarian society, dynastic monarchy, clericalism, and so on, then conservatism today de-

fends the collapsing institutions of the *moderne* that are connected with the national state of classical rationality and with what one might call classical European values against postmodern and contemporary European values.[90]

This reading also makes it possible to reconcile nationalism with conservatism. In the nineteenth century, the concept of the nation-state was viewed as a fellow traveler of emancipation from rule by forces external to the national ethnic group, whereas today liberalism sees the nation-state as an obstacle to cosmopolitanism and globalization. In other words, liberalism had associated itself symbiotically with nationalism for a certain period before moving on and rejecting nationalism as its quintessential opposition. Here, too, conservatism remains loyal to the original sense of modernization, calling for the rehabilitation of the idea that nationalism, as a sense of rootedness, goes hand in hand with emancipation—this time from a globalizing homogenization of the world. Still, it remains unclear from the Young Conservatives' blend of Enlightenment and Romanticism whether they do believe in natural rights that are not dependent on local laws and customs.

Even if the Young Conservative school does not exist anymore as such, Remizov and Mezhuev remain leading public intellectual figures on Russian conservatism. More integrated into official structures, Remizov has been president of the Institute for National Strategy, a think tank close to the Presidential Administration that promotes a foreign policy of sovereignty and technological autonomy for Russia.[91] Further away, Mezhuev was for a few years deputy editor-in-chief of the newspaper *Izvestia* and a prolific commentator on Russian political life; he is at the time of this writing editor-in-chief of the website Russkaya Pravda (The Russian Truth).

The ideological backbone of the Putin regime, conservatism has succeeded in blending the situational conservatism of Russian society after the dramatic transformations of the 1990s and the ruling elite's quest for regime status quo. It has gradually evolved from being a form of centrism against what was seen as the two extremes of Communist reaction and liberal imitation to embody the state ideology shaped by a language of morality, traditional values, and political loyalty.

That state ideology can be broadly defined as *national conservatism*, here referring to a set of fluid philosophical parameters that: (1) insist on the need for a society to respect traditional values, institutions, and practices, and not alter them too rapidly (the conservative part); (2) hold that human experiences are not universal but rather shaped by national cultural contexts (the national part); and (3) expect the state not only to protect the social order but also to coherently formulate it (the *-ism* part). This national conservatism therefore conflates the national and the cultural with the conservative, as it places itself in dichotomous opposition to elements that are interpreted as foreign *and* progressive or liberal. In the Russian case, national is synonymous not with ethnic nationalism but with state patriotism: it is the state that embodies the nation and makes decisions in its name.

NINE

KATECHON
Reaction and Eschatology

The traditional faith of the Russian Federation and the nuclear shield are the components that strengthen the Russian State and create the necessary conditions for internal and external security of the country.
VLADIMIR PUTIN, press conference, 2007[1]

WHILE CONSERVATISM CALLS FOR making changes that are slow and organic, there exist more reactionary interpretations of Russia's counterrevolution. Unlike mainstream conservatives, hardline reactionaries call for going back in time, erasing changes, and recreating a mythologized past—in the Russian case, this can be about pre-Christian, pagan times, Ivan the Terrible's era, nineteenth-century tsarism, or Stalinism. If conservatism is about respect for the status quo, hardline reaction aims to take the country back, if necessary through revolutionary means.

Because it is anchored in Orthodox theology, the Russian reactionary tradition should be read through its religious undertones: those of millenarianism and eschatology.[2] Belief in the imminence of Judgment Day and expectations about the end of the present age of human history are often expressed through apocalypticism—i.e., the idea that the end of the world is near and that this will allow for the reunion of ordinary reality with the divine.[3] The Biblical notion of the *katechon* ("the withholder" in Ancient Greek), comes from the Second Epistle of Paul to the Thessalonians, which describes a force that delays the coming of the Antichrist and protects the world from the kingdom of the Beast (cf. II Thessalonians 2:3–10). Early Church Father and Archbishop of Constantinople John Chrysostom interpreted Paul's words as referring to the emperor, who personified the amalgamation (or symphony) between temporal and spiritual powers. He saw in the Second Roman Empire, the Byzantine one, the antithesis of Anomia that should restrain the chaos preceding the Second Coming.

This more political reading of the katechon passed to Muscovy through the myth of Moscow as the Third Rome. Crafted by the monk Philotheus from the Belozersky Monastery in 1523–24, the Third Rome was officially recorded in the 1589 Founding Deed of the Moscow Patriarchate.[4] In the Tsardom of Muscovy, the notion became even more political: as Maria Engström explains, "Already during Ivan the Terrible's reign it was specified that the two enemies of Moscow as the Katechon are the external Antichrist, that is, all lands beyond Muscovy, and the internal Antichrist, which is no less dangerous than the external one."[5] One may also mention the Old Believers' tradition, in which Russia is the home of the true faith and the West that of Satan.[6]

In the eighteenth and nineteenth centuries the concept entered the more secular foreign policy realm surrounding the idea of Russia's role as protector of Eastern Christians from persecution by the Ottoman Empire. It then informed apocalyptic interpretations of the October Revolution as bringing the world closer to the Judgment Day. Some also read the Soviet regime's messianism and self-proclaimed role of defending the proletariat around the world as a secularist, Marxist take on the former Orthodox Third Rome.[7] The concept reentered Russian political language in 1997 with Alexander Dugin's article "Katechon and Revolution," in which he proposed a Schmittian reading of the former. Indeed in his *Nomos of the Earth*, German philosopher Carl Schmitt (1888–1985) described the securitizing work of the sovereign against the eschaton, the agent that ends time or the temporal order.[8] A former student of Dugin's, Arkady Mahler, created the almanac *Northern Katechon* in 2005 and the intellectual club Katechon in 2007, while the topic of "keeper" (*khranitel'*) rose in visibility in the Russian media landscape.[9]

In her seminal work on today's reinvention of this tradition, Maria Engström translates katechon as the "gatekeeper of chaos":

> Russia sees itself not so much as an empire that holds the power of chaos beyond the borders of the world by its inner order, but rather as a military force that resists a metaphysical enemy, sent by the Antichrist. This metaphysical enemy takes different shapes in different historical periods: the

Tatars, the Turks, freemasons, Napoleon, Hitler, and nowadays American agents, Ukrainian fascists, and the Kiev junta.[10]

In this reading, Russia is the shield, restoring order in the face of an Antichrist embodied by a West that is destroying itself and others. But because restraint can feel threatened, the securitized nature of the katechon can also be linked with expansion, aggression, *Reconquista*. The katechon can therefore be isolationist or expansionist, calling for restraint or for restoration.

THE LOVE AFFAIR BETWEEN THE CHURCH AND THE ARMY

The most explicit katechonic project is called Nuclear or Atomic Orthodoxy (*atomnoe pravoslavie*). This is both the title of a book by Israeli scholar Dmitry Adamsky describing the symbiosis between the church and Russian nuclear power, as well as an intellectual trend promoted by the Izborsky Club (described below). The central idea is that for Russia to succeed against the West, it needs to take the best of tsarism and the Soviet Union, combining Orthodoxy as a spiritual shield and nuclear weapons as a material shield—as expressed in Putin's quote at the beginning of this chapter.

Explored in Adamsky's seminal work, the fusion between the ROC and the Russian Army has its roots in the 1990s. Both had to find a way to rise from the Soviet ashes: the army was demoralized and in search of a new meaning and mission, while the church was looking for a new anchor in society to avoid being erased by an antireligious regime again. Whereas the Soviet Army had long been a stronghold of atheism, in the post-Soviet era a marriage of convenience rapidly emerged before blossoming into a kind of honeymoon. Gradually, the ROC positioned itself "as one of the main guardians of the state's nuclear potential and, as such, claim[ed] the role of one of the main guarantors of Russian nuclear security."[11] The fact that the Soviet A-bomb was developed (on Stalin's orders) on the territory of the Sarov Monastery some three hundred miles east of Moscow was interpreted as a "divine predestination of the Soviet nuclear project," meaning the ROC and the army could rely on each other.[12] The church formalized cooperation with the ministries of defense and internal affairs, as well as the Federal Border Service in the mid-1990s. Patriarch Alexy II explained:

> Orthodox pastors must understand more than anyone else that the army cannot be spiritless. Service to the Fatherland and selfless performance of

military duty presuppose the presence of high moral qualities. And faith is the main source from which a warrior draws moral rules and spiritual health. The need for pastoral care for military personnel is increasingly understood by military leadership.[13]

But it was after 2008, with the enthronement of Kirill as Alexy's successor and the beginning of the Medvedev presidency, that the relationship between church and military became more symbiotic.[14] The ROC recreated the institute of the military priesthood and has since gradually permeated the whole military realm, and especially the nuclear forces. Religious symbols saturate the military space: garrison churches, pastoral care for servicemen, catechization as an integral part of military education, consecration of new materials, processions of the cross, patron saints for each leg of the nuclear triad, etc. The church's priests have sprinkled holy water on the S-400 missile system in Crimea[15] and the MS-11 Soyuz spaceship at the Baikonur Cosmodrome in Kazakhstan,[16] accompanied a polar expedition to the Russian Antarctic Station, and headed an Orthodox procession together with the traffic police in Krasnodar.[17]

The church also works closely with the security services, which have infiltrated it since Soviet times. Metropolitan Tikhon of Simferopol and Crimea for years headed the Sretensky Monastery.[18] Close to the Lubyanka (the headquarters of the KGB and its successor, the FSB), the monastery is seen as the place where many high-ranking FSB officers go to confess, while it also hosts one of Russia's largest publishing houses, producing liturgical texts, along with secular books relating to religious culture. The monastery also manages the site Pravoslavie.ru, the church's most popular internet portal, with several million visitors per month.[19]

The church-army symbiosis was embodied in the Main Cathedral of the Armed Forces of the Russian Federation (the third-largest cathedral in Russia), erected in Patriot Park in the Moscow suburbs and inaugurated in 2020. This edifice sanctifies the relationship between faith and the military. On the ceilings, Soviet war medals are represented in stained glass, while Nazi weapons and tanks taken as trophies by the Soviet Army were melted down for the cathedral's floors. Huge mosaics depict Russia's historical battles, many of these from the Second World War, but also including more recent ones such as the 2008 Russo-Georgian war, the 2014 "return of Crimea," and counterterrorist operations in the Syrian civil war, as well as the faces of prominent military figures from the tsarist period.[20] Some leaks revealed plans to create a mosaic with Stalin, Putin, and Defense Minister Shoigu, though once the information was out, the ROC, which first attributed it to the Orthodox tradition of representing historical figures, got cold feet, apparently under pressure from the Kremlin, and withdrew the idea.

NUCLEAR ORTHODOXY

Intellectually, nuclear Orthodoxy was conceptualized by Yegor Kholmogorov in 2007, but the term itself was coined by Alexey Beliayev-Guintovt, a leading contemporary Russian painter who received the Kandinsky Prize and whose work is admittedly inspired by fascist and radical nationalist themes. *Nuclear Orthodoxy* was the title of one of his works, which depicts a deeply frozen Russia with the rudder of the missile submarine resembling a cross.[21] Kholmogorov, having gradually moved away from moderate conservative figures such as Remizov and Mezhuev, has now been closer to Prokhanov and Dugin and collaborates with Malofeev's Tsargrad TV channel. Advocating for what he calls a "pragmatic imperialism," Kholmogorov argues that Russia needs to be an empire, with an autocratic regime and Orthodox ideology, so that it can fulfill its katechonic mission. Consolidating Russia's military shield is therefore a matter of "sacral industrialization," since high spirituality and high technology go hand in hand. As he explains:

> It is especially important to strengthen the "conceptual shield": As long as the atomic clinch remains . . . the war is being conducted primarily by conceptual [*smyslovymi*] means. That is why, together with a traditional military defense, the Russian State has to protect the nation by conceptual means, to protect it from mental threats.[22]

Not one to shy away from bold language, Kholmogorov describes Russia as "the geopolitical embodiment of the divine" (*geopoliticheskoe ubozhenstvo*), and explains Russia's Third Rome identity in biblical terms: "Because 'there shall not be the fourth one', and if before us there was the Flood, after us there is only the Apocalypse."[23] Worshipping both the Romanov monarchy and the Stalin years, Kholmogorov has also been one of the first to explicitly theorize the idea that Russia always defends itself even when it seems like it is attacking.[24] Over the years, the theme has grown, first implicitly—for instance, pro-Kremlin analysts were nicknamed *okhraniteli* (guardians) as early as the mid-2000s—before becoming an explicit feature of state language.

This katechonic language around a cult of industrialization has been a typical feature of the Izborsky Club, the most vocal institution in the realm of eschatological thinking.[25] Launched in the fall of 2012 in the small town of Izborsk, near Pskov and the borders with Estonia and Latvia, the club has a political identity that is reflected in its name. The town was commemorating its 1,150-year anniversary—a date based on the legendary arrival of Rurik and his brothers in the area—which allowed the club to link itself to Russia's long history of statehood. The town is also situated on the western border of the Russian world, meaning it has resisted an array of invasions—Poland-Lithuania in the sixteenth century, Sweden in the seventeenth century, and Germany during the Second World War. These two facts encapsulate the club's ideological stance: Russia's historical continuity and its fundamental mission as a fortress against Western influences are two sides of the same coin.

The Izborsky Club was born out of the blending of two doctrinal traditions. The first, which Alexander Prokhanov promotes, can be called "Soviet imperialism"—a broad term that also includes, but is not limited to, Alexander Dugin. Nicknamed the "songbird of the Soviet General Staff" since the publication of his writings celebrating the Soviet invasion of Afghanistan in the early 1980s, Prokhanov has since become the patriarch of the so-called "red-brown" realm, blending the cult of Soviet industrial and technological greatness and Orthodoxy. He puts forward the notion of the Fifth Empire (after Kievan Rus, Mongol-dominated Muscovy, the Romanov-led Russian Empire, and the Soviet Union), according to which today's Russia will succeed at blending Orthodox spirituality and Soviet-inspired technological feats.[26]

The second tradition can be defined as political Orthodoxy, exemplified by the now defunct Center for Dynamic Conservatism. The center was led by Vitaly Averyanov, one of the best-known Orthodox publicists and editor-in-chief of Pravoslavie.ru, the most-read Orthodox website. He is also a member of the Writers' Union and several secular councils of the Russian Orthodox Church. Its "Russian Doctrine" manifesto explicitly refers to the concept of the katechon: "The defense of civilization from barbarism, its assimilation, this is the first function of the katechon . . . The katechon as an Orthodox kingdom defends Christians against forces hostile to the salvation of the soul."[27]

The Izborsky Club brings together about thirty major names from the Russian conservative and nationalist scene, among whom, besides the already-mentioned Kholmogorov, are Nataliya Narochnitskaya, Metropolitan Tikhon; Leonid Ivashov, a retired general, influential go-between for nationalist circles and the military, and longtime Dugin supporter; Mikhail Leontyev, the well-known anchor of the weekly news magazine on Channel One, *Odnako*, in the 2000s; Nikolay Starikov, commercial director of Channel One in St. Petersburg, cochair of the Great Fatherland Party, and a prolific publicist; and two famous economists, Sergey Glazyev and Mikhail Deliagin, who share relatively similar statist stances in favor of socialist-type dirigisme. The Izborsky Club serves as the ideological factory of the military-industrial complex and appears to function on a fairly generous budget, largely provided by the main defense firms and the Presidential Administration.[28]

The club argues that the two major catastrophes of twentieth-century Russia—the fall of tsarism in 1917 and the collapse of the Soviet Union in 1991—resulted from the authorities failing to uphold a state ideology and being unable to combine doctrinal fragments into a logical whole. Its mission is thus to reopen the "cultural front" and be "a laboratory where we will elaborate an ideology, an institute to engage in creating a forward-looking theory, a construction site to make an ideological weapon that we will send into combat without delay."[29] The club can therefore be compared with Pamyat, the cadres school of nationalism during the perestroika years—though it probably has engineered fewer new doctrinal products than its infamous predecessor.

One of the most striking features of the club's ideology is its emphasis on a new great mobilization project for Russia, and the name given to it—the "great leap forward" (*bol'shoi ryvok*), an unabashed reference to the policies of forced collectivization and rapid industrialization pursued by Maoist China between 1958 and 1960.[30] It also plays on more Russian references by calling for the creation of an *oprichnina*—Ivan the Terrible's first private militia, which inaugurated the tradition of the security services—to supervise a new mobilization project characterized by a "moral revolution" and the patriotic indoctrination of the elites, a terminology that leaves little doubt about the repressive character of the project.[31]

The Izborsky Club aims to develop a doctrine that would unify Soviet nostalgia and military prowess with Orthodox symbolism while also reconciling the Soviet and tsarist pasts. As Prokhanov has proclaimed, "It is necessary to create a state in which, as Putin has said, one can live as a Red commissar or as a White officer."[32] The effort to sanctify the Soviet Union so as to integrate it with the Orthodox tradition was illustrated in 2015, when the club commissioned a new icon called "The Great Power Virgin Mary"

(*Bogomater' derzhavnaia*), which showed Stalin as a holy figure. The icon was blessed in a small parish and exhibited on a tank for the annual May 9 Victory Day military parade in 2015, a gesture criticized by the patriarchate.[33]

Accompanying the new icon, Prokhanov's article on "Mystical Stalinism" offers a solemn ode to the Soviet leader, who was said to have snatched victory from defeat and, like a phoenix, will be reborn in popular memory as a *bogatyr'* (knight), a revered figure in Russian fairy tales.[34] This "mystical Stalinism" represents the core of Nuclear Orthodoxy, even if it has caused disapproval on the part of the Moscow Patriarchate, for whom Stalinist-era state crimes against religion forbid such easy reconciliation. But the more radical segment of the church supports such a blending, like Metropolitan Tikhon.

HOLY RUS': THE CHURCH'S CONTRIBUTION TO KATECHONIC DISCOURSES

Although the ROC mainstream disapproves of "mystical Stalinism," it has developed its own version of Russia's katechonic identity through the idea of "Holy Rus'" (*Sviataia Rus'*), and connected it to the myth of the Third Rome. This Holy Rus' has been reflected in the ROC's vast canonical territories, which extended beyond Russia's internationally recognized borders.[35]

The term Holy Rus' has its own genealogy, emerging in the late sixteenth century in missives from Prince Andrey Kurbsky opposing Ivan the Terrible and accusing him of bringing violence on "the Holy Rus' land," followed a few decades later by a tale about how Cossacks, besieged by Ottoman troops, looked to Holy Rus'. In its folkloric and literary expressions, the notion of Holy Rus' has no clear geographical boundaries and refers to the community of believers, with in fact more mentions of Palestine and Jerusalem than of Moscow.[36] In the nineteenth century, the concept gradually took on a more political connotation to express in romanticized language the difference between an expanding Russian Empire and a core national Russian territory that encompassed all those embracing the tenth-century baptism of Prince Vladimir/Volodymyr. For Slavophiles, Holy Rus' was mostly an inward-looking project of conservative utopia embodied by traditional peasant communities (in Russian, the word for "peasant" is etymologically connected to that for "Christian": *krestianin* and *khristianin*, respectively).[37]

In the 1990s, the term was rediscovered and promoted by nationalist and conservative forces with a strong katechonic aspect, such as in Gennadi Zyuganov's book *Holy Rus' and Koshchei's Kingdom*,[38] in which he suggests that Russia should resist Western pressures by going back to its religious and autocratic heritage. The church officialized the concept of Holy Rus' during Patriarch Kirill's 2009 enthronement speech, making it a standard ideological currency. Whereas his predecessor Alexy II held closer to the original meaning of the term—Holy Rus' as the metaphorical space of churches and monasteries, the spiritual and transcendental core of Russia—Kirill has decisively politicized and geopoliticized the concept so that it overlaps with the idea of a collective identity based on the Orthodox faith, Russian language, and shared historical memory. As Mikhail Suslov shows, in Kirill's thinking, Russia is a geopolitical entity with the highest relationship to the Deity but also a spiritual space that transcends official state boundaries.[39]

The notion of Holy Rus' thus implies both inward- and outward-looking movements: inward-looking in the sense of defining an ethnically bound identity for Russians and promoting the re-Christianization of Russian society after state atheism and against Western secularism, and outward-looking in the sense of advocating an imperial pan-Russian nation divided into several political entities. Oleksandr Zabirko explains the dual implicit meaning of the concept: the space of Holy Rus' "is understood as both a geographical and metaphysical entity."[40] As often, the muftiates have attempted to follow the church's lead, with the Ufa-based Central Spiritual Administration of Muslims making use of the concept too. In 2015, Chief Mufti Talgat Tadzhuddin, in polemics about the impact of propaganda from the Islamic State of Iraq and Syria (ISIS), went so far as to say that "Russia's Muslims already have a caliphate: Holy Rus',"[41] though the borrowing of this concept for an Islamic context was largely criticized by Russian Muslim communities.

Another semantic overlap of Holy Rus' can be found in the notion of the Russian World (see chapter 11). Both Holy Rus' and the Russian World imply a sacred land that encompasses Belarus, Ukraine, and Russia, born from the same Kievan Rus' cradle, sometimes including Moldova or even Kazakhstan.[42] As stated by Kirill, "Ukraine is not on the periphery of our church. We call Kiev 'the mother of all Russian cities.' For us Kiev is what Jerusalem is for many. Russian Orthodoxy began there, so under no circumstances can we abandon this historical and spiritual relationship."[43] On the Moscow Patriarchate website's archives, which go back to 2004, one can find more than 350 mentions of the "Russian World," including several key texts by Kirill, in particular speeches delivered during the annual World Russian People's Congress. The patriarch regularly stresses the need to conserve the Russian World (*sokhranit' russkii mir*) and reassemble the Russian World (*sobirat' russkii mir*), and since 2014 has also looked aggressively outward, denouncing "Ukrainian nationalism," along with "foreign forces," that want to impede the Russian World.

The concept of Holy Rus' thus justifies the narrative of Russians as a nation divided by contemporary borders and has been put forward by the patriarchate to support the full-scale invasion of Ukraine. In practice, the church's canonical hierarchy has been gradually challenged: first by the autocephaly of the Ukrainian Orthodox Church, granted by the Ecumenical Patriarchate in Constantinople in 2019—though disputed by the Moscow Patriarchate—and more recently by similar processes of severing ties with Moscow launched by the Russian Orthodox churches in the Baltic states and Moldova.[44]

ISOLATIONIST AND EXPANSIONIST KATECHON: FROM THE CITY OF KITEZH TO NOAH'S ARK

While the church's notions of Holy Rus' and Third Rome can be both isolationist and expansionist, another, more clearly and uniquely isolationist, version of the katechon has been theorized by Vadim Tsymbursky (1957–2009), a central yet underappreciated figure in Russian geopolitical thought.[45] An Orientalist by training, Tsymbursky worked in several academic institutions, such as the Institute for the Study of the US and Canada of the Academy of Sciences, the Institute of Oriental Studies, and later the Institute of Philosophy. A liberal in the early 1990s, he was shocked by the NATO bombings of Yugoslavia and moved closer to conservative circles, working with Gleb Pavlovsky's team at APN.ru, Mikhail Remizov's National Strategy Institute, and the Conservative Press Club.

Deeply influenced by civilizationist thinking, Tsymbursky elaborated the isolationist notion of Russia as an "island civilization" to counter the Eurasianist concept of Russia as a "continent-ocean."[46] In his view, there does exist such a thing as Eurasia, though this refers to a "giant inter-civilizational belt,"[47] a "Great Periphery" from which Russia should protect itself. Tsymbursky coined the notion of "Russia First": the country should refocus on a core Russia, which approximately coincides with seventeenth-century Muscovy once it absorbed Siberia, and forget about neighboring territories. Tsymbursky relied in large part on Solzhenitsyn's vision of the national revival of

Russia as entailing a retreat into its own past and territory and a rejection of any global mission.[48] According to Tsymbursky, Russia should focus on modernizing its urban culture and revitalizing Siberia without pursuing broader imperial projects, from which it does not stand to gain.

If there is a Third Rome to build, it is an autarkic, isolated spiritual community closed off from an apostate world. As Tsymbursky explains, "This shrunken Russia is my country and the one in which I want to live."[49] His vision calls for another myth to be reactivated, that of Kitezh, the "invisible city" of Russian folk tales—known through Nikolay Rimsky-Korsakov's opera of the same name. The first reference to Kitezh comes in an anonymous late-eighteenth-century book known as the *Kitezh Chronicle*, which was thought to have originated among the Old Believers. In the thirteenth century, to avoid Mongol raids, the city was believed to have sunk itself into Lake Svetloyar, becoming invisible to its enemies. It would appear to some with pure hearts as a symbol of the passage between different worlds, fated to rise again only on Judgment Day.[50] Tsymbursky's idea of Russia as an island, not a continent, has been continued by his disciple Boris Mezhuev and, to a lesser extent, Mikhail Remizov.

Opposing the isolationist language of "island Russia" have been the neo-Eurasianist and neo-imperialist figures of the Izborsky Club, Alexander Prokhanov and Alexander Dugin, who have offered an expansionist reading of Russia's katechonic status since the early 1990s. Amid growing tensions with the West and emboldened by the war in Ukraine, the club published a new manifesto, *The Ideology of Russian Victory*, in late 2021, presenting it as a new national project.[51] Since the invasion, the club's main figures have been trying to promote it as the official ideology of the special military operation. *The Ideology of Russian Victory* probably offers the most elaborate doctrinal platform for justifying the war, repackaging many of the previous ideological constructs advanced by the Izborsky Club. It defines the battlefield as an existential one, metaphysical rather than geographic, between "Ukrainian fascist codes and the codes of the Russian Victory." One can identify three ideological pillars coming from the club's three main leaders.

First, Prokhanov focuses on economics, calls for Russia's reindustrialization and informational innovations such as AI, and claims that victory is possible only through organizational structures and a new elite—all components inspired by Soviet discursive lines. Indeed, Prokhanov's intellectual brand since the 1970s has been on everything industrial and technological, which at the time clearly set him apart from the more culture- and religion-oriented Russian nationalists. One can also find an explicit reference to Russian Cosmism,[52] which constitutes a mainstay of Prokhanov's worldview: the manifesto criticizes transhumanism as Western technological madness and suggests replacing it with a science "ultimately striving for immortality according to the precepts of Christ and the precepts of Russian Cosmism,"[53] including human superpowers.

Second, the contribution from Dugin revolves around his classic geopolitical themes: Schmittian narratives about larger spaces and authoritarianism, the spatial quality of the conflict with the West (maritime versus continental powers), and Russia's geopolitical projection in the Arctic, Eastern Mediterranean, and Far East. Dugin stresses the idea of Russia embarking upon its "Fifth Empire" and insists on Russia's multinationalism and religious pluralism. All these references are mixed with more Western-inspired fascist language, such as Russia being the heir of the mythical Aryans or Hyperboreans—a typical blending for Dugin's prose.[54]

Third, Vitaly Averyanov offers repackaged biblical themes. The key narrative is that the war is a new biblical Flood sent by God to punish mankind for losing its way in the form of postmodern Western values, while Russia represents a new Noah's Ark, the one place where civilization will survive. Averyanov describes the West as a "golem" civilization led by decadent globalist elites driving the "Great Reset," a classic conspiracy theory about cosmopolitan elites using immigration and the Covid-19 pandemic to destroy the world. Only Russia can offer an answer, as it "feels" the eschatological End of Days more than any other nation in the world and will be the only country to survive the Flood.

The war has allowed the language used by the Izborsky Club to reach a larger audience. The assassination of Dugin's daughter, Darya Dugina, on August 20, 2022 (which was attributed by Moscow to the Ukrainian secret services, and which probably targeted him, not her) was the first assassination of a pro-war figure on Russia's territory. It garnered Dugin wider media exposure and new political recognition: at her funeral, he presented her as a martyr of the special military operation, having "died for Russia and the front, and that front is here."[55] The ceremony was attended by some officials close to the Izborsky Club, such as Leonid Slutsky, who became the leader of the LDPR after the passing of Zhirinovsky, while Putin sent his personal condolences. On his September 30, 2022, speech on the annexation of four

Ukrainian regions, the Russian president mentioned "our philosophers" being killed, signaling that Dugina's assassination had a broader meaning for the Russian elite.[56]

Since then, Dugin has regained the media visibility that he had lost after 2015 and become a regular guest on Russia's most famous television talk shows such as Bol'shaia igra (Great Game). He was also able to secure a two-hour meeting with Belarusian president Alexander Lukashenko and attended the St. Petersburg Economic Forum in 2023—a sign that with the war he was able to secure higher patrons in the Kremlin's ecosystems. He also managed to get himself named director of the new Ivan Ilyin Higher Political School at RGGU, which aims to indoctrinate the higher-education faculty and staff and purge academia of its Western references. For those who follow Russian intellectual history, seeing Dugin chair an institution named after Ilyin, who hated Eurasianism, may seem like a historical irony. Dugin himself criticized and disdained Ilyin for a long time before feeling the tide turn and rallying to him.[57] Yet one cannot say the Izborsky Club's status has been catapulted to officialdom by the war: it has remained in the shadows when compared to the main ideological products built by the regime to deal with the new context.

ISLAMIC-INSPIRED KATECHON

There have been other eschatological voices in Russia, this time rooted not in Russian Orthodoxy but in Islam. Reading Islam as the last fortress able to resist Westernization has indeed been common among Islamic thinkers of many different ideological backgrounds, ranging from Salafists to those inspired by the Muslim Brotherhood, Wahhabis, Iranian Shia revolutionaries, and of course jihadists. As Ghassan El Masri writes, "The Christian *katechon*, sometimes represented in the image of a wall, is not unlike the Islamic wall that the secular world-figure named Dhū al-Qarnayn built to stave off the apocalyptic Gog and Magog (Q 18.83–101ff.)."[58]

A member of the Izborsky Club, Geydar Dzhemal (1947–2016) probably best embodied this Islamic interpretation of Russia's katechonic identity. An esoteric philosopher of Russian and Azeri descent, Dzhemal considered Russia the country best placed to resist US domination because it combines Russian Orthodox nationalism and Islamic renewal. He was not the first figure to state that the "red-brown" (Russian imperialist nationalist) and "green" (Islamic) movements shared common objectives and should combine forces. But his emphasis was an original one, as it articulated an Islamic version of liberation theology linking faith with the fight for social justice. According to him, the enemy is embodied by the US, the "party of Satan," as the symbol of all the evils of the modern world: colonialism, capitalism, and inequality. The "New American World" is said to be engaged in a lethal fight with the Ancient World, which represents the party of God, shaped by the three religions of Abraham, but only Islam has managed to preserve the authentic revolutionary tradition of monotheism and avoid making a compromise with the liberal order. In merging the protest potential of Islam with socialist resistance to the American world, Dzhemal hoped to make Islam the new vanguard of international resistance. His Islamic political philosophy, Sunni but inspired by the Iranian Revolution, was too radical to appeal to a broad audience, but has remained quite visible on the Russian Islamic ideological market.[59]

A similar reading of Islam as the last fortress can be found among Russian converts to Islam. For them, the ROC has lost its capacity to resist Western-inspired modernity and is too controlled by secular state structures, while Islam remains the least touched and closest to the original faith. Many Russian converts to Islam refer to René Guénon and Julius Evola's Traditionalism or Perennialism, a school of thought that inspired both the Western and Islamic far right and advocates a return to a pre-Renaissance vision of faith.[60] Russian converts first unified in the National Organization of Russian Muslims (NORM), created in 2004. One of their main representatives, Ali Polosin, a former Orthodox priest who converted to Islam and now works for the Moscow-based muftiate, has invited Russians to convert to Islam as the only path to moral and physical regeneration after decades of state atheism and Western liberalism.[61] Many converts have then joined the Russian section of the Murabitun World Movement, calling for the recognition of a "White Islam" and asserting that Islam is native to the original European population and should be dissociated from the idea of migration from south of the Mediterranean.[62]

WHEN ESCHATOLOGY HITS THE MAINSTREAM

Direct allusions to religious messianism have been rare in Russian official language. Putin rarely mentions God, but he alluded to the spiritual/religious nature of Russia's identity on several occasions. In 2001, during a visit to the

Solovetsky Islands in the White Sea—a Gulag camp and now monastery—he declared, for instance, that "without Christianity and Orthodox faith, without the culture which grew out of them, there would not be any Russia," and therefore that it was "important, necessary, and timely" to return to the Orthodox faith.[63] In 2007, in the quote introducing this chapter, he plainly declared that "Russia relies on two pillars, nuclear bombs and Orthodoxy."[64]

It is the Syrian civil war and Russia's involvement on the side of Bashar Al-Assad that accelerated the religious tone of Russian political language. State media mostly described the conflict as a war on an Eastern Christian territory toward which Moscow has a special debt/duty to protect. For the Russian public, Syria is the last place in the world where people still speak Jesus's mother tongue, Aramaic, which lends it powerful symbolic value. Inside the church, a form of "militant piety" and rhetoric of political violence, which had always existed on the margins, gradually seeped into the higher hierarchy.[65] Patriarch Kirill, who presented Putin's rule as "a miracle of God" already in 2012,[66] justified Russia's intervention in Syria by stating that it was Russia's historical mission. The head of the church's public affairs department, Vsevolod Chaplin, spoke of a "holy battle" for ancient Christian lands.[67] Archpriest Oleg Trofimov explained, "In this war, Russia is acting as a representative of the civilization of Jesus Christ—Holy Rus'. . . . . No matter how these wars are unleashed upon her, Russia bears the global mission of the Katechon."[68]

Yet it is with the full-scale invasion of Ukraine that the eschatological potential of this katechonic language has materialized.[69] Putin even mentioned the Gospels and Patriarch Kirill called him "a fighter against the Antichrist."[70] The notion of the Antichrist, already operationalized by far-right thinkers such as Dugin and Prokhanov, has now reached official discourse. Connected to this has been the revival of the label of Satan/satanism. Kadyrov and Patrushev advisor Alexey Pavlov have, for instance, commented on the need to "desatanize" Ukraine,[71] while Dmitry Medvedev has declared that the war aims to stop "the supreme ruler of hell, whatever name he uses—Satan, Lucifer, or Iblis."[72] The 24th World Russian People's Congress in 2022 presented the special military operation as a "holy war in which Russia and its people, defending the single spiritual space of Holy Russia, are fulfilling the mission of the 'Katechon,' protecting the world from the onslaught of globalism and victory of a West that has fallen into Satanism."[73] Sergey Naryshkin advised "the Anglo-Saxons to go to their old friend, the Devil."[74] President of the Chechen Academy of Sciences Dzhambulat Umarov went further, linking the supposed denazification of Ukraine with the fight against LGBTQ+ rights by declaring that "sodomy is the core of Satanism, against which our brothers and sons are now dying on Ukrainian soil."[75]

The church, too, has embraced a religious legitimation of the war and has even included in its liturgies a prayer for Russia's victory in the war, "Prayer for Holy Rus'." After some minor hesitations in the first days of the invasion to avoid any schism with its Ukrainian parishes (about one third of the Moscow Patriarchate's parishes are/were located in Ukraine), Kirill delivered a sermon on Forgiveness Day, March 6. In it, he represented Russia's opponents as "evil forces," declared that there cannot be forgiveness without justice (referring to the Donbas), and asserted that "If we see [Ukraine] as a threat, we have the right to use force to ensure the threat is eradicated."[76] He also offered a holy icon to Viktor Zolotov, the commander of the Russian National Guard, a gesture that symbolizes the full ideological companionship of the church and the *siloviki*. Since then, the Moscow Patriarchate has blessed those said to be defending the motherland. The church has thus fully endorsed the concept of spiritual warfare, bringing in arguments close to the notion of a "just war" (as existing in Saint Augustine's theory) protecting Russia to remain a country of the true faith.[77] It has legitimized the war as a fundamental civilizational divide in which allowing or prohibiting a gay pride parade signaled belonging to either Western or Russian civilization, stating: "We are talking about human salvation, something much more important than politics."[78]

Other confessions have followed but with less motivation. The main muftiates have embraced the war too, yet with tensions inside their hierarchy. The two other religions recognized as "traditional" in the Russian legislation, Buddhism and Judaism, have been more divided, with some leaders and institutions supporting the war and others opposing it.[79] Even among the Russian Orthodox Church, there is not absolute unanimity: there have been several hundred cases of Orthodox priests publicly opposing the war, replacing praying for "victory" by praying for "peace" in their sermons. The majority of them have lost their positions, among them the famous protodeacon Andrey Kuraev.[80]

The risk of nuclear escalation has also pushed eschatological references into political language. As early as 2014, Dmitry Kiselyov, chief propagandist and head of the state-controlled media group Rossiya Segodnya, warned of Russia's ability to turn the US into "radioactive ashes."[81] In 2018, Putin explained that though Russia would never be the first to use nuclear weapons: "An aggressor should know that vengeance is inevitable, that he will be annihilated. Whereas we would become the victims of their aggression, and as martyrs, will go to heaven—they will just end up dead. Because they won't even have time to repent."[82] Since 2022, Russian political talk shows, fed on provocations, went further, such as when the infamous Vladimir Soloviev said "we will go to paradise" in the event of a nuclear war.[83] More seriously, Sergey Karaganov has called for Russia to launch limited nuclear strikes in order to terminate the war in a way favorable to Moscow—his controversial statement was criticized by other Russian officials, but the Kremlin's gambling with blurring the nuclear "red lines" has undoubtedly escalated.[84]

The war has led Russian officials to voice plainly a katechonic vision of Russia, which had been present for a long time in radical circles but only implicit in official language. This identity is based on the philosophical principle of an ontological nature of humankind that must be protected against transformations/denaturation, and on messianic arguments that only chosen nations can rescue humankind from the Antichrist's temptations. It allows the use of violence, presented as a legitimate means for the katechon to protect itself.[85] Although this katechonic language is imbued with religious metaphors, it remains deeply secular: "the chosen" refers to the Russian state itself, not to the body of believers.

In this reading of Russia as a shield, one can find both isolationist and expansionist tendencies, which more often coexist than oppose one another. Here, too, that tension is nothing new, as Orthodox Christianity has always been ambivalent toward the universalistic call of Christianity and favorable to religion as national cultures. These ambivalences are explicit in Russia's war narrative, which simultaneously combines the idea to save/protect (Donbas residents, Russian-speaking Ukrainians, historically Russian territories, or Russia itself) *and* to attack first, to isolate itself from the liberal West, *and* to prove itself to the rest of the world.

PART IV
RUSSIA'S GEO-IMAGINARIES

RUSSIA'S POWER PROJECTION REMAINS shaped by the need to move from being on the periphery—of the West—to becoming a new center in its own right. But a new center of what? Four possible answers have emerged: (1) the center of "real" (read: Christian and continental) Europe against a "fake" Europe defined by liberalism, a status embedded in the notion of Russia as the new Byzantium, which we discussed previously; (2) the center of Eurasia, so that Russia would lead a "community of destiny" that would include countries that are contiguous with it; (3) the center of the Russian World, a space that is both de-territorialized—Russia as an archipelago of diasporas—*and* yet still territorialized because it is embodied in the defense of Russian minorities abroad; and (4) an anticolonial center in a multipolar world, engaged in the de-Westernization of the international order in alignment with the Global South.

This type of power projection belongs to the classic toolkit of great-power influence. Yet in the Russian case it has some specific, enduring characteristics: spatial features matter. Russia's empire was historically built on territorial continuity on the Eurasian landmass, in contrast to European powers that projected their colonial mindset across seas and oceans. This alleged link between size and meaning illustrates in an exemplary manner the idea, common in Russia, that the country's destiny is linked to its geographic scope. As argued by Edith Clowes, "The geographical metaphors dominant in current discourse about identity convey the sense that who a Russian is depends on how one defines where Russia is."[1] One could argue that in the Russian case, geography may provide a more powerful source of identity than does history, especially in the post-Soviet period, when a concept of space is easier to promote than a disrupted and traumatic history.[2]

But the idea that Russian identity is largely dependent on space is nothing new: the great Russian philosophers and Russian émigré thinkers of the Silver Age—such as Vladimir Soloviev (1853–1900), Sergey Bulgakov (1871–1944), and Pavel Florensky (1882–1837)—interpreted Orthodox Christianity as a religion that grants particular attention to territory, through the notion of canonical territory and philosophical interpretations thereof, and which seeks to ground its harmony with the universe through the idea of the Kingdom of the Spirit or of the Heavens. All this makes Russia fertile ground for what I have called "geographical metanarratives" (Laruelle 2012), which advance a supposedly comprehensive and teleological explanation of Russia through a master idea: territorial size and location in space are the drivers of the country's mission in the world and of the nature of its political regime.[3]

For today's authorities, projecting power is thus intrinsically connected to spatial self-representation. Eurasia activates the memory of the empire, the *Großraum* celebrated by German geopoliticians such as Friedrich Ratzel (1844–1904) and Karl Haushofer (1869–1946), as well as by Carl Schmitt: being a transcontinental nation acting as a regional hegemon is the most surefire way to claim great-power status. The Russian World activates the vision of a divided nation that needs to overcome that diminished status by recapturing the most symbolic of its lost territories: Crimea and Novorossiya—with potential expansion to the whole of Ukraine. The Global South sketches a picture of a globalized and modernized Russia blossoming in a multipolar world, without reference to a regional sphere of influence.

These repertoires offer different socially constructed spatial realities surrounding Russia, different mental mappings. They create new "imagined communities" in which Russia is the leading power, providing cognitive frameworks for elites but also for public opinion in interpreting international relations and the place of their country on the world scene.[4] Is Russia's uniqueness rooted in its religious heritage (Byzantium), its large territory (Eurasia), its archipelagic nature (the Russian World), or its anticolonial stance (the Global South)? Each of these mental maps implies cultural and political boundaries that do not overlap with state borders, what Franck Billé has called "auratic bodies."[5] Eurasia makes Russia's great-power status dependent on former imperial or Soviet territories; the Russian World implies that parts of Russia's ethnic body lie outside the borders of the Federation; the

Global South suggests that Russia is a great power because it assists in leading a non-Western coalition. These concepts also imply different boundaries of belonging: are the former Soviet republics parts of Russia's body (Eurasia), or is that body composed of Russian-speaking constituencies (the Russian World), or could it be that Russia simply has fellow travelers scattered around the world (the Global South)?

The notion that Russia's identity boundaries do not always align with legal borders is implicit in many of these repertoires. Putin did say that "Russia's borders do not finish anywhere" (*granitsy Rossii ne konchaiutsia nigde*) in 2016—a joke at a children's contest at the Russian Geographical Society, but which can obviously be interpreted as illuminating expansionist undertones.[6] These aspirational narratives all, too, have messianic undertones: they each advance solutions to what is seen as the deadlock of a US-led global order. Eurasia does this by denouncing Western intrusion into Russia's historic sphere of influence along with a containment strategy; the Russian World does so by promoting a particularistic, rather than universalistic, form of soft power; meanwhile, the anticolonial stance projects an anti-imperialist messianism.

All these repertoires were deployed by various nonstate actors from the very early 1990s before being appropriated by the Presidential Administration to varying degrees in the 2000s. The Eurasia concept was promoted by the conservative forces around Zyuganov's Communist Party and Zhirinovsky's LDPR, as well as by Alexander Dugin, Alexander Prokhanov, and myriad lesser-known figures. The Russian World and the notion of Russia as a divided nation were key themes advanced by ethnonationalists who clustered around the Congress of Russian Communities and Rogozin's Rodina party. The anticolonial language was deployed by Russian entrepreneurs of influence and state media targeting foreign audiences, especially those in Africa, before being captured by state language. The fact that these repertoires originated outside of state structures per se is crucial to comprehending the capacity of the regime to absorb and co-opt ideational products emanating from different segments of the elite.

The Presidential Administration's operationalization of these repertoires has occurred in sequence: the Russian World in 2007, Eurasia in 2011, again the Russian World in 2014, and then the anticolonial stance very visibly since 2022. But they may also overlap, as they express different foreign-policy orientations. As geopolitical concepts, they are all floating signifiers that speak to different audiences and are open to rebranding and rearticulations. Their blurred nature is part of their design—hence the contradictions of the official narrative, which celebrates Russia's multiethnic nature while also calling for the defense of ethnic Russians abroad, and its paradoxical policy choices such as having the paramilitary troops of infamous Chechen head of state Ramzan Kadyrov fighting in Ukraine on behalf of the Russian World.[7] The 2023 Russian Foreign Policy Concept attempts to blend all these repertoires into a coherent language. It is this puzzle of overlapping spatial and geopolitical repertoires that the next three chapters aim to solve.

TEN

EURASIA
The Transcontinental Space

Greater Eurasia is not an abstract geopolitical scheme, but, without any exaggeration, a genuinely civilizational project directed toward the future.
VLADIMIR PUTIN, Belt and Road International Forum, Beijing, 2017[1]

RUSSIA'S BEST-KNOWN GEOPOLITICAL REPERTOIRE today is probably that of Eurasia. It is mentioned twenty-four times in the 2023 Russian Foreign Policy Concept (compared to only twice in the 2016 edition), a sign of its semantic elasticity. It is certainly Russia's broadest geographical signifier, offering a kaleidoscope of narratives: Eurasia as a mirror of Europe, a regional space that would collaborate with the European Union as an equal; Eurasia as an alternative to Europe, a way for Russia to exit a failing Europe; Eurasia as the absolute, civilizational opposite of Europe or the West, its essentialist "Other."

The term caps off the pyramid of Russia's geopolitical concepts for want of something better: it expresses conveniently, and in a rather intuitive way, the historical space of Russia and its "peripheries." It is both multiscalar and multiperspectival: it can refer to geography by stressing the country's spatial breadth (with several subniches accentuating either its relationship with Central Asia and the Turkic world, or with China and the Asia-Pacific); to history by emphasizing the shared community of destiny of Eurasian peoples over several centuries; and to tomorrow's global order by envisioning a new pole of regional influence in a multipolar world. It is also attractive because it has risen from being a product of more or less marginal intellectual circles to become the official language of Russia's ambitions to lead regional integration and become a new center—whether alone or together with China—of a post-unilateral international order.[2]

The notion of Eurasia can claim a plethora of spiritual fathers: the founding fathers among the interwar émigrés, Lev Gumilev during the Soviet era, Alexander Dugin and Alexander Panarin in the 1990s, Sergey Glazyev in the 2000s, Sergey Karaganov in the 2010s. Each iteration of the term is thus saturated with different ideological assumptions depending on its author(s) and the historical context. Yet despite its extreme elasticity, one may identify three core shared assumptions: first, that there exists a space called Eurasia united by a shared common destiny and led by Russia (whatever its borders and the nature of the Russian leadership); second, that this space relies on a specific civilizational project which differs from the European or Western one (here too, with different contents to be filled out); and third, that it seeks to compete (whether peacefully or not) with the Western, European, or transatlantic project(s).

THE SERPENTINE DEFINITIONS OF EURASIA

The term "Eurasia" is a revealing example of the constructed character of spatial definitions. It emerged in the nineteenth century to define the Euro-Asian landmass. In 1829, the German geographer and naturalist Alexander von Humboldt (1769–1859), who revolutionized the use of topographic maps, visited Russia at the invitation of Tsar Nicholas I. He traveled to Siberia, making it as far as the Yenissei River, which runs from Mongolia to the Arctic, and the newly conquered Turkestan.[3] He appears to be the first to have used the term "Eurasia" to describe Russia's continental landmass and the continuity between the European and Siberian plains, while maintaining the conventional view that the Urals marked the dividing line between Europe and Asia. At the end of the century, the Austrian geographer Eduard Suess (1831–1914) challenged this division in his book *Das Antlitz der Erde* (*The Face of the Earth*, 1885): according to him, Europe and Asia are, geologically speaking, only one continent, as they share the same tectonic plate.

After that, the term "Eurasia" moved from the sphere of geology into those of culture and race: it was used to denote the children of ethnically mixed couples, including by the French administration in colonial Indochina.[4] In Russia, however, the term was destined for another fate. At the end of the nineteenth century, a new school of geographers emerged that considered the Russian Empire to be a specific geographic entity. This perception of a proper third continent was investigated—without using the term "Eurasia"—by Vladimir Lamansky (1833–1914), Vasily Dokuchaev (1846–1903), and the economist Petr Struve (1870–1944).[5] They insisted on the continuity of geographical features from the European to the Siberian regions, as well as on the specificities of human geography, population patterns, etc., across Russia, with the goal—whether openly stated or not—of justifying the Russian Empire's dominion over its conquered peoples, its civilizing mission in Asia, and its *Sonderweg*, or special path, when compared to European countries.[6]

In the early 1920s, a group of émigrés in Europe led by Petr Savitsky (1895–1968) and Prince Nikolay Troubetzkoy (1890–1938) was the first to unite these scattered elements into a single all-encompassing, well-articulated, and highly sophisticated principle: that of Russia *as* Eurasia.[7] For the founding fathers of Eurasianism, Russia *is* Eurasia in the sense that Russia's geographical and cultural features are intrinsically those of the whole of Eurasia: differences between center and peripheries should be effaced, as they are all part of the same natural entity. In this view, Eurasia is unified by shared spatial features—a dialectic between forest and steppe—and by anthropological, linguistic, and cultural similarities. The movement adhered to a core principle, according to which Eurasia is necessarily an entity all its own—which is explicable through its own internal elements and not in terms of its interaction with the outside world. Savitsky drew on the work of Vladimir Vernadsky (1863–1945), the famous Russian scientist who developed the notion of the noosphere[8] and the tendency of continents toward self-organization—that is, the notion that each cultural world is supposedly moved by an internal centripetal dynamic.[9]

But beyond this ontological view of the world as a holistic and organicist structure, Eurasia displays a very political repertoire aiming to justify the naturalness of Russia's imperial structure. If Eurasia is a "natural" space, then it cannot accept any sort of amputation, which should be regarded as violence against nature: hence the political conclusion that all Eurasian peoples share the same destiny and should live under the same political structure. "The nature of the Eurasian world is very unfavorable to all types of separatism, political, cultural or economic," stated Savitsky, a political message that could not have been clearer in the 1920s, as debates over Ukrainian and Belarussian autonomy raged among émigrés and in the Soviet Union alike.[10] A second conclusion is that Eurasia is not the *overlapping* of Europe and Asia but a unique third continent. As a Eurasianist manifesto of 1926 declared, "Russia's culture is neither a European nor an Asian culture, nor is it the sum or mechanical combination of elements of the one or the other."[11]

Interwar Eurasianists were the first to coin the term "Eurasianism" (*evraziistvo*). The Russian suffix -*stvo* is used to define something abstract: it could perhaps be better translated as "Eurasianness." For Eurasianists, *evraziistvo* means simultaneously the fact of being Eurasian (*evraziistvo*), the science of Eurasia (which could have been *evraziovedenie*), and the political project or ideology of Eurasian unity (which could have been *evrazizm*). But these last two coinages have not been struck; the semantic space has been left open, with just one term to cover three different meanings. Similarly, the Russian language does not distinguish between "Eurasian" (geographically speaking) and "Eurasianist" (ideologically speaking): both are expressed as *evraziiskii*. In other words, a Eurasian, in the sense of a person who lives in Eurasia or was born of a mixed Euro-Asian marriage, and an ideologue of Eurasianism, are both referred to as *Evraziets*. Terminological ambivalences are thus an intrinsic part of the discussion.

With the collapse of the Soviet Union, the term "Eurasia" gained a new lease on life. This second life has been sufficiently distinct from the first to merit describing the current ideologies as *neo*-Eurasianisms (plural), to distinguish them from the interwar one. Neo-Eurasianisms have a complex relationship to classical Eurasianism, and the initial impression of a continuity between that of interwar emigration and the post-Soviet period is debatable. Indeed, the dissident historian Lev Gumilev, the only promoter of Eurasianism in the Soviet Union itself, and then the aforementioned Moscow State University philosophy professor Alexander Panarin, followed by the infamous geopolitician Alexander Dugin, as well as theorists of Turkic or Kazakhstani neo-Eurasianism, often speak harshly of the original Eurasianists. Very few of them see themselves as disciples of the founding fathers (with the sole exception of Gumilev being regularly referred to, but more for his ethnic theories than for his Eurasianist views per se), whom they more often consider, at best, to have only partially anticipated their own ideas.

Neo-Eurasianisms also exhibit great internal diversity. First, they are diverse in terms of space. The implosion of the Soviet Union also imploded narratives on the theme of Eurasia. They can thus be found not only in present-day Russia but also in Kazakhstan, where Eurasianism functioned for decades as an official doctrine for a state that presents itself as the intersection of East and West, Europe and Asia, Russia and the East, placing Kazakhs on a pedestal as the heirs of the leading world civilizations.[12] Since 2020, the Kazakhstani use of "Eurasia" has changed for both domestic and international reasons. First, Astana toned down references to it within the context of the transfer of power from President Nursultan Nazarbayev to Kassym-Jomart Tokayev, who modified Kazakhstan's political language to make it more Kazakh-centric and less Eurasianist. Second, with Russia's full-scale war in Ukraine, Astana had to rhetorically distance itself from everything that smacked of Russian imperialism, and thus could not unburden the notion of "Eurasia" from its Russo-centric baggage.

Even within Russia, there are many neo-Eurasianisms, as political figures and public intellectuals in various ethnic republics have elaborated their own local versions. They inflect it with local colors and wield it as a tool that allows for claims to both local national identity and loyalty to the Russian state. Tatarstan has been at the forefront of this trend, followed by Kalmykia, which, under the leadership of Kirsan Ilyumzhinov (1993–2010), crafted its own combination of Eurasianism, cosmism, and Soviet-inspired ideology.[13] Additional variations have taken shape in Sakha-Yakutia, Bashkortostan, Buryatia, Tuva, and so on.

Second, neo-Eurasianisms are diverse in their thematic foci. In many of the Russian Federation's republics, the Eurasianist motif is inflected with the theme of ethnicity: it is used to celebrate the unique character of the titular ethnic group (*etnos*), as well as its harmonious integration into a larger pan-Russian ensemble. This gives a central place to the Gumilevian ethnic prism and its theory of "passionarity," as well as to narratives of cultural encounters between East and West. Ethnically Russian neo-Eurasianisms, meanwhile, have dropped one of the central criteria of classical Eurasianism—namely, calling for miscegenation between Slavic and Turkic cultures—in favor of a more traditional imperial narrative for whom the country's ethnic diversity is secondary.[14] In Dugin's version of neo-Eurasianism, for instance, Eurasia is seen as a Russian-style formulation of the "Third Way" inspired by the German Conservative Revolution of the interwar period.[15] Thus, while some

Eurasianisms celebrate Russia's multiethnic character and interreligious harmony, others embody a Russian version of European far-right theories.

Last but not least, neo-Eurasianisms have evolved over the course of the post-Soviet era. In the early 1990s, references to Eurasia were used primarily to compensate for the Soviet collapse, and were brandished by the so-called red-brown coalition. At that time, they represented the most convincing way to reintroduce a *longue durée* perspective in the face of an abrupt fragmentation, with the aim of relegitimizing a crumbling community of destiny. In the 2000s, the Kremlin's rehabilitation of the Soviet past as the key common dominator of Russian society made the first neo-Eurasianisms seem comparatively unoriginal, being only one version of a broader nostalgia for the Soviet past. With the emergence of the state-sponsored Eurasian project in the early 2010s, Eurasianism took on a more official stance.

APPLIED EURASIA: FROM THE EURASIAN UNION TO GREATER EURASIA

While playing with the notion of Eurasia was historically the province of intellectual circles and regional elites, the term has gradually been appropriated by the Kremlin, becoming one of the country's main geopolitical narratives. As with every such appropriation by government bodies, it has lost some of its theoretical sophistication and become a more applied formula when deployed at the policy level. Yet despite its incorporation into the official language of Russia's claim to regional hegemony, the term has retained some of its plasticity.

Already in 1992, at the time of a fervent pro-Western mindset among the Russian elites, one of Yeltsin's advisers, Sergey Stankevich, expressed the idea of Russia as a crossroads between East and West:

> As I see it, Russia's mission in the world is to initiate and support a multilateral dialogue of cultures, civilizations, and states . . . This is a perfectly natural role for it, since Russia is in itself, by nature, dialogical . . . Two tendencies, Atlanticism and Eurasianism, have recently made themselves felt in our foreign policy practice.[16]

Once Putin came to power, the Presidential Administration limited itself to speaking about Russia as a "Euro-Asian country" (*evro-aziatskaia strana*), rarely using the adjective "Eurasian" (*evraziiskii*). For a very long time, the term was synonymous with regional integration, referring to nothing beyond

Commonwealth of Independent States (CIS)–related matters and subsequent regional initiatives that existed mostly on paper. As a form of soft power for the near abroad, it was promoted by myriad small associations, either closer to the more ideological forms of Eurasianism (such as Dugin's Eurasian Youth Movement and the Young Eurasia of Yury Kofner), or a more bureaucratic one like the Eurasian Youth Parliament. Things changed, however, in 2011, with the launch of Putin's pet project, the Eurasian Union, just before his return for a third presidential term.[17] From then on, the number of mentions of Eurasia grew steadily, especially in 2015–16, before dropping back down and rebounding in 2020–22 (see fig. 10.1).

Putin's dream of a Eurasian Union functioning in a genuinely supranational manner never became a reality. Only a more limited version of it took shape: the Eurasian Economic Union (EAEU). Established in 2015, from the moment of its inception it was hampered by Russia's recent annexation of Crimea and the ensuing Western sanctions. While Western observers mostly read Russia's Eurasian proposal as a project of restoring the Soviet Union, they missed the neoliberal aspect of the idea: the EAEU remains based on the "four freedoms" (goods, capital, services, and people) of the European Union,

FIG. 10.1. Mentions of "Eurasia" in presidential speeches, 2000–2023.

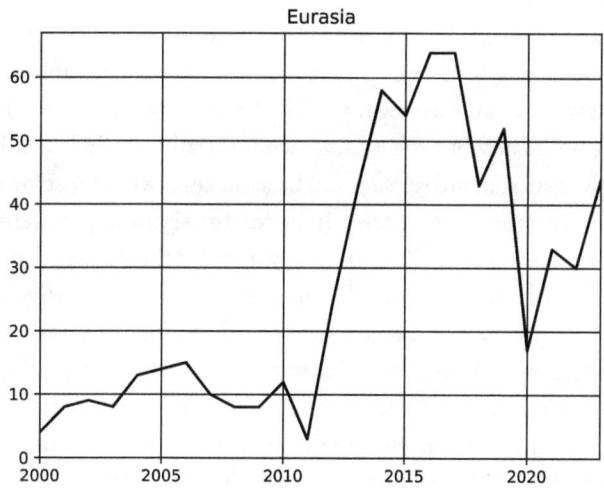

Source: Author's compilation based on Kremlin.ru for *Evraziia, evraziiskii, evroaziatskii, Bol'shaia Evraziia,* and *evraziistvo.*

and it was envisioned by Russia as a way to better integrate the global economic order.[18] Composed of Russia, Belarus, Kazakhstan, Kyrgyzstan, and Armenia, the EAEU project can be considered both a success and a failure. It is a success in the sense that it is the only Russia-led regional economic integration project that has managed to become a real customs union and to persuade its members to make good on at least some of their commitments. Yet the project can also be characterized, at least in part, as a failure: member states have divergent policies, have engaged in trade wars among themselves, and are skeptical about the future of the institution—and all of them have also become particularly concerned about Russia's ambitions.[19] Moreover, the authoritarian nature of the majority of member states makes it difficult to delegate power to supranational bodies.[20]

To use the terms coined by Alexander Libman, the *real* and the *imagined* Eurasian Economic Union do not overlap.[21] Russia's *imagined* EAEU would have been a conduit for its own interests that was able to influence not only its neighbors but also the global economy, and become accepted as a new regional bloc. Moscow was, for instance, hoping to have the European Union recognize the EAEU as the regional umbrella organization under which it would trade with the EAEU's members. Yet the *real* EAEU has been difficult for Moscow to maneuver within: it has sometimes been able to constrain Russia's sovereignty, and has made decisions that favor the smaller countries. Once, the only genuinely supranational EAEU organ, the Commission, even blocked a Russian initiative. As a result, Moscow has been acting increasingly unilaterally and in a protectionist fashion, thereby undermining the legitimacy of its own regional strategy.[22] With the 2022 sanctions, the EAEU has been failing politically but succeeding economically: while Kazakhstan, Armenia, and Kyrgyzstan are reluctant to be associated with Moscow politically, they have all become major transit hubs for Russia to bypass sanctions and acquire Western products, with positive results for their own economies.[23]

In parallel with the Eurasian Economic Union, an *aspirational* Eurasian Union (without the inclusion of any other modifier such as economic, thereby implying that it would promote a more comprehensive integration program that would include both domestic and foreign policy) has been theorized mostly through the works of Sergey Glazyev, the spiritual father of the project.[24] Glazyev has published widely on the Eurasian Union project as a new pole of civilization on the world scene. He advocates for a socialist slate of economic reforms, with calls for the re-nationalization of major parts of the agricultural and industrial sectors, celebrating the collective ownership of land, and support for protectionism that hampers imports and foreign investment. His plan also emphasizes the need for Russia to become competitive in terms of information and network warfare—which would entail massive investment in advanced technologies, but without explaining how Russia could become self-sufficient or how the state could develop the IT and AI sectors.[25]

A former member of the liberal Gaydar government, Glazyev drew closer to the nationalist and Communist opposition in the late 1990s. In the early 2000s he fought with Dugin over control of the term "Eurasia," seeking to move it away from the latter's esoteric interpretation and to rethink it in a pragmatic way that would have policy relevance. That being said, like Dugin, Glazyev has built contacts with the Western far right. Most notable is his personal friendship with Lyndon LaRouche (1922–2019), the founder of an eponymous eclectic movement in the US that denounces the "world oligarchy" that allegedly controls state decisions and promotes neoliberal values in order to destroy world cultures. The friendship was an enduring one: until LaRouche's death, Glazyev's championing of the Eurasian Union and LaRouche's dreams of a transcontinental "Eurasian land-bridge" complemented each another.[26] Glazyev thus represents one of these conveyor belts between the Kremlin and more radical actors and thinkers (both domestic and foreign), and the central node that connects the applied Eurasian Economic Union to a broader far-right ideological framework.

In 2015, just as the Eurasian Economic Union was being launched, a new iteration of the term appeared: "Greater Eurasia" (*Bol'shaia Evraziia*). This term envisions a new geopolitical entity driven by Sino–Russian cooperation. This "pivot toward Asia" is nothing revolutionary—it was already well established and theorized under former prime minister Yevgeny Primakov, who envisioned a Russia-India-China geopolitical triangle that could balance the West—but had to be revamped and adapted to account for the disproportionate rise of China relative to Russia and India.[27]

Among neo-Eurasianist theoreticians, China has long been the object of contradictory statements. Alexander Dugin historically portrayed it as Russia's enemy in Asia, instead favoring Japan, before recognizing some common Russo-Chinese interests and then becoming a fervent supporter of the Russo-Chinese continental alliance.[28] Alexander Panarin, who was strongly opposed to any connection with the Islamic world, was supportive of the idea of Russia joining the "Buddhist-Taoist" realm.[29] Yet it was Mikhail Titarenko (1934–

2016), former director of the Far East Institute of the Russian Academy of Sciences, who embodied the only genuinely Sinophile form of Eurasianism. For years, Titarenko exalted China for its supposed geopolitical complementarity with Moscow, presenting it as the driver of Russia's Eurasian fate and showing the path to follow in terms of political regime, identity, philosophy, and economic development.[30] Titarenko supported the Chinese way of development and publicly lamented the Kremlin's inability to follow the Chinese example of how to successfully transform a Communist regime. He also insisted on the notion of harmony at the core of Taoism and Confucianism, and which the Chinese authorities have popularized by evoking the construction of a "harmonious society"—claiming that this overlapped with one of the central concepts of Orthodox Christianity and Slavophile thinking, namely the idea of conciliation (*sobornost'*).[31]

This official Sinophilia took flight with Russia's new pivot toward Asia, which coincided with a series of major events: the start of Putin's third presidential term in 2012, Chinese president Xi Jinping's taking office in 2013, and Russia's need to find alternative economic partners following the imposition of Western sanctions in 2014.[32] Developed by Sergey Karaganov and a team of experts from the Valdai Discussion Club and the Higher School of Economics in 2015, the notion of Greater Eurasia reveals the willingness of the Russian state to move away from interpreting China's Belt and Road Initiative (BRI) as a competitor and instead find a common language with it, insisting on the "linkage" (*sopriazhenie*) of the Chinese strategy with Russia's Eurasian Union.[33]

The idea behind the concept of Greater Eurasia is also to deal with Russia's subaltern status in relation to Europe. As Karaganov explained, "From being the periphery of Europe, we have turned into the center of Greater Eurasia."[34] He argued, for instance, for the birth of a "Central Eurasian Moment" in which Russia's and China's international stances and regional strategies would converge.[35] This new alliance would offer Moscow several advantages: Chinese investments to support Russian regional economic development, especially in the Far East, Siberia, and the Arctic; the ability to avoid tensions with Beijing over Central Asia; and the legitimization of Russia's claim to be leading a new geopolitical bloc distinct from, even opposed to, the Western one.[36] This narrative has reached the highest spheres of power: head of the Russian Security Council Sergey Naryshkin spoke of a Greater Eurasia "stretching from Murmansk to Shanghai and from New Delhi to Hanoi,"[37] while Putin has asserted that the Eurasian Economic Union and the BRI "are efficiently complementing each other. The harmonization of these projects can lay the foundation for establishing a Greater Eurasian Partnership—an economic cooperation space that is as free as possible from all barriers."[38]

In 2018, members of the Eurasian Economic Union and China signed the Trade and Economic Cooperation Agreement, which covers such areas as customs cooperation and trade facilitation, the elimination of tariff barriers, and intellectual property rights.[39] Besides this agreement, it is difficult to identify any concrete form of cooperation that has resulted from the convergence of the two projects.[40] It seems that the Chinese interpret the "Greater Eurasia" narrative as an empty signifier with no mission other than to restore Russian prestige in the face of the BRI's successes.[41] While the 2018 Foreign Policy Concept of the Russian Federation did not mention the project at all,[42] the idea of a Greater Eurasian Partnership has continued to be enthusiastically promoted within foreign policy circles. Then academic director of the Russian International Affairs Council (RIAC) Andrey Kortunov saw in the Russia-China "Greater Eurasia" concept the first step toward a new history-making construction that will span the whole Eurasian continent, including its European peninsula, and shape a new multipolar order.[43] With the war in Ukraine, the Greater Eurasia narrative had gained in visibility, and in May 2022, Vladimir Putin commented at length on it:

> Greater Eurasia . . . is without exaggeration a huge civilizational project, and its main idea relies on the creation of a common space of equal cooperation for regional organizations. The Greater Eurasia Partnership is called to change the political and economic architecture, become the guarantor of stability and prosperity on the whole continent, and, obviously, take into account the diversity of models of development, culture, and traditions of all peoples.[44]

BEYOND MULTIPLE MEANINGS, WHICH CORE DOCTRINE?

Do all these Eurasianist and neo-Eurasianist ideological trends, in their theoretical and applied diversity, share similar fundamental premises? Two can be pointed to, and they likely constitute the unchangeable core of an otherwise polymorphous ideology.

The first conceptual premise is that there exists something called Eurasia which, different spatial realities notwithstanding, reveals a shared destiny over time. This *longue durée* looks not only to the Soviet past or the expansion of the Russian Empire under the Romanov Dynasty, but as far back as early medieval history. It emphasizes the Golden Horde (usually seen in Russian historiography as a terrible "Tatar yoke" that cut Russia off from Europe), which is reevaluated as the crystalizing moment of Eurasia's future destiny. Neo-Eurasianist movements may have their own ways of defining the borders of the Eurasian entity and who should be considered part of it, but every iteration of the term implies a shared community of destiny.[45] On this premise, even when the Eurasian region appears fragmented, as it does today, this would be only a brief moment in a centuries-long history: the pendulum will eventually swing back toward reintegration.

There are several variants of this shared destiny, each with its own emphasis: a mostly cultural one (regional/ethnic Eurasianisms), a metapolitical one (according to Panarin and Dugin), a more *realpolitik* one (the Eurasian Union project), a purely economic one (the EAEU), and a more multipolar one associated with China (Greater Eurasia). Eurasia can also be seen as coexisting peacefully with other regional integration projects (that is, the Eurasian Union with the EU or with China's BRI) or as being in open competition, even conflict, with them (as in Dugin's version of an eschatological war with the West announcing the End of Days).

As an imagined community, Eurasia's identity is relational, taking on different nuances depending on the context. From the beginning, it has been possible to read Eurasia as both Europe *and* Asia or as *neither* Europe nor Asia. This plasticity allows its promoters to insist on Russia's Eurasian identity either in relation to the Muslim world or toward the Asia-Pacific. For instance, during his first visit to China in 2000, Putin declared, "We know that Russia is both a European and an Asian country. We pay tribute both to European pragmatism and to Oriental wisdom. This is why Russia's foreign policy will be balanced."[46] Two decades later, the new partnership with China encapsulated in the notion of Greater Eurasia confirms the ability of the concept to generate new spatial self-representations: Andrey Bezrukov of the Moscow State Institute of International Relations (MGIMO) argues, for instance, that "Russia is no longer the East of Europe, but the North of Greater Eurasia."[47] In this view, China has replaced Europe as Russia's reference point.

The second conceptual premise shared by all Eurasianist and neo-Eurasianist movements is that Russia should decenter itself from Europe or the West. This decentering was at the core of classical Eurasianism: the movement's first collective volume, published in Sofia, Bulgaria, in 1921, was entitled *Exodus to the East* (*Iskhod k Vostoku*), playing on the double meaning of the word *iskhod*, which expresses the ideas of both "exodus" and "solution."[48] Once again, the persistence of this point in today's neo-Eurasianisms is striking. Most of the experts who came up with the concept of Greater Eurasia are former Westernizers disappointed by the West's inability to accommodate Russia's perceptions and for whom the West no longer holds appeal as a convincing path of development. Echoing the founding fathers of Eurasianism, Sergey Karaganov vividly expresses the feeling that Russia has taken a "Eurasian *exit* [*vykhod*] from the European crisis."[49] Russia's anticolonial narrative should not therefore be seen as a new creation from scratch: it has its roots in the era even before the Soviet narrative, in the Eurasianist interpretation of Europe's epistemological imperialism (see chapter 12).

Depending on how Russia positions itself toward Europe or the West, the concept of Eurasia allows for several possible strategic narratives. If Russia claims it initially wanted to follow Europe's path of development, then the "Eurasian turn" is Russia's response to what it perceives as the political, economic, and cultural failure of Europe. If Russia wants to present itself as Europe's savior, then Eurasia is a messianic project that will rescue Europe from its own liberal demons and absorb it under the Eurasian "healthy conservatism" umbrella. Last but not least, if Russia wants to position itself as the anti-West, then Eurasia is interpreted as Russia's counterhegemonic strategy for challenging the Western neocolonial order and approaching the Global South. As Alexander Panarin asserts,

> The Eurasianist project is postmodern, and in this way, it is reminiscent of the neoconservative wave in the West. It manifests in a kind of "revenge of the provinces," a rehabilitation of the values of rootedness. It does not distinguish between regional cultures in a hierarchical fashion (separating them into "modern" and "non-modern" ones) but perceives them from the point of view of an inalienable diversity that is valuable in and of itself.[50]

This conceptual premise of "decentering" is rooted in the idea that Eurasia represents a specific model of civilization whose definition of pluralism diverges from the conventional European or Western one. Panarin offers the crispest formulation of this idea. According to him, there are two forms of pluralism: the one embodied by the Roman Empire, and the other represented by the Athenian republic. The Greek republican model, which is the one preferred by modern Europe, understands democracy in the narrow and mechanical sense of statistical representation, advancing what Panarin calls a "democratic racism" that limits democracy to its polity's own members while undemocratically imposing its value system on those outside of the community.[51] The West would thus uphold pluralism for individuals but promote a hegemonic approach to relations between nations. The Roman imperial model, preferred by Russia, takes the opposite approach: it does not give rights to individuals but retains them for the collective, thereby fostering a more fair and equal democracy for all nations. To quote Panarin, in the Roman imperial model, "The principle of cultural pluralism, as well as attention to and tolerance for different ethno-cultural experiences, is combined with a monist political authority that tolerates no opposition."[52]

Whether explicitly or implicitly, the perception that Russia offers a non-European or non-Western form of pluralism permeates every iteration of Eurasia. For radical theoreticians like Dugin, this confirms that an imperial and autocratic model is the only viable option for the country against both the idea of a nation-state and that of a democratic model. For the pragmatic experts in charge of promoting the notion of Greater Eurasia, the contrast is not between republic and empire but between liberal and illiberal values in favor of a supposed "sovereign democracy," as expressed by Vladislav Surkov. The partnership between Russia and China, which share a narrative of state sovereignty and noninterference (even if Moscow has violated it several times), provides a new framework for revisiting Panarin's statement. Sergey Karaganov, for instance, presents Greater Eurasia as advocating "the rights of every people and country to choose their own path of development and way of life," while guaranteeing "freedom from external interference" and a genuine "cultural pluralism."[53]

Another, secondary assumption is that the world order is structured by a binary division. For classical Eurasianists, inspired by German geopolitics, the binary opposes maritime and land-based empires (referred to as thalassocracies and tellurocracies, respectively). The maritime mode of development (exemplified by Britain and later by the US) is marked by the predominance of representative democracies, economic and trade relations, as well as by the flattening of the cultures that it dominates (thus overlapping with Panarin's Athenian republican model). The continental mode of development is defined by a more autocratic vision of power which believes that ideas shape reality more than economic issues do and advances a more equalizing vision of other cultures (overlapping with Panarin's Roman imperial model).

Refurbished by the works of Carl Schmitt and his theory of *Großraum*,[54] proponents of Eurasia today believe in a "continental geopolitics" that would oppose the Atlantic-led liberal world order—a theme common both to Alexander Dugin, who constructs a radical, aggressive, and metaphysical version of this idea, and to supporters of the Greater Eurasia concept, who advocate a more moderate and realist version. Fyodor Lyukanov notes, for instance, that a new bipolar world order is emerging between "a collective Trans-Atlantic (which encompasses part of the Pacific Ocean) and the collective Central Eurasia."[55] It should be noted that while this geopolitical binary could easily be replicated in the moral realm, it has rarely been explicitly articulated by the Kremlin. The potential to frame Eurasia in ideological terms to make conservative morality a cause for integration—mostly by speaking a conservative language to the Central Asian and South Caucasian states—has not really taken root. While the ROC and Russia's Islamic institutions do regularly mention their shared values on morality against the decadent West, the Russian state's language has only rarely deployed this argument in its Eurasianist language or its partnership with China.

The fluid repertoire of Eurasia has been used and overused in Russia, from Dugin's prolific writings and its international visibility among the global far right to the Kremlin's malleable projections of power around the Eurasian Union, the Eurasian Economic Union, and Greater Eurasia. Eurasia's plasticity contributed to the popular success of the term, the usage of which has steadily grown in the Russian media space, first slowly in the 2000s, then more prominently after 2011 once it become one of Putin's pet projects, before reaching a second set of high points in 2018–20 and with the full-scale war in Ukraine.

All Eurasia-related formulas draw on a core projection: that of a non-Western, essentialist, multinational Russia with a concentric periphery or sphere of influence and some forms of permeability to Asia. As Samuel Sorokin explains, "By fixing local identities around ethnic, religious, cultural and geographic parameters, the nature of Eurasian multiculturalism is disproportionally built around the defense of the cultural boundaries within, and of the Eurasian collective against the outside world."[56]

Yet there are also numerous semantic gaps. No official text about the Eurasian Union mentions Eurasianism as an ideology. If the founding fathers were all republished with large print runs at the beginning of the 1990s—as were all the authors of the Silver Age and the interwar émigré culture—they enjoy success only in terms of prestige. In Kremlin circles, Troubetzkoy and Savitsky were never on Putin's communication gurus' list of "must-read" or "must-quote" authors. However, the president seems to have some personal affection for Gumilev: he has mentioned him several times in relation to Russia's multiethnic character, especially with reference to Gumilev's "passionarity" concept.[57] In 2023, at a meeting with war correspondents (*voenkory*), Putin declared, for instance: Western nations "have no passionarity, they are fading nations, that's the whole problem. But we have passionarity."[58] As for Dugin, even the officialization of the Eurasian Union or of the Greater Eurasia did not bring him an official status: "Eurasia" has largely escaped his grasp and has taken on a life of its own with more influential figures such as Sergey Glazyev and Sergey Karaganov.

Hence the paradoxical destiny of a movement, Eurasianism, that contributed to shaping Russian intellectual life in the twentieth century, but which is today both central and yet forgotten. The more "Eurasia" invades Russia's public space, from popular culture to state policies, the more forgetful of its Eurasianist founding ideological origins it seems to become. At the level of metapolitics, Eurasia continues to circulate as a successful concept among the international far right due to Dugin's ability to reach out to different audiences.

However, in the post-Soviet space, the term is retreating: the aspirational Eurasian Union began to lose its meaning since 2014, beginning with the conflict in Ukraine, and even more so with Russia's full-scale war since 2022. Countries from Central Asia and the South Caucasus have shifted to a much more open decolonizing mindset toward Russia, and in such a context, any form of Russia-led regional project sounds like a revamped imperialism. The EAEU still functions but has limited the scope of its activities to trade and customs issues, and now appears to be a mere technical project with no broader conceptual reach. One of the many paradoxes of Russia's war in Ukraine is thus to have killed off the legitimacy of the notion of Eurasia in the so-called Eurasian space. Yet the semantic space for Eurasia still exists in relation to China, and Asia will likely be the main and only space left in which it can be successfully deployed. With the war in Ukraine, Eurasia as a regional sphere of influence has largely retreated, to be replaced by Eurasia as a multipolar international positioning.

ELEVEN

THE RUSSIAN WORLD
From Messianism to Irredentism

> The notion of Russian World extends far from Russia's geographical borders and even far from the borders of the Russian ethnicity.
> VLADIMIR PUTIN, World Congress of Compatriots, 2001[1]

AS WITH EURASIA, the concept of "Russian World" (*russkii mir*) is fundamentally blurry by design, allowing for multiple interpretations.[2] Yet unlike Eurasia, it does not feature a spatial core that would unify at least minimally its divergent interpretations, making its semantic overstretch even greater. The concept has been deployed in three directions: as a repertoire of soft power for Russia to brand itself in the world; as a repertoire of spheres of influence to justify what Russia considers to be its right to oversee the evolution of the so-called near abroad; and as a repertoire of the "divided nation" to justify irredentism, especially toward Ukraine. Rooted in the intellectual history of the 1990s, the concept quickly spread into the political lexicon in the 2000s, eventually becoming a central justification of Russian aggression against Ukraine. To highlight the term's multiple meanings, one has to remember that the notion of *world* should be understood in its ancient sense of *realm*—as a kingdom, a civilization, and a sphere of interest. The Russian *world/realm* therefore shares similarities with the notion of empire, and this imperial nature can be expressed with different political objectives: to assert a specific voice in the concert of nations, to lay claim to the geopolitical loyalty of one's neighbors, or to expand borders to include those considered as part of the realm.

THE RUSSIAN WORLD AS MARKETING AND PHILOSOPHICAL BRAND

The concept of the Russian World was born in the 1990s among an intellectually vivid network of mild and pro-government conservative thinkers, all connected to the methodologists and to Gleb Pavlovsky's Foundation for Effective Politics. The concept can then claim multiple intellectual fathers, from Petr Shchedrovitsky (son of the Methodological Circle's founder, Georgy Shchedrovitsky), to Sergey Chernyshev, Yury Krupnov, Sergey Gradirovsky, and to Pavlovsky himself. The concept is also related to the Soviet historian and philosopher Mikhail Gefter (1918–1995), whom Pavlovsky credits with being the first, around 1993, to theorize the notion of the Russian World as a postnational formation similar to a civilization, a structure of several "Russian states" maintaining their irreducible differences from other civilizations.[3]

In 1995, Pavlovsky created what became known as the Russian Institute, which had as its declared mission "the recreation of the Russian as the new" (*vossozdanie russkogo kak novogo*), or in other words, "the collection of personal ideas and individual spiritual findings to found a new Russian consensus."[4] In the Russian Institute's manifesto, Pavlovsky and his colleague Sergey Chernyshev criticized the taboo around the term "Russian" (*russkii*) and the inability to speak serenely about Russian national consciousness (*russkoe samosoznanie*).[5] In order to fill this gap, the institute gave birth to the *Russian Journal*, a high-quality web publishing platform that helped revive the debate on Russian identity. This platform would inspire many additional online media projects and serve as an incubator for a large number of young nationalist-minded publicists, thinkers, and journalists.

In late 1997, Shchedrovitsky and his colleague Efim Ostrovsky authored the paper "An Eagle Spreads Its Wings: 1,111 Signs in 1,111 Days before the New Millennium. Manifesto for a New Generation."[6] In it, they addressed the concept of "Russia's World" (*mir Rossii*), described as a consensual reestablishment of Russia's identity and its reconnection with its past and its diasporas. In Shchedrovitsky's vision, Russia's self-reinvention and globalization could only succeed if the country reintegrated the brightest parts of its identity and intellectual production that had been shaped abroad during the interwar emigration.

The 1997 text spoke of *Russia's World*, not yet of a *Russian World*. It was not until 1999 that the concept emerged in its current form in a new article by the same authors, "Russia: The Country that Does Not Exist," which bore the revealing subtitle, "To Create the Image of Russia Today Is to Create New Connections [*sviazi*] among Russians."[7] The text reads like a manifesto inspired by Gleb Pavlovsky on the necessity for the country to construct an image (*imidzh*) for itself. Aware that they were introducing foreign terms and concepts to the Russian public, the authors explained that the country needed a brand as understood in the sense of "humanitarian technologies" (*gumanitarnye tekhnologii*), then moved on to the more explicit phrasing of "public relations development" (*razvitie obshchestvennykh sviazei*).[8] As a result, the notion of the Russian World has, since its birth, been associated with the idea of a brand for Russia. In their 1999 article, Shchedrovitsky and Ostrovsky elaborated on their definition of the Russian World:

> Over the course of the twentieth century, following tectonic historical shifts, world wars and revolutions, a Russian World was created on Earth—a network of small and large communities, thinking and speaking in Russian. It is not a secret that the territory of the Russian Federation contains only half of this Russian World. The state formation created on the territory of the Russian Federation at the turn of the 1990s did not turn out to be an adequate means for incorporating Russian society into the global historical process... This process of social degradation (the collapse of the Soviet Union) has been compensated for by the formation, over the course of the twentieth century, of a sizable Russian diaspora in the world.[9]

The tone of the article invites readers to move away from a pessimistic view of the Soviet collapse toward a positive view of Russia's transformations and its ability to embrace the future without anxiety. In conclusion, the article highlights the innovative character of the Russian World as a sign of a new, globalized Russia: "A Russian World in a Peaceful World (*russkii mir v mire mirov*), attracting Russians from all over the world to participate in a new global meta-project."[10] The "meta" aspect of the project should not be interpreted as territorial expansion—on the contrary: by taking stock of its diasporas spread all around the world and its fragmented identity, Russia will be able to enter a globalized era of *deterritorialization*. Russian diasporas being better adapted to globalization, and many of them already Europeans, would therefore represent an optimistic developmental path for the country on the whole. As one of the elaborators of this concept, Sergey Gradirovsky, has stated: "Russia has shrunk in order for the Russian Archipelago to expand, for the Russian World to spread."[11]

Shchedrovitsky himself has recontextualized the birth of the concept: he recounted how it had appeared between 1993 and 1997, "gradually crystallizing from a proto-concept, an amorphous sentiment, to a complete concept."[12] He recalled that the term itself was born at the beginning of 1998, after the Foundation for Effective Politics was commissioned to write a concept paper for Russia's CIS policy. "It was the first time that the hypothesis that . . . a similar number of Russians live inside Russia's borders and beyond them was mentioned. . . . The idea of the Russian World was the conceptual backbone of this document. And one month earlier, this idea was presented in our article 'An Eagle Spreads Its Wings.'"[13] In this interview, Shchedrovitsky added a new element to his definition of the Russian World: it is shaped not only by a shared destiny but by a common language, as language structures the mental world of its speakers. He insisted once again on globalization as the driver of Russia's transformation and reinvention: "The Russian World is the means, the instrument to make Russia and the Russian Federation adapt to globalization. Small countries adapt themselves by letting globalization into them; large ones do so by entering the space of globalization."[14]

Two central conclusions can be drawn from this brief analysis of the genesis of the Russian World concept. First, the term Russian/*russkii* (and not Rossian/*rossiiskii*) was at the center of the project on which Pavlovsky and his circle were working in 1995 when they launched the Russian Institute. These individuals were far from ethnonationalists who sought an ethnically pure, minority-free Russia; their definition of "Russian" was not understood as having an ethnocentric character. Still, they did not use the term Rossian/*rossiiskii*, which was overly reminiscent of the Yeltsin political project and its limits. A *rossiiskaia* Russia called to mind a failed liberal ideology, the inability of Russia to be proud of its identity, and the diffuse impression of cloning what the West wanted Russia to be. Unlike Yeltsin's project, Pavlovsky, Chernyshev, and Shchedrovitsky's *russkaia* Russia was called to offer a particular Russian voice, as well as one that would be that of a modern and globalized nation-state.[15] Their goal of overhauling national identity sought to be more broadly encompassing, sketching out a future Russia that would be in dialogue with the world.

Second, the architects of the Russian World were all passionate about Russian philosophy, eager to rediscover Vladimir Soloviev and Nikolay Berdyaev among many others. At the same time, they were specialists in marketing and branding. This merging of genres proved to be a successful mix. It allowed them—just as it has allowed the Presidential Administration since—to combine theoretical and practical talents to shape information: the marketing techniques that Pavlovsky introduced to Russia have since been successfully mastered by generations of "polit-technologists." The genealogical origins of the Russian World are thus characterized by this dual feature that dates back to the birth of the idea: in a marketing sense, it is a brand for establishing Russia's voice in the chorus of nations, but it is also a vessel for a more philosophical or even messianic vision which believes that Russia's message to the world is one of universal value.

THE RUSSIAN WORLD AS SPHERE OF INFLUENCE

While the first genealogy of the concept of the Russian World did not originally stress the presence of Russian or Russian-speaking diasporas in post-Soviet countries, the fact that one of its first iterations was commissioned for Russia's CIS policy had already laid out the kind of overlapping that would take place. And indeed, there emerged a second genealogy of the Russian World, a more bureaucratic one, in which the Russian World became a tool for transitioning from a Russian *presence* in the world to a Russian *influence* over the "near abroad."

The concept of near abroad as a specific region of interest for Moscow was formed and expressed almost immediately after the collapse of the Soviet Union, despite the fact that the Kremlin then lacked the capacity to impose its foreign policy decisions. In 1992, then chairman of the parliamentary Joint Committee on International Affairs and Foreign Economic Relations, Yevgeny Ambartsumov, criticized Russian foreign minister Andrey Kozyrev for lacking a clear policy for the near abroad, explicitly noting: "As the internationally recognized legal successor to the USSR, the Russian Federation should base its foreign policy on a doctrine declaring the entire geopolitical space of the former Union to be the sphere of its vital interests (like the United States' Monroe Doctrine in Latin America) and should strive to achieve understanding and recognition from the world community of its special interests in this space."[16]

The privileged status of the near abroad in Russia's foreign policy grew under the prime ministership of Yevgeny Primakov, who stated that Moscow's attempt to regain its international status involved recovering its role as a center of influence over the post-Soviet space.[17] As early as June 2000, Putin formulated a new foreign policy for the federation that recognized the country's limited capacity and the need to give priority to the near abroad.[18] But it was the waves of color revolutions, particularly the 2004 Orange Revolution in Ukraine, which accelerated the Kremlin's obsession with retaking rhetorical—as well as other forms of—control over the region. Sergey Markov, a professor at the Moscow State Institute of International Relations (MGIMO) known for his role as one of the PR representatives of the regime, stated for instance that Russia had lost Georgia and Ukraine in 2003–4 because its "political technologies" were inferior to those of the West.[19]

The Kremlin's perception that it had been defeated in its own neighborhood had serious repercussions and revived Moscow's will to invest in soft power and image-making. The Presidential Directorate for Interregional and Cultural Relations, led by another influential "polit-technologist," Modest Kolerov, was charged with conceptualizing Russia's new policy toward the near abroad. It gradually became structured under the supervision of the Ministry of Foreign Affairs and its specialized agency, Rossotrudnichestvo (the Federal Agency for the Commonwealth of Independent States, Compatriots Living Abroad, and International Humanitarian Cooperation).[20]

State agencies working on Russia's presence in the near abroad use different concepts such as the Russian World, "compatriots," or "shared information space." In this sense, this second genealogy of the concept is about Russia's sphere of influence—the countries over which Moscow believes it has a right to have a say. This influence policy is based on an extremely wide spectrum of activities and options that can be summarized as follows, listed in order from hard to soft power: annexing territories (Crimea in 2014 and the four occupied territories of eastern Ukraine in September 2022); supporting secessionist regions (Transnistria in Moldova, South Ossetia and Abkhazia in Georgia, Donbas in Ukraine, and in a more complex way, the Nagorno-Karabakh region in Azerbaijan, at least until 2020); promoting regional integration structures (among many failed attempts, the only survivors of which are the Collective Security Treaty Organization and the Eurasian Economic Union); fostering economic investments in key sectors such as energy, infrastructure, and agribusiness so that countries remain economically tied to Russia; launching a generous citizenship policy that allows post-Soviet citizens to acquire a Russian passport quite easily (including distributing passports in secessionist regions); and investing in culture, media, and public diplomacy outreach to Russia-friendly populations.[21]

As previously noted, the need to create a global brand for Russia was present from the very inception of the Russian World concept. Russia's strategy of embracing globalization reached its zenith during Putin's second term and Medvedev's presidency. The country's economy was booming, and the authorities were confident in their rediscovered great-power capabilities and in the country's political and economic globalization. In 2004, the Kremlin launched the Valdai Club, a platform for dialogue among international experts on Russia. In 2007, it founded two Institutes for Democracy and Cooperation, in Paris and Berlin, to promote the notion of "sovereign democracy" crafted by Vladislav Surkov. The Public Diplomacy Foundation was launched in 2008 and the Russian International Affairs Council, another expert platform, in 2010. At the same time, Russia invested massive sums in its information space, launching multiple new media initiatives for Russian-speaking audiences and the international community such as the infamous Sputnik and RT.[22]

It was in such a moment of proliferation of new institutions representing Russia's branding strategies that the concept of Russian World reemerged. In 2006, in a speech at the Derzhavin House in St. Petersburg, Putin mentioned the concept, announcing that 2007 would be the year of the Russian language: "The Russian World can and should unite all those for whom the Russian language and culture are dear, whether they live in Russia or beyond its borders. Use this term, 'Russian World,' more often."[23] A few months later, the authorities established the Russian World Fund, whose leadership was given to a loyal intellectual apparatchik originally close to Pavlovsky, Vyacheslav Nikonov, head of the Politika Foundation.

The fund functions as an umbrella organization for about a dozen other institutions such as the Gorchakov Foundation, the Foundation for the Support of Compatriots, the Moscow House of Compatriots, the World Congress of Russian Compatriots, the International Union of Russian Compatriots, and the Institute of Russian Compatriots.[24] Its core activities relate to promotion of the Russian language and cultural, scientific, and educational exchanges (through Russian Houses and Russian Centers abroad), including the Russian state vision of the Second World War, along with the development of Russia's international aid programs. Indeed, the fund defines the Russian World as consisting of "not only Russians, not only Rossians, not only our compatriots in the near and far abroad, émigrés and their descendants. It also includes foreign citizens, speaking Russian, studying it, and all those who are honestly interested in Russia and care for its future. . . . In forming the Russian World as a global project, Russia is creating for itself a new identity, new possibilities for effective cooperation with the rest of the world, and new incentives for its own development."[25]

THE RUSSIAN WORLD AS IRREDENTISM

A third genealogy of the Russian World will have a more fatal destiny. As Petr Shchedrovitsky noted in his interview, the concept did not immediately convince those who had commissioned it for Russia's CIS policy, who sought a more ethnocentric narrative. As early as 2000, Sergey Gradirovsky, one of the cocreators of the concept with Shchedrovitsky, summed up this tension, criticizing the authorities' vacillation between an ethnocentric defense of fellow ethnic Russians abroad and what he called, borrowing from Dostoyevsky, the "Russian universal" (*russkoe vsemirnoe*).[26] And indeed, the first official use of the term by Vladimir Putin in a speech before the first World Congress of Compatriots Living Abroad in 2001 contained all the ambivalences that would later became so obvious: "Since time immemorial, the notion of the 'Russian World' has grown far from the geographical border of Russia, and even from the borders of the Russian ethnos."[27] Ethnicity and territory, which were not part of the first genealogy of the concept, were then given priority.

To understand why an ethnocentric and territorialized reading of the Russian World won out in official state usage, it is helpful to follow the trajectory of a competing concept: that of the "compatriot" (*sootechestvennik*), itself intimately connected to the notion of the "Russian Question" (*russkii vopros*). The latter's term was coined by Nobel Prize for Literature laureate Alexander Solzhenitsyn in his famous 1994 work, *The Russian Question at the End of the 20th Century*, which followed his 1990 essay, "How Shall We Organize Russia?"[28] According to the dissident writer, the Soviet experiment alienated Russia from itself not only ideologically but territorially: as Russia's domination over the South Caucasus and Central Asia is the fruit of a sick imperial expansion, Moscow should let these regions go their own way in order to resume privileged links with Belarus, Ukraine, and northern Kazakhstan, which should be united in a single state of Eastern Slavs:

> And now, when those twelve [other former Soviet republics] are gone, the only thing that remains is what can be called Rus', as it has been called for a long time (the word "Russian" has embraced the Little Russian, the Great Russians and Belarusians for centuries), or Russia (the name from the 18th century), or, in the right sense now: Russian Union.[29]

The idea of a triune nation of Russians, Ukrainians, and Belarusians was originally coined by Russian tsarist authorities in the mid-nineteenth century to oppose Polish and then Ukrainian nationalism in the western borderlands of the empire. With *The Russian Question*, Solzhenitsyn gave intellectual expression to a worldview that was already present in Russia's political landscape at that time, embodied by the Congress of Russian Communities, led by Dmitry Rogozin (a future Russian ambassador to NATO and deputy prime minister responsible for the military-industrial complex).[30] In the landscape of opponents to Yeltsin's liberalism, the Congress established its own distinctive voice: it did not call for a pure and simple restoration of the Soviet Union like the Communist Party was doing, nor for rebuilding imperial influence across the entire post-Soviet territory like Zhirinovsky's LDPR did. Rather, it called for protecting ethnic Russian minorities abroad and, if possible, for modifying borders in order to integrate Belarus, Transnistria, eastern Ukraine, and northern Kazakhstan into the Russian Federation.[31]

The Congress claimed "the right of the Russian nation to unification in a united state on its historical territory, to the rebirth of the fatherland's great power, to well-being, and to the development of all the peoples of Russia."[32] Despite its failure in the 1995 parliamentary elections, it left behind a considerable political heritage. Its "Manifesto of Russia's Rebirth" and "Declaration of the Rights of Compatriots" directly influenced the first official texts the Duma adopted on the subject. In 1997, a bill on Russia's policy toward compatriots was the first to define precise rights for these individuals, but it was vetoed by Yeltsin. A new bill, "On the Russian Federation's Policy in Its Relations with Foreign Compatriots," passed in 1999 even if the text did not put forward any legally binding definition of compatriots.[33]

Vladimir Putin's rise to the presidency in 2000 created a new dynamic for the compatriot issue. From his first months in power, the president decried the demographic danger that was creeping up on Russia and threatening it with extinction. In 2001, the government adopted the Concept on the Demographic Development of Russia for 2001–15, which defined immigration as one of the country's priorities. A new plan, the Principal Directions of the Federation toward Compatriots Living Abroad, outlined for the first time the range of possible actions that Russia could take on the issue of its compatriots. The document simultaneously played the card of defending Russians abroad and that of their repatriation for demographic and workforce-related reasons. A new policy infrastructure around "compatriots" was born that would later merge with the concept of the Russian World.

As with other concepts, "compatriot" was intended to remain fuzzy in terms of citizenship.[34] As early as 2001, Putin insisted on its fluidity: "The compatriot is not only a legal category. More importantly, it is not an issue of status or favoritism. It is primarily a matter of personal choice. Of self-identification. I would even say, of spiritual self-identification."[35] The term indeed encompasses several concentric circles. According to the 1999 federal law, "compatriots" can be both Russian expatriate citizens, a broader group of people who are culturally and spiritually oriented toward Russia (a formulation that prevents a purely ethnic or linguistic definition of ethnic Russians), an even larger group of all Soviet peoples and people who were part of the tsarist empire (according to which definition citizens of Poland and Finland could apply for compatriot status), as well as all "fellow travelers" who identify with the fate of Russia.

The main programmatic result of the concept of "compatriot" has been the Program of State Assistance for Voluntary Travel of Compatriots to Russia, launched in 2006.[36] The state agencies in charge of the program sought primarily to bring back expatriate citizens as well as those with dual citizenship, whether they lived in the near or far abroad. The implicit model was that of Israel, with the hope that many successful second- or third-generation emigrants would reinvest in Russia and engage in industrial and technological transfers. In reality, the program garnered interest almost exclusively among the most impoverished segments of Russian or Russian-speaking society from within the CIS, mostly in Central Asia and the South Caucasus.[37]

Moreover, the state-sponsored repatriation program came, by and large, too late: the majority of those who wished to settle in Russia had already done so on their own in the early 1990s, while those who remained abroad were now relatively well integrated into their host societies. On top of all this, the program has been very inefficient, especially when it comes to the job and housing opportunities to be provided by regional authorities. Between 2006 and 2022, the repatriation program brought back only about one million people[38]: what looked on paper like a huge pool of tens of millions of people who could contribute to Russia's demographic and economic revival did not take into consideration the fact that many people identified as Russians were not interested in operationalizing this identity to the point of returning to a symbolic home.

If the strategy of reunification of the divided nation through repatriation did not succeed, the irredentist reading thereof grew into an official argument justifying Russia's aggression toward Ukraine. It was seen by the political establishment as Russia's reinterpretation of the UN "Responsibility to Protect" principle, which allows foreign intervention in the name of human rights. Such a parallel was explicitly invoked to justify Russia's interventions in South Ossetia and Abkhazia in 2008, and in Ukraine in 2014 and 2022, each of which was presented as a humanitarian mission aimed at rescuing ethnic Russians, Russian-speakers, or nations friendly to Russia. In his famous March 18, 2014, speech in front of both Duma and Federation Council to announce the annexation of Crimea, Putin declared that "the Russian nation [has become] one of the biggest, if not the biggest, ethnic groups in the world to be divided by borders."[39] With this formula, the Kremlin officially recognized the gap between Russia's legal and imagined national body. Putin asserted: "Millions of Russians and Russian-speaking people live in Ukraine and will continue to do so. Russia will always defend their interests using political, diplomatic, and legal means. But it should be above all in Ukraine's own interest to ensure that these people's rights and interests are fully protected. This is the guarantee of Ukraine's state stability and territorial integrity."[40] Read today, this last point emphasizes the security threat to Ukraine in case of what Moscow would interpret as a lack of respect toward Russian "compatriots."

A month later, commenting on the situation in Donbas, Putin emphasized Russia's relationship to Russian-speakers and Russians abroad, which hits more of an emotive register, playing on an essentially ethnic and/or linguistic sense of nationalism.[41] And around the same time, Kremlin press secretary Dmitry Peskov similarly proclaimed: "Russia is the country that underlies the Russian World, and the president of that country is Putin; Putin himself is the main guarantor of the security of the Russian world."[42] Yet the concept was not fully rigidified in this irredentist position at that time. For instance, minister of foreign affairs Sergey Lavrov, responding to the Lithuanian media in early 2015, advanced a definition of the Russian World that moved the concept from the realm of irredentism to that of cultural diplomacy:

> You began by saying that everyone is afraid of Russia's desire to reestablish the Soviet Union, to seek the reunification of Russian lands. I ask, if you have concrete sources, to show me the official Russian citations proposing to reestablish the Soviet Union or reunify the Russian world [*sobirat' russkii mir*]. The Russian world—it is totally different. The Russian world is about culture, language, values, and religious orientations. One can draw an analogy (albeit imperfectly) with the Francophonie, the Ibero-American community, and Confucius, Goethe, or Cervantes institutes. . . . Like any normal country [we] wish to preserve [our] cultural heritage.[43]

This reading of Russian World has thus zigzagged between a vague definition of compatriots that avoids overly legally binding boundaries and an irredentist interpretation of it. But irredentism has found other semantic spaces in which to express itself, such as "Donbas" and "Novorossiya." The use of "Novorossiya" has been documented since the end of the eighteenth century, designating the regions north of the Black Sea that Catherine the Great won from the Ottoman Empire during the Russo-Turkish wars of 1768–74. In the nineteenth century, Novorossiya was the name of the general governorate in Odesa, a term that survived up to the 1926 census, which grouped under the Novorossiya label Odesa, Mykolaiv, Kirovohrad, Dnipropetrovsk, Kherson, Zaporizhzhia, Donetsk, and Luhansk, the oblasts which today represent most of southern and eastern Ukraine.[44] It then disappeared from use before reemerging briefly in 1994 among Transnistrian separatists who wanted to substantiate their rights to join the Russian Federation.[45]

Putin's first use of the term "Novorossiya" dates from his April 17, 2014 speech, when he described the situation of the Russian-speaking population of Ukraine:

> I would like to remind you that what was called Novorossiya [New Russia] back in the tsarist days—Kharkov, Lugansk, Donetsk, Kherson, Nikolayev, and Odessa—were not part of Ukraine back then. These territories were given to Ukraine in the 1920s by the Soviet government. Why? Who knows. They were won by Potemkin and Catherine the Great in a series of well-known wars. The center of that territory was Novorossiysk, so the region is called Novorossiya. Russia lost these territories for various reasons, but the people remained.[46]

Outside of presidential speeches, "Novorossiya" became widely used to describe the eastern Ukrainian territories whose destiny would be to reunite with Russia. Donbas secessionist authorities used the term too: in May 2014, the self-proclaimed Donetsk and Luhansk People's Republics decided to form a new "Union of Novorossiya." In August of the same year, Putin issued a statement labeled on the Kremlin.ru website "To the militia of Novorossiya," but the actual text of the speech itself does not use that specific phrasing, instead unassumingly mentioning "the representatives of Donbas."[47]

Since then, the semantic space of Novorossiya has displayed multiple, often overlapping, ideological colors. The first, which I have called red, can be defined as post-Soviet, in the sense that it uses Novorossiya to reformulate Russia's great-power status and socialist messianism. The second one, white, is inspired by tsarist nostalgia and the reactivation of ultraconservative Orthodox circles. The third one, brown, comes from the European fascist tradition and claims that Novorossiya will be the battleground that gives birth to a new revolution that will overthrow the current regimes.[48] The concept of Novorossiya has also circulated through a more bottom-up dynamic, with the rapid growth of social media and websites linked to it, all revamping older formulations of Eastern Slavic nationalism.[49] A related but never used in official contexts was the notion of the "Russian Spring" (*russkaia vesna*), which was deployed mostly by the radical imperial and nationalist fringes: with its much more contentious overtones, "Russian Spring" enthusiasts hoped to transform Russian ethnonationalism into a political force capable of shaking up the regime, a process that was swiftly repressed by the Kremlin.

In the semantic continuum between the Russian World, compatriots, Novorossiya, and Donbas, one can notice some discrepancies as shown in figure 11.1. Putin has only used the term "Russian World" episodically, in 2007 during its official launching and then in 2014–15, with no visible increase over time. He mentions "Novorossiya" only a few times per year; "compatriots" has consistently been used around twenty times per year; and only "Donbas," previously modest, has jumped dramatically with the full-scale invasion.

FIG. 11.1. Mentions of "Russian World," "compatriots," "Donbas," and "Novorossiya" in presidential speeches, 2000–2023.

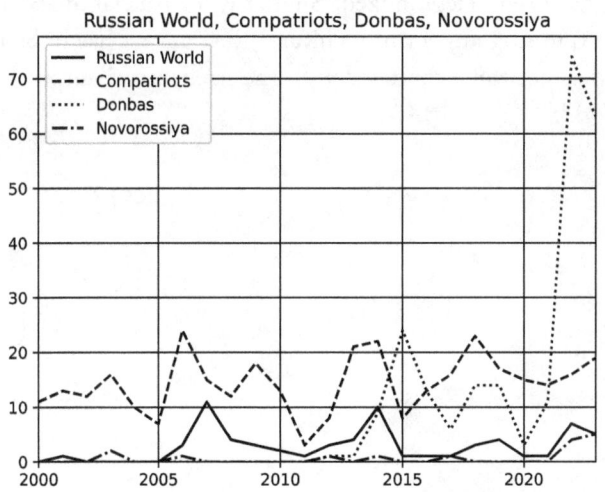

Source: Author's compilation based on Kremlin.ru.

The Russian World concept relies on three different genealogies that are intertwined but do not completely overlap. One, born of a blending of philosophy and marketing techniques, conceives of the Russian World as Russia's entrée into the globalized world by making the best use of its already fragmented and diasporic, deterritorialized identity. A second one, more bureaucratic, has interpreted the Russian World as a reflection of Russia's sphere of influence over its near abroad, and in this case the term intersects with the notion of Eurasia as Moscow's projection of power over its neighbors. A third one, more ethnocentric and territorialized, reads the Russian World as the solution to Russia's status as a divided nation, as visibly crystallized in the conflict over Ukraine. Over the years, the Donbas (and to a lesser extent, Novorossiya) gradually became the quintessential example of this divided-nation status and the need for Moscow to fight—politically, and then literally in the military sense—for the defense of its "compatriots" in Ukraine.

This third, fatal interpretation has definitively colored the other two. The Methodological Circle has been, for instance, accused by Russian liberals of having inspired the war intellectually and bureaucratically.[50] More pragmatically, countries from Central Asia and the South Caucasus, while not interested in severing ties with Moscow and applying Western sanctions, have all tried to keep their distance from Russia in the field of cultural influence, accelerating the end of what was left of the post-Soviet order. The Russian World as Russia's sphere of influence, even more so than the concept of Eurasia, has been delegitimized. Similarly, for Russian diasporas around the world, expressing any form of cultural Russianness has to be negotiated carefully, so as not to be conflated with the irredentist interpretation of the Russian World.

TWELVE

ANTICOLONIALISM
Russia as a Global South Power

[Western countries] do not wish us freedom but want to see us as a colony. They do not want equal cooperation but robbery. They do not want to see us a free society, but a crowd of slaves without souls.
VLADIMIR PUTIN, speech on the annexation of four Ukrainian territories, September 30, 2022[1]

WITH THE FULL-SCALE INVASION of Ukraine, the Russian leadership has reactivated another repertoire of Russia's great-power status: that of being an anticolonial force partnering with countries of the "Global South" (itself a contested notion) to oppose Western hegemony. This strategic narrative is rooted in a long-standing political tradition, that of Soviet anti-imperialist rhetoric. It can also rely on an intellectual tradition going back to the nineteenth century of seeing Russia as having been colonized by Europe, as theorized by the founding fathers of Eurasianism in the 1920s and rearticulated by Russian nationalist dissidents in the Soviet Union in the 1960s–1980s. This anti-imperialist language can therefore benefit from a powerful hold on the imagination of Russian society.

On the international scene, it has met with mixed success: depending on whether one considers the glass half-full or half-empty, one might observe either (a) that Moscow has lost part of its appeal in many societies of the Global South and was widely condemned at the UN General Assembly for the invasion of Ukraine, or (b) that about forty countries still abstained from that General Assembly vote and frame a "positive neutrality" toward Russia and that Moscow has since benefitted from the refusal of the whole non-Western world to apply sanctions.[2]

Unlike the two previous repertoires of Russia's great-power status, the anticolonial one does not imply a Russia whose symbolic boundaries would exceed its legal, territorial borders. It is the only repertoire that is universalistic, in the sense that it is not designed to apply to only one region or group of people: there are no Eurasian spheres of influence, compatriots, or post-imperial regional identity to defend. For once, there is no need for Russia to be a regional hegemon in order to be recognized as a great power: the anticolonial repertoire is genuinely worldwide in scope. It allows Russia to present itself not as a *great* power but as a *global* power—a nuance that matters. It is also the repertoire most anchored in mainstream modernity, encapsulated in a language of economic partnership, shared technologies, and prosperity. It combines leftist undertones surrounding the idea of worldwide social justice with illiberal accents of conservative values to be defended: the decolonization of the world order would indeed avoid "imposing destructive neoliberal ideological orientations contrary to traditional spiritual-moral values" on non-Western civilizations.[3]

Seen from the outside, the core paradox of this anticolonial repertoire is, obviously, Russia's own imperial tone toward its peripheries—a paradox that is nothing new. During the Cold War decades, the socialist Second World justified itself as supporting the developing Third World in its struggle against imperialism from the capitalist First World, while at the same time dominating Central and Eastern Europe. A similar triangle is repeating itself today: Russia is both a country from the Global North still dealing with its imperial mindset, and a country that presents itself as allied with the Global South, resisting the neo-imperialism of what has now become, in the Russian state language, the "collective West."[4] As we can learn from Global South perspectives, Russia's counterhegemonic language against Western domination makes enough sense to be able to partly obfuscate its own local imperialism.

COLONIZED RUSSIA: AN ENDURING FEATURE IN RUSSIA'S INTELLECTUAL TRADITION

The idea of Russia being colonized by the West and having self-colonized has broad roots and has shaped a large part of Russia's political and intellectual history. This tension was already captured by the nineteenth-century historian Vasily Klyuchevsky (1841–1911) in a crisp manner: "The history of Russia is a history of the country, which is colonizing itself. The area of colonization here has been expanding together with its state territory. Sometimes slowing and sometimes rising, this movement is still going on."[5] Russian elites perceived the country as caught between two Others: Europe's status of referential center, and the East's status of being a periphery. In such an in-between situation, they tended to share the idea that the European Other emulated by Russia is still more dangerous than the Eastern Other that it hopes to civilize.[6]

This self-colonization generated two deep-seated visions of Russia by its intellectual elites. First, the interpretation of Russia as colonized by the West through its own elites: at the core of Slavophile thinking lay the idea of the Russian imperial elite being so Westernized that they were disconnected from the real people and forced the whole country to accept foreign values.[7] Peter the Great encapsulates this ambivalence: the Russian emperor brought modernity to Russia and opened it up to Europe, but through top-down, authoritarian methods of "deculturing" the ancient Muscovite elite to force the adoption of European norms and values. As early as 1845, the leading thinker of the Slavophile school, Alexey Khomiakov, denounced the colonizing character of the European Enlightenment in Russia: he saw an acculturation to Europe in the reforms of Peter the Great and their adoption by cosmopolitan Russian elites ("European eclectics") disconnected from the grassroots.[8] A similar perception was expressed by the first generation of *Narodniki* (Populists), inviting nascent urban intellectuals to "go to the people" to rediscover their own Russianness, a push continued by leftists, socialists, anarchists, and conservative *pochvenniki*, as well as Leo Tolstoy's followers.[9]

Second, there is the interpretation of Russia's imperial expansion as an answer to the country's relationship to Europe. The Russian authorities colonized Siberia, the South Caucasus, and Central Asia in the name of a European civilization to be exported to backward nations. Simultaneously, Russia was presented in Europe as a retrograde civilization shaped by Mongol domination. This painful contradiction was grasped in a crude way by Fyodor Dostoyevsky: "In Europe we were hangers-on and slaves, while in Asia we shall be the masters. In Europe we have been Tatars, in Asia it will be our turn to be Europeans."[10] In the late nineteenth century, the Russian authorities even supported a narrative of Aryanness, through which the conquest of Central Asia was presented as the return of the prodigal Slavic son to his civilizational cradle in the steppe world and as victory against the archaism of Turkic nations.[11]

Yet one would have to wait for the catharsis of the Bolshevik Revolution to see Russia's colonial status with regard to Europe entirely reconsidered. This deconstruction came from the Eurasianist circles: in 1920—that is, a year before the famous edited volume *Exodus to the East* and the formation of the movement as such—Prince Troubetzkoy published *Europe and Mankind*. While at this point the author did not yet advocate the idea of Eurasian unity, he did endeavor to deny the West or Europe any universal value. "My book does not have the ambition to put forward concrete positive and directive principles. It must only help to overthrow certain idols and, after confronting the reader with empty pedestals, force him to rack his brains for a solution."[12] By applying its own concepts to the rest of the world, he argued, Europe obfuscates the diversity of civilizations and establishes a benchmark for measuring political and economic backwardness. However, Europe does not represent a *state* of development that all nations must reach, but a specific *mode* of development that cannot be reproduced.[13] Seen through the historicist Western prism, Russia is a backward country; but the Eurasianists suggested that Russia should unlearn the West and perceive itself *geographically*.

The Eurasianist movement therefore aimed to put an end to the "cultural hegemony of the West" by asserting the superiority of the East.[14] It subscribed to a Third Worldism *avant la lettre*: Eurasianists were persuaded not only of non-Western cultures' right to differ but also, and above all, of their ultimate superiority and Europe's decline. This precursor to postcolonialism was always more intense in rejecting Europe than in engaging with Eastern cultures.[15] Still, it explains Eurasianism's partial alliance with Bolshevism: both united against the West, in sympathy with non-European cultures, and condemning the European experience *out of principle*. As Troubetzkoy wrote:

> Eurasianism agrees with Bolshevism in rejecting not just certain political forms, but the entire culture that existed in Russia immediately before the

revolution and continues to exist in the countries of the Romano-Germanic West, as well as in demanding a radical reconstruction of that entire culture. Eurasianism agrees with Bolshevism in its call for the liberation of the peoples of Asia and Africa who are enslaved by the colonial powers.[16]

Indeed, since its inception, Soviet internationalism favored anticolonial movements coming from European colonies. In 1923, at the Twelfth Congress of the Bolshevik Party, Nikolay Bukharin explained that "apart from the only consistent bearer of the Communist uprising, the European and American proletariat, hundreds of millions of the colonial and semi-colonial slaves are taking part in the fight."[17] Paralleling proletarians in the First World and colonized nations in the Third World became a structural element of Soviet internationalist language. In the post–Second World War period, the Soviet Union played a crucial role in supporting anti-imperial movements, both among countries that were fellow travelers of socialism and in the nonaligned world. The Soviet regime gradually developed rules of thumb to follow in deciding whether and how to assist the varied types of anti-imperialist and separatist movements.[18] Visible in Southeast Asia, Latin America, and to a lesser extent in the Middle East, this strategy was epitomized in the 1970s in the support offered to African revolutionary armed movements in the three Portuguese colonies of Angola, Mozambique, and Guinea-Bissau, and the backing of Nelson Mandela's African National Congress (ANC) in apartheid South Africa.[19]

As soon as the Khrushchev thaw allowed it in the second half of the 1950s, the debate about Russia's self-colonialism reappeared in public intellectual life. The theme of Russia being colonized by the West was actively advocated by the so-called Russian Party: for them, the Soviet experiment in itself, because it was inspired by a European ideology, Marxism, should be read as Western colonialism. This colonialism aimed to destroy Russia in three key domains: ruining the old Russian social fabric of estate (*soslovie*) hierarchy,[20] to be replaced by a Western-inspired urban modernity; annihilating Orthodox Christian faith through Western-inspired forms of secularism or atheism; and devastating Russia's nature by means of a Western-inspired industrial frenzy.[21] In different declensions, this language of colonization can also be identified in Solzhenitsyn's works, in the *derevenshchiki* movement (the village-prose literature of the late Soviet Union),[22] as well as among the more "red-brown" authors such as Alexander Prokhanov.

For Russian conservative and nationalist figures, the dismantling of the

Soviet Union by the Gorbachev-Yeltsin elites and the imposition of shock therapy by international financial institutions is interpreted as the culmination of this Western neocolonialism. In the 1990s, a dense network of illiberal civil society groups experimented with "decolonizing" practices around the ancient idea of *zemstvo*, the traditional Russian locally elected council. As Ivan Grek has explored, several conservative initiatives inspired by Alexander Solzhenitsyn used the language of right-wing postcolonialism, denouncing both the Soviet experiment and post-Soviet liberalism as forms of colonialism foisted on the Russian, pan-Slavic, Orthodox national self-consciousness.[23]

THE KREMLIN'S LATEST REPERTOIRE

This dual legacy, coming from the Slavophile tradition as well as from Soviet internationalism, has converged in today's Russia to form a new repertoire of state language. For a long time, the semantic space of coloniality was not mentioned per se, but the tone of denouncing the imposition of foreign norms as deculturing was unambiguously critical. Already in his Millennium Manifesto of December 1999, Putin wrote: "The modernization of our country cannot be achieved only by the simple transfer to Russian soil of abstract models and diagrams drawn in foreign textbooks."[24] While the Russian leader had in mind, at that time, mostly economic neoliberal reforms and the role of foreign actors (corporate or state) in capturing Russia's natural and industrial resources, the idea that the country's transformations have had foreign origins was already widespread. In the early 2000s, the government spoke regularly about the West's attempts to transform Russia into a colony providing raw materials, framing the government's economic recentralization and exertion of pressure on foreign investors as a strategic step to secure the country's sovereignty against Western intrusions.[25] The denunciation of the so-called "golden billion" also became a regular reference in official speeches.[26]

At that time, far-right politician Vladimir Zhirinovsky was among the last to continue the Soviet legacy of the "fight against US imperialism" by organizing international conferences with the shrinking realm of fellow travelers. But with Russia's renewed international assertiveness under Putin and the revival of tensions with the US, new actors emerged. In 2011, the entrepreneur of influence Alexander Yonov launched the Anti-Globalization Movement of Russia, the aim of which was to "[help] countries and individuals in their opposition to the dictate of the unilateral world and in their quest for an alternative agenda."[27] The movement listed thirty-two foreign partner organizations in Syria, Libya, Palestine, Iraq, Lebanon, Egypt, Sudan, Tunisia, Iran, Venezuela, Bolivia, Argentina, El Salvador, and North Korea, as well as nongovernmental organizations (NGOs) from the US, the United Kingdom, Germany, Poland, Italy, and France.

In 2015 and 2016, the movement organized two conferences funded by state money, "Dialogue of Nations: The Right of Peoples to Self-Determination and the Construction of a Multipolar World," bringing together associations with an anti-American or anticolonial agenda: the secessionist movements of Texas, California, Puerto Rico, and Hawaii; the Uhuru movement for the defense of African-Americans (a former fellow traveler of the Soviet Union that called for a Black internationalist socialism); autonomist movements from Catalonia and Sicily, the Republican Sinn Féin in Ireland, and the Polisario Front that advocates for the independence of Western Sahara; and several European far-right representatives. The movement has since ceased its operations but has been replaced by more influential structures and state initiatives.

In a second phase, Russian media outlets aimed at foreign audiences, such as Sputnik and RT, as well as the media empire around Yevgeny Prigozhin, took control of this anticolonial language (see below). Such language also began proliferating at the government level: the bellicose Alexey Pushkov, head of the Duma Committee for Foreign Affairs, commented on the 2013 Foreign Policy Concept by declaring that "Washington has to realize during the 'pause' in the relations between the Russia and the United States that Russia is no longer a 'political colony' of the US."[28]

This theme returned to the forefront in 2019, when Putin made his first explicit mentions of the Western "colonial mindset" toward former colonized countries.[29] "Anticolonialism" then became institutionalized in the short-lived International Agency for Sovereign Development (IASD), which shut its doors in February 2023. The agency presented itself as assisting to raise funds and attract investors outside European markets to contribute to Africa's economic decolonization.[30] It published a report entitled *Conspiracy against Africa: Breaking the Shackles of Colonialism*, which reproduced all the usual clichés about the persistence of European colonialism in Africa and the dictates of the Washington Consensus that purportedly entrench the dependency and exploitation of Africa. This anticolonial stance was supported by important names in the Kremlin's ideological ecosystems such as Konstantin Malofeev, the agency's president; Kirsan Ilyumzhinov, the eccentric former president of the Kalmyk Republic (currently under US sanctions for aiding and abetting Russia's allies in Syria), who traveled to Sierra Leone, Kenya, Togo, and

Burkina Faso in 2019 to help set up investment meetings with Russian firms;[31] and Sergey Glazyev, one of the agency's advisers.[32]

It is only with the country's full decoupling from the West in 2022 that the Russian president has actively appropriated the anticolonial semantic space, as illustrated in figure 12.1. Journalists from Meduza reported that the choice of a new exportable image for Russia was selected by the president himself from among several options.[33] In all his 2022 and 2023 discourses, Putin expressed a sharp binary vision of the world order: "either a country is independent, or it is a colony."[34] He also plainly differentiates between "globalism," by which he means globalization by and for Western interests, and "integration," by which he means the genuine collective work of equal countries seeking the common good.[35] In his September 30, 2022, discourse announcing the annexation of the four (partly) occupied eastern Ukrainian territories, he summarized Western colonialism in broad terms:

> It is worth remembering that the West began its colonial policy already in the Middle Ages, and then with worldwide slavery, the genocide of Native Americans, the robbery of India, Africa, the French and British wars against China... What they did—putting entire nations under drugs, exterminating entire ethnicities in the name of land and resources, organized hunting of human beings as if they were animals. It is against the very nature of mankind, truth, freedom, and justice.[36]

State media and nationalist publicists have echoed and reinforced the idea of Russia having to decolonize itself from the West. The "denazification of Ukraine" is, for instance, articulated within the anticolonial framework: Moscow would be liberating itself from its last layer of European acculturation by forcing Ukraine to come back to Russia's orbit and putting an end to Ukraine's own colonization by the West. Hawkish public intellectuals such as Sergey Karaganov and Nikolay Starikov, who had long denounced Russia as the West's economic colony, have been leading this anticolonial language on state media.[37] In late 2023, Sergey Karaganov and a group of colleagues published a long report, coordinated with the Presidential Administration and the Ministry of Foreign Affairs, on Russia's relationship to what is now called in Russia the "Global Majority" (*global'noe bol'shinstvo*), avoiding the contested notion of the "Global South." The report invites Russia to entirely abandon any relationship with the West, to make dialogue with the Global Majority its main strategic goal, and to prepare these countries for the potentiality of a full war with the West, while also recognizing that the main

FIG. 12.1. Mentions of "colonialism" in presidential speeches, 2000–2023.

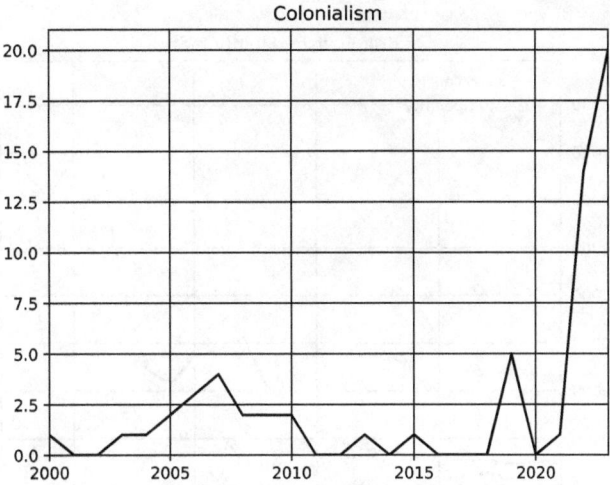

Source: Author's compilation based on Kremlin.ru.

non-Western powers, including its Chinese partner, are not interested in a confrontation with the West.[38]

Russia's anticolonial stance has also been enshrined in official documents. The 2023 Foreign Policy Concept mentions colonialism five times. Russia's historical role in "eliminating the global system of colonialism" is presented as equal to its "contribution to the victory in the Second World War"—the highest status symbol of legitimacy in the Russian worldview. The concept insists on "revolutionary changes" underway so that "sophisticated neocolonial policies" and "vestiges of domination by the US" will be "irrevocably fading into the past."[39] Sergey Lavrov's tour of Latin America and Africa in spring 2023 embodied this new diplomacy around the anticolonial theme. The Russian foreign affairs minister celebrated, for example, the structuring of a multipolar world (*multipoliarnyi*, or *politsentrichnyi*) and denounced the permanence of "colonial methods of interaction" by the US and its allies as a "neocolonial mindset" that is "categorically rejected by Africans as by us."[40] Even for Russian domestic audiences, the themes of colonialism and multipolarity have been growing since the second half of the 2010s, with a big jump in 2019 for the term "colonialism" and a spike for "multipolarity" in 2021 (see fig. 12.2).

FIG. 12.2. **Mentions of "colonialism" and "multipolarity" in Russian media, 2000–2023.**

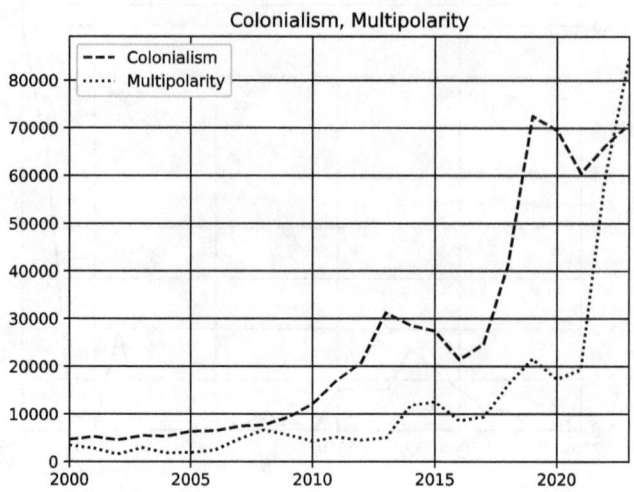

Source: Author's compilation based on Integrum.

There is a subtle difference between brandishing *anticolonialism* as the country's new geopolitical identity and the silence surrounding the concept of *decolonization*. The latter is connected with groups accusing Russia of being an empire and attempting to break up the country in the name of ethnic minorities' self-determination. At the 2023 plenary session of the World Russian People's Congress, Putin mentioned Western discourses on the need to "decolonize" Russia:

> Our diversity and unity of cultures, traditions, languages, and ethnicities simply do not fit into the logic of Western racists and colonizers, into their cruel plans for total depersonalization, separation, suppression, and exploitation. That is why they have started their old rant again: they say that Russia is a "prison of nations" and that Russians are a "nation of slaves." We have heard this many times throughout the centuries. Now we have also heard that Russia apparently needs to be "decolonized." But what do they really want? They want to dismember and plunder Russia. If they cannot do it by force, they sow discord.[41]

ANTICOLONIALISM IN PRACTICE: RUSSIA'S LANGUAGE TO THE GLOBAL SOUTH

Now formally inscribed into Russia's Foreign Policy Concept, the anticolonial stance has roots in several foreign policy strategies. One can locate three core sites of production: around the topic of the BRICS and multipolarity; in Russia's media narrative toward Latin America; and in Russia's renewed presence in Africa.

BRICS: Multipolarity as the Answer to Western Domination

The notion of multipolarity belongs to the anticolonial repertoire but with much more nuanced, reformist, and less confrontational overtones. It allows the Russian leadership and its foreign-policy elites to operationalize the notions, previously discussed, of civilization as normative pluralism and Russia as one of these autonomous civilizational centers.[42] More pragmatically, multipolarity is a way to describe a possible peaceful coexistence of different normative systems on the international scene, and the development of myriad multiregional cooperation mechanisms on specific issues. It is translated in Russian as either multipolar (*multipoliarnyi*) or polycentric (*politsentrichnyi*), with the second term more clearly implying power centers with "spheres of influence" than a balance between all countries' strategic interests.

Russia can claim a key role in today's pushes for multipolarity/polycentrism thanks to Yevgeny Primakov's forward-looking vision of the international order and Russia's place in it: for him, the fact that Russia has weakened during the transition from a bipolar world to a multipolar world has been used by the US to establish a unipolar domination that is destabilizing the whole international order. To fight against that destabilization, Russia should then partner with China and India to create a new multipolar triangle, as well as develop economic interdependencies across the globe as a guarantee for a democratization of the international scene.[43] Primakov's major legacy has inspired Russia's global outreach strategy of the 2010s, transforming his intuition into concrete policies.[44] It fits well Russia's multifaceted foreign policy, able to play different roles depending on regional contexts and evolving circumstances.[45]

While Russia promotes several regional institutions, only BRICS constitutes a genuine multipolar one in which Moscow exists without its regional hegemon status—unlike in the CIS, the Eurasian Economic Union, or even the Shanghai Cooperation Organization, which all have regional, post-Soviet ordering aspects. BRICS thus constitutes Russia's main concrete embodiment of its declared commitment to multipolarity. First, because Russia's economy is too small (about 2 percent of global GDP) to be able to challenge the world order alone, it needs more powerful allies, in particular China, to develop economically credible alternatives to US domination. The launch of the BRICS New Development Bank and the creation of a BRICS Reserve Fund in 2014 were, for instance, intended to challenge the roles of the International Monetary Fund and the World Bank. The BRICS also discussed the creation of their own international rating agency, which could compete with the existing US-based agencies by establishing methods to assess the health of global economies that would be more respectful of domestic social conditions. The de-dollarization of the world economy is another of these projects to reduce US domination and has grown slowly since 2014, to accelerate in 2022 with Russia and China mutually trading increasingly in yuan. Two alternative systems from SWIFT, one Chinese and one Russian, were also launched. Moscow has since pushed for settlement currency for BRICS countries and the introduction of BRICS regulatory functions in areas like standardization, vaccine certification, and cybersecurity regulation, to name a few.[46]

However, for Russia, the ideological component of BRICS matters more than the economic one. Lavrov has repeatedly noted that BRICS has been first and foremost a geopolitical association, and Fyodor Lukyanov has analyzed BRICS as "primarily a political group that emerged in response to the obvious need for a more diverse and less Western-oriented global political structure."[47] And indeed, the existence of multiple power poles in the international system provides additional leverage to the Kremlin. BRICS offers each member greater legitimacy than it would have individually and, as Alexander Sergunin explains, the association can "give way to cumulative soft power capacity."[48] It also guarantees a platform for dialogue with rising countries or regional powers such as Saudi Arabia, Egypt, the United Arab Emirates, Iran, and Ethiopia, which joined in 2024, and others interested in joining such as Turkey, Indonesia, and Nigeria.

Moscow is thus interested in empowering the institution and transforming it into an alternative system of global governance, but this could be done only were the main BRICS powers themselves to be interested in such a transformation. Moreover, if multipolarity amplifies the idea of an unavoidable "decline of the West" and the need for a global power redistribution, Russia's position on this redistribution is ambiguous. It has indeed a dual identity: that of being an old great power representing the Global North imbued with heavy symbolic power, and therefore not interested in, for instance, reforming the UN Security Council to accommodate new powers; and that of being a non-Western power wanting to challenge the international status quo. In any case, for Russia, BRICS has been a crucial tool to gain legitimacy in the Global South and present itself as a constructive, nonconfrontational actor in the transformation of the global order—this, in a sharply contrasting view and strategy with its much more revisionist stance on the European security architecture, and the violence deployed in its war against Ukraine.

Latin America: Sovereignism versus US Imperialism

More explicitly than in the BRICS context, Russia's return to influence in Latin America has been playing on anticolonial sensibilities, with mixed success. Russia is a small-time economic player in the region—especially when compared with the inroads China has been making—and has a major economic partnership only with Brazil (particularly in fertilizers), and a few other countries in specific sectors such as military cooperation, hydrocarbons, civil nuclear power, and hydroelectricity.[49] However, ideological convergences are much more numerous: first, with socialist countries such as Cuba and Nicaragua; second, with countries that experienced the "pink tide" of electoral victories by left-wing populist parties in the 2000s (Venezuela, Brazil under Lula, and to a lesser extent Ecuador and Mexico); and third, with right-wing leaders such as Brazil's former president Jair Bolsonaro.

The late president Hugo Chávez and Venezuelan Bolivarianism have encapsulated a Russia–Latin America honeymoon, but it has not been only a left-leaning one. The continuity of a positive view of Russia in Brazil from Bolsonaro to Lula, even in the middle of the war in Ukraine, confirms that Russia may speak to Latin American elites beyond the usual right-left divide.[50] While Moscow cannot secure full approval of its policies by Latin American governments and has faced declining public approval, it can still rely on at least a "positive neutrality" by many in the region, or even on explicit support from at least Cuba, Venezuela, and Nicaragua. Thanks to them, the Russian Navy now has, for instance, the right to make ports of call and there is a constant rotation of Russian security personnel in Nicaragua and Venezuela. Moscow is also promoting its GLONASS system (the Russian competitor to GPS) to Mexico.[51]

To accompany its return to the region, Russia has deployed its media presence. RT en Español, launched in 2009, has recorded large audience successes, and was then complemented by the launch in 2014 of Sputnik Mundo in Spanish and Sputnik Brasil in Portuguese. According to Diego Soliz, both media outlets have promoted several types of anticolonial narratives that fit Latin American political culture. The first rhetorical line is that of a Soviet legacy for whom anti-imperialism is directly connected with Marxism, socialism, and Soviet support (Sandinismo in Ortega's Nicaragua, Popular Unity for the Chilean Frente Amplio, and the late Cuban president Fidel Castro's fight against the US). The second, broader rhetorical line is that of sovereignism: it denounces (neo)liberal globalization and promotes nationalist, regionalist, and/or indigenous identities as a resistance to any forms of confiscation of sovereignty. In different combinations per country, it mixes critique of neoliberal reforms that impacted Latin American economies in the 1990s, critique of geopolitical liberalism embodied by US interventionism (both Cold War–era military intervention and support for far-right dictatorships), and critique of colonial cultural liberalism.

Parallels made between the US today and the Spanish Empire on one side, and between wars of independence, indigenous revolts for land control, and today's resistance on the other, have been numerous in Russian media, in particular during the postelection crises in Venezuela in 2018, Bolivia in 2019, and Nicaragua in 2020.[52] This anticolonial alliance may not have resulted in economic gains, nor in Russian military intervention to shore up Venezuelan president Nicolás Maduro in 2018, but it produces enough for Moscow's foreign policy: a potential reservoir of votes in the UN General Assembly (especially when an issue can be framed as anti-US or anti-Western), mutual diplomatic support (with both Bolsonaro and Lula in Brazil), and a decentering of Western narratives (for instance, on the war in Ukraine).

In Africa: Russia, the Liberator from European Neocolonialism

Russia has also made a visible return to the African continent. This was epitomized in the first Russia-Africa Summit, held in the fall of 2019 in Sochi, in partnership with Egyptian president Abdel Fattah el-Sisi. The summit confirmed Russia's successful diplomatic outreach in Africa, with the feat of bringing 45 of the 54 African heads of state to the 2014 Winter Olympic Village.[53] Less successful, the Second Russia-Africa Summit, held in July 2023, still generated a lot of political and media coverage on Moscow's role in helping Africa to "decolonize." The 2023 Russian Foreign Policy Concept itself put great emphasis on Africa, stating that "Russia stands in solidarity with the African states in their desire for a more equitable polycentric world and elimination of social and economic inequality . . . and support[s] further the establishment of Africa as a distinctive and influential center of world development."[54]

The indefatigable Sergey Lavrov traveled to Mali, Mauritania, Sudan, and South Africa in spring 2023. Rossotrudnichestvo has been reorienting itself toward Africa, opening new Russian Houses in Sudan, Mali, Egypt, and Algeria to complement those already existing in Morocco, Zambia, the Democratic Republic of the Congo (DRC), Tanzania, and Ethiopia.[55] The number of fellowships offered to African students to study in Russian universities has been growing too: for the 2023–24 academic year, the quota has more than doubled, from 2,300 to 4,700 spots. It is worth noting that the person in charge of this outreach toward the Global South is Yevgeny Primakov Jr., the grandson of the architect of Russian multipolarity.

While Russia's economic presence on the continent remains obviously modest compared to those of China and the West, Moscow still has trade agreements and bilateral relations with more than forty African countries and has become a major supplier of weapons to several of them, including Algeria, Angola, Egypt, Eritrea, Ethiopia, Morocco, Nigeria, and Uganda.[56] Soviet-trained African elites play a key role in this renewal of ties as Moscow tries to revive Soviet transnational networks of professional mobility and training. The Soviet Afro-Asian Solidarity Committee, which was funded by the Soviet Peace Fund, assisted many African countries in their struggle for independence. The Patrice Lumumba People's Friendship University in Moscow and other Soviet higher education institutions provided prestigious training to more than 1.5 million African elites. Sputnik could also benefit from its Soviet predecessors, Sovinformburo and Radio Moscow, which had broadcast in French, English, Bambara, Amharic, Peul, Swahili, Malgash, etc., from the 1960s onward.[57]

Russia's successful reimplantation in Africa has been mostly visible in French-speaking countries. Both RT and Sputnik invested in the French-speaking African landscape in the mid-2010s and have since gone mainstream thanks to a marketing strategy based on clickbait, buzz, and reposts without the payment of royalties.[58] The state agency Rossiya Segodnya signed several cooperation agreements with state media, for instance in the DRC and Ivory

Coast; Sputnik has recruited several African journalists; and two training schools, RT School and SputnikPro, have organized sessions for journalists from the DRC, Ivory Coast, Kenya, and Zimbabwe. As for RT France, it has insisted that its audience is not only France-based but Africa-oriented—and indeed, RT became available via satellite in Algeria, Morocco, and Tunisia in 2019.[59] Like Sputnik, RT social media activities have boomed mostly thanks to African audiences, particularly from Algeria, Morocco, Tunisia, Senegal, Cameroon, and Burkina Faso.[60]

Unlike in Latin America, in Africa RT and Sputnik found themselves working both in tandem and in competition with Prigozhin's media outlets—all dismembered since his failed mutiny and subsequent death by plane crash in the summer of 2023. The Prigozhin universe was founded on three pillars: paramilitaries (the infamous Wagner Group), resource-extraction contracts, and a media and cultural presence that accompanied the most "hard-power influence" techniques. Prigozhin was, for instance, funding several African front organizations such as the Association for Free Research and International Cooperation (AFRIC),[61] and the Central African radio station Lengo Songo, which echo Russian state media narratives. Prigozhin's media and cultural presence has become a central component of Russia's toolkit in some key countries like the DRC and Mali.[62] To this should be added myriad other local media outlets connected to less important entrepreneurs of influence such as Luc Michel—a Belgian and dubious fellow traveler of Russia involved with Afrique Media, a pan-African web-TV channel known for its pro-Russian stance, along with a dozen other smaller radio stations or web-TV channels.[63]

Both RT and Sputnik, as well as Prigozhin's media universe, have made the anticolonial tone one of their articles of faith. Their critique emphasizes the failure of the French military presence in the Sahel, as well as the existence of the CFA (Financial Community of Africa) Franc, or Françafrique—seen as a reminder of the status of many African countries as former colonies of France. This storyline resonates with local resentment toward former colonial powers and narratives on the West's double standards and the bloody legacy of colonial borders. It allows Russian media to become at least an echo chamber of these critiques, and sometimes a spearhead of them.[64] Moscow can then brand itself as a credible alternative to the former colonial powers, and the image of Putin as a leader who has extricated his country from the rut into which Western countries pushed it after the USSR's fall is widespread.[65]

A more caricatural version of this anticolonial storyline can be found in Prigozhin's movies. The opaque Foundation for the Defense of National Values, a paradiplomatic structure promoting Russia abroad, produced fifteen- to twenty-minute documentaries painting a world in which wars and other societal problems in the Middle East and in Africa are caused by the United States and its "satellites" (in particular, France), accused of engaging in neocolonialist politics. The same line was exploited in the animated short film for children, *The Lion and the Bear*, released in 2019 by the Central African Republic company Lobaye Invest, directly linked to Prigozhin. The plot revolves around an elephant (representing Africa) attacked by rebellious hyenas. The Western lion, who leads the elephant's army, is defeated, and only the altruistic intervention of the Russian bear helps the elephant to protect himself and rebuild the lands destroyed by the enemies.[66]

One may obviously mock this unsophisticated storyline, but it would be a mistake to think that Russia's anticolonial language does not find resonance in some local audiences. This strategy has greatly accelerated with the war. Banned from broadcasting in Europe, RT and Sputnik had to reorient themselves toward Africa. RT even opened a new office in South Africa (after an aborted attempt in Kenya) with the hope that it would act as a hub for the whole of English-speaking sub-Saharan Africa.[67] Maxime Audinet's comparative lexicometric analysis has showed that since 2022 especially, RT in English has been using the keywords "colonialism," "colonial," "neocolonialism," and "neocolonial" more than BBC News and Al Jazeera.[68]

Russia's new strategies for Africa also include a nonnegligible role for the church. The Moscow Patriarchate has created a new Exarchate of Africa to compete with the Greek Orthodox Patriarchate of Alexandria, which historically covered the Eastern Christians of Africa. It has also opened new churches in some countries, among them Uganda, and taken over some parishes, as in Kenya.[69] At the Second Russia-Africa Summit of 2023, Patriarch Kirill attempted to play the "traditional values" card with African leaders: "We are united by adherence to traditional values, conservative view of human nature, and rejection of the ideology of permissiveness and overconsumption."[70]

Outside the BRICS, Latin America, and Africa, a new space for Russia's anticolonial narrative has opened with the Israel-Gaza war. While the Russian authorities long balanced a privileged relationship with Israel—due to multiple factors, ranging from the importance of the Russian Jewish diaspora to shared strategic interests in Syria—and support for the Muslim world, since the Hamas attacks of October 7, 2023, Moscow has broken the equilibrium in favor of siding more explicitly with Muslim countries. There are three central reasons for this shift in Russian foreign policy. First, Moscow could not miss the opportunity to side with the Global South while accentuating the divide between "the West and the rest" by presenting the US-Israel-Ukraine triangle as destabilizing the world order; second, Moscow has become too close to and dependent on Iran not to embrace its point of view; and third, the Kremlin must take account Russian Muslim minorities by showcasing support for the Palestinian cause. And indeed, Putin tried to "do the splits," connecting the defense of Palestinians to Russia's war against Ukraine:

> The Muslim Ummah of Russia must understand that our country is not only the most consistent supporter of the rights of the Palestinian people, but the future of Palestine depends on Russia's victory. And even the entire Islamic world—divided, but increasingly striving to free itself from dependence on the West. If Russia loses and is defeated . . . almost the entire two-billion-strong Islamic world will lose hope for consolidation and independent development: the West will continue successfully to divide and conquer.[71]

Russia's anticolonial repertoire may seem to an outside Western observer like an artificial construct, and in such direct contradiction with the Kremlin's imperial language on Ukraine that this branding can only fail. But in countries where both elite and popular political cultures are deeply shaped by anticolonial mindsets and the legacy of the Non-Aligned Movement, Russia's language may resonate. While many are repulsed by Russia's violation of international law and territorial sovereignty, they still see a different equation at stake, one in which Russia's actions are the byproduct of a broader, systemic context of Western domination and normative expansion.[72] Pope Francis's comments on the war being fueled by "imperial interests, not just of the Russian empire, but of empires from elsewhere,"[73] offer a window into that vision of multiple normative empires colliding with each other.

In such a context, Russia's attempt at rebranding itself as an anticolonial power is likely to remain one of the key pillars of any future ideological construct. If Russia's quest for status cannot be achieved through integration with the West on its own terms, or through achieving regional hegemony (under its Eurasian or Russian World scheme), then joining the non-Western world to transform the international order looks like the most promising strategy.

This new repertoire appears not just as a cynical image-repair technique, but is anchored in an enduring tradition a "theology of liberation" from what is seen as Western colonialism. Since the nineteenth century, and more evidently in the twentieth century, Russian intellectual circles have articulated their country's colonized status with respect to Europe or the West with a messianic posture toward other colonized nations in the world.

Today's radical conflict with the West therefore almost automatically moves the pendulum toward identifying Russia with the "Global Majority" against the West. This was made explicit in the 2023 Foreign Policy Concept, which mentions China and India (albeit with some caution), as well as Latin America and Africa (in this case with enthusiasm), and takes a messianic tone according to which Russia has a "unique, historically formed mission of maintaining the global balance of power and shaping a multipolar international system."[74] This anticolonial stance allows the Russian regime to rebrand for its own purposes not only the Soviet legacy of internationalism but also a more socialist language, especially that of a more just world order and that of social justice—the latter being mentioned ten times in the 2023 Foreign Policy Concept. It is one of the paradoxes of the war and the decoupling from the West that a neoliberal Kremlin has been forced to rediscover military Keynesianism and rebrand its foreign policy strategy with a more leftist ideological coloring.

CONCLUSION

OVER THE LAST THIRTY YEARS—and with a deeper continuity between Boris Yeltsin and Vladimir Putin than we usually recognize—the Russian establishment has actively invested in a reordering process that has entailed "digesting" the collapse of the Soviet Union and the birth of a new Russia. This reordering process is both fed by and feeds the idea of an ontological insecurity with regard to Russia's place in Europe. Being unable to integrate the hegemonic Other, the Putin regime opted to confront it. Since the 2010s, it has shifted from seeking to make Russia a "normal" country in the eyes of the prevailing international order—a pursuit that dominated the 1990s and the first decade of the 2000s—to asserting its exceptionality and unique destiny. Having learned from the West, it now seeks to teach the West a lesson.

With the full-scale war, the more hawkish section of the Russian establishment has been triumphing over the more reformist one. The authorities have moved toward a much more rigid ideological structure, to the point that one can now talk about an official ideology, even it has not yet reached the level of a state ideology—which would necessitate changing the Russian Constitution. This ideology sees resistance against Western hostility as the driving force of Russia's history, and believes that having a powerful and unchallenged state is the only way for the country to survive and thrive. It has succeeded, over the years and with the war as the culminating point, in blending two previously diametrically opposed discursive lines that battled each other during the Soviet decades and the 1990s: Soviet greatpowerness— itself a mix of a Marxist-Leninist reading of the world order, and Western geopolitical schools—and the White imperial vision of Russia.

As much as the war against Ukraine can be read as a return of Russian imperialism, it is presented by Russia as decolonization: it is a "liberation war" waged by Holy Rus' against the empire of the "collective West"—with all the religious and messianic undertones this framing implies. The start of the war culminates a broader trend that Krastev and Holmes call the "end of imitation," in the sense that Russia has now broken the supreme taboo inherited from cooperation with the West thirty years ago: the refusal to go to war to challenge the borders inherited from the Soviet Union. Admittedly, cracks in this taboo had been showing since the 2014 annexation of Crimea, but at the time the Kremlin framed that move as a "surgical adjustment" rather than an element of global revisionism. That is not the case in the present war: Moscow seeks a more structural reshaping of Europe's security architecture, at least a symbolic recognition of being an equal creator of it. From the Kremlin's perspective, the war has opened the way for what Yegor Kholmogorov, as early as 2005, called the "restoration of the future": the war has accelerated history, suddenly shuffling geopolitical cards and opening new, unknown futures for Russia.

Long just one of many possibilities for the regime's ideological trajectory, old-fashioned territorial conquest became the only available path following a succession of turning points that closed off alternatives and shaped Putin's (seemingly quite solitary) decision to invade Ukraine. Russian efforts to project soft power—via economic interdependence, political pressures, and societal influence—have failed, increasing the appeal of a more literal reading of power projection as simple territorial annexation. The long-standing idea that part of Russia's symbolic body exists outside its internationally recognized legal borders has now been read verbatim: Russia is rightsizing its territory and assuming its *Großraum* identity. Yet the state's survival remains the main objective of the regime, and acquired territories are subordinated to this state-centric strategy more than having a value in themselves.

While the war is entirely Russia's responsibility, accountability for the strategic deadlock that preceded it should to a certain degree be shared between Russia and the West. Moreover, the deep Eurocentrism of the war has postponed the urgently needed rebalancing of the international scene in favor of the so-called Global South, as well as the shift in economic, political, and societal structures that will be critical to confronting ongoing environmental transformations. As Gerard Toal discusses in *Oceans Rise, Empires Fall*, current tensions on the international scene have sent the world hurtling back to a nineteenth-century vision of geopolitics that is oblivious to twenty-first-century environmental crises.[1]

One can obviously attribute full responsibility for this to Russia, given the Russo-Ukrainian War's terrible human and economic costs. But the West has easily let itself be drawn into a mirroring match with Moscow, one that is full of simplistic rhetoric about the "free world" whose democracies fight the darkness of authoritarian regimes and that takes a binary reading of the Global South as either "with us or against us." A Hollywood-like story of Zelensky as the absolute hero and Putin as the archetypal villain has helped to consolidate the West's strategic identity in opposition to Russia, similar to how it previously used the "Orient" (using Said's language) as a "constituent Other" to construct its own identity.

RUSSIA AS A MICROCOSM OF GLOBAL IDEOLOGICAL TRANSFORMATIONS

The ideological transformation that has taken place in Russia over the last thirty years can also be seen in other countries. Poland, Hungary, and Serbia (to take the most well-known regime cases in Europe) have been playing with similar ideological repertoires, even if—as in the Polish case—they vehemently oppose Russia geopolitically. Slovakia, Bulgaria, and even Slovenia and Croatia have occasionally passed through similar phases, though these have not consolidated into authoritarian regimes. Like Russia's evolution, this illiberal response coming from several Central European countries demonstrates that the political project of the post-1989 European order—namely, the rapid imposition of liberal norms in pursuit of eventual European reintegration—has partially backfired. This is not, of course, to suggest that postcommunist societies were not thirsty for change; they most certainly were, but the scale of this attempted transition and its socioeconomic and cultural impacts were far greater than anticipated.

The polysemic process of joining the "West" institutionally, politically, economically, strategically, and philosophically—that is, of integration into postmodern liberal society—constituted an uncertain pursuit subject to contestation, disappointment, and resentment. This pursuit has generated a reaction framed through a postcolonial lens: progressivist liberal worldviews and values are seen as having been imposed from abroad in a way that has failed to consider the symbolic and material aspects of existing power hierarchies. The way the European Union has envisioned its expansion implies that postcommunist societies are students of the "West" rather than cocreators of a new Europe. The current illiberal backlash stemming from the region should therefore be read as a pursuit effectively aimed at reclaiming agency and subjectivity. While this backlash is massive, it is not present throughout the entire region; one can also identify societies that formulate their agency and subjectivity through and in the name of the Western liberal project, among them Ukraine.

Where there is a backlash, it is often inspired by the West's own ideological production. Indeed, much of the modern Russian perspective can be also found in illiberal movements growing in Western Europe and the United States. Challenges to liberal democracy as we know it have also effectively become mainstream in Europe: France, Italy, Spain, Germany, Sweden, Israel, and others have all witnessed, in recent years, national-populist, illiberal, or far-right parties becoming powerful enough to reshape the prevailing political language, partake in government coalitions, control major ministries, influence policy, or even govern. In the Americas, the US has housed its own illiberal project—one that challenged the constitutional order with the storming of the US Capitol on January 6, 2021—and several major Latin American countries have experienced comparable transformations. The Global South, too, has witnessed illiberal transformations in countries as diverse as India, the Philippines, and South Africa, not to mention the role of Islamism in Muslim countries and the series of coups that have taken place in the Sahel.

What sets the Russian backlash apart are its prominence and scale—it was the first to be so clearly formulated, and Putin's strategies predated the current global trend—as well as the violence that Moscow displays in those conflicts in which it is engaged. But it would be a mistake to imagine that there is a Russian "hidden hand" behind the global shift, even if there is a degree of transnational connections, ideological borrowing, mirroring, and solidarity among illiberal leaders.[2] While the Kremlin was certainly an early representative of this worldview and may have shown the way to some actors, the reasons for this increasingly widespread distaste for liberalism are systemic and unrelated to Russia. There is an ongoing erosion of Enlightenment values and a return to a Schmittian secularized political theology, of which Russia represents just the tip of the iceberg.

To challenge the liberal status quo, it is no longer necessary to follow a coherent doctrine à la Marxism. On the contrary, more polysemic ideological projects—like the Russian one—mesh well with the postmodern global order, enabling countries to maintain their own agency, pick and choose ideological products that fit their specific needs, and build alliances in a purely transactional way—what India calls "multi-alignment." Russia's behavior on the international stage is thus both a product and a catalyst of the current global disorder.

TYPOLOGIZING THE PUTIN REGIME

Trying to impose a typologizing filter on the Putin regime may be morally reassuring, but it does not automatically provide a heuristic approach for scholarship if the typology in question is taken at face value and not itself interrogated.

Take, for instance, the notion of imperialism. Per the neutral definition of Estonian political scientist and historian Rein Taagepera, an empire is a "relatively large sovereign political entity whose components are not sovereign."[3] Although Western European colonialism was a product of a specific period in history (i.e., Europe's overseas expansion from the late fifteenth to the mid-twentieth centuries), empires have existed around the world since ancient times, including in Asia, Africa, and Latin America. Describing Russia's "imperialism" is therefore based on a normative critique that posits Russia's identity as something to dismiss, while thinking of Russia as an "empire" allows for a much-needed decentering from the Western experience and a more globalized view of Russia. It reminds us that the concept of "empire" is not limited to large-scale and straightforward oppression but includes complex forms of globalization and identity hybridity, such as intersectionality between ethnicity, class and territory.

Another example is nationalism. Is Putin's regime nationalistic, or should we view nationalism as the state-initiated version of nationhood, which, in the Russian case, puts statism at the center of any collective construction? The Russian national construction is indeed pyramidal, with ethnic Russians at the top layer and minorities in a second, lower tier. In practice, however, Russia has approached its ethnic and religious diversity in a manner broadly comparable to European practices. In terms of migration policy, too, Russia's experience is fundamentally aligned with that of its European counterparts and not different by nature. Discussing Russia's "nationalism" in dialogue with nation-state, nation-building, and ethnicity brings more to the scholarly table than a simple contemptuous critique of Russia as "nationalist."

The same applies to the notion of conservatism. Advancing a normative definition would entail attributing degrees of authenticity. Yet conservatism is a broad continuum of claims by a diverse range of actors regarding the need for organic and slow changes, and Putin is no less legitimate in his claim to moral conservatism than Ronald Reagan. Russian intellectuals have indeed been reworking the main tenets of conservatism in line with the European continental tradition, in which (unlike in the American and British variants) the state is central, both for its absolute value of embodying the nation and for its redistributive power. A strong statism, combined with an essentialist vision of the nation and its civilizational features or "cultural codes"—what Mikhail Suslov calls communitarianism—constitutes the cornerstone of the regime's construction. More comparative research, for instance with US paleoconservatism (combining nationalism, traditional values, Christian moral principles, celebration of rural life, and a wariness of free markets), and the idea of culture wars as the new battlefield for political subversion would enrich scholarship and avoid the exceptionalization of Russia.

Last but not least, the notion of fascism. Is Russia fascist? The answer largely depends on the definition—extensive or restrictive—of fascism, as well as its perceived "location." Are we looking at individual actors and ecosystems, at entire regimes, at society at large? If fascism is defined by three main criteria—an obsession with matters of identity, a utopia that envisions the regeneration of mankind through war, and an ultra-mobilization of society in everyday life—then Russia, even in the context of its war with Ukraine, is not fascist. While it exhibits an obsession with matters of identity, it boasts of no regenerative utopia and does not engage in ultra-mobilization. Moreover, the notion of rebirth or regeneration, when it appears in public speeches, may find root not in a fascist genealogy but in a religious one: the war as a redemption after having sinned by Westernizing, making Russia a "born-again" state.

Growing elements related to fascism may permeate the political mainstream: the "party of war," or the hawkish ecosystem, often meets the second and third conditions, especially in its call for spiritual warfare. Yet this ecosystem does not represent the Kremlin as a whole; a large part of the state apparatus continues to work hard to preserve "normalcy" for Russian citizens and keep them demobilized despite the war. At the more grassroots level, the paramilitarization of Russian society, and in particular the large segment of society that has experienced the battlefield—the hundreds of thousands of veterans of the "special military operation"—might nurture a powerful grassroots illiberal civil society with fascist tendencies, already visible in a surge of vigilantism and grassroots anti-immigrant activities. Last but not least, the Russian political project for Ukraine fits the three criteria mentioned above: it plans to extirpate the Ukrainianness from Ukrainians and unveil their supposedly hidden Russianness through both physical and symbolic violence. This violence includes biopolitical measures, such as the forced adoption of children, as well as cultural policy aimed at eliminating the symbols of Ukrainian identity, but Moscow also places a lot of effort and emphasis on a more pragmatic economic reconstruction to win the "hearts and minds" in occupied territories.

SHOULD WE TALK ABOUT PUTINISM?

Can Russia's political language be defined as "Putinism"? The term is problematic, as it can variously be read as a synonym of a highly coherent doctrine such as Marxism-Leninism; as analogous to a broader cluster of ideologies, such as liberalism or conservatism; or as a more modest personification of a time and a mindset, other examples being Reaganism and Thatcherism. To which of these three sets of *-ism*s do we want to compare "Putinism"? The term implies that (1) the personality of the president plays a crucial role in Russia's ideological construction, (2) there is clear ideological continuity over the years of Putin's long reign, and (3) there is sufficient ideological coherence to warrant the creation of an *-ism*.

On the first point, the notion of Putinism bears the risk of overemphasizing the personalization of the regime. There is no doubt that Putin "metaphorically condenses in himself the features of a historical period, his name becomes the name of an era."[74] He is obviously crucial as the symbolic tip of the regime (in a vertical representation of power) and its median, equilibrium point (in a horizontal one), and he can take major strategic decisions alone with no accountability. But the regime has been much more of a collective endeavor than an individual construct, and while the president can influence the direction taken by the system as a whole, he himself also represents deeper, more structural realities and vested interests, such as those of the *siloviki*. One can therefore use the notion of Putinism to express the existence of a "collective Putin" but should not become imprisoned by this personalization into psychoanalytical interpretations of what is happening in the head of the president.

On the second point, there have been some forms of unity and continuity of the regime over its more than two decades—both in terms of the sociological continuity of Russia's political and intellectual personnel and in terms of ideology. One could also discuss longer trends, such as the obvious continuity with late Soviet culture, and even more *longue durée* patterns that have their roots in imperial Russia. Yet this continuity should not be used as a tautological strategy to reread the past with the eyes of the present: the regime has its own sedimentation process, and there have been many Putinism*s* over the years, with a plurality of potential futures. War Putinism was only one of the possible options of early Putinism.

On the third point, there is enough ideological coherence in the regime's global political project to merit the *-ism* title, not in a sense of a "thick" ideology like Marxism but in the sense of a cluster of different doctrinal stocks that have been woven into a coherent mythological frame. Over the years, the regime has managed to structure a more stable worldview with greater ideological consistency. The semantic space of the regime's main repertoires has evolved, but the grand narratives have solidified and now appear less open to deep reformulations. That said, we should not underestimate the regime's creative potential to reinvent itself, both concretely (economically to bypass sanctions) and symbolically (in terms of identity narratives by presenting itself as a Global South power). The modernization trope could reappear, as well as the ambivalence of wanting to be the second Europe and therefore reconnecting with Europeans (at least some of them), while the ambivalent relationship to China could evolve in a way less favorable to Moscow. As I have explored in this book, there is both stability and coherence in the core set of beliefs and opportunism in reshaping the strategic narratives. Ideology matters when it reinforces strategic goals, but not enough to force a decision solely on this basis.

MEANING-MAKING ENGINEERING

Returning to the three layers of ideological production proposed in the introduction, one can conclude that the Putin regime does have a mainstream ideology, understood as a belief system. This first level of ideology—a doxa, or a *zeitgeist*—has been cocreated by the establishment and a large part of the population. The regime keeps this *zeitgeist* alive by saturating the public space with narratives and relying heavily on emotions—an ambivalent blend of hope, resentment, disillusion, and pride. At a second level, that of strategic narratives, the regime has long allowed eclecticism and diversity, promoting or demoting repertoires and storylines in line with its own evolving interpretations of the domestic and international scenes. A large market of private and public actors competing for state resources has emerged, regulated by state funding and patronage networks. At the third level, that of topoi, the regime has tested dozens of new ideologemes through state media and empowered influential entrepreneurs of all stripes, building a successful "networked authoritarianism" that circulates narratives of power in a horizontal way, through "active citizens" and patriotic civil society.

This state-sponsored diversity has gradually reduced the space available for framing alternative narratives. With the turning point of 2020–21 and then, obviously, the full-scale war, previously disunited repertoires stemming from different doctrinal stocks—sovereignty, civilization, conservatism, traditional values, Eurasia, Russian world, Byzantium, victory in the Second World War, etc.—have gradually been blended through determined bureaucratic work. The war has provided internal coherence to this ideological puzzle, as demonstrated by the already-mentioned Russia's 2023 Foreign Policy Concept and by Putin's speeches at the World Russian People's Congress, both of which link several long-disconnected repertoires.

Indeed, two major discursive lines that were, prior to the war, largely dissociated from each other have now been joined together. The first is the identitarian line on Russia as a state-civilization, which focuses on the country's historical continuity (its "one-thousand-year-long" history), its multinationality (the national construction that promotes "unity in diversity"), its spatial features (the world's biggest country), and its Eurasian/Russian World destiny. The second is the geopolitical line on the memory of the Second World War and the legitimacy that the 1945 victory gives to Russia; the Soviet Union's legacy on the international scene; and present-day Russia's aspirations to a multipolar world decolonized from the West. The central repertoire of traditional values speaks to both lines: identitarian (conservative values as a component of Russia's state-civilizational identity) and geopolitical (conservative values as a form of *soft power* against the liberal influence promoted by the West).

One can still identify several tensions in this ideological construction. One relates to the mixing of Eurasianist and Russian World notions, which seem to be oppositional (one is imperial, the second is ethnocentric), but these contradictions are encompassed by state-centrism, which allows the state to have multiple identities depending on its audience. A second is connected to Russia's civilizational claim to be both the original Europe and a civilization in its own right—a paradoxical stance that blends the Slavophile and Eurasianist views of Russia's relationship to Europe. A third revolves around the challenge of identifying the alternative world order to be pursued: a multipolar one in which Russia would be one center of gravity among many equals, or a new bipolar world that opposes Russia and China (as the leaders of the non-Western world) to the US and its allies-clients? A fourth is expressed in the regime's economic policy: it continues to see the market economy as desirable, uses market mechanisms as a political tool to generate consensus among elite and oligarch's loyalty, but is also pushing toward a more Soviet-style Keynesianism of sponsoring new industrial projects and better redistributing in the name of social justice.

Retrotopia forms an important part of the regime's political project. That said, retrotopia is not unique to Russia: it can also be found in the West, where the Trente Glorieuses are the implicit or explicit model that one seeks to preserve or recreate. The Russian version focuses on the Soviet Golden Age of the 1960s–1980s, with efforts to recreate it both at home and on the international stage, albeit with certain caveats: private property and the consumer society, for example, are both now social norms coming from the 1990s that Russians do not wish to see called into question. This Soviet Golden Age has become a dreamed-of homeland, promising what Svetlana Boym has called a "guilt-free homecoming," or a return to an idealized past, free from the burden of critical examination—a self-protecting nostalgia.[5] It also relies heavily on the idea of morality—be it socialist or conservative—with the idea that liberalism as experimented in the 1990 has failed precisely as a *moral order.*

There is a social class aspect in this retrotopia. The war in Ukraine is indeed interpreted as the revenge of the forgotten, authentic, blue-collar Russia against its Westernized elites. In the article "Dietetic Sadness," film director Konstantin Bogomolov rejoices at the downfall of cosmopolitan, rich, and glamorized Russians (of which he is one, ironically), whose Westernizing way of life came to an end on February 24, 2022.[6] Mocking such Russians' despair at losing access to Western brands, Bogomolov's diatribe insists on their lack of patriotism and inability to accept material sacrifices for the sake of the war. In contrast, he celebrates the average Russian citizen's readiness to accept the burden of the war, in terms of both casualties and declining standards of living. Like the works of many "Z" authors, Bogomolov's pamphlet may seem opportunistic, but it resonates with some segments of Russian society.

These retrotopian accents reveal hope, fear, and nostalgia, or what Althusser defines as the motor of ideology. A secularized religion around broad concepts such as state-civilization posits itself as an ideological substitute for Communism, the embodiment of Russia's resilience, and a tool for enforcing unity and cohesion. The textbook for the new Russian university course "Fundamentals of Russian Statehood" reproduces for instance, via impressive platitudes, Slavophile clichés about the Russian and Western value systems: morality versus cynicism, community versus individuality, social justice versus profit-obsessed capitalism, spirituality versus consumerism, rooted identity versus global cosmopolitanism. It also counters the West's framing by presenting "backwardness" as positive—a tactic that may resonate strongly in the global context of recalculations of humanity's relationship with nature.

The war has raised questions of moral responsibility and ethical direction. The current ideological construction in Russia bars any prospect of historical change: it freezes the country in time and sometimes even returns it to the past. The Great Patriotic War has become a reenacted myth that transcends precise historical boundaries, as it can be "relived" by successive generations. With its sacralization comes the silencing of the memory of state violence. Recall Renan's definition of the nation as not only what people have in common but also what they want to collectively forget: this certainly applies to Russian society. As Maria Lipman asserts, the Kremlin, under Putin, chose reconciliation over truth.[7] To an external observer or a historian, this may seem to have been the wrong choice, but it has been viewed internally as the right move for a head of state taking power following a decade of deep division.

Yet while the Putin regime has worked hard to "suture" a national identity wounded by the collapse of the Soviet Union and the difficult 1990s, with its war against Ukraine it has created a new stratum of wounds that will need to be healed in the future. The question of moral responsibility for letting this war happen in the name of the Russian people and the issues of recognizing state violence committed against civilians in Ukraine, of addressing the Soviet past, and of rethinking the country's colonial/imperial attitude toward the broader region will haunt Russian society for a long time to come.

RUSSIA AS AN ORPHAN OF EUROCENTRISM

The Russian intellectual and political mainstream has positioned Russia on a continuum of identity that runs from Western Europe to Central Europe to Russia and then to Asia. This perception of Russia as a subaltern empire (following Vyacheslav Morozov) or a case of hybrid exceptionalism (per Kevork Oskanian) explains the longevity of colonial and Eurocentric stereotypes in Russia's views of its neighbors. Russia is portrayed both as the periphery or epigone of the West, and therefore as wanting to exit that humiliating position, and as the legitimate coauthor of European civilization, and therefore entitled to lecture the West about its own values and identity. The substance of these civilizational claims may have changed since the nineteenth century, but the idea that Russia has something significant to say to the rest of the world—a form of universalism through celebrated particularism—has persisted over time, always in tension with isolationism and autarky. (Nor is Russia the only great power to have such cycles of isolationism and expansionism; the US provides another example.)

In a highly personal text written in spring 2023, Fyodor Lukyakov presents the current Russian decoupling from the West as the genuine end of the Petrine period, closing the cycle opened in the eighteenth century by Peter the Great's windows to Europe.[8] What Lukyanov expresses here, and this is a sentiment widely shared among the Russian establishment, is not so much that Russia will not one day reconnect with Europe, but that the Europe that they dream of—a "Eurocentric Europe," the yardstick of classic humanist values—no longer exists. Even if we were to imagine a new perestroika happening in Russia, there is no "European harbor" to which to return. The Europe that Russia might rejoin in the future would be just one pole in a multipolar world, with many features of a declining power demographically and economically (and morally, for those of a conservative persuasion). Westernism as the romantic political myth of the final decades of the Soviet Union cannot simply be revived from the ashes.

From the perspective of the Russian establishment, Europeans have put themselves in a self-defeating position by questioning traditional hierarchies in terms of gender, ethnicity, colonialism, and classical culture. Challenging the Eurocentric episteme is read as a sign of civilizational decline, if not blatant suicide. In that sense, Russians are the last believers in Europe's cultural supremacy—and the Putin regime is an orphan of its own Eurocentrism. This is what intellectuals like Boris Mezhuev express through the idea of Russia's search for "civilizational indifference": the Europe that was supposed to give them meaning and direction having vanished, Russians now wander with no reference point. Save for a few fellow travelers, they are left alone to carry the burden of the classic *moderne* born from a blending of the Enlightenment and Romanticism.

MANUFACTURING CONSENT AND ITS LIMITS

Many observers have wondered about the Russian population's support for the onset of the war. Even if we take into consideration the Kremlin's repressive tools for punishing dissent, the acquiescence of a majority of the population to the war implies that state language is making sense of the world for Russian citizens, even if only partially and implicitly. And indeed, to guarantee cohesion in times of turbulence, a society needs, at a minimum, some shared representation of reality—including common worldviews, language, practices, and rituals.

Western punditry tends to think that nondemocratic regimes do not care about public opinion. On the contrary, they do—a lot. We have seen the importance the Kremlin placed on the March 2024 presidential elections, seeking to ensure a symbolic plebiscite in favor of the president as the embodiment of the nation's fate. Since the early 1990s, the regime has closely monitored public opinion to ensure it can preempt protests: its "polit-technologist" has worked with a vast array of polling agencies providing both political and commercial services.[9] Over the years, the regime has also developed extensive mechanisms of "feedback" (*obratnaia sviaz'*—a tradition coming from Soviet times) to capture public opinion's acceptance or rejection of state-sponsored storylines: the entire realm of military bloggers and social media influencers occupy this niche of "capillarity."

In its relationship to ideology, the Russian regime is thus best classified as a consolidated personalistic authoritarianism but not a totalitarianism: it does not believe that it can recalibrate the brains of its citizens (though it does believe that it can do so when it comes to Ukrainians), but rather aims to marginalize or eliminate the public availability and accessibility of rival ideologies and heavily incentivize public allegiance. Popular acquiescence is sufficient for the regime to function; it does not need to be translated into active support or enthusiasm—on the contrary, too much genuine commitment to the cause can be dangerous, as seen in the Kremlin's ambivalent relationship to the "Z" movement and its simultaneous co-optation and repression. At the core of the relationship to public opinion lie constraints on public discourse: practice and rituals are central to signaling ideological conformity. That people may not believe what they say publicly and may privately dispute the regime's claims is a secondary concern. This is a smart strategy to make citizens uncertain about the representativeness of their views and therefore push them toward self-censorship and feelings of isolation.

This widespread acquiescence is still secured through "manufacturing consent"[10] more than through coercive tools, even if the latter aspect has increased with the war. Western observers tend to project two visions of Russian society. The first is a unified society that has been "brainwashed" by propaganda to the point that either it is entirely supportive of—and even enthusiastic about—the regime's goals, or that it is anesthetized by repression and petrified with fear. The second is that Russian society is full of hidden resistance and movements ready to break the country, if not take arms, as soon as it will be possible. Both are inaccurate.

First, a large part of the Russian population can well dissociate fake news from plausible news, know about the regime's efforts to engage in discursive control, but is just not interested in looking for alternative narratives that would create cognitive dissonance with their world.[11] Second, Russian citizens possess agency. Many of them, especially those over forty—who were raised in late Soviet culture—are accustomed to operating in contradictory normative systems; they have easily relearned how to function with strong cognitive dissonance and double-think. The massive phenomenon that is seen as depoliticization—such as replying "don't know" to surveys, withdrawing into "inner exile," self-censorship, expressing doubts, and using humor and irony—should therefore be interrogated by scholars as "hidden scripts"[12] of dissatisfaction that are not easily interpretable to external eyes.[13]

Moreover, forms of public debate still exist in nondemocratic settings. Authorized forms of social contention, often referred to as "consentful" discontent, challenge the government based on its own ideology and legality and focus on elite-enabling behavior.[14] For instance, aside from voting in elections, filing a citizen appeal and engaging in the formal complaint process is the most common form of political participation among Russian citizens. As Danielle Lussier argues: "In modernizing the citizen appeals process for a large percentage of the Russian population that does not view itself as particularly political, Putin has succeeded in presenting himself as an efficient manager and benevolent protector of citizens' rights."[15] Even in times of war, Russians continue to petition their government to express their anxiety and dissatisfaction regarding socioeconomic issues as well as the ongoing war.[16]

For years, Russian sociologists have emphasized the ideological passivity of the society. In the eyes of Levada Center chief sociologist Lev Gudkov, for instance, "We cannot speak seriously about liberal or conservative values in Russia. There are attitudes and reactions to government actions. . . . Society is not ideologized."[17] Vladimir Petukhov, a sociologist at the Russian Academy of Sciences, takes a similar view: "The majority is an enormous, unstructured mass of the population . . . which doesn't have any ideological or political preferences at all."[18] Gudkov also notes that for the past two decades, whenever Russian citizens have been asked which problems they are the most concerned with, there has been no mention of anything ideological—such as the danger of losing "traditional values" or the "Russophobia" of the "collective West"—but only of concrete issues such as social justice, salaries, pensions, quality of education and healthcare, and corruption.[19]

Yet Russians share, broadly speaking, the *zeitgeist* advocated by the regime: the idea that Russian society is morally "healthier" than the West, the sense that its claim to great-power status is legitimate, and an attitude of disdain toward neighboring countries and internal minorities can all be read as components of a broader ideology. The regime has been able to build on genuine grassroots fears and desires, objectifying them and feeding them back into the public discourse—a form of vicious circle that creates social cohesion. It has continued to both rely on and cultivate social traumas inherited from the 1990s and to present itself as offering society protection from internal and external threats. While the memory of the collapse of the Soviet Union has gradually faded, since younger generations of Russians did not experience it, it has been reimagined and augmented as the fear of an existential threat coming from the "collective West." It should thus come as no surprise that one of Russia's leading cinematographic successes of 2023 was *Cheburashka*, a remake of the famous Soviet children's cartoons,[20] and that the most popular TV show (which also met with huge success among audiences in Ukraine and Kazakhstan) was *The Boy's Word*, a violent drama about the lives of young gang members in Kazan in the late 1980s and early 1990s that reactivated the trauma of the collapse of the Soviet Union.[21]

As such, while citizens, in their everyday life, focus on concrete issues like state public services, living conditions, and corruption, this should not be read to imply that they do not share an ideological background with the regime (whether this is cocreated or a product of the state's hegemonic culture and coercion is a matter for debate). The LEGITRUSS survey conducted in spring 2021 reveals, for instance, a widespread, relatively coherent ideological tendency in public opinion that we can broadly define as national-conservative. Depending on where one draws the line, a majority of Russians strongly (73 percent) or very strongly (58 percent) subscribe to a set of national-conservative attitudes, values, and policy preferences that have a strong positive correlation with one another.[22] While this national-conservatism is filled with many malleable concepts that largely function as empty signifiers, its component values and beliefs indicate a fairly consistent vision of what the social and cultural order ought to be, including in terms of institutional support. Its coherence and salience contradict the mainstream conception of public opinion as ideologically amorphous.

This social order is *conservative* in that it supports the political status quo against perceived chaos, is moderately morally conservative in terms of its prescriptions regarding family values on topics like divorce and abortion, and is radically conservative in its support for heterosexuality and condemnation of LGBTQ+ rights. It also supports stronger imposition of moral norms in the public space. It is *national* in that it believes in the specificity of Russian identity, expressed by different *topoi*, including "statism and patriotism," "traditional Russian values," and the "national values of all the peoples living in Russia." It expects the state to protect this social order and enforce its coherence through a variety of policies and institutions, the most heavily supported being military education in schools and patriotic youth educational organizations.

Within the national-conservative realm, there exist some differences between the different ideational subgroups—mostly in terms of their support for religious education at school and vigilante movements such as the Cossacks—but it would be overreaching to define these variations as clear ideational categories. The main caveat to these findings remains the definition of *state* ideology. We do not know what degree of indoctrination the national-conservative majority would support. People might indeed approve of state policies in theory while rejecting state or church intrusions into privacy in practice.

The Russian regime's ideological production has thus succeeded in creating a popular consensus behind its reading of the world and crafting mental paradigms that make sense of reality from its own perspective. Of course, this consensus is not complete: there has long been a stable minority (usually identified as about 15–20 percent of the population) that disagrees with the regime and exhibits liberal and pro-Western worldviews—as reflected in the large crowds bringing flowers to Navalny's grave, and in support for alternative candidates during the March 2024 presidential elections. For this minority, the free space in which to exist alongside the rest of Russian society has shrunk dramatically with the war, and emigration has only further depleted it. But for a large part of provincial Russia, long forgotten, the war appears as a chance to rise. Millions of Russians at the bottom of the social ladder can picture themselves as the country's true heroes, ready for the ultimate sacrifice, and their material and financial situation has improved thanks to the state's generous funding of those going to the front.

Two groups appear to actively support the regime's reinforced ideological control. The first of these is the older generation (fifty and above), which approves more than any other age bracket of all regime-sponsored initiatives that are inspired by Soviet methods of social control. The second is a hawkish segment of the population—accounting for between 10 and 15 percent of the total, depending on the survey—for whom winning the war against the "collective West" in Ukraine means putting Russian society in a war mood, including full military mobilization, mobilization of the economy for the war effort, and more active popular support.[23] The authorities' ability to find the right balance between, on one side, mobilizing provincial and rural Russia to go to war through ideological and material motivations, and, on the other, shielding the rest of society—and especially the upper and middle classes from big cities—from the impact of the same war will be critical to the long-term success or failure of state ideology.

But perhaps even more important than capturing the society's diversity is the degree of variance among those who largely agree with the state *zeitgeist*. Indeed, ordinary citizens' interpretations of the war are best represented not as a black-and-white binary but as a continuum of shades of gray. While the majority of society interprets the war as the West's war against Russia, and supports the regime in its ideological indoctrination, as soon as one digs a little deeper, the facade of uniformity disappears. Citizens are expressing anxiety about the war, not enthusiasm: this is the big difference with the annexation of Crimea in 2014, which generated genuine elation. People are worried about the suddenly uncertain future, they are confused about the loss of life, and many continue to see Ukraine as a victim of the West, not as an enemy of Russia per se. Moreover, state-sponsored repertoires and ideologemes can take on a life of their own as they are adopted, reinterpreted, or rejected by citizens. Russian public opinion, for instance, largely rejected the state's proposed narrative of the "denazification" of Ukraine; in light of their cognitive and emotional struggle to accept a war against a "brotherly nation," the state media were forced to tone down that narrative in favor of the notion of a war against the "collective West."[24]

Western observers tend to see the Russian ideological construction as weak because it lacks a vision of the future, but one may challenge that interpretation. The retrotopia of a Soviet Union–lite blends a cult of archaic features justifying violence, visible among the hawkish segment, with modernizing aspects: social justice, a welfare state, and a modernizing economy are still major components of state legitimacy, and foreign policy language is open to the future (multipolarity, joining the Global South, etc.). The growing place of leftist ideas inspired by the Soviet doctrinal stock helps the Kremlin combine its retrotopia for Russia with a forward-looking narrative for the world, offering a rebranded messianism at a low cost.

To date, the regime has not recreated a Soviet-type ideological monolith. Even in the context of war, it refuses to formalize a comprehensive doctrine, remaining timid about excessive "true teaching" and preferring a functional, technological understanding of ideology. Of course, this is not the end of the story. The final Soviet generation, raised under Brezhnev, and which is currently in power in Russia, is trying desperately to transmit to Millennial and Gen Z Russians its (reconstructed) memory of what a good society should be. However, the balance between a banal constellation of notions for broader consumption and an appealing ideology is difficult to identify and implement. Ideological routinization is necessary for citizens to blend bottom-up and top-down ideological demands, but it also risks becoming overly verbose and losing its attractiveness—as did Soviet ideology in the late 1970s and 1980s. One may thus wonder if it will have the same effect—namely, significant distanciation and double-think on the part of young people who find themselves indifferent or hostile to this sterile form of coaching.

There is little chance that Soviet-inspired indoctrination through textbooks would work, but other forms of ideological transmission that are anchored in entertainment, cultural production, and prominent real-world institutions—such as the massive military-patriotic education institutions targeting younger people—will likely be more successful. As Ilya Budraitkis accurately explains, the actual content of ideology for popular consumption is secondary to form and place; the regime needs not a "real" ideology that takes itself seriously "but an ideology as an empty form, a technology of domination that works as a set of performative practices."[25] The authorities' capacity to maintain ideological control over the younger generations will thus be critical to the future of the regime: youth may share the state ideological repertoires when it comes to Russia's identity and status, but they are more sensitive to state intrusions into their privacy, more autonomous, less paternalistic, and less willing to sacrifice their well-being in the name of overarching national goals.

The new era that opened with the full-scale invasion of Ukraine has decoupled Russia from the West. As long as Vladimir Putin remains in power—and potentially even after he leaves office, depending on how the succession is conducted—the relationship between Russia and the West will not be normalized. Even when the weapons fall silent, the judicial fights to hold the Russian regime legally responsible for its assault on Ukraine will endure. All the while, Russia will continue to gain prominence in the Global South, actively sponsoring non-Western institutional frameworks, cultivating the language of anti-Western neo-imperialism, and steadily accelerating the de-Westernization of the world.

Putin's departure from power would not necessarily cause the ideological construction elaborated during his reign to collapse. If we define a nation as a "population with a coordinated set of beliefs about their cultural identities," then there is undoubtedly a Russian nation that has voluntarily participated in the cocreation of the Putin regime. As the Nobel Prize–winning writer Svetlana Alexievich succinctly states, "There is a collective Putin, consisting of some millions of people who do not want to be humiliated by the West. There is a little piece of Putin in everyone."[26] Some of these components will surely persist, constituting one more layer of textualities to tap into for generations to come.

As Vladislav Surkov summarizes, "For many years Russia will still be Putin's state. . . . We need to recognize, understand and describe the Putin system of government and the entire complex of ideas and measures of Putinism as the ideology of the future."[27] In Surkov's vision, "the ideology of the future" should not be read as "Putin is the future of Russia"; instead, Putin has left a legacy that will leave heavy footprints on Russian society. Post-Putin Russia could go down many potential paths, including ones leading to peaceful coexistence with its neighbors and the West. However, the deep-seated features that the regime has cultivated for years—such as the notions that Russia offers a unique civilizational contribution to the world, that it should have an autonomous voice on the international stage, and that it will not be an obedient subject of Western interests—are here to stay, in one way or another.

Two years after the launch of the full-scale invasion of Ukraine, the existential war with the West has helped the regime to "find itself" ideologically. Whereas the Ukrainian battlefield can be negotiated in one way or another, the symbolic struggle against the West is here to stay. Russia's relative favorability on the battlefield at the time of this writing could be temporary and the regime may need to reinvent itself to deal with less favorable realities. In 2022, the Funds for Progressive Politics released a report forecasting three possible scenarios for postwar Russia. In the first scenario, USSR 2.0, Russia returns to a situation where a highly rigid ideological regime controls an impoverished society that has largely lost its "creative class" in exchange for a generous welfare state and the nationalization of the economy. In the second, NEP 2.0 (the New Economic Policy, the liberalization of the economy launched by the Bolsheviks in the 1920s), Russia embarks on partial democratization, decreases ideological indoctrination, and relaunches at least some forms of economic modernization and support for the private sector. In the third, the Z-nation, Russia moves toward a nationalist regime focused on natalist policies and vigilante movements—something close to a fascist state.[28] At this stage, the NEP is not in view: Russia seems to be moving toward the first, Soviet-inspired scenario, with some features of the Z-nation, of which the veterans' movements will likely be the leading force.

However, it would be a mistake to portray Russia in an essentialist way as unable to reform and rebalance itself. Over many centuries of history, the country has undergone cycles of reforms following autocratic reigns, and there will surely be periods of reform in the future. Under certain circumstances, the regime could reinvent itself as more open to cooperation with the West and with some features of a new modernization trend. In the event of more structural changes, a new regime could take different directions. A Western-centric liberal-democratic model looks improbable in the near- and medium-term future. But an "Asian" model of self-reform (such as that followed by Singapore) that would maintain some forms of authoritarianism but with a modernizing objective, or an illiberal, communitarian grassroots democracy based on Russian traditional institutions (e.g., *zemstvo*), appears more plausible than a second coming of the 1980s' liberal, pro-Western perestroika.

NOTES

Introduction

1. Georges Balandier, *Le pouvoir sur scènes* (Paris: Balland, 1980), 15.
2. The Russian agency VTsIOM carried out the survey, which was commissioned by Pål Kolstø and Helge Blakkisrud, principal investigators of the University of Oslo's research project "Values-Based Legitimation in Authoritarian States: Top-Down versus Bottom-Up Strategies—The Case of Russia." The project was funded by the Research Council of Norway (project no. 300997). The dataset is currently scheduled to be released to the broader research community in 2025 through the LEGITRUSS website: https://www.hf.uio.no/ilos/english/research/projects/value-based-regime-legitimation-in-russia/index.html.
3. Karen Dawisha, *Putin's Kleptocracy: Who Owns Russia?* (New York: Simon & Schuster, 2004).
4. Sergei Guriev and Daniel Treisman, *Spin Doctors: The Changing Face of Tyranny in the 21st Century* (Princeton, NJ: Princeton University Press, 2022).
5. Andrey Makarychev, "The War in Chechnya in Russian Cinematographic Representations: Biopolitical Patriotism in 'Unsovereign' Times," *Transcultural Studies* 12, no. 1 (2016): 115–135.
6. Charles Clover, *Black Wind, White Snow: The Rise of Russia's New Nationalism (New Haven, CT: Yale University Press, 2016)*; Marcel H. van Herpen, *Putin's Wars: The Rise of Russia's New Imperialism* (Lanham, MD: Rowman and Littlefield, 2014); Michel Eltchaninoff, *Inside the Mind of Vladimir Putin* (London: Hurst, 2018).
7. On this debate, see Marlene Laruelle, *Is Russia Fascist? Unraveling Propaganda East and West* (Ithaca, NY: Cornell University Press, 2021).
8. Timothy Snyder, *The Road to Unfreedom: Russia, Europe, America* (New York: Tim Duggan Books, 2018); Timothy Snyder, "Ukraine Holds the Future: The War between Democracy and Nihilism," *Foreign Affairs*, October 2022, https://www.foreignaffairs.com/ukraine/ukraine-war-democracy-nihilism-timothy-snyder.
9. Mikhail Epstein, "Schizophrenic Fascism: On Russia's War in Ukraine," *Studies in East European Thought* 74, no. 4 (2022): 475–481.

10. Snyder, *The Road to Unfreedom*, 145.

11. Among a rich literature, see Marlene Laruelle, *Russian Eurasianism: An Ideology of Empire* (Woodrow Wilson Press / Johns Hopkins University Press, 2008); Andreas Umland and Anton Shekhovtsov, "Is Dugin a Traditionalist? 'Neo-Eurasianism' and Perennial Philosophy," *Russian Review* 68 (2009): 662–678; Andreas Umland, "Aleksandr Dugin's Transformation from a Lunatic Fringe Figure into a Mainstream Political Publicist, 1980–1998: A Case Study in the Rise of Late and Post-Soviet Russian Fascism," *Journal of Eurasian Studies* 1 (2010): 144–152; Anton Shekhovtsov, "The Palingenetic Thrust of Russian Neo-Eurasianism: Ideas of Rebirth in Aleksandr Dugin's Worldview," *Totalitarian Movements and Political Religions* 9, no. 4 (2008): 491–506; Anton Shekhovtsov, "Aleksandr Dugin's New Eurasianism: The New Right à la Russe," *Religion Compass* 3/4: (2009): 697–716; Dmitry Shlapentokh, *Ideological Seduction and Intellectuals in Putin's Russia* (Cham, Switz.: Palgrave Macmillan, 2021).

12. Paul Robinson, *Russian Conservatism* (Ithaca, NY: Cornell University Press, 2019); Mikhail Suslov and Dmitry Uzlaner, eds., *Contemporary Russian Conservatism: Problems, Paradoxes, and Perspectives* (Leiden: Brill, 2019); Glenn Diesen, *Russian Conservatism: Managing Change under Permanent Revolution* (Lanham, MD: Rowman & Littlefield, 2021); Kristina Stoeckl and Dmitry Uzlaner, *The Moralist International: Russia in the Global Culture Wars* (New York: Fordham University Press, 2022); David Lewis, *Russia's New Authoritarianism: Putin and the Politics of Order* (Edinburgh: Edinburgh University Press, 2020).

13. Among the most recent works, see Olga Malinova, "Constructing the Collective Trauma of 'The Hard 1990s' as a Disregarded Tool of Legitimation for Putin's Authority," *Nationalities Papers: The Journal of Nationalism and Ethnicity* 50, no. 3 (2022): 619–623; "Legitimizing Putin's Regime: The Transformations of the Narrative of Russia's Post-Soviet Transition," *Communist and Post-Communist Studies* 55, no. 1 (2022): 52–75; "Symbolism and the Transformation of the National Historical Narrative in Post-Soviet Russia," in *Routledge Handbook of Russian Politics and Society* (London: Routledge, 2022), 377–387; "Framing the Collective Memory of the 1990s as a Legitimation Tool for Putin's Regime," *Problems of Post-Communism* 68, no. 5 (2021): 429–441; "Politics of Memory and Nationalism," *Nationalities Papers: The Journal of Nationalism and Ethnicity* 49, no. 6 (2021): 997–1007.

14. Jade McGlynn, *Memory Makers: The Politics of the Past in Putin's Russia* (London: Bloomsbury, 2023); Nina Tumarkin, "The Great Patriotic War as Myth and Memorym," *European Review* 11, no. 4 (2003): 595–611; Nikolay Koposov, *Memory Laws, Memory Wars: The Politics of the Past in Europe and Russia* (Cambridge: Cambridge University Press, 2017).

15. Andrey Tsygankov, *Russia's Foreign Policy: Change and Continuity in National Identity* (Lanham, MD: Rowman & Littlefield, 2019); Richard Sakwa, *Russia against the Rest: The Post–Cold War Crisis of World Order* (Cambridge: Cambridge University Press, 2017); Andrej Krickovic and Igor Pellicciari, "From 'Greater Europe' to 'Greater Eurasia': Status Concerns and the Evolution of Russia's Approach to Alignment and Regional Integration," *Journal of Eurasian Studies* 12, no. 1 (2021): 86–99.

16. Among many others, see Stoeckl and Uzlaner, *The Moralist International*; Dmitry Adamsky, *Russian Nuclear Orthodoxy: Religion, Politics, and Strategy* (Stanford, CA: Stanford University Press, 2019); Katja Richters, *The Post-Soviet Russian Orthodox Church: Politics, Culture and Greater Russia* (London: Routledge, 2012); Irina Papkova, *The Russian Orthodox Church and Russian Politics* (New York: Oxford University Press, 2011); Alicja Curanović, "Russia's Mission in the World: The Perspective of the Russian Orthodox Church," *Problems of Post-Communism* 66, no. 4 (2019): 253–267.

17. The most comprehensive being Jardar Østbø, *The New Third Rome: Readings of a Russian Nationalist Myth* (Stuttgart: Ibidem, 2016).

18. Brian Taylor, *The Code of Putinism* (Oxford: Oxford University Press, 2018), 2.

19. Elena Chebankova, *Political Ideologies in Contemporary Russia* (Montréal: McGill-Queen's University Press, 2020).

20. Mikhail Suslov, *Putinism: Post-Soviet Russian Regime Ideology* (London: Routledge, 2024).

21. Gulnaz Sharafutdinova, *The Red Mirror: Putin's Leadership and Russia's Insecure Identity* (Oxford: Oxford University Press, 2020).

22. Cheng Chen, *The Return of Ideology: The Search for Regime Identities in Postcommunist Russia and China* (Ann Arbor: University of Michigan Press, 2016).

23. Bo Petersson, *The Putin Predicament: Problems of Legitimacy and Succession* (Stuttgart: Ibidem, 2021).

24. Marlene Laruelle, "Introduction: Illiberalism Studies as a Field," in Marlene Laruelle, ed., *Oxford Handbook of Illiberalism* (Cambridge, MA: Oxford University Press, 2024), pagination not allocated.

25. Eliot Borenstein, *Plots against Russia: Conspiracy and Fantasy after Socialism* (Ithaca, NY: Cornell University Press, 2019); Ilya Yablokov, *Fortress Russia: Conspiracy Theories in the Post-Soviet World* (New York: Polity Press, 2018).

26. Marlene Laruelle, "Russia's Niche Soft Power: Sources, Targets, and Channels of Influence," *Russie.Nei.Visions* 122, April 2021, https://www.ifri.org/en/publications/notes-de-lifri/russieneivisions/russias-niche-soft-power-sources-targets-and-channels.

27. Marlene Laruelle and John Chrobak, "The Carlson-Putin Interview, or the Limits of Dialogue between the Western Far Right and Russia," *PONARS Eurasia Policy Memo*, no. 881, March 2024, https://www.ponarseurasia.org/the-carlson-putin-interview/.

28. Anna Gryzmala-Busse, "Why Comparative Politics Should Take Religion (More) Seriously," *Annual Review of Political Science* 15 (2012): 421–442.

29. Jan-Willem van Prooijen and Karen M. Douglas, "Conspiracy Theories as Part of History: The Role of Societal Crisis Situations," *Memory Studies* 10, no. 3 (2017): 323–333.

30. In his seminal work, Freeden sees ideology as a process of decontestation offering "temporary stabilities carved out of fundamental semantic instability in the social and political worlds." Michael Freeden, "The Morphological Analysis of Ideology," in Michael Freeden, ed., *The Oxford Handbook of Political Ideologies* (Oxford: Oxford University Press, 2013), 119.

31. Vera Tolz and Stephen Hutchings, *Nation, Ethnicity and Race on Russian Television Mediating Post-Soviet Difference* (London: Routledge, 2015). For Russian media's interna-

tional outreach, see Stephen Hutchings, Vera Tolz, Precious Chatterje-Doody, et al., *Russia, Disinformation, and the Liberal Order: RT as Populist Pariah* (Ithaca, NY: Cornell University Press, 2024).

32. Jade McGlynn, "Illiberal Memory across Borders," *Journal of Illiberalism Studies* 3, no. 3 (2023): 44.

33. Claire Yorke, "Is Empathy a Strategic Imperative? A Review Essay," *Journal of Strategic Studies* 46, no. 5 (2023): 1082–1102.

34. Presidential speeches were collected through the the RuBase data (https://hcss.nl/rubase/), which had cleaned up presidential speeches from all other documents released by the Presidential Administration. There were three possible scenarios: 1. A single-word-expression with only one possible form. In that case we simply counted documents where this form was mentioned. 2. A single-word-expression with several possible forms. In that case we counted a document if we found one of the forms in the document. 3. A two-word-expression with only one possible form. In that case we simply counted documents where this form was mentioned.

35. Olga Malinova and N. V. Karpova, "Deputaty Gosudarstvennoi dumy kak aktory rossiiskoi politiki pamiati," *Politicheskaia nauka* no. 1 (2023) 113–138; Olga Malinova, "Russian Identity and the 'Pivot to the East': An Analysis of Rhetorical References to the American and Chinese 'Others' in Political Elite Discourse," *Problems of Post-Communism* 66, no. 4 (2019): 227–239; Olga Malinova, "Ritorika politicheskogo lidera kak indicator znachimostly Drugogo: Analiz ssylok na SShA I KNP v vystupleniakh prezidentov RF (2000–2015)," *Polis. Politicheskie issledovaniia* no. 2 (2016): 21–37.

36. Oksana Drozdova and Paul Robinson, "A Study of Vladimir Putin's Rhetoric," *Europe-Asia Studies* 71, no. 4 (2019): 1–19.

37. Alicja Curanović, *Russian Foreign Policy: Destined for Greatness!* (Abingdon, UK: Routledge, 2021).

38. Adriana Cuppuleri, "20 Years of LIO Contestation(s): A Computational Text Analysis of Russia's Foreign Policy Discourse (2003–2023)," SCRIPTS Working Paper no. 38 (2024).

39. Georgy A. Borshchevskiy, "'Direct Line with Vladimir Putin' in the Mirror of Sociology and Axiology," *Sotsiologicheskie issledovaniia* 11 (2022): 54–65.

40. Ivan Fomin, "Two Statisms of Putin's Ideology: From Proclamation to Mobilization," forthcoming, https://papers.ssrn.com/abstract=4624081.

Part I

1. Alexei Yurchak, *Everything Was Forever, Until It Was No More: The Last Soviet Generation* (Princeton, NJ: Princeton University Press, 2005).

2. "Constitution of the Russian Federation," official website of the government of the Russian Federation, http://archive.government.ru/eng/gov/base/54.html.

3. Boris Dubin, "Kharakter massovoi podderzhki nyneshnego rezhima," *Emsu.ru*, February 26, 2010, https://emsu.ru/nmsu/2010/0224_levada.htm.

Chapter 1: Actors, Networks, and Structures
1. Vladislav Surkov, *Russkaia politicheskaia kul'tura: Vzgliad iz utopii* (Moscow: BCG Press, 2007), 14.
2. Timothy Frye, "Is Putin's Popularity (Still) Real? A Cautionary Note on Using List Experiments to Measure Popularity in Authoritarian Regimes," *Post-Soviet Affairs* 39 no. 3 (2023): 213–222.
3. Louis Althusser, *Lenin and Philosophy and Other Essays*, trans. Ben Brewster (New York: NYU Press, 2001).
4. Terry Eagleton, *An Introduction to Ideology* (London: Verso, 1991).
5. John Gerring, "Ideology: A Definitional Analysis," *Political Research Quarterly* 50, no. 4 (1997): 980.
6. Teun A. van Dijk, "Principles of Critical Discourse Analysis," *Discourse & Society* 4, no. 2 (1993): 258.
7. Andreas Fagerholm, "Ideology: A Proposal for a Conceptual Typology," *Social Science Information* 55, no. 2 (2016): 144.
8. Fagerholm, "Ideology," 146.
9. John Jost, Christopher Federico, and Jaime Napier, "Political Ideology: Its Structure, Functions, and Elective Affinities," *Annual Review of Psychology* 60 (2006): 307–337.
10. Clifford Geertz, "Ideology as a Cultural System," in David Apter, ed., *Ideology and Discontent* (New York: Free Press, 1964), 47.
11. Juan Linz, *Totalitarian and Authoritarian Regimes* (London: Lynne Rienner, 2000).
12. Fabio de Sa e Silva, "Autocratic Legalism 2.0: Insights from a Global Collaborative Research Project," *Verfassung Und Recht in Übersee* 55, no. 4 (2023): 430.
13. Roland Barthes, *Mythologies*, trans. Annette Lavers (London: Paladin, 1972).
14. Clifford Geertz, *The Interpretation of Cultures* (New York: Basic Books, 1973).
15. Sara Cobb, David Laws, and Carlos Sluzki, "Modeling Negotiation Using 'Narrative Grammar': Exploring the Evolution of Meaning in a Simulated Negotiation," *Group Decision and Negotiation* 23, no. 5 (2014): 1048.
16. Michel Foucault, *The Archaeology of Knowledge* (New York: Harper & Row, 1972), 49.
17. Van Dijk, "Principles of Critical Discourse Analysis," 249–283.
18. Geertz, *The Interpretation of Cultures*, 220.
19. Van Dijk, "Principles of Critical Discourse Analysis," 275.
20. Zygmunt Bauman, *Liquid Modernity* (Hoboken, NJ: John Wiley & Sons, 2013).
21. Alister Miskimmon, Ben O'Loughlin, and Laura Roselle, eds., *Forging the World: Strategic Narratives and International Relations* (Ann Arbor: University of Michigan Press, 2017).
22. Marianne Kneuer, "Legitimation beyond Ideology: Authoritarian Regimes and the Construction of Missions," *Zeitschrift Für Vergleichende Politikwissenschaft* 11, no. 2 (2017): 184.
23. Vladimir Pribylovskii, *Kooperativ Ozero i drugie proekty Putina* (Moscow: Algoritm, 2012).
24. Nikolai Petrov, "Vintiki putinskoi politiki: Nesamostoiatel'nye rossiiskie elity,"

Moscow Times, January 23, 2024, https://www.moscowtimes.ru/2024/01/23/vintiki-putinskoi-politiki-nesamostoyatelnie-rossiiskie-eliti-a119234.

25. Maria Snegovaya and Kirill Petrov, "Long Soviet Shadow: The Nomenklatura Ties of Putin Elites," *Post-Soviet Affairs* 38, no. 4 (2022): 329–348.

26. Vladimir Putin, "Rossiia na rubezhe tysiacheletii," *Nezavisimaia gazeta*, December 31, 1999, https://www.ng.ru/politics/1999-12-30/4_millenium.html. An English-language translation is available at pages.uoregon.edu.

27. Levada Center, "Massovye pokazateli samochustviia i strakhov," February 20, 2024, https://www.levada.ru/tag/strahi/.

28. Kenneth Wilson, "Modernization or More of the Same in Russia: Was There a 'Thaw' under Medvedev?," *Problems of Post-Communism* 62, no. 3 (2015): 145–158; Katja Richters, "The Russian Orthodox Church and Medvedev's Modernisation Policy: Allies or Foes?," *Religion, State & Society* 40, no. 3/4 (2012): 363–378.

29. Vladimir Putin, "The Real Lessons of the 75th Anniversary of World War II," *National Interest*, June 18, 2020, https://nationalinterest.org/feature/vladimir-putin-real-lessons-75th-anniversary-world-war-ii-162982; Vladimir Putin, "On the Historical Unity of Russians and Ukrainians," Kremlin.ru, July 12, 2021, http://en.kremlin.ru/events/president/news/66181.

30. Ivan Krastev, "V chem Zapad oshibaetsia naschet Rossii," *Rossiia v global'noi politike*, August 16, 2015, http://www.globalaffairs.ru/global-processes/V-chem-Zapadoshibaetsya-naschet-Rossii-17643.

31. Mikhail Suslov, Marek Čejka, and Vladimir Đorđević, *Pan-Slavism and Slavophilia in Contemporary Central and Eastern Europe: Origins, Manifestations and Functions* (London: Palgrave Macmillan, 2023).

32. Juliette Faure, "What Role Did Ideology Play in Triggering Russia's Invasion of Ukraine," *Russia Program Online Papers* 8 (2023), 2. See also Juliette Faure, "Russian Modernist Conservatism (1960–2022): The Intellectual and Social Reconstitution of Russia's Alternative to Western Liberal Modernity," PhD defended at Science Po Paris, November 29, 2022.

33. Andrei Kolesnikov, "The Special Ideological Operation Going According to Plan," *Russia.Post*, August 31, 2023, https://russiapost.info/politics/slo.

34. For a biography, see Fiona Hill and Clifford G. Gaddy, *Mr. Putin: Operative in the Kremlin* (Washington, DC: Brookings Institution, 2015).

35. Fiona Hill and Clifford Gaddy, "Putin and the Uses of History," *National Interest*, January 2012; *Kommersant*, "Chto chitaet Vladimir Putin," January 20, 2014, https://www.kommersant.ru/doc/2383840; Aleksei Miller, "Talking Politics: Vladimir Putin's Narrative on Contemporary History (2019–2022)," *Russia in Global Affairs*, no. 2 (2023), https://eng.globalaffairs.ru/articles/putins-narrative/.

36. See Valerie Sperling, *Sex, Politics and Putin: Political Legitimacy in Russia* (Oxford: Oxford University Press, 2014); Elizabeth A. Wood, "Hypermasculinity as a Scenario of Power," *International Feminist Journal of Politics* 18, no. 3 (2016): 329–350.

37. *Izvestia*, "est' Putin—est' Rossiia, net Putina—net Rossii," October 22, 2014, https://iz.ru/news/578379.

38. Martin Kragh and Andreas Umland, "Putinism beyond Putin: The Political Ideas of Nikolai Patrushev and Sergei Naryshkin in 2006–20," *Post-Soviet Affairs* 39, no. 5 (2023): 366–389; Martin Kragh and Andreas Umland, "Ukrainophobic Imaginations of the Russian *Siloviki*: The Case of Nikolai Patrushev, 2014–2023," Center for Democratic Integrity, 2023, https://democratic-integrity.eu/ukrainophobic-imaginations-of-the-russian-siloviki/; Andrei Soldatov and Irina Borogan, "Dead Water: How the Russian Security Services' Paranoid Mindset Justifies the War," *SCEEUS Guest Report* 5 (2022), https://sceeus.se/publikationer/dead-water-how-the-russian-security-services-paranoid-mindset-justifies-the-war.

39. Maria Antonova, "Putin's Great Patriotic Pseudoscience," *Foreign Policy*, November 29, 2016, https://foreignpolicy.com/2016/11/29/putins-great-patriotic-pseudoscience/.

40. See Mikhail Zygar, *All the Kremlin's Men* (New York: PublicAffairs Books, 2016); Mikhail Zygar, "How Vladimir Putin Lost Interest in the Present," *New York Times*, March 10, 2022, https://www.nytimes.com/2022/03/10/opinion/putin-russia-ukraine.html.

41. Jørgen Staun, *Siloviki Versus Liberal-Technocrats: The Fight for Russian and Its Foreign Policy* (Copenhagen: Danish Institute for International Studies, 2007).

42. Ivan Fomin, "Sixty Shades of Statism: Mapping the Ideological Divergences in Russian Elite Discourse," *Demokratizatsiya: The Journal of Post-Soviet Democratization* 30, no. 3 (2022): 305–332.

43. Marlene Laruelle and Laura Howells, "Ideological or Pragmatic? A Data-Driven Analysis of the Russian Presidential Grant Fund," *Russian Politics* 5 (2020): 29–51.

44. At the turn of the twenty-first century, a movement opposing electronic barcodes—in which the church saw the presence of the Antichrist in the world—became so powerful within the church that it began to threaten the unity of the institution. See Marcin Skladanowski, "The Devil in Technologies: Russian Orthodox Neoconservatism versus Scientific and Technological Progress," *Zygon: Journal of Religion and Science* 54, no. 1 (2019): 46–65.

45. More in Laruelle, *Is Russia Fascist?*, 96–97.

46. Sharon Werning Rivera, ed., *Survey of Russian Elites 2020: New Perspectives on Foreign and Domestic Policy* (Hamilton College, 2020), https://www.hamilton.edu/documents/SRE2020ReportFINAL.pdf.

47. Rivera, *Survey of Russian Elites 2020*.

48. Danielle Lussier, "Ideology among Russian Elites: Attitudes towards the United States as a Belief System," *Post-Soviet Affairs* 35, no. 5/6 (2019): 433–449.

49. Among the scant existing research, see Olga Malinova and N. V. Karpova, "Deputaty Gosudarstvennoi dumy kak aktory rossiiskoi politiki pamiati: Na primera transformatsii Federal'nogo zakona 'O dniakh voinskoi slavy i pamiatnykh datakh Rossii,'" *Politicheskaia nauka* no. 1 (2023): 113–138.

50. Julian G. Waller, "Elites and Institutions in the Russian Thermidor: Regime Instrumentalism, Entrepreneurial Signaling, and Inherent Illiberalism," *Journal of Illiberalism Studies* 1, no. 1 (2021): 1.

51. Marlene Laruelle and Kevin Limonier, "'Beyond Hybrid Warfare': A Digital Exploration of Russia's Entrepreneurs of Influence," *Post-Soviet Affairs* 37, no 4 (2021): 318–335.

52. Alena V. Ledeneva, *Can Russia Modernise? Sistema, Power Networks and Informal Governance* (Cambridge: Cambridge University Press, 2013); Vadim Volkov, *Violent Entrepreneurs: The Use of Force in the Making of Russian Capitalism* (Ithaca, NY: Cornell University Press, 2002); Mark Galeotti, *The Vory: Russia's Super Mafia* (New Haven, CT: Yale University Press, 2018); Olga Kryshtanovskaya, *Anatomiia rossiiskoi elity* (Moscow: Zakharov, 2005).

53. Anna Schwenk, *Flexible Authoritarianism Cultivating Ambition and Loyalty in Russia* (Oxford: Oxford University Press, 2024).

54. Ivan Zassourky, *Media and Power in Post-Soviet Russia* (Armonk, NY: M. E. Sharpe, 2004), 136–137.

55. Quoted from Mischa Gabowitsch, "Fascism as Stiob," *Kultura* 4 (2009): 5.

56. Vera Tolz and Yuri Teper, "Broadcasting Agitainment: A New Media Strategy of Putin's Third Presidency," *Post-Soviet Affairs* 34, no. 4 (2018): 213–227.

57. Meduza.io, "State-Controlled 'Autonomy': How the Kremlin Uses 'Independent Organizations' to Do Its Propaganda Dirty Work," February 27, 2024, https://meduza.io/en/feature/2024/02/27/state-controlled-autonomy.

58. Yurchak, *Everything Was Forever, Until It Was No More*.

59. Vadim M. Rozin, "The Moscow Methodological Circle: Its Main Ideas and Evolution," *Social Epistemology* 31, no. 1 (2017): 78–92.

60. Marlene Laruelle, "Conceiving the Territory: Eurasianism as a Geographical Ideology," in Mark Bassin, Sergei Glebov, and Marlene Laruelle, eds., *Between Europe and Asia: The Origins, Theories, and Legacies of Russian Eurasianism* (Pittsburgh: University of Pittsburgh Press, 2015), 68–83.

61. Andrew Wilson, *Virtual Politics: Faking Democracy in the Post-Soviet World* (New Haven, CT: Yale University Press, 2005); Peter Pomerantsev, *Nothing Is True and Everything Is Possible* (New York: PublicAffairs Books, 2015).

62. Sergei A. Samoilenko and Elina Ezikova, "Public Relations in Russia: Formation, Etatization, and Calcification," in Maureen C. Minielli et al., *Media and Public Relations Research in Post-Socialist Societies* (Lanham, MD: Lexington, 2021), 3–46.

63. Ilya Kukulin, "The Sorcerers' Apprentices: Can Georgy Shchedrovitsky Be Responsible for Russia's Invasion of Ukraine?" *Russia.Post*, June 26, 2022, https://russiapost.info/society/the_sorcerers_apprentices.

64. Viktor Pelevin, *Generation P* (Moscow: AST, 2022).

65. Ivan Krastev, "Democracy's 'Doubles,'" *Journal of Democracy* 17, no. 2 (2006): 58.

66. Konstantin Beniumov, and Taisiia Bekbulatova, "Kak Gleb Pavlovskii pridumal sovremennuiu vlast'," *Meduza.io*, August 1, 2018, https://meduza.io/episodes/2018/08/01/kak-gleb-pavlovskiy-pridumal-sovremennuyu-vlast.

67. Max Seddon, "Gleb Pavlovsky, Russian Spin Doctor, 1951–2023," *Financial Times*, March 11, 2023, https://www.ft.com/content/9a101862-7f39-4894-9bf6-ac06365f2e08f.

68. Anton Barbashin et al., *Thinking Foreign Policy in Russia: Think Tanks and Grand Narratives* (Washington, DC: Atlantic Council), November 12, 2019, https://www.atlanticcouncil.org/in-depth-research-reports/report/thinking-foreign-policy-in-russia-think-tanks-and-grand-narratives/

69. Juliette Faure, "Définir le conservatisme russe," *Cahiers du monde russe* 61, no. 3/4 (2020): 573–584.

70. Elias Götz and Jørgen Staun, "Why Russia Attacked Ukraine: Strategic Culture and Radicalized Narratives," *Contemporary Security Policy* 43, no. 3 (2022): 483.

71. Aliaksei Kazharski, *Eurasian Integration and the Russian World: Regionalism as an Identitary Enterprise* (Budapest: Central European University Press, 2019), 30.

72. Among the rich literature on religion, see, for the Orthodox Church, Kristina Stoeckl, "The Russian Orthodox Church as Moral Norm Entrepreneur," *Religion, State & Society* 44, no. 2 (2016): 132–151; Kristina Stoeckl, "Three Models of Church-State Relations in Contemporary Russia," *Constitutions and Religion* 36, no. 3 (2018): 195–223; Curanović, "Russia's Mission in the World"; and for Islam, Gulnaz Sibgatullina, *Languages of Islam and Christianity in Post-Soviet Russia* (Leiden, Brill, 2020); Gulnaz Sibgatullina, "The Muftis and the Myths: Constructing the Russian 'Church for Islam,'" *Problems of Post-Communism*, 2023, pagination not allocated.

73. Margarita Karnysheva, "Writing an Illiberal History of the Russian Revolution: How the Kremlin Projected Policy into the Past, 1985–2011," *Journal of Illiberalism Studies* 3, no. 3 (2023): 47–70.

74. Luke March, *The Communist Party in Post-Soviet Russia* (Manchester: Manchester University Press, 2002).

75. Katharina Bluhm, "Russia's Conservative Counter-Movement: Genesis, Actors, and Core Concepts," in Katharina Bluhm and Mihai Varga, eds., *New Conservatives in Russia and East Central Europe* (London: Routledge, 2018), 25–53.

76. Juliette Faure, "A Russian Version of Reactionary Modernism: Aleksandr Prokhanov's 'Spiritualization of Technology," *Journal of Political Ideologies* 26, no. 3 (2021): 356–379.

77. Marlene Laruelle and Margarita Karnysheva, *Memory Politics and the Russian Civil War: Reds versus Whites* (London: Bloomsbury, 2020).

78. Agnes Wenger, "Return of the Voenkor: The Military as a New Opinion Leader in Russia?" *Russia.Post*, August 15, 2022, https://russiapost.info/politics/voenkor; Ivan Filippov and Yevgeni Senshin, "'The Z-Space Has Unexpectedly Become a Place for Political Thought,'" *Russia.Post*, November 14, 2023, https://russiapost.info/society/zchannel.

79. Faure, "What Role Did Ideology Play in Triggering Russia's Invasion of Ukraine."

Chapter 2: The Sedimentation of Ideology

1. Vladimir Putin, "Rossiia: Natsional'nyi vopros," *Nezavisimaia gazeta*, January 23, 2012, https://www.ng.ru/politics/2012-01-23/1_national.html.

2. Parts of this chapter are updated versions of my already published works, *In the Name of the Nation*, *Is Russia Fascist?*, and *Russia: Great Power, Weakened State*.

3. Eliot Borenstein, *Plots against Russia: Conspiracy and Fantasy after Socialism* (Ithaca, NY: Cornell University Press, 2019); Ilya Yablokov, *Fortress Russia: Conspiracy Theories in the Post-Soviet World* (New York: Polity Press, 2018).

4. Louis Sell, "Embassy under Siege: An Eyewitness Account of Yeltsin's 1993 Attack on Parliament," *Problems of Post-Communism* 50, no. 4 (2003): 43–64.

5. Russian State Duma, "Postanovlenie ob ob' avlenii politicheskoi i ekonomicheskoi amnistii," February 23, 1994, http://api.duma.gov.ru/api/transcriptFull/1994-02-23.

6. Boris Yeltsin, "Poslanie Prezidenta Federal'nomu Sobraniiu RF: "Ob ukreplenii rossiiskogo gosudarstva,'" February 24, 1994, http://www.intelros.ru/2007/02/04/poslanija_prezidenta_rossii_borisa_elcina_federalnomu_sobraniju_rf_1994_god.html.

7. Natasha Singer, "'Russia for Russians' Is the Ominous Battle Cry : Nationalism: Yeltsin's Tour of an Openly Racist Exhibit Signals the Mainstreaming of a Dangerous Radical Movement," *Los Angeles Times*, July 24, 1994, https://www.latimes.com/archives/la-xpm-1994-07-25-me-19573-story.html.

8. Marlene Laruelle, "Inside and around the Kremlin's Black Box: The New Nationalist Think Tanks in Russia," *Stockholm Papers*, October, 2009, 121–123, http://isdp.eu/content/uploads/images/stories/isdp-main-pdf/2009_laruelle_inside-and-around-the-kremlins-black-box.pdf.

9. David A. Strickland, "Overriding Democracy: American Intervention in Yeltsin's 1996 Reelection Campaign," *Footnotes: A Journal of History* 4 (2000): 166–181; Derek S. Hutcheson, "How to Win Elections and Influence People: The Development of Political Consulting in Post-Communist Russia," *Journal of Political Marketing* 5, no. 4 (2009): 47–70.

10. Laruelle, "Inside and around the Kremlin's Black Box."

11. Kathleen E. Smith, *Mythmaking in the New Russia: Politics and Memory during the Yeltsin Era* (New York: Cornell University Press, 2002).

12. Laruelle, "Inside and around the Kremlin's Black Box."

13. *Nezavisimaia gazeta*, "El'tsyn o 'natsional'noi idee," July 13, 1996, 1.

14. E. Sytaia, "Ocherednoi proekt geopolitiki," *Nezavisimaia gazeta*, October 18, 1996.

15. Laruelle, "Inside and around the Kremlin's Black Box."

16. Radio Svoboda, "Rossiane o natsional'noi idee (1996)," October, 16, 2016, https://www.svoboda.org/a/28050704.html.

17. Igor Chubais, *Ot russkoi idei—k idee novoi Rossii: Kak nam preodelet' ideiniy krizis* (Ann Arbor: Izdatel'skii dom Sotsial'naia zashchita, 1997), 6

18. Robin Aizlewood and Ruth Coates, eds., *Landmarks Revisited: The Vekhi Symposium One Hundred Years On* (Boston: Academic Studies Press, 2013).

19. Michael Urban, "Remythologising the Russian State," *Europe-Asia Studies* 50, no. 6 (1998): 969–992.

20. Fiona Hill, *In Search of Great Russia: Elites, Ideas, Power, the State, and the Pre-Revolutionary Past in the New Russia, 1991–1996* (PhD diss., Harvard University, 1998).

21. Aleksei Podberezkin, "Radikal'nyi protest maloproduktiven," *Nezavisimaia gazeta*, April 2, 1997.

22. Aleksandr Lebed, *Ideologiia zdravstvogo smysla* (Moscow, 1995).

23. Robert V. Daniels, "Evgenii Primakov: Contender by Chance," *Problems of Post-Communism* 46, no. 5 (1999): 27–36; Andrei Tsygankov, "Finding a Civilisational Idea: 'West,' 'Eurasia,' and 'Euro-East,'" in Russia's Foreign Policy," *Geopolitics* 12, no. 3 (2007): 375–399.

24. Boris Yeltsin, "Zaiavlenie Borisa El'tsina," Kremlin.ru, December 31, 1999, http://en.kremlin.ru/events/president/transcripts/24080.

25. Gavid Slade and Andrei Nesterov, "Deconstrucing the Millennium Manifesto: The Yeltsin-Putin Transition and the Rebirth of Ideology," *Geohistory*, May 2006.

26. Putin, "Rossiia na rubezhe tysiacheletii."

27. Sanna Turoma and Kåre Johan Mjør, "Introduction: Russian Civilizationism in a Global Perspective," in Kåre Johan Mjør and Sanna Turoma, eds., *Russia as Civilization: Ideological Discourses in Politics, Media, and Academia* (London: Routledge, 2020), 4.

28. Aleksei Ulykaev, *Pravyi povorot: Programma pravil'noi zhizni, zdorovoi ekonomiki i chesnoi politiki* (Moscow: Strelets, 1999), http://traditio.wiki/holmogorov/library/povorot/povorot.htm.

29. Stephen Hanson, "Instrumental Democracy: The End of Ideology and the Decline of Russian Political Parties," in Vicki Hesli and William Reisinger, eds., *Elections, Parties, and the Future of Russia* (Cambridge: Cambridge University Press, 2003), 163–185; Chen, *The Return of Ideology*.

30. Ivan Krastev, "Paradoxes of the New Authoritarianism," *Journal of Democracy* 22, no. 2 (2011): 5–16.

31. Harley Balzer, "Managed Pluralism: Vladimir Putin's Emerging Regime," *Post-Soviet Affairs* 19, no. 3 (2003): 189–227; Sakwa, *Putin: Russia's Choice*; Daniel Treisman. *The Return: Russia's Journey from Gorbachev to Medvedev* (New York: Simon & Schuster, 2011).

32. Vladimir Putin, "Poslanie Prezidenta Rossiiskoi Federatsii," Kremlin.ru, July 8, 2000, http://www.kremlin.ru/acts/bank/22401.

33. BusinessPress.ru, "Prochat v Glavy Soveta po natsional'noi ideologii," December 8, 2003, http://www.businesspress.ru/newspaper/article_mId_33_aId_286900.html.

34. Julie Deschepper, "Le 'patrimoine soviétique' de l'URSS à la Russie contemporaine: Généalogie d'un concept," *Vingtième Siecle: Revue d'Histoire* 137, no. 1 (2018): 88.

35. Maria Omelicheva, "A New Russian Holiday Has More Behind It Than National Unity: The Political Functions of Historical Commemorations," *Australian Journal of Politics & History* 63, no. 3 (2017): 430–442.

36. Sakwa, *Putin: Russia's Choice*.

37. The largest social mobilization the country had known at that time was in January 2005, when the state decided to replace the benefits in kind (mainly free public transport and medications) traditionally granted to the poorest classes with financial compensation. This monetization of social benefits triggered large spontaneous demonstrations from several tens of thousands of persons around the country and forced the Kremlin to reverse its decision.

38. Laruelle, *Russian Eurasianism*, 102–117.

39. Vladimir Putin, "'Proekt' gosudarstvo-tsivilizatsiia," *APN.ru*, February 9, 2005, https://www.apn.ru/index.php?newsid=1280.

40. Sarah E. Mendelson and Theodore P. Gerber, "Soviet Nostalgia: An Impediment to Russian Democratization," *Washington Quarterly* 29, no. 1 (2005): 6.

41. Malinova, "Framing the Collective Memory of the 1990s"; Malinova, "Constructing the Collective Trauma of 'The Hard 1990s'."

42. Aleksei Chadaev, *Putin: Ego Ideologiia* (Moscow: Evropa, 2006).

43. Giuliano da Empori, *The Wizard of the Kremlin* (New York: Penguin, 2023).

44. On Suslov, see Richard Sakwa, "Russian Political Culture through the Eyes of Vladislav Surkov: Guest Editor's Introduction," *Russian Politics and Law* 46, no. 4 (2008): 3–7; Georgii Bovt, "Vladislav Surkov: A Pragmatic Idealism," *Russian Politics and Law* 46, no. 5 (2008): 33–40.

45. Alexander Morozov, "Kazuz Nemtsova i spetspropagandony," *OpenSpace.ru*, January 17, 2011, https://os.colta.ru/media/projects/18065/details/19871/.

46. Andrey Okara, "Sovereign Democracy: A New Russian Idea or a PR Project?" *Russia in Global Affairs*, no. 3 (2007), https://eng.globalaffairs.ru/articles/sovereign-democracy-a-new-russian-idea-or-a-pr-project/.

47. Surkov, *Russkaia politicheskaia kul'tura*, 11.

48. Sirke Mäkinen, "Surkovian Narrative on the Future of Russia: Making Russia a World Leader," *Journal of Communist Studies and Transition Politics* 27, no. 2 (2011): 143–165.

49. Bovt, "Vladislav Surkov: A Pragmatic Idealism"; Sakwa, "Putin's Leadership: Character and Consequences."

50. Clémentine Fauconnier, *Entre le marteau et l'enclume: Russie unie, la fabrication d'une hégémonie partisane dans la Russie de Poutine* (Lille : Éditions du Septentrion, Presses Universitaires de Lille, 2019).

51. More in Laruelle, "Inside and around the Kremlin's Black Box."

52. Sergei Prozorov, "Russian Conservatism in the Putin Presidency: The Dispersion of a Hegemonic Discourse," *Journal of Political Ideologies* 10, no. 2 (2005): 121–143.

53. Laruelle, "Inside and around the Kremlin's Black Box."

54. Boris Gryzlov, "Ni odna politicheskaia partiia poka ne sposobna sozdat' v Rossii usloviia dlia novogo tsivilizatsionnogo ryvka," *RBK*, December 20, 2005.

55. Boris Gryzlov, "Sovremennyi rossiiskii konservatizm," Tsentr Sotsial'no-Konservativnoi Politiki, December 2007, http://www.cscp-pfo.ru/index.php?option=com_content&task=view&id=187&Itemid=34.

56. Lenta.ru, "Vzgliad na Rossiiu s verkhushki Spasskoi bashni. Dmitrii Medvedev ob"iasnil elektoratu zadachi tekushchego momenta," April 4, 2005, https://m.lenta.ru/articles/2005/04/04/medvedev/.

57. Laruelle, "Inside and around the Kremlin's Black Box."

58. Tsentr sotsial'no-konservativnoi politiki, "Predlozheniia k platforme rossiiskogo sotsial'nogo konservatizma," Tsentr Sotsial'no-Konservativnoi Politiki, http://www.cscp.ru/about/manifest/41/.

59. Aleksandra Samarina, Natalia Kostenko, and Ivan Rodin, "Edinaia Rossiia razdelitsia na techeniia," *Nezavisimaia gazeta*, November 2, 2007, http://www.ng.ru/politics/2007-11-02/1_er.html.

60. Laruelle, *In the Name of the Nation*.

61. Km.ru, "Edinaia Rossiia sozdaet russkii proekt," February 5, 2007, https://www.km.ru/glavnoe/2007/02/07/arkhiv/edinaya-rossiya-sozdaet-russkii-proekt. The Movement against Illegal Immigration (DNPI) was at that time the main skinhead political movement, promoting xenophobia and racism, before being banned in 2011. It succeeded in becoming the intermediary between the skinhead movements and more respectable nationalist political personalities and in widely broadcasting the slogan "Russia to the Russians" (more in Laruelle, *In the Name of the Nation*, 74–79).

62. Gosudarstvenno-politicheskii klub, "Politicheskaia deklaratsiia," 2006–2007, http://www.gpclub.ru/news/0x1x2.html (site discontinued).

63. Vladimir Putin, "Zachem ia vozglavil spisok Edinoi Rossii," *Kreml.org*, November 13, 2007, http://www.kreml.org/media/165463628?mode=print.

64. Fauconnier, *Entre le marteau et l'enclume*. See also Anna Zakatnova, "Edinorossy zakrepili klubnuiu zhizn' Kharitiei," *Rossiiskaia gazeta*, April, 10, 2008, https://rg.ru/2008/04/10/edinorossy.html.

65. Sakwa, "Putin's Leadership: Character and Consequences."

66. Richard Sakwa, *The Crisis of Russian Democracy: The Dual State, Factionalism and the Medvedev Succession* (Cambridge: Cambridge University Press, 2011).

67. Katri Pynnoniemi, "Science Fiction: President Medvedev's Campaign for Russia's 'Technological Modernization,'" *Demokratizatsiya: The Journal of Post-Soviet Democratization* 22, no. 4 (2014): 605–625.

68. InoSMI.ru, "Yurgens, Igor: Ia ne izkliuchaiu integratsiiu v NATO," November 18, 2010, http://inosmi.ru/europe/20101118/164327795.html.

69. Edwin Bacon, "Policy Change and the Narratives of Russia's Think Tanks," *Palgrave Communications* 4, no. 1 (2018): 94–106.

70. *Interfax*, "Medvedev nazval SSSR 'slozhnym gosudarstvom' i prizval ne idealizirovat ego," December 5, 2019. https://www.interfax.ru/russia/686800.

71. Andrei Tsyngakov, "Two Faces of Putin's Great Power Pragmatism," *Soviet and Post-Soviet Review* 34, no. 1 (2007): 103–199.

72. Gerard Toal, *Near Abroad: Putin, the West, and the Contest over Ukraine and the Caucasus* (Oxford: Oxford University Press, 2017).

73. Irina Papkova, "Russian Orthodox Concordat? Church and State under Medvedev," *Nationalities Papers* 39, no. 5 (2011): 667–683.

74. BBC Monitoring, "Russian President Outlines Principles of Relations between State and Church," *NTV*, February 2, 2009.

75. Katja Richters, "The Russian Orthodox Church and Medvedev's Modernisation Policy: Allies or Foes?" *Religion, State & Society* 40, no. 3/4 (2012): 363–378.

76. Olga Iakimova, "A Decade of Religious Education in Russian Schools," *PONARS Eurasia Policy Memo*, no. 676, November 2020.

77. US Embassy, "Svetlana Medvedeva Steps into the Spotlight," Cable 08MOSCOW2306 from US Embassy Moscow to Washington," August 8, 2008, https://wikileaks.org/plusd/cables/08MOSCOW2306_a.html.

78. Samuel Greene, *Moscow in Movement: Power and Opposition in Putin's Russia* (Stanford, CA: Stanford University Press, 2014); Graeme Robertson, "The Election Protests of 2011–2012 in Broader Perspective," *Problems of Post-Communism* 60, no. 2 (2013): 11–23.

79. Pål Kolstø, "Marriage of Convenience? Collaboration between Nationalists and Liberals in the Russian Opposition 2011–12," *Russian Review* 75, no. 4 (2016): 645–663.

80. Daniel Weiss, "The New Russian Legislation on Blasphemy and Swearing: The Parliamentary Debates," *Zeitschrift Für Slavische Philologie* 72, no. 2 (2016): 289–321.

81. Eliot Borenstein, *Speaking Punk to Power* (London: Bloomsbury, 2021).

82. Neil Robinson, "Russian Neo-Patrimonialism and Putin's 'Cultural Turn,'" *Europe-Asia Studies* 69, no. 2 (2017): 348–366.

83. Sharafutdinova, *The Red Mirror*, 146.

84. Quoted by Chen, *The Return of Ideology*, 75.

85. Vladimir Putin, "Vladimir Putin Meets with Members of the Valdai International Discussion Club," Kremlin.ru, August 19, 2013, https://rg.ru/2013/09/19/stenogramma-site.html.

86. Damien Sharikov, "Putin nazval Kodeks stroitelia kommunizma 'primitivnoi vydzerzhkoi iz Biblii'," *Nezavisimaia gazeta*, January 14, 2018, https://www.ng.ru/news/604988.html.

87. Egor Mostovshchikov, "Yelena Mizulina: The Creation of a Conservative," *OpenDemocracy*, May 28, 2015, https://www.opendemocracy.net/en/odr/yelena-mizulina-creation-of-conservative/.

88. Irina Tumakova, "Evgenii Fiodorov: Rossiiskaia Konstitutsiia, kolonial'nyi listok upravleniia," *Fontanka.ru*, November 29, 2013, https://www.fontanka.ru/2013/11/29/186/.

89. Julie Ray and Neli Esipova, "Russian Approval of Putin Soars to Highest Level in Years," Gallup, July 18, 2014, http://www.gallup.com/poll/173597/russian-approval-putin-soars-highest-level-years.aspx.

90. Natal'ia Rajbman, "V Rossii smenilas' doktrina informatsionnoi bezopasnosti," *Vedomosti*, December 6, 2016, https://www.vedomosti.ru/politics/articles/2016/12/06/668347-doktrina-informatsionnoi.

91. *Moscow Times*, "Russian Orthodox Priests and Traffic Police March to Remember Road Victims," November 20, 2017, https://www.themoscowtimes.com/2017/11/20/russian-orthodox-priests-and-traffic-police-march-to-remember-road-victims-a59614.

92. *The Economist*, "Russian Culture Wars Take Centre Stage," August 19, 2017, https://www.economist.com/europe/2017/08/19/russian-culture-wars-take-centre-stage.

93. Maria Lipman, "Meet the Second-Rate Academic Who Is Vladimir Putin's Culture Cop," *New Republic*, May 23, 2014, http://www.newrepublic.com/article/117896/vladimir-medinsky-russias-culture-minister-putin-toady.

94. Lev Jakobson et al., "From Liberal to Conservative: Shifting Cultural Policy Regimes in Post-Soviet Russia," *International Journal of Cultural Policy* 24, no. 3 (May 2018), https://www.researchgate.net/publication/303693734_From_liberal_to_conservative_shifting_cultural_policy_regimes_in_post-Soviet_Russia

95. *Nezavisimaia gazeta*, "Novyi zakon o osnovakh preduprezhdeniia pravonarushenii protiv Rossiiskoi Federatsii," June 28, 2016, https://rg.ru/documents/2016/06/28/profilaktika-dok.html.

96. Aleksei Chadaev, *Putin: Nashi tsennosti* (Moscow: Eksmo, 2018).

97. Regina Smyth, "How the Kremlin Is Using the Moscow Renovation Project to Reward and Punish Voters," *PONARS Eurasia Policy Memo*, no. 513, March 2018.

98. Jeremy Morris, Andrei Semenov, and Regina Smyth, eds., *Varieties of Russian Activism: State-Society Contestation in Everyday Life* (Bloomington: Indiana University Press, 2023).

99. Kirill Rogov, "Putin's Reelection: Capturing Russia's Electoral Patterns," *PONARS Eurasia Podcast*, June 2018, https://www.ponarseurasia.org/putin-s-reelection-capturing-russia-s-electoral-patterns-a-discussion-with-kirill-rogov.

100. Filip Kovačević, "The Second Most Powerful Man in Russia," *New Lines Magazine*, March 10, 2022, https://newlinesmag.com/reportage/the-second-most-powerful-man-in-russia.

101. Nikolai Petrov, "The Repressions Spiral," *PONARS Eurasia Commentary*, March 11, 2019, https://www.ponarseurasia.org/the-repressions-spiral.

102. Derek S. Hutcheson and Ian McAllister, "Consolidating the Putin Regime: The 2020 Referendum on Russia's Constitutional Amendments," *Russian Politics* 6, no. 3 (2021): 355–376.

103. Sergei Belov, "The Content of the 2020 Constitutional Amendments in Russia," *IACL-AIDC Blog*, April 4, 2021, https://blog-iacl-aidc.org/2021-posts/2021/04/01-constitutional-amendments-in-russia-content-lhnf7.

104. Zygar, "How Vladimir Putin Lost Interest in the Present."

105. *Bellingcat*, "FSB Team of Chemical Weapon Experts Implicated in Alexey Navalny Novichok Poisoning," December 14, 2020, https://www.bellingcat.com/news/uk-and-europe/2020/12/14/fsb-team-of-chemical-weapon-experts-implicated-in-alexey-navalny-novichok-poisoning/.

106. Jan Matti Dollbaum, Marvan Lallouet, and Ben Noble, *Navalny: Putin's Nemesis, Russia's Future?* 2nd ed. (London: Hurst, 2021).

107. Putin, "Ob istoricheskom edinstve russkikh i ukraintsev."

108. Andrew Roth, "Russia Issues List of Demands It Says Must Be Met to Lower Tensions in Europe," *The Guardian*, December 17, 2021, https://www.theguardian.com/world/2021/dec/17/russia-issues-list-demands-tensions-europe-ukraine-nato.

109. *Holod*, "Sem' sluchaev smertei rossiiskikh top-menedzherov za etot god," September 1, 2022, https://holod.media/2022/09/01/deaths-2022.

110. Wenger, "Return of the Voenkor": Filippov and Senshin, "'The Z-Space Has Unexpectedly Become a Place for Political Thought'."

111. Julian G. Waller, "Public Politics in the Wartime Russian Dictatorship," *War on the Rocks*, January 17, 2023, https://warontherocks.com/2023/01/public-politics-in-the-wartime-russian-dictatorship.

112. *Kommersant*, "Gosduma priniala v 2022 godu rekordnoe chislo zakonov—653," December 22, 2022, https://www.kommersant.ru/doc/5736100.

113. *Roskomsvoboda*, "Monitoring of Registry, February 24, 2022 through December 31, 2023," 2022, https://reestr.rublacklist.net/en/?status=all&gov=all&date_start=24-02-2022&date_end=31-12-2023; *Meduza.io*, "Russian Authorities Blocked More than 885,000 Websites in First Half of 2023," September 7, 2023, https://meduza.io/en/news/2023/09/07/russian-authorities-reportedly-blocked-more-than-885-000-websites-in-first-half-of-2023.

114. *OVD-Info*, "Svodka antivoennykh repressii. Odinnadtsat' mesiatsev voiny," January 2023, https://data.ovd.info/svodka-antivoennyh-repressiy-11.

115. Tat'iana Gurova, "Nuzhna li sovremennoi Rossii ideologiia ?," *Rossiiskaia gazeta*, February 27, 2020, https://rg.ru/2020/02/27/nuzhna-li-sovremennoj-rossii-ideologiia.html.

116. Anastasia Maier, Anna Kiseleva, and Elena Mukhametshina, "Ministr iustitsii nachal diskussiiu ob otmene zapreta na ideologiiu," *Vedomosti*, May 12, 2023, https://www

.vedomosti.ru/politics/articles/2023/05/12/974675-ministr-yustitsii-nachal-diskussiyu-ob-otmene-zapreta-na-ideologiyu; Anastasia Kornia and Andrei Vinokurov, "Ideologicheskie edinoglasiia," *Kommersant*, May 11, 2023, https://www.kommersant.ru/doc/5979267.

Part II

1. BBC, "Vladimir Putin's Interview with the BBC," *Gazeta.ru*, March 13, 2000, http://www.gazeta.ru/2001/02/28/putin_i_bbc.shtml.

2. Ted Hopf, *Social Construction of International Politics: Identities and Foreign Policies* (Ithaca, NY: Cornell University Press, 2002); Jack Snyder, *Myths of Empire: Domestic Politics and International Ambition* (Ithaca, NY: Cornell University Press, 1991).

3. Iver Neuman, *Russia and the Idea of Europe* (London: Routledge, 2017); Edward C. Thaden, *Interpreting History: Collective Essays on Russia's Relations with Europe* (New York: Columbia University Press, 1990); Robert A. Saunders and Vlad Strukov, "The Popular Geopolitics Feedback Loop: Thinking beyond the 'Russia against the West' Paradigm," *Europe-Asia Studies* 69, no. 2 (2017): 303–324.

4. Ella Shohat and Robert Stam, *Unthinking EurocentrismMulticulturalism and the Media* (London: Routledge, 1994), 2.

5. While the Slavophiles saw the people as the core of the nation's legitimacy, the pan-Slavists, *pochvenniki*, and Byzantinist nostalgics emphasized the dynastic power and autocratic structure of the state. See Andrzej Walicki, *The Slavophile Controversy: History of a Conservative Utopia in Nineteenth-Century Russian Thought* (Notre Dame, IN: University of Notre Dame Press, 1989); Laura Engelstein, *Slavophile Empire: Imperial Russia's Illiberal Path* (Ithaca, NY: Cornell University Press, 2009).

6. Edward C. Thaden, *Interpreting History: Collective Essays on Russia's Relations with Europe* (New York: Columbia University Press, 1990); James H. Billington, *Russia in Search of Itself* (Washington, DC: Woodrow Wilson Press / Baltimore: Johns Hopkins University Press, 2004).

7. Fedor Dostoevskii, *Dnevnik pisatelia*, 1876, available at http://dostoevskiy-lit.ru/dostoevskiy/dnevnik/index.htm.

8. Milan Hauner, *What Is Asia to Us? Russia's Asian Heartland Yesterday and Today* (London: Routledge, 1992); Svetlana Gorshenina, *L'invention de l'Asie centrale: Histoire du concept de la Tartarie à l'Eurasie* (Geneva: Droz, 2014).

9. Alfred Evans, "Ideological Changes under Vladimir Putin in the Perspective of Social Identity Theory," *Demokratizatsiya: The Journal of Post-Soviet Democratization* 23, no. 4 (2015): 401–426.

10. Neil Malcolm, "The 'Common European Home' and Soviet European Policy," *International Affairs* 65, no. 4 (1989): 659–676.

11. Mikhail Gorbachev, *Memoirs* (New York: Doubleday, 1996).

12. Lilia Shevtsova, *Yeltsin's Russia: Myths and Reality* (Moscow: Carnegie Center, 1999).

Chapter 3: The Painful Relationship to a Polysemic West

1. Vladimir Putin, "Interview with the Chinese Newspaper Renmin Ribao, the Chinese News Agency Xinhua and the RTR TV Company," Kremlin.ru, July 16, 2000, http://en.special.kremlin.ru/events/president/transcripts/24168.

2. Malinova, "Framing the Collective Memory of the 1990s." See also Veronika Pehe and Joanna Wawrzyniak, eds., *Remembering the Neoliberal Turn: Economic Change and Collective Memory in Eastern Europe after 1989* (London: Routledge, 2023); Malinova, "Legitimizing Putin's Regime"; Olga Malinova, "Encounters with Liberalism in Post-Soviet Russia," in Michael Freeden, Javier Fernández-Sebastián, and Jörn Leonhard, eds., *In Search of European Liberalisms: Concepts, Languages, Ideologies* (New York: Berghahn Books, 2019), 278–301.

3. Leonid Polyakov, "Liberal'nyi Konservator," *Nezavisimaia gazeta*, no. 18, 2000, https://www.ng.ru/ideas/2000-02-02/8_conserve.html.

4. Peter Rutland, "Neoliberalism and the Russian Transition," *Review of International Political Economy* 20, no. 2 (2013): 339.

5. Alexander Etkind, "Barrels of Fur: Natural Resources and the State in the Long History of Russia," *Journal of Eurasian Studies* 2, no. 2 (2011): 164–171; Peter Rutland, "Neoliberalism and the Russian Transition," *Review of International Political Economy* 20, no. 2 (2013): 332–362.

6. Stephen J. Collier, *Post-Soviet Social: Neoliberalism, Social Modernity, Biopolitics* (Princeton, NJ: Princeton University Press, 2011).

7. Jarett Zigon, *"HIV Is God's Blessing": Rehabilitating Morality in Neoliberal Russia* (Berkeley: University of California Press, 2011); Julie Hemment, *Youth Politics in Putin's Russia: Producing Patriots and Entrepreneurs* (Bloomington: Indiana University Press, 2015).

8. Elisabeth Schimpfössl, "Russian Philanthrocapitalism," *Cultural Politics* 15, no. 1 (2019): 105–120.

9. Alexander Bibkov, "Neo-traditionalist Fits with Neo-liberal Shifts in Russian Cultural Policy," in Lena Jonson and Andrei Erofeev, eds., *Russia—Art Resistance and the Conservative-Authoritarian Zeitgeist* (London: Routledge, 2017); Ilya Budraitkis, "Contradictions in Russian Cultural Politics: Conservatism as an Instrument of Neoliberalism," September 12, 2017, https://lefteast.org/russian-contradiction/.

10. Vladislav Surkov, "Suverenitet—eto politicheskii sinonim konkurentosposobnosti," *Edinaia Rossiia*, February, 22, 2006, https://web.archive.org/web/20060418035317/http://www.edinros.ru/news.html?id=111148.

11. Peter Rutland, "The Contradictions in Putin's Economic Nationalism: From Western Partner to Fortress Russia," *Russian Politics 8, no. 1 (2023): 24–47.*

12. Ivan Timofeev, "'Russian Rebellion:' Local and Global Consequences," Russian International Affairs Council, June 15, 2022, https://russiancouncil.ru/en/analytics-and-comments/analytics/russian-rebellion-local-and-global-consequences/.

13. Vadim Visloguzov and Evgenia Kriuchkova, "Biudzhet ushel v priemlemyi minus," *Kommersant*, January 1, 2023, https://www.kommersant.ru/doc/5759937.

14. Timur Batyrov, "'Ne namechaetsia': Putin iskliuchil provedenie deprivatizatsii v

Rossii," *Forbes.ru*, September 12, 2023, https://www.forbes.ru/biznes/496276-ne-name-caetsa-putin-isklucil-provedenie-deprivatizacii-v-rossii.

15. RBK, "Shokhin ob iz"iatii chastnykh aktivov: 'Nikto ne znaet, kto v ocheredi,'" *RBK*, September 11, 2023, https://www.rbc.ru/economics/11/09/2023/64fedbc59a7947a77baeraac.

16. Nikolai Petrov, "The State Machine Redistributing Property into the Right Hands," *Russia.Post*, October 24, 2023, https://russiapost.info/politics/redistributing.

17. Volodymyr Ishchenko, Ivan Matveev, and Oleg Zhuravlev, "Russian Military Keynesianism: Who Benefits from the War in Ukraine?" *PONARS Eurasia Policy Memo*, no. 865, November 27, 2023.

18. Dmitry Dolgin, "Russian Budget Consolidation May Face Obstacles in 2022," *ING*, October 2021, https://think.ing.com/articles/russian-budget-consolidation-may-face-obstacles-in-2022.

19. Fomin, "Two Statisms of Putin's Ideology," 1.

20. Olesya Zakharova, "The Evolution of the Idea of Democracy in Putin's Rhetoric," *Ridl.io*, April 7, 2021, https://ridl.io/ru/jevoljucija-idei-demokratii-v-putinskoj-ritorike/.

21. Dominic Lieven, *Empire: The Russian Empire and Its Rivals* (New Haven, CT: Yale University Press, 2002); Diesen, *Russian Conservatism*.

22. Riccardo Mario Cucciolla, ed., *Dimensions and Challenges of Russian Liberalism: Historical Drama and New Prospects* (Cham, Switz.: Springer, 2019); Paul Robinson, *Russian Liberalism* (Ithaca, NY: Cornell University Press, 2023).

23. Boris Nemtsov, *Ispoved' buntaria* (Moscow: Partizan, 2007).

24. *Moscow Times*, "A Beginner's Guide to Russia's Fragmented Opposition," March 6, 2023, https://www.themoscowtimes.com/2023/03/06/a-beginners-guide-to-russias-fragmented-opposition-a80262.

25. L. G. Byzov, "Tsennostnaia evolutsiia 'putinskogo konsensusa' v pervyi god poslednego prezidentskogo sroka," *Obshchestvennyie nauki i sovremennost'* 4 (2019): 42–56.

26. Lewis, *Russia's New Authoritarianism*.

27. Lionel Barber, Henry Foy, and Alex Barker, "Vladimir Putin Says Liberalism Has 'Become Obsolete,'" *Financial Times*, June 17, 2019, https://www.ft.com/content/670039ec-98f3-11e9-9573-ee5cbb98ed36.

28. Vladimir Putin, "Interv'iu pervomu kanalu i agentstvu Assoshieited Press," Kremlin.ru, September 4, 2013, http://kremlin.ru/events/president/news/19143#sel=127:98:g,127:98:g.

29. Vladimir Putin, "Poslanie Prezidenta Rossiiskoi Federatsii Ot 18.03.2014 g.," Kremlin.ru, March 18, 2014, http://kremlin.ru/acts/bank/39444.

30. Ielena Chernyshova, "V. Putin podtverdil, chto on 'nastoiashchii liberal,'" *RBK*, January 19, 2014, https://www.rbc.ru/politics/19/01/2014/570416189a794761c0ce5bf4.

31. Richard Sakwa, *Russia against the Rest: The Post–Cold War Crisis of World Order* (Cambridge: Cambridge University Press, 2017).

32. John G. Ikenberry, "The Liberal International Order and Its Discontents," *Millennium: Journal of International Studies* 38, no. 3 (2010): 509–521.

33. John G. Ikenberry, "The End of Liberal International Order?" *International Affairs* 94, no. 1 (2018): 11.

34. Andrej Krickovic and Richard Sakwa, "War in Ukraine: The Clash of Norms and Ontologies," *Journal of Military and Strategic Studies* 22, no. 2 (2022): 90–91.

35. Neil Malcolm, "The 'Common European Home' and Soviet European Policy," *International Affairs* 65, no. 4 (1989): 659–676; Neuman, *Russia and the Idea of Europe*.

36. Sakwa, *Russia against the Rest*, 4–5

37. Andrey Tsygankov, "Vladimir Putin's Last Stand: The Sources of Russia's Ukraine Policy," *Post-Soviet Affairs* 31, no. 4 (2015): 279–303.

38. Curanović, "Russia's Mission in the World," 215.

39. John Mearsheimer, *The Great Delusion: Liberal Dreams and International Realities* (New Haven, CT: Yale University Press, 2018).

40. Alexander Lukin, "Eurasian Integration and the Clash of Values," *Survival* 56, no. 3 (2014): 43–60; Sergei S. Karaganov, "S Vostoka na Zapad, ili Bol'shaia Evraziia," *Rossiia v global'noi politike*, October 25, 2016.

41. Sergei S. Karaganov, "Venskii kontsert XXI veka," *Rossiia v global'noi politike*, June 3, 2015, https://globalaffairs.ru/articles/venskij-konczert-xxi-veka/.

42. Sergey Kurginian, "Kurginyan: SShA–Novyi Karfagen, ustraivayushchii khaos po vsemu miru," *Regnum*, September 30, 2015, http://regnum.ru/news/polit/1982223.html, quoted in Elena Chebankova, "Ideas, Ideology and Intellectuals in Search of Russia's Political Future," *Daedalus* 146, no. 2 (2017): 81.

43. Andrey Tsygankov, "Crafting the State-Civilization: Vladimir Putin's Turn to Distinct Values," *Problems of Post-Communism* 63, no. 3 (2016): 146–158.

44. Gregorio Bettiza and David Lewis, "Authoritarian Powers and Norm Contestation in the Liberal International Order: Theorizing the Power Politics of Ideas and Identity," *Journal of Global Security Studies* 5, no. 4 (2020): 559–577.

45. Elena Chebankova, "Russia's Idea of the Multipolar World Order: Origins and Main Dimensions," *Post-Soviet Affairs* 33, no. 3 (2017): 217–234.

46. Xymena Kurowska, Viacheslav Morozov, and Anatoly Reshetnikov, "Why Russia's Strategic Deception Is Popular: The Cultural Appeal of the Trickster," *PONARS Eurasia Policy Memo*, no. 554, December 2018, https://www.ponarseurasia.org/why-russia-s-strategic-deception-is-popular-the-cultural-appeal-of-the-trickster/.

47. Kévin Limonier and Maxime Audinet, "La stratégie d'influence informationnelle et numérique de la Russie en Europe," *Hérodote* 1, no. 164 (2017): 123–144; Maxime Audinet, *Le Lion, l'ours et les hyènes: Acteurs, pratiques et récits de l'influence informationnelle russe en Afrique subsaharienne francophone* (Paris: Institut de Recherche Stratégique de l'École Militaire, 2021).

48. Fedor Luk'ianov, "V teni sovetskogo statusa," *Rossiia v global'noi politike*, January 30, 2017, https://globalaffairs.ru/articles/v-teni-sovetskogo-statusa/.

49. Olga Malinova, "Russia and 'the West' in the 2000s: Redefining Russian Identity in Official Political Discourse," in Raymond Taras, ed., *Russia's Identity in International Relations: Images, Perceptions, Misperceptions* (London: Routledge, 2012), 81.

50. Aleksandr Vasil'ev, "Eksperty rasskazali o griadushchem fundamental'nom sdvige v geopolitike," *Rossiiskaia gazeta*, April 6, 2017, https://rg.ru/2017/04/06/eksperty-rasskazali-o-griadushchem-fundamentalnom-sdvige-v-geopolitike.html.

51. Stephen Holmes and Ivan Krastev, *The Light That Failed: Why the West Is Losing the Fight for Democracy* (New York: Pegasus Books, 2020).

52. Dmitry Bykov, "Andrey Konchalovskii: Chem dol'she budet Putin, tem luchshe," *Sobesednik*, October 17, 2016, https://sobesednik.ru/Dmitryy-bykov/20171017-andrey-kon chalovskiy-chem-dolshe-budet-putin-tem-luchshe.

53. Konstantin Bogomolov, "The Rape of Europe 2.0," Simone Weil Center, March 14, 2021, https://simoneweilcenter.org/publications/2021/3/14/an-introduction-to-bogomo lovs-manifesto-the-rape-of-europe-20.

54. Vladimir Putin, "Zasedanie mezhdunarodnogo diskussionnogo kluba 'Valdai,'" Kremlin.ru. October 27, 2022, http://kremlin.ru/events/president/news/69695.

55. Marlene Laruelle, "Russia as an Anti-Liberal European Civilization," in Pål Kolstø and Helge Blakkisrud, eds., *The New Russian Nationalism: Between Imperial and Ethnic* (Edinburgh: Edinburgh University Press, 2017), 275–297.

56. Nikolai Patrushev, "Nuzhny li Rossii 'universal'nye tsennosti?" *Rossiiskaia gazeta*, June 17, 2020, rg.ru/2020/06/17/nuzhny-li-rossii-universalnye-cennosti.html.

57. Katharina Bluhm, "Russia's Conservative Counter-Movement: Genesis, Actors, and Core Concepts," in Bluhm and Varga, eds., *New Conservatives in Russia and East Central Europe*, 25–53.

58. Karaganov, "Venskii kontsert XXI veka."

59. Ulrich Beck, *Risk Society: Towards a New Modernity* (Thousand Oaks, CA: Sage, 1992), 14.

60. Ted McAlllister, *Revolt against Modernity: Leo Strauss, Eric Voegelin, and the Search for a Post-Liberal Order* (Lawrence: University Press of Kansas, 1996).

61. Stoeckl and Uzlaner, *The Moralist International*.

62. MID.ru, "Kontseptsiia Vneshnei Politiki Rossiiskoi Federatsii," March 31, 2023, https://www.mid.ru/ru/detail-material-page/1860586/.

63. Tsoncho S. Tsonchev, "Russia and the West: Fyodor Tyutchev on Russian Exceptionalism," *Montreal Review*, September 2018, https://www.themontrealreview.com/2009/Russia-and-the-West-Fyodor-Tyutchev-on-Russian-Exceptionalism.php.

64. Dusko Doder, "Soviets Blame Chilled Relations on Reagan-Led Russophobia," *Washington Post*, July 27, 1984, https://www.washingtonpost.com/archive/politics/1984/07/27/soviets-blame-chilled-relations-on-reagan-led-russophobia/6850736a-29b2-4d98-8c61-effa5d089517/.

65. Mimi Reitz, "Weaponised 'Russophobia,'" *Riddle*, August 9, 2023, https://ridl.io/weaponised-russophobia.

66. Douglas Irvin-Erickson, "Genocide Discourses: American and Russian Strategic Narratives of Conflict in Iraq and Ukraine," *Politics and Governance* 5, no. 3 (2017): 130–145.

67. Yitzhak Brudny, *Reinventing Russia: Russian Nationalism and the Soviet State, 1953–1991* (Cambridge, MA: Harvard University Press, 2000).

68. Sergei Glaz'ev, *Genotsid* (Moscow: Terra, 1998).

69. Toal, *Near Abroad*, 181–185, 188–190.

70. Oksana Dudko, "A Conceptual Limbo of Genocide: Russian Rhetoric, Mass Atrocities in Ukraine, and the Current Definition's Limits," *Canadian Slavonic Papers* 64, no. 2–3 (2022): 133–145.

71. Vladimir Putin, "Obrashchenie Prezidenta Rossiiskoi Federatsii," Kremlin.ru, February 21, 2022, http://kremlin.ru/events/president/news/67828.
72. Laruelle, *Is Russia Fascist?*
73. Mischa Gabowitsch, "Fascism as Stiob," *Kultura* 4 (2009): 4.
74. Lenta.ru, "Lavrov: Na pravde o voine nel'z'a spekulirovat'," May 4, 2005, https://lenta.ru/news/2005/05/03/lavrov/.
75. Vladimir Putin, "'Proekt' gosudarstvo-tsivilizatsiia," *APN*, February 9, 2005, https://www.apn.ru/index.php?newsid=1280.
76. Maria Mälksoo, "Liminality and Contested Europeanness: Conflicting Memory Politics in the Baltic Space," in Eiki Berg and Piret Ehin, eds., *Identity and Foreign Policy: Baltic-Russian Relations in the Context of European Integration* (Aldershot, UK: Routledge, 2013), 65–83; Maria Mälksoo. "The Memory Politics of Becoming European: The East European Subalterns and the Collective Memory of Europe," *European Journal of International Relations* 15, no. 4 (2009): 653–680.
77. Piotr Akopov, "Vyshla iz doveriia: Elita velikoi strany polnost'iu diskreditirovana," *RIA Novosti*, October 29, 2020, https://ria.ru/20201029/frantsiya-1581974459.html.
78. Samuel Charap and Timothy Colton, *Everyone Loses: The Ukraine Crisis and the Ruinous Contest for Post-Soviet Eurasia* (London: Routledge, 2017).
79. Ivan Timofeev, "'Russian Rebellion:' Local and Global Consequences," Russian International Affairs Council, June 14, 2022, https://valdaiclub.com/a/highlights/russian-rebellion-local-and-global-consequences/.

Chapter 4: Byzantium

1. Vladimir Putin, "Poslanie Prezidenta Rossiiskoi Federatsii Ot 18.03.2014 g.," Kremlin.ru, March 18, 2014, http://kremlin.ru/acts/bank/39444.
2. Sergei A. Ivanov, "The Second Rome as Seen by the Third: Russian Debates on 'the Byzantine Legacy," in Przemyslaw Marciniak and Dion C. Smythe, eds., *The Reception of Byzantium in European Culture since 1500* (Farnham, UK: Ashgate, 2016), 55–80.
3. Alexander Bitis, *Russia and the Eastern Question: Army, Government and Society, 1815–1833* (London: British Academy, 2006).
4. Konstantin Leont'ev, "Vizantizm i Slavianstvo," 1873, https://azbyka.ru/otechnik/Konstantin_Leontev/vizantizm-i-slavjanstvo/.
5. Leont'ev, "Vizantizm i Slavianstvo."
6. Leont'ev, "Vizantizm i Slavianstvo."
7. Leont'ev, "Vizantizm i Slavianstvo."
8. Fedor Dostoevskii, *Dnevnik pisatelia*, 1876, available at http://dostoevskiy-lit.ru/dostoevskiy/dnevnik/index.htm.
9. Laruelle and Karnysheva, *Memory Politics and the Russian Civil War.*
10. Anton Bryukov, "Aktual'nost' vizantinizma," *Geopolitika.ru*, June 7, 2016, https://www.geopolitika.ru/en/article/relevance-byzantinism
11. Timur Novikov, *Lektsii* (St Petersburg: Novaia akademiia iziashchnykh iskusstv, 2003), 161.
12. One of the only studies devoted to her is by Østbø, *The New Third Rome.*
13. Natal'ia Narochnitskaia, *Rossiia i russkie v mirovoi istorii* (Moscow: Mezhdunarodnye otnosheniia, 2003).

14. Narochnitskaia, *Rossiia i russkie v mirovoi istorii*.

15. More in Suslov, Čejka, and Đorđević, *Pan-Slavism and Slavophilia in Contemporary Central and Eastern Europe*.

16. Mikhail Remizov, "Interview by Paul Robinson," *Irrussianality*, November 2, 2007, https://irrussianality.wordpress.com/2017/11/02/interview-with-mikhail-remizov/.

17. Remizov, "Interview by Paul Robinson."

18. Sergei Chapnin, "Tsarskie ostanki: Obratnyi otchet," *Colta*, July 18, 2017, https://www.colta.ru/articles/media/15442-tsarskie-ostanki-obratnyy-otschet.

19. Leonid Reshetnikov, *Vernut'sia v Rossiiu* (Moscow: Lana, 2019).

20. "Russkii Lemnos," n.d., http://ruslemnos.ru/.

21. Irina Papkova, "Saving the Third Rome: 'Fall of the Empire,' Byzantium and Putin's Russia," in *Reconciling the Irreconcilable*, vol. 24 (Vienna, Austria: Institute for Human Sciences, 2009), http://www.iwm.at/index.php?option=com_content&task=view&id=131&Itemid=125.

22. Ivanov, "The Second Rome as Seen by the Third."

23. Bogoslov, "Vstrecha avtora fil'ma 'Vizantiiskii urok' so studentami moskovskikh dukhovnykh shkol," September 17, 2008, http://www.bogoslov.ru/text/321296.html.

24. Vladimir Putin, "Poslanie Prezidenta Rossiiskoi Federatsii Ot 18.03.2014 g.," Kremlin.ru, March 18, 2014, http://kremlin.ru/acts/bank/39444.

25. Institut politicheskikh issledovanii, "Byzantium Club," http://www.ipi-rf.ru/vizantiya_club.php.

26. Evraziiskoie dvizhenie Rossiiskoi Federatsii, 2016, https://vk.com/russiaeurasia.

27. Maria Engström, "Re-Imagining Antiquity: The Conservative Discourse of 'Russia as the True Europe' and the Kremlin's New Cultural Policy," in Mjör and Turoma, eds., *Russia as Civilization*, 142–163.

28. Bibkov, "Neo-traditionalist Fits with Neo-liberal Shifts in Russian Cultural Policy"; Budraitkis, "Contradictions in Russian Politics."

29. Kommersant, "Kontsert v osvobozhdennoi Pal'mire—prizyv k ob"edineniyu vsego mira," June 6, 2016, https://www.kommersant.ru/doc/2980408.

30. Marlene Laruelle, *Mythe aryen et rêve impérial dans la Russie tsariste* (Paris: CNRS Éditions, 2005).

31. Vladimir Putin, "Direct Line with Vladimir Putin," Kremlin.ru, April 17, 2014, http://eng.kremlin.ru/news/7034.

32. Marlene Laruelle, "Politika pamiati russkoi pravoslavnoi tserkvi: Reabilitiruia, rerekhvatyvaia, vozvrashchaia," in Aleksei Miller and D.V. Efremenko, eds., *Politika pamiati v sovremennoi Rossii i stranakh Vostochnoi Evropy: Aktory, instituty, narativy* (St. Petersburg: European University, 2019), 122–143.

33. Konstantin Malofeev, *Imperiia* (Moscow: ACT, 2021).

34. Stephen J. Flanagan et al., "Russia, NATO, and Black Sea Security," *RAND Corporation*, October 5, 2020, https://www.rand.org/pubs/research_reports/RRA357-1.html.

35. Dmitry Gorenburg, "Russia's Naval Strategy in the Mediterranean," *Security Insights*, no. 35 (2019), https://www.marshallcenter.org/sites/default/files/files/2019-09/SecurityInsights_35_Gorenburg_July2019.pdf.

36. See Russian Federal Statistic Service Rosstat, census of 1989 and 2021, https://eng.rosstat.gov.ru/.

37. Tom Parfitt, "Vladimir Putin's Greek Urns Claim Earns Ridicule," *The Guardian*, August 12, 2011, https://www.theguardian.com/world/2011/aug/12/vladimir-putin-greek-urns-ridicule.

38. Laura Pennisi, *The Katechon and Moscow as Third Rome: Visual Analysis of Russia's Religious Soft Power in Greece* (MA thesis, Uppsala University, 2021).

39. Dmitry Adamsky, "Christ-Loving Diplomats: Russian Ecclesiastical Diplomacy in Syria," *Survival* 61, no. 6 (2019), https://www.tandfonline.com/doi/full/10.1080/00396338.2019.1688564.

40. Mospat, "Presentation by the DECR Chairman Metropolitan Hilarion at the World Summit in Defense of Persecuted Christians," May 12, 2017, https://mospat.ru/en/news/48514/.

41. Kremlin, "Prazdnovanie 1025-letiia kreshcheniia Rusi," July 27, 2013, http://www.kremlin.ru/events/president/news/18958.

42. Gianni Valente, "Russia's 'Protectorate' over Middle Eastern Christians," Orthodox Christian Laity, October 24, 2013, https://ocl.org/russias-protectorate-over-middle-eastern-christians/.

43. Foma, "Russkaia Pravoslavnaia Tserkov' ne ostavit svoikh siriiskikh sobratev: Protoierei Nikolai Balashov," April 24, 2013, https://foma.ru/russkaya-pravoslavnaya-czerkov-ne-ostavit-svoix-sirijskix-sobratev-protoierej-nikolaj-balashov.html.

44. "Joint Declaration of Pope Francis and Patriarch Kirill," also known as the Havana Declaration, Vatican.va, February 12, 2016, https://www.vatican.va/content/francesco/en/speeches/2016/february/documents/papa-francesco_20160212_dichiarazione-comune-kirill.html.

45. Irina du Quenoy, "Christian Geopolitics and the Ukrainian Ecclesiastical Crisis," *War on the Rocks*, October 30, 2018, https://warontherocks.com/2018/10/christian-geopolitics-and-the-ukrainian-ecclesiastical-crisis/; Kathy Rousselet, "Orthodox Churches in the War in Ukraine," *Bulletins de l'Observatoire international du religieux*, no. 36 (2022), https://sciencespo.hal.science/hal-03662947/.

46. Fedor Luk'ianov, " Rossiia ka strana zdravogo smysla—vot eto bylo by zdorovo," *Rossiia v global'noi politike*, February 13, 2023, https://globalaffairs.ru/articles/strana-zdravogo-smysla/.

47. Dmitri S. Moiseev, Aleksei N. Kharin, Maksim I. Sigachev, and Sergei P. Arteev. "Conservative Values as a Bridge between Russia and the West," *Russia in Global Affairs* 21, no. 3 (2023): 38–60.

Chapter 5: Spiritual Security

1. Vladimir Putin, "Poslanie Prezidenta Federal'nomu Sobraniu," Kremlin.ru, December 4, 2014, http://kremlin.ru/events/president/news/47173.

2. Boris Dubin, *Zhit' v Rossii na rubezhe* (Moscow: Progress-Traditsiiaa, 2007), 192.

3. *The Economist*, "The Rewriting of History," November 8, 2007, https://www.economist.com/europe/2007/11/08/the-rewriting-of-history.

4. Malinova, "Politics of Memory and Nationalism."

5. Mikhail Zygar, "How Vladimir Putin Lost Interest in the Present," *New York Times*, March 10, 2022, https://www.nytimes.com/2022/03/10/opinion/putin-russia-ukraine.html.

6. William Pomeranz, "How 'The State' Survived the Collapse of the Soviet Union," *Kennan Cable*, Wilson Center, no. 18, September 2016, https://www.wilsoncenter.org/publication/kennan-cable-no18-how-the-state-survived-the-collapse-the-soviet-union.

7. Vladimir Putin, "Poslanie Prezidenta RF Federal'nomu Sobraniiu," Kremlin.ru, December 12, 2013, http://kremlin.ru/events/president/news/19825.

8. Aliia Samigullina, "Zapros za velichie," *Gazeta.ru*, December 29, 2008, https://www.gazeta.ru/politics/2008/12/29_a_2919791.shtml.

9. *Calvert Journal*, "New Bronze Statue of Stalin to be Unveiled in Moscow," September 12, 2017, https://www.calvertjournal.com/news/show/8955/statues-soviet-leaders-mos cows-alley-rulers.

10. Rogers M. Smith, *Stories of Peoplehood: The Politics and Morals of Political Membership* (Cambridge: Cambridge University Press, 2003).

11. *RIA Novosti*, "Tseremoniia otkrytiia olimpiiskikh igr: Zriteli uvideli sny o Rossii," February 7, 2014, https://ria.ru/20140207/993764277.html.

12. Deutch Gabby, "Russia's Bizarre New Campaign to Define Its National Identity," *The Atlantic*, December 5, 2018, https://www.theatlantic.com/international/archive/2018/12/kremlin-effort-rename-airports-russian-identity/577363/.

13. Alexander Etkind, "Vremia sobirat' kamni : Postrevoliutsionnaia kul'tura politicheskoi skorbi v sovremennoi Rossii," *Ab Imperio* 2 (2004): 70.

14. Calculated by the author based on the state programs in 2001–5, 2006–10, 2011–15, 2016–20, and on annual spending for 2021 and 2022.

15. Paul Goode, "Patriotic Legitimation and Everyday Patriotism in Russia's Constitutional Reform," *Russian Politics* 6, no. 1 (2021), 112–129.

16. Valerie Sperling, "The Last Refuge of a Scoundrel: Patriotism, Militarism, and the Russian National Idea," *Nations and Nationalism* 9, no. 2 (2003): 235–253.

17. *Re:Russia*, "Voina patriotizmov: Razvernutaia v Rossii totalitarnaia kampaniia shkol'nogo militarizma prizvana podavit' modernye ustanovki rossiiskoi molodezhi," July 4, 2023, https://re-russia.net/review/321/; Ian Garner, *Z Generation: Into the Heart of Russia's Fascist Youth* (London: Hurst, 2023).

18. *TASS*, "'Dvizhenie pervykh' ob"edinilo 3 mln chelovek po vsei Rossii," November 6, 2023, https://tass.ru/obschestvo/19214843/amp.

19. Slava Kutenov, "Novoe vserossiiskaia detskaia organizatsiia poluchila nazvanie 'Dvizhenie pervykh'," *RTVI*, December 18, 2022, https://rtvi.com/news/novoe-vserossij skaya-detskaya-organizacziya-poluchila-nazvanie-dvizhenie-pervyh/.

20. *Iunarmiia*, "O Dvizhenii 'Iunarmiia,'" n.d., https://yunarmy.ru/headquarters/about/.

21. Ivan Fomin, "How the Kremlin Uses Schools for Ideological Indoctrination," *Russia. Post*, September 12, 2022, https://russiapost.info/society/putinism_for_kids. See also *Meduza*.io, "Minprosveshcheniia opublikovalo metodichki dlia vneklassnykh zaniiatii 'Razgovory o vazhnom,'" August 26, 2022, https://meduza.io/feature/2022/08/26/minpro svescheniya-opublikovalo-metodichki-dlya-vneklassnyh-zanyatiy-razgovory-o-vazhnom.

22. *Novye izvestiia*, "Senators Want to Make Primary Military Training a Separate School Subject, " April 2, 2023, https://en.newizv.ru/news/2023-04-12/senators-want-to-make-primary-military-training-a-separate-school-subject-404063.

23. *Doxa*, "'Gusi-lebedi' s avtomatami: Kak militarism stal chast'iu shkol'nogo obrazovaniia v Rossii," May 2, 2023, https://doxa.team/articles/gusi-lebedi-s-avtomatami?utm_source=newsletter&utm_medium=email&utm_term=2023-05-08&utm_campaign=+Z.

24. *RTVI*, "Iznezhennyi 'patriot': V Gosdume otreagirovali na prizyv mera Penzy ne prevrashchat' shkoly v 'nekropoli,'" November 25, 2023, https://rtvi.com/news/iznezhennyj-patriot-v-gosdume-otreagirovali-na-prizyv-mera-penzy-ne-prevrashhat-shkoly-v-nekropoli/.

25. Vladimir Rubanov, "Veteranov SVO podgotoviat dlia prepodavaniia novogo predmeta v shkolakh," *TVZvezda*, September 6, 2023, https://tvzvezda.ru/news/2023961556-qOtwR.html.

26. Joseph Zajda and Rea Zajda, "The Politics of Rewriting History: New History Textbooks and Curriculum Materials in Russia," *International Review of Education* 49, no. 3/4 (2003): 361–386.

27. David Brandenberger, "A New Short Course? A.V. Filippov and the Russian State's Search for a 'Useable Past'," *Kritika: Explorations in Russian and Eurasian History* 10, no. 4 (2009): 825–833.

28. Todd Nelson, "History as Ideology: The Portrayal of Stalinism and the Great Patriotic War in Contemporary Russian High School Textbooks," *Post-Soviet Affairs* 31, no. 1 (2015): 37–65.

29. David Brandenberger, "Promotion of a Usable Past: Official Efforts to Rewrite Russo-Soviet History, 2000–2014," in Vladimir Tismaneanu, ed., *Remembrance, History, and Justice: Coming to Terms with Traumatic Pasts in Democratic Societies* (Budapest: Central European University Press, 2015), 212.

30. Maria Mälksoo, "The Memory Politics of Becoming European: The East European Subalterns and the Collective Memory of Europe," *European Journal of International Relations* 15, no. 4 (2009): 653–680.

31. Jack Snyder, "The Historical Reality of Eastern Europe," *East European Politics and Societies* 23, no. 1 (2009): 7–12.

32. Richard Holbrooke, "The End of the Romance," *Washington Post*, February 2005, https://www.washingtonpost.com/archive/opinions/2005/02/16/the-end-of-the-romance/9390d1a5-0242-4318-8540-a20f9b842eb3/.

33. Maria Mälksoo, "In Search of a Modern Mnemonic Narrative of Communism: Russia's Mnemopolitical Mimesis during the Medvedev Presidency," *Journal of Soviet and Post-Soviet Politics and Society* 1, no. 2 (2015): 317–339.

34. Mikhail Zakharov, "Kommissia protiv istorii," *Polit.ru*, May 19, 2009, http://www.polit.ru/country/2009/05/19/history.html.

35. Ivan Kurilla, "The Struggle for the History Textbook in Russia," *Newsnet: News of the Association for Slavic, East European, and Eurasian Studies* 54, no. 5 (2014): 13–15.

36. Ielena Mukhametshina, "Starsheklassnikam s sentiabria 2023 goda budut ob'iasniat', pochemu nachalas' voennaia operatsiia," *Vedomosti*, July 19, 2023, https://www.

vedomosti.ru/society/articles/2023/07/19/985928-starsheklassnikam-budut-obyasnyat-po
chemu-nachalas-voennaya-operatsiya.

37. Nikolay Koposov, *Memory Laws, Memory Wars: The Politics of the Past in Europe and Russia* (New Delhi: Cambridge University Press, 2018); Nikolai Koposov, "'The Only Possible Ideology': Nationalizing History in Putin's Russia," *Journal of Genocide Research* 24, no. 2 (2022): 205–215.

38. Todd Nelson, *Bringing Stalin Back In: Memory Politics and the Creation of a Useable Past in Putin's Russia* (Lanham, MD: Lexington Books, 2021).

39. *Gazeta*, "Dmitri Medvedev: 'Prestupleniiam Stalina protiv sobstvennogo naroda net proshcheniia," May 7, 2010, http://www.gazeta.spb.ru/316694-1/. See Maria Lipman, "The Third Wave of Russian De-Stalinization," *Foreign Policy*, December 16, 2010, https://foreignpolicy.com/2010/12/16/the-third-wave-of-russian-de-stalinization/.

40. Sophia Kishkovsky, "Putin Visits Memorial to Victims of Stalinist Great Terror," *New York Times*, October 30, 2007, https://www.nytimes.com/2007/10/30/world/europe/30iht-putin.4.8118386.html; Kathy Rousselet. "Butovo: La création d'un lieu de pèlerinage sur une terre de massacres," *Politix* 20, no. 77 (2007): 55–78.

41. Sarah Rainsford, "Wall of Grief: Russia Remembers Victims of Soviet Repression," *BBC*, August 17, 2017, https://www.bbc.com/news/world-europe-40948224.

42. Daniel Treisman, "Putin Unbound: How Repression at Home Presaged Belligerence Abroad," *Foreign Affairs*, April 6, 2022, https://www.foreignaffairs.com/articles/ukraine/2022-04-06/putin-russia-ukraine-war-unbound.

43. Andrey Kolesnikov, "The Special Ideological Operation Going According to Plan," *Russia.Post*, August 31, 2023, https://russiapost.info/politics/slo.

44. *RBC*, "Medvedev peredal Pol'she materialy po Katyni," May 8, 2010, https://amp.rbc.ru/rbcnews/society/08/05/2010/5703d9ff9a79470ab50206ac.

45. Mark Edele, "Fighting Russia's History Wars: Vladimir Putin and the Codification of World War II," *History and Memory* 29, no. 2 (2017): 90–124.

46. Vladimir Putin, "75 let Velikoy Pobedy: Obshchaia otvetstvennost' pered istoriei i budushchim," *Rossiiskaia gazeta*, June 19, 2020, https://rg.ru/2020/06/19/75-let-velikoj-pobedy-obshchaia-otvetstvennost-pered-istoriej-i-budushchim.html.

47. Mikhail Suslov, "From Uvarov's 'Triad' to Kiriyenko's 'Pentabasis': Conservative Ideology in Russia," *Russia.Post*, February 20, 2024, https://russiapost.info/page44081013.html.

48. Julian Cooper, "Russia's Updated National Security Strategy," *Russian Studies Series*, no. 21 (2021): 1–6, https://www.ndc.nato.int/research/research.php?icode=704.

49. *RIA Novosti*, "Putin podpisal zakon o zaprete uravnivaniia rolei SSSR i Germanii v voine," July 1, 2021, https://ria.ru/20210701/voyna-1739359047.html.

50. Sergei Ivanov, "What Russia's New History Textbook Reveals," *Russia.Post*, August 18, 2023, https://russiapost.info/politics/new_history. See also Timofei Loginov, "Russkaia nepravda," *Novaia gazeta*, May 4, 2023, https://novaya-media.cdn.ampproject.org/c/s/novaya.media/amp/articles/2023/05/04/russkaia-nepravda.

51. Anna Vasil'eva, "Istoriia stanet tsaritsei nauk," *Kommersant*, February 2, 2023, https://www.kommersant.ru/doc/5798930.

52. For more on their biographies, see Pertsev, "Spasti poteriannoe pokolenie"; Elena Mukhametshina, Maksim Ivanov, and Vladimir Stepanov, "Kurator regionov iz 'Rosatoma' zanialsia voprosami gosideologii na dolzhnosti prorektora RANKhiGS," *Vedomosti*, May 14, 2023, https://www.vedomosti.ru/politics/articles/2023/05/14/974978-kurator-regionov-rosatoma-zanyalsya-voprosami-

53. On Drobinin, see Mikhail Suslov.. "Isolationism, a Broad European Partnership, and a Left Tinge," *Russia.Post*, April 20, 2023, https://russiapost.info/politics/isolationism.

54. Andrey Zaiakin, "Doktor pauk," *Novaia gazeta*, January 29, 2023, https://novayagazeta.eu/articles/2023/01/29/doktor-pauk; Mikhail Rubin et al., "Blizkii po mozgam sibarit: Kak glavnyi v 'Rossii' Iurii Koval'chuk stal doverennym bankirom i ustroitelem dosuga Putina," *Kompromat*, December 9, 2020, https://www.compromat.ru/page_41915.htm.

55. https://zinoviev.info/wps/archives/6835.

56. Marlene Laruelle, "Back from Utopia: How Donbas Fighters Reinvent Themselves in a Post-Novorossiya Russia," *Nationalities Papers* 47, no. 5 (2019): 719–733.

57. Maria Antonova, "State Lays Claim to Geography Society," *St. Petersburg Times*, November 20, 2009, http://www.sptimes.ru/story/30332.

58. Nikolai Petrov, "Vozmozhnyi li peremeny v setevoi Rossii?," *Kontrapunkt* 9 (2017): 1–15.

59. Marlene Laruelle, "A Territory or an Identity? The Far North in Russia's Statehood," in Marlene Laruelle, *Russia's Arctic Strategies and the Future of the Far North* (New York: M. E. Sharpe, 2013), 24–46.

60. John McCannon, *Red Arctic: Polar Exploration and the Myth of the North in the Soviet Union, 1932–1939* (Oxford: Oxford University Press, 1998).

61. See the Russian Geographical Society's website, https://rgo.ru/activity/expeditions/.

62. See its website, wncontest.ru, n.d.

63. See its website, Cha.ru, n.d.

64. Joshua P. Newell and Laura A. Henry. "The State of Environmental Protection in the Russian Federation: A Review of the Post-Soviet era," *Eurasian Geography and Economics* 57, no. 6 (2016) 779–801; Debra Javeline et al., "Russia in a Changing Climate," *Wiley Interdisciplinary Reviews: Climate Change* 15, no. 3 (2023).

65. Lada Kochtcheeva, "Positioning: Russia's Post-Paris Climate Change Actions, Discourse, and Engagement," *Problems of Post-Communism* 69, no. 4–5 (2022): 423–435.

66. Marlene Laruelle and Jean Radvanyi, *Russia: Great Power, Weakened State* (Lanham, MD: Rowman and Littlefield, 2023), 7–32.

67. Vladimir Putin, "Vystuplenie Vladimira Putina na zasedanii popechitel'skogo soveta Russkogo Geograficheskogo Obshchestva (27 aprelia 2018 goda, Sankt-Peterburg)," RGO.ru, April 27, 2018, https://web.archive.org/web/20190308052559/www.rgo.ru/ru/article/vystuplenie-vladimira-putina-na-zasedanii-popechitelskogo-soveta-russkogo-geograficheskogo-o.

68. Charles Sullivan, *Motherland: Soviet Nostalgia in the Russian Federation* (London: Palgrave Macmillan, 2022).

69. Serguei Alex Oushakine, "Remembering in Public: On the Affective Management of History," *Ab Imperio* 1 (2013): 269–302.

Chapter 6: Russia's Imperialness and the Fight for Ukraine

1. Kremlin.ru, "Vstrecha s prezidentom Kazakhstana Kasym-Zhomartom Tokaevym," September 9, 2022, https://kremlin.ru/events/president/news/68606.

2. Matt Janney, "New Bronze Statue of Stalin to Be Unveiled in Moscow," *Calvert Journal*, September 12, 2017, https://www.calvertjournal.com/news/show/8955/statues-soviet-leaders-moscows-alley-rulers; Diana Omarova, "'Rasstreliali neskol'ko chelovek i spokoino khodili na rabotu': Pamiatnik Stalinu otkryli v Volgograde," *Bloknot Volgograd*, February 1, 2023, https://bloknot-volgograd.ru/news/rasstrelyali-neskolko-chelovek-i-spokoyno-khodili--1567602; *Sever.Realii*, "'U Putinskoi vlasti problemy s ideologiei': Ekspolitseiskii protiv pamiatnika Stalinu," August 22, 2023, https://www.severreal.org/a/u-putinskoy-vlasti-problemy-s-ideologiey-eks-politseyskiy-protiv-pamyatnika-stalinu/32558614.html.

3. Kathleen Smith, *Mythmaking in the New Russia* (Ithaca, NY: Cornell University Press, 2002).

4. Kremlin.ru, "Decree of the President of the Russian Federation Dated November 7, 1996 No. 1537," https://web.archive.org/web/20180411073917/http://www.kremlin.ru/acts/bank/10231.

5. Aleksandr I. Lebed, *Za derzhavu obidno* (Kirov: Izdatel'stvo Viatskoe Slovo, 1995).

6. Lenta.ru, "Dokument dnia: platforma natsional'nogo primireniia Rossii," May 20, 2015, https://lenta.ru/articles/2015/05/20/medinskyvoice.

7. *RIA Novosti*, "Naryshkin schitaet stoletie revoliutsii 1917 goda povodom izvlech' uroki," December 27, 2016, https://ria.ru/20161227/1484741774.html.

8. Olga Malinova, "'The Embarrassing Centenary': Reinterpretation of the 1917 Revolution in the Official Historical Narrative of Post-Soviet Russia (1991–2017)," *Nationalities Papers* 46, no. 2 (2018): 272–289.

9. Gazeta.ru, "Peskov ne uvidel neobkhodimosti v prazdnovanii 100-letiya revolyutsii," October 25, 2017, https://m.gazeta.ru/politics/news/2017/10/25/n_10735148.shtml.

10. Sergei Naryshkin, "Revolutsionnye sobytiia 1917 goda bol'she ne raskalyvaiut obshchestvo," *TASS*, November 7, 2017, https://tass.com/interviews/4699298.

11. Marlene Laruelle, "Commemorating 1917 in Russia: Ambivalent State History Policy and the Church's Conquest of the History Market," *Europe-Asia Studies* 71, no. 2 (2019): 249–267.

12. Laruelle and Karnysheva, *Memory Politics and the Russian Civil War*.

13. Imperial House.ru, "Glavnaia," n.d., http://imperialhouse.ru/rus/.

14. *Interfax*, "Volodin predlozhil ispol'zovat' opyt SSSR i tsarskoi Rossii dlia razvitiia obrazovaniia v RF," June 15, 2022, https://www.interfax.ru/russia/846357.

15. Wendy Slater, *The Many Deaths of Tsar Nicholas II: Relics, Remains and the Romanovs* (Abingdon: Routledge, 2007).

16. Mikhail Suslov, "The Genealogy of the Idea of Monarchy in the Post-Soviet Political Discourse of the Russian Orthodox Church," *State, Religion and Church* 3, no. 1 (2016): 28; Marlene Laruelle, "Ideological Complementarity or Competition? The Kremlin, the Church, and the Monarchist Idea in Today's Russia," *Slavic Review* 79, no. 2 (2020): 345–364.

17. Andrey Kamakin, "Konstantin Malofeev: 'Poiavilas´ boiazn, chto Putin uidet'," *MK.ru*, March 13, 2018, https://www.mk.ru/politics/2018/03/13/konstantin-malofeev-poyavilas-boyazn-chto-putin-uydet.html.

18. Kremlin.ru, "Vserossiiskii molodozhnyi forum Seliger-2014," August 29, 2014, http://en.kremlin.ru/events/president/news/46507.

19. *Interfax*, "Putin rasskazal uchenym o podryvnoi roli Lenina v rossiiskoi istorii," January 21, 2016, http://www.interfax.ru/russia/490856.

20. Konstantin Pakhalyuk, "Historical Past as Foundation of Russia's Polity: Assessing Putin's Speeches in 2012–2018," *Politeia* 4 (2018): 6–31.

21. Gazeta.ru, "Putin rasskazal o rabote ego deda u Lenina i Stalina," March 11, 2018, https://www.gazeta.ru/politics/news/2018/03/11/n_11270995.shtml.

22. *Vedomosti*, "Peskov: Putin otnositsia k monarkhii bez optimizma," March 15, 2017, https://www.vedomosti.ru/politics/news/2017/03/15/681255-peskov-putin-monarhiyu.

23. Aleksei Makarkin, "The Radical Rejection of Revolutionism by the Russian Intellectual Class Has Led to a Glorification of State Restoration," *Russia.Post*, January 23, 2023, https://russiapost.info/culture/intellectual_class.

24. Anastasiia Gladil'shchikova, "Soiuz Spaseniia: Zachem rossiianam pokazali novyi obraz dekabristov," *Profile.ru*, December 27, 2019, https://profile.ru/culture/soyuz-spaseniya-zachem-rossiyanam-pokazali-novyj-obraz-dekabristov-208017/; Anton Dolin, "Soiuz Spaseniia: Monarkhicheskii blokbaster o vosstanii dekabristov, kotoryi osuzhdaet i ne zhaleet buntuiushchikh intelligentov," *Meduza.io*, December 24, 2019, https://meduza.io/feature/2019/12/24/soyuz-spaseniya-monarhicheskiy-blokbaster-o-vosstanii-dekabristov-kotoryy-osuzhdaet-buntuyuschih-intelligentov-i-odobryaet-ih-kazn.

25. More in Laruelle and Karnysheva, *Memory Politics and the Russian Civil War*, 35–58.

26. More in Suslov, *Putinism: Post-Soviet Russian Regime Ideology*.

27. Elizaveta Surnacheva, "V poiskakh mudrosti," *Kommersant' Vlast'*, January 20, 2014, https://www.kommersant.ru/doc/2383840.

28. Varvara Vernadskaya, *Ivan Ilyin: White Emigration, Fascist Sympathies, and Post-Mortem Return to Russia* (self-pub., 2024), https://ivanilyin.org/.

29. Ivan Ilyin, "I snova izvestiia s Vostoka," in Ivan Ilyin, *Sobranie sochinenii: Spravedlivost' ili ravenstvo?* (Moscow: PSTGU, 2006), 275.

30. Ivan Ilyin, "Sovetskii Soiuz—ne Rossiia," 1947, republished at http://possev.org/jornal/izbran/?SECTION_ID=23&ELEMENT_ID=928.

31. Ivan Ilyin, "O russkom fashizme," *Russkii Kolokol, Zhurnal Volevoi Idei*, 3 (1928), https://vtoraya-literatura.com/pdf/russky_kolokol_1928_3_text.pdf.

32. Ivan Ilyin, "Natsional-sotsializm, Novyi dux," *Vozrozhdenie*, May 17, 1933, http://www.odinblago.ru/filosofiya/ilin/ilin_i_nacional_sociali.

33. Ivan Ilyin, "O fashizme" (1948), republished in *Sobranie sochinenii*, vol. 1 (Moscow: Russkaia kniga, 1993), 86–89.

34. Laruelle and Karnysheva, *Memory Politics and the Russian Civil War*.

35. Anatoly Chubais, "Chubais: A Liberal Empire Is an Orientation Point Far Beyond 2008," *BBC Monitoring International Reports*, November 25 2003.

36. Laruelle, "Politika pamiati Russkoi Pravoslavnoi Tserkvi," 122–143.

37. We checked that mentions of "empire" were not related to the US and found that while the US is often decried using the notion of "imperializm," it is rarely presented as an "empire" in presidential speeches.

38. Vladimir Putin, "Vystuplenie na tseremonii otkrytiia prazdnika na Neve," Kremlin.ru, May 31, 2003, http://www.kremlin.ru/events/president/transcripts/22016.

39. Dmitri Medvedev, "Interv'iu gazete '*Fainenshl Taims*,'" Kremlin.ru, June 18, 2011, http://kremlin.ru/events/president/news/11630.

40. Vladimir Putin, "Vstrecha s molodymi predprinimateliami, inzhenerami i uchenymi," Kremlin.ru, June 9, 2022, https://kremlin.ru/events/president/news/68606.

41. Serhii Plohii, *The Russo-Ukrainian War: The Return of History* (New York: W.W. Norton, 2023).

42. Olga Allenova, Elena Geda, and Vladimir Novikov, "Blok NATO razoshelsia na blokpakety," *Kommersant*, April 7, 2008, https://www.kommersant.ru/doc/877224.

43. Putin, "75 let Velikoi Pobedy."

44. Putin, "Ob istoricheskom edinstve russkikh i ukraintsev"

45. Vladimir Putin, "Obrashchenie Prezidenta Rossiiskoi Federatsii," Kremlin.ru, February 21, 2022. http://kremlin.ru/events/president/news/67828.

46. Ivan Grek, "What the Istanbul Agreements Reveal about the Future of Russia-Ukraine Negotiations," *Russia.Post*, March 1, 2024, https://russiapost.info/politics/agreements.

47. Marlene Laruelle, Ivan Grek, and Sergei Davydov, "Culturalizing the Nation: A Quantitative Approach to the Russkii/Rossiiskii Semantic Space in Russia's Political Discourse," *Demokratizatsiya: The Journal of Post-Soviet Democratization* 31, no. 1 (2023): 3–27.

48. Vladislav Surkov, "Dolgoe gosudarstvo Putina," *Nezavisimaia gazeta*, February 11, 2019, https://www.ng.ru/ideas/2019-02-11/5_7503_surkov.html.

49. *Interfax*, "Volodin uvidel v sanktsiiakh protiv RF i Belorussii geneticheskoe nepriiatie Zapadom slavian," June 14, 2017, https://www.interfax.ru/world/566540.

50. Andrey Kolesnikov, "Istoki i smysl russkogo national-imperializma: Istoricheskie korni ideologii Putina," Carnegie Endowment for International Peace, November 1, 2023, https://carnegieendowment.org/2023/11/01/ru-pub-90833; Andrei Pertsev, "Kredo razvitogo putinizma: Kak ob' iasniaiut mir 'Osnovy rossiiskoi gosudarstvennosti,'" *Carnegie politika*, July 21, 2023, https://carnegieendowment.org/politika/90247.

51. Among others, see Andrey Makarychev and Sergei Medvedev, *Biopower in Putin's Russia: From Taking Care to Taking Lives* (Vienna: CEU University Press, 2024); Andrey Makarychev and Alexandra Yatsyk, *Critical Biopolitics of the Post-Soviet. From Populations to Nations* (Lanham, MD: Lexington, 2019).

52. Anna-Liisa Heusala and Kaarina Aitamurto, eds., *Migrant Workers in Russia: Global Challenges of the Shadow Economy in Societal Transformation* (London: Routledge, 2016).

53. Jason Stanley, *How Fascism Works: The Politics of Us and Them* (New York: Penguin, 2020).

54. Laruelle, *Is Russia Fascist?*

55. Vladimir Putin, "Putin zaiavil, chto gorditsia byt' chast'iu sil'nogo i mnogonatsional'nogo naroda Rossii," *TASS*, March 3, 2022, https://tass.ru/politika/13955467.

56. Il'ia Budraitkis, "Pereizobretenie natsizma dlia nuzhd gospropagand: Kak moral'

zameniaetsia siloi," *Republic*, April 14, 2022, https://republic.ru/posts/103587?utm_source =republic.ru.

57. Scott Radnitz and Harris Mylonas, *Enemies Within: The Global Politics of Fifth Columns* (New York: Oxford University Press, 2022).

58. *Verstka*, "Ne skuliat i ne ropshchut," November 16, 2022, https://verstka.media/kto-takie-kuzmichi-i-kak-propaganda-ispolzuet-etot-obraz.

59. *Vedomosti*, "Putin ob' asnil slova 'terpi, moya krasavitsa,'" February 10, 2022, https://www.vedomosti.ru/politics/news/2022/02/10/908783-putin-obyasnil-slova.

60. Vladimir Putin, "Vystuplenie na plenarnom zasedanii Peterburgskogo mezhdunarodnogo ekonomicheskogo foruma," Kremlin.ru, June 16, 2023, http://kremlin.ru/events/president/transcripts/72259.

61. Putin, "Vystuplenie na plenarnom zasedanii."

62. Glenn Kessler, "The Roots of the Zombie Claim that Hitler Had Jewish Blood," *Washington Post*, May 3, 2022, https://www.washingtonpost.com/politics/2022/05/03/roots-zombie-claim-that-hitler-had-jewish-blood/?itid=lk_inline_manual_21.

63. Francesca Ebel, "Putin Rails against 'Antisemitism' While Attacking Ukraine's Jewish President," *Washington Post*, September 25, 2023, https://www.washingtonpost.com/world/2023/09/25/putin-antisemitism-zelensky-russia-ukraine/.

64. Timofei Sergeitsev, "Chto Rossiya dolzhna sdelat' s Ukrainoi," *RIA Novosti*, April 5, 2022, https://ria.ru/amp/20220403/ukraina-1781469605.html.

65. Sergeitsev, "Chto Rossiya dolzhna sdelat' s Ukrainoi."

66. Sergeitsev, "Chto Rossiya dolzhna sdelat' s Ukrainoi."

67. Wenger, "Return of the Voenkor."

68. Kristina Hook, *The Russian Federation's Escalating Commission of Genocide in Ukraine: A Legal Analysis* (New Lines Institute, 2023).

69. Jade McGlynn, "Russian Propaganda Tactics in Wartime Ukraine," *Russia Program Online Papers*, no. 10, November 2023.

70. Andrey Pertsev, "Spasti poteriannoe pokolenie: Poznakom'tes' s Andreem Polosinym—polittekhnologom, kotoromu Kreml' poruchil prevratit' rossiiskikh studentov v 'patrioticheskuiu intelligentsiiu," *Meduza.io*, May 22, 2023, https://meduza.io/feature/2023/05/22/spasti-poteryannoe-pokolenie. See also Grigorii Golosov, "Est li u Putina ideologiia?," *Holod*, December 14, 2022, https://holod.media/2022/12/14/pution-idiotology/.

Part III

1. Edmund Fawcett, *Conservatism: The Fight for a Tradition* (Princeton, NJ: Princeton University Press, 2020).

2. Prozorov, "Russian Conservatism in the Putin Presidency," 125.

Chapter 7: Civilization

1. Vladimir Putin, "Poslanie Prezidenta Federal'nomu Sobraniiu," Kremlin.ru, February 20, 2019, http://kremlin.ru/events/president/news/59863.

2. Peter Katzenstein and Nicole Weygandt, "Mapping Eurasia in an Open World: How the Insularity of Russia's Geopolitical and Civilizational Approaches Limits Its Foreign Policies," *Perspectives on Politics* 15 (2017): 428–442.

3. Chebankova, "Russia's Idea of the Multipolar World Order."

4. Sebastian Conrad, *What Is Global History?* (Princeton, NJ: Princeton University Press, 2016).

5. Patrick Sériot, *Structure and the Whole (Semiotics, Communication and Cognition)* (Berlin: De Gruyter Mouton, 2014).

6. M. Hahn Gordon, *Russian Tselostnost': Wholeness in Russian Culture, Thought, History, and Politics* (London: Europe Books, 2022).

7. Andrzej Walicki, *The Slavophile Controversy: History of a Conservative Utopia in Nineteenth-Century Russian Thought* (Notre Dame, IN: University of Notre Dame Press, 1989); Engelstein, *Slavophile Empire*; Peter K. Christoff, *An Introduction To Nineteenth-Century Russian Slavophilism: Iu. F. Samarin* (Abingdon: Routledge, 1991); Aileen M. Kelly, *Toward Another Shore: Russian Thinkers between Necessity and Chance* (New Haven, CT: Yale University Press, 1998).

8. Nikolai Danilevskii, *Rossiia i Evropa: Vzgliad na kul'turnye i politicheskie otnosheniia slavianskogo mira k germano-romanskomu* (St. Petersburg: Glagol, 1995 [1869]).

9. Robert E. MacMaster, *Danilevsky: A Russian Totalitarian Philosopher* (Cambridge, MA: Harvard University Press, 1967).

10. Egyptian, Chinese, Assyrian-Babylonian, Indian, Iranian, Jewish, Greek, Roman, neo-Semitic or Arabian, Romano-Germanic or European, and Slavic.

11. Laruelle, *Russian Eurasianism*; Sergei Glebov. *From Empire to Eurasia: Politics, Scholarship, and Ideology in Russian Eurasianism, 1920s–1930s* (Ithaca, NY: Cornell University Press, 2017).

12. Lev N. Gumilev, "Pis'mo v redaktsiiu 'Voprosov filosofii,'" *Voprosy Filosofii*, no. 5 (1989): 160.

13. Bassin, Glebov, and Laruelle, *Between Europe and Asia*.

14. Gumilev, "Pis'mo v redaktsiiu," 161.

15. Viktor Shnirelman and Sergei Panarin, "Lev Gumilev: His Pretensions as Founder of Ethnology and His Eurasian Theories," *Inner Asia* 3, no. 1 (2001): 1–18.

16. Vesa Oittinen, "From Socio-Economic Formations to Civilizations: Seeking a Paradigm Change in Late Soviet Discussions," in Mjør and Turoma, *Russia as Civilization*, 47–58.

17. Andrey Tsygankov, "Mastering Space in Eurasia: Russia's Geopolitical Thinking after the Soviet Break-Up," *Communist and Post-Communist Studies* 36, no. 1 (2003): 101–127.

18. Marlene Laruelle, "The Discipline of Culturology: A New 'Ready-Made Thought' for Russia," *Diogenes* 51, no. 4 (2004): 21–36; Jutta Scherrer. *Kulturologie: Rußland Auf Der Suche Nach Einer Zivilisatorischen Identität* (Göttingen: Wallstein, Essener kulturwissenschaftliche Vorträge, 2003).

19. Kåre Johan Mjør, "An Eternal Russia: Oleg Platonov, the Institute for Russian Civilization and the Nationalization of Russian Thought," in Kåre Johan Mjør and Sanna Turoma, eds., *Russia as Civilization*, 101.

20. Valentin Bazhanov, "A Note on A. S. Panarin's *Revansh Istorii*," *Europe-Asia Studies* 51, no. 4 (1999): 705–708.

21. Aleksandr S. Panarin, *Iskushenie globalizmom* (Moscow: Algoritm, 2000); Aleksandr S. Panarin, *Strategicheskaia nestabil'nost' v XXI veke* (Moscow: Algoritm, 2003).

22. Aleksandr S. Panarin, *Vtoraia Evropa ili Tretii Rim? Izbrannaia sotsial'no-filosofskaia publitsistika* (Moscow: RAN, 1996), 59.

23. Alexander S. Panarin, "Predeli faustovskoi kul'turi i puti rossiiskoi tsivilizatsii," *Rossiia i Vostok: Geopolitika i tsivilizatsionnie otnosheniia* (Moscow: RAN, 1996), 40.

24. Alexander S. Panarin, *Rossiia v tsiklakh mirovoi istorii* (Moscow: Moscow State University Press, 1999).

25. Panarin, *Rossiia v tsiklakh mirovoi istorii*, 72.

26. Alexander S. Panarin, *Pravoslavnaia tsivilizatsiia v global'nom mire* (Moscow: Algoritm, 2002), 142.

27. Galina Zvereva, "'Civilization' in the Russian Mediatized Public Sphere: Imperial and Regional Discourses," in Mjør and Turoma, eds., *Russia as Civilization*, 87–114.

28. Gleb Pavlovskii and Sergei Chernyshev, "K vozobnovleniiu russkogo," Russkii Institut, June 27, 1996, http://www.archipelag.ru/ru_mir/history/history95-97/chernishov-perepiska/.

29. Andrey Tsygankov, "In the Shadow of Nikolai Danilevskii: Universalism, Particularism, and Russian Geopolitical Theory," *Europe-Asia Studies* 69, no. 4 (2017): 585.

30. Mikhail Suslov and Irina Kotkina, "Civilizational Discourses in Doctoral Dissertations in Post-Soviet Russia," in Mjør and Turoma, eds., *Russia as Civilization*, 164–185.

31. Boris Gryzlov, "Ni odna politicheskaia partiia poka ne sposobna sozdat' v Rossii usloviia dlia novogo tsivilizatsionnogo ryvka," *RBK*, December 20, 2005.

32. MID, "Kontseptsiia vneshnei politiki Rossiiskoi Federatsii," 2008, https://normativ.kontur.ru/document?moduleId=1&documentId=131926.

33. Fabian Linde, "State Civilisation: The Statist Core of Vladimir Putin's Civilisational Discourse and Its Implications for Russian Foreign Policy," *Politics in Central Europe* 12, no. 1 (2016): 21–35; Sanna Turoma, Kaarina Aitamurto, and Slobodanka Vladiv-Glover, eds., *Religion, Expression, and Patriotism in Russia: Essays on Post-Soviet Society and the State* (Stuttgart, New York: Ibidem and Columbia University Press, 2019).

34. Vladimir Medinskii, "Kto ne kormit svoiu kul'turu, budet kormit' chuzhuiu armiiu," *Izvestia*, June 17, 2015, https://iz.ru/export/google/amp/30536.

35. Tsygankov, "Crafting the State-Civilization," 151.

36. MID.ru, "Kontseptsiia Vneshnei Politiki Rossiiskoi Federatsii," March 2023, https://www.mid.ru/ru/detail-material-page/1860586/.

37. Aleksei Drobinin, "Obraz mnogopoliarnogo mira: Tsivilizatsionnyi faktor i mesto Rossii v formiruiushchemsia miroporiadke," *Rossiia v global'noi politike*, February 20, 2023, https://globalaffairs.ru/articles/obraz-mnogopolyarnogo-mira/.

38. Vladimir Putin, "Zasedanie Mezhdunarodnogo Diskussionnogo Kluba 'Valdai,'" Kremlin.ru, October 27, 2022, http://kremlin.ru/events/president/news/69695.

39. Kremlin.ru, "Stenograficheskii otchet o zasedanii Rossiiskogo Organizatsionnogo Komiteta 'Pobeda,'" March 29, 2005, http://kremlin.ru/events/president/transcripts/22888.

40. Vladimir Putin, "Interv'iu rossiiskim i inostrannym SMI," Kremlin.ru, January 19, 2014, http://kremlin.ru/events/president/news/20080.

41. Gleb Pavlovsky, *Agitator Edinoi Rossii* (Moscow: Europa, 2011).

42. Surkov, *Teksty*; Richard Sakwa, "Surkov: Dark Prince of the Kremlin," *OpenDemocracy*, April 7, 2011, https://www.opendemocracy.net/en/odr/surkov-dark-prince-of-kremlin.

43. Sergei Lavrov, "Russia in a Multipolar World: Implications for Russia–EU–US," Washington, DC: Center for Strategic and International Studies, July 16, 2011, http://www.rusembassy.ca/ru/node/589.

44. Dmitrii Rogozin, "Rossiia—krupneishaia chast' Evropy i posledniaia ee nadezhda," *Inosmi*, June 3, 2010, https://inosmi.ru/20100603/160347052.html.

45. Vladimir Medinskii, "Rossiia vynuzhdena kul'turno zashchishchat'sia ot 'anti-Evropy,'" *RBC*, April 15, 2014, https://www.rbc.ru/society/15/04/2014/57041b349a794761c0ce8f51.

46. Vladimir Putin, "Rossiia: Natsional'nyi vopros," *Nezavisimaia gazeta*, January 23, 2012, https://www.ng.ru/politics/2012-01-23/1_national.html.

47. Putin, "Rossiia: Natsional'nyi vopros."

48. Vladimir Putin, "Obrashchenie Prezidenta Rossiiskoi Federatsii," Kremlin.ru, February 21, 2022, http://kremlin.ru/events/president/news/67828.

49. Putin, "Obrashchenie Prezidenta Rossiiskoi Federatsii."

50. Vladimir Putin, "Zasedanie Soveta po mezhnatsional'nym otnosheniiam," Kremlin.ru, July 3, 2014, http://www.kremlin.ru/events/president/news/46144.

51. Vladimir Putin, "Priamaia Liniia s Vladimirom Putinym," Kremlin.ru, April 16, 2015, http://www.kremlin.ru/events/president/transcripts/statements/49261.

52. Vladimir Putin. "Zasedanie Diskussionnogo Kluba 'Valdai,'" Kremlin.ru, October 18, 2018, http://kremlin.ru/events/president/news/58848.

53. TASS, "Putin zaiavil, chto gorditsia byt' chast'iu sil'nogo i mnogonatsional'nogo naroda Rossii," March 3, 2022, https://tass.ru/politika/13955467.

54. Vera Tolz, *Russia: Inventing the Nation* (London: Bloomsbury, 2021); Şener Aktürk, *Regimes of Ethnicity and Nationhood in Germany, Russia, and Turkey* (Cambridge: Cambridge University Press, 2012).

55. Mikhail Remizov, "Proekt 'gosudarstvo-tsivilizatsiia,'" *APN*, February 9, 2005, http://www.intelros.org/drevo/remizov1.htm.

56. Mark R. Beissinger, *Nationalist Mobilization and the Collapse of the Soviet State* (Cambridge: Cambridge University Press, 2002); Dmitry Gorenburg, *Minority Ethnic Mobilization in the Russian Federation* (Cambridge: Cambridge University Press, 2003); Elise Giuliano, *Constructing Grievance: Ethnic Nationalism in Russia's Republics* (Ithaca, NY: Cornell University Press, 2017).

57. Kaarina Aitamurto, "Discussions about Indigenous, National and Transnational Islam in Russia," *Religion, State and Society* 47, no. 2 (2019): 198–213.

58. Vladimir Putin, "'Vystuplenie na torzhestvenom sobranii, posviashchennom 225-letiiu Tsentral'nogo dukhovnogo upravlennia musul'man Rossii," Kremlin.ru, October 22, 2013, http://kremlin.ru/events/president/transcripts/19473.

59. Eren Tasar, *Soviet and Muslim: The Institutionalization of Islam in Central Asia* (Oxford: Oxford University Press, 2017).

60. Tim Epkenhans, "The Islamic Revival Party of Tajikistan: Episodes of Islamic Activism, Postconflict Accommodation, and Political Marginalization," *Central Asian Affairs* 2, no. 4 (2015): 321–346.

61. Kimitaka Matsuzato, "The Regional Context of Islam in Russia: Diversities along the Volga," *Eurasian Geography and Economics* 47, no. 4 (2006): 449–461; Kimitaka Matsuzato. *Islam ot Kaspiia do Urala: Makroregional'nyi podkhod* (Sapporo and Moscow: Rossiiskaia politicheskaia entsiklopediia, 2007).

62. Gulnaz Sibgatullina and Michael Kemper, "Liberal Islamic Theology in Conservative Russia: Taufik Ibragim's 'Qur'ānic Humanism,'" *Die Welt Des Islams: International Journal for the Study of Modern Islam* 61, no. 3 (2019): 279–307; Renat Irikovich Bekkin, "The Renovationist Movement in Contemporary Russian Islam," *Context: Journal of Interdisciplinary Studies / Časopis Za Interdisciplinarne Studije* 6, no. 1 (2019): 65–90.

63. Gulnaz Sibgatullina, "The Muftis and the Myths: Constructing the Russian 'Church for Islam,'" *Problems of Post-Communism* (2023).

64. Sibgatullina, *Languages of Islam and Christianity in Post-Soviet Russia*; Alfrid K. Bustanov and Michael Kemper, "Russia's Islam and Orthodoxy beyond the Institutions: Languages of Conversion, Competition and Convergence," *Islam and Christian–Muslim Relations* 28, no. 2 (2017): 129–139.

65. Timur Rakhmatullin, "Chem otlichilsia Talgat Tadzhuddin za 40 let?" *Real'noe vremia*, June 19, 2020, https://realnoevremya.ru/articles/178095-chem-otlichilsya-talgat-tadzhuddin-za-40-let.

66. Laruelle, Grek, and Davydov, "Culturalizing the Nation."

67. Michael Kemper, "Mufti Ravil Gainutdin: The Translation of Islam into a Language of Patriotism and Humanism," in Alfrid K. Bustanov and Michael Kemper, eds., *Islamic Authority and the Russian Language: Studies on Texts from European Russia, the North Caucasus and West Siberia* (Amsterdam: Pegasus, 2012), 105–141; Michael Kemper, "Religious Political Technology: Damir Mukhetdinov's 'Russian Islam'," *Religion, State & Society* 47, no. 2 (2019): 214–233.

68. Gulnaz Sibgatullina and Michael Kemper, *The Imperial Paradox: Islamic Eurasianism in Contemporary Russia* (Berlin: Frank & Timme, 2019).

69. Damir Mukhetdinov, *Rossiiskoe musul'manstvo: Traditsii Ummy v usloviiakh evraziiskoi tsivilizatsii* (Moscow: Medina, 2016), 6–7.

70. Marlene Laruelle, "Kadyrovism: Hardline Islam as a Tool of the Kremlin," *IFRI Notes, Russie.NEI.Vision*, 99 (2017). See also Alexandra Yatsyk, "Promoting Islam within the 'Russian World': The Cases of Tatarstan and Chechnya," *PONARS Eurasia Policy Memo*, no. 383, August 2015.

Chapter 8: Conservatism

1. Vladimir Putin, "Presidential Address to the Valdai Foundation, presented at the 11th Annual Meeting of the Valdai International Discussion Club, Lake Valdai, Russia," Kremlin.ru, October 24, 2014. http://www.en.kremlin.ru/events/president/news/46860.

2. Arkadii Minakov, "Tipologiia konservatizma v sovremennoi Rossii," *Tetradi russkoi ekspertnoi shkoly*, no. 1 (2017): 8–34.

3. Richard Pipes, *Russian Conservatism and Its Critics: A Study in Political Culture* (New Haven, CT: Yale University Press, 2007); Nicholas V. Riasanovsky, *Nicholas I and Official Nationality in Russia, 1825–1855* (Berkeley: University of California Press, 1969).

4. Nikolai Mitrokhin, *Russkaia partiia: Dvizhenie russkikh natsionalistov v SSSR v 1953—1985* (Moscow: Novoe Literaturnoe Obozrenie, 2003).

5. Kathleen Parthé, *Russian Village Prose: The Radiant Past* (Princeton, NJ: Princeton University Press, 1992); Brudny, *Reinventing Russia*.

6. David Brandenberger, *National Bolshevism: Stalinist Mass Culture and the Formation of Modern Russian National Identity, 1931–1956* (Cambridge, MA: Oxford University Press, 2002).

7. Laruelle and Karnysheva, *Memory Politics*.

8. The *zemstvo* was an institution of local government set up after the emancipation from serfdom by Alexander II. They organized themselves into an All-Russian Zemstvo Union in 1914, siding in favor of more liberal reforms. The *zemstvo* movement was dismantled by the Bolsheviks.

9. Oleg V. Kirichenko, *Granitsy sovetskogo traditsionalizma: Iz opyta russkogo naroda v XX veke* (Moscow: Aleteia, 2021).

10. Guillaume Sauvé, "The Lessons from Perestroika and the Evolution of Russian Liberalism (1995–2005)," in Mario Cucciolla, ed., *Dimensions and Challenges of Russian Liberalism: Historical Drama and New Prospects* (Cham, Switz.: Springer Verlag, 2019), 139–151.

11. John T. Ishiyama, "Strange Bedfellows: Explaining Political Cooperation between Communist Successor Parties and Nationalists in Eastern Europe," *Nations and Nationalism* 4, no. 1 (1998): 61–85.

12. Zoe Knox, "Russian Orthodoxy, Russian Nationalism, and Patriarch Aleksii II," *Nationalities Papers* 33, no. 4 (2005): 533–545; Aleksandr Verkhovsky, "The Role of the Russian Orthodox Church in Nationalist, Xenophobic and Antiwestern Tendencies in Russia Today: Not Nationalism, but Fundamentalism," *Religion, State & Society* 30, no. 4 (2002): 333–345.

13. Luke March, *The Communist Party in Post-Soviet Russia* (Manchester: Manchester University Press, 2002).

14. Roger Eatwell, "The Rebirth of Right-Wing Charisma? The Cases of Jean-Marie Le Pen and Vladimir Zhirinovsky," *Totalitarian Movements and Political Religions* 3, no. 3 (2002): 1–23; Andreas Umland, "Zhirinovsky in the First Russian Republic: A Chronology of Events, 1991–1993," *Journal of Slavic Military Studies* 19, no. 2 (2006): 193–241.

15. Ivan Grek, "The Grassroots of Putin's Ideology: Civil Origins of an Uncivil Regime," *East European Politics* 39, no. 2 (2023): 220–329.

16. Georgiy Il'ichev, "Serafimy, odnako," *Izvestiia*, January 31, 2003, https://iz.ru/news/272449.

17. Dmitry Medvedev, "Interv'iu Informatsionnomu Agentstvu Reiter," *Reuters*, June 25 2008, http://kremlin.ru/events/president/news/542.

18. Vladimir Putin, "Interv'iu gazete 'Fainenshl Taims,'" Kremlin.ru, June 27, 2011, http://kremlin.ru/events/president/news/60836.

19. Vladimir Putin, "Interv'iu pervomu kanalu i agentstvu Assoshieited Press," Kremlin.ru, September 4, 2013, http://kremlin.ru/events/president/news/19143#sel=127: 98:g,127:98:g.

20. Vladimir Putin, "Press-Konferentsiia Vladimira Putina," Kremlin.ru, December 19, 2013, https://rg.ru/2013/12/19/putin-site.html.

21. Vladimir Putin, "Rossiia: natsional'nyi vopros," *Nezavisimaia gazeta*, January 23, 2012, https://www.ng.ru/politics/2012-01-23/1_national.html.

22. Putin, "Press-Konferentsiia Vladimira Putina."

23. Putin, "Presidential Address to the Valdai Foundation."

24. Vladimir Putin, "Prezident Rossii: Bol'shaia press-konferentsiia Vladimira Putina," Kremlin.ru, December 23, 2016, http://kremlin.ru/events/president/news/53573.

25. Vladimir Putin, "Ob istoricheskom edinstve russkikh i ukraintsev," Kremlin.ru, July 12, 2021, http://kremlin.ru/events/president/news/66181.

26. Gulnaz Sharafutdinova, "The Pussy Riot Affair and Putin's Démarche from Sovereign Democracy to Sovereign Morality," *Nationalities Papers* 42, no. 4 (2014): 615–621.

27. Vladimir Putin, "Zasedanie Mezhdunarodnogo Diskussionnogo Kluba 'Valdai,'" Kremlin.ru, September 19, 2013, http://kremlin.ru/events/president/news/19243.

28. Putin, "Rossiia: Natsional'nyi vopros."

29. Vladimir Putin, "Poslanie Prezidenta RF Federal'nomu Sobraniiu," Kremlin.ru, December 12, 2013. http://kremlin.ru/events/president/news/19825.

30. Vladimir Putin, "O Strategii Natsional'noi Bezopasnosti Rossiiskoi Federatsii 2015," Kremlin.ru, December 31, 2015, http://static.kremlin.ru/media/events/files/ru/l8i XkR8XLAtxeilX7JK3XXy6YoAsHD5v.pdf.

31. Putin, "O Strategii Natsional'noi."

32. Ben Noble, "'Traditional Values' and the Limits of Civic Unity," *Russia.Post*, November 21, 2022, https://russiapost.info/politics/traditional_values.

33. Elena Stepanova, "'The Spiritual and Moral Foundation of Civilization in Every Nation for Thousands of Years': The Traditional Values Discourse in Russia," *Politics, Religion & Ideology* 16, no. 2–3 (2015): 119–136.

34. Anna Rotkirch, Anna Temkina, and Elena Zdravomyslova, "Who Helps the Degraded Housewife? Comments on Vladimir Putin's Demographic Speech," *European Journal of Women's Studies* 14, no. 4 (2007): 349–357.

35. Alexandra Novitskaya et al., "Unpacking 'Traditional Values' in Russia's Conservative Turn: Gender, Sexuality and the Soviet Legacy," *Europe-Asia Studies* 75, no. 7 (2023): 1–25.

36. Oleg Riabov and Tatiana Riabova, "The Decline of Gayropa? How Russia Intends to Save the World," *Eurozine.com*, February 5, 2014, https://www.eurozine.com/the-decline-of-gayropa/; Andriy Tyushka, "Weaponizing Narrative: Russia Contesting Europe's Liberal Identity, Power and Hegemony," *Journal of Contemporary European Studies* 30, no. 1 (2022): 115–135.

37. Pjotr Sauer, "Russia Outlaws 'International LGBT Public Movement' as Extremist," *The Guardian*, November 30, 2023, https://www.theguardian.com/world/2023/nov/30/russia-supreme-court-outlaws-lgbt-movement.

38. Novitskaya, "Unpacking 'Traditional Values' in Russia's Conservative Turn."
39. Benoît Vitkine, "En Russie, l'échec démographique de Poutine," *Le Monde*, November 29, 2023, https://www.lemonde.fr/international/article/2023/09/28/en-russie-l-echec-demographique-de-poutine_6191340_3210.html.
40. WHO, "Deaths by Sex and Age Group for a Selected Country or Area and Year [caused by injury]," WHO Mortality Database, accessed January 24, 2024, https://www.who.int/data/gho/data/themes/mortality-and-global-health-estimates.
41. Boris Mezhuev, "Razumnyye konservatory protiv novoy etiki i 'patriotov ne po umu'," Vzglyad.ru, October 25, 2021, https://vz.ru/opinions/2021/10/25/1125804.html.
42. Petr Akopov, "Chetvertyi vizit v tret'emu pape," *Vzgliad*, November 26, 2013, https://vz.ru/politics/2013/11/26/661301.html.
43. Putin, "Ob istoricheskom edinstve russkikh i ukraintsev."
44. Putin, "Rossiia: Natsional'nyi vopros."
45. Alexander Agadjanian, "Tradition, Morality and Community: Elaborating Orthodox Identity in Putin's Russia," *Religion, State & Society* 45, no. 1 (2017): 39–60; Kristina Stoeckl. "Russian Orthodoxy and Secularism," *Brill Research Perspectives in Religion and Politics* 1, no. 2 (2020): 1–75.
46. Mikhail Antonov, "Church-State Cooperation and Its Impact on Freedom of Religion or Belief and on Gender Issues in Russia," *Review of Faith & International Affairs* 20, no. 3 (2022): 32–46.
47. Stoeckl, "Russian Orthodox Church as Moral Norm Entrepreneur." See also Petr Kratochvíl and Gaziza Shakhanova, "The Patriotic Turn and Re-Building Russia's Historical Memory: Resisting the West, Leading the Post-Soviet East?," *Problems of Post-Communism* 68, no. 5 (2021): 442–456.
48. Pål Kolstø, "The Russian Orthodox Church and Its Fight against Abortion: Taking on the State and Losing," *Religion, State & Society* 51, no. 2 (2023): 153–173.
49. Pal Kolstø and Helge Blakkisrud, "Not So Traditional After All? The Russian Orthodox Church's Failure as a 'Moral Norm Entrepreneur," *PONARS Eurasia Policy Memo*, no. 710, October 4, 2021, https://www.ponarseurasia.org/not-so-traditional-after-all-the-russian-orthodox-churchs-failure-as-a-moral-norm-entrepreneur/. See also Aleksei Makarkin, "Sem' problem 'tserkovnogo vozrozhdeniia," *Sotsiodigger* 8, no. 13 (2021): 35–39.
50. *TASS*, "Rossiiskie shkol'niki chashche vybiraiut izuchenie etiki, chem osnov pravoslaviia," July 12, 2019, https://tass.ru/obschestvo/6659493.
51. Katharina Bluhm and Martin Brand, "'Traditional Values' Unleashed: The Ultraconservative Influence on Russian Family Policy," in Bluhm and Varga, eds., *New Conservatives in Russia and East Central Europe*, 223–244; Marlene Laruelle, "Values Entrepreneurship and Ideological Reaction: The Case of Konstantin Malofeev," in Pal Kolstø and Helge Blakkisrud, eds., forthcoming.
52. *RBK*, "V. Milonov o Madonne: Ne dopustim skarmlivaniia nam 'pomoev iz adskoi kukhni imperii zla,'" April 7, 2012, https://www.rbc.ru/spb_sz/07/08/2012/55929c6f9a794719538c4b01.
53. Boris Butylin, "Milonov: Mesto Rammstein—na korporative v bane!" *Natsion-*

al'naia Sluzhba Novostei, August 1, 2019, https://nsn.fm/music/milonov-normalnym-ludy am-rammstein-ne-nravitsya.

54. Vladimir Putin, "Milonov predlozhil vozrodit' politsiiu nravov," *RBK*, March 31, 2014, https://www.rbc.ru/politics/31/03/2014/5704ia559a794761c0ce874d.

55. Zolotoi Most, "Deputat Gosdumy Vitalii Milonov: Nam nuzhna politsiia nravov," *Zolotoi Most*, April 8, 2018, https://goldenmost.ru/deputat-gosdumyi-vitaliy-milonov-nam-nuzhna-politsiya-nravov/.

56. Elena Agafonova, "Deputat Milonov vnes zakonoproekt o zaprete smeny pola bez meditsinskikh pokazanii," *Gazeta.ru*, November 24, 2022, https://www.gazeta.ru/social/news/2022/11/24/19113049.shtml.

57. Daria Kozlova, "Kanon otnyne tam," *Novaia gazeta*, October 28, 2021, https://novayagazeta.ru/articles/2021/10/28/kanon-otnyne-tam; Viktoriia Sapunova, "Detskim Ombudsmenom ozhidaiut podrugu Kuznetsovoi: Senatorshu iz Penzy s 'peremennym' chislom detei," *Bloknot.ru*, October 22, 2021, https://bloknot.ru/obshhestvo/detskim-om budsmenom-stanet-podruga-kuznetsovoj-senator-iz-penzy-s-peremenny-m-chislom -detej-827639.html.

58. Ivan Akimov, "Na strazhe blagopoluchiia detei," *Gazeta.ru*, September 9, 2021, https://www.gazeta.ru/social/2021/09/09/13966910.shtml?updated.

59. Lou Roméo, "Mother Russia: Maria Lvova-Belova, the Putin Ally Deporting Ukrainian Children," *France 24*, January 13, 2024, https://www.france24.com/en/europe/20230113-mother-russia-maria-lvova-belova-the-putin-ally-deporting-ukrainian-children.

60. International Criminal Court, "Situation in Ukraine: ICC Judges Issue Arrest Warrants against Vladimir Vladimirovich Putin and Maria Alekseyevna Lvova-Belova," March 17, 2023, https://www.icc-cpi.int/news/situation-ukraine-icc-judges-issue-arrest -warrants-against-vladimir-vladimirovich-putin-and.

61. Iwona Kaliszewska, *For Putin and for Sharia: Dagestani Muslims and the Islamic State* (Ithaca, NY: Cornell University Press, 2023).

62. Kirill Antonov, "Konstitutsii khotiat dobavit' dukhovnosti," *Kommersant*, January 30, 2020, https://www.kommersant.ru/doc/4235335.

63. Spiritual Administration of Muslims of Russia, "Sovremennaia sem'ia trebuet novykh podkhodov dlia ee sokhraneniia: Pri mechetiakh nachnut deistvovat' komnaty semeinoi konsultatsii," DUMRB.ru, August 20, 2021, https://dumrb.ru/sovremennaja -semja-trebuet-novyh-podhodov-dlja-ee-sohranenija-pri-mechetjah-nachnut-dejstvovat -komnaty-semejnoj-konsultacii/.

64. Egor Lazarev, "Laws in Conflict: Legacies of War, Gender, and Legal Pluralism in Chechnya," *World Politics* 71, no. 4 (2019): 667–709.

65. *Meduza.io*, "Territoriia 'Matil'dy': gde mozhno i gde nel'zia smotret' fil'm v Rossii. Karta," August 10, 2017, https://meduza.io/feature/2017/08/10/territoriya-matildy-gde -mozhno-i-gde-nelzya-smotret-film-v-rossii-karta.

66. *Interfax*, "Muftii Moskvy predlozhil sniat' blokbaster o Nikolae II v otvet na 'Matil'Du,'" August 9, 2017, http://www.interfax.ru/moscow/574154.

67. Anna Shamanska, "Chechen 'Spiritual-Moral Passports' Rebranded as Question-

naires," *RFE/RL*, March 3, 2016, https://www.rferl.org/a/chechnya-spiritual-moral-passports-questionnaires/27587868.html.

68. Lazarev, "Laws in Conflict."

69. Oksana Skripnikova, "Vezhlivyi konservatism' vnedriat progressivnymi metodami," *Nezavisimaia gazeta*, May 19, 2014, http://www.ng.ru/politics/2014-05-19/2_berdiaev.html.

70. *Tetradi po konservatizmu*, "Politika zhurnala," http://essaysonconservatism.ru/politika/.

71. Alexander Pavlov, "The Great Expectations of Russian Young Conservatism," in Suslov and Uzlaner, *Contemporary Russian Conservatism*, 153–176; Marlene Laruelle, "The Emergence of the Russian Young Conservatives," in A. James McAdams and Alejandro Castrillon, eds., *Contemporary Far-Right Thinkers and the Future of Liberal Democracy* (Abingdon: Routledge), 149–166.

72. Robinson, *Russian Conservatism*.

73. Valerii V. Aver'ianov, "Dva konservativnykh manifesta," *Zolotoi Lev* 91, no. 10 (2006). http://www.zlev.ru/91_10.htm.

74. Sergius of Radonezh, canonized in 1452, is famous for having blessed Prince Dmitry Donskoi before his battle against the Mongols in 1380, which marked the beginning of the liberation of Muscovy from the "Tatar yoke."

75. Pravaya.ru, "Imperativy natsional'nogo vozrozhdeniia: Manifest russkikh konservatorov," March 21, 2006, http://www.pravaya.ru/book/120/7943.

76. Pål Kolstø, "Russia's Nationalists Flirt with Democracy," *Journal of Democracy* 25, no. 3 (2014): 120–134; Nicu Popescu, "Putinism under Siege: The Strange Alliance of Democrats and Nationalists," *Journal of Democracy* 23, no. 3 (2012): 46–54; Marlene Laruelle, "Alexei Navalny and Challenges in Reconciling 'Nationalism' and 'Liberalism,'" *Post-Soviet Affairs* 30, no. 4 (2014): 276–297.

77. Mikhail Remizov, "Revoliutsiia dolzhna byt' konservativnoi," *Russkii zhurnal*, September 22, 2003, http://old.russ.ru/politics/20030922-rem.html.

78. Anders Åslund, "Sergei Glazyev and the Revival of Soviet Economics," *Post-Soviet Affairs* 29, no. 5 (2013): 375–386.

79. Prozorov, "Russian Conservatism in the Putin Presidency."

80. Irina Karlsohn, "From Expansion to Seclusion and Back Again: Boris Mezhuev's Isolationism and Its Roots in Solzhenitsyn and Tsymbursky," in Suslov and Uzlaner, *Contemporary Russian Conservatism*, 257–279.

81. Boris Mezhuev, *Politicheskaia kritika Vadima Tsymburskogo* (Moscow: Evropa, 2012), 138–139.

82. Boris Mezhuev, "Civilizational Indifference," *Russia in Global Affairs* 20, no. 4 (2022): 10–27.

83. Mikhail Remizov, *Russkie i gosudarstvo* (Moscow: Eksmo, 2016), 96.

84. Mikhail Remizov, "Apologiia natsionalizma," *Russkaia Narodnaia Liniia*, November 28, 2006, https://ruskline.ru/monitoring_smi/2006/11/28/apologiya_nacionalizma.

85. Remizov, "Apologiia natsionalizma," 366.

86. Mikhail Remizov, "Interview by Paul Robinson," *Irrussianality*, November 2, 2007, https://irrussianality.wordpress.com/2017/11/02/interview-with-mikhail-remizov/.

87. Kholmogorov, *Russkii proekt*.

88. Pravaya.ru, "Imperativy Natsional'nogo Vozrozhdeniia."
89. Remizov, "Interview by Paul Robinson."
90. Remizov, "Interview by Paul Robinson."
91. Katharina Bluhm, "Russia's Conservative Counter-Movement: Genesis, Actors, and Core Concepts," in Bluhm and Varga, *New Conservatives in Russia and East Central Europe*, 25–53.

Chapter 9: Katechon

1. Vladimir Putin, "Stenograficheskii otchet o press-konferentsii dlia rossiiskikh i inostrannykh zhurnalistov," Kremlin.ru, February 1, 2007, http://www.kremlin.ru/events/president/transcripts/24026.
2. Victor Shnirelman, "Russian Neoconservatism and Apocalyptic Imperialism," in Suslov and Uzlaner, *Contemporary Russian Conservatism*, 347–378.
3. Christopher Rowland, "Imagining the Apocalypse," *New Testament Studies* 51, no. 3 (2005): 303–327.
4. Dmitry Sidorov, "Post-Imperial Third Romes: Resurrections of a Russian Orthodox Geopolitical Metaphor," *Geopolitics* 11, no. 2 (2006): 317–347.
5. Maria Engström, "Contemporary Russian Messianism and New Russian Foreign Policy," *Contemporary Security Policy* 35, no. 3 (2014): 356–379.
6. The Old Believers are schismatic groups that retain the liturgical and ritual practices of the church as they existed before the reforms carried out by Patriarch Nikon in the mid-seventeenth century. They have been now reintegrated into the church but are allowed to preserve their unique features. They are often branded in Russian political culture as the guardians of pre-Petrine Russia, that of Moscovy before the Europeanization launched by Peter the Great.
7. Shnirelman, "Russian Neoconservatism and Apocalyptic Imperialism"; Peter J. S. Duncan, *Russian Messianism: Third Rome, Revolution, Communism and After* (London: Routledge, 2002).
8. Matilda Arvidsson, "From Teleology to Eschatology: The Katechon and the Political Theology of the International Law of Belligerent Occupation," in Matilda Arvidsson, Leila Brännström, and Panu Minkkinen, eds., *The Contemporary Relevance of Carl Schmitt* (London: Routledge, 2015), 223–236.
9. Sergei V. Perevezentsev and Aleksandr A. Shiriniants, *Ocherki istorii russkogo khranitelstva: Monografiia, chast 1* (Moscow: Izdatel'stvo Moskovskogo universiteta, 2021).
10. Engström, "Contemporary Russian Messianism and New Russian Foreign Policy," 365.
11. Adamsky, *Russian Nuclear Orthodoxy: Religion, Politics, and Strategy*.
12. Michael Kofman, "Blessed Be Thy Nuclear Weapons: The Rise of Russian Nuclear Orthodoxy," *War on the Rocks*, June 21, 2019, https://warontherocks.com/2019/06/blessed-be-thy-nuclear-weapons-the-rise-of-russian-nuclear-orthodoxy/.
13. Patriarkh Alexy II, "Doklad Sviateishego Patriarkha Aleksiia na Arkhiereiskom Sobore 1997 goda," Patriarchia.ru, June 6, 2008, http://www.patriarchia.ru/db/text/421718.html.
14. Kratochvíl and Shakhanova, "The Patriotic Turn and Re-Building Russia's Historical Memory."

15. Miranda Aldersley, "Orthodox Priest Blesses Russian Missiles in Annexed Crimea as Ukrainian President Claims Putin Has Massed Tanks on His Border and Is Preparing to Seize More Land," *Daily Mail Online*, November 30, 2018, https://www.dailymail.co.uk/news/article-6448013/Orthodox-priests-blesses-Russian-missiles-Crimea-amid-heightened-tensions-Ukraine.html.

16. Radio Free Europe/Radio Liberty, "Svoboda Today," *RFE/RL*, December 3, 2018, https://pressroom.rferl.org/a/svobodatoday-12-03-2018/29635492.html.

17. *Moscow Times*, "Russian Orthodox Priests and Traffic Police March to Remember Road Victims," November 20, 2017, https://www.themoscowtimes.com/2017/11/20/russian-orthodox-priests-and-traffic-police-march-to-remember-road-victims-a59614.

18. Charles Clover, "Putin and the Monk," *Financial Times*, January 25, 2013, https://www.ft.com/content/f2fcba3e-65be-11e2-a3db-00144feab49a.

19. Anastasia Mitrofanova, "Russian Ethnic Nationalism and Religion Today," in Kolstø and Blakkisrud, *The New Russian Nationalism*, 104–131.

20. Shaun Walker, "Angels and Artillery: A Cathedral to Russia's New National Identity," *The Guardian*, October 20, 2020, https://www.theguardian.com/world/2020/oct/20/orthodox-cathedral-of-the-armed-force-russian-national-identity-military-disneyland.

21. Maria Engström, "Apollo against Black Square: Conservative Futurism in Contemporary Russia," in Günter Berghaus, ed., *International Yearbook of Futurism Studies* (Berlin: Walter de Gruyter, 2016), 328–353.

22. Quoted by Engström, "Contemporary Russian Messianism and New Russian Foreign Policy," 370.

23. Engström, "Contemporary Russian Messianism," 368

24. Kholmogorov, *Russkii proekt: Restavratsiia budushchego*, 267.

25. Marlene Laruelle, "The Izborsky Club, or the New Conservative Avant-Garde in Russia," *Russian Review* 75, no. 4 (2016): 626–644.

26. Juliette Faure, "A Russian Version of Reactionary Modernism: Aleksandr Prokhanov's 'Spiritualization of Technology," *Journal of Political Ideologies* 26, no. 3 (2021): 356–379.

27. Russkaia doktrina, "Russkaia Doktrina," 2007, http://www.rusdoctrina.ru/page95507.html.

28. Laruelle, "The Izborsky Club."

29. Sergei Gogin, "Izborskii Klub: Back in the USSR?" *Ezhednevnyi Zhurnal*, January 2013. http://www.ej.ru/?a=note&id=12560#.

30. Aleksandr Prokhanov, ed., "Mobilizatsionnyi proekt—osnovnaia predposylka strategii 'Bol'shogo ryvka' (Ustanovochnaia stat'ia)," *Izborskii klub: Russkie strategii* 1 (2013): 41.

31. Engström, "Apollo against Black Square."

32. Alexander Prokhanov, "Rozhdenie Izborskogo kluba," *Izborskii Klub: Russkie Strategii* 1 (2013): 6.

33. Valentina Brykalina and Dmitrii Kozurov, "Na moleben na aviabaze pod Saratom privezli ikonu s izobrazheniem Stalina," *Komsomol'skaia pravda*, June 16, 2015, https://www.saratov.kp.ru/daily/26393/3271092/.

34. Alexander Prokhanov, "Misticheskii Stalinizm," *Izborskii klub: Russkie Strategii* 4 (2015): 78–81.

35. The Moscow Patriarchate's canonical territories include, in theory, the whole of the post-Soviet space except Armenia and Georgia, which have their own historical patriarchates, as well as Ukraine, given its newly asserted jurisdictional autonomy. They include China, Mongolia, Japan, and the Russian Orthodox Church Outside of Russia (ROCOR), which rejoined the patriarchate in 2007. Canonical territories have different statuses: some are autonomous churches inside the patriarchate, while others have a much lower degree of autonomy on the level of their being an exarchate, eparchy, or diocese.

36. Oleksandr Zabirko, "The Concept of Holy Rus' in Russian Literary and Cultural Tradition: Between the Third Rome and the City of Kitezh," *Entangled Religions* 13, no. 8 (2022): 1–30.

37. John Strickland, *The Making of Holy Rus': The Orthodox Church and Russian Nationalism before the Revolution* (Jordanville, NY: Printshop of St. Job of Pochaev, 2013).

38. Koschei is a figure from Russian mythology who represents evil or death.

39. Mikhail Suslov, "Mapping 'Holy Rus'": Ideology and Utopia in Contemporary Russian Orthodoxy," *Russian Politics and Law* 52, no. 3 (2014): 67–86; Mikhail Suslov, "The Utopia of 'Holy Rus' in Today's Geopolitical Imagination of the Russian Orthodox Church: A Case Study of Patriarch Kirill," *PLURAL: Journal of the History and Geography Department, Ion Creangă State Pedagogical University* 2, no. 1/2 (2014): 81–97.

40. Zabirko, "The Concept of Holy Rus' in Russian Literary and Cultural Tradition," 1.

41. IslamNews.ru, "Tadzhuddin anonsiroval khalifat 'Sviataia Rus," November 10, 2015, https://islamnews.ru/news-tadzhuddin-anonsiroval-xalifat-svyataya-rus.

42. Daniel P. Payne, "Spiritual Security, the Russian Orthodox Church, and the Russian Foreign Ministry: Collaboration or Cooptation?" *Journal of Church and State* 52, no. 4 (2010): 712–727.

43. *TASS*, "Russian Patriarch Likens Kiev for Russian Orthodoxy to Jerusalem for Global Christianity," January 31, 2019, https://tass.com/society/1042662.

44. Ksenia Luchenko, "Why the Russian Orthodox Church Supports the War in Ukraine," Carnegie Endowment for International Peace, January 31, 2023, https://carnegieendowment.org/politika/88916.

45. On Tsymbursky, see Igor Torbakov, *After Empire: Nationalist Imagination and Symbolic Politics in Russia and Eurasia in the Twentieth and Twenty-First Century* (Stuttgart: Ibidem-Verlag, 2018).

46. The notion of Russia as a "continent-ocean" was crafted by one of the founding fathers of Eurasianism, Petr Savitsky (1895–1968). See Laruelle, "Conceiving the Territory," 68–83.

47. Dmitry S. Moiseev, Alexei N. Kharin, Maksim I. Sigachev, and Sergei P. Arteev, "Conservative Values as a Bridge between Russia and the West," *Russia in Global Affairs* 21, no. 3 (2023): 38–60.

48. Ben A. McVicker, "The Creation and Transformation of a Cultural Icon: Aleksandr Solzhenitsyn in Post-Soviet Russia, 1994–2008," *Canadian Slavonic Papers* 53, no. 2–4 (2011): 305–333.

49. Vadim Tsymburskii, *Rossiia-Zemlia za Velikim Limitrofom: Tsivilizatsiia i ee geopolitika* (Moscow: URSS, 2009), 102.

50. N. A. Krinichnaia, "Etnos i kul'tura: Legendy o nevidimom grade Kitezhe—Kontakty mezhdu mirami," *Etnograficheskoe obozrenie* 5 (2003): 87–99.

51. Vitalii Aver'ianov, "Ideologiia Pobedi kak natsional'nii proekt (integral'nii doklad Izborskogo kluba, 2021)," Averianov.net, http://averianov.net/doc/846/?h=834.

52. Assuming that scientific progress and the spiritual quest go hand in hand, Cosmism is the Russian version of space utopia. It maintains that there is only one real goal of humanity, the resurrection of the dead, and that all of humanity's intellectual, spiritual, and scientific activity is directed, wittingly or otherwise, toward this accomplishment. This quest for immortality will be achieved through faith, but also through technological knowledge and the conquest of space. See George M. Young, *The Russian Cosmists: The Esoteric Futurism of Nikolai Fedorov and His Followers* (Cambridge, MA: Oxford University Press, 2012).

53. Aleksandr Prokhanov, "Ideologiia russkoi pobedy," Izborsky-klub.ru, January 26, 2022, https://izborsk-club.ru/22260.

54. Laruelle, *Is Russia Fascist?*, 100–120; Viktor Shnirel'man, *Ariiskii mif v sovremennoi Rossii* (Moscow: NLO, 2020).

55. Oleg Adamovich, "Mama vse vremia tikho plakala, papa ves' osunulsia: Kak proshchalis' s Dar'ei Duginoi," *Komsomol'skaia pravda*, August 23, 2022, https://www.kp.ru/daily/27435/4636691.

56. Vladimir Putin, "Podpisanie dogovorov o priniatii DNR, LNR, Zaporozhskoi i Khersonskoi oblastei v sostav Rossii," Kremlin.ru, September 30, 2022, http://www.kremlin.ru/events/president/transcripts/statements/69465.

57. Alexander Dugin, "Poslanie vo fruktovykh tonakh," *Evrazia: Informatsionno-Analiticheskii Portal*, April 27, 2005, http://evrazia.org/modules.php?name=News&file=article&sid=2400.

58. Ghassan El Masri, "The European Katechon: A Note on the Political Theology of Present-Day Christian–Muslim Engagement," *Islam and Christian–Muslim Relations* 33, no. 4 (2022): 377–402.

59. Gulnaz Sibgatullina and Michael Kemper, "Between Salafism and Eurasianism: Geidar Dzhemal and the Global Islamic Revolution in Russia," in Alfrid K. Bustanov and Michael Kemper, eds., *Russia's Islam and Orthodoxy beyond the Institutions: Languages of Conversion, Competition and Convergence* (London: Routledge, 2018), 91–108; Marlene Laruelle, "Digital Geopolitics Encapsulated. Geidar Dzhemal between Islamism, Occult Fascism and Eurasianism," in Mikhail Suslov and Mark Bassin, eds., *Eurasia 2.0. Russian Geopolitics in the Age of New Media* (Lanham, MD: Lexington, 2016), 81–100; Maria Engstrom, "Orientation—North: Geidar Dzhemal's Metaphysics of Politics," *Russia Program Online Papers*, no. 7 (2023).

60. Mark Sedgwick, *Against the Modern World: Traditionalism and the Secret Intellectual History of the Twentieth Century* (New York: Oxford University Press, 2004).

61. Marlene Laruelle, "Islamic Political Ideologies in Post-Soviet Russia," in Gregory Simons, Marat Shterin, and Eric Shiraev, eds., *Islam in Russia: Religion, Politics, and Soci-*

ety (Boulder, CO: Lynne Rienner, 2023), 31–48.

62. Gulnaz Sibgatullina and Tahir Abbas, "Political Conversion to Islam among the European Right," *Journal of Illiberalism Studies* 1, no. 2 (2021): 1–17.

63. Vladimir Putin, "Vystuplenie na otkrytii Kongressa sootechestvennikov," Kremlin.ru, October 11, 2001, http://www.kremlin.ru/events/president/transcripts/21359.

64. *RIA Novosti*, "Pravoslavie i iadernii shchit ukrepliaiut Rossiiu—schitaet Putin," February 1, 2007, https://ria.ru/20070201/60050923.html.

65. Boris Knorre and Aleksei Zygmont, "'Militant Piety' in 21st-Century Orthodox Christianity: Return to Classical Traditions or Formation of a New Theology of War?" *Religions* 11, no. 2 (2019): 1–17.

66. Gleb Bryanski, "Russian Church under Attack after Backing Putin" *Reuters*, April 3, 2012, https://www.reuters.com/article/us-russia-church-statement/russian-church-under-attack-after-backing-putin-idUSBRE83214B20120403/.

67. Ishaan Tharoor, "The Christian Zeal behind Russia's War in Syria," *Washington Post*, October 1, 2015, https://www.washingtonpost.com/news/worldviews/wp/2015/10/01/the-christian-zeal-behind-russias-war-in-syria/.

68. Pravoslavie.fm, "Slovo Russkoi tsivilizatsii v sviashchennoi voine v Sirii: Protoierei Oleg Trofimov," December 2023 https://pravoslavie.fm/articles/slovo-russkoy-civilizacii-v-svyashhennoy-voine-v-sirii-protoierey-oleg-trofimov/.

69. Niels Drost and Beatrice de Graaf, "Putin and the Third Rome: Imperial-Eschatological Motives as a Usable Past," *Journal of Applied History* 4, no. 2 (2022): 28–45.

70. Patriarch Kirill, "Doklad Sviateishego Patriarkha Kirilla na plenarnom zasedanii XXIV Vsemirnogo Russkogo Narodnogo Sobora," Patriarchia.ru, October 25, 2022, http://www.patriarchia.ru/db/text/5971182.html.

71. *RBK*, "V Sovbeze Rossii prizvali k 'desatanizatsii' Ukrainy," October 25, 2022. https://www.rbc.ru/politics/25/10/2022/63581bbe9a7947dfb157c030.

72. Dmitri Medvedev, Telegram channel, November 4, 2022, https://t.me/medvedev_telegram/206.

73. World Russian People's Congress, "Nakaz XXIV Vsemirnogo russkogo narodnogo soveta," October 25, 2022, https://vrns.ru/documents/nakaz-xxiv-vsemirnogo-russkogo-narodnogo-sobora/.

74. *TASS*, "Naryshkin nazval Anglosaksov 'starymi priiateliami d'iavola,'" May 24, 2023. https://tass.ru/politika/17827999.

75. *Kommersant*, "Parlamentarizm protiv satanizma," October 17, 2022, https://www.kommersant.ru/doc/5619814.

76. Patriarch Kirill, "Patriarshaia propoved' v nedeliu syropustnuiu posle liturgii v Khrame Khrista Spasitelia," Patriarchia.ru, March 6, 2022, http://www.patriarchia.ru/db/text/5906442.html#:~:text=6%20марта%202022%20года%2C%20в,Русской%20Православной%20Церкви%20произнес%20проповедь.

77. Cyril Hovorun, "Enmity between the Orthodox Churches in Ukraine as Collateral Damage of the Russian Aggression," *Russia.Post*, April 11, 2023, https://russiapost.info/politics/enmity.

78. Patriarch Kirill, "Patriarshaia propoved.'"

79. *Novye izvestiia*, "Novye raskol'niki: sobytiia v Ukraine rassorili rossiiskih buddistov," October 13, 2022, https://newizv.ru/news/2022-10-13/novye-raskolniki-sobytiya-v-ukraine-rassorili-rossiyskih-buddistov-368810; *Radio Svoboda*, "Glavnyi ravvin Moskvy uekhal iz Rossii posle otkaza podderzhat' voinu v Ukraine," June 8, 2022, https://www.svoboda.org/a/glavnyy-ravvin-moskvy-uehal-iz-rossii-posle-otkaza-podderzhatj-voynu-v-ukraine/31888833.html.

80. Sergei Romashenko, "Gruppa sviashchennikov RPC prizvala prekratit' voinu v Ukraine," *Deutsche Welle*, March 1, 2022, https://www.dw.com/ru/gruppa-svjashhennikov-rpc-prizvala-prekratit-vojnu-v-ukraine/a-60960423.

81. Adam Taylor, "Russian TV Host: Russia Is the Only Country with Capability to Turn U.S. into 'Radioactive Ashes,'" *Washington Post*, March 16, 2014, https://www.washingtonpost.com/news/worldviews/wp/2014/03/16/russian-tv-host-russia-is-the-only-country-with-capability-to-turn-u-s-into-radioactive-ashes/.

82. *RIA Novosti*, "Putin rasskazal na Valdae: 'My popadem v rai, a oni—prosto sdokhnut,'" October 18, 2018, https://ria.ru/20181018/1530999011.html.

83. Elena Rasenko, "Propagandist Solovyov Stated that Life Is Greatly Overestimated," *Korrespondent.net*, January 3, 2023, https://korrespondent.net/world/4549561-propahandyst-solovev-zaiavyl-chto-zhyzn-sylno-pereotsenena.

84. Steven Pifer, "Russia, Nuclear Threats, and Nuclear Signaling," Brookings, October 13, 2023, https://www.brookings.edu/articles/russia-nuclear-threats-and-nuclear-signaling/

85. François Debrix, "Katechonic Sovereignty: Security Politics and the Overcoming of Times," *International Political Sociology* (2015):143–157.

Part IV

1. Edith W. Clowes, *Russia on the Edge: Imagined Geographies and Post-Soviet Identity* (Ithaca, NY: Cornell University Press, 2011), xii.

2. David Hooson, *Geography and National Identity* (Oxford: Blackwell).

3. Mark Bassin, "Nationhood, Natural Region, Mestorazvitie: Environmentalist Discourses in Classical Eurasianism," in Mark Bassin, Chris Ely, and Melissa Stockdale, eds., *Space, Place and Power in Modern Russia: Essays in the New Spatial History* (De Kalb: Northern Illinois University Press, 2010), 49–80.

4. Gearóid O'Tuathail (Gerard Toal), *Critical Geopolitics* (Minneapolis: University of Minnesota Press, 1996).

5. Franck Billé, "Auratic Geographies: Buffers, Backyards, Entanglements," Academia.edu, 2021, https://www.academia.edu/46672204/Auratic_Geographies_Buffers_Backyards_Entanglements.

6. *TASS*, "Putin poiasnil svoe vyrazhenie o tom, chto granitsy Rossii nigde ne zakanchivaiutsia," October 5, 2023, https://tass.ru/politika/18921495.

7. Adam Lenton, "Who Is Dying for the 'Russian World'?" *Riddle*, April 22, 2022, https://ridl.io/who-is-dying-for-the-russian-world/.

Chapter 10: Eurasia

1. Vladimir Putin, "Mezhdunarodnyi forum 'Odin Poias, Odin Put'," Kremlin.ru, May 14, 2017, http://www.kremlin.ru/events/president/news/54491.

2. Jeremy Smith and Paul Richardson, "The Myth of Eurasia: A Mess of Regions," *Journal of Borderlands Studies* 32, no. 1 (2017): 1–6; Chris Hann, "A Concept of Eurasia," *Current Anthropology* 57, no. 1 (2016): 1–27.

3. Mehmet Akif Okur, "Classical Texts of the Geopolitics and the 'Heart of Eurasia,'" *Türk Dünyası İncelemeleri Dergisi / Journal of Turkish World Studies* 14, no. 2 (2014): 73–104.

4. Yves Denéchère, "Les 'Rapatriements' En France Des Enfants Eurasiens de l'ex-Indochine: Pratiques, Débats, Mémoires," *Revue d'histoire de l'enfance Irrégulière* 14 (2012): 123–141.

5. Sériot, *Structure and the Whole*.

6. Laruelle, *Russian Eurasianism*.

7. Bassin, Glebov, and Laruelle, eds., *Between Europe and Asia*.

8. The noosphere is defined as the new state of the biosphere, shaped by human reason and scientific thought, which are creating a new geological layer. The notion was developed not only by Vernadsly but also by Jesuit priest Pierre Teilhard de Chardin.

9. Laruelle, *Russian Eurasianism*, 31–40.

10. Petr N. Savitsky, "Geograficheskie i geopoliticheskie osnovy evraziistva," original from 1933, republished in *Kontinent Evraziia* (Moscow: Agraf, 1997), 301.

11. *Evraziistvo: Opyt sistematicheskogo izlozheniia* (Paris: Evraziiskoe knigoizdatel'stvo, 1926), 32.

12. Luca Anceschi, *Analysing Kazakhstan's Foreign Policy: Regime Neo-Eurasianism in the Nazarbaev Era* (London: Routledge, 2017).

13. Baasanjav Terbish, "State Ideology, Science, and Pseudoscience in Russia," *Journal of Illiberalism Studies* 2, no. 1 (2022): 73–90.

14. Laruelle, *Russian Eurasianism*, 40–46.

15. Anton Shekhovtsov and Andreas Umland, "Aleksandr Dugin's Neo-Eurasianism: The New Right à la Russe," *Religion Compass*, no. 3/4 (2009): 697–716.

16. Sergei Stankevich, "Derzhava v poskakh sebia: Sametki o rossiiskoi vneshnei politike," *Nezavisimaia gazeta*, March 28, 1992, 4.

17. Putin, "Interv'iu gazete 'Fainenshl Taims.'"

18. Alexander Libman and Evgeny Vinokurov, *One Eurasia or Many? Regional Interconnections and Connectivity Projects on the Eurasian Continent* (Washington, DC: Central Asia Program, 2021).

19. The literature on the Eurasian Union project is immense. See, among others, Piotr Dutkiewicz and Richard Sakwa, eds., *Eurasian Integration: The View from Within* (London: Routledge, 2014)

20. Alexander Libman and Evgeny Vinokurov, "Autocracies and Regional Integration: the Eurasian Case," *Post-Communist Economies* 30, no. 3 (2018): 334–364.

21. Alexander Libman, "Russian Power Politics and the Eurasian Economic Union: The Real and the Imagined," *Rising Powers Quarterly* 2, no. 1 (2017): 81–103.

22. Richard Connolly, "The Empire Strikes Back: Economic Statecraft and the Secu-

ritisation of Political Economy in Russia," in Derek Averre and Katarina Wolzcuk, eds., "The Ukrainian Crisis and the Post-Post-Cold War Europe," special issue, *Europe-Asia Studies* 68, no. 4 (June 2016); Irina Busygina, "Russia's Changing Role in the Post-Soviet Space," PONARS Eurasia Podcast, March 2019, https://www.ponarseurasia.org/russia-s-changing-role-in-the-post-soviet-space/.

23. Peter Rutland, PONARS, forthcoming.

24. Dutkiewicz and Sakwa, *Eurasian Integration*.

25. Åslund, "Sergey Glazyev and the Revival of Soviet Economics."

26. Helga Zepp-LaRouche, Michael Billington, and Rachel Douglas, *The New Silk Road Becomes the World Land-Bridge* (Leesburg, VA: Executive Intelligence Review, 2014).

27. Akihiro Iwashita, "Primakov Redux? Russia and the 'Strategic Triangles' in Asia," *Eager Eyes Fixed on Eurasia, vol. 1, Russia and Its Neighbors in Crisis* (Sapporo: Slavic Research Center, 2007), 165–194.

28. John B. Dunlop, "Aleksandr Dugin's 'Neo-Eurasian' Textbook and Dmitry Trenin's Ambivalent Response," *Harvard Ukrainian Studies* 25, no. 1–2 (2001): 91–127.

29. Andrey Tsygankov, "Aleksandr Panarin kak zerkalo rossiiskoi revoliutsii," *Vestnik MGU: Sotsiologiia i Politologiia* 4 (2005): 166–177.

30. Marlene Laruelle, ed., *China's Belt and Road Initiative (BRI) and Its Impact in Central Asia* (Washington, DC: GW's Central Asia Program, 2017).

31. Mikhail L. Titarenko, *Geopoliticheskoe znachenie Dal'nego Vostoka: Rossiia, Kitai i drugie Azii* (Moscow: Pamiatniki Istoricheskoi Mysli, 2008), 196.

32. David G. Lewis, "Geopolitical Imaginaries in Russian Foreign Policy: The Evolution of 'Greater Eurasia,'" *Europe-Asia Studies* 70, no. 10 (2018): 1612–1637.

33. Karaganov, "Venskii kontsert XXI Veka."

34. Leonid Khairemdinov, "Rossiia chustvuet sebia uverenno i komfortno," *Krasnaia zvezda*, March 6, 2017.

35. Valdai Discussion Club, "Toward the Great Ocean-3: Creating Central Eurasia: The Silk Road Economic Belt and the Priorities of the Eurasian States' Joint Development," Valdaiclub, June 2015, 4, http://valdaiclub.com/a/reports/toward_the_great_ocean_3_creating_central_eurasia.

36. Silviana Malle, Julian Cooper, and Richard Connolly, "Greater Eurasia: More Than a Vision?" *Post-Communist Economies* 32, no, 5 (2020): 561–590; Marina Glaser (Kukartseva) and Pierre-Emmanuel Thomann, "The Concept of 'Greater Eurasia': The Russian 'Turn to the East' and Its Consequences for the European Union from the Geopolitical Angle of Analysis," *Journal of Eurasian Studies* 13, no. 1 (2021): 3–15.

37. Minval.az, "Glava Gosdumy prigrozil ierevanu sanktsiiami," April 1, 2015, https://minval.az/news/79713

38. Vladimir Putin, "Vystuplenie Vladimira Putina na zasedanii popechitelskogo soveta Russkogo Geograficheskogo Obshestva," *Rgo.ru*, April 27, 2018, https://rgo.ru/ru/article/vystuplenie-vladimira-putina-na-zasedanii-popechitelskogo-soveta-russkogo-geo graficheskogo-o.

39. Chris Devonshire-Ellis, "China-Russia Great Eurasian Partnership on Development Track as EAEU Agree to Regional Free Trade," *Silk Road Briefing*, February 2019.

40. Malle, Cooper, and Connolly, "Greater Eurasia: More Than a Vision?"

41. Yongquan Li, "The Greater Eurasian Partnership and the Belt and Road Initiative: Can the Two Be Linked?," *Journal of Eurasian Studies* 9, no. 2 (2018): 94–99.

42. MID.ru, "Kontseptsiia Vneshnei Politiki Rossiiskoi Federatsii," 2016, http://static.kremlin.ru/media/acts/files/0001201612010045.pdf.

43. Andrey Kortunov et al., "The Coming Bipolarity and Its Implications: Views from China and Russia," RIAC, November 23, 2020, https://russiancouncil.ru/en/analytics-and-comments/analytics/the-coming-bipolarity-and-its-implications-views-from-china-and-russia/?sphrase_id=133251320.

44. Kremlin.ru, "Pervyi evraziiskii ekonomicheskio forum," May 26, 2022, http://kremlin.ru/events/president/news/68484.

45. All Eurasianists and neo-Eurasianists consider the Baltic states to be part of Europe but not Eurasia. The Eurasianists tend to add Mongolia to their definition but subtract the South Caucasus, while the Eurasian Union project aims to hold onto the South Caucasus but does not have much interest in Mongolia.

46. Vladimir Putin, "Interview by David Frost," *Breakfast with Frost, BBC*, March 5, 2000. http://news.bbc.co.uk/hi/english/static/audio_video/programmes/breakfast_with_frost/transcripts/putin5.mar.txt.

47. Andrei Bezrukov, "Spasti i sokhranit': Rossiia kak eksporter bezopasnosti," *Rossiia v global'noi politike*, no. 1 (2017), https://globalaffairs.ru/articles/spasti-i-sohranit/.

48. Nicholas V. Riasanovsky, "The Emergence of Eurasianism," *California Slavic Studies* 4 (April 1967): 39–72.

49. Karaganov, "Venskii kontsert XXI veka."

50. Alexander S. Panarin and Boris B. Il'in, eds., *Rossiia: Opyt natsional'no-gosudarstvennoi ideologii* (Moscow: MGU, 1994), 185.

51. Alexander S. Panarin, *Pravoslavnaia tsivilizatsiia v global'nom mire* (Moscow: Algoritm, 2002), 16.

52. Panarin, "Predely faustovskoi kul'tury i puti rossiiskoi civilizatsii," 49.

53. Sergei Karaganov, "From East to West, or Greater Eurasia," *Russia in Global Affairs*, October 25, 2016, https://eng.globalaffairs.ru/articles/from-east-to-west-or-greater-eurasia/.

54. Lewis, *Russia's New Authoritarianism*

55. Fedor Luk'ianov, "Zapros na poriadok," *Rossiiskaia gazeta*, October 20, 2015, https://www.rg.ru/2015/10/21/lukjanov.html.

56. Samuel Sorokin, *Eurasianism and Political Islam in Russia: Ethnoreligious Identities in Transformation, 1990–2020* (PhD diss., European University Institute, 2021), 225.

57. Putin, "Ob istoricheskom edinstve russkikh i ukraintsev," MID.ru, "The Foreign Policy Concept of the Russian Federation, 2023."

58. Vladimir Putin, "Vstrecha s voennymi korrespondentami," Kremlin.ru, June 13, 2023, http://www.kremlin.ru/events/president/news/71391.

Chapter 11: The Russian World

1. Vladimir Putin, "Vystuplenie na otkrytii Kongressa Sootechestvennikov," Kremlin.ru, October 11, 2001, http://www.kremlin.ru/events/president/transcripts/21359.

2. Luke March, "Nationalism for Export? The Domestic and Foreign-Policy Implications of the New 'Russian Idea,'" *Europe-Asia Studies* 64, no. 3 (2012): 401–425; Igor Zevelev, "The Russian World Boundaries: Russia's National Identity Transformation and New Foreign Policy Doctrine," *Russia in Global Affairs*, June 2014; Michał Wawrzonek, "The Concept of 'Russkii Mir,'" in Giuseppe Motta, ed., *Dynamics and Policies of Prejudice from the Eighteenth to the Twenty-First Century* (Cambridge, UK: Cambridge Scholars, 2018), 289.

3. Mikhail Gefter, *Tret'ego tysiacheletiia ne budet. Russkaia istoriia igry s chelovechestvom. Opyty politicheskie istoricheskie i teologicheskie o revoliutsii i sovetskom mire kak russkom. Razgovory s Glebom Pavlovskim* (Moscow: Evropa, 2015).

4. Gleb Pavlovskii and Sergei Chernyshev, "K vozobnovleniiu russkogo," Russkii Institut, June 1996, http://www.archipelag.ru/ru_mir/history/history95-97/chernishov-perepiska/.

5. Pavlovskii and Chernyshev, "K vozobnovleniiu russkogo."

6. Efim Ostrovskii and Petr Shchedrovitskii, "Orel raspravliaet kryl'ia. 1111 znakov za 1111 dnei do novogo tysiacheletiia. Manifest novogo pokoleniia," *Russkiy Arkhipelag*, December 1997.

7. Efim Ostrovskii and Petr Shchedrovitskii, "Rossiia: Strana, kotoroi ne bylo. Sozdat' 'imidzh' Rossii segodnia oznachaet postroit' novoiu sistemu sviazei mezhdu russkimi," *Russkiy Arkhipelag*, 1999, http://www.archipelag.ru/ru_mir/history/history99-00/shedrovicky-possia-no/.

8. Samoilenko and Erzikova, "Public Relation in Russia."

9. Ostrovskii and Shchedrovitskii, "Rossiia: Strana, kotoroi ne bylo."

10. Ostrovskii and Shchedrovitskii, "Rossiia: Strana, kotoroi ne bylo."

11. Sergei Gradirovskii, "Rossiia i postsovetskie gosudarstva: Iskushenie diasporal'noi politikoi," *Diaspory*, no. 2/3, 1999, https://archipelag.ru/ru_mir/rm-diaspor/diaspor-politic/iskus/.

12. Petr Shchedrovitskii, "Russkii mir: Vosstanovlenie konteksta," *Russkiy Arkhipelag*, September 2001, http://www.archipelag.ru/ru_mir/history/history01/shedrovitsky-russmir/.

13. Shchedrovitskii, "Russkii mir."

14. Shchedrovitskii, "Russkii mir."

15. Marlene Laruelle, ed., *Eurasianism and the European Far Right: Reshaping the Europe-Russia Relationship* (Lanham, MD: Lexington, 2015).

16. Konstantin Eggert, "Rossiya v roli 'yevraziyskogo zhandarma,'" *Izvestiia* 6 (1992).

17. Robert V. Daniels, "Evgenii Primakov: Contender by Chance," *Problems of Post-Communism* 46, no. 5 (1999): 27–36.

18. Vladimir Putin, "Kontseptsiia Vneshnei Politiki Rossiiskoi Federatsii," *Nezavisimaia gazeta*, July 11, 2000, https://www.ng.ru/world/2000-07-11/1_concept.html.

19. Sinikukka Saari, "Russia's Post-Orange Revolution Strategies to Increase Its Influ-

ence in the Former Soviet Republics: Public Diplomacy Po Russki," *Europe-Asia Studies* 66, no. 1 (2014): 50–66.

20. Saari, "Russia's Post-Orange Revolution Strategies."

21. Jakov Hedenskog and Robert L. Larsson, *Russian Leverage on the CIS and the Baltic States* (Stockholm: FOI, Swedish Defence Research Agency, 2007); Michael Gorham, "Virtual Rusophonia: Language Policy as 'Soft Power' in the New Media Age," *Studies in Russian, Eurasian and Central European New Media*, no. 5 (2011): 23–48; Gerard Toal, *Near Abroad*.

22. Mikhail Suslov, "'Russian World' Concept: Post-Soviet Geopolitical Ideology and the Logic of 'Spheres of Influence,'" *Geopolitics* 23, no. 2 (2018): 330–353.

23. Putin, "Stenograficheskii otchet."

24. Orysia Lutsevych, "Agents of the Russian World Proxy Groups in the Contested Neighbourhood," *Russia and Eurasia Programme (Blog)*, April 2016, https://policycommons.net/artifacts/613721/agents-of-the-russian-world/1593810/.

25. See Russkii Mir Foundation, "Russian World Foundation," *Russkiymir.ru*, n.d., http://russkiymir.ru/fund/.

26. Sergei Gradirovskii, "Rossiia i postsovetsksie gosudarstva: Iskushenie diasporal'noi politikoi," *Diaspory*, no. 2/3 (1999), http://www.archipelag.ru/ru_mir/history/history98-00/gradirovsky-diasporpolit/; Sergei Gradirovskii, "Bez kart, bez kompasa, bez postavlennykh zadach, ili na chto obrechena," *Russkiy Arkhipelag*, 2000, https://archipelag.ru/ru_mir/rm-diaspor/diaspor-politic/gradirovsky-bezkart/.

27. Putin, "Vystuplenie na otkrytii kongressa sootechestvennikov."

28. Aleksandr Solzhenitsyn, *The Russian Question at the End of the Twentieth Century* (New York: Farrar Straus & Giroux, 1995).

29. Alexander I. Solzhenitsyn, *Publitsistika. Tom 1* (Yaroslavl: Verkhne-bolzhskoe knizhnoe izdatel'stvo, 1995), 26.

30. Alan Ingram, "A Nation Split into Fragments: The Congress of Russian Communities and Russian Nationalist Ideology," *Europe-Asia Studies* 51, no. 4 (1999): 687–704.

31. Laruelle, *In the Name of the Nation*; Wayne Allensworth, *The Russian Question: Nationalism, Modernization, and Post-Communist Russia* (Lanham, MD: Rowman and Littlefield, 1998).

32. Dmitri Rogozin, "Kongress russkikh obshchin: V bor'be za interesy sootechestvennikov," *Daidzhest materialov Rosinformbiuro KRO*, 1994, http://www.rau.su/observer/N18_94/18_21.htm.

33. Laruelle, ed., *Eurasianism and the European Far Right*.

34. Oxana Shevel, "Russian Nation-Building from Yelt'sin to Medvedev: Ethnic, Civic or Purposefully Ambiguous?," *Europe-Asia Studies* 63, no. 2 (2011): 179–202.

35. Putin, "Vystuplenie na otkrytii kongressa sootechestvennikov."

36. Marthe Handa Myhre, "The State Program for Voluntary Resettlement of Compatriots: Ideals of Citizenship, Membership, and Statehood in the Russian Federation," *Russian Review* 76, no. 4 (2017): 690–712.

37. Sebastien Peyrouse, "Former 'Colonists' on the Move? The Migration of Russian-Speaking Populations," in Marlene Laruelle, ed., *Migration and Social Upheaval as the Face of Globalization in Central Asia* (London: Brill, 2013), 215–238.

38. *RIA Novosti*, "Volodin prizval uchest' opyt obrazovatel'noi sistemy tsarskoi Rossii," June 14, 2022, https://ria.ru/20220614/obrazovanie-1795209804.html.

39. Vladimir Putin, "Prezident Rossii Vladimir Putin obratilsia k Opolcheniiu Novorossii," Kremlin.ru, August 29, 2014, http://kremlin.ru/events/president/news/46506.

40. Putin, "Prezident Rossii Vladimir Putin obratilsia k Opolcheniiu Novorossii."

41. Vladimir Putin, "Presidential Address to the Valdai Foundation," Kremlin.ru, October 24, 2014, http://www.en.kremlin.ru/events/president/news/46860.

42. Lenta.ru, "Peskov rasskazal o zashkalivaiushchem reitinge Putina," March 7, 2014, http://lenta.ru/news/2014/03/07/rating/.

43. Russian Embassy in Washington, DC, "Vystuplenie i otvety na voprosy SMI ministra Inostrannykh Del Rossii S.L. Lavrova v khode sovmestnoi press-konferentsii po itogam peregovorov s ministrom Inostrannykh Del Latvii E. Rinkevich," January 13, 2015, http://www.russianembassy.org/node/1854.14:4712.01.2015.

44. Toal, *Near Abroad*.

45. Dmitri Trenin, *Post-Imperium: A Eurasian Story* (Moscow: Carnegie Center, 2011).

46. Vladimir Putin, "Zasedanie Soveta po mezhnatsional'nym otnosheniiam," Kremlin.ru, July 3, 2014, http://www.kremlin.ru/events/president/news/46144.

47. Putin, "Prezident Rossii Vladimir Putin obratilsia k Opolcheniiu Novorossii."

48. Laruelle, ed., *Eurasianism and the European Far Right*.

49. Samuel Greene and Graeme Robertson, "State-Mobilized Movements after Annexation of Crimea: The Construction of Novorossiya," in Grzegorz Ekiert, Elizabeth J. Perry, and Yan Xiaojun, eds., *Ruling by Others Means: State-Mobilized Movements* (Cambridge: Cambridge University Press, 2020), 193–216

50. Andrei Pertsev, "Stantsuem val's bol'shoi voyny," *Meduza.io*, June 8, 2022, https://meduza.io/feature/2022/06/09/stantsuem-vals-bolshoy-voyny.

Chapter 12: Anticolonialism

1. Putin, "Podpisanie dogovorov o priniatii DNR, LNR, Zaporozhskoi i Khersonskoi oblastey v sostav Rossii."

2. Maria Repnikova, "Russia's War in Ukraine and the Fractures in Western Soft Power," *Place Branding and Public Diplomacy* 19 (2023): 190–194; Vadim Grishin, "Russia, Global South, or the Mystery of Political Semantic," *Russia Program Online Papers*, March 15, 2024, https://therussiaprogram.org/page44928741.html.

3. MID.ru, "Kontseptsiia Vneshnei Politiki Rossiiskoi Federatsii."

4. Maxim Khomyakov, "Russia: Colonial, Anticolonial, Postcolonial Empire?" *Social Science Information* 59, no. 2 (2020): 225–263.

5. Vasilii Kliuchevskii, *Kratkoe posobie po russkoi istorii* (Moscow: G. Lissner and D. Sobko, 1908): 24.

6. On this topic, see the seminal works of Alexander Etkind, *Internal Colonization: Russia's Imperial Experience* (New York: Polity, 2011); Vyacheslav Morozov, *Russia's Postcolonial Identity: A Subaltern Empire in a Eurocentric World* (London: Palgrave Macmillan, 2015); Kevork Oskanian, *Russian Exceptionalism between East and West: The Ambiguous Empire* (London: Palgrave Macmillan, 2021)

7. And for good reason, as many of the Romanov family members were of German origin, and a large part of the aristocratic elites were so-called Baltic Germans, that is, native German-speakers forming the majority of landowning nobility, merchants, and clergy in the Baltic region.

8. Aleksei Khomyakov, *Polnoe sobranie sochinenii* (Moscow: Universitetskaia tipografia na Strastnom bul'vare, 1900), 24.

9. The *pochvennichestvo*—from *pochva*, the soil—movement of late nineteenth-century intellectuals with conservative perspectives, insisting on Russia's natural autocracy and Orthodoxy, combined with Slavophile statements, and on the importance of preserving national cultures. Its authors such as Apollon Grigoriev, Nikolai Strakhov, Nikolai Danilevsky, and Konstantin Leontiev have often expressed xenophobic and antisemitic views.

10. Fedor Dostoevskii, *Dnevnik pisatelia*, 1876, available at http://dostoevskiy-lit.ru/dostoevskiy/dnevnik/index.htm.

11. Marlene Laruelle, *Mythe aryen et rêve impérial dans la Russie tsariste* (Paris: CNRS-Editions, 2005).

12. Roman Jakobson, ed., *N. S. Trubetzkoy's Letters and Notes* (Berlin: Mouton, 1975), 12.

13. Laruelle, "Conceiving the Territory."

14. Georgii Vernadskii, "Mongol'skoe igo v russkoi istorii," *Evraziiskaia khronika*, no. 5 (1927): 155.

15. Sergei Glebov, *From Empire to Eurasia: Politics, Scholarship, and Ideology in Russian Eurasianism, 1920s–1930s* (Ithaca, NY: Cornell University Press, 2017); Sergei Glebov, "Wither Eurasia? History of Ideas in an Imperial Situation," *Ab Imperio* 2 (2008): 345–376.

16. N. Trubetskoi, "My i drugie," *Evraziiskii vremennik*, no. 4 (1925): 66–81.

17. "XXII S' ezd kommunisticheskoi partii Sovetskogo Soiuza," *Stenographicheskii otchet*, vol. 1 (Moscow: Politizdat, 1968), 272, quoted in Khomyakov, "Russia: Colonial, Anticolonial, Postcolonial Empire?"

18. Galia Golan, *The Soviet Union and National Liberation Movements in the Third World* (London: Unwin Hyman, 1988).

19. Alvin Rubinstein, *Moscow's Third World Strategy* (Princeton, NJ: Princeton University Press, 1989); Carol Savietz, *The Soviet Union and The Gulf in The 1980s* (New York: Routledge, 1989).

20. In fact the Soviet social engineering project only partly destroyed the old social fabric, as new research shows; see Tomila Lankina, *The Estate Origins of Democracy in Russia: From Imperial Bourgeoisie to Post-Communist Middle Class* (Cambridge: Cambridge University Press 2022).

21. Brudny, *Reinventing Russia*.

22. Anna Razuvalova, *Pisateli-'derevenshchiki': Literatura i konservativnaia ideologiia 1970-kh godov* (Moscow: NLO, 2015).

23. Grek, "The Grassroots of Putin's Ideology."

24. Vladimir Putin, "Rossiia za rubezhe tysiatseletii."

25. Peter Rutland, "The Place of Economics in Russian National Identity Debates," in Kolstø and Blakkisrud, *The New Russian Nationalism*, 336–360.

26. *TASS*, "Putin nazval ideiu 'zolotogo milliarda' neokolonial'noi i rasistskoi," July 20, 2022, https://tass.ru/politika/15264159.

27. More in Laruelle and Limonier, "Beyond 'Hybrid Warfare'," 10–11.

28. Gazeta.ru, "Pushkov: Rossiia uzhe perestala byt' politicheskoi koloniei SshA," August 10, 2013, https://www.gazeta.ru/social/news/2013/08/10/n_3102425.shtml.

29. Gazeta.ru, "Putin raskryl tseli Rossii v Afrike," October 21, 2019, https://www.gazeta.ru/politics/2019/10/21_a_12767696.shtml.

30. Konstantin Malofeev, "Rossiia dlia afrikanskikh stran iavliaetsia prioritetnym partnerom," Roskongress, October 15, 2019, https://roscongress.org/materials/konstantin-malofeev-rossiya-dlya-afrikanskikh-stran-yavlyaetsya-prioritetnym-partnerom/.

31. Matt Maldonaldo, "Russia's Hardest Working Oligarch Takes Talents to Africa," *PONARS Eurasia Policy Memo*, no. 672, September 2020.

32. Irina Parfent'eva and Vyacheslav Kozlov, "Investor Malofeev stal konsul'tantom afrikanskikh pravitel'stv," *RBK*, September 11, 2019, https://www.rbc.ru/business/11/09/2019/5d7796cc9a794731b3800996.

33. Meduza.io, "Minprosveshcheniia opublikovalo metodichki dlia vneklassnykh zaniatii 'Razgovory o vazhnom,'" August 26, 2022, https://meduza.io/feature/2022/08/26/minprosvescheniya-opublikovalo-metodichki-dlya-vneklassnyh-zanyatiy-razgovory-o-vazhnom.

34. Vladimir Putin, "Obrashchenie Prezidenta Rossiiskoi Federatsii," Kremlin.ru, February 24, 2022, http://kremlin.ru/events/president/news/67843.

35. Vladimir Putin, "Putin zaiavil, chto gorditsia byt' chast'iu sil'nogo i mnogonatsional'nogo naroda Rossii," *TASS*, March 3, 2022, https://tass.ru/politika/13955467.

36. Putin, "Putin zaiavil."

37. Vera Tolz and Stephen Hutchings, "Truth with a Z: Disinformation, War in Ukraine, and Russia's Contradictory Discourse of Imperial Identity," *Post-Soviet Affairs* 39, no. 5 (2023): 347–365.

38. Sergei S. Karaganov et al., *Politika Rossii v otnoshenii mirovogo bol'shinstva*, Moscow, 2023, https://globalaffairs.ru/wp-content/uploads/2023/12/doklad_politika-rossii-v-otnoshenii-mirovogo-bolshinstva.pdf.

39. MID.ru, "Kontseptsiia Vneshnei Politiki Rossiiskoi Federatsii," March 2023.

40. Sergei Lavrov, "Speech and Answers to Media Questions by the Minister of Foreign Affairs of the Russian Federation," *Posol'skaia zhizn'* , October 12, 2023, https://embassylife.ru/en/post/36179.

41. Kremlin.ru, "Plenarnoe zasedanie Vsemirnogo russkogo narodnogo sobora," November 28, 2023, http://kremlin.ru/events/president/news/72693.

42. Chebankova, "Russia's Idea of the Multipolar World Order."

43. Thomas Ambrosio, "Russia's Quest for Multipolarity: A Response to US Foreign Policy in the Post-Cold War Era," *European Security* 10, no. 1 (2001): 45–67.

44. Eugene Rumer, "The Primakov (Not Gerasimov) Doctrine in Action," *Carnegie Papers* (Washington, DC: Carnegie Endowment for International Peace, 2019).

45. Emel Parlar Dal and Emre Erşen, eds., *Russia in the Changing International System* (London: Palgrave Macmillan, 2020).

46. Grishin, "Russia, Global South, or the Mystery of Political Semantic."
47. Fyodor Lukyanov, "BRICS Goes from Fantasy to Reality," *Russia in Global Affairs*, April 17, 2011, https://eng.globalaffairs.ru/articles/brics-goes-from-fantasy-to-reality/.
48. Alexander Sergunin et al., "International Relations Theory and the BRICS Phenomenon," *Journal of China and International Relations* (2020): 67–88.
49. Alexei Kuznetsov, "Russian Direct Investment in Countries of Latin America," *Herald of the Russian Academy of Sciences* 92(Suppl 9) (2022): S859–64.
50. Bárbara Vasconcellos de Carvalho Motta and David Paulo Succi Jr., "Brazilian Foreign Policy for the War in Ukraine: Changing Non-Alignment, Counterfactual, and Future Perspectives," *Globalizations* 20, no. 7 (2023): 1227–1240.
51. Ivan U. Klyszcz, "Russia's Changing Latin America Strategy," *PONARS Policy Memo*, no. 875, February 2024.
52. Diego Soliz, "From Counter-Hegemonic Dialogue to Illiberal Understanding: Russia-Latin America Relations (2000–2023)." *Journal of Illiberalism Studies* 3, no. 3 (2023): 87–109.
53. Russia-Africa Summit and Economic Forum, Summit Africa, 2023, https://summitafrica.ru.
54. MID.ru, "Kontseptsiia Vneshnei Politiki Rossiiskoi Federatsii."
55. Alena Nefedova, "Savanna nebesnaia: Rossotrudnichestvo otkryvaet novye tsentry v Afrike," *Iz.ru*, November 2022, https://iz.ru/1420557/alena-nefedova/savanna-nebesnaia-rossotrudnichestvo-otkryvaet-novye-tcentry-v-afrike.
56. SIPRI (Stockholm International Peace Research Institute), "Arms Transfer Database," 2021.
57. Philo C. Wasburn, "Voice of America and Radio Moscow Newscasts to the Third World," *Journal of Broadcasting & Electronic Media* 32, no. 2 (1988): 197–218.
58. Maxime Audinet and Kevin Limonier, "Le dispositif d'influence informationnelle de la Russie en Afrique subsaharienne francophone: Un écosystème flexible et composite," *Questions de Communication* 41, no. 1 (2022): 129–148.
59. Maxime Audinet, *Un média d'influence d'Etat*: Enquête sur la chaine russe RT (Paris: INA, 2024).
60. Audinet, *Un média d'influence d'Etat*.
61. Michael Weiss, "Russia Is Using Undercover Racists to Exploit Africa's Anti-Racist Political Revolt," *Daily Beast*, September 8, 2020, https://www.thedailybeast.com/prigozhin-is-using-afric-to-exploit-africas-anti-colonial-political-revolt.
62. Maxime Audinet and Emmanuel Dreyfus, *A Foreign Policy by Proxies? The Two Sides of Russia's Presence in Mali*, IRSEM, Report 97, September 2022, updated January 2023.
63. Kevin Limonier and Marlene Laruelle, "Russia's African Toolkit: Digital Influence and Entrepreneurs of Influence," *Orbis* 65, no. 3 (2021): 403–419.
64. Audinet and Limonier, "Le dispositif d'influence informationnelle."
65. Dmitri M. Bondarenko, "In the Red Banner's Shade: The Image of Post-Soviet Russia in Africa," *Africa Review* 2, no. 1 (2010): 1–14.
66. Marlene Laruelle and Kelian Sanz Pascual, "The Wagnerverse: Pop Culture and

the Heroization of Russian Mercenaries," *Russia.Post*, June 28, 2022, https://russiapost.info/politics/wagnerverse.

67. Anthony Sguazzin, "Banned in Europe, Kremlin-Backed RT Channel Turns to Africa," *Bloomberg*, July 22, 2022, https://www.bloomberg.com/news/articles/2022-07-22/banned-in-europe-kremlin-backed-rt-channel-turns-toafrica#xj4y7vzkg.

68. Audinet, *Un média d'influence d'Etat*, 272.

69. Ksenia Luchenko, "Propaganda in Holy Orders: Africa, Ukraine, and the Russian Orthodox Church," *European Council on Foreign Relations*, September 20, 2023, https://rb.gy/4omszs.

70. Patriarchal Press Service, "Address by His Holiness Patriarch Kirill at the 2nd Russia–Africa Summit," *Patriarchia.ru*, July 27, 2023, http://www.patriarchia.ru/en/db/text/6045854.html.

71. Petr Akopov, "Budushchee Palestiny reshaetsia na Ukraine," *RIA Novosti*, October 31, 2023. https://ria.ru/20231030/palestina-1906305434.html.

72. Igor Delanoë, "Un 'retour' inachevé: La relation entre la Russie et l'Afrique à l'épreuve de la guerre en Ukraine," *Paix et Sécurité Européenne et Internationale* 13 (2023).

73. Reuters, "Pope Says Ukraine War Fuelled Not Just by 'Russian Empire,'" March 10, 2023, https://www.reuters.com/world/pope-says-ukraine-war-fuelled-not-just-by-russian-empire-2023-03-10/.

74. MID.ru, "Kontseptsiia Vneshnei Politiki Rossiiskoi Federatsii."

Conclusion

1. Gerard Toal, *Oceans Rise, Empire Fall* (Oxford: Oxford University Press, 2024).

2. On mutual learning for the Eurasian region, see Stephen Hall, *The Authoritarian International* (Cambridge: Cambridge University Press, 2023).

3. Rein Taagepera, "Size and Duration of Empires: Growth-Decline Curves, 600 B.C. to 600 A.D.," *Social Science History* 3, no. 3/4 (1979): 119.

4. Ilya Kalinin, "Putin' as a Metaphor and/or Metonymy for Russia," *Russia.Post*, March 18, 2024, https://russiapost.info/politics/metaphor.

5. Svetlana Boym, *The Future of Nostalgia* (New York: Basic Books, 2002).

6. Konstantin Bogomolov, "Dieteticheskoe gore," *Ekho*, May 24, 2023, https://echofm.online/documents/konstantin-bogomolov-dieticheskoe-gore.

7. Maria Lipman, "Putin's Nation-Building Project Offers Reconciliation without Truth," *Open Democracy*, April 12, 2017, https://www.opendemocracy.net/od-russia/maria-lipman/putins-nation-building-project-reconciliation-without-truth.

8. Fedor Luk'ianov, "Rossiia ka strana zdravogo smysla—vot eto bylo by zdorovo," *Rossiia v global'noi politike*, February 13, 2023, https://globalaffairs.ru/articles/strana-zdravogo-smysla/.

9. Kirill *Rogov* and Maxim *Ananyev*, "The New Autocracy: Information, Politics, and Policy in Putin's Russia," in Daniel Treisman, ed., *The New Autocracy: Information, Politics, and Policy in Putin's Russia* (Washington, DC: Brookings Institution Press, 2018), 191–216.

10. Edward S. Herman and Noam Chomsky, *Manufacturing Consent: The Political Economy of the Mass Media* (New York: Pantheon, 1988).

11. Anton Shirikov, "Filtering the News: Why Russians Prefer Propaganda and Shield

Themselves from Independent Reporting," *PONARS Eurasia Policy Memo*, no. 873, January 29, 2024, https://www.ponarseurasia.org/filtering-the-news-why-russians-prefer-propaganda-and-shield-themselves-from-independent-reporting/.

12. James C. Scott, *Domination and the Arts of Resistance; Hidden Transcripts* (New Haven, CT: Yale University Press, 1992).

13. Jeremy Morris, *Intimate Autocracy* (New York: Bloomsbury, 2024); Jeremy Morris, "Political Ethnography and Russian Studies in a Time of Conflict," *Post-Soviet Affairs* 39, no. 1/2 (2023): 92–100; Guzel Yusupova, "Critical Approaches and Research on Inequality in Russian Studies: The Need for Visibility and Legitimization," *Post-Soviet Affairs* 39, no. 1/2 (2023): 101–107.

14. Ammon Cheskin and Luke March, "State–Society Relations in Contemporary Russia: New Forms of Political and Social Contention," *East European Politics* 31, no. 3 (2015): 261–273.

15. Danielle Lussier, "The Political Participation that Enables Putin," *PONARS Eurasia Policy Memo*, no. 699, May 2021, https://www.ponarseurasia.org/wp-content/uploads/2021/05/Pepm699_Lussier_May2021.pdf.

16. Guillaume Sauvé and Maxime Duchâteau, "Petitioning War: How Russians Speak Up Collectively about the Invasion of Ukraine," *Russia.Post*, September 29, 2022, https://russiapost.info/society/petitioning_war.

17. Lev Gudkov, "Eto ne konservatizm! Eto nevroticheskaia reaktsiia," Levada-Center, February 26, 2014, https://www.levada.ru/2014/02/26/eto-ne-konservatizm-eto-nevroticheskaya-reaktsiya/.

18. Vladimir Petukhov, "Autentichnykh konservatorov v Rossii ochen' malo. A te, chto est'- eto, skoree, traditsionalisty (prichem, sovetskie), a ne konservatory. Tstenogramma vystupleniia V.V. Petukhova na kruglom stole-ekspertize Gorbachev-fonda 'Proekt sozdaniia konservativnogo cheloveka dlia sovremennoi Rossii: sotsial'nye realii i perspektivy (May 15, 2014)," Gorbachev-Fond, 2014, p. 2, http://www.gorby.ru/userfiles/o2_petuhov_red_.pdf.

19. Lev Gudkov, "Times Change, but Problems Worrying Ordinary Russians Stay the Same," *Russia.Post*, November 16, 2023, https://russiapost.info/society/problems_worrying.

20. Mikhail Zygar, "What Does Popular Culture Reveal about Russians' Feelings?," *Russia.Post*, April 7, 2023, https://russiapost.info/culture/popular_culture.

21. Sofia Sorochinskaia, "Russian Series on Perestroika-Era Youth Gangs Breaks Popularity Records, Defying Attempts to Ban It," *Russia.Post*, January 10, 2024, https://www.russiapost.info/digest/slovo_pacana.

22. Marlene Laruelle, "Russian Public Opinion on State Ideology and the Predominance of National-Conservatism," *Russian Politics*, forthcoming.

23. Russian Field, "Support for Non-Support of Peace and War," March 9, 2023, https://re-russia.net/en/analytics/059/. See also all waves of the Chronicles survey, available at www.chronicles.report. See also Svetlana Erpyleva and Sasha Kappinen, eds., "Resigning Themselves to Inevitability: How Russians Justified the Military Invasion of Ukraine (Fall-Winter 2022)," Russia Program and PS Lab report, October 2023, https://therussiaprogram.org/ps_lab_1.

24. Paul Goode, "How Russian Television Normalizes the War," *Riddle*, July 14, 2023.

25. Iliya Budraitkis, "The Kremlin's Theory of Ideology: A Very Short Introduction," *Russia.Post*, May 4, 2023, https://russiapost.info/politics/ideology_introduction.

26. Quoted in Rachel Donadio, "Svetlana Alexievich, Nobel Laureate of Russian Misery, Has an English-Language Milestone," *New York Times*, May 26, 2016, https://www.nytimes.com/2016/05/21/books/svetlana-alexievich-a-nobel-laureate-of-russian-misery-has-her-english-debut.html.

27. Surkov, "Dolgoe gosudarstvo Putina."

28. Oleg Bondarenko, Ili'a Grashchenkov, and Sergei Serebrennikov, "Obrazy budushchego dlia Rossii: Stsenarii, razvilki i ocenki," *Fond progressivnoi politiki*, 2022, https://progresspolicy.ru/wp-content/uploads/2022/11/Prezentatsiya-OB3.pdf.

SELECTED BIBLIOGRAPHY

Adamsky, Dmitry. (2019) *Russian Nuclear Orthodoxy: Religion, Politics, and Strategy* (Stanford, CA: Stanford University Press).
Agadjanian, Alexander. (2017) "Tradition, Morality and Community: Elaborating Orthodox Identity in Putin's Russia," *Religion, State & Society* 45, no. 1: 39–60.
Aitamurto, Kaarina. (2019) "Discussions about Indigenous, National and Transnational Islam in Russia," *Religion, State & Society* 47, no. 2: 198–213.
Aktürk, Şener. (2012) *Regimes of Ethnicity and Nationhood in Germany, Russia, and Turkey* (Cambridge: Cambridge University Press).
Alexeev, Michael, and William Pyle. (2023) "A Blind and Militant Attachment: Russian Patriotism in Comparative Perspective," *Post-Soviet Affairs* 39, no. 5: 309–328.
Allensworth, Wayne. (1998). *The Russian Question: Nationalism, Modernization, and Post-Communist Russia* (Lanham, MD: Rowman and Littlefield).
Ambrosio, Thomas. (2001) "Russia's Quest for Multipolarity: A Response to US Foreign Policy in the Post-Cold War Era," *European Security* 10, no. 1: 45–67.
Anceschi, Luca. (2017) *Analysing Kazakhstan's Foreign Policy: Regime Neo-Eurasianism in the Nazarbaev Era* (London: Routledge).
Antonov, Mikhail. (2022) "Church-State Cooperation and Its Impact on Freedom of Religion or Belief and on Gender Issues in Russia," *Review of Faith & International Affairs* 20, no. 3: 32–46.
Åslund, Anders. (2013) "Sergey Glazyev and the Revival of Soviet Economics," *Post-Soviet Affairs* 29, no. 5: 375–386.
Audinet, Maxime. (2021) *Le Lion, l'ours et les hyènes: Acteurs, pratiques et récits de l'influence informationnelle russe en Afrique subsaharienne francophone* (Paris: Institut de Recherche Stratégique de l'École Militaire).
Audinet, Maxime. (2024) *Un média d'influence d'Etat: Enquête sur la chaine russe RT* (Paris: INA).
Audinet, Maxime, and Emmanuel Dreyfus. (2022) *A Foreign Policy by Proxies? The Two Sides of Russia's Presence in Mali*, IRSEM, Report 97, September 2022, updated January 2023.

Audinet, Maxime, and Kevin Limonier. (2022) "Le dispositif d'influence informationnelle de la Russie en Afrique subsaharienne francophone: Un écosystème flexible et composite," *Questions de Communication* 41, no. 1: 129–148.

Bacon, Edwin. (2018) "Policy Change and the Narratives of Russia's Think Tanks," *Palgrave Communications* 4, no. 1: 94–106.

Barbashin, Anton et al. (2019) *Thinking Foreign Policy in Russia: Think Tanks and Grand Narratives*, Washington, DC: Atlantic Council, November 12, 2019, https://rb.gy/40mszs.

Barthes, Roland. (1972) *Mythologies* (London: Paladin).

Bassin, Mark, Sergei Glebov, and Marlene Laruelle, eds. (2015) *Between Europe and Asia: The Origins, Theories and Legacies of Russian Eurasianism* (Pittsburgh: University of Pittsburgh Press).

Bauman, Zygmunt. (2013) *Liquid Modernity* (Hoboken, NJ: John Wiley & Sons).

Beissinger, Mark R. (2002) *Nationalist Mobilization and the Collapse of the Soviet State* (Cambridge: Cambridge University Press).

Bekkin, Renat Irikovich. (2019) "The Renovationist Movement in Contemporary Russian Islam," *Context: Journal of Interdisciplinary Studies / Časopis Za Interdisciplinarne Studije* 6, no. 1: 65–90.

Bettiza, Gregorio, and David Lewis. (2020) "Authoritarian Powers and Norm Contestation in the Liberal International Order: Theorizing the Power Politics of Ideas and Identity," *Journal of Global Security Studies* 5, no. 4: 559–577.

Bibkov, Alexander. (2017) "Neo-traditionalist Fits with Neo-liberal Shifts in Russian Cultural Policy," in Lena Jonson and Andrei Erofeev, eds., *Russia—Art Resistance and the Conservative-Authoritarian Zeitgeist* (London: Routledge), 65–84.

Billington, James H. (2004) *Russia in Search of Itself* (Washington, DC: Woodrow Wilson Press and Baltimore: Johns Hopkins University Press).

Bluhm, Katharina, and Mihai Varga, eds. (2019) *New Conservatives in Russia and East Central Europe* (London: Routledge).

Bondarenko, Dmitri M. (2010) "In the Red Banner's Shade: The Image of Post-Soviet Russia in Africa," *Africa Review* 2, no. 1: 1–14.

Borenstein, Eliot. (2019) *Plots against Russia: Conspiracy and Fantasy after Socialism* (Ithaca, NY: Cornell University Press).

Borenstein, Eliot. (2021) *Speaking Punk to Power* (London: Bloomsbury).

Borshchevskiy, Georgy A. (2022) "'Direct Line with Vladimir Putin' in the Mirror of Sociology and Axiology," *Sotsiologicheskie issledovaniia* 11: 54–65.

Bovt, Georgii. (2008) "Vladislav Surkov: A Pragmatic Idealism," *Russian Politics and Law* 46, no. 5: 33–40.

Boym, Svetlana. (2002) *The Future of Nostalgia* (New York: Basic Books).

Brandenberger, David. (2002) *National Bolshevism: Stalinist Mass Culture and the Formation of Modern Russian National Identity, 1931–1956* (Cambridge, MA: Oxford University Press).

Brandenberger, David. (2009) "A New Short Course? A.V. Filippov and the Russian State's Search for a 'Useable Past,'" *Kritika: Explorations in Russian and Eurasian History* 10, no. 4: 825–833.

Brandenberger, David. (2015) "Promotion of a Usable Past: Official Efforts to Rewrite Russo-Soviet History, 2000–2014," in Vladimir Tismaneanu, ed., *Remembrance, History, and Justice: Coming to Terms with Traumatic Pasts in Democratic Societies* (Budapest: Central European University Press), 191–212.

Brudny, Yitzhak. (2000) *Reinventing Russia: Russian Nationalism and the Soviet State, 1953–1991* (Cambridge, MA: Harvard University Press, 2000).

Budraitkis, Ilya. (2017) "Contradictions in Russian Cultural Politics: Conservatism as an Instrument of Neoliberalism," LeftEast, September 12, https://lefteast.org/russian-contradiction/.

Bustanov, Alfrid K., and Michael Kemper. (2017) "Russia's Islam and Orthodoxy beyond the Institutions: Languages of Conversion, Competition and Convergence," *Islam and Christian–Muslim Relations* 28, no. 2: 129–139.

Byzov, L. G. (2019) "Tsennostnaia evolutsiia 'putinskogo konsensusa' v pervyi god poslednego prezidentskogo sroka," *Obshchestvennyie nauki i sovremennost'* 4: 42–56.

Charap, Samuel, and Timothy Colton. (2017) *Everyone Loses: The Ukraine Crisis and the Ruinous Contest for Post-Soviet Eurasia* (London: Routledge).

Chebankova, Elena. (2017) "Russia's Idea of the Multipolar World Order: Origins and Main Dimensions," *Post-Soviet Affairs* 33, no. 3: 217–234.

Chebankova, Elena. (2020) *Political Ideologies in Contemporary Russia* (Montréal: McGill-Queen's University Press).

Chen, Cheng. (2016) *The Return of Ideology: The Search for Regime Identities in Postcommunist Russia and China* (Ann Arbor: University of Michigan Press).

Christoff, Peter K. (1991) *An Introduction to Nineteenth-Century Russian Slavophilism: Iu. F. Samarin* (Abingdon: Routledge, 1991).

Clover, Charles. (2016) *Black Wind, White Snow: The Rise of Russia's New Nationalism* (New Haven, CT: Yale University Press).

Clowes, Edith W. (2011) *Russia on the Edge: Imagined Geographies and Post-Soviet Identity* (Ithaca, NY: Cornell University Press).

Collier, Stephen J. (2011) *Post-Soviet Social: Neoliberalism, Social Modernity, Biopolitics* (Princeton, NJ: Princeton University Press).

Connolly, Richard. (2016) "The Empire Strikes Back: Economic Statecraft and the Securitisation of Political Economy in Russia," *Europe-Asia Studies* 68, no. 4: 750–773.

Cucciolla, Riccardo Mario, ed. (2019) *Dimensions and Challenges of Russian Liberalism: Historical Drama and New Prospects* (Cham, Switz.: Springer).

Curanović, Alicja. (2019) "Russia's Mission in the World: The Perspective of the Russian Orthodox Church," *Problems of Post-Communism* 66, no. 4: 253–267.

Curanović, Alicja. (2021) *The Sense of Mission in Russian Foreign Policy: Destined for Greatness!* (London: Routledge).

Daniels Robert V. (1999) "Evgenii Primakov: Contender by Chance," *Problems of Post-Communism* 46, no. 5: 27–36.

Dawisha, Karen. *Putin's Kleptocracy: Who Owns Russia?* (New York: Simon & Schuster, 2004).

Deschepper, Julie. (2018) "Le 'patrimoine soviétique' de l'URSS à la Russie contemporaine. Généalogie d'un concept," *Vingtième Siecle: Revue d'Histoire* 137, no. 1: 77–98.

Diesen, Glenn. (2021) *Russian Conservatism: Managing Change under Permanent Revolution* (Lanham, MA: Rowman & Littlefield).
Drost, Niels, and Beatrice de Graaf. (2022) "Putin and the Third Rome: Imperial-Eschatological Motives as a Usable Past," *Journal of Applied History* 4, no. 2: 28–45.
Drozdova, Oksana, and Paul Robinson. (2019) "A Study of Vladimir Putin's Rhetoric," *Europe-Asia Studies* 71, no. 4: 1–19.
Dudko, Oksana. (2022) "A Conceptual Limbo of Genocide: Russian Rhetoric, Mass Atrocities in Ukraine, and the Current Definition's Limits," *Canadian Slavonic Papers* 64, no. 2/3: 133–145.
Duncan, Peter J. S. (2002) *Russian Messianism: Third Rome, Revolution, Communism and After* (London: Routledge).
Dunlop, John B. (2001) "Aleksandr Dugin's 'Neo-Eurasian' Textbook and Dmitry Trenin's Ambivalent Response," *Harvard Ukrainian Studies* 25, no. 1/2: 91–127.
Dutkiewicz, Piotr, and Richard Sakwa, eds. (2014) *Eurasian Integration: The View from Within* (London: Routledge).
Eatwell, Roger. (2002) "The Rebirth of Right-Wing Charisma? The Cases of Jean-Marie Le Pen and Vladimir Zhirinovsky," *Totalitarian Movements and Political Religions* 3, no. 3: 1–23.
Edele, Mark. (2017) "Fighting Russia's History Wars: Vladimir Putin and the Codification of World War II," *History and Memory* 29, no. 2: 90–124.
Eltchaninoff, Michel. (2018) *Inside the Mind of Vladimir Putin* (London: Hurst).
Engelstein, Laura. (2009) *Slavophile Empire: Imperial Russia's Illiberal Path* (Ithaca, NY: Cornell University Press).
Engström, Maria. (2014) "Contemporary Russian Messianism and New Russian Foreign Policy," *Contemporary Security Policy* 35, no. 3: 356–379.
Engström, Maria. (2016) "Apollo against Black Square: Conservative Futurism in Contemporary Russia," in Günter Berghaus, ed., *International Yearbook of Futurism Studies* (Berlin: Walter de Gruyter), 328–353.
Engstrom, Maria. (2023) "Orientation—North: Geidar Dzhemal's Metaphysics of Politics," *Russia Program Online Papers*, no. 7.
Epstein, Mikhail. (2022) "Schizophrenic Fascism: On Russia's War in Ukraine," *Studies in East European Thought* 74, no. 4: 475–481.
Etkind, Alexander. (2004) "Vremia sobirat' kamni: Postrevoliutsionnaia kul'tura politicheskoi skorbi v sovremennoi Rossii," *Ab Imperio* 2: 33–77.
Etkind, Alexander. (2011) "Barrels of Fur: Natural Resources and the State in the Long History of Russia," *Journal of Eurasian Studies* 2, no. 2: 164–171.
Etkind, Alexander. (2011) *Internal Colonization: Russia's Imperial Experience* (New York: Polity).
Evans, Alfred. (2015) "Ideological Changes under Vladimir Putin in the Perspective of Social Identity Theory," *Demokratizatsiya: Journal of Post-Soviet Democratization* 23, no. 4: 401–426.
Fauconnier, Clémentine. (2019) *Entre le marteau et l'enclume: Russie unie, la fabrication d'une hégémonie partisane dans la Russie de Poutine* (Lille: Éditions du Septentrion, Presses Universitaires de Lille).

Faure, Juliette. (2020) "Définir le conservatisme russe," *Cahiers du monde russe* 61, no. 3/4: 573–584.
Faure, Juliette. (2021) "A Russian Version of Reactionary Modernism: Aleksandr Prokhanov's 'Spiritualization of Technology," *Journal of Political Ideologies* 26, no. 3: 356–379.
Faure, Juliette. (2022) "Russian Modernist Conservatism (1960–2022): The Intellectual and Social Reconstitution of Russia's Alternative to Western Liberal Modernity," PhD defended at Science Po Paris, November 29, 2022.
Faure, Juliette. (2023) "What Role Did Ideology Play in Triggering Russia's Invasion of Ukraine," *Russia Program Online Papers* no. 8, 2.
Fomin. Ivan. (2022) "Sixty Shades of Statism: Mapping the Ideological Divergences in Russian Elite Discourse," *Demokratizatsiya: The Journal of Post-Soviet Democratization* 30, no. 3: 305–332.
Fomin, Ivan. (Forthcoming) "Two Statisms of Putin's Ideology: From Proclamation to Mobilization," https://papers.ssrn.com/abstract=4624081.
Foucault, Michel. (1972) *The Archaeology of Knowledge* (New York: Harper & Row).
Freeden, Michael. (2013) "The Morphological Analysis of Ideology," in Michael Freeden, ed., *The Oxford Handbook of Political Ideologies* (Oxford: Oxford University Press), 115–137.
Galeotti, Mark. (2018) *The Vory: Russia's Super Mafia* (New Haven, CT: Yale University Press).
Geertz, Clifford. (1964) "Ideology as a Cultural System," in David Apter, ed., *Ideology and Discontent* (New York: Free Press), 47–76.
Geertz, Clifford. (1973) *The Interpretation of Cultures* (New York: Basic Books).
Giuliano, Elise. (2017) *Constructing Grievance: Ethnic Nationalism in Russia's Republics* (Ithaca, NY: Cornell University Press).
Glaser (Kukartseva), Marina, and Pierre-Emmanuel Thomann. (2021) "The Concept of 'Greater Eurasia': The Russian 'Turn to the East' and Its Consequences for the European Union from the Geopolitical Angle of Analysis," *Journal of Eurasian Studies* 13, no. 1: 3–15.
Glebov, Sergey. (2008) "Wither Eurasia? History of Ideas in an Imperial Situation," *Ab Imperio* 2: 345–376.
Glebov, Sergey. (2017) *From Empire to Eurasia: Politics, Scholarship, and Ideology in Russian Eurasianism, 1920s–1930s* (Ithaca, NY: Cornell University Press).
Goode, Paul. (2021) "Patriotic Legitimation and Everyday Patriotism in Russia's Constitutional Reform," *Russian Politics* 6, no. 1: 112–129.
Gordon, Hahn M. (2022) *Russian Tselostnost': Wholeness in Russian Culture, Thought, History, and Politics* (London: Europe Books).
Gorenburg, Dmitry. (2003) *Minority Ethnic Mobilization in the Russian Federation* (Cambridge: Cambridge University Press).
Gorham, Michael. (2011) "Virtual Rusophonia: Language Policy as 'Soft Power' in the New Media Age," *Studies in Russian, Eurasian and Central European New Media*, no. 5: 23–48.
Gorshenina, Svetlana. (2014) *L'invention de l'Asie centrale: Histoire du concept de la Tartarie à l'Eurasie* (Geneva: Droz).

Götz, Elias, and Jørgen Staun. (2022) "Why Russia Attacked Ukraine: Strategic Culture and Radicalized Narratives," *Contemporary Security Policy* 43, no. 3: 482–497.
Greene, Samuel. (2014) *Moscow in Movement: Power and Opposition in Putin's Russia* (Stanford, CA: Stanford University Press).
Greimas, Julien. (1969) "Éléments d'une grammaire narrative," *L'Homme* 9, no. 3: 71–92.
Grek, Ivan. (2023) "The Grassroots of Putin's Ideology: Civil Origins of an Uncivil Regime," *East European Politics* 39, no. 2: 220–329.
Grishin, Vadim. (2024) "Russia, Global South, or the Mystery of Political Semantic," *Russia Program Online Papers*, March 15.
Guriev, Sergei, and Daniel Treisman. (2022) *Spin Doctors: The Changing Face of Tyranny in the 21st Century* (Princeton, NJ: Princeton University Press).
Hall, Stephen. (2023) *The Authoritarian International* (Cambridge: Cambridge University Press).
Hann, Chris. (2016) "A Concept of Eurasia," *Current Anthropology* 57, no. 1: 1–27.
Hauner, Milan. (1992) *What Is Asia to Us? Russia's Asian Heartland Yesterday and Today* (London: Routledge).
Hedenskog, Jakov, and Robert L. Larsson. (2007) *Russian Leverage on the CIS and the Baltic States* (Stockholm: FOI, Swedish Defence Research Agency).
Hemment, Julie. (2015) *Youth Politics in Putin's Russia: Producing Patriots and Entrepreneurs* (Bloomington: Indiana University Press).
Hill, Fiona. (1998) *In Search of Great Russia: Elites, Ideas, Power, the State, and the Pre-Revolutionary Past in the New Russia, 1991–1996* (PhD diss., Harvard University).
Hill, Fiona, and Clifford G. Gaddy. (2015) *Mr. Putin: Operative in the Kremlin* (Washington, DC: Brookings Institution).
Holmes, Stephen, and Ivan Krastev. (2020) *The Light That Failed: Why the West Is Losing the Fight for Democracy* (New York: Pegasus Books).
Hutcheson, Derek S. (2009) "How to Win Elections and Influence People: The Development of Political Consulting in Post-Communist Russia," *Journal of Political Marketing* 5, no. 4: 47–70.
Hutcheson, Derek S., and Ian McAllister. (2021) "Consolidating the Putin Regime: The 2020 Referendum on Russia's Constitutional Amendments," *Russian Politics* 6, no. 3: 355–376.
Hutchings, Stephen, Vera Tolz, Precious Chatterje-Doody, et al. (2024) *Russia, Disinformation, and the Liberal Order: RT as Populist Pariah* (Ithaca, NY: Cornell University Press).
Ingram, Alan. (1999) "A Nation Split into Fragments: The Congress of Russian Communities and Russian Nationalist Ideology," *Europe-Asia Studies* 51, no. 4: 687–704.
Ishiyama, John T. (1998) "Strange Bedfellows: Explaining Political Cooperation between Communist Successor Parties and Nationalists in Eastern Europe," *Nations and Nationalism* 4, no. 1: 61–85.
Ivanov, Sergei A. (2016) "The Second Rome as Seen by the Third: Russian Debates on 'the Byzantine Legacy,'" in Przemyslaw Marciniak and Dion C. Smythe, eds., *The Reception of Byzantium in European Culture since 1500* (Farnham, UK: Ashgate), 55–80.

Karnysheva, Margarita. (2023) "Writing an Illiberal History of the Russian Revolution: How the Kremlin Projected Policy into the Past, 1985–2011," *Journal of Illiberalism Studies* 3, no. 3: 47–70.

Kazharski, Aliaksei. (2019) *Eurasian Integration and the Russian World: Regionalism as an Identitary Enterprise* (Budapest: Central European University Press), 30.

Kelly, Aileen M. (1998) *Toward Another Shore: Russian Thinkers between Necessity and Chance* (New Haven, CT: Yale University Press).

Kemper, Michael. (2012) "Mufti Ravil Gainutdin: The Translation of Islam into a Language of Patriotism and Humanism," in Alfrid K. Bustanov and Michael Kemper, eds., *Islamic Authority and the Russian Language: Studies on Texts from European Russia, the North Caucasus and West Siberia* (Amsterdam: Pegasus), 105–141.

Kemper, Michael. (2019) "Religious Political Technology: Damir Mukhetdinov's 'Russian Islam,'" *Religion, State & Society* 47, no. 2: 214–233.

Khomyakov, Maxim. (2020) "Russia: Colonial, Anticolonial, Postcolonial Empire?" *Social Science Information* 59, no. 2: 225–263.

Kirichenko, Oleg V. (2021) *Granitsy sovetskogo traditsionalizma: Iz opyta russkogo naroda v XX veke* (Moscow: Aleteia).

Kneuer, Marianne. (2017) "Legitimation beyond Ideology: Authoritarian Regimes and the Construction of Missions," *Zeitschrift Für Vergleichende Politikwissenschaft* 11, no. 2: 181–211.

Knorre, Boris, and Aleksei Zygmont. (2019) "'Militant Piety' in 21st-Century Orthodox Christianity: Return to Classical Traditions or Formation of a New Theology of War?" *Religions* 11, no. 2: 1–17.

Knox, Zoe. (2005) "Russian Orthodoxy, Russian Nationalism, and Patriarch Aleksii II," *Nationalities Papers* 33, no. 4: 533–545.

Kolstø, Pål. (2014) "Russia's Nationalists Flirt with Democracy," *Journal of Democracy* 25, no. 3: 120–134.

Kolstø, Pål. (2016) "Marriage of Convenience? Collaboration between Nationalists and Liberals in the Russian Opposition 2011–12," *Russian Review* 75, no. 4: 645–663.

Kolstø, Pål. (2023). "The Russian Orthodox Church and Its Fight against Abortion: Taking on the State and Losing," *Religion, State & Society* 51, no. 2: 153–173.

Kolstø, Pål, and Helge Blakkisrud, eds. (2016) *The New Russian Nationalism: Imperialism, Ethnicity and Authoritarianism 2000–2015* (Edinburgh: Edinburgh University Press).

Koposov, Nikolai. (2018) *Memory Laws, Memory Wars: The Politics of the Past in Europe and Russia* (New Delhi: Cambridge University Press).

Koposov, Nikolai. (2022) "'The Only Possible Ideology': Nationalizing History in Putin's Russia," *Journal of Genocide Research* 24, no. 2: 205–215.

Kragh, Martin, and Andreas Umland. (2023) "Putinism beyond Putin: The Political Ideas of Nikolai Patrushev and Sergei Naryshkin in 2006–20," *Post-Soviet Affairs* 39, no. 5: 366–389.

Kragh, Martin, and Andreas Umland. (2023) "*Ukrainophobic Imaginations of the Russian Siloviki: The Case of Nikolai Patrushev, 2014–2023,*" *Center for Democratic Integrity*, https://democratic-integrity.eu/ukrainophobic-imaginations-of-the-russian-siloviki/.

Krastev, Ivan. (2006) "Democracy's 'Doubles'," *Journal of Democracy* 17, no. 2: 58.
Krastev, Ivan. (2015) "V chem Zapad oshibaetsia naschet Rossii," *Rossiia v global'noi politike*, August 16.
Kratochvíl, Petr, and Gaziza Shakhanova. (2021) "The Patriotic Turn and Re-Building Russia's Historical Memory: Resisting the West, Leading the Post-Soviet East?" *Problems of Post-Communism* 68, no. 5: 442–456.
Krickovic, Andrej, and Igor Pellicciari. (2021) "From 'Greater Europe' to 'Greater Eurasia': Status Concerns and the Evolution of Russia's Approach to Alignment and Regional Integration," *Journal of Eurasian Studies* 12, no. 1: 86–99.
Krickovic, Andrej, and Richard Sakwa. (2022) "War in Ukraine: The Clash of Norms and Ontologies," *Journal of Military and Strategic Studies* 22, no. 2: 89–109.
Kryshtanovskaya, Olga. (2005) *Anatomiia rossiiskoi elity* (Moscow: Zakharov).
Kukulin, Ilya. (2022) "The Sorcerers' Apprentices: Can Georgy Shchedrovitsky Be Responsible for Russia's Invasion of Ukraine?," *Russia.Post*, June 26, https://russiapost.info/society/the_sorcerers_apprentices.
Laruelle, Marlene. (2008) *Russian Eurasianism: An Ideology of Empire* (Woodrow Wilson Press; Johns Hopkins University Press).
Laruelle, Marlene, ed. (2015) *Eurasianism and the European Far Right: Reshaping the Europe-Russia Relationship* (Lanham, MD: Lexington).
Laruelle, Marlene. (2016) "Digital Geopolitics Encapsulated. Geidar Dzhemal between Islamism, Occult Fascism and Eurasianism," in Mikhail Suslov and Mark Bassin, eds., *Eurasia 2.0: Russian Geopolitics in the Age of New Media* (Lanham, MD: Lexington), 81–100.
Laruelle, Marlene. (2019) "Commemorating 1917 in Russia: Ambivalent State History Policy and the Church's Conquest of the History Market," *Europe-Asia Studies* 71, no. 2: 249–267.
Laruelle, Marlene. (2019) *Russian Nationalism. Imaginaries, Doctrines, and Political Battlefields* (London: Routledge).
Laruelle, Marlene. (2020) "Ideological Complementarity or Competition? The Kremlin, the Church, and the Monarchist Idea in Today's Russia," *Slavic Review* 79, no. 2: 345–364.
Laruelle, Marlene. (2021) "The Emergence of the Russian Young Conservatives," in A. James McAdams and Alejandro Castrillon, eds., *Contemporary Far-Right Thinkers and the Future of Liberal Democracy* (London: Routledge), 149–166.
Laruelle, Marlene. (2021) *Is Russia Fascist? Unraveling Propaganda East and West* (Ithaca, NY: Cornell University Press).
Laruelle, Marlene. (2021) "Russia's Niche Soft Power: Sources, Targets, and Channels of Influence." *Russie.Nei.Visions* 122, April, https://www.ifri.org/en/publications/notes-de-lifri/russieneivisions/russias-niche-soft-power-sources-targets-and-channels.
Laruelle, Marlene. (2024) "Russian Public Opinion on State Ideology and the Predominance of National-Conservatism," *Russian Politics*, forthcoming.
Laruelle, Marlene, and Laura Howells. (2020) "Ideological or Pragmatic? A Data-Driven Analysis of the Russian Presidential Grant Fund," *Russian Politics* 5: 29–51.

Laruelle, Marlene, and Margarita Karnysheva. (2020) *Memory Politics and the Russian Civil War: Reds versus Whites* (London: Bloomsbury).
Laruelle, Marlene, and Kevin Limonier. (2021) "'Beyond Hybrid Warfare': A Digital Exploration of Russia's Entrepreneurs of Influence," *Post-Soviet Affairs* 37, no 4: 318–335.
Laruelle, Marlene, Ivan Grek, and Sergei Davydov. (2023) "Culturalizing the Nation: A Quantitative Approach to the Russkii/Rossiiskii Semantic Space in Russia's Political Discourse," *Demokratizatsiya: The Journal of Post-Soviet Democratization* 31, no. 1: 3–27.
Ledeneva, Alena V. (2013) *Can Russia Modernise? Sistema, Power Networks and Informal Governance* (Cambridge: Cambridge University Press).
Lewis, David G. (2018) "Geopolitical Imaginaries in Russian Foreign Policy: The Evolution of 'Greater Eurasia,'" *Europe-Asia Studies* 70, no. 10: 1612–1637.
Lewis, David. (2020) *Russia's New Authoritarianism. Putin and the Politics of Order* (Edinburgh: Edinburgh University Press).
Libman, Alexander. (2017) "Russian Power Politics and the Eurasian Economic Union: The Real and the Imagined," *Rising Powers Quarterly* 2, no. 1: 81–103.
Libman, Alexander, and Evgeni Vinokurov. (2018). "Autocracies and Regional Integration: The Eurasian Case," *Post-Communist Economies* 30, no. 3: 334–364.
Libman, Alexander, and Evgeny Vinokurov. (2021) *One Eurasia or Many? Regional Interconnections and Connectivity Projects on the Eurasian Continent* (Washington, DC: Central Asia Program).
Limonier, Kévin, and Maxime Audinet. (2017) "La stratégie d'influence informationnelle et numérique de la Russie en Europe," *Hérodote* 1, no. 164: 123–144.
Limonier, Kevin, and Marlene Laruelle. (2021) "Russia's African Toolkit: Digital Influence and Entrepreneurs of Influence," *Orbis* 65, no. 3: 403–419.
Linde, Fabian. (2016) "State Civilisation: The Statist Core of Vladimir Putin's Civilisational Discourse and Its Implications for Russian Foreign Policy," *Politics in Central Europe* 12, no. 1: 21–35.
Linz, Juan. (2000) *Totalitarian and Authoritarian Regimes* (London: Lynne Rienner).
Luchenko, Ksenia. (2023) "Propaganda in Holy Orders: Africa, Ukraine, and the Russian Orthodox Church." *European Council on Foreign Relations*, September 20, https://rb.gy/4omszs.
Luchenko, Ksenia. (2023) "Why the Russian Orthodox Church Supports the War in Ukraine," Carnegie Endowment for International Peace, January 31, https://carnegieendowment.org/politika/88916.
Lussier, Danielle. (2019) "Ideology among Russian Elites: Attitudes towards the United States as a Belief System," *Post-Soviet Affairs* 35, no. 5/6: 433–449.
Lutsevych, Orysia. (2016) "Agents of the Russian World Proxy Groups in the Contested Neighbourhood," *Russia and Eurasia Programme (Blog)*, April, https://policycommons.net/artifacts/613721/agents-of-the-russian-world/1593810/.
MacMaster, Robert E. (1967) *Danilevsky: A Russian Totalitarian Philosopher* (Cambridge, MA: Harvard University Press).
Makarychev, Andrey, and Sergey Medvedev. (2024) *Biopower in Putin's Russia: From Taking Care to Taking Lives* (Vienna: CEU University Press).

Makarychev, Andrey, and Alexandra Yatsyk. (2019) *Critical Biopolitics of the Post-Soviet. From Populations to Nations* (Lanham, MD: Lexington).
Mäkinen, Sirke. (2011) "Surkovian Narrative on the Future of Russia: Making Russia a World Leader," *Journal of Communist Studies and Transition Politics* 27, no. 2: 143–165.
Malcolm, Neil. (1989) "The 'Common European Home' and Soviet European Policy," *International Affairs* 65, no. 4: 659–676.
Malinova, Olga. (2012) "Russia and 'the West' in the 2000s: Redefining Russian Identity in Official Political Discourse," in Raymond Taras, ed., *Russia's Identity in International Relations: Images, Perceptions, Misperceptions* (London: Routledge), 73–90.
Malinova, Olga. (2018) "'The Embarrassing Centenary': Reinterpretation of the 1917 Revolution in the Official Historical Narrative of Post-Soviet Russia (1991–2017)," *Nationalities Papers* 46, no. 2: 272–289.
Malinova, Olga. (2019) "Encounters with Liberalism in Post-Soviet Russia," in Michael Freeden, Javier Fernández-Sebastián, and Jörn Leonhard, eds., *In Search of European Liberalisms: Concepts, Languages, Ideologies* (New York: Berghahn Books), 278–301.
Malinova, Olga. (2021) "Framing the Collective Memory of the 1990s as a Legitimation Tool for Putin's Regime," *Problems of Post-Communism* 68, no. 5: 429–441.
Malinova, Olga. (2021) "Politics of Memory and Nationalism," *Nationalities Papers* 49, no. 6: 997–1007.
Malinova, Olga. (2022) "Legitimizing Putin's Regime: The Transformations of the Narrative of Russia's Post-Soviet Transition," *Communist and Post-Communist Studies* 55, no. 1: 52–75.
Malinova, Olga, and N. V. Karpova. (2023) "Deputaty Gosudarstvennoi dumy kak aktory rossiiskoi politiki pamiati: Na primera transformatsii Federal'nogo zakona 'O dniakh voinskoi slavy i pamiatnykh datakh Rossii," *Politicheskaia nauka* 1: 113–138.
Mälksoo, Maria. (2009) "The Memory Politics of Becoming European: The East European Subalterns and the Collective Memory of Europe," *European Journal of International Relations* 15, no. 4: 653–680.
Mälksoo, Maria. (2015) "In Search of a Modern Mnemonic Narrative of Communism: Russia's Mnemopolitical Mimesis during the Medvedev Presidency," *Journal of Soviet and Post-Soviet Politics and Society* 1, no. 2: 317–339.
Malle, Silviana, Julian Cooper, and Richard Connolly. (2020) "Greater Eurasia: More Than a Vision?" *Post-Communist Economies* 32, no, 5: 561–590.
March, Luke. (2002) *The Communist Party in Post-Soviet Russia* (Manchester: Manchester University Press).
March, Luke. (2012) "Nationalism for Export? The Domestic and Foreign-Policy Implications of the New 'Russian Idea'," *Europe-Asia Studies* 64, no. 3: 401–425.
McGlynn, Jade. (2023) "Illiberal Memory across Borders," *Journal of Illiberalism Studies* 3, no. 3: 44.
McGlynn, Jade. (2023) "Russian Propaganda Tactics in Wartime Ukraine," *Russia Program Online Papers*, no. 10, November.
McGlynn, Jade. (2023) *Memory Makers: The Politics of the Past in Putin's Russia* (London: Bloomsbury).

McGlynn, Jade. (2023) *Russia's War* (New York: Polity Press).
McVicker, Ben A. (2011) "The Creation and Transformation of a Cultural Icon: Aleksandr Solzhenitsyn in Post-Soviet Russia, 1994–2008," *Canadian Slavonic Papers* 53, nos. 2–4: 305–333.
Miller, Aleksei. (2023) "Talking Politics: Vladimir Putin's Narrative on Contemporary History (2019–2022)," *Russia in Global Affairs*, no. 2, https://eng.globalaffairs.ru/articles/putins-narrative/.
Miller, Aleksei, and D. V. Efremenko, eds. *Politika pamiati v sovremennoi Rossii i stranakh Vostochnoi Evropy: Aktory, instituty, narativy* (St. Petersburg: European University), 122–143.
Miskimmon, Alister, Ben O'Loughlin, and Laura Roselle, eds., (2017) *Forging the World: Strategic Narratives and International Relations* (Ann Arbor: University of Michigan Press).
Mitrokhin, Nikolai. (2003) *Russkaia partiia: Dvizhenie russkikh natsionalistov v SSSR v 1953—1985* (Moscow: Novoe Literaturnoe Obozrenie).
Mjør, Kåre Johan, and Sanna Turoma, eds. (2020) *Russia as Civilization: Ideological Discourses in Politics, Media, and Academia* (London: Routledge).
Morozov, Vyacheslav. (2015) *Russia's Postcolonial Identity: A Subaltern Empire in a Eurocentric World* (London: Palgrave-Macmillan).
Morris, Jeremy. (2023). "Political Ethnography and Russian Studies in a Time of Conflict," *Post-Soviet Affairs* 39, no. 1/2: 92–100.
Morris, Jeremy. (2024). *Intimate Autocracy* (New York: Bloomsbury).
Morris, Jeremy, Andrei Semenov, and Regina Smyth, eds. (2023) *Varieties of Russian Activism: State-Society Contestation in Everyday Life* (Bloomington: Indiana University Press).
Myhre, Marthe Handa. (2017) "The State Program for Voluntary Resettlement of Compatriots: Ideals of Citizenship, Membership, and Statehood in the Russian Federation," *Russian Review* 76, no. 4: 690–712.
Nelson, Todd. (2015) "History as Ideology: The Portrayal of Stalinism and the Great Patriotic War in Contemporary Russian High School Textbooks," *Post-Soviet Affairs* 31, no. 1: 37–65.
Nelson, Todd. (2021) *Bringing Stalin Back In: Memory Politics and the Creation of a Useable Past in Putin's Russia* (Lanham, MD: Lexington Books).
Neuman, Iver. (2017) *Russia and the Idea of Europe* (London: Routledge).
Novitskaya, Alexandra, et al. (2023) "Unpacking 'Traditional Values' in Russia's Conservative Turn: Gender, Sexuality and the Soviet Legacy," *Europe-Asia Studies* 75, no. 7: 1–25.
Okara, Andrey. (2007) "Sovereign Democracy: A New Russian Idea or a PR Project?" *Russia in Global Affairs*, no. 3, https://eng.globalaffairs.ru/articles/sovereign-democracy-a-new-russian-idea-or-a-pr-project/.
Okur, Mehmet Akif. (2014) "Classical Texts of the Geopolitics and the 'Heart of Eurasia'," *Türk Dünyası İncelemeleri Dergisi / Journal of Turkish World Studies* 14, no. 2: 73–104.

Omelicheva, Maria. (2017) "A New Russian Holiday Has More behind It than National Unity: The Political Functions of Historical Commemorations," *Australian Journal of Politics & History* 63, no. 3: 430–442.

Oskanian, Kevork. (2018) "A Very Ambiguous Empire: Russia's Hybrid Exceptionalism," *Europe-Asia Studies* (January): 26–52.

Oskanian, Kevork. (2021) *Russian Exceptionalism between East and West: The Ambiguous Empire*. London: Palgrave Macmillan.

Østbø, Jardar. (2016) *The New Third Rome: Readings of a Russian Nationalist Myth* (Stuttgart: Ibidem Verlag).

Pakhalyuk, Konstantin. (2018) "Historical Past as Foundation of Russia's Polity: Assessing Putin's Speeches in 2012–2018," *Politeia* 4: 6–31.

Papkova, Irina. (2009) "Saving the Third Rome: 'Fall of the Empire,' Byzantium and Putin's Russia," in *Reconciling the Irreconcilable*, vol. 24 (Vienna: Institute for Human Sciences), http://www.iwm.at/index.php?option=com_content&task=view&id=131&Itemid=125.

Papkova, Irina. (2011) "Russian Orthodox Concordat? Church and Atate under Medvedev," *Nationalities Papers* 39, no. 5: 667–683.

Papkova, Irina. (2011) *The Russian Orthodox Church and Russian Politics* (New York: Oxford University Press).

Parthé, Kathleen. (1992) *Russian Village Prose: The Radiant Past* (Princeton, NJ: Princeton University Press).

Payne P., Daniel. (2023) "Spiritual Security, the Russian Orthodox Church, and the Russian Foreign Ministry: Collaboration between Russia and the West," *Russia in Global Affairs* 21, no. 3: 38–60.

Pehe, Veronika, and Joanna Wawrzyniak, eds. (2023) *Remembering the Neoliberal Turn: Economic Change and Collective Memory in Eastern Europe after 1989* (London: Routledge).

Pennisi, Laura. (2021) *The Katechon and Moscow as Third Rome: Visual Analysis of Russia's Religious Soft Power in Greece* (MA thesis, Uppsala University).

Perevezentsev, Sergei V., and Aleksandr A. Shiriniants. (2021) *Ocherki istorii russkogo khranitelstva: Monografiia, chast 1* (Moscow: Izdatel'stvo Moskovskogo universiteta).

Petersson, Bo. (2021) *The Putin Predicament: Problems of Legitimacy and Succession* (Stuttgart: Ibidem).

Pipes, Richard. (2007) *Russian Conservatism and Its Critics: A Study in Political Culture* (New Haven, CT: Yale University Press);

Plohii, Serhii. (2023) *The Russo-Ukrainian War: The Return of History* (New York: W.W. Norton).

Pomerantsev, Peter. (2015) *Nothing Is True and Everything Is Possible* (New York: PublicAffairs Books).

Popescu, Nicu. (2012) "Putinism under Siege: The Strange Alliance of Democrats and Nationalists," *Journal of Democracy* 23, no. 3: 46–54.

Prozorov, Sergei. (2005) "Russian Conservatism in the Putin Presidency: The Dispersion of a Hegemonic Discourse," *Journal of Political Ideologies* 10, no. 2: 121–143.

Pynnoniemi, Katri. (2014) "Science Fiction: President Medvedev's Campaign for Russia's 'Technological Modernization,'" *Demokratizatsiya: The Journal of Post-Soviet Democratization* 22, no. 4: 605–625.

Radnitz, Scott, and Harris Mylonas. (2022) *Enemies Within: The Global Politics of Fifth Columns* (New York: Oxford University Press).

Razuvalova, Anna. (2015) *Pisateli-'derevenshchiki': Literatura i konservativnaia ideologiia 1970-kh godov* (Moscow: NLO).

Repnikova, Maria. (2023) "Russia's War in Ukraine and the Fractures in Western Soft Power," *Place Branding and Public Diplomacy* 19: 190–194.

Riasanovsky, Nicholas V. (1969) *Nicholas I and Official Nationality in Russia, 1825–1855* (Berkeley: University of California Press);.

Richters, Katja. (2012) "The Russian Orthodox Church and Medvedev's Modernisation Policy: Allies or Foes?," *Religion, State & Society* 40, no. 3/4: 363–378.

Richters, Katja. (2012) *The Post-Soviet Russian Orthodox Church: Politics, Culture and Greater Russia* (London: Routledge).

Rivera, Sharon Werning, ed. (2020) *Survey of Russian Elites 2020: New Perspectives on Foreign and Domestic Policy* (Hamilton College), https://www.hamilton.edu/documents/SRE2020ReportFINAL.pdf.

Robinson, Neil. (2017) "Russian Neo-Patrimonialism and Putin's 'Cultural Turn'," *Europe-Asia Studies* 69, no. 2: 348–366.

Robinson, Paul. (2019) *Russian Conservatism* (Ithaca, NY: Cornell University Press).

Robinson, Paul. (2023) *Russian Liberalism* (Ithaca, NY: Cornell University Press).

Rogov, Kirill, and Maxim *Ananyev*. (2018) "The New Autocracy: Information, Politics, and Policy in Putin's Russia," in Daniel Treisman, ed., *The New Autocracy: Information, Politics, and Policy in Putin's Russia* (Washington, DC: Brookings Institution Press), 191–216.

Rotkirch, Anna, Anna Temkina, and Elena Zdravomyslova. (2007) "Who Helps the Degraded Housewife? Comments on Vladimir Putin's Demographic Speech," *European Journal of Women's Studies* 14, no. 4: 349–357.

Rousselet, Kathy. (2007) "Butovo: La création d'un lieu de pèlerinage sur une terre de massacres," *Politix* 20, no. 77: 55–78.

Rousselet, Kathy. (2022) "Orthodox Churches in the War in Ukraine," *Bulletins de l'Observatoire international du religieux*, no. 36, https://sciencespo.hal.science/hal-03662947/.

Rozin, Vadim M. (2017) "The Moscow Methodological Circle: Its Main Ideas and Evolution," *Social Epistemology* 31, no. 1: 78–92.

Rumer, Eugene. (2019) "The Primakov (Not Gerasimov) Doctrine in Action," *Carnegie Papers* (Washington, DC: Carnegie Endowment for International Peace).

Rutland, Peter. (2023) "Neoliberalism and the Russian Transition," *Review of International Political Economy* 20, no. 2: 332–362.

Rutland, Peter. (2023) "The Contradictions in Putin's Economic Nationalism: From Western Partner to Fortress Russia," *Russian Politics* 8, no. 1: 24–47.

Saari, Sinikukka. (2014) "Russia's Post-Orange Revolution Strategies to Increase Its Influence in the Former Soviet Republics: Public Diplomacy Po Russki," *Europe-Asia Studies* 66, no. 1: 50–66.

Sakwa, Richard. (2007) *Putin: Russia's Choice*, 2nd ed. (London: Routledge, 2007).
Sakwa, Richard. (2008) "Russian Political Culture through the Eyes of Vladislav Surkov: Guest Editor's Introduction," *Russian Politics and Law* 46, no. 4: 3–7.
Sakwa, Richard. (2011) *The Crisis of Russian Democracy: The Dual State, Factionalism and the Medvedev Succession* (Cambridge: Cambridge University Press).
Sakwa, Richard. (2017) *Russia against the Rest: The Post–Cold War Crisis of World Order* (Cambridge: Cambridge University Press).
Sakwa, Richard. (2024). *The Lost Peace: How the West Failed to Prevent a Second Cold War* (New Haven, CT: Yale University Press).
Samoilenko, Sergei A., and Elina Erzikova. (2021) "Public Relation in Russia: Formation, Etatization, and Calcification," in Maureen C. Minielli et al., eds., *Media and Public Relations Research in Post-Socialist Societies* (Lanham, MD: Lexington), 3–46.
Saunders, Robert A., and Vlad Strukov. (2017) "The Popular Geopolitics Feedback Loop: Thinking beyond the 'Russia against the West' Paradigm," *Europe-Asia Studies* 69, no. 2: 303–324.
Sauvé, Guillaume. (2019) "The Lessons from Perestroika and the Evolution of Russian Liberalism (1995–2005)," in Mario Cucciolla, ed., *Dimensions and Challenges of Russian Liberalism: Historical Drama and New Prospects* (Cham, Switz.: Springer Verlag), 139–151.
Schimpfössl, Elisabeth. (2019) "Russian Philanthrocapitalism," *Cultural Politics* 15, no. 1 (2019): 105–120.
Schwenk, Anna. (2024) *Flexible Authoritarianism Cultivating Ambition and Loyalty in Russia* (Oxford: Oxford University Press).
Sedgwick, Mark. (2004) *Against the Modern World: Traditionalism and the Secret Intellectual History of the Twentieth Century* (New York: Oxford University Press).
Sell, Louis. (2003) "Embassy under Siege: An Eyewitness Account of Yeltsin's 1993 Attack on Parliament," *Problems of Post-Communism* 50, no. 4: 43–64.
Sériot, Patrick. (2014) *Structure and the Whole (Semiotics, Communication and Cognition)* (Berlin: De Gruyter Mouton).
Sharafutdinova, Gulnaz. (2020) *The Red Mirror: Putin's Leadership and Russia's Insecure Identity* (Oxford: Oxford University Press).
Shekhovtsov, Anton. (2008) "The Palingenetic Thrust of Russian Neo-Eurasianism: Ideas of Rebirth in Aleksandr Dugin's Worldview," *Totalitarian Movements and Political Religions* 9, no. 4: 491–506.
Shekhovtsov, Anton, and Andreas Umland. (2009) "Aleksandr Dugin's Neo-Eurasianism: The New Right à la Russe." *Religion Compass*, no. 3/4 (June): 697–716.
Shlapentokh, Dmitry. (2021) *Ideological Seduction and Intellectuals in Putin's Russia* (Cham, Switz.: Palgrave Macmillan).
Sibgatullina, Gulnaz. (2020) *Languages of Islam and Christianity in Post-Soviet Russia* (Leiden: Brill).
Sibgatullina, Gulnaz. (2023) "The Muftis and the Myths: Constructing the Russian 'Church for Islam,'" *Problems of Post-Communism*, pagination forthcoming.
Sibgatullina, Gulnaz, and Tahir Abbas. (2021) "Political Conversion to Islam among the European Right," *Journal of Illiberalism Studies* 1, no. 2: 1–17.

Sibgatullina, Gulnaz, and Michael Kemper. (2018) "Between Salafism and Eurasianism: Geidar Dzhemal and the Global Islamic Revolution in Russia," in Alfrid K. Bustanov and Michael Kemper, eds., *Russia's Islam and Orthodoxy beyond the Institutions: Languages of Conversion, Competition and Convergence* (London: Routledge), 91–108.

Sibgatullina, Gulnaz, and Michael Kemper. (2019) "Liberal Islamic Theology in Conservative Russia: Taufik Ibragim's 'Qur'ānic Humanism,'" *Die Welt Des Islams: International Journal for the Study of Modern Islam* 61, no. 3 (2019): 279–307.

Sibgatullina, Gulnaz, and Michael Kemper. (2019) *The Imperial Paradox: Islamic Eurasianism in Contemporary Russia* (Berlin: Frank & Timme).

Sidorov, Dmitry. (2006) "Post-Imperial Third Romes: Resurrections of a Russian Orthodox Geopolitical Metaphor," *Geopolitics* 11, no. 2: 317–347.

Slade, Gavid, and Andrei Nesterov. (2006) "Deconstrucing the Millennium Manifesto: The Yeltsin-Putin Transition and the Rebirth of Ideology," *Geohistory*, May 31.

Slater, Wendy. (2007) *The Many Deaths of Tsar Nicholas II: Relics, Remains and the Romanovs* (Abingdon: Routledge).

Smith, Jeremy, and Paul Richardson. (2017) "The Myth of Eurasia—A Mess of Regions," *Journal of Borderlands Studies* 32, no. 1: 1–6.

Smith, Kathleen E. (2002) *Mythmaking in the New Russia: Politics and Memory during the Yeltsin Era* (Ithaca, NY: Cornell University Press).

Smith, Kathleen. (2002) *Mythmaking in the New Russia* (Ithaca, NY: Cornell University Press).

Snegovaya, Maria, and Kirill Petrov. (2022) "Long Soviet Shadow: The Nomenklatura Ties of Putin Elites," *Post-Soviet Affairs* 38, no. 4: 329–348.

Snyder, Jack. (2009) "The Historical Reality of Eastern Europe," *East European Politics and Societies* 23, no. 1: 7–12.

Snyder, Timothy. (2018). *The Road to Unfreedom: Russia, Europe, America* (New York: Tim Duggan Books).

Soldatov, Andrei and Irina Borogan. (2022) "Dead Water: How the Russian Security Services' Paranoid Mindset Justifies the War," *SCEEUS Guest Report* 5, https://sceeus.se/publikationer/dead-water-how-the-russian-security-services-paranoid-mindset-justifies-the-war/.

Soliz, Diego. (2023) "From Counter-Hegemonic Dialogue to Illiberal Understanding: Russia–Latin America Relations (2000–2023)." *Journal of Illiberalism Studies* 3, no. 3: 87–109.

Solzhenitsyn, Aleksandr. (1995) *The Russian Question at the End of the Twentieth Century* (New York: Farrar Straus & Giroux).

Sorokin, Samuel. (2021) *Eurasianism and Political Islam in Russia: Ethnoreligious Identities in Transformation, 1990–2020* (PhD diss., European University Institute).

Sowa, Jan. (2012) "An Unexpected Twist of Ideology: Neoliberalism and the Collapse of the Soviet Bloc," *Praktyka Teoretyczna* 5: 153–180.

Sperling, Valerie. (2003) "The Last Refuge of a Scoundrel: Patriotism, Militarism, and the Russian National Idea," *Nations and Nationalism* 9, no. 2: 235–253.

Sperling, Valerie. (2014) *Sex, Politics and Putin: Political Legitimacy in Russia* (Oxford: Oxford University Press).

Stanley, Jason. (2020) *How Fascism Works: The Politics of Us and Them* (New York: Penguin).

Staun, Jørgen. *Siloviki Versus Liberal-Technocrats: The Fight for Russian and Its Foreign Policy* (Copenhagen: Danish Institute for International Studies, 2007).

Stepanova, Elena. (2015) "'The Spiritual and Moral Foundation of Civilization in Every Nation for Thousands of Years': The Traditional Values Discourse in Russia," *Politics, Religion & Ideology* 16, no. 2–3: 119–136.

Stoeckl, Kristina. (2016) "The Russian Orthodox Church as Moral Norm Entrepreneur," *Religion, State & Society* 44, no. 2: 132–151.

Stoeckl, Kristina. (2018) "Three Models of Church-State Relations in Contemporary Russia," *Constitutions and Religion* 36, no. 3: 195–223;

Stoeckl, Kristina. (2020) "Russian Orthodoxy and Secularism," *Brill Research Perspectives in Religion and Politics* 1, no. 2: 1–75.

Stoeckl, Kristina, and Dmitry Uzlaner. (2022) *The Moralist International: Russia in the Global Culture Wars* (New York: Fordham University Press).

Strickland, David A. (2000) "Overriding Democracy: American Intervention in Yeltsin's 1996 Reelection Campaign," *Footnotes: A Journal of History* 4: 166–181.

Strickland, John. (2013). *The Making of Holy Rus': The Orthodox Church and Russian Nationalism before the Revolution* (Jordanville, NY: The Printshop of St. Job of Pochaev).

Sullivan, Charles. (2022) *Motherland: Soviet Nostalgia in the Russian Federation* (London: Palgrave Macmillan).

Suslov, Mikhail. (2014) "Mapping 'Holy Rus'": Ideology and Utopia in Contemporary Russian Orthodoxy," *Russian Politics and Law* 52, no. 3: 67–86;

Suslov, Mikhail. (2014) "The Utopia of 'Holy Rus'sia' in Today's Geopolitical Imagination of the Russian Orthodox Church: A Case Study of Patriarch Kirill," *PLURAL: Journal of the History and Geography Department, Ion Creangă State Pedagogical University* II, no. 1/2: 81–97.

Suslov, Mikhail. (2016) "The Genealogy of the Idea of Monarchy in the Post-Soviet Political Discourse of the Russian Orthodox Church," *State, Religion & Church* 3, no. 1: 28.

Suslov, Mikhail. (2018) "'Russian World' Concept: Post-Soviet Geopolitical Ideology and the Logic of 'Spheres of Influence,'" *Geopolitics* 23, no. 2 (2018): 330–353.

Suslov, Mikhail. (2024) *Putinism: Post-Soviet Russian Regime Ideology* (London: Routledge).

Suslov, Mikhail, and Dmitry Uzlaner, eds. (2019) *Contemporary Russian Conservatism: Problems, Paradoxes, and Perspectives* (Leiden: Brill).

Suslov, Mikhail, Marek Čejka, and Vladimir Đorđević. (2023) *Pan-Slavism and Slavophilia in Contemporary Central and Eastern Europe: Origins, Manifestations and Functions* (London: Palgrave Macmillan).

Taylor, Brian. (2018) *The Code of Putinism* (Oxford: Oxford University Press).

Terbish, Baasanjav. (2022) "State Ideology, Science, and Pseudoscience in Russia," *Journal of Illiberalism Studies* 2, no. 1: 73–90.

Thaden, Edward C. (1990) *Interpreting History: Collective Essays on Russia's Relations with Europe*. New York: Columbia University Press.

Toal, Gerard. (2017) *Near Abroad: Putin, the West, and the Contest over Ukraine and the Caucasus* (Oxford: Oxford University Press).

Tolz, Vera. (2021) *Russia: Inventing the Nation* (London: Bloomsbury).

Tolz, Vera, and Stephen Hutchings. (2015) *Nation, Ethnicity and Race on Russian Television Mediating Post-Soviet Difference* (London: Routledge).
Tolz, Vera, and Stephen Hutchings. (2023) "Truth with a Z: Disinformation, War in Ukraine, and Russia's Contradictory Discourse of Imperial Identity," *Post-Soviet Affairs* 39, no. 5: 347–365.
Tolz, Vera, and Yuri Teper. (2018) "Broadcasting Agitainment: A New Media Strategy of Putin's Third Presidency," *Post-Soviet Affairs* 34, no. 4: 213–227.
Torbakov, Igor. (2018) *After Empire: Nationalist Imagination and Symbolic Politics in Russia and Eurasia in the Twentieth and Twenty First Century* (Stuttgart: Ibidem-Verlag).
Trenin, Dmitri. (2011) *Post-Imperium: A Eurasian Story* (Moscow: Carnegie Center).
Tsygankov, Andrey. (2003) "Mastering Space in Eurasia: Russia's Geopolitical Thinking after the Soviet Break-Up," *Communist and Post-Communist Studies* 36, no. 1: 101–127.
Tsygankov, Andrey. (2005) "Aleksandr Panarin kak zerkalo rossiiskoi revoliutsii," *Vestnik MGU: Sotsiologiia i Politologiia* 4: 166–177.
Tsygankov, Andrey. (2007) "Finding a Civilisational Idea: 'West,' 'Eurasia,' and 'Euro-East,' in Russia's Foreign Policy," *Geopolitics* 12, no. 3: 375–399.
Tsygankov, Andrey. (2007) "Two Faces of Putin's Great Power Pragmatism," *Soviet and Post-Soviet Review* 34, no. 1 (2007): 103–199.
Tsygankov, Andrey. (2015) "Vladimir Putin's Last Stand: The Sources of Russia's Ukraine Policy," *Post-Soviet Affairs* 31, no. 4: 279–303.
Tsygankov, Andrey. (2016) "Crafting the State-Civilization: Vladimir Putin's Turn to Distinct Values," *Problems of Post-Communism* 63, no. 3: 146–158.
Tsygankov, Andrey. (2017) "In the Shadow of Nikolai Danilevskii: Universalism, Particularism, and Russian Geopolitical Theory," *Europe-Asia Studies* 69, no. 4: 585.
Tsygankov, Andrey. (2019) *Russia's Foreign Policy: Change and Continuity in National Identity* (Lanham, MD: Rowman & Littlefield).
Tumarkin, Nina. (2003) "The Great Patriotic War as Myth and Memory," *European Review* 11, no. 4: 595–611.
Turoma, Sanna, Kaarina Aitamurto, and Slobodanka Vladiv-Glover, eds. (2019) *Religion, Expression, and Patriotism in Russia: Essays on Post-Soviet Society and the State* (Stuttgart and New York: Ibidem and Columbia University Press).
Tyushka, Andriy. (2022) "Weaponizing Narrative: Russia Contesting Europe's Liberal Identity, Power and Hegemony," *Journal of Contemporary European Studies* 30, no. 1: 115–135.
Umland, Andreas. (2006) "Zhirinovsky in the First Russian Republic: A Chronology of Events 1991–1993," *Journal of Slavic Military Studies* 19, no. 2: 193–241.
Umland, Andreas. (2010) "Aleksandr Dugin's Transformation from a Lunatic Fringe Figure into a Mainstream Political Publicist, 1980–1998: A Case Study in the Rise of Late and Post-Soviet Russian Fascism," *Journal of Eurasian Studies* 1: 144–152.
Umland, Andreas, and Anton Shekhovtsov. (2009) "Is Dugin a Traditionalist? 'Neo-Eurasianism' and Perennial Philosophy," *Russian Review* 68: 662–678.
Urban, Michael. (1998) "Remythologising the Russian State," *Europe-Asia Studies* 50, no. 6: 969–992.
van Dijk, Teun A. (1993) "Principles of Critical Discourse Analysis," *Discourse & Society* 4, no. 2: 258.

van Herpen, Marcel H. (2014) *Putin's Wars: The Rise of Russia's New Imperialism* (Lanham, MD: Rowman and Littlefield).

Vernadskaya, Varvara. (2024) *Ivan Ilyin: White Emigration, Fascist Sympathies, and Post-Mortem Return to Russia* (self-pub.), https://ivanilyin.org/.

Volkov, Vadim. (2002) *Violent Entrepreneurs: The Use of Force in the Making of Russian Capitalism* (Ithaca, NY: Cornell University Press).

Walicki, Andrzej. (1989) *The Slavophile Controversy: History of a Conservative Utopia in Nineteenth-Century Russian Thought* (Notre Dame, IN: University of Notre Dame Press).

Waller, Julian G. (2021) "Elites and Institutions in the Russian Thermidor: Regime Instrumentalism, Entrepreneurial Signaling, and Inherent Illiberalism," *Journal of Illiberalism Studies* 1, no. 1: 1–23.

Wawrzonek, Michał. (2018) "The Concept of 'Russkii Mir'," in Giuseppe Motta, ed., *Dynamics and Policies of Prejudice from the Eighteenth to the Twenty-First Century* (Cambridge: Cambridge Scholars), 289–305.

Weiss, Daniel. (2016) "The New Russian Legislation on Blasphemy and Swearing: The Parliamentary Debates," *Zeitschrift Für Slavische Philologie* 72, no. 2 (2016): 289–321.

Wilson, Andrew. (2005) *Virtual Politics: Faking Democracy in the Post-Soviet World* (New Haven, CT: Yale University Press).

Wilson, Kenneth. (2015) "Modernization or More of the Same in Russia: Was There a 'Thaw' under Medvedev?," *Problems of Post-Communism* 62, no. 3: 145–158.

Wood, Elizabeth A. (2016) "Hypermasculinity as a Scenario of Power," *International Feminist Journal of Politics* 18, no. 3: 329–350.

Yablokov, Ilya. (2018) *Fortress Russia: Conspiracy Theories in the Post-Soviet World* (New York: Polity Press).

Yurchak, Alexei. (2005) *Everything Was Forever, Until It Was No More: The Last Soviet Generation* (Princeton, NJ: Princeton University Press).

Yusupova, Guzel. (2023) "Critical Approaches and Research on Inequality in Russian Studies: The Need for Visibility and Legitimization," *Post-Soviet Affairs* 39:1–2: 101–107.

Zabirko, Oleksandr. (2022) "The Concept of Holy Rus' in Russian Literary and Cultural Tradition: Between the Third Rome and the City of Kitezh," *Entangled Religions* 13, no. 8: 1–30.

Zajda, Joseph, and Rea Zajda. (2003) "The Politics of Rewriting History: New History Textbooks and Curriculum Materials in Russia," *International Review of Education* 49, no. 3/4: 361–386.

Zassourky, Ivan. (2004) *Media and Power in Post-Soviet Russia* (Armonk, NY: M.E. Sharpe), 136–137.

Zevelev, Igor. (2014) "The Russian World Boundaries: Russia's National Identity Transformation and New Foreign Policy Doctrine," *Russia in Global Affairs*, June.

Zigon, Jarett. (2011) *"HIV Is God's Blessing": Rehabilitating Morality in Neoliberal Russia* (Berkeley: University of California Press).

Zygar, Mikhail. (2016) *All the Kremlin's Men* (New York: PublicAffairs Books).

INDEX

Italic page numbers indicate material in tables or figures.

Abkhazia, 59, 92, 104, 236, 241post
abortion, 59, 179, 180, 182
academia, academics, 33, 34, 38
Africa, 6, 153, 213, 249, 251, 252; Lavrov's tour of, 253; Russia-Africa Summits, 258, 261; Russian messaging in, 261; Russian presence in, 255, 258–263
African National Congress (ANC), 249
Afrique Media, 260
agitprop, 32, 38
Agrarian Party, 42
A Just Russia–For Truth (political party), 53, 69
Alexander I, *136*, 171
Alexander II, 135, *136*, 171
Alexander III, 132, 135, *136*, 171
Alexy II. *See* Patriarchs of Moscow
Alley of Rulers, 111
Algeria, 259, 260
All-Russian Social-Christian Union for the Liberation of the People (VSKhSON), 172
Althusser, Louis, 15
Ambartsunov, Yevgeny, 235
Americans, 44, 195
anarchism, 171
Anglo-Saxon countries, 89, 91: characterized as friends of the Devil by Naryshkin, 207

Angola, 249, 259
annexation of Ukrainian territories by Russia: control over the Black Sea, 104; display of Russian hard power, 236; impediment to Eurasian Economic Union, 221; inspired by Kovalchuk, 26; Kremlin's plotting to eventually reconquer Crimea from Ukraine, 138, 212; as depicted in the Main Cathedral of the Armed Forces of the Russian Federation, 196; memory wars over Grand Prince Vladimir/Volodymyr, 161; occurrence of protests, 65; Putin approval ratings, 63; Putin quoting Ilyin to justify, 132; Putin's speech on, 204–205; Putin's speech to the Federation Council on, 241; Putin's taking Peter the Great as a role model for annexationism, 136; as response to Ukraine's refusal to negotiate on Russia's terms, 139; not initially evident in Russian strategic thought, 137; Russia's European heritage, 103; supported by war correspondents, 69; tensions with the West over, 163, 221. *See also* Crimean Peninsula
annual addresses. *See* presidential addresses
anthem, 50, 51

363

anti-Americanism: Ilyin on, 133; Islamic, 205; Naryshkin on, 25; Patrushev on, 25; *siloviki* on, 29
Antichrist, 193, 194, 195, 207, 209
anticolonialism, 19, 20, 76, 99, 211, ch. 12 (245–263)
anticommunism, 138, 172, 186
Anti-Corruption Foundation (FBK), 65
antifascism, 19, 20, 93, 133
Anti-Globalization Movement of Russia, 250
antiliberalism, 28, 61, 78, 88
Antioch, 106
antiracism, 18, 180
antisecularism, 171
antisemitism, 42, 92, 143, 171
anti-Westernism: Dugin, 76; Global South, 76, ch. 12 (245–263); Islamic, 166, 185, 205, 206; Kremlin ideology and, 61; Medvedev's presidency, 59; multipolar world order and, 211; Primakov, 223; Putin, 6; Russian, 73, 76, 77, 91, 213; Russia's millennial-historical continuity as a state and, 198, 205; *siloviki*, 29, 70. *See also* pro-Westernism; West, the
anti-*zapadniki*. *See* anti-Westernism
apocalypticism, 28, 193, 194, 197, 205
apostasy, 203
Aramaic, 207
asceticism, 156
Arctic, 122, 123, 204, 216, 224
Argentina, 251
Armenia, 104, 222
Asia: Asia-Pacific region, 215, 226; civilization of, 160, *160*, 162, 169, 217; Dostoyevsky on, 99; empires of, 269; Russia's Far Eastern geopolitics, 153, 204; Russia's growing search for partnerships in, 169, 230; Russian identity and, 54, 75, 76, 101; Troubetzkoy on, 249. *See also* Central Asia; Southeast Asia

Askenov, Sergey, 130
Assad, Bashar al-, 106, 207
Association for Free Research and International Cooperation (AFRIC, Wagner front organization), 260
Astakhov, Pavel, 183
Astrakhan, 162
Atheism: Russian, 201; Soviet, 35, 172, 195
Atlanticism, 220
ATON (investment fund), 60
attitudes, 17. *See also* mentalities
autarky, 158, 168, 189, 203
authoritarianism: Dugin, 204; EAEU member states, 222; empire not necessarily seen as a form of, 134; liberalism, 6; policies, 47; power relations, 17; regimes, 16, 23, 42, 54, 78; Russian, 141, 145; Schmitt, 204; socially networked, 273; sovereignty, 6; Young Conservatives, 190
autocephaly, 106, 202
autocracy, 28, 66, 98, 99–100, 129: defense of, 132, 171; Dugin, 99–100; Khomolgorov, 197; Leontyev, 98; regime, 28; seen by Putin as an admirable trait for a tsar to possess, 135; theory that Russia cannot maintain its territorial integrity under any other form of government, 139; under the tsars, 66, 129, 134, 171; Zyganov, 201
Aven, Peter, 68
Averintsev, Sergey, 99, 154
Averyanov, Vitaly, 188, 198, 204
Azerbaijan, 104, 236

Baburin, Sergey, 103
Badovsky, Dmitry, 186
backwardness (Russian), 118, 134, 248
Balashov, Nikolay, 106
Balkans, 98, 104
Baltic states: anti-Russian policies, 91; history, 116, 117; investigative journalist platform Delfi, 31; Russian Orthodox

churches' schism from the Moscow Patriarchate, 202; war crimes in, 119
Baptism of the Rus', 102, 106, 127, 161, 200. See also Vladimir/Volodymyr the Great, Grand Prince
barbarism, 78, 152, 198
Bashkortostan, 184, 219
"Basic Values—Fundamentals of National Identity, The," (Moscow Patriarchate), 182
Bastrykin, Alexander, 70
Beast, Kingdom of the, 193
behavior, 7, 17
Belarus, 43, 201, 218, 222, 238–239
Beliayev-Guintovt, Alexey, 197
Belkovsky, Stanislav, 187
Belovezha Accords, 43
Belozersk Monastery, 98, 194
beliefs, 22
Belt and Road Initiative (BRI), 224, 225, 226
Berdyaev, Nikolay, 45, 132, 157, 175, 186: promoter of the Russian World, 235
Berlin, 43, 237
Bezrukov, Andrey, 226
Bible, 101, 193–194, 197, 204
bipolar world order, 151, 255
Black Sea, 97, 104–107, 162, 242
Blagovest (organization), 184
blasphemy, 62, 65, 185
blogs, bloggers, 36, 69, 142
bogatyr'. *See* knights
Bogomelov, Konstantin, 89
Bolshevik Revolution: anniversary of, 51; as a catastrophe according to Yeltsin, 127; Eurasianism and, 248; interpreted apocalyptically by Christians, 194; lack of commemoration in modern Russia, 128, 129
Bolsheviks/Bolshevism: accepted in modern Russia as long as they admit some of Lenin's mistakes, 132; anti-Bolsheviks, 43, 99; internationalism of, 171; Kerensky, 111; murder of royal family by, 129; as a potential revolutionary threat in interwar Germany, 133; as traitors who wanted Russia to lose in World War I, 130; narratives, 130; National-Bolshevism, 35, 99; post-Soviet efforts to promote reconciliation with Whites, 127–128, 199; responsibility for generating Russia-Ukraine territorial controversies, 138; Stalin's promotion of nationalism with, 172
Bolivia, 251
Bolsonaro, Jair Messias, 257–258
Bortnikov, Alexander
Brazil, 257
Brezhnev, Leonid, 125, 166
BRICS, 255–257, 261
British Empire, 252
Bucharest NATO summit (2008), 137
Budapest Uprising. *See* Hungarian revolution
Buddhism, 166, 181, 208, 223
Bukharin, Nikolay, 249
Bulgakov, Sergey, 45, 211
Bulgaria, 102, 104, 226, 267
Bulgars, 167
bureaucracy, 29, 33, 56, 58, 130
Burke, Edmund, 188
Burkina Faso, 252, 260
Buryatia, 219
Business Russia, 56
Byzantine Empire, 75
Byzantinists, 74, 75. *See also* neo-Byzantinism
Byzantium, ch. 4 (97–108), 162, 212, 273
Byzantium and Slavdom (Leontyev), 98

Cameroon, 260
cancel culture, 90, 91, 180
capitalism: economic system, 134; equated with democracy, 41; Russian regime critique of, 87; viewed as a source of social ills by Russian economic leftists, 188; Western, 99

Carlson, Tucker, 7
Cathedral of Christ the Savior (Moscow), 62
Catholicism. *See* Christianity
Catherine II, the Great, 74, 98, 134, *136*, 138, 242
Caucasus Federal Districts (North and South), 104
Caucasus, North, 185
Caucasus, South, 139, 141, 230, 240, 244; Russian imperial expansion into a competitive response to Europe, 247. *See also* Abkhazia; Armenia; Azerbaijan; Georgia, Republic of; Ossetia, South
Center for Dynamic Conservatism, 188, 198
Center for Social Conservative Policy, 56
Center for Strategic Development, 47–48
censorship, 116, 172
Central Africa, 260
Central Asia, 139, 141, 215, 224, 230, 240; distancing from Russia, 244; Russian Empire in, 247–248. *See also names of individual Central Asian republics*
Central Europe. *See* Europe
centrism: as blended with conservatism, 191; Kiriyenko, 65; political, 40–49, 50, 83; United Russia, 55
Chadaev, Alexey, 53, 64
Chaplin, Vsevolod, 207
Chávez, Hugo, 257
Cheburashka (film), 279
Chechnya: Asia, 162; calls to ban *Matilda* in, 185; Chechen Wars, 42, 46, 52; Kadyrov's dictatorial rule in, 30, 168, 214; radicalism in, 185; security challenge, 47; "spiritual" passports in, 185
Chernomyrdin, Viktor, 43
Chernyshev, Sergey, 232, 234
Chesnakov, Alexey, 53
Children's Ombudsman (Russian Commissioner for Children's Rights), 182–184
Chile, 258
China, 5, 35, 47, 88, 199, 215, 216, 226; economic relations with Africa, 259; economic relations with Latin America, 257; Sino-Russian cooperation, 223, 230, 253, 255, 256, 263, 272; Titarenko on, 224; Trade and Cooperation Agreement (with EAEU), 225; wars with France and Britain, 252
Christianity, 6, 27, 56, 75, 78, 90, 95, ch. 4 (97–108), 162: All-Russian Social-Christian Union for the Liberation of the People, 172; and civilization, 5, 95, 97–108, 160, *160*, 161, 168, 177, 180; Catholicism, 75, 180; conservatism, 56; culture, 75, 78; dissident and reformist traditions under the USSR, 173; East African, 261; ethics, 90; Islamic world and, 226; Levantine (Middle Eastern), 106, 207; Orthodox (Eastern), 75, ch. 4 (97–108), 118, 180, 209, 211; Protestantism, 75; re-Christianization, 27, 201, 207; traditional values and, 6, 169, 177; Western Christianity (Catholicism and Protestantism viewed jointly from the East), 97, 98, 177, 249
Chubais, Anatoly, 45, 49, 68, 79; and shock therapy, 79; as a marginalized figure, 68; branded as a Jewish traitor by Putin for leaving Russia, 143; church attendance, 182; his brother Igor, 45; his concept of Russia's future as a "liberal empire," 134; Union of Right Forces, 49
Chubais, Igor, 45
Chubaryan, Alexander, 120
Churchill, Sir Winston, 43
Chuychenko, Konstantin, 70
citizenship, 67
Civic Chamber, 29
civic consciousness, 178

civic organizations, 26, 174. *See also* civil society
civilization: alliances between, 86; Christian, 6, 160, *160*, 177, 180, 204; Eurasian, 101, 160, *160*, 161, 162, 167, 202, 215, 222; European, 36, 90, 160, *160*, 162, 177, 180, 189, 216; in presidential speeches, 158, *159*; Islamic, 223; Mongol legacy an impediment to the development of Russian, 247–248; multipolarity, 87; Nile River's role in giving rise to, 153; non-Western, 246; Russian rejection of Western civilization as a model for the world, 40, 73, 148, ch. 7 (151–169); Russo-Byzantine, 98; threatened by globalist elites, 204; Western, 6, 78, 94, 177, 180, 216
civilizational awareness: delegitimization of Marxism, 154; Russian framework, 8
civilization-state (Russia as a): debate as to whether Russia is a, 156; Eurasianism and, 217, 220; following the West, 74; Leontyev, Konstantin, on, 98; non-Russian peoples' choice to join Russia's, 134; non-Western, 76, 89; in presidential speeches and writings, *160*, 161, 163, 164; relationship to Islam, 166; Russian reception of Huntington, 155; Russian unique civilizational identity, 19, 20, 21, 49, 151, 158, 160, 169; Tsymbursky's concept of Russia as an "island civilization," 202–203
civilizing mission, 75, 153, 217, 247
civil society, 26, 28, 112, 174, 273. *See also* civic organizations
civil war, risk of, 42, 43, 71
clash of civilizations, 22, 151–152, 155–156, 208
classicism, 64, 103
clericalism, 190
co-citizenship (*sograzhdanstvo*), 42. *See* citizenship
Cold War, 47, 77, 91, 95, 133; bipolar world order of, 151, 246; followed by clash of civilizations, 152; United States in, 258. *See also* post-Cold War
Collective Security Treaty Organization (CSTO), 58, 236
collectivism: collective ownership, 222; in *Novye vekhi*, 46; Russian civilization, 155; Russian identity, 45, 49; Russian values, 178
colonialism, 75, 134, *253*, *254*
color revolutions: 1956 Hungarian revolution cast by Russia as, 120; critique of US support for, 86; Gryzlov on, 55; Naryshkin on, 128; Patrushev on danger of, 25; Russian fear of, 52, 236; Surkov's response to, 54; tsarism indirectly rehabilitated by modern resistance to, 130. *See also specific revolutions*
commissioned works (*goszakazy*), 122
Commonwealth of Independent States (CIS), 221, 234, 235, 238, 240: Russian hegemony within, 255
communes (peasant), 98
Communism, 6, 13, 18, 35, *37*, 41, 42, 43, 51, 55, 74: and autocracy, 129; and opposition to Yeltsin, 42; China as a model form of, 223; collapse of 13, 74; in the Duma, 43; Islam under, 166; on moral equivalency between Nazism and, 119; as an ideology, 18; *nomenklatura*, 41; opposition to in United Russia party, 55; references in anthem, 51; Russian ideology, 6, 35, *37*. *See also* Bolshevism; Communist Party of the Russian Federation (CPRF); decommunization; Marxism; Marxism-Leninism; Soviet Union
Communist Party of the Russian Federation (CPRF): anti-Westernism, 40; and Byzantium, 99; conservative Eurasian forces within, 213; doctrine, 35; as loyal opposition, 69; calls for

restoration of the USSR, 239; media demonization of, 44; Podberezkin, 46; Soviet patriotism, 43
Communist Party of the Soviet Union (CPSU): economic competition and, 80; members benefitting from privatization, 41; predecessor to CPRF, 40
conceptual ideologues, 36
Concept on the Demographic Development of Russia, 239
Confucianism, 223
Confucius Institutes, 241
Congress of Russian Communities (Kongress Russkikh Obshchin: KRO), 44, 52, 92, 213, 239: Declaration of the Rights of Compatriots, 239; Manifesto of Russia's Rebirth, 239
Congress of Vienna, 74, 171
conservatism: American, 79, 270; British, 79, 270; Dugin, 32; European, 186 270; Global South, 186; Medvedev, 58–60; Mizulina, 63; national-conservatism, 89; Pavlovsky, 33; as an ideology, 17, 18, 47, 55; as pragmatism, 174–175, 187; in presidential speeches, *175*, 176; as rootedness, 148, 189–190; right-conservatism (*pravokonservativnyi*), 174; Putin, 6, 22, 82, 175, 176; Russian, 4, 8, 64, 65, 73, 76, 77, 78, 84, 91, 94, 95, 107, 141, ch. 8 (170–192), ch. 9 (193–209); Russian Club, 57; Russian Orthodox, 261; Russian Orthodox and Islamic, 168, 181–185; social, 148; Young Conservative school, *37*, 101, 190. *See also* neoconservatism
Conservative Assembly (Young Conservatives discussion club), 187, 188. *See also* Young Conservatives
conservative liberals. *See* United Russia (political party); *For the article by Polyakov, see* "Liberal Conservative, The"
Conservative Party, 55

Conservative Press Club, 202
conservatives: Alexander III, 171; Bogomolov's critique of, 89; Leontyev, Konstantin, 98; Moro, 55; Russian, 94. *See also names of individuals. See also* Young Conservative school
conservative turn: foreign policy, 85; led by Ernst and Mikhalkov, 31; Medvedev, 22, 59, 60; support from Muslims for, 184; Putin, 61–63, 178; Surkov, 54
conspiracy theories about the globalist elite, 204, 223; anti-Western narratives in Russian political culture, 91; ethical considerations as mechanisms for making sense of the world, 7; Kovalchuk, 121; Starikov, 64; Russia's ideological construction, 77; *siloviki*'s conspiracy mindset and anti-Westernism, 29; teachers of Marxism-Leninism, 154. *See also* antisemitism
Constantinople, 97, 99, 153
Constantinople Patriarchate, 106
constitutional amendments, 22, 63, 66, 70. *See also* Russian Constitution
Continental System, 74
cosmism, 155, 204, 219
cosmopolitanism, 63, 191, 204
Cossacks, 131–132, 183, 200
Council for Foreign and Defense Policy, 33, *37*, 86
Council for National Ideology (proposed), 50
counterculture, 32, 53
counterhegemonic narratives, 14, 148, 246. *See also* hegemonic narratives
Counter-Reformation: Report of the Conservative Assembly (2005), 187
counterrevolution, 11, 49. *See also* Part III (147–209), especially ch. 9 (193–209)
Covid-19 pandemic, 66–68
Crimean Peninsula: annexation of, 63; Byzantine symbolism, 102; consensus and new politics, 64–66; constitutional

amendments prohibiting separatism and addressing territorial integrity, 67; debates on opening casinos on the, 62; debates on restoring monarchism, 130; exhibitions on Russia's European heritage, 103; investments and symbolic integration into Russia, 105; Khrushchev's act of giving to Ukraine, 138; Kremlin's plotting to eventually reconquer from Ukraine, 138; Putin's speech to the Federation Council on annexation, 241; recapture by Russia, 212, 266; Russian Orthodox Church's sprinkling of holy water on the S-400 missile system, 195; tensions with the West following annexation, 163, 221. *See also* annexation of Ukrainian territories by Russia

Croatia, 267
Cuba, 257
cult of personality, 24
cultural change, 148
culture wars, 91, 179, 185, 270
culturology (*kul'turologiia*), 155
customary law (*adat*), 185
czarism. *See* tsarism

Dagestan, 185
Damascus, 106
Danilevsky, Nikolay, 153, 157, 159
Danilov Monastery (Moscow), 168
Day of the Family, Love, and Fidelity, 60
decadence (cultural decline), 97, 174, 204
Decembrists, 130, 131
decision-making processes, 8
Declaration of Sovereignty of the Russian Federation Day. *See* Russia Day; *see also* sovereignism
decline of the West, 256
Decline of the West, The (Spengler), 152, 158
decommunization, 138
decolonization, 254
de-kulakization, 142

denazification, 142, 144
deep people, the (*glubinnyi narod*), 140–141
Deliagin, Mikhail, 199
defamation law, 62
de Gaulle, Charles, 94
Demidov, Ivan, 56, 57
democracy: challenges to liberal-democratic framework, 5; democratic patriotism, 44; European values of, 161; Karaganov, 86; liberal democracy, 55, 77, 85; managed democracy, 50, 62; non-democratic versus liberal democratic societies, 16; notion of Europe, 95; power relations in, 17; presidential speeches, 83; rejection of imposed state ideology in Russia, 48; Russia's economic dissatisfaction, 80; Russia's post-Soviet transition, 41; Russian Orthodox Church's shift away from support for, 173; Russia's reaction to democratic contestation in the near abroad, 52; shift from voting processes to broader legality, 82; social democracy, 43, 45; sovereign democracy, 54, 148, 237; threats to, 90; universal values, 78; views of Young Conservatives on, 190. *See also zakonnost'* (legality)
Democratic Republic of the Congo (DRC), 259–260
Democratic Choice of Russia (political party), 42, 43
demographics, 50, 176, 177–180, 239, 240
demonstrations. *See* protest
denialism, 144
Denikin, Anton, 131, 132
Derzhavin House, 237
Destruction of an Empire: Lesson from Byzantium, The (film), 102
dialectical materialism, 154
dictatorship of the law, 50
Dima Yakovlev law, 62
diplomats, 121. *See also* names of individual foreign ministers

diplomacy, 236, 241
Direct Line (TV program), 9, 24
discussion clubs, 26, 56, 57. *See also* think tanks; *and individual organization names*
disinformation, 88, 144
dissent, 2, 14, 15, 23, 32, 40, 50, 52, 70, 71, 91, 111. *See also* protests
dissidents: anti-Soviet, 171, 245; antiwar, 70; Christian, 173; culture of, 120; dissident voices, 2, 40, 64, 69; former dissidents, 41; historiographic, 154, 218; ideological, 71; as a form of opposition, 15; intellectual production of, 32; marginalization, 14; of the nationalist Rodina Party, 52; Pavlovsky as, 33; political, 50, 149; Russia viewed as one with respect to the global order, 189; Russian religious leaders opposed to the war against Ukraine, 208; Shafarevich as, 92; Solzhenitsyn as, 238; tsarists under the Soviet regime, 172; underground subculture, 23; Young Conservatives as with respect to the global order, 191. *See also names of individuals*
division of labor, 80
divorce, 179, 180
Dnipropetrovsk, 242
Dokuchaev, Vasily, 217
domestic violence, 182
Donbas region, 92, 105, 121, 144, 208, 209; occupied territories: in presidential speeches, *243*; Russian designs on, 239, 242–244; Russian display of hard power in, 235; Russian occupation of, 252. *See also* Donetsk; Luhansk; Novorossiya
Donetsk, 105, 138, 242. *See also* Donbas region
donors, 41
Donskoy, Dmitry, 110
Dostoyevsky, Fyodor, 75, 99, 238, 248
double-headed eagle, 51

Drobinin, Alexey, 121, 158
Dubin, Boris, 14
Dugin, Alexander: Antichrist instrumentalized by, 207; assassination of his daughter Darya, 204–205; Byzantine metaphorical framing of Russia's geopolitical mission, 99; on China, 223; esotericism of, 187, 223; Eurasia Party, 167; Eurasian Youth Movement, 221; Eurasianism of, 213, 216, 219, 226, 230; as leader of the Ivan Ilyin Higher Political School (Russian State Humanities University: RGGU), 133, 205; contacts with the European far right, 223; contradictions of relating to Ilyin, 205; connection to Ivashov, 199; Kholmogorov and, 197; membership in Izborsky Club, 203; the Kremlin's vision of Russia inspired by, 37; differences with certain Muslim leaders, 168; imperial-Eurasianist school, 36; influence of Moscow and Leningrad intellectual circles on ideology of, 32; International Eurasia Movement, 167–168; "Katechon and Revolution" (article), 194; neo-Eurasianism, 45; neo-imperialism, 64; Prokhanov and, 189; promotion of a "Fifth Empire," 204; radical Eurasianism, 76; Tadzhuddin and, 167
Dugina, Darya, 204–205
Duma (lower house of Russian parliament): amnesties granted by, 42; Committee for Foreign Affairs, 251; Committee for Geopolitics, 44; Committee on Family, Women, and Children, 63, 182, 183; conservative legislation, 178; contrast between Putin's speeches to the, 9; debates on casino legalization and protection of religion, 62; definition of Russianness and criticism of neo-Eurasianism, 45; Gryzlov as speaker of, 55; as part of ideological ecosystem, 10; imperialist

ideology of, 134; KRO's influence on legislation, 239; legislation on false information about military operations, 69; Narochnitskaya as an MP, 100; ideologemes in, 19; Putin's address to, 241; radicalism in, 144; recognition of Soviet responsibility for the Katyn massacre, 119; repeal of Belovezha Accords and validation of the 1991 Soviet Union referendum by, 43; representatives in World Russian People's Congress, 27; Naryshkin as former chairman of, 25; People's Unity Day replacing November 7 celebrations, 52; Volodin as speaker, 129, 141
Dyukov, Alexander, 118
Dzemal, Geydar, 205

East Slavs, 139, 161, 243
Eastern Europe. *See* Europe
Economic Council (Presidential Administration), 65
economic liberalism. *See* market economy
Ecuador, 257
Ecumenical Patriarchate of Constantinople, 202
egalitarianism, 41
Egypt, 106, 251, 256, 259
Ekspert (magazine), 56, 174
elections, 43, 43–44, 61, 65, 88, 278
Electoral Commission, 61
elites: African, 259; anti-Westernism and conspiracy mindset among, 29; around Putin reading Ilyin, 133; cognitive frameworks of, 212; Communist Party, 41; consolidation of, 68; conspiracy theories about, 204; contemporary, 74; corruption among, 278; cosmopolitanism among, 247; criticism of elite moral and political conscience, 50; debate on top-down versus bottom-up creation of ideology, 16; seen as deficient in patriotism, 174; relationship to the "deep people," 141; divided opinion on Article 13 of the Constitution, 70; Eurasianism among, 220; hypocrisy among, 3; ideational products of, 213; impact of war on, 2; intellectual, 97; Latin American, 257; liberal, 90; patriotic indoctrination of, 199; political, 20; populist criticism of corruption of, 36; preference for status quo, 191; repressive apparatus to enforce ideological constraints among, 13; Russian, 205; Soviet, 76; "special military operation" and, 142; Surkov, 53, 80; technocratic, 28; van Dijk on, 17; undoing the Soviet Union under Gorbachev and Yeltsin, 249–250; views on Russian historical figures, 125; Yeltsin-era pro-Westernism of, 173. *See also names of individuals*
El Salvador, 251
empire, 134, *135*
End of Days, 204, 226
Enlightenment, the, 78, 90, 99, 161, 191: Russian resistance to, 268; Slavophiles' opposition to, 247
entrepreneurs of influence, 10, 30, *37*, 213
Erdoğan, Recep Tayyip, 108
Ernst, Konstantin, 31, 131
equality, 98
Eritrea, 259
eschatology, 11, 148, 156, ch. 9 (193–209), 226
esotericism, 187, 205, 223
establishment, the: competing with United Russia, 35; role in ideological construction, 28; lack of interest in Chubais' idea of Russia becoming a "liberal empire," 134; "methodologists'" influence on, 32; patriotic centrism, 49; preference for avoiding full mobilization of society, 142, 270; political, 86; Russian, 10, 26, 76, 80, 85, 88, 89, 95, 96; vision of Russia among, 37
Estonia, 198

ethics, 90
Ethiopia, 256, 259
ethnic republics, 46, 65, 164, 219
ethnonationalism, 45, 62, 98: antisemitism and, 171; church, 35; Komsomol and, 171; narratives as seen by the regime, 10; Putin's criticism of, 164; Rogozin, 162; Russian World and, 213; Russophobia argument's use by groups, 92; Solzhenitsyn, 162; State-Patriotic Club, 57
Eurasia, ch. 10 (215–230), *221*; as a concept, 8; as a continent of its own between Europe and Asia, 218; definitions of, 216–220; destiny for Russia, 54; geopolitical mission of, 100; Greater Eurasia (*Bol'shaia Evraziia*), 20, 223, 224, 226; in the post-Cold War, 134; Russian uniqueness within, 212; Russian World and, 244; State-Patriotic Club, 57
Eurasian Economic Union (EAEU), 221–222; as a "Muslim Union," 168; Glazyev as one of the architects of, 188; limited scope of, 230; Russian hegemony within, 255; and Trade and Cooperation Agreement (with China), 225, 226
Eurasianism generally, 36, 75, 107, ch. 10 (215–230); bid to become a new state ideology, 220; Bolshevik Revolution and, 248; civilizational thinking, 154; concept of Russia as a "continent-ocean," 202–203; containment strategy against Western intrusion, 213, 245; contested by Dugin, Glazyev, and Karaganov, 230; Ilyin's opposition to, 205; failure to take gain traction with Muslims, 168; Leontyev, Konstantin, on 99; literature on, 4; promoted by Dugin and Prokhanov, 213; Russian hegemony and, 262; Troitsky's synthesis of, 155. *See also* neo-Eurasianism

Eurasian Union (proposal), 220–225, 226, 230
Eurasian Youth Movement, 221
Eurasian Youth Parliament, 221
Eurasia Party, 167
Eurocentrism, 74, 76, 266
Euromaidan, 63, 138
Europe: Central Europe, 41, 91, 93, 116, 119, 179, 246, 267; civilization, 90, 153, 160; Eastern Europe, 57, 91, 93, 116, 246; far-right forces in, 94; Kremlin's insistence on right to shape post–Cold War order in, 134; neo-fascism in, 95; pan-European political community, 85; right-wing ideology in, 56; Russia as part of, 73–74; Russia's relationship to, 159, 265; Satarov and rapprochement with, 45; Western Europe, 75, 100, 165, 179, 182, 269
Europe and Mankind (Troubetzkoy), 248
European Union (EU): Christian Europe, 211; consequences of expansion, 267; expansion into Russian sphere of strategic interest, 95; four freedoms of, 221; notion of Europe, 78; Russia criticized for subservience to the US, 91; Russian opposition to Ukraine's potential membership, 137, 139
Evola, Julius, 100
Exarchate of Africa, 261
exceptionalism, 91
expansionism, 195, 202–205, 209, 213
extremism, 46, 62, 179

Fadeev, Valery, 56, 174
fabrika obrazov (image factory), 53
Face of the Earth, The [*Das Antlitz der Erde*] (Suess), 216
faith, 45, 182
family policy 66, 172; church as a legitimate partner in discussing societal and family relation, 59, 170; Duma Committee on Family, Women, and

Children, 182; dysfunctional families, 183; single-parent families, 180; traditional values in Russia, 60, 176–181; wives of Orthodox priests' administration of, 184
family values. *See* values
far left, 6
far right, 6, 56, 89, 94, 162: Dugin's and Glazyev's contacts with European, 223; neo-Eurasianism and, 220
fascism, 3, 31, 55, *94*, 94, 95; Beliayev-Guintovt's painterly inspiration, 197; debate on whether the Putin regime is an example of, 141, 270; dearth of calls for fascist revolution in Russia, 145; Ilyin's relationship to, 133; in Portugal, 133; Russian accusations of against Ukrainians, 195; Russian strategic narratives on, 91–95; Russian undercurrents of, 142, 144, 204; "Seventeen Moments of Spring" and Soviet views on, 31; in Spain, 133; Ukrainian "fascism," 293; van Dijk's definition of, 18
Fateyev, Sergey, 46
Fatherland (Otechestvo, political party), 47, 56
February 24, 2024 speech announcing the "Special Military Operation" in Ukraine (Putin), 92
February Revolution (1917), 199
Federal Agency for the Commonwealth of Independent States, Compatriots Living Abroad, and International Humanitarian Cooperation (Rossotrudnichestvo), 236, 259
Federal Assembly (joint session of parliament), 70, 109, 151, 160
Federal Border Service, 195
Federal Security Service (FSB): Bortnikov as director of, 25; Navalny poisoned by, 67; Patrushev as former director of, 20, 66; Putin as interim director of, 47;

Sretensky Monastery, 196; transfer of essential functions to the government, 58
Federation Council (upper house of Russian legislature): approval a law allowing the Soviet flag to be used once more at major ceremonies, 51; Committee on Social Policy, 184; as a part of the ideological ecosystem, 10; ideological production in, 29; Putin's address to, 241; Shumeyko as chairman of, 44
Federation of Independent Unions of Russia, 56
Feodorov, Evgenii, 63
feminism, 18
Filatov, Vladimir, 46
Finland, Finns, 131, 240
flag, 50–51
Flood, The, 197, 204. *See also* Noah
Florensky, Pavel, 211
freedom, 13, 161, 178, 182. *See also* liberty: EU's four freedoms (goods, capital, services, and people), 221
Freemasons, 195
foreign agents, 48, 62, 65, 69
Foreign Intelligence Service (SVR), 25, 102
foreign policy: Atlanticism and Eurasianism in, 220; toward EAEU member states, 222; Foreign Policy Concept of the Russian Federation, 91, 157, 158, 214, 215, 225, 251, 252, 255, 259, 263; Institute for National Strategy, 191; Karaganov and perspectives of *siloviki*, 121; patriarchate's most successful area of cooperation, 181; Russia's role as protector of Eastern Christians, 194; toward Syria, 207; theology-based doctrine in today's Russia, 35; variability of, 213
Forgiveness Day (March 6)
Foundation for the Defense of National Values, 261

Foundation for Effective Politics, 33, 187, 232, 234
Foundation for the Support of Compatriots, 237
Françafrique, 260
France, 112, 251, 260, 268
Francis, Pope, 180, 262
Francophonie, 241
Frank, Semyon, 45
French Empire, 252, 260
Frente Amplio (Chile), 258
Fridman, Mikhail, 68
Front Philosophy (*Frontovaia filosofia*), 121, 122
frozen conflicts, 59. See also individual conflicts
Fukuyama, Francis, 156
full-scale invasion of Ukraine by Russia, 149; apocalypticism, 207; Eurasian Union proposals overshadowed by, 230; family policy, 179; Kazakhstani distancing from, 219; Patriarch Kirill's blessing of, 202; pushing the Putin regime in the direction of fascism, 142; as Putin's sole decision, 266; Russian historical narrative of the invasion, 127–128; Russian textbook on the history of twentieth-century and, 120; as turning point for ideology, 158, 164, 273. See also Russo-Ukrainian War

Gagarin, Yuri, 110, 127
Gaydar, Yegor, 43, 79, 223
Gaynutdin, Ravil, 168
gay propaganda law, 62, 183
Gayropa, 19, 20, 179
Gefter, Mikhail, 232
Gelman, Vladimir, 145
Generation P (Pelevin), 33
gender politics, 89, 178, 179, 181, 183
genocide, 19, 20, 91–95, 143–144
Genocide (Glazyev), 92
geography, 122–125, 169, 200, 203, 211; narratives about, 212, 215, 248

geopolitics: Black Sea in Russian, 104; BRICS and, 256; collapse of Soviet Union seen as the greatest geopolitical catastrophe, 52; concepts, 213; criticisms of political and societal liberalism, 78; divine mission and, 197; Dugin's theories of, 204; Duma Committee for Geopolitics, 44; Eurasia's mission, 100; Eurasian, 156, 220; hegemony, 6; Holy Rus', 201; infrastructure, 123; interests, 27, 46; liberalism, 49, 89, 91; Orthodox realm's division, 106; reality, 73; Russian ambitions and/or identity, 8, 21; Russian expectations of continued loyalty from countries in its near abroad, 137; Serbia, 101; tensions of, 141, 203, 224; traditional values in, 95; Tsymbursky's contributions to, 202; the West in, 224
Georgia, Republic of: authorities, 92; North Ossetia's border with, 52; Mchedlov, Georgian-born scholar, 154; national history of rewritten, 116; NATO partners, 104; Russian display of hard power in Abkhazia and South Ossetia, 236; Russian fears of losing ground to US in, 236; Russian intervention in, 59. See also Abkhazia; Ossetia, South
Germany, 93, 116, 251; challenges to liberal democracy in, 268; Conservative Revolution (interwar period), 219; Navalny's hospitalization in, 67; Nazi regime in, 118, 120, 131, 159, 198; in World War I, 130
Girkin-Strelkov, Igor, 36, 278
Glazunov, Ilia, 42
Glazyev, Sergey, 92, 188, 199, 216, 222, 252; contestation with Dugin over Eurasia, 223, 230; drifting between liberalism, nationalism, Communism, and the European far right, 223; friendship with conspiracy-monger Lyndon LaRouche, 223
Glinka, Mikhail, 51

globalism, 168, 174, 252; identified with Satanism by the World Russian People's Congress, 207
Global North, 246, 257
Global South, 6, 76, 87, 152, 211, 212; balancing in favor of, 266; reframed by Russia as the "Global Majority," 252, 263; illiberalism in, 268; Russia's ambiguous relationship to, 257, 272; as Russia's fellow travelers, 213
globalization: of culture wars, 90; as dangerous, 121; economic legacy of the 1990s, 49; geopolitical West, 78; Global South, 87; nation-state viewed as an obstacle to deepening, 191; neoliberalism and, 188; Putin regime, 109; resistance to, 156, 189, 250; Russian, 212; Russian Orthodox Church's perception of as a threat, 173; Russian society, 13; Surkov's vision for Russia's role, 54, 80; Western-led, 158, 189
God, 67, 154, 177, 201, 204, 207
Golden Horde. *See* Mongols
Going Back to Russia (Reshetnikov), 102
Gorbachev, Mikhail: memoirs, 76; opposition to reforms put forth by, 173; overthrow of (1991), 40; *perestroika*, 85; undoing of the Soviet Union, 249–250
Gorchakov Foundation, 237
gospels, 207
Gradirovsky, Sergey, 232, 234, 238
grand narratives, 6, 18, 81
Greater Eurasia (*Bol'shaia Evraziia*). *See* Eurasia
Great Fatherland Party, 64, 199
Great Patriotic War. *See* World War II
greatness of the state, 122, 139
Great Northern War, 126
great powers, 48, 49; ambiguity of Russia's status as a, 257; balance of, 85; center of influence, 87; demotion of Russia from such status in the 1990s, 148; *derzhavnost'*, 46, 110; European powers, 75; hegemony, 212, 245; more legitimate than small countries, 86, 279; power projection, 211; Russia's expansion, 134; Russia as one of the European, 74 160, 211; Russia's Byzantine model theorized by Konstantin Leontyev, 186; Russia's Pontic identity, 106; Russia's status as a secondary great power, 80; Russia's status as a, 21, 40, 47, 95; Russia's status confirmed by its leadership of a non-Western coalition, 213; Russian Orthodox Church's support for Russia's continued status as, 173; Russian state language, 77; Surkov's vision for Russia's role in the world, 54; transcontinental nationhood, 212

Greco-Roman culture, 97
Greece, Greeks, 101–102, 106
Greek Orthodox Patriarchate of Alexandria, 261
Gref, German, 47
Großraum (great space), 212, 229, 266
Gryzlov, Boris, 55, 157
Goreslavsky, Alexey, 31
Guénon, René, 100
Guinea-Bissau, 249
Gulag system, 118, 207
Gumilev, Lev, 154, 157, 216, 218, 219,
Gurova, Tatyana, 70

Hagia Sophia, 104
Hamas, 262
hammer and sickle, 51
Hanoi, 224
Haushofer, Karl, 212
hawks (the "party of war"), 66, 68: conquest of Ukraine called for by, 142, 144; element closest to fascism in Russian society, 144; hardcore faction that pushes for more radical indoctrination, 27–28; Karaganov and Starikov, 252; spiritual warfare called for by, 270; tsarist references, 129
Hegel, Georg Wilhelm Friedrich, 154

hegemonic narratives, 49, 50, 54, 55, 71, 95.
  See also counterhegemonic narratives
hegemony, 212, 220, 262
Helsinki, 145
Herder, Johann Gottfried von, 152, 154
heterosexuality, 179, 184
hierarchies, 5, 21, 22–26
Higher School of Economics, 86, 120, 224
historical materialism, 154
Historical Memory Foundation, 118
Historical Perspective Foundation, 100, 118
history, 24, 25
Hitler, Adolph: and Adamkus, 116; antisemitic comparison with Zelensky by Lavrov, 143; as an embodiment of the Antichrist, 195; Ilyin's article, 133
Holy Alliance, 171
Holy Rus' (*Sviataia Rus'*), 200–202, 207, 208, 266
Holy Rus' and Koshchei's Kingdom (Zyuganov), 201
homosexuality, 55, 84, 172, 177, 179, 182–183, 208
humanism: failure to gain traction within Islam, 166–167; Kremlin's references, 95; presidential decree on the "Fundamentals of State Policy to Preserve and Strengthen Traditional Russian Spiritual and Moral Values," 178; Russia celebrated for, 76
"How Shall We Organize Russia?" (Solzhenitsyn), 238
human dignity, 177, 178
human rights, 78, 85, 161, 178
Humboldt, Alexander von, 216
Hungarian revolution, 22, 120, 138
Hungary, 267
Huntington, Samuel P., 152, 156
hybrid warfare, 136

Ibero-America, 241
Ibragim, Taufik, 166
identity, 81, 94, 95, 109; civic identity, 114, 165; civilizational, 89; cultural, 126, 177; dual, 26; ethnic, 165; European, 75; identity politics, 90; identity politics, 90; ideologues, 36; Islamic, 35; metanarratives in presidential speeches, 82; national, 177, 270; new identity language, 13; Putin's masculine virility, 24; religious, 177; Russian, 120, 133, 139–145, 158, 160, 162, 166, 168, 173, 187, 207, 211, 270; sexual, 177; Ukraine as a Russian identity project, 136–139; unique, 49
ideological construction, 53–54, 77, 169, 188, 199, 203, 262
ideological diversity, 54
ideological ecosystems, 26–29
ideological entrepreneurs, 14, 26, 29–30. See also entrepreneurs of influence
ideological evolution, 39
ideological production, 22–26, 63, 145, 205, 268
ideological sedimentation, 39–71
ideologues, 145. See also *names of individuals*
Ideology of Common Sense (Lebed), 47
Ideology of Russian Victory, The (Izborsky Club), 203
image factory (*fabrika obrazov*), 53
immigration, 57, 239, 269
INDEM, 45
Information Security Doctrine, 64
illiberalism, 5, 18, 88, 141, 268: in Muslim countries, 268
Ilyin, Ivan, 36, 37, 57, 132: antisemitism, 133; Eurasianism opposed by, 205; far-right ideologue, 37; reactionary ideology, 36, 57, 132, 172
Ilyumzhinov, Kirsan, 219, 251
imperialism, 36, 47, 75, 76, 95, ch. 6 (126–145); Dugin's "Fifth Empire," 204; epistemological, ch. 12 (245–263); philosophical underpinnings of, 187;

Russian, 133–136, 165, 217; Solzhenitsyn's opposition to, 172; Soviet (promoted by Kholmogorov, Prokhanov, and Dugin), 197–198; viewed as natural, 131, 217. *See also* neo-imperialism

Imperatives of National Renaissance: Manifesto of Russian Conservatives (Young Conservatives), 188, 190

Imperium (Malofeev), 104

India, 47, 252, 255, 263, 268: policy of "multi-alignment," 269

individualism, 45, 155

individual rights, 19

Indochina, 217

indoctrination: higher education, 205; ideological, 9, 28; mechanisms, 14, 23; methods, 22; nostalgia in the population, 125; patriotic, 199; program of forced, 13

Indonesia, 256

infotainment, 31

insurgents, 42

Institute for Cooperation and Democracy, 100

Institute for Internet Development, 31

Institute for National Strategy, 33, *37*, 187, 191

Institute for Political Research, 103

Institute for Social Forecasting, 56

Institute for the Study of the US and Canada, 202

Institute of Contemporary Development (INSOR), 58–59

Institute of History at the Academy of Sciences, 33

Institute of Oriental Studies, 202

Institute of Philosophy, 202

Institute of Russian Civilization, 155

Institute of Russian Compatriots, 237

Institute of Socio-Economic and Political Research (ISEPI), 33, *37*, 186

Institute of Sociological Analysis, 45

Institute of World Economy and International Relations (IMEMO), 33

institutions: agencies, 24; divisions of power, 23; dominant, 17; ecosystem, 26; educational, 182; intermediary, 68; international, 88; Islamic, 166, 181–185; NATO, 78; Russian, 106; Russian Orthodox, 181–185; social, 148; Soviet, 122; state, 22, 30, 174; state and non-state, 117–118; supranational, 86; targeting, 62; traditional, 192; trans-Atlantic, 85. *See also names of individual institutions*

intellectual history, 10, 16, 19, 32–34, 205

intellectuals: Council for National Ideology, 50; elites, 73, 97, 98; Eurasianism among, 216, 219, 220; figures, 35, 36, 54; German influence upon Russian, 152–153; history, 10, 74; Methodology School and, 244; national idea, 44; production, 32, 34; rejection of revolution, 130; Russian, European, British, and American, 270; *samizdat*, 121; Silver Age, 211. *See also names of individuals*

intellectual traditions, 5, 6, 7, 31, 186–191, 247–250

intelligentsia, 45, 83, 88, 172

International Agency for Sovereign Development (IASD), 251

International Criminal Court, 86, 184

International Eurasia Movement, 168

international law, 262

International Monetary Fund, 87, 256

International Union of Russian Compatriots, 237

Interreligious Council of Russia, 51

Iran, 74, 251, 256, 262

Iraq, 251. *See also* Islamic State of Iraq and Syria (ISIS)

irredentism, 92, 126, 137, ch. 11 (231–244)

irregular warfare, 223

Isaev, Andrey, 56

Isaev, Maksim (code name: Max Otto von Stierlitz), 30–31. See also *Seventeen Moments of Spring* (TV series)
Islam, 35, 59, 97, 166; anti-Westernism, 205; Chechnya, 185; Crimea, 97; failure of liberal, European, and humanist undercurrents within, 166–167; Fundamentals of Religious Cultures and Secular Ethics, 59; gambling forbidden, 185; Hadiths, 185; honor killings, 185; identity, 35; institutional contributions to conservatism, 181–185; political, 166; polygamy, 185; promotion of revolution within USSR, 166; Prophet Muhammad, 185; Quran, 185; Salafism, 185; Sharia law, 184, 185; Sufism, 185; veiling of women, 185. *See also* Hamas; jihad; muftiates; Muslims; Palestine; Sharia law; Spiritual Administrations of Muslims; *as well as names of individual Muslim-majority countries*
Islamic Renaissance (political party), 166
Islamic State of Iraq and Syria (ISIS), 201
Islamic world, 226, 261–262
Isolationism: civilizationist, 36; conservative, 169–170; globalization and, 189; Izborsky Club, 203–205; *katechon*, 195; Russia as an "island civilization," 202; Russia's view of itself as "chosen" and, 209; from the West, 163
Israel, 142, 152, 261, 262, 268
Italy, 251, 268
Ivan III, 98, 103
Ivan IV, the Terrible: hero of national history, 127; mythologized past, 193; Old Believers' tradition, 194; opposed by Prince Andrey Kurbsky for bringing violence on Holy Rus' land, 200; private militia, 199
Ivanov, Sergey, 25, 98
Ivashov, Leonid, 199
Ivory Coast, 259–260

Izborsky Club, *37*: conservative and nationalist scene, 198, 199; doctrinal production, 37; intellectual trend, 195; neo-imperialist figures, 203; Russo-Ukrainian War's expansion of influence, 204–205

Japan, 66, 223
Jerusalem, 97, 106, 153, 200, 201
Jesus Christ, 97, 102, 194, 204, 207. *See also* Second Coming of Christ
jihad, 205. *See also* Islam
Joint Committee on International Affairs and Foreign Economic Relations, 235
Judaism, 97, 101, 166, 181, 208, 261
Judgement Day, 193, 194, 203
Justice: European culture, 161; juvenile, 182; Russian traditional values, 178, 181
Justification of the Good (Soloviev), 132
just war doctrine, 133, 208

Kaczynski, Lech, 119
Kadyrov, Ramzan, 30, 185, 207, 214; dressing as Ilya Muromets, 168. *See also* Chechnya
Kalmykia, 219, 251
Karachay-Cherkessia, 123
Karaganov, Sergey, 33, 86, 89, 90, 121, 209, 216, 224; contestation with Dugin over Eurasianism, 230; as a hawk, 252
Kara-Murza, Vladimir, 70
Karamzin, Nikolay, 74, 171
Karichev, Alexander, 120, 121
Karpov, Sergey, 103
katechon (bulwark, shield, gatekeeper), 19, 20, ch. 9 (193–209)
Katechon (club), 194
Katkov, Mikhail N., 186
Kazakhstan, 196, 201, 218, 219, 222: relationship to Eastern Slavic nations, 238; Russian minority in north, 239
Kazan, 162
Kenya, 251, 260, 261

Kerch Strait Bridge, 105, 123
Kerensky, Alexander, 111
Keynes, John Maynard (Keynesianism), 189, 263
KGB (Committee for State Security), 20, 33, 196
Khasavyurt Accords, 46
Khasbulatov, Ruslan, 42
Kiev/Kyiv, 92, 98
Kievan Rus', 188, 201
Kherson, 105, 242
Khersones, 102
Khodorkovsky, Mikhail, 50
Kholmogorov, Yegor: conservative-reactionary intellectual circles, 57; Izborsky Club membership, 198; move away from more moderate figures to collaborate with radicals, 197; pragmatic imperialism, 197; reactionary groups, 188; Russia as a conservative power, 187, 189; prescience regarding a future Ukraine War, 266; Young Conservatives, 186
Khomiakov, Alexey, 247
Khrushchev, Nikita, 138, 171, 249
Kirill, Patriarch of Moscow and all Rus'. *See* Patriarch Kirill
Kiriyenko, Sergey: conservative, 55; Foundations of Russian Statehood, 141; and ideological indoctrination, 28, 144; patriotic centrism, 49; Presidential Administration chief, 65; Rosatom, 120; serving as a bridge between hawks and the technocratic establishment, 142
Kirovohrad, 242
Kiselyov, Dmitry, 31, 143, 208; antisemitism of, 143
Kitezh (folk myth), 202–205
Kitezh (opera by Rimsky-Korsakov), 203
Kitezh Chronicle (anonymous work), 203
kleptocracy, 2
Klyuchevsky, Vasily, 247
knights (*bogatyr'*), 168, 200
Kofner, Yury, 220

Kokoshin, Andrey, 46
Kolchak, Alexander, 131
Kolerov, Modest, 236
Konchalovsky, Andrey, 89
Korea, North, 74, 251
Korea, South, 89
Kortunov, Andrey, 225
Kosachev, Konstantin, 116
Kosovo, 101
Kostikov, Vyacheslav, 44
Kostin, Konstantin, 53
Komsomol (All Union Leninist Young Communist League: VLKSM), 114, 171
Kovalchuk, Mikhail, 121
Kovalchuk, Yury, 26, 67, 121, 132
Kozyrev, Andrey, 235
Krasnodar, 196
Krasnoyarsk krai, 43, 123
Krastev, Ivan, 33, 49, 89
Krganov, Albir, 185
Krickovic, Andrej, 4, 85
Krupnov, Yury, 232
Krylov, Konstantin, 187, 188
Kudrin, Alexey, 28, 33, 65, 174
Kurbsky, Prince Andrey, 200
Kurchatov Institute, 121
Kuril Islands, 66
Kurayev, Protodeacon Andrey, 208
Kutuzovsky Avenue, 43
Kuznetsova, Anna, 183, 184
Kyiv/Kiev, 92, 98, 102
Kyrgyzstan, 222

Lamansky, Vladimir, 217
LaRouche, Lyndon, 223
Last Address (human rights organization), 119
Latin America, 6, 235, 249, 253, 255; empires of, 269; challenges to liberal democracy in, 268; political culture of, 258; Russian messaging in, 260, 261; Russian promotion of sovereignism in, 257–258; Russian relations with, 263
Latvia, 198

Lavrov, Sergey, 93, 143: antisemitism, 143; Africa, 259; BRICS geopolitics, 256; concept of Europe, US, and Russia as the three branches of the West, 162; irredentism defended by, 241; Russia's foundational myth, 93
law and order, 30, 81, 148
Law on Foundations of the Cultural Policy of the Russian Federation, 64
Law on the Fundamentals of the Prevention of Offenses against the Russian Federation, 64
Law on the Russian Federation's Policy in Its Relations with Foreign Compatriots, 239
Lebanon, 106, 251
Lebed, Alexander, 43, 47, 127
leftists. *See also* names of specific groups: Communist Party, 46; economic, 188; leftist conservatism, 188
legality (*zakonnost'*), 82
Lengo Songo, 260
Lenin, Vladimir Ilich (Vladimir Ilyich Ulyanov), 111, 125, 127, 132; Bolshevism, 132; monuments to, 111, 138; nation's reconciliation, 127; Russian elite, 125
Leontyev, Konstantin: Byzantine ideology, 99; civilizationist thinking, 157; conservative thought, 98; pan-Slavism, 153; Putin quoted, 159; Russia as a conservative great power, 186
Leontyev, Mikhail, 174, 199
Le Pen, Marine, 94
Levada Center, 14, 21, 109, 279
"Liberal Conservative, The" (Polyakov), 79
liberal democracy. *See* democracy
Liberal-Democratic Party of Russia (LDPR): new ideology, 44, 46; reviving the Russian Empire in the near abroad, 239; Russia's unique spirituality, 174; Slutsky, 204; systemic opposition, 69; Zhirinovsky's leadership of, 40, 213, 239
liberal internationalism / liberal international order: conflict with Russia's interests, 84; Putin's Munich speech, 59, 85, 86; Russia's minor role, 74; strategic interests, 87–91; universalism, 95; Western, 78
liberalism: authoritarian, 6, 7; classical ("old-fashioned") liberalism, 73, 78, 90; consensus, 49; elites, 10; European, 180; failure to take root in Russia, 171; geopolitical, 89, 91; ideologies of, 55; Islam and, 166–167; national-conservative opposition to, 192; radical, 26; reforms, 42; Russian official language, 77; and sexual perversion, 173; societal, 78; Western donors, 41; Western Europe, 76, 95; Western model, 52, 127, 129, 148, 178, 209, 268; Yeltsin era (1990s), 166
liberals. *See also names of individuals*: Alexander II as, 171; American firms interested in supporting, 32; antiliberalism and, 61; elections, 43–44; Kudrin as, 33; elites, 90; imitative of the West, 191; liberal agenda, 65; liberal camp, 54; liberal opposition, 89; liberal think tank, 58; liberal views, 84; private business and, 26; pro-Western discourse, 48; reforms, 42; Russian Idea, 46; Russian, 244; systemic liberals, 27; Yeltsin-era problems driving many back into conservatism as a reaction, 173. *See also* systemic liberals (*sislibs*)
liberalization, 22, 32, 84. *See also* market economy
liberty, 98. *See also* freedom
Libya, 251
life expectancy, 179
Lion and the Bear, The (Prigozhin-sponsored film), 261
Lithuania, 116, 119, 241. *See also* Polish-Lithuanian Commonwealth
Lobaye Invest (Prigozhin front company), 261

logocentrism, 7
loyalty, 52, 66, 69, 137, 191, 219
Lubyanka Building (former KGB, now FSB, headquarters), 196
Luhansk, 105, 138, 242. *See also* Donbas
Lukyanov, Fyodor, 88, 256
Lula (Luiz Inácio "Lula" da Silva), 257
lustration, 116, 143
Luzhkov, Yuri, 47, 56
Lvova-Bulova, Maria, 183, 184

machismo, 24–25
mafia, 30; condemned by Russian Orthodox Church, 173. *See also* thieves-in-law (*vory v zakone*)
Mahler, Arkady, 194
Main Cathedral of the Armed Forces of the Russian Federation, 196
majoritarianism, 5
Mali, 259, 260
Malofeev, Konstantin: dependency conspiracy theories promoted by, 251; entrepreneur of influence, 30; Kholmogorov, 197; media tycoon, 36, 132; Metropolitan Tikhon, 104; Putin support, 129; monarchism and Russian Orthodoxy, 182
managed democracy. *See* democracy
managerial governance, 32, 54
Mandela, Nelson, 249
Manege Square, 43
manifestos, 17, 239. *See also* Millennium Manifesto
Mao Zedong, 199
market economy, 27, 30, 41, 42, 46, 56, 78, 79–84, 95
marketing, 32, 53
marketplace of ideas, 14
Markov, Sergey, 103, 236
marriage, 184–185
Marxism, 4, 35, 38, 55, 74, 155; illiberalism of, 268; Latin American, 258; Russia Party's criticism of as a form of Western colonialism, 249; thick ideology, 272; Marxism-Leninism: collapse of, 154–155; doctrine of, 271; forced indoctrination program, 13; legacy of, 265; Russian Communism, 35; state ideology, 48; teleological interpretation of the world, 38; USSR's enforcement of, 172

Marx, Karl, 154
Maslin, Mikhail, 186
material values. *See* values
Matilda (film), 65, 185
Mauritania, 259
Mchedlov, Miran, 154–155
Medinsky, Vladimir: Ministry of Culture, 64; presidential adviser, 70; production of presidential decree on "Basics of State Cultural Policy," 157; proposal for reconciliation between Reds and Whites, 127–128; proximity to presidency, 67; rejection of Russia being part of Europe after fallout over Crimea, 163; Russian Military Historical Society, 117; textbook for the history, 120, 121
Mediterranean Sea, 97, 104–107, 204
Meduza, 252
Medvedev, Dmitry, 9, 21, 25, 28, 56, 57, 58–60, 65, 70, 93, 116; Church-military relations strengthened by, 196; corrupt practices of, 65; creation of Commission to Fight Against Falsifications of History to the Detriment of Russia's Interests, 116; creation of Commission to Fight Against Falsifications of History to the Detriment of Russia's Interests, 116; declaration that Russian foreign policy was neither liberal nor conservative, 174; decreased references to Russia's European civilizational belonging, 161; deputy chairman of the Security Council of Russia, 25, 70; "empire" referred to less often than by

Medvedev, Dmitry (*cont.*)
    Putin, 134; frequent references to history and culture, 140; presidency, 9, 21, 58, 59, 60, 93, 119; Russia's height of global integration under, 237; Russian World policy under, 237; "Satanic" accusations in Ukraine, 207; totalitarianism criticized by, 118
Medvedeva, Svetlana, 59
mentalities, 16. *See also* attitudes; mindset
mental maps, 17, 212
Memorial (human rights organization), 67, 119
memory wars, 4, 93, 116, 119
memory policy: historical references, 112; Pamyat and, 199; political history, 110; Russian geopolitical ambitions, 8; Russian Orthodox Church, 35; securitization of Russian history, 115–122; traditional values, 178
mercy, 178, 182
messianism: ch. 11 (231–244); Byzantium as a powerful source of, 99; Communist, 74; Curanović, 9; imperial-Eurasianist school, 36; Remizov's opposition to, 189; Russia's aspirations to undo the US-led global order, 213, 216, 262, 263; Russia's war on Ukraine, 209; Solzhenitsyn's opposition to, 172, 202–203; Soviet Union, 194; Third Rome, 4
meta-ideologies 18. *See also* conservatism; liberalism; illiberalism
metanarratives, 19, 81, 82, 91
metaphysics, 193, 201, 203
methodology, 8, 9
metodologi (methodologists), 32, 244
Metropolitan Tikhon (Shevkunov): confessors to the president and religious figures, 59; historical park celebrating Crimea's Byzantine past, 103–104; Izborsky Club membership, 199; Patriarch Kirill's potential successor, 27; Russia as the second Byzantium, 102; Sretensky Monastery, 196
Mexico, 257
Mezhuev, Boris: European-inspired conservatism, 36; intellectual figures, 187; Kholmogorov's finding it too moderate for him, 197; radicalism of, 200; Russo-Ukrainian War viewed as a civilizational conflict, 189; thought leader, 191; traditional-values agenda, 180; Tsymbursky's disciple, 203; Young Conservatives, 186
MGIMO. *See* Moscow State Institute of International Relations
Michel, Luc, 260
Middle Ages, 74, 226, 252
middle class, 35, 55, 62, 66, 142
Middle East, 86, 153, 249, 261
Migranyan, Andranik, 55
mindset, 14, 89, 93, 140, 211; Putinism, 271. *See also* attitudes; mentalities
militarism/militarization: children, 115; interpretative tool, 8; military, 27, 68; patriotic movements, 114; Putin's regime, 3; understanding of patriotism, 113; youth training, 114. *See also* military bloggers
military-industrial complex, 26, 27, 80, 199, 239
millenarianism, 193
Millennium Manifesto ("Russia at the Turn of the Millennium"), 21, 47–49, 81, 250
military: equipment, 68; industries, 27; youth training, 114
military bloggers, 36, 69, 142, 277
Milonov, Vitaly, 183
Milošević, Slobodan, 101
Mikhalkov, Nikita, 31, 36, 64, 132
Ministry of Agriculture, 20
Ministry of Culture, 64, 103, 127, 132, 158
Ministry of Defense: policy of reappropriation of Europe's legacy, 103; Putin as a

prime minister, 58; Russian Orthodox Church's formal cooperation with, 195; Russian political construction, 112–113; Shoigu, 25, 122
Ministry of Education, 59, 113, 114, 115, 171
Ministry of Finance, 28, 33, 65, 174
Ministry of Foreign Affairs: Cuppuleri, 9; Drobinin, 158; Lavrov, 93, 162; new foreign policy language, 121; Primakov, 47; reports of, 252; Rossotrudnichestvo and, 236
Ministry of the Interior, 45, 58, 121
Ministry of Internal Affairs, 195
Ministry of Justice, 70, 92
Minsk II agreements, 67, 143
miscegenation, 219
Mizulina, Ekaterina, 182
Mizulina, Elena, 63, 182
modernity (classical, non-postmodern), 73, 78, 90–91, 98
modernization: 1917 revolutions' interruption of, 172; compatibility with mainstream Russian conservatism, 148; discussion on, 59–60; economic and technological, 58; European culture, 100; gradual reforms, 55; Kremlin, 95; Medvedev presidency, 22; nationalism, 191; Peter the Great's promotion of, 135; Putin regime, 79–84; Russian official language, 77; Russian, 212; state's central role in, 54; warfighting, 118; Western, 78, 87–88, 109
modernism, 103
modernizers, 28
Moldova, 104, 116, 139, 201, 236; Congress of Vienna and Holy Alliance, 171; French, 112; Leontyev, Konstantin, 98; Malofeev, 182; Mikhalkov, 64; nostalgic, 28; Putin's mocking of monarchists, 130; Remizov, 190; Reshetnikov, 102; Russia's twentieth-century history, 44; Transnistria's Russian population, 239, 242

Mongols, 43, 110, 167, 203; Golden Horde, 74, 225; retrograde influence on Russian civilization, 247–248; Tatar-Mongols, 167
Mongolia, 216
monism, 153
Monroe Doctrine, 235
moral values. *See* values
mores, 35, 50, 64, 185. *See also* values
Moro, German, 55
Morocco, 259, 260
Morozov, Alexander, 5
mortality, 180
Moscow, 105
Moscow House of Compatriots, 237
Moscow Methodological Circle, 32, 232, 244
Moscow Patriarchate: administrative body, 40; African relations, 261; "Basic Values—Fundamentals of National Identity, The," 182; blessing of the Russian Armed Forces and *siloviki*, 208; conservatism, 27; founded as the "Third Rome," 194; mission, 181; Moscow Patriarchate's authority over its churches in Ukraine, Moldova, and the Baltic states, 202; post-Soviet individualists, 45; Russia as the third Rome, 98; Russian Club, 57; support for *Serge's Project*, 188; Synodal Department of Church-State Relations, 182; Syrian civil war, 106; Yeltsin criticized by, 173
Moscow principality (Muscovy), 74, 98, 103, 194, 202, 247
Moscow State Institute of International Relations (MGIMO), 33, 120, 226, 236
Moscow State University: Panarin, 155, 218; Byzantine esthetics, 99; conservative philosophers, 186; intellectual production, 33; new Front Philosophy, 121; Karpov, 103
Mount Athos, 101, 106
Movement of the First, 113–114

Mozambique, 249
muftiates: conservatism, 181; culture wars, 185; doctrine-producers, 37; Holy Rus' and, 201; Islamic identity, 34–35; Kazan, 167; mores and values, 184; Moscow, 166; support for Russia's war on Ukraine, 208; unique institutional intermediary, 167. *See also* Islam
Mukhetdinov, Damir, 168
multiculturalism: civilizational choice, 134; condemned as a failed project, 163; gender politics, 89
multilateralism, 85, 95
multipolar world order: against the West, 25, 156; alliances in, 47; anticolonialism and, 211, 254; civilizational global order, 151; decolonization and, 254, 259; presidential speeches' mentions of, *254*; Russia and China working toward, 225, 226; Russia benefiting from, 212; Russia's promotion of, 216, 263; Russian potential, 178; system, 87; Western hegemonic normativity rejected, 169
Munich speech (Putin), 59, 85
Murmansk, 224
Muromets, Ilya (folk character), 168
Muscovy. *See* Moscow principality
museums, 103; Gulag History Museum, 118; Hermitage Museum, 121; Russia's cultural exhibition policy, 103
Muslims, 6, 167, 168, 262. *See also* Islam
Muslim world. *See* Islamic world
Mykolaiv, 242
mysticism, 99, 140

Nabiullina, Elena, 28
Nagorno-Karabakh region, 236
Name of Russia (television series), 111
Narochnitskaya, Nataliya, 100, 101, 118, 180, 198
Narodniki (Populists), 247
Naryshkin, Sergey, 25, 117, 128, 224
Nashi (youth movement), 53

National Assembly, 44
National-Bolshevism. *See* Bolshevism
National Committee of Byzantinologists, 103
national-conservatism. *See* conservatism
national-democratic movement (*Natsdem*), 188
national idea, 14, 48, 63, 64. *See also* state ideology
nationalism: constitution, 41; ideologies, 18; imperial, 46; interpretative tools, 8; language around new values, 33; national idea, 63; patriotic conservatism, 56; populist figures, 89; Putin's regime, 3; Russia's ideological construction, 77; Russian, 35, 92, 269; specificities, 186; Ukrainian, 202; United Russia, 54, 57. *See also* ethnonationalism
nationalists, 42, 44, 46, 64, 186; Baburin, 103; Glazunov, 42; Holy Rus' concept's appropriation by, 200–201; Medinsky, 64; Putin's claim to be the true example of a good, 164; radical, 173; Rodina party, 52, 100;Yeltsin's opponents, 44. *See also names of individuals*
national security, 80, 88; demographic outlook of country weakening, 50; demographic trends and, 141, 179; guaranteed by nuclear weapons, 193; law on "undesirable" organizations, 62
National Security Strategy, 119, 178
National Strategy Institute, 202
nation-building, 4, 50
nation-state, 191
NATO. *See* North Atlantic Treaty Organization
natural law, 148
Navalny, Alexei, 61, 65, 67, 70, 188
Nazarbayev, Nursultan, 219
Nazis/Nazism, *94*; Article 354.1 of the Penal Code, "On the Rehabilitation of

Nazism," 117; civilization threatened by, 159; consensus against, 132; Ilyin's relationship to, 133; Putin's accusation that Ukraine's Jewish president is serving as cover for supposed neo-Nazis, 143; Putin's unfounded allegations against Ukraine of harboring, 164; Russia's defeat of invasion, 128; Russia's historic victories over, 43; Russian narrative on Central Europe, 119; Russian narrative on the West and Ukraine, 121; Soviet domination, 116; West as Russia's eternal enemy, 92–94

near abroad, the (and Russia's assertion of strategic sovereignty over it), 44, 52, 58; disrupting the European order, 95; Eurasianism and, 213, 217 LDPR's calls for revival of Russian Empire in, 239; narratives, 21; post-Soviet citizens given Russian passports, 236; post-Soviet space and interests, 47; Primakov's view of, 235–236; recognition of Russia's strategic sovereignty by the West, 39; Russian dispute over legitimacy of nations having left the Soviet orbit, 137; Russian-speaking diasporas in, 235, 239; soft power and, 220

Nemtsov, Boris, 83
neo-Byzantinism, 99–104. *See also* Byzantinists
neocolonialism, 258–262
neoconservatism, 6, 79, 186, 188
neo-Eurasianism, 45, 167, 187, 203, 218–220, 226
neo-imperialism, 64, 203, 246
neoliberalism: economic legacy, 49, 78; economic tools, 79; Eurasian Economic Union and, 220; individualism and globalization under, 188; integration, 87; marketplace of ideas, 38, 70; political language, 35; principles, 54; state, 66; strategy, 29; structure, 30;

Valdai summit, 90; values of, 223; Van Dijk's definition, 18; Western ideological and economic standards, 74
neo-Nazism. *See* Nazis/Nazism
neo-paganism, 187, 193
Neo-Sovietism, 53
Nevsky, Alexander, 110
New Delhi, 224
New Development Bank (BRICS), 256
New Jerusalem Monastery, 59
Nicaragua, 257, 258
Nicholas I, 122, 130, 135, *136*, 171, 216
Nicholas II: in *Matilda* (film), 185; mentions, 136; nostalgia for, 99, 127; seen by Putin as too weak, 135; symbols of the nation's reconciliation, 127; tsar's family, 102, 129
Nigeria, 256, 259
Night Wolves, 65
Nikonov, Vyacheslav, 237
NKVD (People's Commissariat of Internal Affairs), 119
Noah, 103, 204
Nobel Prize, 238
nomenklatura, 20, 41, 45, 79
Nomos of the Earth (Schmitt), 194
nongovernmental organizations (NGOs), 118–119, 251. *See also names of individual organizations*
noosphere, 217
Non-Aligned Movement, 262
norms, 74, 90. *See also* values
North Atlantic Treaty Organization (NATO); bombings in the former Yugoslavia, 202; enemy status, 73; expansion into Russian near abroad, 95, 126; prospect of Russian membership in, 58; security arrangements against, 104; trans-Atlantic institutions, 78
nostalgia, 28, 35, 50–53, 59, 93, 99; for Ivan IV, The Terrible, 193; for Nicholas II and the imperial family, 28, 99, 129; for

nostalgia (*cont.*)
  paganism, 193; for Stalinism, 193; for state socialism, 188; for the Brezhnev era, 125; for the Russian Empire, 125, 127, 145; for the Soviet regime, 35, 50–53, 59, 93, 127, 173, 174, 199, 220; for tsarism, 193; Rogozin as Russian Ambassador, 239; Russian Eurasianism as a counter response to, 216; Russian opposition to Ukraine's potential membership, 137, 139
November 4 Club, 56
Novikov, Timur, 100
Novorossiya, 138, 212, 242–244, *243*. *See also* Donbas
Novye vekhe (New Milestones), 45, 46, 188
Northern Katechon (Mahler), 194
North Korea. *See* Korea, North
North Ossetia. *See* Ossetia, North
nuclear weapons, 193, 197–200, 208–209
Nuremburg Trials, 117

occupied territories (Ukraine), 28, 142, 144, 252
October Revolution. *See* Bolshevik Revolution
Odesa/Odessa, 242
okhraniteli (pro-Kremlin analysts, or "guardians"), 197
Old Believers, 194
Olympics, 105, 111
"On Fascism" (Ilyin), 133
On Resistance to Evil by Force (Ilyin), 132–133
"On the Historical Unity of Russians and Ukrainians" (Putin), 137
ontology, 25, 85, 147–148, 209, 217
Operation Successor, 47
oprichnina, 199
Orange Revolution (Ukraine), 52, 82, 236
Ortega, Daniel, 258
Orthodox Christianity (Eastern Orthodoxy). *See* Christianity

Orthodox Church of Ukraine. *See* Ukrainian Orthodox Church–Kyiv Patriarchate
Orwell, George, 109–110
Orwellian language, 142
Ossetia, North, 52
Ossetia, South, 59, 92, 104, 236, 241
Otechestvo (Fatherland, political party), 47, 56
Ottoman Empire, 98, 105, 138, 194, 200
Our Home-Russia (political party), 43
Our Tasks (Ilyin), 132

Paleologue, Zoe, 98, 103
Palestine, 251, 262
Pamyat ("memory"), 199
pan-Africanism, 6
Panarin, Alexander, 155, 157, 216, 218, 226; on Buddhist-Taoist world, 223; on China, 223; on Islamic world, 223
pan-Slavism: civilizational notion of, 153; division of Europe, 100; Historical Perspective Foundation, 118; ideology, 98; "specific path" of Russia, 74; Suslov, 23, 101; Troitsky's synthesis of, 155. *See also* Slavophiles
paramilitary groups, 30, 69, 142, 214, 270–271. *See also names of individual groups*
Paris, 131, 237
parliament, 41, 42, 44, 63, 161; MPs, 100, 116. *See also* Duma
passionarity, 154, 219, 230
parliamentarianism, 41, 171
"party of war," the. *See* hawks
Patriarchs of Moscow: Alexy II, 51, 60, 102, 167, 195–196, 201; Kirill (Vladimir Mikhailovich Gundyaev), 27, 59, 106, 168, 201–202, 207, 261
patriarchy, 18, 98
Patrice Lumumba People's Friendship University, 259
particularism, 5, 21

patriotic conservatism. *See* United Russia, patriotic conservative wing

patriotism: backward-looking currents within, 187; centrism, 49; civil society, 273; conceptualization, 8; cultural turn, 31; democratic, 44; education, 110, 113, 123; elites seen as deficient in, 174; healthy, 46; ideological, 63; Ilyin's assertion that it was nonexistent in the USSR, 133; Kuznetsova's promotion of, 184; militant, 168; military, 195–196; nation-building and, 177; Patriot Park, 196; Putinism, 50; Russian Civil War, 128; Russian Orthodox values, 182; Soviet, 43; statism, 81; World War I, 132; Z-patriotism, 36, *37*, 278

Patrushev, Dmitry, 20

Patrushev, Nikolay, 20, 25, 66, 90, 207

Pavlov, Alexey, 207

Pavlovsky, Gleb: calls for a new state ideology, 162; father of political communication in Russia, 22; Kremlin's main spin doctor, 53; polit-technology, 33, 235; "Putin's silent majority" idea, 50; Russian World Fund connections, 237; "Russian world" conceptualization, 231, 232, 234; "specific civilization" idea, 156, 157; work on *Russian Journal*, 188; work with the Young Conservatives, 187; work with Tsymbursky, 202

Peace and Reconciliation Day (November 7), 51, 127

Pelevin, Viktor, 32

Penza region, 184

People's Unity Day (November 4), 52

perestroika (restructuring): debate over Stalinism, 118; failure of discourse on repentance for past crimes, 43; Gorbachev's aims, 76; morality and, 171, 173; "normal country" being established under, 40; Pamyat nationalism during, 199; pan-European political community, 85; Russia's sense of history, 13; Russia's twentieth-century history, 44; Russian regrets over, 120; Satarov, 45

Perevezentsev, Sergey, 186

Peskov, Dmitry, 63, 128, 130, 241

Petersson, Bo, 5

Peter I, the Great: civilizational ambivalence of, 247; conquest of new territories, *136*; modernizing "window on Europe," 135; Putin's admiration for as a personal role model, 136; Soviet official pantheon, 134; top-down approach to modernization, 110; top-down authoritarian approach to governance, 247; war with Sweden, 126

petitions, 279

Petrov, Nikolay, 20, 80

philhellenism, 99

Philippines, 268

philosemitism, 143

philosophers, 212. *See also names of individuals*

philosophy, 45, 57, 90, 218

Philosophy of Inequality (Berdyaev), 132

Philotheus, 98, 194

pink tide (Latin America), 257

Piotrovsky, Mikhail, 121

Pipes, Richard, 77

Platonov, Oleg, 155, 156

Pligin, Vladimir, 55

pluralism, 168; celebration of Russia's ethnic, 214; Dugin's view of, 204; ethnic and religious, 152, 163, 164, 169; ideological marketplace, 71; Russian Orthodox Church's shift away from support for, 173

Pobedonostev, Konstantin, 171

pochennichestvo, 48

pochvenniki, 74

Podberezkin, Alexey, 46, 173

Poklonnaya Gora, 43

Poland, 91, 116, 119, 131, 239, 251; ideological relationship to Russia, 267. *See also* Polish-Lithuanian Commonwealth
polarization, 40, 42, 50, 70, 83
Poles, 119, 240
Polish-Lithuanian Commonwealth, 52, 128, 198
Politburo, 26
political class, the, 32
political communication, 22
political correctness, 89
political culture, 18, 84, 91
political rights, 41
political violence, 42
politicians, 17, 20, 35, 44, 166. *See also names of individuals*
Politika Foundation, 237
polit-technologies, 32–34, 53, 120, 235, 236, 277
Polosin, Andrey, 120, 121
Polyakov, Leonid, 79
polycentrism. *See* multipolar world order
polygamy, 185
popular culture, 30–31
populism, 6, 36, 69, 90, 98, 247. See also *Narodniki*
Portuguese Empire, 249
post-Cold War, 134. *See also* Cold War
post-industrial society, 156
postliberalism, 88
postmodernism: Europe viewed through lens of, 78; ideological fluidity, 7; managed democracy, 62; polit-technology culture, 33; political construction of the Russian regime, 73; regime's ideological production, 23 state elites, 53; Western values, 90, 204; world, 18
post-Soviet countries. *See* near abroad
Potemkin, Grigory, 242
power vertical, 23, 50, 68
Prague Spring, 22, 138
premarital sex, 172

presidential addresses: annual, 81; "conservatism" mentioned in, *175*; Medvedev, 174; national idea, 63; Putin, 175; references to Russia's European connections, 160; *rossiiskaia* preferred over *russkaia* in, 163; Soviet antisemitism, 42
Presidential Commission to Counter Attempts to Falsify History to the Detriment of Russia's Interests, 100, 117
Presidential Council for Culture, 31
Presidential Directorate for Interregional and Cultural Projects, 236
Presidential Directorate for Social Projects, 31
Prigozhin, Yevgeny, 30, 36, 69, 251, 260; death in plane crash viewed as a Kremlin-backed assassination, 278
Prilepin, Zagar, 36, 278
Primakov, Yevgeny, 47, 56, 223, 235, 255
Primakov Jr., Yevgeny, 259
primitivism, 177
Principal Directions of the Federation toward Compatriots Living Abroad, 239
Privalov, Alexander, 174
private/personal property (or lack thereof), 79, 99
private sector, 56
privatization, 35, 41, 45, 49, 79, 80
Program of State Assistance for Voluntary Travel of Compatriots to Russia, 240
progress, 78, 178
progressivism: criticized as being hegemonically status quo, 190; human nature as a constraint on, 148; mainstream ideology, 17; national conservative opposition to, 192; Putin regime, 6
Project for a New American Century, 188
Prokhanov, Alexander: alliance between Communist forces and the Russian Orthodox Church, 173; Antichrist

instrumentalized by, 207; Cosmist belief system of, 204; Dugin and, 189; Eurasianism, 213; imperial-Eurasianist school, 36; Izborsky Club, 203; Kholmogorov and, 197; "Mystical Stalinism" article, 200; neo-imperialism, 64; "red-brown" author, 198, 249; "red-brown" ideologists, 45; Soviet nostalgia, 187; support for Soviet imperialism, 198

propaganda: alternative point of view, 90; communication strategy, 7; doublethink and, 278; Islamist, 201; Kremlin as propaganda operator, 3; propaganda move, 105; Russian propaganda drawing analogies between Muslim support for Palestine and support for Russian-occupied territories in Ukraine, 262; Russian textbooks and, 120; Stalinist, 91; state, 16; targeting Ukraine, 144

prosperity, 81, *82*, 95, 182

protectionism, 189, 223

Protestantism. *See* Christianity

protests: against liberal musical performers, 183; against the war, 70; Bolotnaya protests, 61–63, 82, 131; public, 65; Rodina party, 52. *See also* dissent

providence, 73

Provisional Government (1917), 111

pro-Westernism, 75; consensus, 40, 41; discourse, 47; liberal experiment, 46; model, 52; Putin regime, 48; right is the new center, 49; Western-style modernization, 62; Yeltsin-era elites, 173, 220

pseudoscience, 25, 32, 121

Pskov, 198

Public Diplomacy Foundation, 237

public opinion: cognitive frameworks of, 212; infrastructure projects and, 123; Institute of Contemporary Development (INSOR), 58–59; intellectual production, 36; post-Crimea consensus, 65–66; prescriptive ideology for, 45; Putin and Medvedev exchange, 61; special ideological operation, 23

public policy, 21, 27

public relations, 44, 47, 70; intellectual production, 33; Markov, 236; pro-Russia politicians in Ukraine, 143; PR firms, 32; regime's tools, 53

puppet regimes, 138

Pushkov, Alexey, 251

Pussy Riot, 62, 183

putsch attempt of August 1991, 40, 42

Putin girls, 24–25

Putinism, ch. 3, (p. 77–96); Putinism, early, 21, 39, 49–57, 82, 88, 134, 148, 160, 178; Putinism, middle, 21, 39, 58–60; Putinism, late (including war Putinism), 21, 39, 61–68, 71, 82, 88; war Putinism (specifically) 68–70, 71, 272; state ideology, 4; top-down and bottom-up encounter, 6

Putin: His Ideology (Chadaev), 53

"Putin's Long State" (Surkov), 140

Putin's silent majority, 50, 89

racialism, 155

racism, 18, 180, 254

Radio Moscow, 259

rally-round-the-flag effect, 63, 65

RANXiGS (Presidential Administration University), 120

Ratzel, Friedrich, 212

raw materials, 80

reactionaries, 82, ch. 9 (p. 193–209); agenda, 27; Astakhov, 183; Communists in the post-Soviet era as, 191; counterrevolutionary script, 11; family policy, 28; Ilyin, 36, 57 132; imperialism, 145, 171; Kholmogorov's affiliation with, 188; Kuznetsova, 183; Lvova-Belova, 183; monarchism, 131; Putin's promotion of a brand of conservatism

reactionaries (*cont.*)
  that would not involve, 176; reactionary conservatism, 170–171; reactionary language, 149; Russian reactionary tradition, 193–209; Starikov, 64. *See also names of individuals*
recentralization, 50, 63, 80. *See also* renationalization
"red-brown" coalition (of Communists and nationalists): CPRF, 44; Dugin and Prokhanov, 45; Eurasianism and, 220; existential danger to democracy, 42; Gorbachev's reforms opposed by, 173; Islam and, 205–206; promoted by Prokhanov, 198, 249
Reds. *See* Bolsheviks
Red Square, 123, 128
referendums, 41, 43, 119
renationalization, 35, 222
repression: competing historical narratives, 118; fear of, 21; hegemony of the regime, 18; Izborsky Club's reinforcement of, 199; key figures, 36; legislation, 69; legislative apparatus, 63; muftiates, 185; necessary evil, 116; of the opposition, 61, 67; political, 2; Stalinism, 115; technocrats' moderation of, 145
reactionaries, 47
realism (international relations), 86
"Real Lessons of the 75th Anniversary of World War II, The" (Putin), 119, 138
realpolitik, 226
referendum, 66
reformers: Christian, 173; Chubais, 79; Gaidar, 79; healthy patriotism, 46; reformist tradition, 83. *See also* perestroika, *and specific groups of reformers*
reforms: conservatism, 47; conservative liberalism, 82; conservative, 174; constitutional, 66; Decembrist demands for, 130; Gorbachev, 173; institutional, 58; liberal, 42; referendum on, 41; right as the new center, 49;

Russia's loss of influence over Ukraine blamed on, 136; socioeconomic reform program, 79; tsarist rejection of, 132; Western-style modernization, 62; Yeltsin, 43; Yeltsin's failures at consolidating liberalism, 127;
regime change, 66
religion, 59, 63, 97, 98, 177–178. *See also specific religions, religious leaders and institutions*
religious philosophy, 45
Remizov, Mikhail: civilizationist isolationism for Russia, 36; defense of classical modernity in opposition to postmodernism, 190–191; editor of the *Russian Journal*, 188; Institute for National Strategy, 33; key intellectual figure, 187; Kholmogorov's view as being too moderate for him, 197; leadership at the National Strategy Institute, 202; Young Conservative movement, 101, 165, 186
Renaissance, 74, 100, 103
renationalization, 80. *See also* recentralization
repentance, 209
republicanism, 112
Reshetnikov, Leonid, 102
Responsibility to Protect Principle (UN), 241
revanchism, 3
Revenge of History, The (Panarin), 155
reverse discrimination, 180
revolution, 55, 176. *See also names of specific revolutions*
revolutionaries, 45, 128, 132, 135, 171
RIA Novosti, 121, 143
Ribbentrop-Molotov Pact, 119
"Right Turn, The" (Ulykaev), 49
Rimsky-Korsakov, Mikail, 203
rituals, 17
Rodina (political party), 52, 56, 213
Rogozin, Dmitry, 44, 52, 56, 162, 213; Congress of Russian Communities,

239; deputy prime minister for military-industrial complex, 239; Russian Ambassador to NATO, 239
Roman Empire, 75
Romania, 104
Rome, 99, 153, 163
Romanticism, 152–153, 191
romanticization, 130
Romanov Dynasty, 28, 52, 129, 197, 226
rootedness, 152–157, 189
Rosatom State Atomic Energy Corporation, 65, 120
Roskomnadzor (Federal Service for Supervision of Communications, Information Technology, and Mass Media), 70
Rosneft, 25
Rossiya Segodnya (media group), 208, 259
Rossotrudnichestvo. *See* Federal Agency for the Commonwealth of Independent States, Compatriots Living Abroad, and International Humanitarian Cooperation
RT (Russia Today), 53, 88, 121, 237, 258, 259–260, 261
rule of law, 44
Runet (Russian internet), 191, 198; Afrique Media and, 260; conservative project, 187; Kremlin and, 242; Moscow Patriarchate and, 201; Pavlovsky, 202; Pravoslavie.ru, 196; public intellectual figures close to the regime, 53–54
Rurik, 111, 198
Rurikid Dynasty, 52
Rus', 100. *See also* Holy Rus'
Russia and Europe (Danilevsky), 153
Russia and the Russians in World History (Narochnitskaya), 100
Russia, My History (park), 134
Russian Academy of Sciences, 33, 117, 120, 166, 202, 279; Far East Institute, 223
Russian Antarctic Station, 196
Russian Armed Forces: discrediting the, 70; flag of, 51; pseudodocumentary film

The Destruction of an Empire: Lesson from Byzantium, 102; relationship with the Russian Orthodox Church, 195–197; "war correspondents," 69. *See also* military
Russian Centers, 237
Russian Civil War, 99, 128, 131
Russian Club, 57
Russian Constitution: adoption of then new, 40–42; alternative proposal for replacing, 187; debates over amending, 265; ideological plurality, 13, 44, 63, 70; marriage defined as between a man and a woman, 184. *See also* constitutional amendments
Russian Empire: "Autocracy, Nationality, Orthodoxy" as the slogan for, 171; "reassembly of Russian lands", 98; confronted with internal revolutions, 130; continental nature of, 211, 217; cultural legacy of, 272; European power, 74; expansion of, 75, 225–226, 247; great power, 110; Holy Rus' and, 200; interpretations of Russia and, 76; neo-Byzantinism, 99, 103; nostalgia for, 125, 127, 145; philosophical underpinnings of, 186; Soviet approach to peripheral nations contrasted with, 138; tsarism, 128
Russian Geographical Society, 105, 122, 123, 213
Russian Historical Society, 117
Russian Houses, 237, 259
Russian Idea, 44, 45, 46
Russian International Affairs Council (RIAC), 33, 80, 225, 237
Russian Institute, 232, 234
Russian Institute for Strategic Studies (RISI), 33, 102
Russian language, 45; emotional aspects of, 124–125; Eurasia and, 217; foundations promoting use of, 237; immigrants' degradation of, 141; Muslims' growing use of, 167; politicized by

Russian language (cont.)
  Patriarch Kirill, 201; Russian ethnic core of, 87; Russian World and, 213, ch. 11 (231–244); spoken in Ukraine, 209, 241, 242, 244; state-forming people's language, 67
Russian Lemnos, 102
Russian Military Historical Society, 117, 121
Russian National Guard, 208
Russian Navy, 257
Russian Orthodox Church: conservative ideology of, 57, 58, 63; contribution to making Russia a civilization-state, 156, 161; defrocking of priests who refuse to lead prayers in support of Russia's war on Ukraine, 208; democratization and pluralism's decline in support from, 173; European cultural and institutional legacies in, 161; fundamentalism within, 172; globalization perceived as a threat, 173; Ilyin's writings aligned with, 132; institutional contributions to conservatism, 181–185; Kovalchuk, 26; mafias and oligarchs condemned by, 173; Marxism opposed by, 249; Medvedev's presidency and, 22; Ministry of the Interior and, 45; moral values of the Russian nation, 59; Moscow Patriarchate's contested authority over churches in Ukraine, Moldova, and the Baltic states, 202; Neo-Byzantinism of, 97–108; Orthodox realm, 27–28; patriotism and, 168; philanthrocapitalism, 79; place in society, 4; relationship with Russian Armed Forces, 195–197; Runet, 198;
Russia as a normal country and, 40; Russia as an exemplary nation, 157; Russian identity defended by, 173;
Russian national identity cornerstone, 187, 188, 205; Social Doctrine of, 167; Stalinist legacies criticized by, 118; symbolic dominance of religious landscape, 167; theological doctrines in today's Russia, 34–35, 37; theology of, 193; tsarist tendencies, 129; under the tsars, 171; Yuriev, 60. *See also* Moscow Patriarchate
Russian Project (*Russkii proekt*), 56, 57. *See also* State-Patriotic Club
Russian Question (*russkii vopros*), 238
Russian Question at the end of the 20th Century (Solzhenitsyn), 238, 239
Russian Spring, 243
Russian State Archives, 33
Russian State Humanities University (RGGU), 133, 205
Russian Supreme Court, 179
Russian Union (proposal), 238
Russian Union of Industrialists and Entrepreneurs (RSPP), 58, 80
Russian universal, the (*russkoe vsemirnoe*): Dostoyevsky, 238
Russian World (*russkii mir*), 33, 158, 198, 211, ch. 11 (231–244), 273; central repertoires for Russia, 33; civilizational community of, 158; ethnonationalism and, 213; Eurasia and, 244; Holy Rus' and, 200–202; Izborsk, 198; presidential speeches, *243*; Russian hegemonic designs for, 262; Russian hegemony over, 212
Russian World Fund, 237
Russia Today. *See* RT
russkii mir. *See* Russian World
"Russia at the Turn of the Millennium." *See* Millennium Manifesto
Russification, 143, 166
Russocentrism, 35
Russo-Georgian war, 196
Russophiles, 106
Russophobia, 19, 20, 91–95, 279
Russo-Turkish Wars, 242

Russo-Ukrainian War 1, 26, 126–145; assassination of Dugin's daughter Darya, 204; civilizational conflict, 189; context of, 96, 107; debate over whether Russia is fascist, 270; decline of Russian political figures identifying Russia as European, 162; fascism, 93; genocide, 92; high human and economic costs of, 266; military patriotism, 113; ontology of power, 25; path for the future of Russia, 2; privatization and, 49; Putin's attempts to justify, 130; Putinism and, 21, 22, 68–70; regime technocrats and, 80; Russia's belligerence, 3; Russian designs for a Greater Eurasia, 225, 230; Russian establishment and, 76 Russian imperialism and, 265–266; Russian political perception of the West and, 91; Russian propaganda drawing analogies between Muslim support for Palestine and support for Russian-occupied territories in Ukraine, 262; Russian public opinion, 23; *siloviki*, 29; state ideology and, 13, 14, 20; strategic object, 105; tensions with the West and, 203, 257, 258; worldviews on, 277; violence of, 34
Rutskoy, Alexander, 42

Saakashvili, Mikheil, 59
Sahel, 260, 268
Saint Augustine, 208
Saint John Chrysostom, Archbishop of Constantinople, 194
Saint Paul the Apostle, 193–194
Saint Sergius of Radonezh, 188
Sakha-Yakutia, 219
salvation, 99
samizdat (underground banned literature), 121
Samigullin, Kamil, 184
samobytnost' (unique national identity), 49.

sanctions (Western), 62, 68, 80, 91, 107; against Ilyumzhinov, 251; ignored by Central Asian republics, 244; ignored by Global South, 246; pushing Putin closer to Xi, 224; Russia's position within the EAEU and, 222
Sandinismo, 258
Sarov Monastery, 195
Satan/satanism, 177, 194, 207–208
Satarov, Georgy, 45
Saudi Arabia, 256
Savitsky, Petr N., 157, 217, 218, 230
Savvidis, Ivan, 106
Scientology, 32
Schmitt, Carl, 84, 194, 204, 212, 229
Sea of Azov, 105, 144
Sechin, Igor, 25
Second Coming of Christ, 194. *See also* Jesus Christ
Second World War. *See* World War II
secularism, 78, 201. *See also* antisecularism
Security Council of Russia, 20, 25, 47, 66, 68, 224
security services: church work with, 196; Kremlin ecosystem, 27; mobilization coalition, 26; private militia, 199; regime's equilibrium, 68; Valdai Club and, 33. *See also* individual agency names
Senegal, 260
Seraphim Club, 174
Serbia, 101, 102, 267
Sergeytsev, Timofey, 143
Sergunin, Alexander, 256
Sevastopol, 105
Seventeen Moments of Spring (television series), 30–31
Shanghai, 224
Shanghai Cooperation Organization (SCO), 256
Sharia law. *See* Islam
Shavarevich, Igor, 92
Shchedrovitsky, Georgy, 32, 231

Shchedrovitsky, Petr, 232, 234, 238
shock therapy, 40, 45, 79
Sierra Leone, 251
silent majority, 62
siloviki (power agencies): Bastrykin, 70; calls for total conquest of Ukraine, 142; civilians, 58; ideology, 121; Kremlin's ecosystem, 37; power agencies, 27; Putin and, 59; relations with the Russian Orthodox Church, 208; Russia-Ukraine unification, 29; structural interests of, 271; systemic liberals, 28. *See also* FSB; military-industrial complex; Ministry of Defense; Ministry of the Interior; National Guard; security services
Silver Age, 57, 186, 211, 230
Sinophilia, 224
Shoigu, Sergei, 25, 122
Shumeyko, Vladimir, 44
Shuvalov, Yury, 56
Siberia, 131, 216, 217, 224, 247
Skobeeva, Olga, 31
Skolkovo, 58
Slavic world, 100, 101, 139, 153, 155, 219
Slavophiles, 74, 98, 100, 103, 153, 155: conservative thinkers, 153; Europe divided, 100; Holy Rus' and, 200; Khomiakov, 247; liberal way of thinking, 98; relationship to Confucian culture, 224; Russia's destiny, 103; Russia's specific path, 74; Russian civilization, 155; state language and, 250; village prose movement (*derevenshchiki*) of, 172, 249; Western Enlightenment values opposed by, 247. *See also* pan-Slavism
Slovakia, 267
Slovenia, 267
Slutsky, Leonid, 204
Sobchak, Anatoly, 20, 56
sobornost', 98
Sobyanin, Sergey, 28

Sochi, 105, 111
social conservatism, 55, 56, 62, 78, 171. *See also* traditional values
social contract, 4, 69, 81
social democracy. *See* democracy
social doctrine: of Kazan Muftiate, 167; of Russian Orthodox Church, 167
social engineering, 32, 142
Social Research Expert Institute (EISI), 33, 37,
socialism: Glazyev's advocacy of, 222; ideology of, 18; Latin American, 258; modernity and, 134; nature of, 54; nostalgia for, 188; Slavic, 155; USSR's enforcement of, 172
soft power, 6, 7, 54, 134, 221; Sergunin on, 256
Sokolov, Maxim, 174
Solonevich, Ivan, 102, 186
Solovetsky Islands, 207
Soloviev, Vladimir (TV host), 31, 132, 186; antisemitism of, 143; *Justification of the Good*, 132; nuclear warmongering by, 209; political talk shows, 31; promoter of the Russian World, 235; views on Russia's uniqueness, 186
Soloviev, Vladimir (Silver Age philosopher), 211
Sonderweg (special path), 5, 153, 217
sograzhdanstvo. *See* co-citizenship
solidarity, 48, 182
Solzhenitsyn, Alexander: Congress of Russian Communities, 44; contemporary thinker, 187; historical figure, 125; "How Shall We Organize Russia?" 238; Marxism opposed by, 249; narrative, 137; Nobel Prize for Literature, 57, 238; Russian messianism opposed by, 172, 202–203; *Russian Question in the 20th Century, The*, 238–239
Sophia (television series), 103
South Africa, 249, 259, 261, 268
South Caucasus. *See* Caucasus, South
Southeast Asia, 249

South Korea. *See* Korea, South
South Ossetia. *See* Ossetia, South
sovereign democracy. *See* democracy
sovereignism, 5, 86
sovereignty: cultural, 176, *177*; EAEU framework constraints on Russia, 222; geopolitical West, 78; global economy and, 80; Institute for National Strategy's promotion of, 191; rules of coexistence, 85; Russia's violations of other countries', 262; Serbian, 86; state, 94; statism, 111; survival, 109; traditional European values and, 90
Soviet army, 51
Soviet space, former or post-. *See* near abroad, the
Soviet Union: ambivalence of modern Russians toward, 129–130, 131; anti-imperialist rhetoric of, 245; Arctic presence, 123; borders between Russia and Ukraine, 137; cast as humanitarian for liberating Nazi-held territories, 120; collapse of, 21, 30, 41, 43, 50, 68, 70, 74, 85, 99, 125, 147, 217, 219, 220, 233, 249–250, 260, 265, 279; consensus on Soviets' heroic role in World War II, 127, 132; conservative social practices under, 172; contrasted with Russian Empire's approach to peripheral nations, 138; CPRF, 46, 63; culture of, 272; diplomatic policy, 92, 93; feedback (*obratnaia sviatz'*) in, 277; historiographic ideology under, 154; imperial logic, 47; imperialism of, 198; institutions of, 122; international affairs, 33; internationalism of, 249, 250; Islam in, 166; Katyn massacre, 119; Khrushchev's rhetoric about a single Soviet nation, 171; Latin American relations with, 258; Lavrov's response to foreign fears of attempts to reestablish, 241; legacy, 32, 84; Marxism-Leninism of, 13, 26, 27, 38, 54, 79; memory policy toward, 115–122; messianism of, 194; nostalgia for, 127, 173, 174, 199, 220, 239; patriotic youth movement, 114; *perestroika*, 40; Pipes, Richard, leading scholar on, 77; post-Soviet period, 57; repression under, 14; Russia as the legal successor to, 235; Russia's historical continuity and, 188; Russian public opinion on, 23; selective praise and scorn for past tsars/tsarinas, 134; Solzhenitsyn's critique of, 238; Soviet Afro-Asian Solidarity Committee, 259; Soviet Peace Fund, 259; state crimes, 67; territories formerly controlled by, 139; village prose (*derevenshchiki*) movement in, 249; war medals awarded by, 196; worldview persistence in post-Soviet Russia, 145, 277
Sovimformburo (Sovietskoe informatsionnoe byuro), 259
Spain, 268
Spanish Empire, 258
Spas (television channel), 56
Special Military Operation: crisis of, 68; fake information and, 69; genocide, 92; great civilizational war with the West, 22; Izborsky Club's support for, 203; large segment of society that has fought in, 270; modeled on Soviet interventions in Budapest and Prague, 138; "Nazism" in Ukraine used as a justification for, 121; patriotic and pro-family themes, 114; preference by technocrats and establishment figures for containing the conflict, 142; Russian public opinion and, 23; "Satanism" in Ukraine used by Pavlov as a justification for, 207. *See also* Russo-Ukrainian War
Spengler, Oswald, 152, 154, 158
spin doctors, 32, 50, 53
Spiritual Administrations of Muslims, 166, 167, 184, 201

spiritual values. *See* values
Sputnik (Russian news agency), 88, 237, 258, 259–260, 261
Sretensky Monastery, 196
Stalin, Joseph: Adamkus and, 116; crimes, 43; historical figure, 111, 125; Kholmogorov's reverence for, 197; nostalgia for, 127; partial rehabilitation of, 118; persecution of religious believers, 200; political repressions, 115; role in creating a Ukrainian state, 138
Stalinism: A-bomb's development, 195; family policy under, 179; National-Bolshevism, 35; nostalgia for, 193; political repressions, 115; propaganda, 91; "Red Arctic" myth, 123; regime, 118
Stankovich, Sergey, 220
Starikov, Nikolay, 64, 199, 252
State Council, 120
statehood (Russian): academic coursework on, 141; "deep people's" relationship to, 141; disruption of Russia's, 50; geography and, 122; historical continuity, 109–119; imperial, 103; millennial-historical continuity, 125, 133, 139, 158, 198; national, 120; presidential speeches, 112; Rurikid Dynasty's foundation, 198
state ideology: aggressive, 36; conservatism and, 191; constitution, 70; Eurasianism's bid to become the new, 220; existence of, 39; ideational products, 14; national, 44–46; patriotism, 63; Pavlovsky's call for a new, 162; portrayed as necessary to prevent state collapse, 199; presidential administration, 53; Putinism, 71; regime construction, 2, 4; restoration of an official's, 48; Russia's unique identity, 49; Russian Constitution's prohibition on, 13, 265; Western, 41. *See also* national idea
State-Patriotic Club, 57
state seal. *See* great seal

statism (*gosudartvennichestvo*), 192; authority over historical memory, 118; defended above all else, 131; Ilyin's promotion of, 133; indirectly supported by leaders' rejection of revolution, 130; patriotic, 81; patriotism, 112–115; preservation of Russian nationhood, 120; radical, 26; Russian values, 48; socialist economics, 199; "The Right Turn," 49; semantic space of, 110–111
status signaling, 148
Stierlitz, Max Otto von. *See* Isaev, Maksim. See also *Seventeen Moments of Spring* (TV series)
St. Basil's Cathedral, 104
St. Petersburg: Derzhavin House, 237; Economic Forum (2023), 205; federal city, 105; International Legal Forum (2023), 70; Pligin as lawyer for the mayor, 56; protests in, 183; Sobchak's mayorship in, 20; Starikov's work for Channel One in, 199; tricentennial, 160
St. Petersburg Economic Forum, 205
St. Petersburg International Legal Forum, 70
Struve, Peter, 45, 217
Study of History, A (Toynbee), 152
Sudan, 251, 259
Suess, Eduard, 216
Sufism. *See* Islam
Surkov, Vladislav: concept of sovereign democracy, 148, 237; globalization and international competition; canceling out the West's normative advantage, 80; Nashi youth movement, 53; project of a "managed democracy," 62; "Putin's Long State," 140; Russian political lexicon, 15
survival values. *See* values
Suslov, Mikhail, 4, 23, 100, 132, 201
Stolypin, Pyotr, 127
Strakhov, Nikolay, 153
strategic narratives, 19

Strugatsky brothers (Arkady and Boris), 33
Suvorov Military Schools, 114
Svalbard Archipelago, 123
Sviataia Rus'. *See* Holy Rus'
Sweden, 126, 136, 198, 268
Syria. *See also* Islamic State of Iraq and Syria (ISIS), 251; Christians in, 106; Russia's strategic and foreign policy goals, 97; Syrian civil war, 103, 104, 106, 261
systemic liberals (*sislibs*): ecosystem inside the Kremlin, 27; ideological production, 37; managing state finances and the economy, 68–69; path to the West, 76; Russia's normalization and integration into the world order, 28

Tadzhuddin, Talgat, Mufti of All Russia, 167, 201
Tajikistan, 166
Tanzania, 259
Taoism, 223
Tarkovsky, Andrey, 99
Tatar-Mongols. *See* Mongols
Tatarstan, 166, 167, 184, 185, 219
Tatars, 195, 248
teachers' unions, 59
technocrats: bureaucracy, 58; conservative values, 59; economic policy, 170; elite, 28; ideological production, 145; Kiriyenko, 65; loyalty to the system, 66; managing state finances and the economy, 68; power as a managerial technique with an ideological façade, 32; preference for avoiding full mobilization of society, 142; Russia's fiscal advantages, 80; way of thinking, 49
teleology, 22, 38, 109, 134, 212
television, 31, 53, 56, 67, 68. *See also* names of television channels, programs, and personalities
theocracy, 98

theology, 132, 175, 262; doctrines in today's Russia, 34; Islamic, 206; Orthodox, 193
thieves-in-law (*vory v zakone*), 30. *See also* mafia
think tanks, 26, 33, 37, 58, 186. *See also* discussion clubs; *and individual organization names*
Third Rome (Russia as), ch. 4 (97–108); autarky and, 203; in biblical terms, 197; as new Byzantium, 98–108; Holy Rus' and, 200; isolationism and expansionism, 202; messianism, 4; myth of, 74; post-industrial era, 156; Russia's role as protector of Eastern Christians, 194; Russia's strategic and foreign policy goals, 97
third way, 48, 219
Tikhon (Shevkunov), Metropolitan of Crimea and Sevastopol. *See* Metropolitan Tikhon (Shevkunov)
Time of Troubles (1598–1613), 49, 52
Timofeev, Ivan, 80, 96
Titarenko, Mikhail, 223–224
Togo, 251
Tokayev, Kassym-Jomart, 219
tolerance, 178
Tolstoy, Leo, 247
Torkunov, Anatoly, 120
totalitarianism: Medvedev's denunciation of, 118; overlaps with both fascism and Communism, 142; post-totalitarian system, 13; regime type, 16, 24; Russia's history, 44; totalitarian sects, 183; Yeltsin's resignation speech, 47
Tower of Babel, 154
Toynbee, Arnold J., 152
trade, international, 87
trade unions, 38
Traditionalism, 100
traditional values. *See* values
transcontinental nationhood, 212
transitional justice, 116
transhumanism, 204

Transnistria, 236, 239, 242. *See also* Moldova
Treaty of Brest-Litovsk, 130
Trofimov, Archpriest Oleg, 207
Troitsky, Yevgeny, 155
Troubetzkoy, Prince Nikolay, 154, 157, 217, 230, 248–249
truth commissions, 116
Tsargrad. *See* Constantinople
tsarism: collapse of, 199; conservatism, 171; double-headed eagle of, 51; legacy in modern Russia, 145; Main Cathedral of the Armed Forces of the Russian Federation's depiction of, 196; modernizing trends toward the end of the old regime, 172; monarchism, 36; nostalgia for, 125, 193, 199; old regime itself not rehabilitated in the same way as tsarist conquests have been, 129, 139; old regime, 50; "Orthodoxy, Autocracy, Nationality," slogan 66; Russia's history shaped by, 44; Russia's multiethnic character shaped by, 100; Soviet regime precursor, 127; tsars as saviors of the nation, 52. *See also* monarchy
Tsymbursky, Vadim, 187, 189, 202–203
Tunisia, 251, 260
Turcophilia, 99
Turkey, Turks, 104, 107, 195, 256
Turkestan, 216
Turkic world, 215, 218, 219, 248
Tuva, 162, 219
Tyutchev, Fyodor, 91
tzarism. *See* tsarism

Ubozhko, Lev, 55
Ufa, 167, 201
Uganda, 259, 261
Ulykaev, Alexey, 49
Ukraine, 11, 21, 25, 26, 28, 63, 67, 82, 92, 95, 97, 104, 105; Bolsheviks' initial acceptance of the secession of, 131; Eastern Slavic nations' relationship to each other, 238–239; "fascism" as alleged by Putin in, 203; independence or autonomy from Russia, 120, 218; national memory, 116, 117; nationalism in, 202, 239; NATO partnership, 104; Novorossiya, 242, 244; occupied territories, 28; Orange Revolution, 82; point of friction, 67; pro-Russian figures and movements in, 63; re-Russification called for, 143–144; Russia's obsession with, 11; Russia's strategic and foreign policy goal, 97; Russian aggression toward, 240–241; Russian World and, 201–202, 212, 231, 244; Russian-speakers in, 209, 241, 242, 244; "Satanism" as alleged by Medvedev and Pavlov in, 207; submission to Russia, 25–26; torn between East and West, 137, 236. *See also* full-scale invasion of Ukraine by Russia
Ukraine War. *See* Russo-Ukrainian War
Ukrainian Armed Forces, 92, 119
Ukrainian language, 67
Ukrainian Orthodox Church–Kyiv Patriarchate, 106, 202
Ukrainian Orthodox Church–Moscow Patriarchate, 106
Ukrainians, 195
Ukrainian Secret Services, 204
Umarov, Dzhambulat, 208
Union of Right Forces (UFR, political party), 49, 56
Union of Salvation (film), 130
Union of Soviet Socialist Republics (USSR). *See* Soviet Union
United Arab Emirates (UAE), 256
United Kingdom (UK), 91, 251
United Nations (UN), 245–246, 257
United Russia (political party): civilizational thinking within, 157; conservatism and centrism within, 174; conservative liberal wing, 55, 56;

distribution by Kremlin of conservative philosophers' works to members of, 132; ideological content, 55–57; patriotic conservative wing, 56; polit-technological activities, 53; political structure, 49; presidential party, 35, 54; social conservative wing, 56. *See also* Unity (political party)

United States (US), 251; alliance, 95; challenges to liberal democracy in, 268; civilizational preeminence in the Americas, 153; confrontation with Soviet-backed Cuba, 258; diplomatic policy, 91–92; global hegemon, 156, 189, 213, 216, 251, 253; Russia's strategic sovereignty and, 39; Russian nuclear threats against, 208–209; social conservatism in, 179; universalism, 6; war between the Soviet Union and, 133

Unity (political party), 47, 55. *See also* United Russia (political party)

Unity Day. *See* People's Unity Day (November 4)

universalism, ch. 7 (151–169); American, 6; Kremlin's references to, 95; national conservative opposition to, 192; rootedness contrasted with, 189–190; Troubetzkoy's rejection of Western/ European, 248; Western, 5, 152. *See also* universal values

Ural Mountains, 216

USSR (Union of Soviet Socialist Republics). *See* Soviet Union

utopianism, 142, 145, 270

Uvarov, Sergey, 171

Valdai Club: conservatism as a gradual development, 170, 175; customs of peoples and civilizations, 159; Institutes for Democracy and Cooperation, 237; leading think tank, 33, *37*, 224; liberalism's absurdity, 90; Lukyanov as research director of, 88; moral conservatism, 176, 177; nationalism, 164; Putin's call for a new national idea, 63; societal changes in the West, 180

values, 16, 19, 29, 30, 33, 35, 42, 48, 55, 59, 64, 73, 88, 101, 157; Christian values, 177–178, 180, 187, 270; Communist values, 173; conservative values, 79, 172, 173, 175, 261, 279; Enlightenment values, 268; ethical values, 158, 181; Eurasianist values, 174; European values, 161, 187, 187; family values, 60, 114, 172, 181, 182; Foundation for the Defense of National Values, 261; ideology and, 16; intergenerational transmission and evolution of, 139–140, 178, 179; Islamic values, 184; language of, 33; liberal values, 42, 279; material values, 45, 76, 155, 178; moral values, 30, 55, 57, 59, 62, 63, 107, 114, 158, 170, 172, 176–181, *177*, 178, 179, 180, 181, 182, 184, 185, 191, 195–196, 246, 270; neoliberal values, 223; Orthodox values, 173; postmodern values, 90, 94, 107, 204; Russian values, 120, 151, 157–158, 172; spiritual values (spirituality), 45, 76, 78, 110, 114, 155, 176, 177, *177*, 178, 181, 196, 197, 246; survival values, 41; system of, 73, 157; traditional values, 19, 20, 30, 31, 50, 55, 59, 63, 65, 78, 90, 95, 107, 141, 148, 149, 151, 168, 169, 176–181, *177*, 182, 184, 187, 191–192, 261, 273, 279; universal values, 5, 6, 11, 48, 54, 78, 79–84, *82*, 90, 95, 107, 108; Western values, 88. *See also* mores; norms

Vanchugov, Vasily, 186

Venezuela, 251, 257

Vernadsky, Vladimir, 217

Vatican, 103, 106, 162

Vekhi (Milestones), 45

Veniavkin, Ilya, 5

veterans, 36

victimhood, 90, 101
victory (World War II), Victory Day (May 9, 1945): Baltic states' views of, 116; censorship of revisionist writings about, 117; ceremonies commemorating, 51; civilizational victory, 159; Europe accused by Russia of once again becoming "fascist," 94–95; legitimizing the socialist regime, 92–93; Orthodox controversy over Stalin on, 200; Russia's demands for recognition of its role in, 119
Virgin Mary, 199
Vladimir/Volodymyr the Great, Grand Prince, 98, 102, 127, 161. *See also* Baptism of the Rus'
Vladivostok, 162
Voegelin, Eric, 90
voenkory. *See* war correspondents; military bloggers
Volga-Urals region, 162, 166, 167
Volgin, Father Vladimir 59
Volodin, Vyacheslav, 25, 62, 65, 129, 132
volunteers, 36
vory v zakone. *See* thieves-in-law
Vučić, Aleksandar, 101

Wagner Group (private military company), 69, 260
Wall of Grief memorial (Moscow), 118
war correspondents (*voenkory*), 69
war economy, 80; Russian self-sufficiency and, 158, 168
war literature, 121
warlords, 63, 69
Washington Consensus, 251
welfare state, 35, 65, 66, 69
Weltanschauung. *See* worldview
West, the: African economic relations with, 259; anti-Westernism, 78–145; Antichrist's personification as, 195; cancel culture in, 180; collective West, 19–20; colonial history, 260; confrontation with, 47; crisis of, 90; elite revenues accumulated in, 2; interaction with, 22; liberalism in, 127, 129, 148, 178, 209; multipolar world, 25; Old Believers' personification as Satan, 194; preeminence of, 151, 246, 256; pro-Western consensus, 40–41; response to Russian propaganda in, 262; Russia against, 21; Russia as part of a European civilization, Part II (73–77); Russia's strategic sovereignty recognized by, 39; Russian confrontation with, 246, 250, 262–263, 265; Russian president as archvillain of, 5; secularism in, 201; sovereign democracy, 54; symbol of freedom, 13; tensions with Russia, 67, 203, 204; Western countries, 42; Western ideas, 70; Western interpretative; framework for Russia, 8; Western liberalism, 7; Western predictions, 58; Western-inspired think tanks, 33; white civilization and, 6; World Russian People's Congress's identification of with "Satanism," 207. *See also* anti-Westernism; pro-Westernism; Westernizers
Western Europe. *See* Europe
Westerners, 1, 3, 5; as invaders, 110; perceived colonial threat from, ch. 12 (245–263)
Westernism. *See* pro-Westernism
Westernization, 40–41
Westernizers (*zapadniki*). *See* pro-Westernism
Westphalian order, 86
"What Russia Should Do with Ukraine" (Sergeytsev), 143
Whites (White Russians, anti-Bolsheviks), 36, 37, 43, 99, 102; Byzantine legacy, 99; cult of the military, 43; ideological production of, 37; Ilyin, 36; Italian Fascism, 133; legacy of, 265; post-Soviet efforts to promote

reconciliation with Reds, 127–128, 199; rehabilitation of, 131–133; Russian Lemnos, 102; views on Ukraine, 126
White Sea, 207
working class, 134
World Bank, 87, 256
World Congress of Russian Compatriots Living Abroad, 237, 238
World Cup soccer hosted by Russia, 183
World Russian People's Congress, 27, 254
worldview; Barthes, 16; de Gaulle's, 94; European, 107; Russian, 13; Russian, 7, 15, 89, 114, 253, 277; Western values, 90
World War II; Cossacks in, 131–132; cult of, 4; Europe as neo-fascist, 94–95; interpretations of, 22; Main Cathedral of the Armed Forces of the Russian Federation representation of, 196; national military traditions, 51; national sentiment, 42–43; postwar period, 249; Putin's interpretative article about, 138; Russia's heroic role memorialized, 67, 127, 132; Russia's history, 92–93; Russia's imperial conquest of other nations, 127; Russian contribution to victory in, 153, 253; Soviet worldview, 145; various countries' national memories, 116, 118, 119; Russian attempts to justify the Ukraine War by drawing parallels with, 273

xenophobia, 164
Xi Jinping, 224

Yabloko (political party), 43
Yalta, 87, 94
Yamalo-Nenets autonomous district, 123
Yashin, Ilya, 70
Yavlinsky, Grigory, 43
Yeltsin, Boris; admiration of the West, 234; centrist political positioning, 47; condemnation of the Bolshevik Revolution, 127; confrontation with Zyuganov, 43; conservative opposition to, 173; control of the ideological marketplace, 70–71; demonization of the Communist opposition, 42; economic achievements, 79; emergence of "systemic liberals," 28; legacy of, 265; liberalism of, 239; new ideology for the Russian Federation, 45–46; patriotic centrism, 49; policy contrast between Putin and, 40; referendum on continued reforms (1993), 41; Russian national identity, 44; Russian regime, 10; veto of legislation, 239
Yeltsin era (1990s); authoritarian means of imposing liberalism, 190; contentious ethnic relations, 165; criminality in, 173; generally, 148, 191; introduction of capitalism in, 173; liberalism of, 166; undoing of the Soviet Union, 249–250
Yenissei River, 216
Yonov, Alexander, 250
Young Army (Iunarmiia), 114
Young Conservative school (*mladokonservativy*); civilizationist isolationism for Russia, 36, 37; disbandment of, 170; expansion and schisms in the 2000s, 187; involvement with the Presidential Administration, 188; Remizov, 101, 165, 186
Young Eurasia, 221
Young Pioneers, 114
youth, 35, 60; patriotic youth movement, 53, 113–114; subculture, 31; traditional, Soviet-inspired system, 27
Yugoslavia, 101, 202
Yurgens, Igor, 58
Yuriev, Yevgeny, 60
Yuzhinsky-Golovin circle, 32

zakonnost' (legality), 82
Zambia, 259
zapadniki. See Westernizers

Zaporizhzhia, 105, 242
Zaryadye Park (Moscow), 123
zemstvo assemblies, 172, 174, 250
zeitgeist, 18, 272, 279
Zelensky, Volodymyr, 67, 267; accused by Putin officials of being a Jewish conspirator against East Slavs, 143
Zhirinovsky, Vladimir, 40, 43, 134, 174, 204; far-right politics, 250; leadership of the LDPR, 213, 239
Zhukov, Georgy, 43
Zimbabwe, 260
Zinoviev, Alexander, 121
Zinoviev Club, 121

Zolotov, Viktor, 208
Z-patriotism. *See* patriotism
Zvezda (television channel), 56
Zygar, Mikhail, 67
Zyuganov, Gennadi, 35, 40, 43, 44, 99; 1995 legislative elections, 43–44; Communist Party of the Russian Federation, 40; competition with Yeltsin, 127; diplomatic exchanges between Russia and China, 35; *Holy Rus' and Koshchei's Kingdom*, 201; leadership in the Communist Party of the Russian Federation, 213; neo-Byzantinism, 99